THE MULTILATERALIZATION
OF INTERNATIONAL
INVESTMENT LAW

Attempts at developing a theory of international investment law are complicated by the fact that this field of international law is based on numerous, largely bilateral treaties and is implemented by arbitral panels established on a case-by-case basis. This suggests a fragmented and chaotic state of the law, with different levels of protection depending on the sources and targets of foreign investment flows. This book, however, forwards the thesis that international investment law develops, despite its bilateral form, into a multilateral system of law that backs up the functioning of a global market economy based on converging principles of investment protection. In discussing the function of most-favored-nation clauses, the possibilities of treaty-shopping and the impact of investor-State arbitration with its intensive reliance on precedent and other genuinely multilateral approaches to treaty interpretation, it offers a conceptual framework for understanding the nature and functioning of international investment law as a system.

STEPHAN W. SCHILL is a senior research at the Max Planck Institute for Comparative Public Law and International Law in Heidelberg. Formerly, he assisted the Honourable Charles N. Brower of 20 Essex Street Chambers, London in international commercial and investor-State arbitrations under various arbitral rules and clerked at the International Court of Justice. He is admitted to the bars in Germany and New York.

THE MULTILATERALIZATION
OF INTERNATIONAL
INVESTMENT LAW

STEPHAN W. SCHILL

CAMBRIDGE UNIVERSITY PRESS
Cambridge, New York, Melbourne, Madrid, Cape Town, Singapore, São Paulo, Delhi

Cambridge University Press
The Edinburgh Building, Cambridge CB2 8RU, UK

Published in the United States of America by Cambridge University Press, New York

www.cambridge.org
Information on this title: www.cambridge.org/9780521762366

First published 2009

Printed in the United Kingdom at the University Press, Cambridge

A catalogue record for this publication is available from the British Library

Library of Congress Cataloging in Publication data
Schill, Stephan (Stephan W.)
The multilateralization of international investment law / Stephan W. Schill.
p.   cm.
ISBN 978-0-521-76236-6 (hardback)   1. Investments, Foreign–Law and
legislation.   2. Investments, Foreign (International law)   3. Arbitration and
award, International.   I. Title.
K3830.S34 2009
346.07–dc22
2009020685

ISBN 978-0-521-76236-6 hardback

Meinen Eltern

CONTENTS

PREFACE

International investment law is one of the fastest-growing and most vibrant fields of international law and dispute settlement today. It is both shaped by, and is shaping, the economic and social processes associated with globalization. In fact, it grows at a rate that makes authoring and publishing a book on international investment law an endeavor that evokes Achilles' footrace against the tortoise: an infinite struggle of catching up to a place and point in time that will be past present. Since the initial manuscript of this book was finalized in August 2008 the developments in arbitral jurisprudence, investment treaty making and scholarship have not paused. Instead, they have continued their exponential growth to now over 2,600 bilateral, regional and sectoral investment treaties and over 300 known investment treaty arbitrations that cover increasingly complex procedural and substantive issues and are accompanied by proliferating scholarship on various facets of international investment law. Although the most relevant subsequent developments in arbitral jurisprudence up to March 2009 have been worked into the book, in particular developments concerning the interpretation of most-favored-nation clauses, it can offer no more than a snapshot of where arbitral jurisprudence, investment treaty making and scholarship on international investment law currently stand, or will stand once this book courts for the attention of counsels and arbitrators in investment treaty disputes, scholars and students of international law and international relations, as well as officials in international organizations, domestic governments and non-governmental organizations active in the field.

While one of its core claims deals with the importance of arbitral jurisprudence for the interpretation and development of international investment law, the present book goes beyond a static perspective of investment jurisprudence and rather attempts to make a contribution towards developing a theory of international investment law that conceptualizes the dynamics of arbitral jurisprudence and investment treaty making. It concentrates on resolving one of the primary obstacles to developing a theory of international investment law, namely the apparently fragmented, disintegrated and chaotic state of the law that is embedded in numerous, largely bilateral treaties and implemented by arbitral tribunals which, established on a case-by-case basis, generate increasing jurisprudential inconsistencies. In analyzing investment treaty making and investment arbitration in a framework that focuses on bilateralism and multilateralism as institutional forms of international cooperation, the book argues that one can observe, despite the existing potential for fragmentation, convergence rather than divergence in this field of international law. In consequence, one can perceive of international investment law as a proper subsystem of international law and dispute resolution that provides a systematic legal framework for structuring, promoting and protecting investment activities in a global economic system that is based on largely uniform principles of investment protection and applies rather independently of the sources and targets of foreign investment flows. Elements of this thesis are the inclusion of most-favored-nation clauses, the possibilities of treaty-shopping through corporate structuring, and the contribution of investor-State dispute settlement through the intensive use of precedent and other genuinely multilateral approaches to treaty interpretation. The book therefore argues that investment treaties in their entirety function largely similar to a genuinely multilateral system and serve a constitutional function for the global economy by establishing institutions that enable economic actors to unfold their activities and to structure economic exchange in the field of foreign investment.

Similar to solving Zeno's problems, the thesis of the multilateralization of international investment law is intended to shift the thinking about ordering paradigms in international investment law away from bilateral – and necessarily limited – rationales towards a more principled theory of international investment law and thereby attempts to explain the paradoxical tension between the fragmentation of sources and dispute settlement institutions, on the one hand, and the creation of convergence, on the other. This thesis, it is hoped, provides a conceptual framework for understanding the nature and functioning of international investment law as a genuine system of law and dispute resolution and offers solutions to numerous practical and theoretical problems regarding, *inter alia*, questions of treaty interpretation, of the use of sources in international investment law and regarding the relationship between arbitral tribunals and States. It may also form the basis for developing a *Rechtsdogmatik* of the principles of substantive international investment law and arbitration which can guide the decision-making of arbitral tribunals and investment treaty makers in a more principled way than solely relying on arbitral precedent, as largely is the case in the current investment jurisprudence and scholarship. Moreover, understanding international investment law as a multilateral order is not only a descriptive claim; it also expresses the normative claim that multilateralism is a sensible and desirable perspective that investment treaty makers and arbitral tribunals should adopt.

The present book is the product of my PhD research that I conducted since the summer of 2004. It was accepted, in April 2008, as an inaugural dissertation at Johann Wolfgang Goethe-Universität Frankfurt am Main. The initial idea for the topic formed during a placement in a law firm in Buenos Aires from February to April 2002 which confronted me, then a legal trainee at the Court of Appeals of Munich, with researching, in the midst of the Argentine financial crisis, for a memorandum on the conformity of some of Argentina's emergency measures with the German–Argentine bilateral investment treaty. Then, unlike today, the material on investor rights, such as fair and equitable treatment, full protection and security or the prohibition of indirect expropriations without compensation, was rather scarce: there was virtually no investment treaty jurisprudence around and the soon-to-come explosion of investment treaty arbitrations was hardly predictable. Then, international investment law seemed like exotic, but quiet waters to explore. It is thus all the more exciting to see the development this area of international has embarked on over the past years.

My PhD research has benefitted from manifold professional, academic and personal experiences and thanks are due to the many friends, colleagues and mentors that have accompanied, supported and inspired me during these years. They are too numerous to mention and have helped, each in their own special way, to help the project go through. I owe special gratitude to my supervisor, Professor Dr. Armin von Bogdandy of the Max Planck Institute for Comparative Public Law and International Law in Heidelberg for his support and constructive criticism, and his reiterated demands that a doctoral thesis needed to explain the functioning of law not only in terms of lawfulness and unlawfulness, but also in terms of its contribution to and interaction with the underlying social, economic and ideological reality. This often daunting challenge and his encouragement throughout the entire period have helped immensely to focus my research, thinking and analysis. Likewise, thanks are due to the other members of my examination committee, in particular Professor Dr. Dr. Rainer Hofmann for his enthusiastic report, and Professor Dr. Peter von Wilmowsky for chairing the committee.

Critical for my research was a two-year stay at New York University where I first pursued the LL.M. program in International Legal Studies and later finalized the original manuscript. NYU's academic community and unique program in international law, as well as working as a research assistant with Professor Benedict Kingsbury, were particularly forming. The stay was made possible by a Hauser Global Scholarship, by a scholarship of the Studienstiftung des deutschen Volkes under the European Recovery Program and by the Lovells Scholarship. Of invaluable support and intellectual stimulus was further the mentorship of the late Professor Dr. Thomas Wälde who personally, and through the many participants of the OGEMID listserv, has strengthened my interest in and understanding of international investment law. Finally, the last revisions and updates of the book have benefitted from a clerkship at the International Court of Justice with Judge Abdul G. Koroma and a further clerkship with the Honorable Charles N. Brower of 20 Essex Street Chambers, London, during which I gained unparalleled insights into the real world of investor-State arbitration.

All of the above have contributed to the fact that the thesis was awarded the Baker & McKenzie Prize for the best doctoral dissertation with an economic law background at Johann Wolfgang Goethe-Universität as well as an Otto Hahn Medal for outstanding scientific achievements. I am honored and humbled by these awards and am grateful to the sponsors, the Frankfurt office of Baker & McKenzie and the Max Planck Society. I hope that this book will prove to be stimulating and contribute to a deeper understanding and the further development of international investment law and arbitration in its pioneering times.

LIST OF FIGURES

TABLE OF TREATIES, DRAFT INSTRUMENTS, AND RELATED DOCUMENTS

Multilateral treaties

Bilateral treaties

In addition to any sources indicated below, the texts of bilateral investment treaties can be found at www.unctadxi.org/templates/DocSearch_779.aspx

Draft instruments and other non-binding instruments and related material

TABLE OF CASES

Permanent Court of International Justice

International Court of Justice

International Tribunal for the Law of the Sea

GATT/WTO Dispute Settlement Body

European Court of Human Rights

European Court of Justice

Iran–United States Claims Tribunal

Arbitral awards and decisions by claims commissions

In addition to any source indicated below, most investment treaty awards can be found at: www.investmentclaims.com *or* http://ita.law.uvic.co

Decisions of Domestic Courts

I

Introduction: globalization and international investment law

> And the more important international economic interests grow, the more International Law will grow.
>
> Lassa Oppenheim, *International Law*, vol. I, § 51 (1905)

Economic interests are among the driving forces for creating and forging legal rules. Law, as a consequence, does not impose only normative guidance for individual behavior, but is itself a product of society, its needs, and preferences, and has the objective of sustaining social exchange. This holds true not only in the domestic realm but also at the international level. In fact, international law is developing, growing, and being refined at an unprecedented pace as the need for international legal rules abounds in reaction to the social and economic phenomenon of globalization.[1] Indeed, globalization, as one of the formative processes which affects today's cultural, political, and economic life virtually anywhere in the world, is gradually transforming international law from a simple tool to coordinate inter-State relations to an instrument that provides a legal structure for truly global social orders.

One of the characteristics of globalization is the growth of transborder economic activities: goods, services, and capital have progressively cast off territorial ties and circulate increasingly freely across borders.[2] This development not only enhances the options and choices of individual economic actors, both consumers and producers, but leads to expanding economic interdependences and to the increasing, yet still incomplete, integration of national economies into a global economic system.[3] At

---

[1] On the notion and concept of globalization from a sociological perspective see Beck, *What is Globalization?* (2000).

[2] For an historical account of economic globalization see Rourke and Williamson, *Globalization and History* (1999).

[3] Even though economic globalization is not a linear, nor necessarily an irreversible development, but rather an evolutionary process towards economic integration which has, up to this moment, not abided in a unitary and borderless economic space, we can

the same time, the release of economic activity from territorial linkages challenges both the ability of States to regulate their economy[4] and their capacity to provide the legal institutions that are necessary for the functioning of a global economy.[5] Such institutions include, for example, the legal concepts of contract and property rights, as well as regulatory frameworks, compliance procedures and dispute settlement mechanisms that enable economic actors to unfold their activity and to structure economic exchange.

As a consequence, the demand for law as an ordering structure progressively shifts from the national to the international level. This shift can be witnessed with regard to international trade and monetary law, where the World Trade Organization (WTO) and the International Monetary Fund (IMF) and their respective legal regimes establish legal and institutional infrastructures that enable and enhance transborder economic exchange.[6] International trade law, for instance, contains principles of non-discrimination and anti-protectionism that, to a certain extent and subject to exceptions, enable competition in order for a global market to function. Similarly, international monetary law attempts to stabilize exchange rates in order to achieve monetary stability as a basis for international financial transactions and capital markets. International cooperation is necessary in these instances, because individual States struggle to provide the rules and institutions that are necessary for global economic exchange.

---

nevertheless understand such transborder economic activities as forming part of the economic system of the *Weltgesellschaft* ("global society"). On the understanding of the economy as a functional sub-system of society see Luhmann, *Die Wirtschaft der Gesellschaft*, pp. 43–90 (1988). On the concept of the "global society" see Luhmann, *Die Gesellschaft der Gesellschaft*, pp. 145–71 (1997); Luhmann, *Die Weltgesellschaft*, 57 Archiv für Rechts- und Sozialphilosophie 1 (1971).

[4] von Bogdandy, *Globalization and Europe*, 15 Eur. J. Int'l L. 885, 886 (2004).

[5] Institutions are understood in North, *Structure and Change in Economic History*, pp. 201 *et seq.* (1981), as "a set of rules, compliance procedures, and moral and ethical behavioral norms designed to constrain the behavior of individuals in the interests of maximizing the wealth or utility of principals," or more plastically: "Institutions are the rules of the game in a society or, more formally, are the humanly devised constraints that shape human interaction." (North, *Institutions, Institutional Change, and Economic Performance*, p. 3 [1990]). Institutions are characterized by constraints with a certain permanence and durability which are imposed on actors of any kind. Legal rules that impose restrictions on the behavior of individuals as well as legal requirements that concern the exercise of public power, therefore, qualify as institutions in this sense.

[6] See Jackson, *Global Economics and International Economic Law*, 1 J. Int'l Econ. L. 1 (1998).

A   International investment law as a building block of the global economy

The shift from national to international level holds equally true for international investment relations, where the demand for international investment law has amplified parallel to an increase in foreign investment flows since the end of the Second World War – and even more so since the end of the Cold War.[7] In fact, foreign investment often takes place in a situation that requires international cooperation as an ordering structure, not so much because of the element of transborder flows of investment, but due to the involvement of the host State as a sovereign actor. While host State and investor initially have largely converging interests in attracting and making investments, the situation changes once an investment has been made. As the investor's option to simply withdraw his investment and re-employ it elsewhere without severe financial loss is limited, the host State has an incentive to change unilaterally the original investment terms by changing an investment contract, amending the law governing the investment, or even expropriating the investor without compensation.[8] This so-called political risk stemming from opportunistic behavior of the host State not only increases the cost of investment for investors and consumers, it may even prevent the flow of foreign investment completely.[9] As a consequence, promoting and protecting foreign investment behooves the establishment of institutions that reduce political risk and outweigh incentives for the host State to act opportunistically in order for private actors to unfold foreign investment activities.

In the domestic context, the task of establishing institutions in order to ensure the proper functioning of the economy, and of imposing constraints on the government's power to regulate and to interfere in economic activities, is largely, but not exclusively, performed by the State and its domestic legal system.[10] Liberal legal systems, in particular, limit government to

---

[7] On the development of foreign investment flows see UNCTAD, *World Investment Report 2007*, pp. 3 *et seq.* (2007).

[8] This change in incentives after one party has started performing or placed an asset under the control of the other party is also described as a hold-up or dynamic inconsistency problem. See Williamson, *The Economic Institutions of Capitalism*, pp. 52 *et seq.* (1985); Guzman, *Why LDCs Sign Treaties that Hurt Them*, 38 Va. J. Int'l L. 639, 658 *et seq.* (1998). Unlike contractual situations where mutual obligations are carried out in a directly reciprocal and simultaneous manner, foreign investment is, therefore, comparable to contracts involving the performance of continuing obligations.

[9] See Cooter and Ulen, *Law and Economics*, pp. 195–200 (4th edn. 2004).

[10] See Furubotn and Richter, *Institutions and Economic Theory*, pp. 265–434 (1997); on the relation between the State and the economy in particular, see also pp. 265–78, 413–20;

acting in accordance with pre-established rules and procedures and restrict its activity by granting rights to individuals and companies.[11] Adherence to the rule of law and the prohibition of expropriations, for example, seek to avoid public opportunism and rent-seeking behavior. At the same time, liberal legal systems allow private parties to engage in economic exchange by delineating property rights, by recognizing enforceable contracts, and by providing dispute settlement mechanisms in courts.

The existence of these institutions is crucial not only for individual investment decisions,[12] but also positively impacts economic growth and development. In fact, the link between the protection of property rights, contract enforcement, government according to the rule of law, and dispute settlement by independent courts, on the one hand, and macroeconomic growth, on the other hand, is stressed by institutional economics and buttressed by theoretical and empirical studies.[13] Conversely, the lack of these institutions is widely regarded as one of the reasons for low levels of foreign investment, for low income levels, and underdevelopment.[14] Even though increases in foreign investment inflows may in and of themselves not create growth,[15] protecting property rights, contract enforcement,

North, *Institutions,* pp. 27–69 (both pointing out that formal and informal, public and private arrangements provide the institutional backbone of any economic system).

[11] See Luhmann, *Grundrechte als Institution* (1965) (outlining an understanding of fundamental rights as performing a specific social function).

[12] World Bank, *World Development Report 1997,* pp. 34 *et seq.* (1997) (reporting the results of a survey concluding that investors primarily make their investment decisions dependent upon the credibility of States to ensure a predictable and stable legal framework).

[13] See Buscaglia, Ratcliff and Cooter, *The Law and Economics of Development* (1997); Platteau, *Institutions, Social Norms, and Economic Development* (2000). More recently on the connection between institutions and growth see Rodrik, Subramanian and Trebbi, *Institutions Rule,* 9 J. Econ. Growth 131 (2004); Acemoglu, Johnson and Robinson, *Institutions as the Fundamental Cause of Long-Run Growth,* in Aghion and Durlauf (eds.), *Handbook of Economic Growth,* vol. 1A, p. 385 (2005); Bénassy-Quéré, Coupet and Mayer, *Institutional Determinants of Foreign Direct Investment,* 30 World Econ. 764 (2007). Critical on the causality between political institutions and growth Glaeser *et al.,* *Do Institutions Cause Growth?,* 9 J. Econ. Growth 271 (2004).

[14] See *supra* footnote 13.

[15] On the causality relations between foreign investment and growth see Hansen and Rand, *On the Causal Links between FDI and Growth in Developing Countries,* 29 World Econ. 21 (2006); Chowdhury and Mavrotas, *FDI and Growth: What Causes What?,* 29 World Econ. 9 (2006) (both suggesting bidirectional causality between foreign direct investment and growth). See also Prasad *et al.,* *Effects of Financial Globalization on Developing Countries,* IMF Occasional Paper 220, paras. 45–70 (2003); Carkovic and Levine, *Does Foreign Direct Investment Accelerate Economic Growth?,* in Moran, Graham and Blomström, *Does Foreign Direct Investment Promote Development?,* p. 195 (2005). See further *infra* Ch. III.C.1.

government according to the rule of law, and dispute settlement by independent courts is crucial for increased economic activity through foreign and local investment and economic growth more generally. Foreign investment activity, in turn, is thus widely regarded as having positive impacts on the host State economy.[16]

Yet, the legal systems of many developing and transitioning economies do not provide the institutions that are necessary to attract and sustain foreign investment and to integrate developing economies into a global market. Their national legal systems often struggle to provide a sufficiently stable and predictable legal framework that protects property and effectively restricts opportunistic conduct of the executive and the legislator. Furthermore, a significant number of countries have difficulties in setting efficient court-based dispute settlement mechanisms in place that are independent vis-à-vis the government and enable investors to enforce their rights against the State and private parties alike.

Against the backdrop of such insufficiencies in many domestic legal systems, international legal instruments have developed to accompany the worldwide increase in foreign investment flows. They respond to the need and interests of foreign investors and their home States for protection and to the desire of host States to attract foreign investment. The international legal framework consists of international treaties providing for the settlement of disputes between foreign investors and host States, instruments providing for investment guarantees, and more than 2,500 bilateral, regional and sectoral investment treaties that contain substantive standards for the protection of foreign investors against undue government interference.[17] These treaties typically grant national treatment, most-favored-nation treatment, fair and equitable treatment, and full protection and security, prohibit direct and indirect expropriations without compensation, and contain the consent of host States to investor-State arbitration.[18] By doing so, they provide a substitute for the

---

[16] Bhagwati, *Why Multinationals Help Reduce Poverty*, 30 World Econ. 211 (2007); but see Axarloglou and Pournarakis, *Do All Foreign Direct Investment Flows Benefit the Local Economy*, 30 World Econ. 424 (2007) (arguing that benefits from foreign investment inflows also depend on the specific industry sector affected in the host State). See also *infra* Ch. III.C.1.

[17] On the statistical increase of investment treaties see UNCTAD, *Bilateral Investment Treaties in the Mid-1990s*, p. 9 (1998); see further UNCTAD, *Recent Developments in International Investment Agreements (2006–June 2007)*, p. 2 (2007) (recording an aggregate of 2,573 bilateral investment treaties at the end of 2006).

[18] For general accounts of investment treaties and related instruments of investment protection see, for example, Dolzer and Stevens, *Bilateral Investment Treaties* (1995);

failure of many domestic legal systems to provide institutions necessary for sustainable economic activities and economic growth.[19]

B International investment law, economic ideology and hegemony

Certainly, this function of international investment law is closely connected to the interests of those foreign investors and States that push for increasingly globalized markets and the legal framework that accompanies them. In particular, the economic and political power of capital-exporting States translates into structures that favor the economic system they prefer, that is, essentially the liberal, market-based model that relies on property rights and government according to the rule of law. This model of global economics is, in turn, a prolongation and projection of the models prevailing in the national economies of traditional capital-exporting States. Accordingly, in the political and legal debate about globalization, its benefits and discontents, international investment law has been the focus of much criticism. Not only the scope of property protection under international law[20] and the tension between investment protection and other competing policy concerns, such as environmental protection or labor standards, have attracted critical attention.[21] Also

Sacerdoti, *Bilateral Treaties and Multilateral Instruments on Investment Protection*, 269 Recueil des Cours 251 (1997); Sornarajah, *The International Law of Foreign Investment*, pp. 204–314 (2nd edn. 2004); McLachlan, Shore and Weiniger, *International Investment Arbitration – Substantive Principles* (2007); Lowenfeld, *International Economic Law*, pp. 467–591 (2nd edn. 2008); Dolzer and Schreuer, *Principles of International Investment Law* (2008); Muchlinski, Ortino and Schreuer (eds.), *The Oxford Handbook of International Investment Law* (2008).

[19] See also Ginsburg, *International Substitutes for Domestic Institutions*, 25 Int'l Rev. L. & Econ. 107 (2005).

[20] See, for example, Been and Beauvais, *The Global Fifth Amendment?*, 78 N.Y.U. L. Rev. 30 (2003); Porterfield, *An International Common Law of Investor Rights?*, 27 U. Pa. J. Int'l Econ. L. 79 (2006) (both criticizing the ambiguity of investor rights, such as fair and equitable treatment and the concept of indirect expropriation).

[21] On the tensions between investment protection and environmental protection see, for example, Strazzeri, *A Lucas Analysis of Regulatory Expropriations under NAFTA Chapter Eleven*, 14 Geo. Int'l Envtl. L. Rev. 837 (2002); Gantz, *Potential Conflicts Between Investor Rights and Environmental Regulation Under NAFTA's Chapter 11*, 33 Geo. Wash. Int'l L. Rev. 651 (2001); Verhoosel, *Foreign Direct Investment and Legal Constraints on Domestic Environmental Policies*, 29 L. & Pol'y Int'l Bus. 451 (1998); Stone, *NAFTA Article 1110: Environmental Friend or Foe?*, 15 Geo. Int'l Envtl. L. 763 Rev. (2003); Gudofsky, *Shedding Light on Article 1110 of the North American Free Trade Agreement (NAFTA) Concerning Expropriations*, 21 Nw. J. Int'l L. & Bus. 243 (2000); Wagner, *International Investment: Expropriation and Environmental Protection*, 29 Golden Gate U. L. Rev. 465 (1999).

the way international investment rules are negotiated, concluded, and implemented has been criticized as constituting the product of hegemonic behavior of capital-exporting countries that aim at preserving their dominance in relation to politically and economically weaker States.[22]

To a certain extent, this critique is a prolongation of the battle of ideologies between more liberal and more communitarian approaches to the relationship between the individual and society in general, and to the gestalt of the global economy in particular. On the level of international investment law, this debate often crystallizes in opposing views on State sovereignty and societal self-determination versus the protection of property, in particular foreign property. Accordingly, much of the critique of international investment treaties focuses on the substantive balance – or, better, the alleged imbalance – between investment protection and competing interests of host States and their constituencies. It concentrates on the content and scope of the rules and principles contained in investment treaties and asserts that they carry unwarranted advantages for foreign investors and capital-exporting States. This critique, therefore, engages in a moral debate about the desirability, the advantages, and the disadvantages that a system of international investment protection has and which interests it favors.

The current study, by contrast, does not focus primarily on the substantive scope of international investment protection and the question of how a proper balance with competing interests of host States can or should be achieved. It does not engage in a moral and philosophical apology of property protection and liberal economics, but is based on the assumption that the liberal market model informs the development and functioning of global economics and international investment law, without however making investment protection immune from competing policy concerns.[23] The focus of this book is much more to show to what

---

[22] See Benvenisti and Downs, *The Empire's New Clothes*, 60 Stan. L. Rev. 595, 611–12 (2007). See also Chimni, *International Institutions Today: An Imperial Global State in the Making*, 15 Eur. J. Int'l L. 1, 7 *et seq.* (2004); Chimni, *Marxism and International Law*, Economic and Political Weekly, p. 337 (February 6, 1999); see also Chung, *The Lopsided International Investment Law Regime and Its Effect on the Future of Investor-State Arbitration*, 47 Va. J. Int'l L. 953 (2007). See further *infra* Ch. III.B.3.

[23] See Vandevelde, *The Political Economy of a Bilateral Investment Treaty*, 92 A.J.I.L. 621, 627 (1998) (arguing that "BITs present themselves as quintessentially liberal documents"); see also Vandevelde, *Investment Liberalization and Economic Development*, 36 Colum. J. Transnat'l L. 501 (1998) (emphasizing that BITs form part of a movement to liberalize the international economy while leaving States considerable leeway for intervention); Vandevelde, *Sustainable Liberalism and the International Investment Regime*,

extent it is possible to perceive international investment law as part of the legal framework that emerges from and, at the same time, drives economic globalization.

While political and economic factors play a role in the development of international investment law, just as moral, political, and economic power shapes municipal societies and the legal and political rules they endorse for the organization of national economies, this book proposes to understand investment treaties in terms of the function they perform for the global economic system. Accordingly, it contrasts the hegemonic critique of investment law with the aspiration and objective of this field of international law to establish institutions that support the functioning of a market-based global economy and stresses that the body of investment law applies indiscriminately to capital-exporting and capital-importing States. This view becomes increasingly apposite the more the distinction between capital exporters and capital importers dissolves, and the more national economies integrate into a global economy.[24] In this perspective, it is less States and their economies that interact with each other in the international economic system but private actors engaging in competition. International investment law, in turn, is about providing the framework for private economic activity in an emerging global economic space.[25]

C   The choice between bilateralism and multilateralism

The development of international investment law after the Second World War on the basis of bilateral treaties contrasts significantly with the multilateral development in other areas of international economic law, in particular international trade and international monetary law. While multilateralism dominated international relations in these fields through the establishment of international organizations, such as the General Agreement on Tariffs and Trade (GATT) and later the WTO, as well as the IMF, several approaches to establish a multilateral investment regime based on a multilateral treaty failed.[26] Instead, international investment

---

19 Mich. J. Int'l L. 373 (1998) (arguing that BITs represent at least a temporary consensus on a liberal order for international investment relations).

[24] See *infra* Ch. III B.3.

[25] *Cf.* Vandevelde, *A Brief History of International Investment Agreements*, 12 U.C. Davis J. Intl L. & Pol'y 157, 183 (2005) (considering pointing investment agreements as "instruments of globalization").

[26] See *infra* Chs. II. B and II E.

law has developed on the basis of a myriad of bilateral, regional, and sectoral investment treaties. The structure of the international economy thus came to be compared with an unbalanced and unstable two-legged stool supported only by international trade and monetary law.[27] Indeed, this choice for bilateralism in international investment law seems surprising compared with the general decision for multilateralism in the other main areas of international economic relations.[28]

Both bilateralism and multilateralism are forms of international cooperation. The major differences between both forms relate to the number of parties to an international agreement and the nature of the rules governing inter-State conduct. From a purely formal perspective, bilateralism refers to ordering relations between States on a dyadic basis, whereas multilateralism concerns "the practice of coordinating national policies in groups of three of more states."[29] More importantly, however, multilateralism differs with respect to the nature of the obligations it creates. Unlike, for example, the imposition of unilaterally favorable standards of conduct by one hegemon upon several other States, a behavior that would qualify as multilateralism under the purely formal understanding, "multilateralism is an institutional form that coordinates relations among three or more states on the basis of generalized principles of conduct: that is, principles which specify appropriate conduct for a class of actions, without regard to the particularistic interests of the parties or the strategic exigencies that may exist in any specific occurrence."[30] It is thus primarily the nature of the rules that regulate inter-State relations rather than their pedigree that characterizes multilateralism.

Multilateralism in this understanding draws a clear distinction between form and content and posits that the core characteristic of multilateral rules is their generalized and non-discriminatory application to all participating actors, rather than the creation of these rules in two-party or multi-party settings. A classic example of such generalized principles are notions of equal treatment and non-discrimination that subject all States

---

[27] See Kline, *International Regulation of Transnational Business*, 2 Transnat'l Corp. 153, 154 (February 1993).

[28] It bears, however, noting that other areas of international economic law also know countermovements in the form of bilateralism and regionalism. See, for example, the contributions in Demaret, Bellis and García Jimenez (eds.), *Regionalism and Multilateralism after the Uruguay Round* (1997); Okediji, *Back to Bilateralism?*, 1 U. Ottawa L. & Tech. J. 125 (2003–2004).

[29] Koehane, *Multilateralism: An Agenda for Research*, 45 Int'l J. 731 (1990).

[30] Ruggie, *Multilateralism: The Anatomy of an Institution*, in Ruggie (ed.), *Multilateralism Matters*, pp. 3, 11 (1993).

to the same standard of conduct independent of their relative factual power. In addition, multilateralism is characterized by "diffuse reciprocity," meaning that benefits from international cooperation are expected to derive over time without the participants being able to determine at the outset who the benefitting participants will be.[31] It thus presupposes uniform rules and standards of conduct for the States participating in a multilateral regime and equal participatory rights under the rules of the regime. Multilateralism thus has the aspiration of ordering international relations on the basis of universal principles.[32] Bilateralism, by contrast, is characterized by specific reciprocity, or *quid pro quo* bargains, and usually manifests itself in rules that favor the interest of the more powerful States.[33]

Consequently, multilateralism is also an alternative concept to a hegemonic order that is characterized by rules that unilaterally favor the hegemon's self-interests without placing other participating actors on an equal footing. However, it is necessary to distinguish between hegemonic elements in the realization of certain rules and principles governing international relations, and the hegemonic nature of the rules that emerge. In other words, even though hegemony may have influenced the process of establishing international cooperation in a specific context, the result of such hegemonic behavior is not necessarily a regime based on hegemonic and, therefore, non-multilateral rules and principles.[34] Instead, multilateralism, as it is understood in the context of this study, distinguishes between procedure and content and is premised on the content-based definition. Legal rules and principles, and the relation between States under a certain regime, are therefore considered as multilateral if they are based on non-discriminatory principles, independent of whether their generative process was influenced by hegemonic conduct.

The core difference between multilateralism and bilateralism as forms of international cooperation, therefore, concerns the nature of the relations among States. While bilateralism puts the State and its sovereignty center stage, assumes a primacy of national interests, and allows for preferential and discriminatory treatment among States depending

---

[31] Ruggie, *ibid.*

[32] *Cf.* Caporaso, *International Relations Theory and Multilateralism: The Search for Foundations*, in Ruggie (ed.) (*supra* footnote 30), pp. 51, 55 (1993).

[33] Ruggie, in Ruggie (*supra* footnote 30), p. 11 (1993).

[34] *Cf.* Ruggie (*supra* footnote 30), pp. 24–31 (1993) (analyzing the influence of American hegemony on multilateralism after the Second World War).

on their relative power,[35] multilateralism views States as embedded in an international community,[36] stresses the primacy of international law over national interests,[37] and presupposes that international relations are ordered on the basis of non-discriminatory principles that apply to all States. The difference between bilateralism and multilateralism is thus comparable to the difference between private law contracts, that order two-party relationships, and statutes or constitutions that provide generally applicable rules and principles for the organization of society as a whole. While contracts concern the exchange of specific performances, general statutes and constitutions establish a general framework, a public order within which specific transactions can take place.

D Investment treaties – instruments of bilateralism or elements of a multilateral system?

The mere number of more than 2,500 bilateral investment treaties (BITs) suggests a chaotic and unsystematic aggregate of substantive rules governing international investment relations. Rather than constituting a consistent and coherent system of law, one would expect an extreme divergence and fragmentation in this area of international cooperation. The fragmentation into bilateral treaties should in fact compromise any attempts at understanding international investment law as providing uniform institutions for the functioning of a global economy. Instead, differentiated standards, such as preferential and discriminatory treatment, should be the result of bilateral treaty-making.

However, what one can observe is a convergence, not a divergence, in structure, scope, and content of existing investment treaties. This material convergence is particularly surprising in view of the continuous failure of multilateral investment treaties and the greater flexibility bilateralism offers in tailoring international obligations to the specific relationship between two States.[38] It also contrasts with the phenomenon in

---

[35] See Simma, *From Bilateralism to Community Interest in International Law*, 250 Recueil des Cours 217, 230–33 (1994).

[36] *Ibid.*, pp. 233–49.

[37] *Cf* J. Alvarez, *Multilateralism and Its Discontents*, 11 Eur. J. Int'l L. 393, 394 (2000) (referring to multilateralism as a "shared secular religion" that "requires preferring ... 'the international over the national, integration over sovereignty'" – quoting from Koskenniemi, *International Law in a Post-Realist Era*, 16 Australian Ybk. Int'l L. 1 [1995]).

[38] See more generally, on the variables that explain the institutional choice between bilateralism and multilateralism, Rixen and Rohlfing, *The Institutional Choice of Bilateralism*

international trade relations where bilateralism, respectively regionalism, is generally viewed as a departure from non-discriminatory treatment and a threat to multilateralism.[39]

The setback of multilateralism in international investment relations and the proliferation of virtually identical BITs therefore confront the observer with a startling conundrum. How can we explain these seemingly contradictory phenomena? What are the implications for a theory of international investment law and what are the consequences for the practice of investment treaty arbitration? Can we perceive of international investment law as ordering international investment relations on the basis of uniform and, therefore, multilateral principles that respond to the needs of a global economy? Or does international investment law remain in the bilateralist tradition of international law that considers State sovereignty as pre-eminent and perceives of international treaties purely as products of national interests backed by the power of the States in question? BITs would then merely constitute instruments of bilateral and, therefore, discriminatory and disintegrative strategies instead of a harmonized framework for international investment relations.[40]

The difference between bilateralism and multilateralism is relevant not only with respect to aspects concerning the organization and conduct of international relations. The difference also plays out concerning the application and interpretation of investment treaties. Above all, the apparent fragmentation of the sources of international investment law entails a number of methodological concerns relating to the application and interpretation of investment treaties. What weight should, for instance, be attached to variations in the wording of different treaties? What is the value, if any, of a decision of an investment tribunal interpreting the BIT between the United States and Argentina for the interpretation

---

and Multilateralism in International Trade and Taxation, 12 Int'l Negotiation 389 (2007).

[39] See Bhagwati, The World Trading System at Risk, pp. 58–79 (1991); Bhagwati, Regionalism and Multilateralism, in de Melo and Panagariya (eds.), New Dimensions in Regional Integration, pp. 22 et seq. (1993). But see Pomfret, Is Regionalism an Increasing Feature of the World Economy?, 30 World Econ. 923 (2007) (suggesting that the threat to the multilateral trading system does not appear as big as is often feared). Similarly, Baldwin, Multilateralising Regionalism, 29 World Econ. 1451 (2006); Abbott, A New Dominant Trade Species Emerges, 10 J. Int'l Econ. L. 571 (2007).

[40] In this sense Sornarajah, A Coming Crisis: Expansionary Trends in Investment Treaty Arbitration, in Sauvant (ed.), Appeals Mechanism in International Investment Disputes, pp. 39, 45–48 (2008); similarly Juillard, Variations in the Substantive Provisions and Interpretation of International Investment Agreements, in Sauvant, ibid., pp. 81, 88–93 (2008); see also Drahos, BITs and BIPs, 4 J. World Int. Prop. 791 (2001).

of the BIT between Germany and China? Can we presume that identically worded standards contained in different investment treaties have the same meaning? For example, is the meaning of fair and equitable treatment in the BIT between Peru and the United Kingdom identical to the one in the BIT between the Netherlands and Kenya? Or do they have to be applied and interpreted independently?

The dynamics between bilateralism and multilateralism in international investment relations also affect the determination of the nature of investment treaties. Do they resemble contracts or do they constitute elements of a multilateral system that organizes international investment relations on the basis of general principles that overarch the individual bilateral treaty relationships and serve a constitutional function for the global economy?[41] Do they constitute a sub-system of international law or a patchwork without an inherent logic that is far from backing an international economic order? If investment treaties merely constituted bilateral bargains between two States, they should be interpreted according to primarily bilateral rationales that take into account the

---

[41] The reference to a "constitutional function" of investment treaties is not related to the democratic understanding of constitutionalism by proponents of "political constitutionalism," but to the notion of "economic constitutionalism" that views the function of constitutions in establishing principles and rights for the organization of the economy. See Jayasuriya, *Globalization, Sovereignty, and the Rule of Law*, 8 Constellations 442 (2001). Specifically on the constitutional function of international investment law see Schneiderman, *Investment Rules and the New Constitutionalism*, 25 L. & Soc. Inquiry 757 (2000); Schneiderman, *Investment Rules and the Rule of Law*, 8 Constellations 521, 523 *et seq.* (2001); Schneiderman, *Constitutionalizing Economic Globalization* (2008); Afilalo, *Constitutionalization Through the Backdoor*, 34 N.Y.U. J. Int'l L. & Pol. 1 (2001); Behrens, *Wirtschaftsverfassungsrechtliche Ansätze im völkerrechtlichen Investitionsschutz*, in Engel and Möschel (eds.), *Recht und spontane Ordnung – Festschrift für Ernst-Joachim Mestmäcker*, p. 53 (2006); Behrens, *Towards the Constitutionalization of International Investment Protection*, 45 AVR 153 (2007); Tams, *Konstitutionalisierungstendenzen im Recht des internationalen Investitionsschutzes*, in Tietje and Nowrot (eds.), *Verfassungsrechtliche Dimensionen des Internationalen Wirtschaftsrechts*, p. 229 (2007). For related discussions in international trade law, European law, and domestic legal systems, see Hilf and Petersmann (eds.), *National Constitutions and International Economic Law* (1993); Trachtman, *The Constitutions of the WTO*, 17 Eur. J. Int'l L. 646 (2006); Dunoff, *Constitutional Conceits*, 17 Eur. J. Int'l L. 675 (2006); E. Petersmann, *Constitutional Functions and Constitutional Problems of International Economic Law* (1991); E. Petersmann, *Constitutionalization and WTO Law*, in Kennedy and Southwick (eds.), *The Political Economics of International Trade Law*, p. 32 (2002); Müller-Graff, *Die konstitutionelle Rolle der binnenmarktrechtlichen Grundfreiheiten im neuen Europäischen Verfassungsvertrag*, in Köck, Lengauer and Ress (eds.), *Europarecht im Zeitalter der Globalisierung – Festschrift für Peter Fischer*, p. 363 (2004); Posner, *The Constitution as an Economic Document*, 56 Geo. Wash. L. Rev. 4 (1987).

interests of the parties concerned exclusively. Investment treaties would then essentially constitute the international law pendant of contracts. Multilateral considerations in interpretation would, by contrast, stress elements of providing an objective order for States on the basis of treaty-overarching principles similar to domestic constitutions.

The distinction between bilateralism and multilateralism also has repercussions for the function and objective of investor-State dispute settlement and the decisions rendered by arbitral tribunals. It relates to the question of whether investment treaty disputes are simply concerned with the resolution of a dispute between two parties to an arbitration, or whether investment treaty arbitration has a broader impact on, and serves a wider purpose for, an international system of investment protection and thus involves a different responsibility of arbitrators? This question is closely related to the determination of the nature of investment treaty arbitration as constituting either a special form of international commercial arbitration that backs up a private law order between investors and States without touching upon points of concern for the international community, or as constituting a sub-category of dispute resolution under public international law that forms part of the institutional framework of a public international order that encompasses aims beyond purely economic interests in bilateral inter-State relations.

The distinction between bilateralism and multilateralism also lurks behind an increasingly voiced concern about the risk of inconsistent decisions in investment treaty arbitration that could compromise the stability and predictability of international investment law. Commentators, in this context, frequently allude to a "legitimacy crisis" in investment arbitration.[42] Again, what this critique obviously presupposes is that, notwithstanding the fragmentation of its sources, international investment law is based on the premise that an overarching system of investment protection exists.

---

[42] C. N. Brower, *A Crisis of Legitimacy*, Nat'l L. J., October 7, 2002; C. H. Brower, *Structure, Legitimacy, and NAFTA's Investment Chapter*, 36 Vand. J. Transnat'l L. 37 (2003); C. H. Brower, C. N. Brower and Sharpe, *The Coming Crisis in the Global Adjudicative System*, 19 Arb. Int'l 415 (2003); Afilalo, *Towards a Common Law of International Investment*, 17 Geo. Int'l Envt'l L. Rev. 51 (2004); Afilalo, *Meaning, Ambiguity and Legitimacy*, 25 Nw. J. Int'l L. & Bus. 279, 282 (2005); Franck, *The Legitimacy Crisis in Investment Treaty Arbitration*, 73 Fordham L. Rev. 1521 (2005); Sornarajah (*supra* footnote 40), pp. 41–44 (2008); see also Gurudevan, *An Evaluation of Current Legitimacy-based Objections to NAFTA's Chapter 11 Investment Dispute Resolution Process*, 6 San Diego Int'l L. J. 399 (2005).

If this was indeed the case, is it possible that the bilateral form of most investment treaties in fact constitutes a misnomer that obscures the multilateral nature of the governing regime for international investment relations? Or, should we not take the failure of multilateralism in international investment relations on its face, interpret it as an expression of the lack of uniform standards, and consequently discard concerns about inconsistencies? Is the quest for coherence not merely a remnant of the romanticized belief of lawyers in the consistency of legal norms that blends out that States have not managed to create a genuinely multilateral system of investment protection and therefore have no interest in it? Or do we instead witness the emergence of a system of investment protection that follows uniform rationales despite its being based on bilateral treaties?

E The multilateralization of international investment law on the basis of bilateral treaties

The form of investment treaties as bilateral treaties suggests that this area of international law and relations is coined by bilateral rationales. It suggests not only that the content of these treaties contains *quid pro quo* bargains that follow the relative negotiating power of the two contracting State parties and provide for unbalanced solutions to questions of investment protection, but also that international investment law is subject to an infinite fragmentation into unconnected and chaotic dyadic treaty relations. This would make it impossible to understand this area of law as a system of law or perceive it as part of an overarching order for international economic relations. As a consequence, it would be impossible to develop theories and doctrines concerning principles of international investment protection that could help to develop systemic solutions for recurring problems in investment law and arbitration.

However, the consistent failure of multilateral instruments and the rise of bilateral treaties do not imply that multilateralism as an institution in investment relations has not materialized to a certain extent or does not serve as an ordering paradigm for this field of international relations. Unlike genuinely bilateral treaties, that is, treaties that are bilateral in form and substance, BITs do not stand isolated in governing the relation between the two contracting States only; they rather develop multiple overlaps and structural interconnections that, it is argued, create a uniform and treaty-overarching regime for international investments. BITs in their entirety, it is argued, function analogously to a truly multilateral system as they establish rather uniform general principles that order the relations between foreign investors and host States in a relatively uniform manner independently of the sources and targets of specific transborder investment flows. Instead of being prone to almost infinite fragmentation, international investment law is thus developing into a uniform governing structure for foreign investment with only limited room for insular deviation by individual States.

Certainly, the texts of all investment treaties are not identical – and differences in wording can matter. Consequently, the argument is not that the BIT regime is fully equivalent to a multilateral treaty with complete uniformity among all individual investment treaties. The argument is instead that there is sufficient convergence among them, namely that investment treaties follow uniform rationales, they are based on rather uniform investment law principles, and are implemented through rather uniform institutional mechanisms. It is thus possible to understand the web of investment treaties, whether bilateral, regional or sectoral, as part of a treaty-overarching legal framework that backs up the functioning of an international investment market within the emerging global economy. While investment treaties do not, therefore, represent an emulation of a multilateral system, the BIT framework, it is argued, shows sufficient parallels to a multilateral investment regime in order to support the thesis that international investment law is multilateralizing on the basis of bilateral treaties.

From a broader perspective and against the widespread concerns uttered in various other fields of international law, such as international trade law, international criminal law, international environmental law or the law on the use of force, that multilateralism is under challenge, partly by unilateralism, partly by bilateralism,[43] the argument presented here involves the paradoxical claim that the conclusion of bilateral treaties may have the effect of resulting in a system that possesses very similar, if not the same, essential features as a multilateral system. While this multilateralism is not procedural in nature or connected to the claim that bilateral or multilateral treaty-making would not result in different substantive contents, it claims that bilateral treaty-making in the context of international investment law nevertheless results in the implementation of generally applicable rules and principles, just as if these rules were enshrined in a

---

[43] Newman, Thakur and Tirman (eds.), *Multilateralism under Challenge? Power, International Order, and Structural Change* (2006) (with numerous contributions on challenges to multilateralism in recent years).

formal multilateral treaty. They do not, by contrast, aim at establishing preferential treatment between specific bilateral sets of States.

The claim connected with this multilateralization is twofold. First, it involves a descriptive claim that suggests that it is possible to understand international investment law as a sub-system of international law that progresses, on the basis of bilateral treaties, towards a universal system which is not based on specific reciprocity, but orders investment relations objectively on the basis of general principles. In this context, it provides a theoretic foundation to a claim that is often made, but rarely explicitly conceptualized, namely that it is possible to speak of a system of international investment protection.[44] It follows that investment treaties do not aim primarily at protecting and promoting investment flows in bilateral relationships, but have a broader function in creating institutions that back up an international market economy in which capital flows in an increasingly liberal fashion between different national economies to wherever it is allocated most efficiently.

Investment treaties are, therefore, not designed to function like private law contracts that order the relationship between a limited number of parties and contain the exchange of specific transactions, but have a constitutional function in providing a legal framework within which international investment activities can take shape and expand. As such, investment treaties are embedded in a larger framework of international law that overarches the individual bilateral treaty relations and establishes uniform rules for the conduct of host States that consist in adopting a liberal attitude vis-à-vis market mechanisms and that accept the limited role of the State vis-à-vis the economy.[45] Notwithstanding, international investment law is primarily concerned with granting protection to foreign investments, rather than regulating their access to foreign countries and thus allowing the free circulation of capital.

Second, the claim that international investment treaties constitute a multilateralized system is normative in the sense that multilateralism rather than bilateralism should inform the application and interpretation of investment treaties. In their interpretation of investment treaties, arbitral tribunals should thus give appropriate weight to the multilateral aspirations of investment law. As a normative claim, the evolving multilateralization of international investment law justifies existing practices in

---

[44] See Van Harten, *Investment Treaty Arbitration and Public Law*, pp. 24 *et seq.* (2007); Van Harten, *Private Authority and Transnational Governance*, 12 Rev. Int'l Pol. Econ. 600 (2005).

[45] See *supra* footnote 23.

investment treaty arbitration, namely the extensive use of precedent and other interpretative techniques that favor uniformity instead of diversity among investment treaties. At the same time, the normative aspect of a multilateralization of international investment law provides a theoretical foundation for the concern regarding inconsistent decision-making. Likewise, the normative claim of a multilateralized investment treaty system supports institutional reforms in investment treaty arbitration that help to avoid multiple proceedings and inconsistent decisions and to suppress other side-effects that stem from residues of bilateralism.

Understanding international investment law as a multilateral system forms part of an attempt to establish a general legal theory of international investment law. Based on the observation that investment treaties converge considerably, the related claim that investment law is continuously multilateralizing allows the reconstruction of international investment law to form a sub-system of international law that follows rationalities that apply independently of the specific bilateral treaty relationship. It enables, for example, an understanding of investor rights, such as fair and equitable treatment or the concept of indirect expropriation, as part of investment law principles that are not only binding in a bilateral treaty relationship, but govern, as treaty-overarching principles, every investment treaty-based relationship. This facilitates the development of a theory of investment law principles and helps rationalize a critical discourse about the appropriate function of these principles in structuring and governing the relationship between foreign investors and host States. This empowers a rational debate about how far States have restricted and should restrict their sovereignty in order to achieve the goal of protecting and promoting foreign investment. Similarly, developing a theory of investment law principles allows for a better understanding of the relationship between international investment law and other areas of international law. This concerns the increasingly frequent tensions between investment protection and international environmental law or human rights.

In sum, the claim that investment protection constitutes a multilateral system allows for the provision of systemic solutions to systemic problems. It helps to conceptualize international investment law as a legal discipline, to assess it in relation to other legal disciplines, and to open it up for evaluation and critique to other political, moral or legal approaches. It also suggests, however, that the continuing efforts in establishing a truly multilateral system might not be as pressing as is often suggested in order to remedy existing imbalances or ambiguities. Instead, they can arguably be tackled within the existing system by means of a careful balance between judicial restraint and judicial activism of arbitral tribunals that remains faithful to the principles established in international investment treaties, but, at the same time, gives room for a careful development of international investment law.[46]

F The course of the argument

In order to advance the thesis that international investment law is multilateralizing on the basis of bilateral treaties, Chapter II revisits the historic development of international investment protection. It focuses in particular on the institutional choice between bilateralism and multilateralism as ordering paradigms for international investment relations. It shows that multilateralism has been largely unsuccessful, whereas bilateral and regional investment treaties have proliferated since the 1960s. While the history of international investment law shows that multilateralism initially failed because States were unable and unwilling to agree on the appropriate standards of treatment of foreign investors, it also shows that over the past two decades a more stable consensus on the content and scope of international investment protection has developed, a consensus which is reflected in the proliferation of bilateral and regional investment treaties since the early 1990s.

Chapter II argues that the move towards bilateralism in international investment relations was initially conditioned by the rejection of international investment protection by capital-importing countries. Bilateralism was thus geared towards breaking the negotiation deadlock that existed in multilateral settings. This strategy of sequential bilateralism had, however, exclusively procedural aspects and did not aim at establishing regimes based on specific reciprocity that impose rules and principles that unilaterally favor capital-exporting countries. Instead, the substantive investment rules that were initially intended to serve as the basis of a multilateral system were embedded without material changes into the bilateral treaties that subsequently took shape. These bilateral treaties are now concluded between developed and developing countries as well as among developing and among developed countries. This suggests a broad acceptance of the principles on which international investment law is based, even if disputes about the proper scope of these principles in individual cases persist.

---

[46] *Cf.* Kooijmans, *The ICJ in the 21st Century*, 56 Int'l & Comp. L. Q. 741 (2007).

Despite their bilateral form, investment treaties remain multilateral in their scope and aspirations. They do not establish preferential and discriminatory treatment for investors from specific countries, but corroborate general principles that restrain host States in their conduct vis-à-vis foreign investors in general. Accordingly, Chapter III presents the argument that bilateral and regional investment treaties are based on essentially converging treaty texts that establish principles and institutions for investor-State relations. Unlike the bilateral form of investment treaties suggest, bilateralism in international investment relations has not resulted in a spread of tailor-made treaties with flexible and diverging content, but has resulted in investment relations being based on uniform principles. Furthermore, Chapter III argues that the convergence of treaty texts is not purely coincidental, but reflects, as in other areas of international economic relations, an interest by States in establishing uniform rules for the regulation of international investment relations. At the same time, Chapter III claims that, even though elements of economic hegemony have played a role in the pedigree of international investment treaties, this did not translate into rules that exclusively favored specific countries, or even ensured the dominance of developed over developing countries. Rather, the content of international investment treaties remains multilateral in that the treaties establish general principles that govern international investment relations independent of which country at a specific point in time is the net capital-exporter or -importer.

Chapter IV subsequently turns to one of the normative bases for the multilateralization of international investment law: the most-favored-nation (MFN) clauses contained in virtually every BIT. These clauses have the effect of adjusting the level of investment protection in any given host State to the highest level offered in any of the host State's BITs. MFN clauses have the effect of multilateralizing the substantive standards of treatment and prevent differentiated, preferential, and discriminatory treatment among investors from different States. Under MFN treatment, uniform standards apply to all investors whose home States have entered into an investment treaty with the host State in question. MFN treatment, therefore, counteracts the possibility of flexible and tailor-made BITs. As will be argued, MFN clauses do not only apply to the substantive treatment of foreign investors, but also multilateralize investor-State arbitration to a certain extent. Chapter IV thus shows that there was not only an abstract interest in States having uniform rules on foreign investment, but that this interest is also firmly built into the texts of the treaties themselves.

Chapter V subsequently analyzes the relationship between investment protection and corporate structuring. As will be argued, corporate
structuring has the effect of dissociating the relation between a foreign
investor and a specific home State and, therefore, aggravates or even
prevents the use of investment treaties in order to accord preferential
treatment to a specific group of investors based on their nationality. The
mechanisms at work in this respect are twofold. First, the broad notion
of "investment" endorsed by most investment treaties encompasses the
protection of shareholders in companies incorporated in the host State.
This in effect multilateralizes BITs independent of the existence of MFN
clauses because the host State has to adapt its measures against a company
to the most expansive BIT protection offered to any of the shareholders in
that company. As a consequence, investors, even if not themselves covered
by any or only a less favorable BIT, indirectly benefit from the treatment
required vis-à-vis other investors in the same corporate structure under
their BIT. Secondly, the broad notion of "investor" enables investors to
actively use corporate structuring to influence the level of investment protection. Instead of remaining under the BIT of their original home jurisdiction, corporate structuring often effectively allows them to choose the
governing investment treaty for their investment activity. By channeling
an investment through a corporate vehicle that is set up in another jurisdiction an investor can opt into the investment treaty it considers most
suitable for its purposes independent of the operation of an MFN clause.

Chapter VI turns to the procedural mechanism for enforcing international investment treaties and analyzes the impact on the system of
investment protection of allowing foreign investors to initiate investor-
State arbitration and to seek damages for the violation of BITs, instead of
relying on traditional inter-State enforcement of investment treaties. This
enforcement structure essentially shifts compliance with investment
treaties from power-based to law-based mechanisms. It enables the law
governing the substantive relations between investors and host States
to be enforced independently of the actual power of the host State and
of the willingness of the home State to grant diplomatic protection. It
also excludes bilateral post-breach negotiations between home and host
States. Furthermore, the institutionalization of investor-State arbitration
develops into a mechanism to solve uncertainty in the substantive framework of international investment law. As will be argued in Chapter VI,
investment tribunals effectively assume a function for adapting investment treaties to changing circumstances and for progressively developing
international investment law. Tribunals regularly not only assume this

function with respect to a specific BIT, but also in relation to the whole system of investment treaties. This introduces an element of multilateral law-making through arbitration into international investment law.

Subsequently, Chapter VII provides a closer look at the contribution of the jurisprudence of investment tribunals to the multilateralization of international investment law. It illustrates how investment tribunals perceive and develop international investment law as a uniform body of law despite the myriad number of BITs and despite being established on a case-by-case basis. In particular, this chapter analyzes how various interpretative approaches used by arbitral tribunals create unity across the different investment treaties rather than divergence and fragmentation. Furthermore, Chapter VII shows the extensive use of arbitral precedent as a source of law. This leads to investment tribunals functioning in a similar manner to a standing institution, even though their constitution on a case-by-case basis would suggest the creation of conflict and inconsistencies rather than coherence.

Finally, Chapter VIII summarizes the claim that international investment law is emerging as a multilateral system and provides an outlook on how international investment law is developing towards a universal system that can serve a constitutional function for the global economy. This perspective offers a framework for the critical analysis of existing international investment law and presents a direction for its future development.

II

The dynamics of multilateralism and bilateralism in international investment relations

The history of international investment law in the post-Second World War period is characterized by repeated failures to establish multilateral treaty rules that govern relations between foreign investors and host States. In particular, imposing substantive limitations on the public authority of host States on a multilateral basis, such as rules concerning expropriations and other investor rights, has proved to be futile. Since 1945 several attempts to conclude a multilateral investment treaty have failed in various fora, caused primarily by the opposition of developing countries who considered that such rules would infringe their sovereignty. Only two multilateral conventions relating to questions of foreign investment succeeded, without, however, imposing any substantive limitations on the host State's treatment of foreign investors. Consequently, multilateralism in international investment relations appears to be a rather limited phenomenon. In sharp contrast, we have witnessed a veritable proliferation of bilateral and regional treaties that impose the very same substantive restrictions on host States regarding treatment and regulation of foreign investment that have failed to materialize on a multilateral basis.

These clearly contradictory developments may be explained by two hypotheses. Either States, in particular developing countries, derive specific benefits from bilateral cooperation that cannot materialize in multilateral settings, or multilateral negotiations allow developing countries to pool their negotiating power in order to resist legal standards that they are not able to decline in bilateral negotiations. Bilateralism and multilateralism in investment cooperation would thus be a function of the varying relative negotiation powers of capital-exporting and capital-importing States, depending on whether they negotiate individually or collectively. Either of these explanations would suggest that BITs succeed because they involve some sort of preferential treatment between two States that does not emerge in multilateral settings. Either the capital-exporting State benefits from preferential protection because it manages to impose obligations upon the capital-importing State in a hegemonic fashion, or the capital-importing State accepts the rules voluntarily because they entail advantages compared with multilateral and uniform rules. Both explanations suggest that international investment relations are dominated by bilateral rationalities of *quid pro quo* bargains, entail preferential treatment and do not base international investment relations on equal and uniform rules.

However, an historic account of the development of international investment law suggests that the failure of multilateral investment rules and the success of bilateral treaties are more closely linked than it appears. Instead of viewing multilateralism and bilateralism in international investment relations as two opposing currents, it is possible to understand non-multilateral investment treaties as pursuing the same goals as multilateral investment treaties. While the proliferation of BITs and similar regional instruments was caused by the failure of genuine multilateralism, it did not modify the underlying multilateral aspiration to arrive at non-discriminatory and uniform standards of investment protection.

This chapter, therefore, traces the history of international investment law in view of the dynamics between multilateralism and bilateralism in international investment relations, and argues that BITs constitute a functional substitute for genuine multilateralism. It shows that the foundations of international investment protection developed from a multilateral basis in customary international law before the First World War. Yet, customary international law soon proved to be incapable of meeting the need of the business sector for protection and stability, in view of increasing international investment flows and challenges to its content in the inter-war period and in the decades after the Second World War. This sparked the interest of Western capital-exporting countries in establishing treaty-based rules for protection of foreign investment.

Attempts at a treatification of investment law focused on multilateral conventions until the late 1960s. They failed, however, because of the resistance of developing countries and socialist States, and prompted capital-exporters to conclude bilateral treaties for the promotion and protection of foreign investment. Yet, capital-exporting States continued to push for multilateral investment rules in various for a, particularly encouraged by the widespread permeation of market economics after the end of the Cold War. Even though multilateral conventions containing substantive investor rights continued to fail, the number of BITs surged between developed and developing countries as well as between developing countries. Consequently, this chapter suggests that bilateralism in investment relations is not opposed to, but rather substitutes genuinely multilateral rules.

A   The state of international investment law until 1945

International investment law developed steadily and in parallel to increases in transborder economic activity. While foreign investment was relatively scarce before 1870, the subsequent industrialization in Europe and a change in paradigm in international economic theory, heralded by Adam Smith, David Hume, David Ricardo, and John Stuart Mill, who opposed mercantilist thinking and advocated international economic cooperation,[1] brought about the first wave of globalization before 1914.[2] At the same time, international law rules concerning the protection and treatment of aliens developed. These rules were primarily part of customary international law, but were complemented by bilateral and multilateral treaty rules. Their aspirations toward bolstering the promotion of international trade and investment were, however, mostly multilateral in nature and were not limited to purely economic objectives. Rather, they formed part of a broader architecture for international relations, peace, and security.

1   Customary international law

Customary international law comprised rules for the protection of aliens on foreign territory as part of the law of State responsibility.[3] These rules were not limited to the protection of property against unlawful expropriation, but equally comprised standards of treatment of aliens as regards their life, security, and property more generally.[4] The basis for the development of these standards was the idea of generally accepted standards of

---

[1] See. E. Petersmann, *International Economic Theory and International Economic Law*, in: Macdonald and Johnston (eds.), *The Structure and Process of International Law*, pp. 227, 235 *et seq.* (1983). See also Vandevelde, *Sustainable Liberalism and the International Investment Regime*, 19 Mich. J. Int'l L. 373, 375 *et seq.* (1998).

[2] See Rourke and Williamson, *Globalization and History*, pp. 29–55 (1999). See also Schularick, *Finanzielle Globalisierung in historischer Perspektive*, pp. 22 *et seq.* (2006); Bloomfield, *Patterns of Fluctuation in International Investment Before 1914* (1968).

[3] On a more comprehensive history of the protection of property by international law including earlier periods see Müller, *Der völkerrechtliche Eigentumsschutz* (1981).

[4] See Roth, *The Minimum Standard of International Law Applied to Aliens*, pp. 127 *et seq.* (1949); see also Borchard, *The Diplomatic Protection of Citizens Abroad* (1915).

civilization. Writing in 1910, Elihu Root stated the rule and basis for customary international law concerning the treatment of aliens as follows:

> The rule of obligation is perfectly distinct and settled. Each country
> is bound to give to the nationals of another country in its territory the
> benefit of the same laws, the same administration, the same protection,
> and the same redress for injury which it gives to its own citizens, and
> neither more nor less: provided the protection which the country gives to
> its own citizens conforms to the established standard of civilization.
>
> There is a standard of justice, very simple, very fundamental, and of
> such general acceptance by all civilized countries as to form a part of the
> international law of the world. The condition upon which any country is
> entitled to measure the justice due from it to an alien by the justice which
> it accords to its own citizens is that its system of law and administration
> shall conform to this general standard. If any country's system of law and
> administration does not conform to that standard, although the people
> of the country may be content or compelled to live under it, no other
> country can be compelled to accept it as furnishing a satisfactory meas-
> ure of treatment to its citizens.[5]

The standard of treatment of aliens was primarily and, with respect to
certain subject-matters, one of national treatment. It was complemented by
what came to be known as the international minimum standard. National
treatment was insufficient to the extent that it did not reach the standards
generally accepted by civilized nations.[6] While customary international
law did not grant aliens the right to acquire property, exercise a profession
or work on foreign territory,[7] the minimum standard protected alien
property against expropriations: "Wherever the alien enjoys the privilege
of ownership of property international law protects his rights insofar as
his property may not be expropriated under any pretext, except for moral
or penal reasons, without adequate compensation."[8]

The existence of the international minimum standard formed the
object of a famous exchange of notes concerning the standard of compensation between US Secretary of State, Cordell Hull, and the Mexican
Minister of Foreign Affairs in 1938. In it, the United States complained

---

[5] Root, *The Basis of Protection to Citizens Residing Abroad*, 4 A.J.I.L. 517, 521 (1910).
[6] The basis for the international minimum standard alludes to the existence of general
principles of law in this field. See Borchard, *The "Minimum Standard" of Treatment of
Aliens*, 38 Mich. L. Rev. 446, 448 *et seq.* (1940).
[7] Roth (*supra* footnote 4), pp. 156 *et seq.*, 161 *et seq.* (1949).
[8] Roth (*supra* footnote 4), p. 177 (1949). See further Friedman, *Expropriation in International Law*, pp. 204 *et seq.* (1953); Foighel, *Nationalization: A Study in the Protection
of Alien Property in International Law*, pp. 85 *et seq.* (1957); Wortley, *Expropriation in
Public International Law*, pp. 12 *et seq.* (1959); White, *Nationalisation of Foreign Property*,
pp. 183 *et seq.* (1961).

of expropriations of agrarian land and oil fields owned by American citizens by Mexico in the 1920s and 1930s.[9] While Mexico took the position that it had treated American citizens on an equal footing with its own nationals, Hull asserted that it was:

> a self-evident fact ... that the applicable precedents and recognized authorities on international law support ... that, under every rule of law and equity, no government is entitled to expropriate private property, for whatever purpose, without provision for prompt, adequate, and effective payment therefor.[10]

This statement – which became widely known as the Hull Formula – encapsulated the standard of compensation that was considered to form part of customary international law at the time.[11] While permitting a host State to expropriate aliens under certain circumstances, it required the payment of compensation and thereby protected the value of property against government interference.

The Mexican position, by contrast, was representative of a movement which started after the First World War that challenged the existence of an international minimum standard and the requirement of "prompt, adequate, and effective" compensation. It asserted that the only treatment an alien was entitled to receive was national treatment.[12] This position gained ground due to the successful communist revolution in Russia in 1917 and communism's rejection of private property in land and the means of production.[13] It was further supported by the endorsement of the Calvo Doctrine by several Latin American countries. Under this doctrine, national treatment, not an international minimum standard, was all an aggrieved foreign investor could invoke and national courts were the only forum competent for disputes between foreigners and host States.[14]

Notwithstanding these challenges, international courts and tribunals in the inter-war period did not accept that national treatment independent of a specific minimum standard was sufficient to conform to

---

[9] The exchange of notes between the two governments is reprinted in Hackworth, *Digest of International Law*, vol. III, pp. 655 *et seq.* (1942).

[10] *Ibid.*, pp. 658 *et seq.*

[11] Dolzer, *Eigentum, Enteignung und Entschädigung im geltenden Völkerrecht*, pp. 20 *et seq.* (1985).

[12] See Roth (*supra* footnote 4), pp. 62 *et seq.* (1949).

[13] Dolzer (*supra* footnote 11), pp. 18 *et seq.* (1985).

[14] On the Calvo Doctrine see Shea, *The Calvo Clause* (1955); Oschmann, *Calvo-Doktrin und Calvo-Klauseln* (1993); Zagel, *Auslandsinvestitionen in Lateinamerika*, pp. 71 *et seq.* (1999); Lipstein, *The Place of the Calvo-Clause in International Law*, 22 Brit. Ybk. Int'l L. 139 (1945).

international law.[15] Nevertheless, these political controversies illustrated the shaky foundations of the standards of customary international law with regard to the protection of aliens and their property and foreshadowed future conflicts about the appropriate standards of treatment of foreign investment that continued to influence international relations after the Second World War.[16]

In any case, the scope of application of the international minimum standard was rather vague and restricted to curtail clearly excessive State measures. It required, as put by the Mexican General Claims Commission in the *Neer* case, that:

> the treatment of an alien, in order to constitute an international delinquency, should amount to an outrage, to bad faith, to wilful neglect of duty, or to an insufficiency of governmental action so far short of international standards that every reasonable and impartial man would readily recognize its insufficiency.[17]

Both the challenges to the international minimum standard in the interwar period and its inherent limitations already reflected the political struggle between capital-exporting and capital-importing countries in finding a consensus on the appropriate standards of investment protection. For capital-exporting countries, the challenges pointed to the need for a treatification of international investment law. Notwithstanding, the historical development also shows that the basis of international investment law was multilateral at the outset, consisting in customary international law rules with a universal scope of application.

2 Treaty rules

Besides customary international law, several treaties concerned questions of foreign investment. Some of these treaties concerned the standards of

---

[15] See *Certain German Interests in Polish Upper Silesia (Germany v. Poland)*, Merits, Judgment, May 25, 1926, P.C.I.J. Series A, No. 7 (1926), p. 33; *Treatment of Polish Nationals and Other Persons of Polish Origin or Speech in the Danzig Territory*, Advisory Opinion, February 4, 1932, P.C.I.J. Series A/B, No. 44 (1932), p. 28; *Harry Roberts (United States) v. Mexico*, Opinion, November. 2, 1926, U.N.R.I.A.A., vol. IV, p. 80; *George W. Hopkins (United States) v. Mexico*, Opinion, March 31, 1926, U.N.R.I.A.A., vol. IV, p. 47; *Marguerite de Joly de Sabla (United States) v. Panama*, Decision of the Commission, June 29, 1933, 28 A.J.I.L. 602 (1934).

[16] Still today, the existence of an international minimum standard under customary international law is cast into doubt by some scholars. Critical, for example, is Sornarajah, *The International Law on Foreign Investment*, pp. 148, 328 (2nd edn. 2004).

[17] *L. F. H. Neer and Pauline E. Neer (United States) v. Mexico*, Opinion, October 15, 1926, U.N.R.I.A.A., vol. IV, pp. 61–62.

treatment of foreign investors, others questions of access and admission of investment into foreign territory. Treaties relating to foreign investment fall into two categories: bilateral and multilateral treaties. Among the first are treaties of friendship, commerce and navigation which the United States started concluding. Furthermore, a number of multilateral treaties ensuring access to commerce and investment in certain territories existed.

(a)   Treaties of friendship, commerce, and navigation

Historically, the first form of bilateral treaties containing rules on investment protection were the friendship, commerce, and navigation (FCN) treaties concluded by the United States starting in the late eighteenth century with several European powers, including France, the Netherlands, Sweden, Prussia, the United Kingdom, and Spain.[18] Subsequently, the United States concluded FCN treaties with various Latin American, European, and Asian States until 1966.[19] While these treaties contained provisions protecting against expropriation, requiring full protection and security, and fair and equitable treatment, their primary purpose was to establish closer commercial and political relations between the contracting parties.[20] This reflected their original design as instruments for the United States, as a then newly independent State, to participate in international trade relations.[21] Accordingly, their scope went beyond the standards of treatment of foreign investors and included shipping

---

[18] Vandevelde, *U.S. Bilateral Investment Treaties: The Second Wave*, 14 Mich. J. Int'l L. 621, 624 (1993); Vandevelde, *A Brief History of International Investment Agreements*, 12 U.C. Davis J. Int'l L. & Pol'y 157, 158 (2005).

[19] Vandevelde (*supra* footnote 18), 14 Mich. J. Int'l L. 621, 624–25 (1993). For a discussion of the later US FCN treaties see Hawkins, *Commercial Treaties and Agreements* (1951); Walker, *Modern Treaties of Friendship, Commerce and Navigation*, 42 Minn. L. Rev. 805 (1958); Walker, *Treaties for the Encouragement and Protection of Foreign Investment: Present United States Practice*, 5 Am. J. Comp. L. 229 (1956); Wilson, *A Decade of Commercial Treaties*, 50 A.J.I.L. 927 (1956); Wilson, *Postwar Commercial Treaties of the United States*, 43 A.J.I.L. 262 (1949); Wilson, *Property-Protection Provisions in United States Commercial Treaties*, 45 A.J.I.L. 83 (1951); Wilson, *The International Law Standards in Treaties of the United States* (1953).

[20] Walker (*supra* footnote 19), 5 Am. J. Comp. L. 229, 231 (1956) (pointing out that "following World War I, such treaties were designed especially to promote international trade").

[21] See Schuyler, *American Diplomacy and the Furtherance of Commerce*, pp. 421 *et seq.* (1886); Frick, *Bilateraler Investitionsschutz in Entwicklungsländern*, p. 77 (1975). See also US Department of State, *Commercial Treaty Program of the United States*, Publication 6565, Commercial Policy Series No. 163, p. 1 (1958) (observing that after 1945 the aim of the FCN treaty program is not only "to assure a greater measure of security for US citizens and US interests in foreign countries," but also "to advance the general objectives of the Nation's foreign policy").

and trading rights.[22] Yet, even though these treaties were bilateral in form, they did not aim at establishing preferential treatment between the contracting parties, but envisaged – as illustrated by the most-favored-nation (MFN) clauses they contained – participation in international commerce on a non-discriminatory basis.[23]

(b)   Treaties establishing equality of opportunity in certain territories

Access to commerce also played a role in a number of multilateral treaties that were modeled after the Congo General Act of February 26, 1885.[24] These treaties provided for "equality of opportunity" concerning commerce in certain territories. Such treaties were concluded with respect to the Congo in 1885, Morocco in 1906, China in 1922, and Turkey in 1923. Similarly, the regime established for the so-called A- and B-mandates under the League of Nations mandate system after the First World War contained comparable provisions on equal opportunity.[25]

The core idea of these treaties was to secure non-discriminatory treatment between the contracting parties, mostly European powers. They aimed at preventing the parties from seeking preferential treatment in trade and investment in the specified territories and were based on a common mind-set:

> *First*, each of the territories involved was coveted by one or more Powers as an object of colonial or imperialist solicitude. *Secondly*, other Powers were anxious to prevent outright annexation of the territory or its transformation into a sphere of exclusive influence. *Thirdly*, in all but one case – that of China which was too big a prize – the other Powers concerned were prepared to grant to the best placed among them the substance of its claim, but not necessarily in the desired form and, in any case, only on condition of equality of commercial opportunity for themselves.[26]

---

[22] Avramovich, *The Protection of International Investment at the Start of the Twenty-First Century*, 31 John Marshall L. Rev. 1201, 1233 (1998); Vandevelde (*supra* footnote 18), 12 U.C. Davis J. Int'l L. & Pol'y 157, 158 (2005). Their enforcement mechanism was, however, limited and did not include investor-State dispute settlement.

[23] On the function of the MFN clause see *infra* Ch. IV.A.

[24] In this context, see Schwarzenberger, *Equality and Discrimination in International Economic Law*, 25 Ybk. World Affairs 163, 174 *et seq.* (1971).

[25] Article 22(5), Covenant of the League of Nations, entered into force January 10, 1920, established the principle of equal opportunity for the so-called B-mandates, i.e., former African colonies except South-West Africa. With respect to the so-called A-mandates, the respective mandate treaties provided for the same standard. See Gerig, *The Open Door and the Mandates System* (1930).

[26] Schwarzenberger (*supra* footnote 24), 25 Ybk. World Affairs 163, 174 *et seq.* (1971) (emphasis in the original).

Thus, the purpose of these treaties was not purely economic. They also attempted to create an inter-State order by establishing a balance of power between States that were struggling for hegemony in order to prevent one State from becoming too powerful in the territories in question.[27] The colonial power structures notwithstanding, that denied political self-determination to the colonized territories, it is noteworthy that these multilateral treaties attempted to reduce international conflict and to contribute to peaceful relations between States by allowing for equal access for trade and investment. Rules for economic non-discrimination were implemented with the larger objective of disassociating economic activity from political and military power.

In sum, the principles of international economic cooperation at the time were to a large extent based on general non-discriminatory principles and uniform standards. Their objective was not only to enable market forces to work, but also to limit the political power and influence of powerful States. They combined the regulation of economic matters with the objective of setting up an international order for inter-State relations more generally. The Great Depression and the advent of the Second World War, however, brought an end to international cooperation based on multilateral principles. Instead, discriminatory and preferential treatment became the order of the day.[28]

B   The failures of multilateralism I: 1945–1974

Renewed efforts to establish multilateral rules on investment protection were made with the proposed International Trade Organization as part of the Havana Charter in 1948, and with the 1967 OECD Draft Convention on the Protection of Foreign Property.[29] Both projects originated in the desire of Western developed countries to establish substantive treaty

---

[27] Cf. Bileski, Der Grundsatz der wirtschaftlichen Gleichberechtigung in den Mandats-gebieten, 16 ZöR 214, 228 et seq. (1936) (pointing out that this also protected smaller States from excessive influence by one or several bigger States).

[28] See Pomfret, Unequal Trade: The Economics of Discriminatory International Trade Policies, pp. 29 et seq. (1988); Kindleberger, Commercial Policy between the Wars, in Mathias and Pollard (eds.), The Cambridge Economic History of Europe, vol. VIII, p. 161 (1989); Oye, Economic Discrimination and Political Exchange, pp. 71–133 (1992).

[29] The focus in the present context is solely on the main multilateral approaches containing substantive obligations relating to the treatment of foreign investors, i.e., treaties concerning investor rights and/or their enforcement. For a more comprehensive discussion of other multilateral approaches regarding foreign investment aspects see Tschofen, Multilateral Approaches to the Treatment of Foreign Investment, 7 ICSID Rev – For. Inv. L. J. 384 (1992).

obligations for the treatment of foreign investors by capital-importing States. Two factors played a dominant role in this process: a genuinely economic one and one relating to international relations. First, the interest in re-establishing international economic ties and prosperity after the Second World War through trade and investment required clear and stable investment rules. This prompted a move toward treaty-based investment protection that could remedy the limitations of customary international law and counter existing and impending threats to international investment protection in view of the nascent decolonization.

Secondly, the move towards multilateralism in investment relations after the end of the Second World War was in line with the general trend, supported above all by the United States, to establish multilateral institutions that would include and bind all major powers, including the emerging superpowers, in order to create a peaceful, stable, and sustainable post-war international order.[30] Creating multilateral investment rules was thus in line with the aspiration to create a different world order for inter-State relations that was not based on the power of single players but on the creation of multilateral institutions. However, capital-exporting countries faced major opposition from developing and socialist countries as regards multilateral investment rules.

1   The Havana Charter – 1948

Attempts to establish multilateral rules on investment protection were made immediately following the end of the Second World War as part of the negotiations for an International Trade Organization (ITO) which took place under the auspices of the United Nations in Havana from November 1947 to March 1948.[31] It was envisaged that the ITO would constitute, together with the IMF and the International Bank for Reconstruction and Development (now the World Bank), the third pillar of the Bretton-Woods system and was originally conceived as an international organization that encompassed competences regarding both trade and investment.[32] The main support for establishing a liberal investment

---

[30] See Ruggie, *Multilateralism: The Anatomy of an Institution*, in Ruggie (ed.), *Multilateralism Matters*, pp. 3, 24 *et seq.* (1993).

[31] For an overview of the negotiations leading to the Havana Charter see Wilcox, *A Charter for World Trade*, pp. 37–50 (1949). See also Dattu, *A Journey from Havana to Paris*, 24 Fordham Int'l L. J. 275, 286 *et seq.* (2000); Shenkin, *Trade-Related Investment Measures in Bilateral Investment Treaties and the GATT*, 55 U. Pitt. L. Rev. 541, 555 *et seq.* (1994).

[32] Kurtz, *A General Investment Agreement in the WTO?*, 23 U. Pa. J. Int'l Econ. L. 713, 718 (2002).

regime as part of a multilateral international organization that contains rules for the protection of foreign investors against discrimination and expropriation came from the United States and its investment-oriented industry.[33]

However, the finally negotiated text, the so-called Havana Charter for an International Trade Organization, contained only embryonic rules on foreign investment protection.[34] Although the Charter acknowledged the need for investment as a driving force for economic development,[35] it did not contain substantive obligations for the protection of foreign investment. Due to significant resistance from developing countries who demanded protection for capital-importing countries rather than capital-exporters, the position of the United States to liberalize foreign investment and to provide for effective protection did not find a consensus.[36] Instead, the Havana Charter emphasized that:

> a Member State has the right: (i) to take any appropriate safeguards necessary to ensure that foreign investment is not used as a basis for interferences in its internal affairs or national policies; (ii) to determine whether and to what extent and upon what terms it will allow future foreign investment; (iii) to prescribe and give effect on just terms to requirements as to the ownership of existing and future investment; (iv) to prescribe and give effect to other reasonable requirements with respect to existing and future investments.[37]

Concerning the protection of foreign investment, the Havana Charter merely set out an unenforceable symbolic undertaking of Members to "provide reasonable opportunities for investment acceptable to them and adequate security for existing and future investments, and ... to give due regard to the desirability of avoiding discrimination as between foreign investments."[38] In addition, it contained provisions on restrictive business practices in international trade, such as measures restricting competition and fostering monopolies.[39] Overall, under the Havana

---

[33] Vandevelde (*supra* footnote 18), 12 U.C. Davis Int'l L. & Pol'y 157, 162 (2005).

[34] The relevant portions of the Havana Charter for an International Trade Organization are reprinted in UNCTAD, *International Investment Instruments: A Compendium, Volume I – Multilateral Instruments*, p. 3 (1996).

[35] See Article 11(1), Havana Charter (stating that "[p]rogressive industrial and economic development, as well as reconstruction, requires among other things adequate supplies of capital funds, materials, modern equipment and technology and technical and managerial skills").

[36] Spero and Hart, *The Politics of International Economic Relations*, p. 156 (6th edn. 2003).

[37] Article 12(1)(c), Havana Charter.

[38] Article 12(2), Havana Charter.

[39] See Articles 46 *et seq.*, Havana Charter.

Charter "domestic policy goals were to be prioritized over international standards for investment policy."[40]

Ultimately, the creation of the ITO and its investment provisions in the Havana Charter failed. The reasons for this lay primarily in domestic US politics and in the emergence of the Cold War.[41] In view of the meager outcome of the ITO negotiations, the US Government prioritized its interests in international trade over interests in international investment. Unlike the GATT framework that promised considerable trade liberalization, and which had entered into force in January 1948 as the sole surviving element of the ITO negotiations,[42] the limited provisions on investment protection in the Havana Charter were disapproved by the US business sector. They were thus unlikely to pass ratification in the Senate.[43] As a consequence, President Truman, a Democrat facing a Republican majority in Congress, decided not to submit the ITO Charter to Congress for ratification, and instead focused on renewing his authority to negotiate further tariff reductions within the GATT under the Trade Agreements Act that was about to expire.[44] Since the participation of the United States was considered crucial for establishing the ITO, this first effort to order international investment relations under the aegis of an international organization also failed to receive sufficient support from other States.[45]

The reason why the negotiating parties at the Havana Conference were unable to agree on more comprehensive and effective rules on investment protection, in turn, already reflected the smoldering North–South conflict about the proper scope of investment protection under international law that would gain momentum in the coming decades as well as the conflict between East and West in the emerging Cold War. As such, the failure of the Havana Charter was not only "a shift away from multilateralism in the coverage of investment instruments,"[46] but also an expression of the fundamental political and ideological conflicts about the place of investment protection in the post-Second World War order.

---

[40] See Dattu (*supra* footnote 31), 24 Fordham Int'l L. J. 275, 288 (2000).
[41] See Shenkin (*supra* footnote 31), 55 U. Pitt. L. Rev. 541, 555 *et seq.* (1994).
[42] The GATT was structured as a Reciprocal Trade Agreement and could thus be passed under the Trade Agreement Act without the Senate's consent. See Brand, *GATT and the Evolution of United States Trade Law*, 18 Brook. J. Int'l L. 101, 117 *et seq.* (1992).
[43] See, comprehensively, Diebold, *The End of the ITO*, in Anderson and Hoekman (eds.), *The Global Trading System*, vol. I, pp. 81 *et seq.* (2002). See also Ostry, *Looking Back to Look Forward*, in WTO Secretariat (ed.), *From GATT to the WTO*, pp. 97, 100 (2000).
[44] Shenkin (*supra* footnote 31), 55 U. Pitt. L. Rev. 541, 557 (1994).
[45] Diebold (*supra* footnote 43), p. 99 (2002).
[46] Kurtz (*supra* footnote 32), 23 U. Pa. J. Int'l Econ. L. 713, 719 (2002).

As such, the failure of the Havana Charter foreshadowed the waves of expropriations that affected foreign investors in many socialist and communist countries,[47] as well as in numerous newly independent States that emerged from the process of decolonization. Growing numbers of expropriations until the mid-1970s[48] were responsible for the preoccupation of Western developed countries with expropriation risks in developing countries and explain their efforts to establish firm international rules on investment protection.[49] For many developing countries, by contrast, expropriations were part of their newly gained independence, complementing formal political independence with substantive control over their economies which were previously often controlled by nationals of the former colonial power.[50]

2   OECD Draft Convention on the Protection of Foreign Property – 1967

As a reaction to the worldwide increase in expropriations, a number of proposals for multilateral conventions were made in the course of the 1950s.[51] They originated primarily from within the business communities that had the greatest interest in the protection of foreign investment, such as the oil industry or the banking sector that financed many foreign investment projects. The most influential of these proposals was the Draft Convention on Investments Abroad, the so-called Abs–Shawcross Draft.[52] It constituted a combination of two earlier draft conventions

---

[47] See, for example, Baklanoff, *Expropriation of U.S. Investments in Cuba, Mexico, and Chile* (1975).

[48] See Minor, *The Demise of Expropriation as an Instrument of LDC Policy, 1980–1992*, 25 J. Int'l Bus. Stud. 177 (1994).

[49] Kurtz (*supra* footnote 32), 23 U. Pa. J. Int'l Econ. L. 713, 719 *et seq.* (2002).

[50] Juillard, *L'évolution des sources du droit des investissements*, 250 Recueil des Cours 9, 138 (1994–VI).

[51] See Brandon, *An International Investment Code*, 3 J. Bus. L. 7, 12 *et seq.* (1959); Brandon, *Recent Measures to Improve the Investment Climate*, 9 J. Pub. L. 125 (1960); Brandon, *Survey of Current Approaches to the Problem*, in *The Encouragement and Protection of Investment in Developing Countries*, Int'l & Comp. L. Q. Suppl. No. 3, p. 1 (1962); Miller, *Protection of Private Foreign Investment by Multilateral Conventions*, 53 A.J.I.L. 371 (1959); Metzger, *Multilateral Conventions for the Protection of Private Foreign Investment*, 9 J. Pub. L. 133 (1960); Fatouros, *An International Code to Protect Private Investment*, 14 U. Toronto L. J. 77 (1961); Sohn and Baxter, *Responsibility of States for Injuries to the Economic Interests of Aliens*, 55 A.J.I.L. 545 (1961).

[52] Draft Convention on Investments Abroad (Abs–Shawcross Convention), reprinted in UNCTAD, *International Investment Instruments: A Compendium – Volume V*, p. 395 (2000).

by Hermann Abs, the then Chairman of Deutsche Bank,[53] and Lord Shawcross, the former British Attorney-General and then Director of the Shell Petroleum Company.[54]

The Abs–Shawcross Draft, which largely mirrored the content of modern international investment treaties, proposed a regime that aimed at the comprehensive protection of foreign investment and contained provisions on fair and equitable treatment, most constant protection and security, on the protection against direct and indirect expropriation, and on investor-State dispute settlement.[55] As a contemporary commentator noted, however, the Draft faced the problem "that even moderate governments of capital-importing countries find it impossible to pay the political price involved in becoming parties to conventions on the Abs–Shawcross lines."[56] Although it was never implemented, it heavily influenced another intergovernmental process that aimed at establishing a multilateral convention on foreign investment protection by serving as the basis for the 1967 OECD Draft Convention on the Protection of Foreign Property.[57]

Similar to the Abs–Shawcross Draft, the 1967 OECD Draft Convention closely resembled the content of modern BITs and provided for fair and equitable treatment, most constant protection and security, protection against direct and indirect expropriation, and investor-State dispute settlement.[58] It failed, however, to gain sufficient support from OECD Members and was never opened for signature. As it was planned as a multilateral convention that was to be open for signature to non-OECD Members also, it failed, like the Havana Charter, due to the ensuing North–South conflict on the appropriate level of protection of foreign investment under international law.

In fact, the international climate at the time could hardly have been less favorable for a multilateral project for the protection of foreign

---

[53] See Abs, *Proposals for Improving the Protection of Private Foreign Investments*, p. 33 (1958) (cited after A. Sinclair, *The Origins of the Umbrella Clause in the International Law of Investment Protection*, 20 Arb. Int'l 411, 418 [2004]).

[54] See, on the Shawcross Draft, Brandon (*supra* footnote 51), 3 J. Bus. L. 7, 12 *et seq.* (1959).

[55] See, for evaluations of the Abs–Shawcross Draft, the contributions in 9 J. Pub. L. 115–87 (1960); see also Schwarzenberger, *Foreign Investments and International Law*, pp. 109–34 (1969).

[56] Schwarzenberger (*supra* footnote 55), p. 134 (1969).

[57] Brandon (*supra* footnote 51), Int'l & Comp. L. Q. Suppl. No. 3, p. 10 (1962).

[58] Draft Convention on the Protection of Foreign Property and Resolution of the Council of the OECD on the Draft Convention, reproduced in 7 I.L.M. 117 (1968). See, on the content of the Draft Convention, Schwarzenberger (*supra* footnote 55), pp. 153–69 (1969).

investment. Instead, in the 1970s a coalition of developing countries, as well as socialist and communist countries, even attempted to openly challenge customary international law rules on property protection in the United Nations General Assembly which it dominated.[59] Both groups were opposed to the protection of foreign investment by customary international law, because they saw it either as an obstacle to their political independence or as an impediment to the organization of their economy according to socialist–communist ideology. In two UN General Assembly resolutions both groups aimed at doing away with the customary international law requirement to provide compensation for the expropriation of foreigners, a position that was still reflected in UN General Assembly Resolution 1803 on the "Permanent Sovereignty over Natural Resources" of December 14, 1962.[60]

UN General Assembly Resolution 3201 of May 1, 1974 contained the "Declaration on the Establishment of a New International Economic Order." The resolution declared "the right of nationalization or transfer of ownership to its nationals, this right being an expression of the full permanent sovereignty of the State."[61] It did so without specifying an obligation to pay compensation. The resolution's thrust in aiming to abrogate the protection of property by international law was further strengthened by the "Charter of Economic Rights and Duties of States," passed as UN

---

[59] See, on the developments in the UN General Assembly, Dolzer (*supra* footnote 11), pp. 24 *et seq.* (1985).

[60] UN General Assembly Resolution 1803 (December 14, 1962), reprinted in 2 I.L.M. 223 (1963) (stating that "4. Nationalization, expropriation or requisitioning shall be based on grounds or reasons of public utility, security or the national interest which are recognized as overriding purely individual or private interests both domestic and foreign. In such cases the owner shall be paid appropriate compensation, in accordance with the rules in force in the State taking such measures in the exercise of its sovereignty and in accordance with international law."). The Resolution thus stressed the significance of international law for questions of compensation for expropriation. The use of the term "appropriate compensation" constituted a compromise that enabled the reading of both the Hull standard into it as well as the emerging view that expropriations required a lesser standard; see Dolzer (*supra* footnote 11), p. 22 (1985); Schwebel, *The Story of the U.N.'s Declaration on Permanent Sovereignty over Natural Resources*, 49 Am. Bar Ass. J. 463 (1963); Gess, *Permanent Sovereignty over Natural Resources*, 13 Int'l & Comp. L. Q. 398 (1964).

[61] § 4(e), UN General Assembly Resolution 3201 (May 1, 1974), reprinted in 13 I.L.M. 715 (1974). More generally on the politics and economics connected with the New International Economic Order, see Bhagwati, *The New International Economic Order* (1978); J. Hart, *The New International Economic Order* (1983); see also Wälde, *A Requiem for the "New International Economic Order"*, in Hafner and Loibl (eds.), *Liber Amicorum: Professor Ignaz Seidl-Hohenveldern*, p. 771 (1998).

General Assembly Resolution 3281 on December 12, 1974 with 120 votes in favor, six rejections and ten abstentions.[62] It stated that every State had

> the right to nationalize, expropriate or transfer ownership of foreign property, in which case appropriate compensation should be paid by the State adopting such measures, taking into account its relevant laws and regulations and all circumstances that the State considers pertinent. In any case where the question of compensation gives rise to a controversy, it shall be settled under the domestic law of the nationalizing State and by its tribunals, unless it is freely and mutually agreed by all States concerned that other peaceful means be sought on the basis of the sovereign equality of States and in accordance with the principle of free choice of means.[63]

Both resolutions triggered vigorous debates on the status of property protection and the requirement to compensate for expropriations as part of customary international law.[64] In the practice of international arbitration, the resolutions were, however, accorded little or no weight and largely disregarded in determining the scope of property protection under customary international law.[65] Instead, Resolution 1803 that provided for adequate compensation continued to be regarded as an authoritative expression of customary international law.[66]

While the development leading up to the proclamation of the New International Economic Order illustrates that developing countries were almost unanimously opposed to the protection of property and would, therefore, not adhere to the 1967 OECD Draft Convention, even some of the OECD Member States were reluctant to support it. In particular Greece, Portugal, and Turkey, considered certain provisions of the 1967 Draft to be too favorable to capital-exporting countries and foreign investors.[67] Similarly, the United States did not actively push toward the

---

[62] UN General Assembly Resolution Res. 3281 (December 12, 1974), reprinted in 14 I.L.M. 251 (1975). States rejecting the Charter were Belgium, Denmark, the Federal Republic of Germany, Luxemburg, the United Kingdom, and the United States; abstentions came from Australia, Canada, France, Israel, Italy, Japan, the Netherlands, Norway, and Spain.

[63] Article 2.2(c), GA Res. 3281.

[64] See C. N. Brower and Tepe, *The Charter of Economic Rights and Duties of States*, 9 Int'l Law 295 (1975); Weston, *The Charter of Economic Rights and Duties of States and the Deprivation of Foreign Owned Wealth*, 75 A.J.I.L. 437 (1981); Dolzer (*supra* footnote 11), pp. 28 *et seq.* (1985) (with further references).

[65] Dolzer (*supra* footnote 11), pp. 35 *et seq.* (1985). See also Norton, *A Law of the Future or a Law of the Past?*, 85 A.J.I.L. 474 (1991) (focusing on the jurisprudence of international tribunals after the proclamation of the New International Economic Order).

[66] Dolzer (*supra* footnote 11), pp. 53 *et seq.* (1985).

[67] A. Sinclair (*supra* footnote 53), 20 Arb. Int'l 411, 432 (2004).

conclusion of a multilateral convention within the OECD as the prospect of successfully integrating developing countries, where the protection of foreign investment was more needed than among OECD Members themselves, was marginal. Consequently, the failure of the 1967 OECD Draft Convention was a result of the ideological divide between capital-exporting and capital-importing countries about the appropriate principles of foreign investment protection.[68] The necessary "consensus concerning the sanctity of private property, the advantages of private enterprises, and the acceptability of alien participation in the country's economy" was simply non-existent at the time.[69]

Despite its failure, the 1967 OECD Draft Convention and its direct precursors had significant influence on the development of the bilateral investment treaties that the OECD Member States started negotiating and concluding in the 1960s and 1970s. Instead of being opened for signature, the 1967 OECD Draft Convention was recommended to OECD Members as a model for the conclusion of bilateral treaties with developing countries. As such, the 1967 Draft demonstrably influenced the Model BITs of France,[70] the United Kingdom,[71] and the United States.[72] Germany's BITs, in turn, developed in parallel to the intergovernmental process within the OECD and also reflected the same structure and content.[73] The pedigree of many BITs is, therefore, linked to the efforts within the OECD in

---

[68] See Dolzer and Stevens, *Bilateral Investment Treaties*, p. 2 (1995) (stating that "[t]he reason for this was in part due to the fact that the Convention was originally intended to be a multilateral instrument applicable to all countries, not only to OECD members ... The controversy surrounding other well known multilateral instruments of that period, however, reflected more accurately the deep divisions in the international community on what in fact constituted 'recognized principles' in the area of foreign investment law.").

[69] Walker (*supra* footnote 19), 5 Am. J. Comp. L. 229, 241 (1956).

[70] Juillard, *Le reseau français des conventions bilatérales d'investissements: à la recherche d'un droit perdu?*, 13 Droit et Pratique du Commerce International 9, 16 (1987).

[71] Denza and Brooks, *Investment Protection Treaties: United Kingdom Experience*, 36 Int'l & Comp. L. Q. 908, 910 (1987).

[72] Gudgeon, *United States Bilateral Investment Treaties*, 4 Int'l Tax & Bus. L. 105, 111 (1986).

[73] On the German treaty practice that arguably served as a model for other European States and itself influenced the processes within the OECD see Alenfeld, *Die Investitionsförderungsverträge der Bundesrepublik Deutschland* (1971); Banz, *Völkerrechtlicher Eigentumsschutz durch Investitionsschutzabkommen* (1988); Frick (supra footnote 21), pp. 171 *et seq.*; Karl, *The Promotion and Protection of German Foreign Investment Abroad*, 11 ICSID Rev. – For. Inv. L. J. 1 (1996); Füracker, *Relevance and Structure of Bilateral Investment Treaties – The German Approach*, 4 SchiedsVZ 236 (2006); Krajewski and Ceyssens, *Internationaler Investitionsschutz und innerstaatliche Regulierung*, 45 AVR 180 (2007).

the 1960s to establish an investment framework on a multilateral basis. The multilateral endeavor within the OECD also largely explains the homogeneity of many BITs.[74] Although the failure of this second major attempt to establish multilateral investment rules was again due to political conflicts about the proper level of investment protection by international law, the progeny of the 1967 OECD Draft Convention illustrates the close linkage between the BIT movement and attempts to establish a multilateral investment treaty.

C   The rise of bilateral and regional investment treaties

In sharp contrast to the failure of multilateral agreements, bilateral and regional treaties containing substantive law on international investment protection came into existence, starting in the late 1950s. The first BIT was concluded in 1959 between the Federal Republic of Germany and Pakistan.[75] The conclusion of this bilateral treaty coincided with the attempts within the OECD in the 1960s to mount a multilateral framework for the protection of foreign investment. Being based on the preparatory work by Abs and Shawcross, the content of this first BIT closely resembled the 1967 OECD Draft Convention.

The motivation for concluding a bilateral treaty, instead of awaiting the developments on the multilateral level, were arguably less due to the desire to depart from a multilateral solution, but rather reflected Germany's strong interest in establishing protection of its foreign investors abroad. As such, the conclusion of the first BIT constituted a test case for the acceptance of the content of the multilateral projects discussed at the time, rather than a departure from multilateralism as a general ordering paradigm for international investment relations.[76] Hence, with respect

---

[74] Dolzer and Stevens (*supra* footnote 68), pp. 2 *et seq.* (1995) (pointing out that "OECD countries have continued to review their policies in this respect within the OECD Committee on International Investment and Multinational Enterprises").

[75] Treaty between the Federal Republic of Germany and Pakistan for the Promotion and Protection of Investments, signed on November 25, 1959, entered into force on April 28, 1962.

[76] This interpretation is suggested by the fact that it was Germany who submitted the Abs–Shawcross Draft to the OECD as a basis for the negotiations on the 1967 OECD Draft Convention. See Brandon (*supra* footnote 51), Int'l & Comp. L. Q. Suppl. No. 3, p. 10 (1962). Furthermore, post-Second World War Germany was firmly attached to multilateralism as an ordering principle for international relations more generally. See Baumann, *Der Wandel des deutschen Multilateralismus*, pp. 26–44 (2006). It would thus

to the historic pedigree of BITs, there seems to be a closer connection to multilateralism than the form of BITs as bilateral treaties might suggest.

Multilateralism as a political agenda behind the conclusion of BITs also surfaces in the BIT practice of the United States which started in the 1970s. As pointed out by Vandevelde who negotiated several of the US treaties:

> one of the most important [purposes], at least in the minds of the early proponents of these treaties, was to counter the claim made during the 1970s by many developing countries that customary international law no longer required that expropriation be accompanied by prompt, adequate, and effective compensation.[77]

BITs initially faced political problems similar to the earlier multilateral projects and consequently remained relatively scarce until about 1990. Between 1959 and 1969, the total number of BITs concluded came up to only 75 treaties, another 92 BITs were concluded between 1970 and 1979, and 219 BITs between 1980 and 1989.[78] From 1959 until 1989, the total number of BITs summed-up to 386, and accordingly covered only a relatively small number of bilateral investment relationships worldwide. To a certain extent, this reflected the negative attitude of developing countries vis-à-vis foreign investment and its protection.

In the 1990s, however, the situation changed rather drastically. Between 1990 and 2006, the number of BITs rose significantly to a total of more than 2,500, with almost every country having entered into usually several of such treaties.[79] In addition, provisions protecting foreign investment, that are often identical to those in BITs, are included in an increasing number of bilateral preferential trade agreements.[80]

Parallel to the number of treaties, the territorial scope of BITs broadened and now comprises countries from every region of the world. BITs have become a popular and accepted instrument to promote and protect

---

be surprising, if Germany departed from this general foreign policy in its international investment relations.

[77] Vandevelde (*supra* footnote 18), 14 Mich. J. Int'l L. 621, 625 (1993).

[78] UNCTAD, *Bilateral Investment Treaties in the Mid-1990s*, p. 9 (1998).

[79] UNCTAD, *Recent Developments in International Investment Agreements (2006–June 2007)*, p. 2 (2007).

[80] By the end of 2006, already over 240 such agreements existed, *ibid.*, p. 6; see also UNCTAD, *Investment Provisions in Economic Integration Agreements* (2006). The United States, for example, has largely shifted away from isolated investment treaties and rather concludes treaties that comprise investment and trade rules; see Hilaire and Yang, *The United States and the New Regionalism/Bilateralism*, 38 J. World Trade 603 (2004); see also Gantz, *The Evolution of FTA Investment Provisions*, 19 Am. U. Int'l L. Rev. 679 (2004).

the inflow of foreign investment and are frequently used by countries in Africa,[81] Asia,[82] and Latin America.[83] The acceptance of BITs in the latter region is particularly noteworthy, since Latin American countries have long relied on the Calvo Doctrine in their foreign relations practice.[84] The acceptance of international law standards in BITs and opening recourse to investor-State dispute settlement, therefore, constitutes a fundamental change in Latin American foreign policy.

Furthermore, BITs ceased to be restricted to pairing developed and developing countries, but were increasingly concluded between and among developing and transitioning economies. By the end of 2004, one-fourth of all BITs were so-called South–South BITs concluded between developing countries.[85] This does not only reflect that the lines between capital-exporting and capital-importing countries are becoming increasingly blurred,[86] it also suggests that the protection of foreign investment by international law and the content of BITs are increasingly recognized by developing and transitioning economies as an appropriate mechanism to promote and protect foreign investment, contrary to the positions taken in the 1970s in the UN General Assembly.[87] Meanwhile, investment protection by international law receives almost universal recognition, with only very few countries not having entered into and ratified a single investment treaty.[88]

Parallel to the rise of BITs, a considerable number of partly existing, partly projected agreements concerning regional economic integration emerged, many of which include provisions on the protection of foreign

[81] See Mosoti, *Bilateral Investment Treaties and the Possibility of a Multilateral Framework in Investment at the WTO: Are Poor Countries Caught in Between?*, 26 Nw. J. Int'l L. & Bus. 95 (2005) (focusing specifically on the BIT practice of African countries).

[82] See Schill, *Tearing Down the Great Wall – The New Generation Investment Treaties of the People's Republic of China*, 15 Cardozo J. Int'l & Comp. L. 73 (2007) (focusing on the development of the investment treaty practice of the People's Republic of China); Reading, *The Bilateral Investment Treaty in ASEAN*, 42 Duke L. J. 679, 693 *et seq.* (1992) (comparing BITs by Member States of ASEAN with the provisions of US BITs).

[83] On BITs and the changing attitudes of Latin American countries see Peters and Schrijver, *Latin America and International Regulation of Foreign Investment*, 39 Neth. Int'l L. Rev. 355 (1992); Oschmann, *Investitionsschutzverträge in Lateinamerika*, 42 RIW 494 (1996); Herdegen, *Investitionsschutz in Lateinamerika*, 94 ZVglRWiss 341 (1995); Escobar, *An Introductory Note on Bilateral Investment Treaties Recently Concluded by Latin American States*, 11 ICSID Rev. – For. Inv. L. J. 86 (1996).

[84] See *supra* footnote 14.

[85] UNCTAD, *South–South Cooperation in International Investment Arrangements*, p. 6 (2005).

[86] Vandevelde (*supra* footnote 18), 12 U.C. Davis J. Int'l L. & Pol'y 157, 182 (2005).

[87] See *supra* footnotes 59–64 and accompanying text.

[88] The most prominent example is Brazil which, although having entered into a few BITs, has so far not ratified them.

investment.[89] The most prominent example is the North American Free Trade Agreement (NAFTA) that was concluded in 1992 between Canada, Mexico, and the United States.[90] Other regional regimes that contain provisions on investment protection were established under the aegis of Mercado Común del Sur (MERCOSUR) and the Caribbean Community (CARICOM) in South and Central America,[91] under the Asia-Pacific Economic Cooperation (APEC) and the Association of Southeast Asian Nations (ASEAN) in Asia,[92] under the Common Market for Eastern and Southern Africa (COMESA) and the Southern African Development Community (SADC) in Africa,[93] and under several regional agreements in the Middle East.[94] Finally, with the Energy Charter Treaty (ECT)[95] one important sectoral agreement exists that contains provisions for the promotion and protection of investment in the energy sector.[96] Overall, the provisions of many of the regional and sectoral investment treaties closely resemble the standard content of BITs, including provision on expropriation, fair and equitable treatment, national and MFN treatment, and investor-State arbitration.

These developments reflect a fundamental change in attitude towards the protection of foreign investment under international law of developing and transitioning economies. It was mainly caused by two factors.[97] First, after the end of the Cold War and the decline of socialism, market ideology became the prevailing model for organizing the economy.

---

[89] See te Velde and Fahnbulleh, *Investment Related Provisions in Regional Trade Agreements* (October 2003).

[90] North American Free Trade Agreement (NAFTA), signed on December 17, 1992, entered into force on January 1, 1994, 32 I.L.M. 289 and 605 (1993).

[91] On the mechanisms of investment protection and dispute settlement in South and Central America see comprehensively Leathley, *International Dispute Resolution in Latin America* (2007).

[92] See generally, on APEC and ASEAN, Kodama, *Asia-Pacific Region: APEC and ASEAN*, 30 Int'l Law 367 (1996). On the respective instruments and principles of investment protection in the Asia-Pacific region see Sornarajah, *Protection of Foreign Investment in the Asia-Pacific Economic Co-operation Region*, 29(2) J. World Trade 105, 122–25 (1995).

[93] See generally on COMESA and SADC Khandelwal, *COMESA and SADC* (December 2004).

[94] See Peters, *Dispute Settlement Arrangements in Investment Treaties*, 22 Neth. Ybk. Int'l L. 91, 160 (1991) (listing three regional agreements on the promotion and protection of investment among Arab countries).

[95] Energy Charter Treaty (Annex I of the Final Act of the European Energy Charter Conference) (ECT), signed December 17, 1994, 34 I.L.M. 373 (1995).

[96] See Wälde (ed.), *The Energy Charter Treaty* (1996).

[97] See Vandevelde (*supra* footnote 18), 12 U.C. Davis J. Int'l L. & Pol'y 157, 177 *et seq.* (2005).

Secondly, it became widely accepted that foreign investment constituted a main factor in stimulating economic development in transitioning and developing economies. The debt crisis in the 1980s and the scarcity of public loans available to developing countries further facilitated the emergence of a positive attitude to foreign investment.[98] Similarly, with developing countries increasingly transforming into emerging markets, the actual practice of developing States to employ expropriation as a policy instrument vanished,[99] and the rhetoric of the New International Economic Order disappeared.[100] Accordingly, "in the Global Era investment agreements … have become instruments of globalization, removing barriers to trade and investment, much in the same way that the FCN treaties of the Eighteenth and Nineteenth Centuries sought to establish commercial relations between countries."[101]

D   Limited success of multilateralism: ICSID and MIGA

Instruments of international investment protection are, however, not restricted to bilateral and regional conventions. Instead, two international conventions have been concluded that express a desire by developed and developing countries to order international investment relations multilaterally. In the mid-1960s the Convention on the Settlement of Investment Disputes between States and Nationals of Other States (ICSID Convention)[102] was concluded and established a multilateral framework containing procedural rules for conducting arbitrations between host States and foreign investors. In addition, the Convention Establishing the Multilateral Investment Guarantee Agency (MIGA Convention) which was finalized in 1985 constitutes a second successful incidence of genuine multilateralism in the investment context.[103] It created a multilateral insurance framework for foreign investment projects.[104] Both conventions support the conclusion that a basic

---

[98] Kurtz (*supra* footnote 32), 23 U. Pa. J. Int'l Econ. L. 713, 720 (2002); see comprehensively on the debt crisis, Corbridge (ed.), *International Debt* (1999).

[99] Minor (*supra* footnote 48), 25 J. Int'l Bus. Stud. 177 (1994).

[100] Wälde (*supra* footnote 61) (1998).

[101] Vandevelde (*supra* footnote 18), 12 U.C. Davis J. Int'l L. & Pol'y 157, 183 (2005).

[102] 575 U.N.T.S. 159 (entered into force on October 14, 1966).

[103] Convention Establishing the Multilateral Investment Guarantee Agency of October 11, 1985, entered into force on April 12, 1988, 1508 U.N.T.S. 99.

[104] On both instruments see also Rowat, *Multilateral Approaches to Improving the Investment Climate of Developing Countries*, 33 Harv. Int'l L. J. 103 (1992).

consensus between capital-importing and capital-exporting countries exists on the desirability of the promotion and protection of foreign investment. Furthermore, they illustrate the potential and the general willingness of States to establish multilateral orders for international investment relations.

1 The International Centre for Settlement of Investment Disputes (ICSID)

Despite the earlier failure of multilateral approaches in establishing substantive obligations on the treatment of foreign investment and parallel to the wave of uncompensated expropriations in many developing countries in the decades following their independence, the ICSID Convention[105] was successfully concluded as early as 1965. This multilateral treaty created the International Centre for Settlement of Investment Disputes (ICSID) – an international organization closely tied to the World Bank – and established a procedural framework for the settlement of investment disputes between foreign investors and States through binding arbitration. As recognized by the Preamble of the ICSID Convention, the conclusion of this multilateral treaty arose out of and reflected "the need for international cooperation for economic development, and the role of private international investment therein."[106] Currently, 143 of the 155 signatory States have ratified the Convention, including many of the most important capital-importing countries.[107]

While the Centre does not arbitrate investment disputes itself, it provides the institutional infrastructure for administering investment arbitrations. Under Article 25 of the ICSID Convention, the Centre has jurisdiction over "any legal dispute arising directly out of an investment, between a Contracting State … and a national of another Contracting State, which the parties to the dispute consent in writing to submit to the Centre." During ongoing investment arbitration under the ICSID Convention, the investor's home State is prevented from granting

---

[105] See, on the ICSID Convention, comprehensively, Schreuer, *The ICSID Convention* (2001); Schöbener and Markert, *Das International Centre for Settlement of Investment Disputes (ICSID)*, 105 ZVglRWiss 65 (2006).
[106] See the Preamble of the ICSID Convention.
[107] See the list of Contracting States (as of November 4, 2007), available at: http://icsid. worldbank.org/ICSID/FrontServlet?requestType=ICSIDDocRH&actionVal=Contract ingStates&ReqFrom=Main.

diplomatic protection, from bringing a claim in its own name,[108] or from otherwise interfering with the settlement of the dispute between investor and host State.[109] Disputes are usually settled by a panel of three arbitrators, two of whom are party-appointed.[110]

Recourse to arbitration under the ICSID Convention is, however, entirely voluntary. Namely, the ratification of the ICSID Convention does not *per se* entail the signatory's acceptance of the Centre's jurisdiction for investment disputes. Instead, host State and investor have to consent separately to ICSID arbitration. Originally drafted in order to offer a forum for contractual arbitration between foreign investors and host States, consent to ICSID arbitration nowadays is most often contained in BITs under which host States extend a standing offer to covered investors that they can accept by initiating arbitration under the Convention.[111]

The specificities of ICSID arbitration are the finality of ICSID awards and their automatic recognition in the Convention's Member States. Unlike awards in international commercial arbitration, ICSID awards are subject only to Convention-specific annulment proceedings,[112] not, however, to domestic review according to the law of the arbitration's situs. Furthermore, the enforcement State is prevented from invoking its public policy (*ordre public*) against the enforcement of an ICSID award.[113] Instead, every Member State has to "recognize an award … as binding and enforce [it] within its territory as if it were a final judgment of a court in that State."[114] Recourse to ICSID arbitration, therefore, enables foreign investors to settle disputes with host States in an independent forum, and is particularly salient in

---

[108] Schreuer, *Investment Protection and International Relations*, in Reinisch and Kriebaum (eds.), *The Law of International Relations*, pp. 345, 350 *et seq.* (2007).

[109] Article 27, ICSID Convention.

[110] See Article 37, ICSID Convention.

[111] Paulsson, *Arbitration Without Privity*, 10 ICSID Rev. – For. Inv. L. J. 232 (1995); Cremades, *Arbitration in Investment Treaties: Public Offer of Arbitration in Investment-Protection Treaties*, in Briner *et al.* (eds.), *Law of International Business and Dispute Settlement in the 21st Century*, p. 149 (2001); Bjorklund, *Contract Without Privity: Sovereign Offer and Investor Acceptance*, 2 Chi. J. Int'l L. 183 (2001).

[112] See Article 52, ICSID Convention.

[113] Schreuer (*supra* footnote 105), Article 54, para. 71 (2001). This differs from arbitral awards enforced under the United Nations Convention on the Recognition and Enforcement of Foreign Arbitral Awards, done at New York on June 10, 1958 ("New York Convention"), 330 U.N.T.S. 38, whose Article V allows the enforcement State to invoke its *ordre public* in order to deny enforcement of an award.

[114] Article 54(1), ICSID Convention. The only loophole enabling States to refuse recognition and enforcement of an ICSID award is State immunity (see Article 55, ICSID Convention). See, on State immunity as a bar to enforcement of ICSID awards, comprehensively, Schreuer (*supra* footnote 105), Article 55.

promoting and protecting investments in countries with an underdeveloped, politically biased, corrupt or inefficient court system.

Somewhat surprisingly, the ICSID Convention has developed into one of the most successful multilateral instruments in the field of international investment protection and governs most BIT-based investor-State disputes,[115] although multilateral instruments containing substantive investment rules have failed and continue to fail even today. Notwithstanding the strong antipathies of most developing countries relating to foreign investment in the 1960s and 1970s, the early success of the ICSID Convention can be ascribed to the absence of any substantive investment protection and the voluntary recourse to investment arbitration under the Convention.

Instead, the ICSID Convention merely created a forum for direct recourse of investors against host States and thereby aims at depoliticizing the settlement of investment disputes.[116] The Convention also left the decision about the applicable law to the arbitrating parties,[117] and did not impose direct obligations relating to the treatment of foreign investors that could have been perceived as limiting the sovereignty of host States.[118] Its apparent neutrality vis-à-vis the sovereignty of capital-importing countries and its apolitical approach to investor-State relations were arguably the decisive factors for the success of this multilateral framework at a time when substantive investment protection standards were highly controversial. Overall, however, it reflects a general interest of States to order international investment relations on a multilateral basis. In fact, the importance of the ICSID Convention as a mechanism for the settlement of investor-State disputes and its impact on the compliance with, and the enforcement of, obligations under international investment agreements cannot be underestimated.[119]

2 The Multilateral Investment Guarantee Agency (MIGA)

The second successful multilateral agreement relating to the promotion and protection of foreign investment was the MIGA Convention.[120]

---

[115] See UNCTAD, *Investor-State Disputes Arising from Investment Treaties: A Review*, p. 5 (2005).

[116] See Shihata, *Towards a Greater Depoliticization of Investment Disputes: The Role of ICSID and MIGA*, 1 ICSID Rev. – For. Inv. L. J. 1 (1986).

[117] See Article 42, ICSID Convention.

[118] See Broches, *The Convention on the Settlement of Investment Disputes between States and Nationals of Other States*, 136 Recueil des Cours 331, 348 (1972–II); Lowenfeld, *Investment Agreements and International Law*, 42 Colum. J. Transnat'l L. 123, 124 *et seq.* (2003).

[119] See *infra* Ch. VI.

[120] On the Convention generally see, for example, Alsop, *The World Bank's Multilateral Investment Guaranty Agency*, 25 Colum. J. Transnat'l L. 101 (1986); Chatterjee, *The*

Having entered into force in 1988 and counting 172 Member States as of April 2008,[121] the Convention established an international organization whose objective is to "encourage the flow of investments for productive purposes among member countries."[122] Apart from activities like research and information about foreign investment,[123] MIGA's primary tool for promoting and protecting foreign investment projects consists in offering an insurance scheme for foreign investors in developing countries.[124]

MIGA's insurance covers currency transfer risks, expropriations and measures tantamount to expropriations, unenforceable breaches of investor-State contracts, and damages from war and civil disturbances.[125] In addition, the investor and MIGA can agree on broader insurance protection against other non-commercial risks.[126] In case of an insured event, MIGA can pursue the rights the investor may have against the host State by means of subrogation in the MIGA's own name.[127] From the point of view of the foreign investor, purchasing MIGA insurance covers against the most salient foreign investment risks and was thus expected to contribute to additional investment flows into developing countries.

As with the ICSID Convention, the MIGA Convention does not, however, impose any direct obligations upon the Member States relating to the treatment of foreign investment. This is considered as one of the reasons why MIGA was accepted by numerous States, including many foreign investment critical Latin American countries, at a time when these countries still

Convention Establishing the Multilateral Investment Guarantee Agency, 36 Int'l & Comp. L. Q. 76 (1987); Ebenroth and Karl, *Die multilaterale Investitions-Garantie-Agentur* (1989); H. Petersmann, *Die Multilaterale Investitions-Garantie-Agentur (MIGA)*, 46 ZaöRV 758 (1986); Oschmann, *Investitionsschutz durch internationale Investitionsversicherung*, 41 RIW 972 (1995); Rowat (*supra* footnote 104), 33 Harv. Int'l L. J. 103 (1992); Shihata (*supra* footnote 116), 1 ICSID Rev. – For. Inv. L. J. 1 (1986); Shihata, *The Multilateral Investment Guarantee Agency*, 20 Int'l Law. 487 (1986); Shihata, *The Multilateral Investment Guarantee Agency (MIGA) and the Legal Treatment of Foreign Investment*, 203 Recueil des Cours 95 (1987–III); Shihata, *MIGA and Foreign Investment* (1988).

[121] See the list of Member States, available at the website of MIGA at www.miga.org/sitelevel2/level2.cfm?id=1152.

[122] Article 2(1), MIGA Convention.

[123] Article 23, MIGA Convention.

[124] See Articles 11–22, MIGA Convention.

[125] See Article 11(a), MIGA Convention.

[126] Article 11(b) and (c), MIGA Convention.

[127] See Article 18, MIGA Convention. The subrogated claims are enforced according to Article 57, MIGA Convention in connection with the dispute settlement provisions in Annex II of the Convention.

rejected entering into BITs.[128] Unlike substantive investment obligations, an insurance framework was viewed as involving fewer restrictions on State sovereignty.[129] Notwithstanding, the accession to the MIGA Convention suggests a positive attitude of States vis-à-vis foreign investment and the desirability of its protection by international law, in particular when compared with the rhetoric of the New International Economic Order.

Furthermore, as with the ICSID Convention, the conclusion of the MIGA Convention illustrates the willingness of developing countries to organize international investment relations on a multilateral basis. Not only is MIGA itself a multilateral international organization, it also actively contributes to fostering multilateral structures in international investment relations. Thus, MIGA has a mandate to conclude, based on MFN treatment, agreements with developing countries that assure MIGA and the investments it insures certain standards of treatment.[130] Furthermore, MIGA is charged with promoting and facilitating the conclusion of international investment treaties among its Member States.[131] This mandate of promoting and protecting foreign investment in a multilateral forum further manifests the potential for multilateralism in international investment relations.[132]

E   The failures of multilateralism II: 1990–2004

Encouraged by the proliferation of bilateral treaties after the end of the Cold War, as well as the success of the ICSID and MIGA Conventions, capital-exporting countries continued to make efforts to establish multilateral rules concerning the treatment of foreign investment by host States. This included endeavors within the various negotiation rounds of the GATT, and later the WTO, as well as a major project at the end of the

---

[128] Germany had in fact requested the inclusion of substantive rules on investment protection into the MIGA Convention. This was, however, rejected because it could have endangered the success of the Convention. See Schlemmer-Schulte, *The World Bank Guidelines on the Treatment of Foreign Direct Investment*, in Bradlow and Escher (eds.), *Legal Aspects of Foreign Direct Investment*, pp. 87, 89 (1999); see on the drafting history of the MIGA Convention, Shihata, *MIGA and Foreign Investment*, pp. 31–99 (1988).

[129] *Cf.* H. Petersmann (*supra* footnote 120), 46 ZaöRV 758, 765 (1986).

[130] Article 23(b)(ii), MIGA Convention.

[131] Article 23(b)(iii), MIGA Convention.

[132] *Cf.* H. Petersmann (*supra* footnote 120), 46 ZaöRV 758, 771 (1986) ("Dadurch dürfte die MIGA in erheblichem Umfang zur Multilateralisierung und Konsolidierung bereits geltender Verträge und Rechtsgrundsätze und zu einer Depolitisierung des internationalen Investitionsschutzes beitragen können.").

1990s in the OECD. Even though the content of this multilateral draft convention closely resembled the content of the then already numerous and widespread BITs, the project failed to reach a consensus among OECD Members. Similarly, renewed efforts to launch negotiations of multilateral investment rules within the WTO in the new millennium brought about no results. Despite the parallel proliferation of BITs, multilateral projects relating to investment protection thus continued to fail.

1   Earlier attempts to introduce investment issues into the GATT/WTO

Instruments of multilateral investment protection became somewhat exceptional after the failure of the 1967 OECD Draft Convention and the proclamation of the New International Economic Order. The United States did, however, launch various attempts to bring the topic back to the forefront in the 1980s, this time within the GATT system.[133] Despite its primary focus on international trade, this platform had already been used as a forum to address, albeit with limited success, issues concerning foreign investment. In 1955, a resolution on International Investment for Economic Development was passed that called upon Member States to "ente[r] into bilateral and multilateral agreements to provide for security for investments, avoidance of double taxation, and facilitation of the repatriation of funds of foreign investments."[134] During the Tokyo Round, a proposal by the United States to deal with investment-related issues was not taken up for further consideration.[135]

In 1982, awareness of GATT Members of the need for trade-related investment measures was created by a dispute concerning the Canadian Foreign Investment Review Act in which a GATT Panel found that certain local content and export performance requirements imposed by Canada on certain foreign investments constituted trade-related measures and violated the GATT national treatment provision.[136] This led ultimately to the conclusion of the Agreement on Trade-Related Investment Measures (TRIMs) in the Uruguay Round.[137] Its scope of application was, however,

---

[133] See Dattu (*supra* footnote 31), 24 Fordham Int'l L. J. 275, 288 *et seq.* (2000).

[134] See Dattu (*supra* footnote 31), 24 Fordham Int'l L. J. 275, 288 (2000).

[135] See Mashayekhi and Gibbs, *Lessons from the Uruguay Round Negotiations on Investment*, 33(6) J. World Trade 1, 4 (1999); see also Brewer and Young, *The Multilateral Investment System and Multinational Enterprises*, p. 122 (1998).

[136] See *Canada – Administration of the Foreign Investment Review Act*, GATT Panel Report, February 7, 1984.

[137] See Shenkin (*supra* footnote 31), 55 U. Pitt. L. Rev. 541, 559 *et seq.* (1994). See also Kurtz (*supra* footnote 32), 23 U. Pa. J. Int'l Econ. L. 713, 722 *et seq.* (2002).

limited to "investment measures related to trade in goods only,"[138] and left issues of foreign investment protection untouched. The reason for such limited scope was again a "compromise reached between the two opposing positions within GATT on investment measures:"[139] one represented by the position of the United States to achieve a strong protection of foreign investment; and the other by developing countries reflecting their concern about restricting their own development goals and their liberty to regulate foreign investment.[140] Not surprisingly, the TRIMs Agreement had only a limited effect as a tool of multilateral investment protection.[141]

Some success concerning multilateral investment liberalization was, however, achieved by the General Agreement on Trade in Services (GATS) that provided for national and MFN treatment as principles governing international trade in services. It applies *inter alia* to the trade in services through the presence of a foreign service-provider in the host State and thus, to a certain extent opened access to foreign markets and foreign investment.[142] Although the negotiations on GATS proposed by the United States were originally opposed by developing countries,[143] the latter finally conceded to negotiate on the condition that GATS would remain separate from trade in goods and would provide for a clear development perspective.[144]

Yet, the impact of GATS on investment liberalization and protection is limited as it applies only to matters upon a specific commitment by a

---

[138] Article 1, TRIMs.

[139] Dattu (*supra* footnote 31), 24 Fordham Int'l L. J. 275, 291 (2000).

[140] See Stewart (ed.), *The GATT Uruguay Round*, pp. 2068 *et seq.* (1993); Price and Christy, *Agreement on Trade Related Investment Measures (TRIMS)*, in Stewart (ed.), *The World Trade Organization*, pp. 439, 447 *et seq.* (1996) (for a description of the positions of the opposing factions in the negotiation of the TRIMs Agreement).

[141] See, for example, Quillin, *The World Trade Organization and its Protection of Foreign Direct Investment*, 28 Okla. City U. L. Rev. 875, 888 *et seq.* (2003); Civello, *The TRIMs Agreement: A Failed Attempt at Investment Liberalization*, 8 Minn. J. Global Trade 97 (1999); Dattu (*supra* footnote 31), 24 Fordham Int'l L. J. 275, 292 *et seq.* (2000); Sauvé, *Regional Versus Multilateral Approaches to Services and Investment Liberalization: Anything to Worry About?*, in Demaret *et al.* (eds), *Regionalism and Multilateralism after the Uruguay Round: Convergence, Divergence and Interaction*, pp. 429, 437 (1997) (criticizing the TRIMs Agreement as "extremely limited in scope, and ... largely attuned to the concerns of an era in policy-making characterized more by suspicion of – and the need to control – foreign investment than by keenness to compete for and attract such investment").

[142] The GATS has thus been called the WTO's "real investment agreement," see Price and Christy (*supra* footnote 140), pp. 439, 454 (1996).

[143] Stewart (*supra* footnote 140), *The GATT Uruguay Round*, pp. 2354 *et seq* (1993).

[144] Kurtz (*supra* footnote 32), 23 U. Pa. J. Int'l Econ. L. 713, 722 (2002).

host State (opt-in) and allows for numerous exceptions.[145] While encompassing national and MFN treatment and establishing an obligation on the host State not to restrict the transfer of funds earned in rendering the services, GATS does not contain other standards of treatment in respect to the protection of foreign investment. Furthermore, the enforcement of GATS remains within the traditional inter-State dispute settlement framework and, therefore, left open various aspects that traditionally play an essential role in the protection of foreign investment.

Finally, the Agreement on Trade-Related Aspects of Intellectual Property Rights (TRIPS) covers some aspects related to foreign investment by according protection for intellectual property. Although foreign investment projects regularly involve issues of intellectual property protection,[146] TRIPS does not provide rules for the protection of foreign investment in more comprehensive terms. It concerns but one aspect of foreign investment activities.

In sum, the achievements within the GATT/WTO to introduce foreign investment protection were barely satisfactory for capital-exporting countries, because they did not achieve the conclusion of substantive rules of investment protection. Instead, investment-related provisions within the GATT/WTO merely constituted a patchwork of isolated aspects that were relevant for foreign investment activity without, however, establishing any systematic or comprehensive framework. Similar to the situation surrounding the failure of the Havana Charter as well as the 1967 OECD Draft Convention, a breakthrough for an encompassing framework for foreign investment in the GATT/WTO collapsed due to the incompatible positions of capital-exporting and capital-importing countries.

Nevertheless, the conclusion of TRIMs, GATS, and TRIPS was viewed as an encouraging sign for the negotiation of further multilateral investment rules. Accordingly, developed countries persisted in pushing to keep this issue on the WTO agenda during the 1990s.[147] Yet, due to reservations by several developing countries,[148] the First Ministerial Meeting in Singapore decided only "to establish a working group to

---

[145] Dattu (*supra* footnote 31), 24 Fordham Int'l L. J. 275, 293 *et seq.* (2000).

[146] See, on the connections between intellectual property and foreign direct investment, Drahos, *BITs and BIPs*, 4 J. World Int. Prop. 791 (2001); Selting, *FDI and International Protection of Intellectual Property*, in Bradlow and Escher (*supra* footnote 128), p. 205 (1999).

[147] See Burt, *Developing Countries and the Framework for Negotiations on Foreign Direct Investment in the World Trade Organization*, 12 Am. U. Int'l L. Rev. 1015 (1997).

[148] See Burt (*supra* footnote 147), 12 Am. U. Int'l L. Rev. 1015, 1049 *et seq.* (1997).

examine the relationship between trade and investment" without, how-ever, granting a mandate for future negotiations.[149]

2   The OECD Multilateral Agreement on Investment (MAI) – 1998

Since hopes of quickly succeeding in negotiations on a multilateral invest-ment treaty in the WTO were dampened during the First Ministerial Meeting in 1996, several developed countries decided to shift negoti-ations for a multilateral investment treaty back to the OECD. Starting in 1996, negotiations for the Multilateral Agreement on Investment (MAI) were launched. The decision to shift forum was a direct reaction to the frictions concerning multilateral investment rules within the WTO and constituted an attempt to break the negotiation deadlock there.[150] In par-ticular, the OECD was chosen in order to avoid the impact of developing countries in watering down the substantive protection to be offered by a multilateral investment treaty.[151]

After preparatory work by the Committee on International Investment and Multinational Enterprises and the Committee on Capital Movements and Invisible Transactions,[152] the OECD Council decided in May 1996 to commence negotiations for the MAI. This agreement was intended to result in a free-standing multilateral treaty that established a comprehen-sive framework for the protection and promotion of foreign investment, open to OECD Members and non-members alike.[153] The negotiations were expressly geared towards existing international investment agree-ments, such as NAFTA Chapter 11, the Energy Charter Treaty, and the

---

[149] World Trade Organization, Ministerial Declaration, December 13, 1996, 36 I.L.M. 218 (1997), para. 20.

[150] See Dattu (*supra* footnote 31), 24 Fordham Int'l L. J. 275, 295 *et seq.* (2000). For the debate about which forum was the appropriate place for negotiation see also Smythe, *Your Place or Mine? States, International Organizations and the Negotiation of Investment Rules,* 7 Transnat'l Corp. 85 (December 1998). On the strategy by the United States to shift forums as a mechanism to achieve its aims on the international level see Braithwaite, *Methods of Power for Development: Weapons of the Weak, Weapons of the Strong,* 26 Mich. J. Int'l L. 297, 310 *et seq.* (2004).

[151] Canner, *The Multilateral Agreement on Investment,* 31 Cornell Int'l L. J. 657, 666 (1998); Kurtz (*supra* footnote 32), 23 U. Pa. J. Int'l Econ. L. 713, 714 (2002).

[152] See Dattu (*supra* footnote 31), 24 Fordham Int'l L. J. 275, 297 (2000).

[153] See OECD, *A Multilateral Agreement on Investment: Report by the Committee on International Investment and Multinational Enterprises (CIME) and the Committee on Capital Movements and Invisible Transactions (CMIT)* (May 5, 1995).

various BITs.[154] Similar to these existing investment treaties, the MAI's negotiation text included a broad definition of investment, protection for investors against direct and indirect expropriation, standards of fair and equitable treatment, and full protection and security, as well as provisions for investor-State dispute settlement.[155] Differences to existing BITs were rather marginal.

Despite its close similarity to existing international investment treaties, the MAI ultimately failed for a number of reasons. While immediately triggered by the decision of France to retract from the negotiations because of concerns over the impact of investment liberalization on its cultural industry that was perceived to be threatened by Hollywood,[156] the impossibility of achieving a viable consensus on a multilateral investment treaty among OECD Members was more closely related to the political costs of such an agreement.

First, OECD Members were unable to achieve a consensus on several contentious issues. In particular, there was an unresolved and continuing disagreement between the United States and EU Member States regarding the extraterritorial effect of the US Helms–Burton Act,[157] a debate about exceptions for cultural industries, demanded primarily by Canada

---

[154] OECD, *ibid.*

[155] OECD, *The Multilateral Agreement on Investment, Draft Consolidated Text* (April 22, 1998) (with commentary). See, on the MAI, Dattu (*supra* footnote 31), 24 Fordham Int'l L. J. 275, 298 *et seq.* (2000); Kurtz (*supra* footnote 32), 23 U. Pa. J. Int'l Econ. L. 713, 756 *et seq.* (2002). See further Böhmer, *The Struggle for a Multilateral Agreement on Investments,* 41 German Ybk. Int'l L. 268 (1998); Canner (*supra* footnote 151), 31 Cornell Int'l L. J. 657 (1998); Engering, *The Multilateral Investment Agreement,* 5 Transnat'l Corp. 147 (December 1996); Graham, *Fighting the Wrong Enemy* (2000); Henderson, *The MAI Affair: A Story and Its Lessons* (1999); Karl, *Das multilaterale Investitionsabkommen (MAI),* 44 RIW 432 (1998); Muchlinski, *The Rise and Fall of the Multilateral Agreement on Investment: Where Now?,* 34 Int'l Law. 1033 (2000); Picciotto, *Linkages in International Investment Regulation,* 19 U. Pa. J. Int'l Econ. L. 731 (1998); Stumberg, *Sovereignty by Subtraction: The Multilateral Agreement on Investment,* 31 Cornell Int'l L. J. 491 (1998); UNCTAD, *Lessons from the MAI* (2000); Valliantos, *De-Fanging the MAI,* 31 Cornell Int'l L. J. 713 (1998); Witherell, *The OECD Multilateral Agreement on Investment,* 4 Transnat'l Corp. 1 (August 1995).

[156] More closely on the impact of domestic French politics see Graham, *Regulatory Takings, Supranational Treatment, and the Multilateral Agreement on Investment,* 31 Cornell Int'l L. J. 599, 613 (1998); Schittecatte, *The Politics of the MAI,* 1 J. World Inv. 329, 349 (2000).

[157] See, on the Helms–Burton Act and its conformity with international law, Clagett, *Title III of the Helms–Burton Act Is Consistent with International Law,* 90 A.J.I.L. 434 (1996); Lowenfeld, *Congress and Cuba: the Helms–Burton Act,* 90 A.J.I.L. 419 (1996); Ratchik, *Cuban Liberty and the Democratic Society Act of 1995,* 11 Am. U. J. Int'l L. & Pol'y 343 (1996). The Act expands the US embargo against Cuba by barring US foreign aid to countries supporting Cuba, allowing US nationals to sue owners of property

and France, the EU's proposal to include an exception for regional economic organizations, and controversy about labor and environmental standards.[158] Second, the MAI negotiations were criticized as a deliberate choice to deny developing countries a voice in the negotiations. Although some non-OECD Members had observer status,[159] they could not formally participate in the negotiations. For this reason, several developing countries, in particular India, opposed the MAI.[160]

Third, the MAI negotiations received considerable opposition from non-governmental organizations (NGOs) that were concerned with the impact of investment protection on issues like environmental protection and labor standards.[161] Actively using the internet for their purposes, NGOs organized massive political opposition by civil society because the negotiations were perceived as fostering the authority of global capital and multinational corporations, while remaining shortsighted on social and environmental standards. The OECD and its Member States, by contrast, were ill-prepared to meet and counter this opposition. They particularly showed a considerable lack in communicating the proper scope, content, and objectives of the MAI to the general public and their domestic constituencies in order to clear misunderstandings.[162] One of these misunderstandings was the widespread perception that the MAI would disable any legislative changes that negatively affected foreign investors. For instance, the MAI's "standstill" principle which would have prevented the introduction of new discriminatory measures against foreign investors was perceived as an absolute prohibition of any new regulation, including measures to protect the environment; the "rollback"

expropriated by Cuba in US courts and visa restrictions for aliens dealing with property expropriated by Cuba.

[158] See further on these deal breakers, Muchlinski, *The Rise and Fall of the Multilateral Agreement on Investment*, in Fletcher, Mistelis and Cremona (eds.), *Foundations and Perspectives of International Trade Law*, pp. 114, 129 *et seq.* (2001). See also Canner (*supra* footnote 151), 31 Cornell Int'l L. J. 657, 667 *et seq.* (1998).

[159] These countries were Argentina, Brazil, Chile, Estonia, Latvia, Lithuania, the Slovak Republic, and Hong Kong. See Karl, *Internationaler Investitionsschutz – Quo vadis?*, 99 ZVglRWiss 143, 147 (2000).

[160] Kelley, *Multilateral Investment Treaties: A Balanced Approach to Multinational Corporations*, 39 Colum. J. Transnat'l L. 483, 494 *et seq.* (2001) (showing that India was opposing the MAI at several occasions); see also Karl (*supra* footnote 159), 99 ZVglRWiss 143, 146 *et seq.* (2000).

[161] See Kelley (*supra* footnote 160), 39 Colum. J. Transnat'l L. 483, 496 (2001); Graham (*supra* footnote 156), 31 Cornell Int'l L. J. 599 (1998); see also Kobrin, *The MAI and the Clash of Globalizations*, 112 Foreign Pol'y 97 (1998); Schittecatte (*supra* footnote 156), 1 J. World Inv. 329, 330 *et seq.* (2000).

[162] Karl (*supra* footnote 159), 99 ZVglRWiss 143, 149 *et seq.* (2000).

principle which would have obliged States to continuously abolish existing discriminations was misunderstood as an obligation to abolish any restriction on investment.[163] This opposition, in tandem with the opposition by developing countries, essentially crippled the MAI.[164]

In addition, the negotiations also assumed a complexity that prevented a successful conclusion in the relatively short timeframe that was originally envisaged.[165] Part of the difficulties in negotiating the substantive provisions was the challenge of finding an appropriate balance between investment protection and the States' right to regulate in the public interest. This complexity was, for example, reflected in the positions taken by many of the NGOs that criticized the adverse relationship and imbalance between investment protection and other competing public interests.[166] They criticized, *inter alia*, that the MAI encroached upon State sovereignty through its investor-State dispute settlement mechanism.[167] Furthermore, the negotiations were opposed based on the position that comprehensive investment protection would disrupt federal regulatory systems,[168] disable States from enacting rules protecting the environment,[169] weaken labor standards,[170] and impact negatively on human rights protection, as the MAI only contained restrictions for host States without imposing obligations on investors concerning the protection of the environment, social standards, and human rights.[171] For instance, the vague concept of

---

[163] Karl (*supra* footnote 159), 99 ZVglRWiss 143, 150 (2000).

[164] See, on the formation of coalitions between developing countries and NGOs despite their often different and opposing interests, Braithwaite (*supra* footnote 150), 26 Mich. J. Int'l L. 297, 315 *et seq.* (2004). See also Hurrell and Narlikar, *A New Politics of Confrontation? Brazil and India in Multilateral Trade Negotiations*, 20 Global Society 415, 424 (2006) (for the same observation concerning the WTO negotiations in the Doha Round).

[165] Karl (*supra* footnote 159), 99 ZVglRWiss 143, 146 (2000).

[166] See, for the following, Kelley (*supra* footnote 160), 39 Colum. J. Transnat'l L. 483, 496 *et seq.* (2001).

[167] Ganguly, *The Investor-State Dispute Mechanism (ISDM) and a Sovereign's Power to Protect Public Health*, 38 Colum. J. Transnat'l L. 113 (1999). MAI chose ad hoc investor-State dispute settlement because a standing judicial body was considered too costly; see Geiger, *Regulatory Expropriations in International Law*, 11 N.Y.U. Envt'l L. J. 94, 106 (2002).

[168] Stumberg (*supra* footnote 155), 31 Cornell Int'l L. J. 491 (1998).

[169] Graham (supra footnote 156), 31 Cornell Int'l L. J. 599 (1998); McDonald, *The Multilateral Agreement on Investment: Heyday or Mai-Day for Ecologically Sustainable Development?*, 22 Melbourne U.L.R. 617 (1998).

[170] Compa, *The Multilateral Agreement on Investment and International Labor Rights*, 31 Cornell Int'l L. J. 683 (1998).

[171] On the need to link investment protection and the requirement for foreign investors to respect human rights, Kelley (*supra* footnote 160), 39 Colum. J. Transnat'l L. 483 (2001). On the imbalance between investment protection and the obligation to respect human

indirect expropriation gave the impression that investment protection was prioritized over other legitimate concerns.[172] That investment protection under the MAI, however, was "not intended to supersede national legislation or specific international agreements on matters such as competition, intellectual property rights, health and consumer protection, labor standards, industrial relations, or environmental protection,"[173] was too difficult to communicate to the general public in the light of the massive NGO opposition. Although the OECD negotiators responded to much of the criticism,[174] a change in public opinion about the MAI's benefits could not be achieved. Negotiations therefore ceased in late 1998.

The reservations against the MAI of developing countries, as well as the opposition of Western NGOs, might lend support to the view that the failure of this multilateral investment instrument essentially replicated the traditional North–South conflicts on the desirability of foreign investment protection by international law. Yet, that the traditional North–South divide continued to be operative in structuring international relations in this context seems to be contradicted by the tentative multilateral achievements in the WTO and, above all, by the numerous BITs developing countries had already concluded by the end of the 1990s. These developments rather suggest that the desirability of foreign investment and the necessity for its protection by international law were, in principle, accepted by developing and transitioning countries. Viewing the MAI as a prolongation of the older North–South conflicts that had obstructed earlier multilateral investment projects does not, therefore, seem convincing.

Instead, the failure of the MAI rather reflects the general complexity of the issues surrounding international investment protection, in particular the problem of how to resolve conflicts with the State's legitimate right to

rights also J. Alvarez, *Critical Theory and the North American Free Trade Agreement's Chapter Eleven*, 28 U. Miami Inter-Am. L. Rev. 303, 307 *et seq.* (1996–97).

[172] See Wälde and Kolo, *Environmental Regulation, Investment Protection and "Regulatory Taking" in International Law*, 50 Int'l & Comp. L. Q. 811 (2001); see also Geiger (*supra* footnote 167), 11 N.Y.U. Envt'l L. J. 94 (2002).

[173] Geiger, *Towards a Multilateral Agreement on Investment*, 31 Cornell Int'l L. J. 467, 472 (1998). Similarly placating concerns of NGOs about labor standards, environmental concerns and the scope of regulatory takings, Graham (*supra* footnote 156), 31 Cornell Int'l L. J. 599 (1998).

[174] See in particular, OECD Negotiating Group on the Multilateral Agreement on Investment (MAI), *The Multilateral Agreement on Investment (Report by the Chairman of the Negotiating Group)* (May 4, 1998) (containing a more balanced approach that intended to introduce elements for the protection of the signatories' legitimate right to regulate). See, for a discussion of the Report, Geiger (*supra* footnote 167), 11 N.Y.U. Envt'l L. J. 94, 97 *et seq.* (2002).

regulate. These conflicts, that had long accompanied and structured the domestic public welfare debate about property protection and competing public interests,[175] ultimately crystallized at the international level. As a symbol for the political struggle between neo-liberalist and communitarian positions about the gestalt of globalization, the MAI and its failure thus became "a litmus test in a battle to decide the shape and direction of the global economy."[176] In the first place, the failure of the MAI should, therefore, be taken as a function of the difficulty and complexity of the substantive issues international investment protection entails for the regulatory leeway of States rather than as evidence for, or as a result of, persisting conflicts in the international community about the general desirability of the protection of foreign investment by international law. The failure of the MAI is less a case against true multilateralism in investment relations as such, but an illustration of the problems relating to the fine-tuning of investment protection in light of competing and legitimate public interests.

3   Multilateral investment rules in the WTO: Doha – Cancun – and beyond

After the failure of the MAI the quest for multilateral investment rules lay dormant, yet surfaced again in another intermezzo within the WTO. After the First Ministerial Meeting in Singapore had established a Working Group on Trade and Investment,[177] the Fourth Ministerial Meeting in Doha in 2001 "[r]ecogniz[ed] the case for a multilateral framework to secure transparent, stable and predictable conditions for long-term cross-border investment, particularly foreign direct investment, that will contribute to the expansion of trade, and the need for enhanced technical assistance and capacity-building in this area" and "agree[d] that negotiations will take place after the Fifth Session of the Ministerial Conference on the basis of a decision to be taken, by explicit consensus, at that session on modalities of negotiations."[178] This declaration suggested a welcoming attitude of developing countries vis-à-vis multilateral rules on investment protection within the WTO.[179]

---

[175] See, for example, Epstein, *Takings: Private Property and the Power of Eminent Domain* (1985).

[176] Canner (*supra* footnote 151), 31 Cornell Int'l L. J. 657, 681 (1998).

[177] See *supra* footnotes 147–49 and accompanying text.

[178] World Trade Organization, Ministerial Declaration, November 14, 2001, 41 I.L.M. 746 (2002), para. 20.

[179] See, on the prospects concerning a multilateral investment treaty within the WTO, Wallace, *The Legal Environment for a Multilateral Framework on Investment and the*

However, in view of the vigorous confrontation between developed and developing countries at the Cancun Summit, further negotiations of investment rules during the Doha Round were taken off the negotiation agenda.[180] Consequently, this decision could be interpreted as a renewed failure of multilateralism in international investment relations along the lines of the old North–South conflicts. In fact, some observers have attributed the failure of the Cancun Summit in a significant part to disagreements on issues of investment protection.[181]

Yet, it seems inadequate to view the resistance of developing countries to multilateral investment rules at the Cancun Summit as their continued opposition to multilateral investment protection. Instead, developing countries were primarily concerned with the elimination of agricultural subsidies, with anti-dumping and countervailing duties, with the liberalization of the trade in textiles, and with the reform of the TRIPS Agreement in order to expand possibilities of compulsory licensing for quintessential medical drugs.[182] Compared with the fundamental disagreements on these trade-related questions, a rather solid consensus existed between developed and developing countries as regards the content of a potential investment agreement. Such a consensus had, in fact, already crystallized during the preparatory work of the Working Group on Trade and Investment which had been established as part of the Singapore Issues.[183]

That interests of developing countries in issues of agriculture, textiles, TRIPS, etc. trumped all other interests is also reflected in the structure of

Potential Role of the WTO, 3 J. World Inv. 289 (2002); Karl, On the Way to Multilateral Investment Rules, 17 ICSID Rev. – For. Inv. L. J. 293 (2002); Kennedy, A WTO Agreement on Investment: A Solution in Search of a Problem?, 24 U. Pa. J. Int'l Econ. L. 77 (2003). It remained unclear, however, whether the so-called Doha Declaration already contained an agreement to commence negotiations on a multilateral investment treaty within the WTO. See, on this controversy, Kurtz (supra footnote 32), 23 U. Pa. J. Int'l Econ. L. 713, 777 et seq. (2002).

[180] World Trade Organization, Decision by the General Council, August 1, 2004, available at: www.wto.org/english/tratop_E/dda_E/ddadraft_31jul04_E.pdf.

[181] See, for example, Wolf, Welthandelsrechtliche Rahmenbedingungen für die Liberalisierung ausländischer Direktinvestitionen, Beiträge zum Transnationalen Wirtschaftsrecht, vol. 61, p. 11 (2006). See also Jawara and Kwa, Behind the Scenes at the WTO, pp. 239–42 (2004).

[182] Kurtz (supra footnote 32), 23 U. Pa. J. Int'l Econ. L. 713, 773 et seq. (2002).

[183] See, on the work of the Working Group and the results they had reached, Sauvé, Multilateral Rules on Investment: Is Forward Movement Possible?, 9 J. Int'l Econ. L. 325, 329–40 (2006) (pointing out that the existing disagreements were not of a fundamental nature, but related to the scope of non-discrimination and pre-establishment commitments).

the bargaining coalitions themselves, that often united developing countries with overall diverse interests and partly conflicting preferences. In particular, liberalization in the agricultural sector and the elimination of subsidies by the EU and the United States formed a common target for many developing countries that was strong enough to outweigh other potential differences. The interest in a common market for agriculture that would have above all benefited developing countries, therefore, served as an aspect uniting them under a common agenda and structured the blocking coalition of developing countries.[184] Opposition to investment rules, by contrast, seems to have played a much less important role in forging developing country opposition. As put by one commentator, "there is little denying that both the appearance and tactical bargaining of such an 'anything but agriculture' coalition hampered the quest for consensus on investment."[185]

In sum, the failure to proceed with negotiations on a multilateral investment treaty under the auspices of the WTO cannot be attributed to persisting fundamental conflicts between capital-exporting and capital-importing countries about the appropriate scope of international investment protection similar to the position taken by developing countries in the 1970s.[186] Instead, a consensus on investment issues was doomed because of the more fundamental concern of developing countries about the lack of a sustainable and comprehensive development perspective in international trade relations. The subsequent decision to remove investment issues from the negotiation agenda, therefore, also reflects the desire to scale down future trade negotiations in the WTO and separate investment and trade issues in order to avoid distributive compromises between both sectors.

F   Conclusion

Although international investment law departed from a genuinely multilateral basis in customary international law before the First World

---

[184] See Hurrell and Narlikar (*supra* footnote 164), 20 Global Society 415, 422–24 (2006) (observing that, instead of employing "value-creative-strategies" that aim at consensus in less contentious areas by partitioning negotiations into several packages, the developing countries' coalitions insisted on strong "distributive strategies" that aimed at reaching agreement on various issues *en bloc*).

[185] Sauvé (*supra* footnote 183); 9 J. Int'l Econ. L. 325, 341 (2006). See also Hurrell and Narlikar (*supra* footnote 164), 20 Global Society 415 (2006).

[186] See Hurrell and Narlikar (*supra* footnote 164), 20 Global Society 415, 423 (2006) (arguing that the behavior of developing countries "fitted within the normative framework of the WTO [and] suggest[s] that the discourse underlying the new politics of fragmentation is fundamentally different from its predecessor of the 1970s").

War, its limited scope was not able to sustain changes in the emergence of an international economy and withstand the political challenges liberal notions of property protection were facing from both communist countries attempting to abolish private property, and from newly independent States that sought to complement their political independence with economic empowerment. Both factors brought about the desire by Western capital-exporting countries to establish international investment rules based on international treaty law. The difficulties in establishing such rules resulted in intense dynamics between multilateral and bilateral approaches to ordering international investment relations.

Multilateralism through instruments that aspired to comprehensively govern investment relations by creating binding substantive obligations concerning the treatment of foreign investors failed without exception to materialize. This was the fate of the Havana Charter in 1948 as well as the 1967 OECD Draft Convention on the Protection of Foreign Property. Similarly, in 1998 the negotiation for a Multilateral Agreement on Investment within the OECD failed. More recently, renewed efforts to launch negotiations on a multilateral investment treaty in the WTO ended without success. Only two multilateral conventions in the investment realm succeeded and continue to enjoy broad support among developed and developing countries: the ICSID and MIGA Conventions. Both conventions do not, however, contain substantive obligations relating to the treatment of foreign investment.

At the same time, bilateral, regional, and sectoral treaties on the promotion and protection of foreign investment flourish. Since Germany and Pakistan concluded the first BIT in 1959, this treaty type has risen to a total number of more than 2,500 by the end of 2006. In addition, a number of other international treaties, such as free trade agreements and various regional agreements relating to economic cooperation, contain substantive rules on the protection of foreign investment. Surprisingly, the content of these treaties does not differ substantially from the content of the conventions proposed on the multilateral level. Above all, the substantive obligations concerning the treatment of foreign investors contained in modern BITs are similar (and often identical) to the rules proposed in the 1960s and 1990s within the framework of the OECD.

Initially multilateral solutions to international investment protection failed because of two, partly independent, partly overlapping, but equally fundamental conflicts. First, the process of decolonization and the accession of former colonies into the arena of international relations created tensions about the protection of foreign property. The emerging North–South conflict essentially understood the protection of foreign investment as an instrument of hegemony, or even prolonged imperialism, by means of which developed countries could foster their power over developing countries. Developing countries, therefore, not only declined to accept new multilateral rules for investment protection but actively opposed existing customary international law until about 1990. The declaration of a New International Economic Order was paradigmatic of this position.

The second conflict that prevented multilateral rules from materializing was the East–West conflict, in particular the underlying ideological differences on the organization of economic affairs and the importance of private property. While Western economies were based on notions of individual freedom, property, and contract protection, socialist and communist countries based the organization of their national economies on notions of collective ownership and a State-run planned economy that was incompatible with individual ownership and private economic activity. These opposing positions prevented consensus on universal international norms governing the protection of foreign investment. In sum, the failures of multilateralism in international investment relations, until 1990, have to be attributed to the lack of a consensus in the international community about the desirability of protecting foreign investment by international law. Even though foreign investment as such was not necessarily opposed by all States, developing and socialist States asserted their sovereignty in regulating entry, treatment, and exit of foreign investors without any limitations by international law.

However, the opposition of many developing and transitioning countries crumbled with the end of the Cold War and the continuing permeation of an economic ideology that favored a liberal conception of market economics. In addition, many developing countries gave up their restrictive attitudes towards protecting foreign investment by international law due to their need for capital as a factor for economic growth and development, in particular after the debt crisis had reduced the availability of public funds. Both developments gave way to the insight that foreign investment inflows had beneficial impacts for host States. This resulted in the increasing openness of developing and transitioning economies to the conclusion of BITs and other instruments of regional economic cooperation starting in the 1990s. The widespread acceptance of these instruments documents a fundamental change of attitude vis-à-vis the protection of foreign investment by international law compared with the zenith of foreign investment scepticism in the wake of the New International Economic Order. In substance, BITs and other international instruments thus represent a basic consensus on the appropriate level of investment protection by international law.

The consensus that the content of BITs constitutes the basis of generally acceptable substantial rules on international investment protection is also not invalidated by the failure of the more recent multilateral attempts in the OECD and the WTO. While the failure of earlier multilateral projects, such as the Havana Charter and the 1967 OECD Draft Convention, was due to the ideological divide between capital-exporting and capital-importing countries, the negotiations on the MAI and attempts to launch negotiations on a multilateral investment treaty in the WTO primarily failed for reasons that did not reflect continuing disagreements between developed and developing countries about the general framework of investment protection by international law. Instead, these projects failed mainly because of the difficulties in resolving the tension between investment protection and competing public interests, as was the case with the MAI, or due to factors outside the investment realm, as was the case within the WTO.

The failure of multilateral solutions and the reappearance of apparently identical rules on a bilateral basis present a puzzling challenge for the political gestalt of international investment relations and the legal structures supporting them. The failure of all multilateral conventions seemingly lends itself to the conclusion that universally accepted rules on international investment protection do not exist. BITs would then simply contain bilateral bargains that follow contract-like rationalities rather than present a regulatory approach for governing international investment relations. However, the counterclaim against such a view, as it was presented in this chapter, is that international investment law only formally developed on the basis of bilateral treaties while in substance these treaties remained multilateral in creating uniform rules for the protection of foreign investment on the basis of general principles. Even the recent failure of multilateralism and the ongoing success of bilateralism in international investment relations do not appear as insurmountable contradictions. Instead, the continuing growth of bilateral, regional, and sectoral investment treaties can be seen as reflecting a general consensus on the level of investment protection by international law. In contrast to the positions associated with the New International Economic Order, bilateralism in international investment law can, therefore, be viewed as part of a development towards the creation of a uniform international investment regime rather than a dynamic that counters multilateralism. Instead, the shift from multilateralism to bilateralism concerned only the form of investment treaties not their substance. The argument that BITs, in fact, aspire to establish uniform rules for the protection of foreign investment will be illustrated more closely in the following chapter.

III

Treaty negotiation and multilateralization of international investment law

The bilateral form of investment treaties suggests that the treaties differ significantly in content and structure, and rather resemble *quid pro quo* bargains than establish a uniform framework governing international investment relations. Although there is widespread agreement that capital-exporting as well as capital-importing States derive benefits from foreign investment through gains in cooperation based on the theory of comparative advantage, capital-exporting States should be expected to aim primarily at the protection of the interests of their nationals investing abroad and restrict the host States' regulatory leeway as far as possible, while capital-importing States should be interested in upholding their sovereignty. Depending on the relative negotiating power of the two parties negotiating a BIT, it should be expected that the different, and partly opposing, interests of States result in radically different and disparate negotiation outcomes in bilateral relations and counteract the creation of uniformity in international investment law.

Contrary to this intuitive expectation, however, international investment treaties have, to a significant extent, developed a surprisingly uniform structure, often converging in their wording and endorsing uniform principles of investment protection.[1] Certainly, the levels of investment protection in different bilateral relationships differ: some treaties may include certain investor rights, while others may not; some treaties may offer recourse to investor-State arbitration, others may not; some treaties may contain specific exceptions to certain principles of investment protection, others may not. Notwithstanding these differences, investment treaties conform to archetypes and converge considerably with regard to the principles of investment protection that they establish. In addition, they often also converge with respect to other elements, such as the definitions of investment or investor. As a result of this, investment treaties offer a surprisingly uniform protection against political risk,

---

[1] See, for an older empirical study, Khalil, *Treatment of Foreign Investment in Bilateral Investment Treaties*, 7 ICSID Rev. – For. Inv. L. J. 339 (1992) (reviewing 335 BITs).

independent of whether the treaties are concluded between developed and developing States or among developing States.

Relying on rather standardized treaty language, their object and purpose is the "promotion and protection of [foreign] investment";[2] they intend to "create favourable conditions for investments in both States and to intensify the cooperation between nationals and companies in both States with a view to stimulating the productive use of resources."[3] In general, they contain a prohibition of direct and indirect expropriation, establish national treatment, MFN treatment, fair and equitable treatment, contain "umbrella clauses" for the protection of specific undertakings and guarantee the free transfer of capital from the host State. Apart from these standards of substantive investment protection, they also provide for the arbitration of investment disputes between investors and host States. Investment treaties, however, do not contain obligations concerning specific investment projects. They merely create a framework that aims at establishing an institutional infrastructure, an economic constitution, within which private economic actors are able to operate. The argument is thus, not that investment treaties are identical nor that there would be no differences among them. The argument is rather that one can observe convergence above all with respect to the principles of investment protection, such as national treatment, fair and equitable treatment, protection against direct and indirect expropriation, and investor-State arbitration.

This convergence may be purely coincidental and, therefore, of little influence in the understanding of bilateral investment treaties and investment treaty arbitration as a uniform international law system. The convergence of treaties could, for example, be explained in view of the transaction costs resulting from the drafting, negotiation, and conclusion of the treaties.[4] By taking pre-existing BITs as a model, the similarity

---

[2] Preamble, Agreement between the People's Republic of China and the Federal Republic of Germany on the Encouragement and Reciprocal Protection of Investments, signed on December 1, 2003, entered into force on November 11, 2005.

[3] Preamble, Agreement between the People's Republic of China and the Government of the Kingdom of Denmark concerning the Encouragement and the Reciprocal Protection of Investments, signed and entered into force on April 29, 1985.

[4] On the influence of negotiation and drafting costs on contracts see Dye, *Costly Contract Contingencies*, 26 Int'l Econ. Rev. 233 (1985); Williamson, *The Economic Institutions of Capitalism*, Ch. 3 (1985); Anderlini and Felli, *Incomplete Written Contracts*, 109 Quart. J. Econ. 1085 (1994); O. Hart and Moore, *Foundations of Incomplete Contracts*, 66 Rev. Econ. Stud. 115 (1999); Maskin and Tirole, *Unforeseen Contingencies and Incomplete Contracts*, 66 Rev. Econ. Stud. 83 (1999); Tirole, *Incomplete Contracts: Where Do We Stand?*, 67 Econometrica 741 (1999); Battigalli and Maggi, *Rigidity, Discretion, and the Costs of Writing Contracts*, 92 Am. Econ. Rev. 798 (2002).

between the different bilateral treaties could thus be explained by cost-saving behavior in drafting and negotiating BITs. If this were the reason for their similarities, the convergence of investment treaties could not be translated into an intention to establish uniform rules. Instead, BITs would remain characterized by a mutual taking and giving in a two-party relationship. This would be particularly true with respect to wholly unrelated BITs. For example, if the People's Republic of China (PRC or China) used a BIT between Germany and Argentina as a basis for its negotiation with Botswana, China and Botswana might attribute a completely different meaning to the term fair and equitable treatment than would Germany and Argentina, even though the wording is identical. If BITs followed this logic, the convergence in treaty texts would not necessarily translate into a uniform system of investment protection.

Similarly, the content of international investment treaties could be solely a function of the hegemonic behavior of capital-exporting countries vis-à-vis their capital-importing counterparts.[5] If this were the case, BITs could hardly be understood as a system of law. The apparent convergence of international investment treaties would then simply conceal differences stemming from different understandings of the standards of treatment contained in the treaties, but would nevertheless endorse preferential benefits of stronger vis-à-vis weaker capital-exporting States. If hegemony were operative with respect to the content of BITs, it would indeed be likely that stronger capital-exporting States would seek specific benefits in BITs in relation to other competing capital-exporters.

In fact, historically, developed States have frequently engaged in anti-competitive behavior in their bilateral economic relations and have used their influence and negotiating power vis-à-vis weaker States to impose specific obligations upon them and extract preferential benefits from bilateral relations to the exclusion and detriment of other, including developed, States.[6] It would thus be surprising if developed countries

---

[5] Distinctively in this sense, Chimni, *International Institutions Today: An Imperial Global State in the Making*, 15 Eur. J. Int'l L. 1, 7 *et seq.* (2004); Chimni, *Marxism and International Law*, Economic and Political Weekly, p. 337 (February 6, 1999); see also Benvenisti and Downs, *The Empire's New Clothes*, 60 Stan. L. Rev. 595, 611–12 (2007).

[6] An example of such behavior can be found in the time leading up to the Second World War where international protectionism and bilateralism were the mainstream ideology in international economic relations. See, for example, Sommer, *Die Voraussetzungen des staatsideologischen Kampfes gegen die Meistbegünstigungsklausel*, 16 ZöR 265 (1936). See also Pomfret, *Unequal Trade: The Economics of Discriminatory International Trade Policies*, pp. 29 *et seq.* (1988); Kindleberger, *Commercial Policy between the Wars*, in

behaved like a single hegemon in international investment relations vis-à-vis developing countries, even though they could derive benefits from entering into investment treaties with developing countries that ensure them an advantage over their competitors from developed countries.

We do not, however, observe such behavior. Instead, investment treaties are grounded on notions of equality and non-discrimination between States, reflected above all in the principles of national treatment and MFN treatment. In addition, they apply the same standards to capital-importing and capital-exporting countries. Although initially this left capital-exporting countries largely unaffected due to the primarily unidirectional flows of capital from developed into developing countries, the directions of these flows are becoming increasingly bidirectional. Finally, the expanding number of South–South BITs, concluded between developing countries, also endorse the same standard terms. International investment law, therefore, develops increasingly from an instrument of development politics to a framework governing international investment flows independent of the character of the host State as a net capital-importing or net capital-exporting country.[7]

That both hegemonic explanations for the convergence of investment treaties as well as explanations focusing on the transaction cost benefits stemming from converging treaty texts are unconvincing will be discussed more in depth in this chapter. In addition, this chapter puts forward an alternative explanation for the convergence of international investment treaties. It argues that the convergence is not merely coincidental but reflects the common interest of States in establishing uniform and universal rules for the protection of foreign investment. The reason for this is that uniform and universal rules are in principle in the interest of all States because they further global welfare. The claim is that uniform rules based on equal and non-discriminatory conditions in international investment relations are not only beneficial for developed countries as a group, but allow every single country, whether developed or developing, to derive benefits from participating in the investment treaty framework. The claim is, therefore, that the myriad number of bilateral treaties is an offspring of the intention of States to establish multilateral investment rules.

The explanation advanced for the convergence of investment treaties is thus that it is rational and efficient to establish uniform standards

---

Mathias and Pollard (eds.), *The Cambridge Economic History of Europe*, vol. VIII, p. 161 (1989); Oye, *Economic Discrimination and Political Exchange*, pp. 71–133 (1992).

[7] See *supra* Ch. II.C on the spread of BITs.

of investment protection. It is argued that uniform rules that impose uniform transaction costs upon every foreign investor, independent of the source or the target of the capital, enable investments to be allocated as efficiently as possible, further international competition, and ultimately maximize overall wealth. The uniformity is particularly salient as it is the prerequisite for competition in a global market. From this point of view, establishing uniform rules is in the long-term interests of all States and explains why bilateral investment treaties are concluded so as to endorse a uniform system of investment protection that can be seen as a substitute for a single multilateral investment treaty. In addition, uniform rules help to counter negative externalities stemming from host State interventions with foreign investment and contribute to the larger international security architecture by decreasing the likelihood of international conflict through increased economic integration.

The first step in advancing the thesis that international investment relations are ordered multilaterally despite their basis in bilateral treaties, requires demonstration that the existing bilateral and regional treaties actually establish an investment regime that in principle follows multilateral rationales, and does not merely enshrine bilateral *quid pro quo* bargains that follow strong distributive rationales. In the first section, this chapter therefore provides an overview of typical clauses that can be found across a wide range of bilateral and regional investment treaties. The objective of this section is less to treat variances in the drafting of investment treaties exhaustively and in detail, but to set out the framework and the principles of investment protection they reference. Again, the argument put forward is not that bilateral treaties do not diverge at all, but instead that they converge to a large degree so that it is permissible to carve out principles that govern international investment relations. These principles are more or less identical across the myriad of BITs. In addition, divergences in the treaty texts are arguably limited enough so as to allow the conclusion that one can observe the existence of relatively uniform treaty texts that form the basis of any international investment treaty.

Subsequently, the question will be raised whether this convergence is purely coincidental or whether it reflects an intention to generate uniform investment rules. For this purpose, the second section of this chapter illustrates how the negotiation process of BITs is structured in order to bring about these relatively uniform treaty texts. It shows that bilateral treaties actually find their origin in multilateral aspirations and approaches and do not coincidentally resemble each other. This section also addresses the frequently raised argument that BITs cannot be viewed as appropriately expressing the attitude of developing countries on the desired level of investment protection, because they constitute promises that are extracted from them by developed countries and, therefore, yield to hegemonic rationales and economic pressure rather than informed consent. Finally, the third section of this chapter presents an explanation, based on rational choice, for why the textual resemblances of bilateral treaties results from a genuine interest in multilateral and thus uniform rules.

A   The standard content of bilateral investment treaties

BITs regularly follow a standard structure, beginning with definitions about their scope of application, followed by rules concerning the admission of investments, principles concerning the treatment of foreign investors once they are admitted to invest in a foreign State, and finally rules on the settlement of disputes between investors and host States. Certainly, differences in the wording of investment treaties exist and commentators and tribunals emphasize that specific attention has to be paid to such differences. The Tribunal in *AES Corporation* v. *Argentina*, for example, emphasized that "each BIT has its own identity."[8] It also warned that the "striking similarities in the wording" of BITs should not lead to an unreflected reference to the interpretation of other treaties that "dissimulates real differences in the definition of some key term concepts ... or for the precise definition of rights and obligations for each party."[9]

Certainly, differences in the wording of investment treaties have to be taken seriously. Yet an analysis of BITs shows that, to a considerable extent, they contain similar, if not identical wording, have the same object and purpose, and follow a rather standard structure. In addition, even if there are differences in wording between different investment treaties concerning the precise formulation of certain investor rights, it has to

---

[8] *AES Corporation* v. *Argentina*, Decision on Jurisdiction, April 26, 2005, para. 24.
[9] *AES Corporation* v. *Argentina*, Decision on Jurisdiction, April 26, 2005, para. 25. Likewise, Argentina stressed in this case that "each bilateral Treaty for the protection and promotion of investments has a different and defined scope of application. It is not a uniform text" (*ibid.*, para. 20). See also Tudor, *The Fair and Equitable Treatment Standard in the International Law of Foreign Investment*, pp. 19–52 (2008); Yannaca-Small, *Fair and Equitable Treatment Standard in International Investment Law*, p. 2 (2004) (both stressing that differences exist concerning the wording of fair and equitable treatment standards in different treaties).

be assessed cautiously whether such differences actually translate into a different content of the legal rights and obligations between the contracting parties in question. In other words, differences in wording do not necessarily translate into differences in content – just as an identity of wording does not necessarily mean an identity of content. The argument forwarded in this section, however, is not that there is identity among investment treaties, but merely sufficient convergence that suggests considerable uniformity in the level of investment protection.

1   The scope of application of BITs

In order for an investor to benefit from the substantive and procedural rights of an investment treaty, the treaty in question has to be applicable *ratione materiae, ratione personae,* and *ratione temporis.* This requires that a covered investment has been made by a covered investor and that the State's measure that interferes with the investment in question is subject to the treaty in time. The definition of investment, the definition of investor, and the specifications of the temporal component, therefore, determine the scope of application of the obligations States incur under their investment treaties.

While there is no uniform definition of investment that is endorsed by every single investment treaty – and nothwithstanding the fact that some treaties contain exceptions for portfolio investments, for investments below a certain value, or for investments in certain economic sectors – the large majority of investment treaties define investment broadly.[10] For this purpose, most treaties rely on a non-exhaustive list of rights and interests that are covered. Thus, the notion of investment often encompasses:

> every kind of asset in the territory of one Contracting Party owned or controlled, directly or indirectly, by an investor of the other Contracting Party, including:
> (a) an enterprise (being a legal person or any entity constituted or organised under the applicable law of the Contracting Party, whether or not for profit, and whether private or government owned or controlled, including a corporation, trust, partnership, sole proprietorship, branch, joint venture, association or organization);
> (b) shares, stocks and other forms of equity participation in an enterprise, and rights derived therefrom;

---

[10] See UNCTAD, *International Investment Agreements: Key Issues – Volume I*, pp. 77–81, 118–26 (2004).

(c) bonds, debentures, loans and other forms of debts and rights derived
     therefrom;
(d) rights under contracts, including turnkey, construction, manage-
     ment, production or revenue-sharing contracts;
(e) claims to money and claims to performance pursuant to a contract
     having an economic value;
(f) intellectual and industrial property rights as defined in the multi-
     lateral agreements concluded under the auspices of the World
     Intellectual Property Organization, including copyright, trade-
     marks, patents, industrial designs and technical processes, know-
     how, trade secrets, trade names and goodwill;
(g) any rights conferred by law or contract or by virtue of any conces-
     sions, licenses, authorisations or permits to undertake an economic
     activity;
(h) any other tangible and intangible, movable and immovable prop-
     erty, or any related property rights, such as leases, mortgages, liens,
     pledges or usufructs.[11]

This wide definition of investment ensures that all essential rights and interests necessary for engaging in economic activities in a host State are covered by the substantive protection of the relevant investment treaty.[12] It covers not only classical property rights, but also includes protec-tion for investor-State contracts, intellectual property, and investments in locally incorporated companies. The open-ended list also allows the adaptation of the scope of application to changing forms and patterns of foreign investment. Similar to the concept of property under consti-tutional law or human rights instruments, the notion of investment is flexible and covers all rights and interests that have a monetary value.[13]

[11] See Article 1(1), Agreement between the Republic of Austria and the Republic of Uzbekistan for the Promotion and Protection of Investments, signed on June 2, 2000, entered into force on August 18, 2001.
[12] Further on the jurisprudence that has developed on the notion of investment see Rubins, *The Notion of "Investment" in International Investment Arbitration*, in Horn and Kröll (eds.), *Arbitrating Foreign Investment Disputes*, p. 283 (2004); Dolzer, *The Notion of Investment in Recent Practice*, in Charnovitz, Steger and von den Bossche (eds.), *Law in the Service of Human Dignity*, p. 261 (2005); Yala, *The Notion of "Investment" in ICSID Case Law: A Drifting Jurisdictional Requirement?*, 22 J. Int'l Arb. 105 (2005); Wolters, *The Meaning of "Investment" in Treaty Disputes: Substantive or Jurisdictional?*, 8 J. Word Inv. & Trade 175 (2007); McLachlan, Shore and Weiniger, *International Investment Arbitration – Substantive Principles*, pp. 163–96 (2007); Dolzer and Schreuer, *Principles of International Investment Law*, pp. 60–71 (2008); Schlemmer, *Investment, Investor, Nationality and Shareholders*, in Muchlinski, Ortino and Schreuer (eds.), *The Oxford Handbook of International Investment Law*, pp. 49, 51–69 (2008).
[13] *Cf. Amoco International Finance Corporation v. Iran et al.*, Award, July 14, 1987, 15 Iran–U.S. C.T.R. 189, 220, para. 108; *Libyan American Oil Company (LIAMCO) v. Libya*, Award, April 12, 1977, 20 I.L.M. 153 (1981).

Similarly, as regards the personal coverage of investment treaties, there is no uniform approach in every investment treaty. Yet the scope of investors who are covered is generally wide. The notion of investor regularly encompasses natural persons and legal entities that have the nationality of the other contracting State, that is, the nationality of the State where the investment is not located.[14] Concerning legal entities, their nationality is usually determined in view of their place of incorporation or based on their principal place of business, but is rarely based on the nationality of their controlling shareholder.[15] Frequently, the treaties also accord protection to investors whose investment is not effectuated directly in the host country, but structured by means of one or several subsidiaries.[16]

With respect to their temporal applicability, BITs usually stay in force for a considerable period of time, sometimes as significant as thirty years.[17] In addition, after a possible termination of the BIT, most treaties protect the covered investment for an additional period of usually ten to twenty years.[18] Most BITs protect both investments that have been made prior to and after the entry into force of the treaty in question.[19] However, as a general matter they protect only against measures taken by the host State after the respective treaty has entered into force.[20]

While all treaties protect investments against measures of the host State in the post-establishment phase, major differences exist with respect to the protection during the admission phase.[21] While the BITs

---

[14] UNCTAD (*supra* footnote 10), pp. 126–30 (2004). Dolzer and Schreuer (*supra* footnote 12), pp. 46–59 (2008); McLachlan, Shore and Weiniger (*supra* footnote 12), pp. 131–62 (2007); Schlemmer, in Muchlinski, Ortino and Schreuer (*supra* footnote 12), pp. 49, 69–86 (2008).

[15] See Dolzer and Stevens, *Bilateral Investment Treaties*, pp. 34–42 (1995).

[16] See in more detail *infra* Chs. V.A.3 and V.A.5.

[17] Dolzer and Stevens (*supra* footnote 15), p. 45 (1995).

[18] See, for example, Article 12(2), Agreement between the Government of the Kingdom of Thailand and the Government of the Kingdom of Bahrain for the Promotion and Protection of Investments, signed on May 21, 2002, entered into force on July 17, 2002 (providing for protection for ten years after the treaty's termination); Article 14(3), Treaty between the Federal Republic of Germany and the Co-operative Republic of Guyana concerning the Encouragement and Reciprocal Protection of Investments, signed on December 6, 1989, entered into force on March 8, 1994 (providing for a period of twenty years of protection after the treaty's termination).

[19] Dolzer and Stevens (*supra* footnote 15), pp. 45–47 (1995).

[20] Moreover, some treaties may even provide for transitional periods in order to allow States to adapt their conduct to the obligations they incurred; see UNCTAD (*supra* footnote 10), p. 72 (2004).

[21] UNCTAD (*supra* footnote 10), pp. 143–60 (2004). See also Gomez-Palacio and Muchlinski, *Admission of Investment and Right of Establishment*, in Muchlinski, Ortino and Schreuer (*supra* footnote 12), p. 227 (2007).

concluded, for example, by the United States impose obligations on the host State concerning the admission of investment,[22] the BITs of most other countries do not restrict the host State's sovereignty at all, or only require compliance with the domestic legislation in place.[23] Consequently, most investment treaties contain relatively weak obligations concerning investment liberalization and market access, and instead grant broad discretion to the host State's decisions as to whether and how far to open up its national economy to foreign investments.[24] Most investment treaties leave States, for example, largely unrestricted in subjecting foreign investors to pre-establishment approval or excluding them from specific sectors of the economy. Notwithstanding the limited regulation of investment access, it is noteworthy that "the nearly universal desire to attract FDI [i.e., foreign direct investment] has [also] led to a convergence of the policies and standards exercised by states with respect to the admission and establishment of FDI."[25]

2   Substantive investor rights conferred under BITs

With respect to the substantive protection offered to covered investments, investment treaties usually contain a number of standard investor rights. These rights regularly feature in investment treaties, independent of the nature of the contracting parties as developed or developing countries, and independent of the political ideology these countries endorse. While not all investment treaties always endorse the identical canon of investor rights, they regularly include non-discrimination provisions, such as national treatment and MFN treatment, require fair and equitable treatment and full protection and security of the covered investors, contain restrictions on direct and indirect expropriation, and grant free transfer of capital in the context of foreign investment activity. Many investment treaties also contain umbrella clauses that offer specific protection to investor-State contracts and similar undertakings. Certainly, the wording of specific treaty provisions that incorporate these

---

[22] See McKinstry Robin, *The BIT Won't Bite: The American Bilateral Investment Treaty Program*, 33 Am. U. L. Rev. 931, 947–50 (1984).

[23] Dolzer and Stevens (*supra* footnote 15), pp. 50–57 (1995).

[24] *Cf.* Vandevelde, *Investment Liberalization and Economic Development*, 36 Colum. J. Transnat'l L. 501, 514 (1998) (concluding that "BITs are very limited tools for liberalization").

[25] Geist, *Toward a General Agreement on the Regulation of Foreign Direct Investment*, 26 L. & Pol'y Int'l Bus. 673, 676 (1995).

substantive standards of treatment is not always identical. Yet variations in treaty texts often do not merit the conclusion that the State parties intended to base their investment relations on standards that diverge from general treaty practice.

The substantive rights the treaties endorse can be grouped into relative standards, that is, non-discrimination provisions and absolute standards of treatment, including rules on expropriation, contract protection, and capital transfer.[26] In view of the function accorded to international investment treaties in providing institutions for the functioning of a global market economy,[27] the standards of treatment contained in the treaties can be linked to specific legal institutions that provide the framework for allowing and stabilizing private economic activity and restricting the host State's power vis-à-vis such private activity. Against this background, national and MFN treatment aim at ensuring a level playing field for competition between foreign and domestic economic actors. The protection against expropriation guarantees respect for property rights as an essential institution for market transactions. Capital transfer guarantees ensure the free flow of capital and contribute to the efficient allocation of resources. Umbrella clauses back up private ordering between foreign investors and the home State. Fair and equitable treatment and full protection and security ensure basic due process rights for foreign investors, and require adequate police protection, features that are equally essential for the functioning of the market. Finally, recourse to international arbitration represents a mechanism that allows foreign investors to actually enforce compliance with these institutions.

---

[26] Apart from these core investor rights, BITs often include a number of miscellaneous provisions that relate to ancillary aspects of foreign investment. By way of example, various treaties contain provisions concerning the granting of visas and working permits for nationals engaged in activities associated with investments (e.g., Article 2(4), Agreement between the People's Republic of China and the Federal Republic of Germany on the Encouragement and Reciprocal Protection of Investments, signed on December 1, 2003, entered into force on November 11, 2005) or specific provisions for national and MFN treatment in matters of compensation "owing to war or other armed conflict, revolution, a State of national emergency" (see, e.g., Article 8, Accord entre la Confédération suisse et la République du Ghana concernant la promotion et la protection réciproque des investissements, signed on October 8, 1991, entered into force on June 16, 1993). They may also contain provisions concerning the subrogation of the investor's home State for compensations paid out of foreign investment insurances. See, for example, Article 8, Agreement between the Republic of India and the Kingdom of the Netherlands for the Promotion and Protection of Investments, signed on November 6, 1995, entered into force on December 1, 1996.

[27] See *supra* Ch. I.A.

(a)   Non-discrimination, national treatment
and MFN treatment

BITs are generally based on notions of non-discrimination.[28] They often contain specific provisions prohibiting discriminatory treatment of foreign investors, or more generally, require national and MFN treatment,[29] at least with respect to the post-establishment phase of an investment.[30] Non-discrimination aims at creating a level playing field between local and foreign investors and among investors from different home States as a prerequisite for equal competition. Most investment treaties contain either a specific clause that prohibits "discriminatory measures [concerning] the management, operation, maintenance, use, enjoyment, acquisition, expansion, or disposal of investments,"[31] or a general non-discrimination clause that either separates between national and MFN treatment or frames them as part of a single treaty provision. Like constitutional protections of equality, such clauses are regularly drafted in a broad and general way. A typical clause thus stipulates:

> Each Party shall accord investments in its territory, and associated activities in connection with these investments of nationals or companies of the other Party, treatment no less favorable than that accorded in like situations to investments of its own nationals and companies or to investments of nationals and companies of any third country, whichever is most favorable.[32]

Other national treatment provisions do not mention the requirement of "like circumstances," but simply require that:

[28] Yet older Chinese BITs only provide for national treatment "to the extent possible" or refer back to treatment in accordance with the stipulations of domestic laws and regulations. See, for example, Article 3(3), Agreement between the Government of the United Kingdom of Great Britain and Northern Ireland and the Government of the People's Republic of China concerning the Promotion and Protection of Investments, signed and entered into force on May 15, 1986. This essentially invalidated national treatment as an independent international law standard. The PRC's treaty practice has, however, changed with respect to national treatment. See Schill, *Tearing Down the Great Wall – The New Generation Investment Treaties of the People's Republic of China*, 15 Cardozo J. Int'l & Comp. L. 73, 94–100 (2007).

[29] Dolzer and Stevens (*supra* footnote 15), pp. 63–76 (1995). UNCTAD (*supra* footnote 10), pp. 161–208 (2004).

[30] See *supra* footnotes 21–25 and accompanying text.

[31] See Article 2(b), Treaty between United States of America and the Argentine Republic concerning the Reciprocal Encouragement and Protection of Investment, signed on November 14, 1991, entered into force on October 20, 1994.

[32] Article 2(a), Treaty between the United States of America and the Arab Republic of Egypt concerning the Reciprocal Encouragement and Protection of Investments, signed on March 11, 1986, entered into force on June 27, 1992.

Each Contracting Party shall accord to investments and activities associated with such investments by the investors of the other Contracting Party treatment not less favourable than that accorded to the investments ... by its own investors.[33]

Occasionally, non-discrimination provisions are subject to exceptions. Some BITs, for example, contain so-called "grandfather clauses" that only forbid the introduction of new discriminatory measures, while allowing the retention of existing discriminations.[34] However, on the level of principle, non-discrimination is a deeply embedded concept of international investment law.

The precise scope of non-discrimination provisions has so far not been settled in treaty practice or arbitral jurisprudence.[35] Similar to non-discrimination provisions in international trade law or domestic constitutional law, they pose problems relating to their proper interpretation, in particular regarding the standard of comparison (the *tertium comparationis*) and the admissibility of, and possible justifications for, differentiations between different groups of investors.

Such questions have, in fact, only started to surface in the jurisprudence of investment tribunals. In particular, tribunals have not yet found a consistent approach on whether the standard of comparison has to be drawn narrowly or whether non-discrimination provisions, such as national treatment, also prohibit different treatment across different

---

[33] Article 3(2), Agreement between the People's Republic of China and the Federal Republic of Germany on the Encouragement and Reciprocal Protection of Investments, signed on December 1, 2003, entered into force on November 11, 2005.

[34] See, for example, Article 3, Protocol to the Agreement between Japan and the People's Republic of China concerning the Encouragement and Reciprocal Protection of Investment, signed on August 27, 1988, entered into force May 14, 1989. See also Ad. Articles 2 and 3, Agreement between the People's Republic of China and the Federal Republic of Germany on the Encouragement and Reciprocal Protection of Investments, signed on December 1, 2003, entered into force on November 11, 2005.

[35] See Dolzer and Schreuer (*supra* footnote 12), pp. 178–91 (2008); McLachlan, Shore and Weiniger (*supra* footnote 12), pp. 254–57 (2007); Tabet, *Application de l'obligation de traitement national et de traitement de la nation la plus favorisée dans la jurisprudence arbitrale en matière d'investissement*, in Kahn and Wälde (eds.), *New Aspects of International Investment Law*, p. 353 (2007). Frequently, however, arbitral tribunals draw parallels to the non-discrimination provisions in international trade law; see Kurtz, *National Treatment, Foreign Investment and Regulatory Autonomy: The Search for Protectionism or Something More?*, in Kahn and Wälde (eds.), p. 311 (2007); DiMascio and Pauwelyn, *Nondiscrimination in Trade and Investment Treaties: Worlds Apart or Two Sides of the Same Coin?*, 102 A.J.I.L. 48 (2008) (both critical that such parallels should be drawn due to the different objectives and the different contexts the non-discrimination provisions both fields operate in). Specifically on the interpretation of MFN clauses see *infra* Ch. IV.

sectors of the economy. Indeed, some arbitral decisions point in this direction,[36] while others handle national treatment more restrictively and allow only for a sector-specific comparison between foreign and domestic investors.[37] Likewise, it is not settled whether non-discrimination in investment treaties only prohibits *de iure* discriminations between investors or whether it encompasses *de facto* discrimination. These unsettled issues about the scope of non-discrimination provisions do not, however, suggest that the principle of non-discrimination is understood differently by the various investment treaties. Indeed, its very purpose of providing competitive structures implies uniformity concerning its general structure and content.

(b)   Fair and equitable treatment and full protection and security

While national and MFN treatment constitute relative standards that depend on the treatment accorded to a reference group, investment treaties also impose standards of treatment on host States, such as fair and equitable treatment and full protection and security, that are absolute in character and grant protection to foreign investors independent of the host State's treatment of its own nationals or of third-party nationals.[38] In this context, BITs regularly provide that "[i]nvestments of investors of each Contracting Party shall at all times be accorded fair and equitable

---

[36] See *Occidental Exploration* v. *Ecuador*, Final Award, July 1, 2004, paras. 167 *et seq.*; *LG&E* v. *Argentina*, Decision on Liability, October 3, 2006, paras. 164 *et seq.*

[37] *Methanex* v. *United States*, Final Award, August 3, 2005, Part IV, Chapter C, para. 25; *CMS* v. *Argentina*, Award, May 12, 2005, paras. 285 *et seq.*

[38] Generally on fair and equitable treatment see Vasciannie, *The Fair and Equitable Treatment Standard in International Investment Law and Practice*, 70 Brit. Ybk. Int'l Law 99, 144 (1999); Yannaca-Small (*supra* footnote 9) (2004); Schreuer, *Fair and Equitable Treatment in Arbitral Practice*, 6 J. World Inv. & Trade 357 (2005); Choudhury, *Evolution or Devolution? – Defining Fair and Equitable Treatment in International Investment Law*, 6 J. World Inv. & Trade 297 (2005); Dolzer, *Fair and Equitable Treatment*, 39 Int'l Law. 87 (2005); Schill, *Fair and Equitable Treatment under Investment Treaties as an Embodiment of the Rule of Law* (2006); Klein Bronfman, *Fair and Equitable Treatment*, 10 Max Planck U.N. Ybk. 609 (2006); Snodgrass, *Protecting Investors' Legitimate Expectations*, 21 ICSID Rev. – For. Inv. L. J. 1 (2006); Tudor (*supra* footnote 9) (2008); Mayeda, *Playing Fair: The Meaning of Fair and Equitable Treatment in Bilateral Investment Treaties*, 41 J. World Trade 273 (2007); Dolzer and Schreuer (*supra* footnote 12), pp. 119–49 (2008); McLachlan, Shore and Weiniger (*supra* footnote 12), pp. 226–47 (2007); Kalicki and Medeiros, *Fair, Equitable and Ambiguous*, 22 ICSID Rev. – For. Inv. L. J. 24 (2007); Orakhelashvili, *The Normative Basis of "Fair and Equitable Treatment"*, 46 AVR 74 (2008); Picherack, *The Expanding Scope of the Fair and Equitable Treatment Standard*, 9 J. World Inv. & Trade 255 (2008).

treatment and full protection and security in the territory of the other Contracting Party."[39] Alternatively, some treaties explicitly provide that under fair and equitable treatment and full protection host States "shall in no case accord treatment less favorable than that required by international law."[40]

In view of the little specific obligation to accord fair and equitable treatment and to provide full protection and security, the exact content of both standards has not been authoritatively determined and remains contested. In particular, a vivid debate has developed as to whether both standards are equivalent to the international minimum standard of treatment under customary international law or whether they constitute a free-standing treaty obligation that can be interpreted and applied autonomously.[41] In practice, however, this debate seems to have little impact on the interpretation of fair and equitable treatment and the actual application of this standard to specific cases.[42] In general, arbitral tribunals only rarely take a principled approach to interpretation of fair and equitable treatment. They regularly apply fair and equitable treatment in a broad manner, using it as a yardstick for the conduct of the national legislator, of domestic administrations, and of domestic courts. They do tackle it, however, primarily on a case-by-case basis.

Yet, from a more conceptual perspective, fair and equitable treatment can be understood as embodying the concept of the rule of law (*Rechtsstaat, état de droit*) as it is widely recognized as an administrative or constitutional law concept in most liberal legal systems. As such it imposes certain procedural and substantive standards on all branches of domestic government.[43] In fact, the jurisprudence of investment tribunals interpreting fair and equitable treatment regularly has recourse to certain sub-elements that run parallel to the concept of the rule of

---

[39] Article 2(2), Agreement between the Government of the United Kingdom of Great Britain and Northern Ireland and the Government of the Republic of Bulgaria for the Promotion and Reciprocal Protection of Investments, signed on December 11, 1995, entered into force on June 24, 1997.

[40] Article 3(a), Treaty between the Government of the United States of America and the Government of the Hashemite Kingdom of Jordan concerning the Encouragement and Reciprocal Protection of Investment, signed on July 2, 1997, entered into force on June 12, 2003. On varying formulations of fair and equitable treatment see also Tudor (*supra* footnote 9), pp. 19–52 (2008).

[41] On this debate see, for example, Dolzer and Schreuer (*supra* footnote 12), pp. 124–28 (2008) (with further references).

[42] See also *infra* Ch. VI.B.3 (concerning the debate in the NAFTA context).

[43] Schill (*supra* footnote 38), pp. 9–28 (2006).

law in domestic legal systems. In this context, fair and equitable treatment is interpreted to include the requirement of stability and predictability of the legal framework, consistency in the host State's decision-making, the principle of legality, the protection of confidence or legitimate expectations, procedural due process and the prohibition of denial of justice, the protection against discrimination and arbitrariness, the requirement of transparency, and the concept of reasonableness and proportionality.[44]

Based on a violation of fair and equitable treatment, arbitral tribunals have, for instance, ordered host States to pay damages to foreign investors for the refusal to grant or to prolong an operating license,[45] for committing a denial of justice in domestic courts,[46] for unpredictable, frequent, and conflicting changes in domestic laws,[47] for inconsistent government action,[48] for violating an obligation of cooperation in negotiations,[49] for the misuse of administrative authority,[50] or for fundamentally changing the regulatory framework of gas distribution in times of economic crises contrary to the legitimate expectations of investors in the stability of the legal framework.[51] Overall, fair and equitable treatment has developed into the single most important standard of international investment protection, which moreover has the potential to shape domestic administrative law, influence the deployment of judicial proceedings, and serve as a quasi-constitutional standard that sets limits to the activity of national legislators.

The standard of full protection and security, in turn, is closely connected to the fair and equitable treatment standard. Unlike fair and equitable treatment, which primarily protects the investor against interferences

---

[44] See Schill (*supra* footnote 38), pp. 11–23 (2006).

[45] See *Tecmed* v. *Mexico*, Award, May 29, 2003, paras. 152 *et seq.* (concerning the non-prolongation of an operating license for a waste landfill); *Metalclad* v. *Mexico*, Award, August 30, 2000, paras. 74 *et seq.* (concerning the refusal to grant a construction permit for a waste landfill).

[46] See *Compañia de Aguas del Aconquija* v. *Argentina*, Award, November 21, 2000, para. 80; *Loewen* v. *United States*, Final Award, June 26, 2003, para. 132; *Waste Management* v. *Mexico*, Award, April 30, 2004, para. 132. See comprehensively, on the concept of denial of justice in international law, Paulsson, *Denial of Justice in International Law* (2005).

[47] *Eastern Sugar* v. *Czech Republic*, Partial Award, March 27, 2007, paras. 222–338; *Occidental Exploration* v. *Ecuador*, Award, July 1, 2004, para. 183; *PSEG Global* v. *Turkey*, Award, January 19, 2007, para. 250.

[48] *MTD* v. *Chile*, Award, May 25, 2004, para. 163; *PSEG* v. *Turkey*, Award, January 19, 2007, para. 248.

[49] *PSEG* v. *Turkey*, Award, January 19, 2007, para. 246.

[50] *PSEG* v. *Turkey*, Award, January 19, 2007, para. 247.

[51] See *CMS* v. *Argentina*, Award, May 12, 2005, para. 279; *LG&E* v. *Argentina*, Decision on Liability, October 3, 2006, paras. 100 *et seq.*

by the host State, full protection and security requires positive action by the host State in establishing and enforcing a legal framework for the protection of foreign investment and in protecting the physical integrity and safety of foreign investments against interference by private actors, such as demonstrating or rioting individuals.[52] Apart from providing police protection, full protection and security is also violated if State conduct actually infringes upon the physical safety of foreign investments outside the scope of law enforcement.[53] This investor right was, therefore, held to be violated in a case of destruction of foreign-owned property by the host State's armed forces.[54]

Both fair and equitable and full protection and security, therefore, ensure basic requirements connected to the concept of the rule of law, namely that the State has to act vis-à-vis individual economic actors through the means of the law, but also has an obligation to protect the physical and economic integrity, safety, and security of its subjects against unlawful interference by private and government actors. It is this principle of government according to the rule of law that fair and equitable treatment and full protection and security reference as a unitary concept in the various BITs.

(c)   Protection against direct and indirect expropriation

Since the various large-scale expropriations that occurred after the First World War,[55] one of the core investor rights under virtually all investment treaties is the protection against expropriation. As with the other standards of treatment, the formulations concerning the prohibition of expropriation in the various BITs are very similar, if not identical.[56] A typical provision is contained, for example, in the BIT between Finland and China that provides:

> Neither Contracting Party shall expropriate, nationalise or take other measures having similar effects, (hereinafter referred to as "expropriation") against the investments of the investors of the other Contracting Party in its territory, unless the following conditions are met. The expropriation is done:

---

[52] See Zeitler, *The Guarantee of "Full Protection and Security" in Investment Treaties Regarding Harm Caused by Private Actors*, Stockholm Int'l Arb. Rev. 1 (2005) (with references to and discussion of the case law on full protection and security).

[53] *Cf. PSEG* v. *Turkey*, Award, January 19, 2007, paras. 256–58.

[54] *American Manufacturing & Trading* v. *Zaire*, Award, February 21, 1997, paras. 6.04 *et seq.*; *Asian Agricultural Products* v. *Sri Lanka*, Final Award, June 27, 1990, paras. 45 *et seq.*

[55] See *supra* Ch. II.A.   [56] Dolzer and Schreuer (*supra* footnote 12), pp. 92–96 (2008).

(a) in the public interest;
(b) under domestic legal procedure;
(c) without discrimination; and
(d) against compensation.[57]

Expropriation does not comprise only direct expropriations or nationalizations that involve the transfer of title from the foreign investor to the State or a third party. It also covers so-called indirect, creeping or *de facto* expropriations involving State measures that do not interfere with the owner's title, but negatively affect the property's substance or void the owner's control over it.[58] In light of receding numbers of direct expropriations,[59] the protection against indirect expropriations is an important instrument that enables foreign investors to challenge not only disguised expropriations, that is, measures taken with the intention of making an investor abandon its investment in order to avoid the financial consequences of a direct expropriation, but also "regulatory takings," that is, measures taken in the context of the modern regulatory State, such as strangulating taxation, overly burdensome measures protecting the environment, disproportionate zoning restrictions, etc.

---

[57] Article 4(1), Agreement between the Government of the Republic of Finland and the Government of the People's Republic of China on the Encouragement and Reciprocal Protection of Investments, signed on November 15, 2004, entered into force on November 15, 2006.

[58] On the concept of indirect expropriation see Christie, *What Constitutes a Taking of Property under International Law?*, 38 Brit. Ybk. Int'l L. 307 (1962); Weston, *"Constructive Takings" under International Law*, 16 Va. J. Int'l L. 103 (1975); Higgins, *The Taking of Property by the State: Recent Developments in International Law*, 176 Recueil des Cours 259, 322 *et seq.* (1982); Dolzer, *Indirect Expropriation of Alien Property*, 1 ICSID Rev. – For. Inv. L. J. 41 (1986); Wälde and Kolo, *Environmental Regulation, Investment Protection and "Regulatory Taking" in International Law*, 50 Int'l & Comp. L. Q. 811 (2001); Yannaca-Small, *"Indirect Expropriation" and the "Right to Regulate" in International Investment Law* (2004); Paulsson and Douglas, *Indirect Expropriation in Investment Treaty Arbitrations*, in Horn and Kröll (eds.), *Arbitrating Foreign Investment Disputes*, p. 145 (2004); Fortier and Drymer, *Indirect Expropriation in the Law of International Investment*, 19 ICSID Rev. – For. Inv. L. J. 293 (2004), Newcombe, *The Boundaries of Regulatory Expropriation*, 20 ICSID Rev. – For. Inv. L. J. 1 (2005); Kunoy, *Developments in Indirect Expropriation Case Law in ICSID Transnational Arbitration*, 6 J. World Inv. & Trade 467 (2005); Leben, *La liberté normative de l'etat et la question de l'expropriation indirecte*; Leben, *Le contentieux arbitral transnational relatif à l'investissement international* (2006); Dolzer and Schreuer (*supra* footnote 12), pp. 92–115 (2008); McLachlan, Shore and Weiniger (*supra* footnote 12), pp. 291–313 (2007); Reinisch, *Expropriation*, in Muchlinski, Ortino and Schreuer (*supra* footnote 12), p. 407 (2008).

[59] See Minor, *The Demise of Expropriation as an Instrument of LDC Policy, 1980–1992*, 25 J. Int'l Bus. Stud. 177 (1994).

Although it is not settled how to draw a distinction between compensable indirect expropriation and non-compensable regulation,[60] the emerging arbitral jurisprudence tends to view unreasonable destruction of the value of foreign investment, interference with the management of a company or the repudiation of an investor-State contract as compensable indirect expropriations.[61] Similarly, the cancellation and the non-prolongation of operating licenses have been classified as indirect expropriations by investment tribunals.[62]

In general, both direct and indirect expropriations are lawful under international investment treaties only if they fulfill a public purpose, are implemented in a non-discriminatory manner, and observe due process of law.[63] Some BITs expressly state that this includes the possibility of judicial review in national courts concerning the legality of an expropriatory measure.[64] Finally, and most importantly, both direct and indirect expropriations require compensation.[65] While the amount of expropriation is still contested and BITs use varying formulations ranging from "reasonable" to "appropriate,"[66] modern treaty practice increasingly accepts the Hull formula of "prompt, adequate and effective" compensation as applicable. The Sino-German BIT, for example, stipulates that the "compensation shall be equivalent to the value of the investment immediately before

---

[60] See Dolzer, *Eigentum, Enteignung und Entschädigung im geltenden Völkerrecht*, pp. 186 *et seq.* (1985); Dolzer, *Indirect Expropriation: New Developments?*, 11 N.Y.U. Envt'l L. J. 64 (2002) (both with further references).

[61] See *supra* footnote 58.

[62] See *Tecmed* v. *Mexico*, Award, May 29, 2003, paras. 95 *et seq.*; *Metalclad* v. *Mexico*, Award, August 30, 2000, paras. 102 *et seq.*

[63] See Reinisch, *Legality of Expropriations*, in Reinisch (ed.), *Standards of Protection in International Investment Law*, pp. 171, 176–78 (2008).

[64] Concerning domestic due process see, for example, Article 4(1), Acuerdo para la promoción y fomento recíprocos de inversiones entre el Reino de España y la República Popular de China, signed on February 6, 1992, entered into force on May 1, 1993; concerning review in national Chinese courts see, for example, Article 4(2), Agreement between the People's Republic of China and the Federal Republic of Germany on the Encouragement and Reciprocal Protection of Investments, signed on December 1, 2003, entered into force on November 11, 2005.

[65] For the question of whether the level of compensation differs for indirect expropriation see Nouvel, *L'indemnisation d'une expropriation indirecte*, 5 Int'l L. Forum du droit int. 198 (2003); Merrill, *Incomplete Compensation for Takings*, 11 N.Y. U. Envt'l L. J. 110 (2002). See also Reisman and Sloane, *Indirect Expropriation and Its Valuation in the BIT Generation*, 74 Brit. Ybk. Int'l L. 115 (2003).

[66] See, for example, on the earlier BIT practice of the People's Republic of China, Shan, *The Legal Framework of EU–China Investment Relations*, p. 200 (2005).

the expropriation is taken or the threatening expropriation has become publicly known" and that "[t]he compensation shall be paid without delay and shall carry interest at the prevailing commercial rate until the time of payment; it shall be effectively realizable and freely transferable."[67]

Despite the endorsement of provisions on direct and indirect expropriation in bilateral treaties, States generally view these provisions as a uniform concept not only of treaty law, but equally of customary international law. For this reason, it is safe to conclude that provisions on expropriation in investment treaties reference a uniform concept of customary international law. Accordingly, tribunals interpret expropriation provisions in investment treaties as a uniform concept. The Tribunal in *S. D. Myers* v. *Canada*, for example, observed that "The term 'expropriation' in Article 1110 [of NAFTA] must be interpreted in light of the whole body of state practice, treaties and judicial interpretations of that term in international law cases."[68]

(d)   Umbrella clauses

Investment treaties often also contain clauses providing that "each Contracting Party shall observe any obligation it may have entered into with regard to investments of investors of the other Contracting Party."[69] Such clauses are most commonly designated as umbrella clauses, because they create a separate obligation under the investment treaty in question to observe obligations the host State has assumed in relation to foreign investors, in particular obligations under investor-State contracts.[70]

---

[67] See Article 4(2), Agreement between the People's Republic of China and the Federal Republic of Germany on the Encouragement and Reciprocal Protection of Investments, signed on December 1, 2003, entered into force on November 11, 2005.

[68] *S. D. Myers* v. *Canada*, Partial Award, November 13, 2000, para. 280.

[69] Article 3(5), Agreement between the Kingdom of the Netherlands and the Hungarian People's Republic for the Encouragement and Reciprocal Protection of Investments, signed on September 2, 1987, entered into force on June 1, 1988.

[70] On umbrella clauses see Dolzer and Schreuer (*supra* footnote 12), pp. 153–62 (2008); Schreuer, *Travelling the BIT Route*, 5 J. World Inv. & Trade 231, 249–55 (2004); Sinclair, *The Origins of the Umbrella Clause in the International Law of Investment Protection*, 4 Arb. Int'l 411 (2004); Alexandrov, *Breaches of Contract and Breaches of Treaty*, 5 J. World Inv. & Trade 555 (2004); Wälde, *The "Umbrella" Clause in Investment Arbitration*, 6 J. World Inv. & Trade 183 (2005); Kunoy, *Singing in the Rain*, 7 J. World Inv. & Trade 275 (2006); Wong, *Umbrella Clauses in Bilateral Investment Treaties*, 14 Geo. Mason L. Rev. 135 (2006); Gaffney and Loftis, *The "Effective Ordinary Meaning" of BITs and the Jurisdiction of Treaty-Based Tribunals to Hear Contract Claims*, 8 J. World Inv. & Trade 5 (2007); Gallus, *An Umbrella just for Two?*, 24 Arb. Int'l 157 (2008); Schill, *Enabling Private Ordering – Function, Scope and Effect of Umbrella Clauses in International Investment Treaties*, 18 Minn. J. Int'l L. 1 (2009).

In practice, the interpretation of umbrella clauses has, however, developed into one of the most contentious aspects of international investment law. Triggered by the incompatible construction of comparable clauses in the Swiss–Pakistani and the Swiss–Filippino BITs by two ICSID tribunals,[71] contrary views are fostered in regard to the function and effect of umbrella clauses in investment treaties.[72] These views can be roughly grouped into two camps. One line of jurisprudence supports a broad application of umbrella clauses which allows foreign investors to use investment treaty arbitration in order to seek relief for any breach of an investment-related promise by the host State, independent of the nature of the obligation and independent of the nature of the breach.[73] It applies to commercial as well as sovereign conduct of host States. In this view, umbrella clauses go beyond customary international law by permitting foreign investors to bring claims for the breach of the host State's promises as a violation of the umbrella clause under the respective investment treaty without limiting it to expropriatory conduct or breaches of a sovereign nature.[74]

The competing approach attributes a narrower function to umbrella clauses and restricts their operation to breaches of investor-State contracts resulting from sovereign acts of the host State.[75] This approach views umbrella clauses essentially as a declaratory codification of customary international law that clarifies that rights of an investor under an investor-State contract can form the object of an expropriation and accordingly require compensation if they are taken.[76] Most importantly, this position reads the distinction between contract claims and treaty claims into the interpretation of umbrella clauses and thus excludes "simple," or

---

[71] See also *infra* Ch. VII, footnotes 173–98 and accompanying text, on the decisions in the two *SGS* cases.

[72] *SGS* v. *Pakistan*, Decision on Jurisdiction, August 6, 2003, paras. 163–73; *SGS* v. *Philippines*, Decision on Jurisdiction, January 29, 2004, paras. 113–28.

[73] Supporting the broader view *SGS* v. *Philippines*, Decision on Jurisdiction, January 29, 2004, paras. 113–28; *Eureko* v. *Poland*, Partial Award, August 19, 2005, paras. 244–60; *Noble Ventures* v. *Romania*, Award, October 12, 2005, paras. 46–62; *LG&E* v. *Argentina*, Decision on Liability, October 3, 2006, paras. 169–75; *Siemens* v. *Argentina*, Award, February 6, 2007, paras. 204–6.

[74] See on the limited protection of investor-State contracts by customary international law, for example, F. A. Mann, *State Contracts and State Responsibility*, 54 A.J.I.L. 572 (1960); Jennings, *State Contracts in International Law*, 37 Brit. Ybk. Int'l L. 156 (1961).

[75] Supporting the narrower view, *CMS* v. *Argentina*, Award, May 12, 2005, paras. 296–303; *El Paso* v. *Argentina*, Decision on Jurisdiction, April 27, 2006, paras. 71–88; *Pan American Energy* v. *Argentina* and *BP America* v. *Argentina* (consolidated claims), Decision on Preliminary Objections, July 27, 2006, paras. 100–16; *Sempra* v. *Argentina*, Award, September 28, 2007, paras. 305–14.

[76] See Wälde (*supra* footnote 70), 6 J. World Inv. & Trade 183 (2005).

commercial, breaches of investor-State contracts from the scope of application of the clauses.

Investment jurisprudence and international law doctrine have not yet settled on how to interpret umbrella clauses. However, it is noteworthy that the different views on interpretation are formulated in a principled way.[77] The interpretative problems that arise out of the considerable vagueness of umbrella clauses are rarely addressed in terms of what provisions containing umbrella clauses could mean for a specific bilateral treaty. Instead, the controversies are framed in terms of how umbrella clauses should be interpreted as part of the general framework of investment protection. This suggests, as with other provisions in BITs containing principles of investment protection that umbrella clauses make reference to a uniform, treaty-overarching concept.

(e)   Capital transfer provisions

Capital transfer provisions complement the protection of foreign investors. They ensure that the host State does not constrain an investor in repatriating its profits and does not restrict the investor's exit options.[78] Likewise, BITs grant free capital transfer to maintain or increase an admitted investment. These protections are important because capital transfer restrictions could result in effectively depriving an investor of its investment. A typical capital transfer provisions reads:

> Each Contracting Party shall assure to investors of the other Contracting Party, without delay and on a non-discriminatory basis, the unrestricted transfer *inter alia* of: (a) Capital and additional capital amounts used to maintain or increase investments; (b) Net operating profits including dividends and interest; (c) Repayments of any loan, including interest thereon, relating to the investment; (d) Payment of royalties and service fees as far as it is related to the investment; (e) Proceeds of sale or liquidation of the investment; (f) The earnings of nationals of one Contracting Party or of any third State who work in connection with investments in the territory of the other Contracting Party.[79]

---

[77] See *infra*, Ch. VII footnotes 175–98 and accompanying text.

[78] See generally Dolzer and Stevens (*supra* footnote 15), pp. 85–95 (1995); UNCTAD (*supra* footnote 10), pp. 257–79 (2004); Dolzer and Schreuer (*supra* footnote 12), pp. 191–94 (2008); Kolo, *Investor Protection vs Host State Regulatory Autonomy during Economic Crisis*, 8 J. World Inv. & Trade 457 (2007); Kolo and Wälde, *Economic Crises, Capital Transfer Restrictions and Investor Protection under Investment Treaties*, 3 Capital Markets L. J. 154 (2008).

[79] Article 7(1), Agreement between the Republic of India and the Kingdom of the Netherlands for the Promotion and Protection of Investments, signed on November 6, 1995, entered into force on December 1, 1996.

Treaty practice generally varies little concerning guarantees of free capital transfer. Yet, the scope of application of capital transfer provisions usually depends on the type of investment covered by the treaty in question. Therefore, capital transfer provisions vary in scope depending, for example, on whether the treaty in question grants a right of establishment to foreign investors or not.[80] Apart from that, capital transfer provisions are, however, framed as a general and principled obligation that suggests a uniform understanding of States as regards their material content.

3   Dispute settlement mechanisms under BITs

By far the most important provisions in investment treaties concern the procedural protection offered to foreign investors. Regularly, BITs provide not only for State-to-State dispute resolution but also allow for direct investor-State arbitration. Compared with traditional means of enforcing public international law through diplomatic protection, this empowerment of private investors has accurately been described as a "change in paradigm in international investment law."[81] Instead of depending on its home State to grant diplomatic protection, most BITs confer on the investor a right to unilaterally initiate arbitral proceedings against the host State without the host State's renewed consent.[82]

BITs vary concerning the forum and the procedure that govern investor-State disputes. Disputes may be conducted, *inter alia*, under the rules of the ICSID Convention, under UNCITRAL Arbitration Rules, or by means of ad hoc non-institutional arbitration. Likewise, the scope of the host State's consent to arbitration may vary.[83] While earlier BITs of socialist and formerly socialist countries, for example, regularly limited consent to arbitration to disputes concerning the amount of compensation for expropriation,[84] most other BITs allow for disputes concerning the violation of any substantive investor right. Some BITs even contain

---

[80] UNCTAD (*supra* footnote 10), pp. 258–59 (2004).

[81] Schreuer, *Paradigmenwechsel im Internationalen Investitionsrecht*, in Hummer (ed.), *Paradigmenwechsel im Völkerrecht zur Jahrtausendwende*, p. 237 (2002).

[82] See *infra* Ch. VI.A.1.b on the insufficiencies of diplomatic protection for effective investment protection.

[83] See Dolzer and Stevens (*supra* footnote 15), pp. 129–56 (1995).

[84] See, for example, Article 13(3), Agreement between the Government of the People's Republic of China and the Government of the Republic of Singapore on the Promotion and Protection of Investments, signed on November 21, 1985, entered into force on February 7, 1986; Article 11, Agreement between the Government of the Kingdom of Norway and the Government of the Republic of Hungary on the Promotion and

consent to arbitration covering any dispute arising between a contracting party and an investor of the other contracting party, thus including
claims based purely on contract.[85] While recourse to arbitration is in itself
not a question of the standard of treatment of foreign investors, investor-
State dispute settlement has a specific function not only with respect to
settling disputes and making host States comply with their promises
under investment treaties. Investor-State arbitration itself has a significant impact on the multilateralization of international investment law.
This influence will be discussed more closely in Chapters VI and VII. At
this point, it is sufficient to observe that investment treaties largely allow
for such recourse to arbitration.

B   The dynamics of treaty negotiation: the creation of homogeneous treaty texts

Above all with respect to the standards of treatment of foreign investment, investment treaties display considerable convergence in their
structure, object and purpose, and content. These similarities are particularly striking as one of the advantages of ordering international relations
on a bilateral basis, compared with multilateral orders, is the flexibility
bilateral treaties offer to respond to the specific needs and interests of
States. Bilateral relationships offer greater flexibility, especially concerning the distribution of mutual rights and obligations in ways the parties
consider beneficial.

Multilateral ordering, by contrast, necessarily entails less flexibility
in reacting to the specific interests of individual States. Being usually
characterized by applying uniform and non-discriminatory rules to all
participating actors, multilateral regimes are less flexible with respect
to maximizing the benefits from international coordination for a specific State. Instead, some States may have to make more concessions
in a multilateral as compared with a bilateral setting because a greater
number of demands has to be taken into account in finding a solution

Reciprocal Protection of Investments, signed on April 8, 1991, entered into force on
December 4, 1992.
[85] See, for example, Article 7(1), Agreement between the Government of the Arab
Republic of Egypt and the Government of Malaysia for the Promotion and Protection of
Investments, signed on April 14, 1997, entered into force on February 3, 1999. *Cf.* Griebel,
*Jurisdiction over "Contract Claims" in Treaty-Based Investment Arbitration on the Basis
of Wide Dispute Settlement Clauses in Investment Agreements*, 4(5) Transnat'l Disp.
Mgmt. (2007).

among a greater number of players. Against this background, it is therefore surprising that BITs display such striking similarities. Apparently, the lack of flexibility, in the sense of the inability to conclude *quid pro quo* bargains, was therefore not a reason why multilateral investment rules did not materialize.

On the contrary, the development of international investment law, and in particular the negotiation process of investment treaties, display several elements that specifically aim at avoiding diverging treaty texts. The similarities between BITs, even among wholly unrelated parties, are thus not coincidental, but result from various processes on the international level that embed bilateral treaties into multilateral frameworks. Instead of being negotiated in isolated bilateral settings, the negotiation and conclusion of bilateral treaties is entrenched in multilateral processes that coordinate investment treaty negotiations and ensure their uniformity. This suggests that a genuine interest of States in uniform investment rules is at play. This is all the more true since alternative explanations, namely lower transaction costs and hegemony, can be ruled out as decisive factors for the uniformity of BITs.

1   The entrenchment of bilateralism in multilateral settings

Unlike pure bilateral bargains, negotiation and conclusion of BITs are channeled by several processes that aim at creating uniformity among the treaties. First, the convergence of treaty texts of many capital-exporting countries finds its origin in national model treaties that serve as a basis for negotiations. The BITs of one capital-exporting country, such as Germany or the United States, are therefore worded similarly or even identically, because the treaty texts derive from a uniform model treaty.

Secondly, the convergence among the various national model treaties is based on their common historic pedigree. They have not been developed independently by every capital-exporting country, but go back to developments in the 1950s and 1960s that culminated in the proclamation of international draft conventions, in particular the 1967 OECD Convention on the Protection of Foreign Property. These international processes had, even though they never resulted in binding international instruments, a harmonizing effect for the BIT programs of the capital-exporting countries involved. This historic pedigree, therefore, illustrates how multilateral processes on the international level influenced the outcome of bilateral negotiations of investment treaties.

The convergence of treaty texts is thus not coincidental, but stems from intentional multilateral planning, above all by traditional capital-exporting countries, initially mostly within the OECD. This effect-ively transforms BITs into functional substitutes for the multilateral conventions that failed earlier. Even though the procedure of investment treaty negotiation switched from multilateral to bilateral forms, the con-tent of the rules and principles that emerged remained multilateral, as they based international investment relations on non-discriminatory prin-ciples that were uniform across the various bilateral treaty relationships.

(a)   The use of model treaties

Historically, the first generation of BITs was concluded between developed capital-exporting countries and developing capital-importing countries.[86] The specificity of these negotiations was – and often still is – that they were mostly based on model treaties developed by capital-exporting coun-tries.[87] Many countries, including Germany, the Netherlands, the United Kingdom, the United States, France, or Canada, use model BITs that are updated and refined on a regular basis.[88] Although divergences between these model treaties and the BITs actually concluded occasionally occur, "[t]ypically, the agreement was drafted by the developed country and offered to the developing country for signature, with the final agreement

[86]   The first BIT was concluded between the Federal Republic of Germany and Pakistan. Other European countries like France, Switzerland, the Netherlands, Italy, the Belgium-Luxemburg Economic Union, Sweden, Denmark, and Norway followed in the 1960s. The United Kingdom, Austria, Japan, and the United States started concluding BITs in the 1970s. See Vandevelde, *A Brief History of International Investment Agreements*, 12 U.C. Davis J. Int'l L. & Pol'y 157, 169 *et seq.* (2005).

[87]   See Dolzer and Stevens (*supra* footnote 15), p. 13 (1995).

[88]   Various model BITs of Austria, China (People's Republic), Denmark, France, Germany, Hong Kong, the Netherlands, Switzerland, the United States, and the United Kingdom, are reprinted in Dolzer and Stevens (*supra* footnote 15), pp. 165 *et seq.* (1995); Dolzer and Schreuer (*supra* footnote 12), pp. 352–419 (2008). On the development of the United States model BITs see Vandevelde, *The Bilateral Investment Treaty Program of the United States*, 21 Cornell Int'l L. J. 201 (1988); Vandevelde, *U.S. Bilateral Investment Treaties: The Second Wave*, 14 Mich. J. Int'l L. 621 (1993). On the 2004 Model BIT of the United States see Kantor, *The New Draft Model U.S. BIT*, 21 J. Int'l Arb. 383 (2004); Schwebel, *The United States 2004 Model Bilateral Investment Treaty*, 3(2) Transnat'l Disp. Mgmt. (2006). On French investment treaties see Juillard, *Le reseau français des conventions bilatérales d'investissements: à la recherche d'un droit perdu?*, 13 Droit et Pratique du Commerce International 9 (1987). On the German Model BIT see Karl, *The Promotion and Protection of German Foreign Investment Abroad*, 11 ICSID Rev. – For. Inv. L. J. 1 (1996); Füracker, *Relevance and Structure of Bilateral Investment Treaties – The German Approach*, 4 SchiedsVZ 236 (2006); Krajewski and Ceyssens, *Internationaler Investitionsschutz und innerstaatliche Regulierung*, 45 AVR 180 (2007).

reflecting only minor changes from the original draft."[89] Some countries, such as the United States, at times, were even generally unwilling to compromise much on the content of their BITs.[90]

The use of model treaties did not only serve the purpose of facilitating the negotiations about the content of a BIT and thus of reducing the drafting and negotiation costs.[91] It also aimed at ensuring a certain level of uniformity with respect to the standards governing the investment relations between the home State and varying host States. That uniformity of investment treaties was among the concerns of capital-exporting countries can be illustrated, for example, with respect to the position of the United States. When it started its BIT program in the late 1970s, the country did not understand BITs only as a tool to channel and to protect investment flows abroad, but also, and maybe foremost, as an instrument to counteract the potentially negative impact on customary international law of the movement to establish a New International Economic Order that was supported by a large number of developing and socialist countries.[92] The US BITs thus also aimed at re-establishing the state of customary international law on the protection of foreign investment that was under siege on the global level during the 1970s. For this reason, the United States only accepted minor changes to the drafts it proposed to developing countries for signature.[93] Against this background, it was essential for the United States that the content of its BITs aimed at a uniform level of investment protection that aspired to general validity. Similarly, the repeated moves to establish a multilateral investment treaty reflect the interest of capital-exporting States in uniform principles of investment protection.[94]

(b)   Multilateral draft conventions as guidance for model BITs

Although the use of model drafts for the negotiation of investment treaties explains the relative uniformity of BITs concluded by a particular capital-exporting country, and suggests an inclination towards multilateralism, this uniformity could still be coincidental in the sense that States

---

[89] See Vandevelde (*supra* footnote 86), 12 U.C. Davis J. Int'l L. & Pol'y 157, 170 (2005).
[90] Vandevelde (*supra* footnote 88), 14 Mich. J. Int'l L. 621, 628 (1993).
[91] On drafting and negotiating costs see *infra* Ch. III.B.2.
[92] On the New International Economic Order and its impact on international investment protection see *supra* Ch. II.B.2.
[93] See Vandevelde (*supra* footnote 88), 14 Mich. J. Int'l L. 621, 628 (1993).
[94] See *supra* Chs. II.B and II.E.

associate different understandings with identical wording. Yet the content of the model treaties itself is influenced not simply by copying the language of another model treaty. Instead, the similarity between model treaties of different capital-exporting countries is intentional and can be traced back to common origins. In fact, the national model treaties are themselves heavily influenced by multilateral processes and take guidance from failed multilateral conventions. Particularly influential in this context were the 1967 Draft Convention on the Protection of Foreign Property and its predecessor, the Abs–Shawcross Draft. Even though both projects never materialized as multilateral conventions, they heavily influenced the position taken by capital-exporting countries in their BIT negotiations, and often translated directly into the formulation of their model drafts.[95]

This influence is well documented, for instance, as regards the inclusion of umbrella clauses in investment treaties.[96] The concept of an umbrella clause as such was first developed by *Elihu Lauterpacht* in a legal opinion given in the context of the Anglo-Iranian oil dispute in the 1950s. It then made its way into the Abs–Shawcross Draft and was later included in the 1967 OECD Draft Convention. From there, it found its way into the model treaties of the United Kingdom, France, Germany, and the United States. This phenomenon does not, however, only hold true with respect to specific treaty clauses, but constitutes a phenomenon that affects the entire structure and content of BITs. Accordingly, the preparation of the OECD Draft Convention "explains in large part the homogeneity in the form and substance of most BITs, and it may be noted that OECD countries have continued to review their policies in this respect within the OECD Committee on International Investment and Multinational Enterprises."[97] The common historic origin of national model treaties, and the influence that failed multilateral projects on investment protection had on them, thus illustrates the existence of a common intention among capital-exporting States to base investment relations on uniform standards.

(c)   Multilateral treaties as frameworks for BITs

Apart from influencing the model BITs of capital-exporting countries, in some instances multilateral treaties also served as a direct framework for the subsequent conclusion of BITs and forged the uniformity of these

---

[95] On the 1967 OECD Draft Convention and the Abs–Showcross Draft, see, *supra* Ch. II.B.2.
[96] See A. Sinclair (*supra* footnote 70), 20 Arb. Int'l 411 (2004).
[97] Dolzer and Stevens (*supra* footnote 15), pp. 2–3 (1995).

BITs. This is, for example, the case with the Fourth Lomé Convention between the Member States of the European Economic Community (EEC) and sixty-eight developing countries from Africa, the Caribbean, and the Pacific.[98] It "affirm[ed] the importance of concluding between States, in their mutual interest, investment promotion and protection agreements …"[99] and specified that these treaties would be based on the States' "particular attention to the following issues: i. legal guarantees to ensure fair and equitable treatment and protection of foreign investors; ii. the most-favoured-investor clause; iii. protection in the event of expropriation and nationalization; iv. the transfer of capital and profits; and v. international arbitration in the event of disputes between investor and host."[100]

This mechanism illustrates how capital-exporting States used multilateral instruments as a means of ensuring convergence among to-be-concluded bilateral treaties between the EEC Member States and many of their former African, Caribbean, and Pacific dependencies. It created a multilateral framework that was responsible for the homogeneity of future BITs between the contracting parties of the multilateral framework. Overall, the various dynamics between bilateralism and multilateralism thus show that the uniformity of BITs was the result of intentional planning by capital-exporting countries. The bilateral form was, therefore, arguably a means to arrive at the type of uniform multilateral order that could not be achieved with multilateral negotiations.

2 Uniformity of investment rules and transaction costs

Not all countries, however, approach the negotiation of BITs by relying on a model draft. This is particularly true with regard to the more recent phenomenon of South–South BITs, that is, BITs among developing and transitioning economies.[101] Still, in form and substance these agreements differ little compared with the BITs negotiated on the basis of model drafts used by capital-exporting countries.[102] Furthermore, unlike in the

---

[98] See Fourth ACP–EEC Convention (Lomé Convention), signed on December 15, 1989, 29 I.L.M. 809 (1990). On the investment rules in this Convention see Juillard, *Lomé III et l'investissement international*, 29 Revue du Marché Commun 217 (1986).

[99] Article 260(1), Lomé Convention, 29 I.L.M. 864 (1990).

[100] See Annex LIII, Final Act concerning the Lomé Convention, 29 I.L.M. 802 (1990).

[101] *Cf.* Dolzer and Stevens (*supra* footnote 15), p. 14 (1995) ("Not all countries, however, rely on model agreements for treaty negotiations but even so a review of recent BITs suggests that the use of individually negotiated agreements has not led to important divergences.").

[102] UNCTAD, *South–South Cooperation in International Investment Arrangements*, p. 31 (2005) (observing that South–South BITs "differ from other (in particular

times of the New International Economic Order, economic and political ideology does not seem to have a significant impact on the content of South–South BITs. The BIT between Cuba and Mexico, for example, both countries that have a pronounced history of expropriating foreign investors and, in the case of Cuba still adhere to a socialist economic system, closely mirrors the BITs between capitalist countries.[103] Similar to other BITs, its Preamble recognizes the "necessity of promoting and protecting foreign investment with the objective of fomenting their [i.e., the Contracting States] economic prosperity;" it contains the guarantee of "fair and equitable treatment and full protection and security, in conformity with international law", national and most-favored-nation treatment, prohibitions on local content requirements and export minimums, a provision on free capital transfer, a prohibition on direct and indirect expropriations without compensation, and provides for investor-State dispute settlement. Similarly, the BIT between Cuba and the Socialist Republic of Vietnam contains almost identical investor rights.[104] Independent of political and economic ideology and breaking with traditional hesitations vis-à-vis international law, the structure and content of these treaties, as with most other South–South BITs, closely resemble – or are even largely identical to – the treaties encountered in the first generation of BITs between developed and developing countries.

The question, however, is whether the similarities between South–South and North–South BITs reflect an intention and an interest of developed and developing countries to have uniform rules of investment protection. The similarities in treaty texts of South–South BITs and North–South BITs could also be due to simple "copy–paste" effects. The convergence of BITs would then stem from the efficiency gains resulting from the use of existing models for drafting and negotiation.[105] The similarity between different bilateral treaties would then simply result

North–South) IIAs [i.e., International Investment Agreements] not so much in their overall objective, which is to promote and facilitate investment flows, but rather in terms of the depth and breadth in which they cover investment issues"); Dolzer and Stevens (*supra* footnote 15), pp. 4–10 (1995) (noting also that South–South BITs are almost identical with other investment treaties).

[103] Acuerdo entre los Estados Unidos Mexicanos y la République de Cuba para la Promoción y Protección de las Inversiones, signed on May 30, 2001, entered into force on March 29, 2002.

[104] See Agreement on the Promotion and Protection of Investment between the Government the Socialist Republic of Vietnam and the Government of the Republic of Cuba, signed on October 12, 1995, entered into force on October 1, 1996.

[105] See *supra* footnote 4.

from cost-saving behavior, but could, despite similar wording, not be directly translated into a convergence of the States' intentions on uniform standards of investment protection. Instead, the similarity of treaty texts would merely conceal that BITs remain the expression of bilateral *quid pro quo* bargains, and would frustrate any assumption of an interest in uniformity and in the existence of uniform standards across different bilateral treaty relationships. This would be particularly true with respect to wholly unrelated BITs. The meaning attributed to the content of fair and equitable treatment in treaty negotiations between State A and State B could thus be completely different from the meaning attributed to the same terms in a BIT between State C and State D, which served as a model, even though the wordings are identical. In fact, in some instances capital-exporting countries provided their model drafts as a starting point for the negotiation and conclusion of BITs between developing countries.[106]

However, model treaties for the negotiation and conclusion of BITs are not only available from capital-exporting States. Instead, a number of international organizations and NGOs have drafted non-binding instruments that can be used as alternative models for ordering international investment relations. While these models usually follow the general pattern of traditional BITs and make reference to the same principles of investment protection, they also aim at remedying what developing countries and critics have targeted as a one-sided imposition of investment rules by capital-exporting countries. For this purpose, these alternatives supplement the language and concepts of standard BITs with exceptions and additional content, or even respond to the widely voiced call to not only lay down investor rights but also investor obligations vis-à-vis the host State.[107] Developing countries, therefore, had, and continue to have, ample instruments at hand in order to structure their investment relations and are not required to revert to model treaties of capital-exporting countries.

---

[106] *Cf.* Elkins, Guzman and Simmons, *Competing For Capital*, 60 Int'l Org. 811, 818–19 (2006) (reporting on conferences sponsored by capital-exporting countries and international organizations that resulted in the conclusion of a number of South–South BITs).

[107] See, for an overview of such non-binding multilateral approaches, Tschofen, *Multilateral Approaches to the Treatment of Foreign Investment*, 7 ICSID Rev. – For. Inv. L. J. 384 (1992); McGhie, *Bilateral and Multilateral Investment Treaties*, in Bradlow and Escher (eds.), *Legal Aspects of Foreign Direct Investment*, pp. 107, 123, footnote 66 (1999) (for a list of partly binding, partly non-binding multilateral investment instruments). See, for a more recent model draft by a non-governmental organization, H. Mann *et al.*, *The IISD Model International Agreement on Investment for Sustainable Development*, 20 ICSID Rev. – For. Inv. L. J. 84–145 (2005).

In actual BIT practice, however, alternative models have had little to no influence. Such was, for example, the fate of the United Nations Code of Conduct on Transnational Corporations, a project that started in 1977.[108] Ideologically connected to the struggle about the New International Economic Order,[109] the Code aimed at balancing the interest of developed countries in protecting their foreign investors and the interest of developing countries in maintaining their sovereignty and economic independence. As a counterweight to rules concerning the treatment of transnational enterprises, the Code extensively addressed the obligations of foreign investors to respect human rights, to abstain from corrupt practices, not to interfere with internal political affairs, and to abide by national laws. While consensus existed concerning these obligations, disagreements persisted between developed and developing countries concerning the protection of foreign investors.[110] While capital-exporting countries were aiming at an extensive protection of their investors abroad, capital-importing countries emphasized the rights of the State to regulate and control foreign investment.[111] In particular, there was disagreement about conditions for the lawfulness of expropriations and about the standard of compensation. Despite the Code's "effort to draw up a universally accepted instrument of the treatment and the duties of foreign investors,"[112] the project had, however, little influence on actual BIT practice, mainly because of the deadlock that persisted between capital-importing and capital-exporting countries.

Similarly, the Asian–African Legal Consultative Committee (AALCC) produced, in 1984, a set of different model treaties in order to facilitate "negotiating texts for bilateral agreement on Promotion and Protection of Investments primarily in the context of economic cooperation between the countries of the Asian–African region."[113] The Committee proposed a set of three different model treaties that were intended for use "by a large number of states with different backgrounds and adhering to differing

---

[108] See Draft United Nations Code of Conduct on Transnational Corporations, 1985, reprinted in UNCTAD, *International Investment Instruments: A Compendium, Volume I – Multilateral Instruments*, pp. 161–80 (1996). See further Ebenroth, *Code of Conduct* (1987).

[109] Ebenroth (*supra* footnote 108), pp. 65 *et seq.* (1987).

[110] Ebenroth (*supra* footnote 108), pp. 410 *et seq.* (1987).

[111] Ebenroth (*supra* footnote 108), pp. 413 *et seq.*, 431 *et seq.* (1987).

[112] Tschofen (*supra* footnote 107), 7 ICSID Rev. – For. Inv. L. J. 384, 393 (1992).

[113] Asian–African Legal Consultative Committee (AALCC), *Models for Bilateral Agreements on Promotion and Protection of Investments*, 23 I.L.M. 237 (1984).

political and economic philosophies."[114] Model A of the Committee's proposal essentially endorsed the traditional North–South BIT model. Model B, in turn, stressed the control of host States over market access for foreign investments and transfer of capital, explicitly recognized the right of the host State to expropriate against "appropriate compensation" and provided for the exhaustion of local remedies before investor-State arbitration. Finally, Model C largely corresponded to the liberal provisions of Model A, but was tailored to apply only to specific economic sectors.[115] While Model A, therefore, endorsed the approach of capital-exporting countries to investment treaty practice, Models B and C mirrored the hesitations of developing countries against investment protection and liberalization. Nevertheless, the AALCC model treaties, in particular Models B and C, did not translate into the actual BIT practice of developing countries.[116]

Another prominent example of an international model instrument is the non-binding World Bank Guidelines on the Treatment of Foreign Direct Investment that were prepared under the auspices of the Development Committee of the World Bank and the IMF and unanimously adopted by it in 1992.[117] Similar to traditional BITs, the Guidelines contain provisions on fair and equitable treatment, national treatment, and free capital transfer, restrict direct and indirect expropriations, protect investor-State contracts, and provide for the settlement of disputes between investors and States by arbitration. The main difference from earlier BITs is, above all, the more detailed way in which the Guidelines regulate the treatment of foreign investors. They contain, for example, more specific rules on promptly granting licenses and permits for admitted investments. In general, the Guidelines were not, however, meant as a replacement of existing binding investment rules, but rather thought to "complement ... bilateral and multilateral treaties and other

---

[114] AALCC (*supra* footnote 113), 23 I.L.M. 238 (1984).
[115] AALCC (*supra* footnote 113), 23 I.L.M. 239 *et seq.* (1984).
[116] Dolzer and Stevens (*supra* footnote 15), p. 13 (1995).
[117] Guidelines on the Treatment of Foreign Direct Investment, 7 ICSID Rev. – For. Inv. L. J. 297 (1992). See further Shihata, *Legal Treatment of Foreign Investment: The World Bank Guidelines* (1993); Schlemmer-Schulte, *The World Bank Guidelines on the Treatment of Foreign Direct Investment*, in Bradlow and Escher (*supra* footnote 107), p. 87 (1999); Wendrich, *Ten Years After: The World Bank Guidelines on Foreign Direct Investment*, 3 J. World Inv. 831 (2002); Wendrich, *The World Bank Guidelines as a Foundation for a Global Investment Treaty*, 2(5) Transnat'l Disp. Mgmt. (2005); Protopsaltis, *Les principes directeurs de la Banque mondiale pour le traitement de l'investissement étranger*, in Kahn and Wälde (eds.) (*supra* footnote 35), p. 151 (2007).

international instruments ... and as a possible source on which national legislation governing the treatment of private foreign investment may draw."[118] As the Guidelines largely reflected the same thrust in approaching the protection of foreign investment as earlier BITs, namely by setting up rights for the protection of foreign investment, while providing for more detailed positions and solutions to tensions that have crystallized between investment protection and competing public concerns, they did not materially alter the BIT practice of States, but rather reinforced it.[119]

In sum, international organizations have been very active in drafting model treaties and guidelines for the protection and treatment of foreign investment. Most instruments had, however, little or no impact on the actual investment treaty practice of States, including the BITs practice among developing and transitioning countries. The almost universally prevailing models remained those that developed on the basis of the 1967 OECD Draft Convention.[120] This suggests that the convergence of South–South BITs with the traditional treaty practice was not due to a lack of alternative models. This further suggests that cost-saving behavior by using model treaties as a basis for the negotiation and conclusion of BITs was not the decisive factor for the treaties' uniformity, as saving costs could also have been achieved by using one of the alternative model treaties. Instead, it suggests that the content of the prevailing model was considered to constitute an appropriate basis for ordering international investment relations by both developed and developing countries.

3   Uniformity of investment rules and North–South hegemony

As the foregoing analysis suggests, the uniformity between investment treaties is not merely coincidental, but can be traced back to a close interconnectedness between bilateral and multilateral processes. BITs display a rather uniform structure and content because they are regularly based on model treaties of capital-exporting countries that serve as a basis for

---

[118] Guideline I(1).

[119] Cf. Wendrich (*supra* footnote 117), 3 J. World Inv. 831, 833 (2002) (pointing out that the Guidelines "constituted one of the precedents for the investment provisions of the Energy Charter Treaty" and "proved useful in the preparation of modern national investment laws and some BITs").

[120] Recently, however, one can witness changes in the treaty practice of various capital-exporting countries, including the United States, in reaction to undesired interpretations of investment treaties in arbitration proceedings. These changes do not, however, depart fundamentally from the traditional BIT practice. See further *infra* Ch. III footnotes 134–45 and accompanying text.

bilateral treaty negotiations. These models in turn go back to multilateral processes, above all within the OECD in the 1960s. Due to the negotiation deadlock that existed in multilateral settings between capital-exporting and capital-importing countries, the former decided to abandon multilateral and switch to bilateral negotiations. This strengthened the relative negotiation position of capital-exporting countries and allowed them to push for a level of investment protection in bilateral settings that developing countries as a group rejected. To a significant extent, the switch from multilateralism to bilateralism can, therefore, be explained with power asymmetries among the contracting parties.[121]

A related explanation for why developing countries concluded investment treaties bilaterally, while rejecting them when acting as a group, is the theory that developing countries face a prisoner's dilemma as soon as a single developing country defects from the opposition to international investment protection.[122] Once a single developing country has entered into a BIT, the argument goes, other developing countries are forced, as a matter of competition for foreign investment, to conclude similar treaties in order to receive any foreign investment inflows at all. The conclusion of BITs is, therefore, viewed as a competitive race to the bottom as developing countries have to give up substantial parts of their sovereignty in return for receiving foreign investment.

Both approaches view BITs as instruments of hegemonic behavior of developed vis-à-vis developing countries.[123] The reproach of the thesis relying on the prisoner's dilemma of developing countries is that developed countries are instrumentalizing the need of developing countries for investment inflows as a bargaining tool to extract promises regarding the treatment of foreign investment that developing countries would not agree to if they had a stronger negotiation position. Similarly, the theory hinging on power asymmetries considers the dissection of the conclusion of investment treaties into sequential bilateralism as a mechanism of strong countries to impose their preferences upon weaker States.[124]

---

[121] *Cf.* Morin and Gagné, *What Can Best Explain the Prevalence of Bilateralism in the Investment Regime?*, 36 Int'l J. Pol. Econ. 53, 54–57 (2007); Benvenisti and Downs (*supra* footnote 5), 60 Stan. L. Rev. 595, 611–12 (2007).

[122] See Guzman, *Why LDCs Sign Treaties that Hurt Them*, 38 Va. J. Int'l L. 639, 669 *et seq.* (1998); Elkins, Guzman and Simmons (*supra* footnote 106), 60 Int'l Org. 811 (2006) (both arguing that host States are under competitive pressure to sign BITs when other host States have done so).

[123] See also Chimni (*supra* footnote 5), 15 Eur. J. Int'l L. 1, 7 *et seq.* (2004); Chimni (*supra* footnote 5), Economic and Political Weekly, p. 337 (February 6, 1999).

[124] Benvenisti and Downs (*supra* footnote 5), 60 Stan. L. Rev. 595, 611–12 (2007).

Ultimately, this hegemonic critique would invalidate the claim that both capital-importing and capital-exporting States have a genuine interest in uniform rules of investment protection. Instead, if BITs were solely a product of hegemonic behavior of capital-exporting countries, the apparent convergence of investment treaties would only conceal that these treaties actually endorse preferential benefits and do not order investment relations on the basis of uniform principles of investment protection.

The view that international investment law is hegemonic in nature is, however, unconvincing for a number of reasons. First, if international investment law were hegemonic, and therefore anti-multilateral, we should expect that the most powerful hegemon secures benefits for itself to the detriment not only of developing countries but also to the detriment of other developed capital-exporting countries. We should thus witness more patterns of imperialism that aim at establishing preferential treatment for certain countries to the exclusion of others, including developed States.[125] Yet we do not observe such behavior. Instead, BITs include and are based on notions of non-discrimination and on uniform standards of investment protection.

To assume that capital-exporting countries behave like a single hegemon in relation to developing countries is, therefore, unconvincing. The hegemonic critique rather remains short in supplementing its formal critique of BIT negotiations with a critique of the substantive bargaining outcome. Apart from the general argument that BITs restrict the sovereignty of host States with respect to the treatment of foreign investors in their territory, and that they might not fully achieve their policy goal of attracting additional foreign direct investment,[126] this criticism does not manage to show that the substantive standards of international investment treaties are in fact detrimental to the interests of developing countries and their populations. Even if the pedigree of international investment law and the conclusion of BITs are forged by the political and economic power of capital-exporting States, this critique of the forms of

---

[125] Such patterns could include either preferential systems like the one established by the United Kingdom under the Imperial Free Trade initiative in the 1930s (see Cone, *The Promotion of Free-Trade Areas Viewed in Terms of Most-Favored-Nation Treatment and "Imperial Preference"*, 26 Mich. J. Int'l L. 563, 573 [2005]; J. Gallagher and Robinson, *The Imperialism of Free Trade*, 6 Econ. Hist. Rev. 1 [1953]) or preferential investment agreements parallel to the recent spread of preferential trade agreements (*cf.* Bhagwati, *Preferential Trade Agreements: The Wrong Road*, 27 L. & Pol'y Int'l Bus. 865 [1996]).

[126] See, however, *infra* Ch. III footnote 147 on the empirical link between the conclusion of BITs and actual flows.

international investment relations would not necessarily invalidate the substantive protection of these treaties.

Second, the hegemonic critique neglects the fact that developing countries obviously attribute a certain value to concluding BITs. Apart from the fact that, on occasion, developing countries were eager to enter into investment treaties with developed countries and actively sought their conclusion,[127] the more recent spread of South–South BITs suggests that traditional capital-importing countries consider investment treaties to constitute an appropriate instrument for governing their international investment relations more generally. Certainly, many developing countries are competing for foreign investment. However, this competition does not primarily take place in relation to the content of investment treaties, in particular the principles of investment protection they contain, but rather with regard to other investment incentives, such as preferential tax treatment and various other investment subsidies.[128] This, as a result, casts doubt on the argument that the content of BITs has been shaped by a competitive race to the bottom.

Third, the hegemonic critique juxtaposes in an oversimplifying manner the interests of capital-exporting and capital-importing States. It disregards the point that the interests among and within both groups can differ considerably. Neither all capital-exporting nor all capital-importing countries are in the same negotiating position and have identical interests concerning the regulation of their international investment relations. Rather the parties' interests and their relative negotiating power in a bilateral relationship depend upon their respective geographic, geological, social, cultural, and economic situations. One should, for example, expect that host States that dispose of monopolized or quasi-monopolized natural resources, or attractive domestic markets, enter into investment treaties that contain less restrictive standards of treatment, whereas countries without such characteristics consent to more extensive standards of investment protection. If BITs simply constituted distributive *quid pro quo* bargains, one should thus expect more variety with regard to the standards of investment protection.

---

[127] Vandevelde (*supra* footnote 88), 14 Mich. J. Int'l L. 621, 635–36 (1993) (noting that the BIT between the United States and the People's Republic of Congo was concluded after the Congolese Government had notified the US Government just prior to a State visit that it was interested in concluding a BIT. Negotiation and conclusion took place during the visit. The BIT was identical to the 1987 US Model BIT.).

[128] See Kurtz, *A General Investment Agreement in the WTO?*, 23 U. Pa. J. Int'l Econ. L. 713, 729 *et seq.* (2002); Nov, *The "Bidding War" to Attract Foreign Direct Investment: The Need for a Global Solution*, 25 Va. Tax Rev. 835 (2003).

Yet only few developing countries have concluded investment treaties that differ substantially from the standard model. The first generation BITs of the People's Republic of China (PRC) are such an example, as they systematically did not contain national treatment provisions and restricted investor-State dispute settlement to disputes about expropriation-related compensation.[129] However, even the PRC has, beginning in the late 1990s, started adapting its treaty practice to reflect international standards. While China's earlier BIT practice can be explained by the country's strong negotiating position, the recent changes arguably reflect China's acceptance that these standards constitute an overall beneficial trade-off between attracting foreign investment and restricting State sovereignty. This is particularly true as China, a net capital-importer, is also becoming a significant and increasing source of outward foreign investment and thus has to find a balance between her interests as a capital-importer, that aims at upholding sovereignty and regulatory leeway as far as possible, and her interests as a capital-exporter that aims at comprehensive protection of her investors abroad.[130] This illustrates that the growing convergence of investment treaty practice can be taken as an indicator that BITs strike an appropriate balance between the protection of foreign investment and State sovereignty and are not due to a competitive race to the bottom that is fueled by the interest of developing countries in attracting foreign investment. Host country-specific factors and their differing negotiation power, therefore, seem to have only minor influence on the content of investment treaties.

Equally, capital-exporting countries are not a uniform group and do not have identical interests in imposing a certain level of investment protection on developing countries. Instead, differences in the structure of their domestic industries and constituencies should influence the respective benefits they expect to derive from investment outflows and, consequently, affect the conclusion and content of their investment treaties.[131]

---

[129] Schill (*supra* footnote 28), 15 Cardozo J. Int'l & Comp. L. 73, 89–91, 94–97 (2007). Furthermore, only a few countries have not entered into any investment treaties at all, such as Brazil which has concluded but not ratified such treaties, or entered into investment treaties that substantially diverge from standard treaty practice.

[130] For a parallel analysis concerning treaties dealing with rules on the international sale of goods see Gilette and Scott, *The Political Economy of International Sales Law*, 25 Int'l Rev. L. & Econ. 446, 447 (2005) (arguing that the State parties to the Convention on the International Sale of Goods cannot be considered to favor either sellers' or buyers' interests, because both groups are likely to be represented in any given country).

[131] *Cf.* in the context of international trade relations Altieri, *Trade and Economic Affairs*, 21 Berkeley J. Int'l L. 847 (2003).

Capital-exporting States, for example, with industries that seek active engagement in foreign countries by exploiting natural resources or by engaging in commodity trade, should be expected to demand a higher level of investment protection than countries where outward foreign investment is less important. Similarly, internal political processes in capital-exporting countries should influence foreign investment policy. Countries with strong unions that instrumentalize the widespread fear that outward foreign investment is connected with a relocation of domestic production and destroys domestic employment should, for example, be expected to take a different position on matters of investment protection than countries where such internal political pressure is absent. Yet, such domestic factors seem to have little influence in compromising the uniformity of the BITs all these countries conclude.

Fourth, the hegemonic critique neglects that investment treaties are equally in force among traditional capital-exporting countries, such as NAFTA or the ECT, without, however, diverging significantly from the level of investment protection of classical North–South BITs. This suggests that capital-exporting States generally also consider the content of international investment treaties as an appropriate yardstick for their own behavior vis-à-vis foreign investors. This is true in relation to investors from other developed countries, as well as investors from developing countries. Although, initially, traditional North–South BITs de facto only imposed unilateral obligations upon developing States because of the lack of investment flows from developing into developed countries,[132] the obligations incumbent upon capital-exporting countries under these treaties assume increasing practical relevance. The more investment flows are becoming bidirectional, the more the effect of BITs on developed countries is actually felt. This is particularly reflected in investment treaty arbitration, where developed countries appear more and more often as respondents and are ordered to pay damages to foreign investors.[133]

Certainly, the fact that developed countries have become respondents in investment treaty arbitrations has had an impact on their investment

---

[132] Cf. Salacuse and Sullivan, Do BITs Really Work?, 46 Harv. Int'l L. J. 67, 78 (2005).

[133] See, for example, Maffezini v. Spain, Award, November 13, 2000; S. D. Myers v. Canada, Final Award, December 30, 2002; Pope & Talbot v. Canada, Award in Respect of Damages, May 31, 2002. The United States also frequently appears as a respondent in NAFTA arbitration, so far, however, without having been ordered to pay damages. More generally on the phenomenon of developed countries as respondents in investment treaty arbitration see G. Alvarez and Park, The New Face of Investment Arbitration, 28 Yale J. Int'l L. 365 (2003).

treaty practice. The United States, for example, has introduced, in direct reaction to investment awards that it considered as too restrictive for State sovereignty, changes both to its model treaty as well as to some recently concluded investment treaties.[134] The NAFTA award in *Metalclad* v. *Mexico*,[135] and some other proceedings,[136] have, for example, triggered a vivid debate about the proper scope of the concept of indirect expropriation and its influence on the State's regulatory power. Against this background, the United States included more specific language in its 2004 Model BIT, and in recent investment treaties, in order to clarify that *bona fide* general regulation did not regularly constitute a compensable indirect expropriation.[137] As a reaction to the decision in *Maffezini* v. *Spain*,[138] the United States introduced a clause in some subsequent investment treaty negotiations aiming specifically at excluding the application of MFN clauses to investor-State dispute settlement.[139] Likewise, in reaction to the interpretation of the fair and equitable treatment standard in *Pope & Talbot* v. *Canada*,[140] the United States pushed for a clarification of this concept in its recent investment treaties.[141] Finally, the United

---

[134] See Gagné and Morin, *The Evolving American Policy on Investment Protection*, 9 J. Int'l Econ. L. 357 (2006); Kantor (*supra* footnote 88), 21 J. Int'l Arb. 383 (2004); Legum, *Lessons Learned from the NAFTA*, 19 ICSID Rev. – For. Inv. L. J. 344 (2004); Schwebel (*supra* footnote 88), 3(2) Transnat'l Disp. Mgmt. (2006). More generally on the interaction between investment arbitration and investment treaty practice see UNCTAD, *Investor–State Dispute Settlement and Impact on Investment Rulemaking*, pp. 71–89 (2007).

[135] *Metalclad* v. *Mexico*, Award, August 30, 2000 (considering that the refusal of an operating license for a hazardous waste landfill and the proclamation of a natural protection zone for cacti that prevented the operation of the landfill constituted an indirect expropriation).

[136] See, in particular, *Ethyl Corporation* v. *Canada*, Award on Jurisdiction, June 24, 1998, and *Methanex* v. *United States*, Final Award, August 3, 2005. Both cases created considerable concerns as to whether product bans for protecting the environment constituted an indirect expropriation under Article 1110, NAFTA and required compensation of affected foreign investors.

[137] See, for example, Article 15.6, United States–Singapore Free Trade Agreement, signed on January 15, 2003, entered into force on January 1, 2004, in connection with an exchange of letters on the scope of the concept of indirect expropriation.

[138] See extensively *infra* Ch. IV.C.1.a.

[139] See Article 10.4(2), footnote 1, Draft of the Central America–United States Free Trade Agreement, January 28, 2004 (stating that the parties agree that the MFN clause they include in their treaty "does not encompass international dispute resolution mechanisms such as those contained in Section C of this Chapter, and therefore could not reasonably lead to a conclusion similar to that of the Maffezini case").

[140] See extensively *infra* Ch. VI.B.3.

[141] See Article 10.5(2)(a), Central America–Dominican Republic–United States Free Trade Agreement, signed on August 5, 2004 (stipulating that "fair and equitable treatment

States is pressing towards procedural changes to the implementation of international investment treaties through investor-State arbitration by advocating, *inter alia*, for the introduction of an appeals mechanism for investment treaty awards.[142] This behavior could indeed be interpreted as the retreat of one of the biggest capital-exporting countries from the standards that it has always considered as appropriate for the restriction of other, notably weaker States, but as too burdensome for its own treatment of foreigners.

However, the recent changes in US BIT practice are of a secondary rather than a fundamental character. They often merely reflect a clarification of how the existing standards should be interpreted and do not constrain the core of existing principles of investment protection. The changes regarding fair and equitable treatment, for example, appear as a declaratory clarification of the existing normative content of this treaty standard rather than as its restriction.[143] Likewise, the changes concerning the concept of indirect expropriation are an explicit confirmation of customary international law's acceptance of a police power for the regulation of property and not a restriction of the current scope of the concept.[144] Finally, restrictions with respect to the scope of MFN clauses have to be considered as minor changes that concern a specific aspect of international investment law without undermining the general framework that international investment protection is based on. Overall, even though the United States amended its treaty practice in reaction to the novel situation of being confronted with investor-State disputes as a respondent, it did not do so in a ground-breaking manner. Instead, its continuous efforts at concluding investment treaties confirm the general position of the United States and other developed countries that the principles of investment protection are appropriate rules for the protection

includes the obligation not to deny justice in criminal, civil, or administrative adjudicatory proceedings in accordance with the principle of due process embodied in the principal legal systems of the world").

[142] See, for example, Article 29(9b) in connection with Annex E, Treaty between the United States of America and the Oriental Republic of Uruguay concerning the Encouragement and Reciprocal Protection of Investment, signed on September 7, 2004, entered into force on November 1, 2006 (providing for the potential introduction of an appeals mechanism for investor-State arbitration under the treaty three years after the treaty entered into force). See also Legum (*supra* footnote 134), 19 ICSID Rev. – For. Inv. L. J. 344 (2004).

[143] *Cf.* Schill (*supra* footnote 38), pp. 11–23. (2006)

[144] *Cf.* Schill, *Do Investment Treaties Chill Unilateral State Regulation to Mitigate Climate Change?*, 24 J. Int'l Arb. 469, 471 *et seq.* (2007); Schill, *Revisiting a Landmark*, 3(2) Transnat'l Disp. Mgmt. 1 *et seq.*, 5 *et seq.* (2006).

of investors in developed and developing countries. Changes to its earlier treaty practice, therefore, suggest that the United States continue to recognize the value of uniform investment rules, while at the same time viewing the bilateral form of investment treaties as a tool for the slow evolution of the system of investment protection.[145]

Overall, the hegemonic critique that the content of investment treaties is imposed on developing countries, and motivated by the desire of developed countries to dominate them, is not convincing. Instead, the broad dispersion of BITs as tools to regulate investment relations between developed and developing countries, and among developed and developing countries, respectively, illustrates the claim of the principles of international protection to universal application, even though they are enshrined in bilateral treaties.

C   Multilateralism and the specific interest in uniform investment rules

Rather than constituting a mere coincidence, the convergence of investment treaties suggests the existence of a genuine interest by States, both developed and developing, in uniform rules of investment protection that is independent of any hegemonic behavior of developed countries and of the motivation to save transaction costs in the drafting of BITs. Reasons supporting a multilateral agreement on investment are usually seen in a number of factors.[146] A multilateral investment agreement is considered to: (1) attract foreign investments, which transfer technology and managerial skills and improve the competitiveness of the host country; (2) lead to greater transparency, predictability and legal security; (3) replace insufficient domestic institutions that prevented attracting more FDI in the past; (4) bring consistency to the fragmented bilateral and regional investment treaties; (5) avoid recourse to inefficient investment incentives; and (6) allow the host State to make more credible commitments with respect to foreign investors.

Many of these objectives can in fact be achieved on the basis of bilateral treaties. In particular, creating the stability, predictability, and legal security needed by foreign investors in order to invest in a specific host country can be reached on the basis of BITs. Like a multilateral treaty, a BIT can establish institutions that can serve as a substitute for insufficient

---

[145] Similarly Morin and Gagné (*supra* footnote 121), 36 Int'l J. Pol. Econ. 53, 64–69 (2007).
[146] See Kennedy, *A WTO Agreement on Investment: A Solution in Search of a Problem?*, 24 U. Pa. J. Int'l Econ. L. 77, 79–80 (2003).

domestic institutions. Investor-State dispute settlement, for example, can replace insufficient domestic dispute settlement mechanisms between investors and host States; the substantive obligations under BITs can replace insufficient domestic property rights and substitute for shortcomings regarding the domestic rule of law. By entering into a BIT, host States are, therefore, able to commit to investment-friendly policies and to give credible commitments to foreign investors. BITs can therefore achieve the aim of protecting foreign investment. Likewise, recent empirical studies show that BITs seem to achieve their objective of attracting foreign investment and thus to contribute to economic growth in developing countries.[147] The effectiveness of BITs in both respects, coupled with the persistent failure of multilateralism, might, therefore, indeed suggest that "the world is not ready for, does not want, and/or does not need a multilateral agreement on investment."[148]

However, the conclusion of bilateral treaties does not mean that States have no interest in uniform and thus multilateral investment rules.

---

[147] Initially, there was quite some skepticism as to whether BITs have the effect of stimulating investment flows between the contracting States. Two earlier studies in particular have found no significantly positive relationship between the conclusion of BITs and an increase in investment inflows; see Hallward-Driemeier, *Do Bilateral Investment Treaties Attract Foreign Direct Investment?* (2003); Tobin and Rose-Ackerman, *Foreign Direct Investment and the Business Environment in Developing Countries* (2005); more recently also, Aisbett, *Bilateral Investment Treaties and Foreign Direct Investment: Correlation and Causation*, in (2007); Sauvant and Sachs (eds.), *The Effect of Treaties on Foreign Direct Investment: Bilateral Investment Treaties, Double Taxation Treaties, and Investment Flows*, p. 395 (2009) (finding no positive relationship). Most recent studies, by contrast, including one by Tobin and Rose-Ackermann, find a positive relationship between signing BITs and FDI flows; see Tobin and Rose-Ackerman, *When BITs Have Some Bite*, in Alford and Rogers (eds.) *The Future of Investment Arbitration*, p. 131 (2009); Egger and Pfaffermayr, *The Impact of Bilateral Investment Treaties on Foreign Direct Investment*, 32 J. Comp. Econ. 788 (2004); Neumayer and Spess, *Do Bilateral Investment Treaties Increase Foreign Direct Investment to Developing Countries?*, 33 World Development 1567 (2005); Salacuse and Sullivan (*supra* footnote 132), 46 Harv. Int'l L. J. 67 (2005); Büthe and Milner, *The Politics of Foreign Direct Investment into Developing Countries*, 52 Am. J. Pol. Sc. 741 (2008); Swenson, *Why Do Developing Countries Sign BITs?*, 12 U.C. Davis J. Int'l L. & Pol'y 131 (2005); Kim, *Bilateral Investment Treaties, Political Risk, and Foreign Direct Investment*, 11 Asia Pac. J. Econ. & Bus. 1 (2007); K. Gallagher and Birch, *Do Investment Agreements Attract Investment?*, 7 J. World Inv. & Trade 961, 969 (2006); Büthe and Milner, *Bilateral Investment Treaties and Foreign Direct Investment: A Political Analysis*, in Sauvant and Sachs (eds.), *The Effect of Treaties on Foreign Direct Investment: Bilateral Investment Treaties, Double Taxation Treaties, and Investment Flows*, p. 171 (2009); Egger and Merlo, *The Impact of Bilateral Investment Treaties on FDI Dynamics*, 30 World Econ. 1536 (2007). See also Yackee, *Conceptual Difficulties in the Empirical Study of Bilateral Investment Treaties*, 33 Brook. J. Int'l L. 405 (2008) (pointing to problems in the empirical studies so far conducted).

[148] Kennedy (*supra* footnote 146), 24 U. Pa. J. Int'l Econ. L. 77, 186 (2003).

Instead, there are at least three specific reasons why uniform rules with respect to investment protection are preferable to a conglomerate of fragmented and diverging bilateral rules. First, multilateral and thus uniform rules concerning the protection of foreign investment are in the interest of States because they create a framework for equal competition among foreign investors and require the same treatment independent of the source or the target of the investment. Enhanced competition, in turn, enhances innovation which, in turn, leads to economic growth and development. At the same time, however, competition benefits from the participation of larger numbers of actors. In this respect, multilateral rules have long-term benefits compared with ordering investment relations bilaterally, because they can effectively implement the legal infrastructure necessary for the functioning of a competitive market with a broader geographic coverage and a larger number of participants.

Second, uniform rules can be necessary to react to negative externalities in an increasingly globalized economy. Some measures passed by host States, that directly affect foreign investors in one country, may also have indirect effects that interfere with the business activities of economic actors in third countries. Large-scale expropriations in one country could, for example, result in a domino effect that destabilizes the global economy beyond the immediate effects of the measures on the directly affected investors. Multilateral rules thus respond to a collective action problem in international investment relations. Third, multilateral investment rules prevent the creation of discriminations based on nationality and the isolation of countries or blocs of countries from the rest of the world. In this respect, multilateral investment rules, much like multilateral trade rules, contribute to an international relations structure that increases international security and peace through economic interdependence.

These reasons, it is submitted, suggest an explanation for why States have, independent from the content of the substantive obligation under investment treaties, an interest in establishing uniform investment rules. This interest ultimately also allows the conclusion that the content of BITs is not only coincidentally similar, but that such similarities reflect an interest of States in uniform standards of international investment protection.

1   Investment cooperation, comparative advantage and competition in a global market

While the outcomes of investment treaty arbitrations, in particular if host States are ordered to pay damages to foreign investors, regularly give rise to criticism about the negative consequences of investment treaties for State sovereignty, the treaties carry long-term benefits for capital-exporting and capital-importing States alike. These gains lie in increased foreign investment flows among States[149] and the increase in economic growth connected to increased international economic cooperation. Similar to the justification for the welfare increases stemming from international trade,[150] foreign investment flows increase the welfare of capital-exporting and capital-importing States based on the theory of comparative or competitive advantage.[151] Similar to international trade scenarios, liberal foreign investment policies enable foreign investors to invest wherever capital is used most efficiently in order to produce the best goods and services at the lowest possible price.

While the macroeconomic determinants of foreign investment flows are varied and still require additional research and study,[152] under the theory of competitive advantage, foreign investment will flow into the sectors among different national economies where countries have an advantage over other economies.[153] This will lead to additional

---

[149] See *supra* footnote 147.

[150] Economic concepts relating to international trade are transferable to international investment, since both trade and investment are not only partly interchangeable, but also mutually supportive. If trade barriers to foreign markets, including quotas, tariffs or domestic subsidies, render trade in goods or services inefficient and uncompetitive, foreign direct investment may be a way to tap a foreign market and create turnover. In this case, investment is a substitute for trade. In other instances, international trade and foreign investment are mutually supportive, as foreign investment enables market actors to relocate their production to a different country, where less expensive labor or the proximity to raw material makes production cheaper, and subsequently trade goods and services back to the country of origin (or any other country). In this case, international trade and international investment are correlative. *Cf.* Kojima, *Direct Foreign Investment*, pp. 119–33 (1978).

[151] See, on the economic theory of comparative advantage, Kenen, *The International Economy*, pp. 19–62 (4th edn. 2000); Södersten and Reed, *International Economics*, pp. 3–71 (3rd edn. 1994) and see also pp. 467–93 (containing a framework explaining foreign investment activities); see further Porter, *The Competitive Advantage of Nations*, pp. 18–21 (1990) (arguing for a more comprehensive model that takes into account that trade and investment are both strategies for the economic success of companies and that focuses rather on the potential of nations for innovation and other country-specific advantages).

[152] In fact, the phenomenon of foreign direct investment is mostly studied from the perspective of the multinational firm; see Navaretti and Venables, *Multinational Firms in the World Economy*, pp. 23–98 (2004); see also Kojima (*supra* footnote 150), pp. 59–67 (1978). Macroeconomic approaches, by contrast, seem to be much less frequent and not yet fully understood; see Navaretti and Venables, *ibid.*, p. 182 (2004).

[153] See on this and the following, Vandevelde, *The Economics of Bilateral Investment Treaties*, 41 Harv. Int'l L. J. 469, 472 *et seq.* (2000); Navaretti and Venables (*supra* footnote 152),

product- and industry-specific specialization, further enable the development of economies of scale, and enhance international competition which will, in turn, result in innovation of products, services and production, reduce costs, and expand customer choice. Instead of investing in its home State, an investor will be able to invest in a foreign country and benefit from cheaper production costs. By transferring industries abroad, the investor can profit from the comparative advantage of the host State and make its economic activity more efficient.

Likewise, the host State benefits from foreign investment inflows. The advantages of foreign investment inflows lie mainly in the efficient use of the host country's resources, in the creation of employment and the payment of higher wages, in improving productivity of local companies and enhancing export performance, and in the transfer of managerial skills and technology from the investor's home State into the host State.[154] In the long run, foreign investment thus enhances economic efficiency in host States. In this context, it is important to note that the contribution of foreign investment to the host State's economy, its economic growth, and development, are not primarily through the additional capital inflow, but mainly through the transfer of technology and managerial skills and the increase in competition and innovation.[155] Economic growth in host States is, therefore, primarily caused through the increase in technological innovation and competition connected to increases in foreign investment inflows.[156]

Foreign investment also has advantages for the investor's home State. The competition effects of foreign investment have repercussions on

pp. 127–50 (2004) (discussing various factors influencing foreign investment flows, including country determinants, such as trade costs and barriers, tax differentials and policies to attract foreign investment, market size, regional integration, agglomeration and herding, i.e., proximity to other firms, and proximity to customers). See also Kojima (*supra* footnote 150), p. 107 (1978) (arguing that "direct foreign investment should follow the direction indicated by comparative investment profitabilities, which in turn are a reflection of comparative advantage under competitive conditions").

[154] See Navaretti and Venables (*supra* footnote 152), pp. 151–85 (2004); see also OECD, *Open Markets Matter*, pp. 25–58 (1998).

[155] See Easterly, *The Elusive Quest for Growth*, pp. 47 *et seq.* (2002); Solow, *Technical Change and the Aggregate Production Function*, 39 Rev. Econ. & Stat. 312 (1957). On competition as the central factor that stimulates innovation and economic development, see Kerber and Schwalbe, *Economic Foundations of Competition Law*, in Säcker, Montag and Hirsch (eds.), *Competition Law: European Community Practice and Procedure*, p. 202 (2007), paras. 66–78; Porter (*supra* footnote 151), pp. 45–49 (1994).

[156] On the relations between foreign investment, institutions and economic growth see *supra* Ch. I, footnotes 12–16 and accompanying text.

capital-exporting countries, because it allows – and requires – them to adjust to changes in competitive advantage by transferring industries abroad that have become comparatively inefficient and instead attract investment into sectors where the home State has competitive advantages over other economies. For the capital-exporting State, this also results in further technical, scientific, and industrial innovation, and creates economic growth.[157]

Ultimately, the free flow of investment should generate global welfare both in capital-exporting as well as capital-importing countries. Again, the crucial factor is not so much the capital flows among national economies, but the potential for innovation and enhanced competition between investors, whether foreign or domestic. All this is not to say that foreign investment flows do not involve risks for home and host States,[158] but rather that it carries advantages that generally favor investment liberalization and investment protection and outweigh existing risks.

The theory of competitive advantage also explains why the interest of States is not limited to bargaining for specific advantages in bilateral relationships, but rather that there is a general advantage in creating uniform standards of treatment for foreign investment. While resources may already be allocated more efficiently if two States benefit from their respective competitive advantage and draw benefits from closer economic relations on a bilateral basis, the larger an investment space is for investors, and the more participants there are with different specializations, the more efficiently will resources be allocated, and the greater will be the benefits that derive from economic cooperation in general and investment cooperation in particular. The more national economies participate in a common investment area and the greater international competition is, the greater the potential for specialization, innovation and economic efficiency will be.[159]

---

[157] While the effects of foreign investment on home States are still not fully understood, there is evidence that outward foreign investment enhances domestic investment, technological upgrading, and the productivity of firms that invest abroad. See Navaretti and Venables (*supra* footnote 152), pp. 217–40 (2004). On the positive correlations between outward foreign investment and domestic investment see Desai, Foley and Hines, *Foreign Direct Investment and the Domestic Capital Stock*, 95(2) Am. Econ. Rev. 33 (2005); Desai, Foley and Hines, *Domestic Effects of the Foreign Activities of U.S. Multinationals*, Am. Econ. J.: Econ. Pol'y 181 (2009).

[158] *Cf.* OECD (*supra* footnote 154), pp. 59–64 (1998).

[159] That multilateralism is economically more beneficial in terms of overall welfare is also the claim of the parallel discussion in the context of international trade about the potentially negative impact of increasing regionalism. See Bhagwati, *The World Trading*

The interest in the participation of the greatest possible number of players, and in the efficiency gains stemming from it, requires, however, that the framework conditions of participation in an international investment market are uniform for all investors and with respect to all investments. In other words, the basic institutions necessary for the functioning of a market must be uniform for all market actors in order for competition to take place on the basis of a level playing field. Otherwise, the competitive advantage of nations is prone to be distorted by differences in political risk. This would result in different transaction costs being imposed on different economic actors and result in losses of competition and a reduction in economic efficiency.

While discriminatory (or differentiated) investment rules and the non-existence of competition may in the short term be interests of some States, a genuine long-term interest among capital-exporting and capital-importing States exists in creating uniform standards of treatment that avoid a distortion of the investment market and the competitive advantage of different national economies. It is this interest that also explains why there has been a strong movement since the end of the Second World War towards concluding multilateral investment treaties, even if the conclusion of these treaties has always failed. While the failure may be interpreted as a lack of a common interest of States, the very fact that these projects have been brought on their way, and the willingness of States to participate in their negotiation, suggest a preference for a multilateral system with equal standards of treatment, even though the preferences about the standards of investment protection may have differed between States in the past and may differ at present. The theory of competitive advantage explains why there is a common and mutual interest in uniform international investment law between capital-exporting and capital-importing countries and within the different groups of contracting States. This mutual interest explains why investment treaties converge significantly in their structure and content, although they are the result of bilateral negotiations.

2   Multilateral investment rules and negative externalities

Uniform rules that impose limits on the way in which States treat foreign investors, or interfere with or regulate economic activities on

System at Risk, pp. 58–79 (1991); Bhagwati, Regionalism and Multilateralism, in de Melo and Panagariya (eds.), New Dimensions in Regional Integration, pp. 22 et seq. (1993); Baldwin, Multilateralising Regionalism, 29 World Econ. 1451 (2006).

their territory more generally, may also be beneficial in avoiding negative externalities of host State measures on economies other than their own. Potentially, the negative effects of some host State measures, such as large-scale expropriations and nationalizations, or certain unpredictable and fundamental policy changes that can affect the host State's economy as a whole, may be significant enough to have negative spillover effects even on the national economies of other States. They may, in other words, trigger a domino effect that destabilizes national economies outside the host State's territory and beyond the immediate effects of the measures. This could be the case, for example, because the mother company of a foreign subsidiary affected by a measure in the host State or financing bank could suffer financial difficulties or even become insolvent. Such effects are increasingly likely the more national economies become interconnected and integrate. Multilateral rules that restrict host State interference of this kind thus respond to a collective action problem in international investment relations.

Even though such situations have not yet occurred in the context of host State interference with foreign investment, analogous domino effects have taken place in the banking sector in the 1970s and 1980s, and have resulted in major economic turbulence not only in the country where the crisis originally arose, but also in third countries.[160] One of the aggravating factors of this crisis, and a reason for the domino effects, was the lack of a multilateral regulatory regime with uniform rules for international financial markets.

After the Second World War, financial markets operated as rather closed national markets. They began, however, to open in the 1960s. This led to increasing competition between financial markets and the regulatory regimes in place in the different national economies, as financial transactions could be conducted in places like London, Frankfurt, Tokyo, New York, etc., depending on where capital transactions could be conducted at the lowest cost. While this competition enhanced the efficiency of international financial markets and lowered the costs for financial transactions, it also increased their vulnerability, as banks had an incentive to relocate their business to wherever regulation was least costly and least restrictive and imposed fewest compliance costs.

---

[160] See, on this and the following, Genschel and Plümper, *Wenn Reden Silber und Handeln Gold ist*, 3 Zeitschrift für Internationale Beziehungen 225, 230–39 (1996); Genschel and Plümper, *Regulatory Competition and International Co-operation*, 4 J. Eur. Pub. Pol'y 626, 628–31 (1997). It may also be noted that the current financial crisis developed in a similar fashion and involved the same type of transborder domino effects.

As a consequence, it became increasingly difficult for States to effectively impose regulatory standards for the banking sector because banks could relocate their business activity to a jurisdiction that imposed less costly restrictions. This led to a race to the bottom with respect to the regulation of banks, in particular their equity-to-assets ratio. However, the negative effects of this race to the bottom, particularly bank insolvencies which were facilitated by lax regulatory regimes, affected banking sectors in every economy. This became apparent with the collapse of several banks on different occasions in the 1970s and the 1980s. Although originally only one bank became insolvent, this insolvency triggered a chain reaction that affected banks in other national economies and ultimately threatened the banking systems of entire countries.

This phenomenon occurred for the first time in 1974 when the German Herstatt Bank and the US-American Franklin National Bank suffered a loss of liquidity because of business activities abroad. Likewise, in 1982, the biggest private Italian bank, Banco Ambrosiano, was threatened by insolvency, because its Luxemburg subsidiary experienced financial difficulties. The problem of chain reactions also became apparent when Mexico and other developing countries declared a default on their foreign debt in 1982. This threatened not only the immediate institutional lenders, but whole groups of banks and the financial markets globally. Again in 1984, the eighth biggest bank in the United States, Continental Illinois, became bankrupt and threatened to destabilize the entire US economy. Ultimately, the Federal Reserve took over the debts of Continental Illinois in order to prevent the further spread of this crisis to other banks both within and outside the United States.

Meaningful governmental reaction to these crises was complicated by the fact that unilateral intervention by increasing the regulatory supervision of banks by a single State would have led to competitive disadvantages of that State's domestic banks or even a dislocation of banking activities to less regulated jurisdictions. However, this would not have prevented the danger of a future chain reaction of the kind to be avoided. Instead, coordinated reactions of the States with major financial markets were necessary. Ultimately, the lack of global regulation of financial markets was solved through the introduction of a multilateral regime that prescribed uniform capital standards for banks and furnished mechanisms for concerted actions that helped to avoid chain reactions in internationally, closely intertwined financial markets due to the under-capitalization of banks.[161]

---

[161] Notably, this regime was brought into existence after the central banks of the United States and the United Kingdom had entered into a bilateral agreement that was subsequently

A justification for uniform rules that regulate and restrict the host States' powers to interfere with foreign investments can be analogous. Parallel to the example discussed above, it is perceivable that some actions by host States vis-à-vis foreign investors, in particular large-scale nationalization without adequate compensation, or interference in sensitive economic sectors like the banking sector or capital markets, may not only negatively impact on the foreign investors directly affected. Instead, similar to the chain reactions in the international financial markets described above, it is possible that the economic destruction of a foreign subsidiary can lead to a financial crisis of the subsidiary's mother company in a third State. This could go as far as causing the insolvency of the mother company, which in turn could have additional negative consequences for the creditors of this company and their creditors, etc. Such consequences could be particularly harsh if nationalizations concern core industries like the banking sector.

Due to the increasing inter-linkages of domestic economies in a globalized market and production processes that span plants in several countries, the consequences of government interference with foreign investors might, therefore, not remain restricted to the companies directly affected, but may have negative consequences upon other share- and stakeholders and eventually even entire foreign economies. Ultimately, massive interference by just one host State could have tremendous impacts on the global economy as a whole. Against this background, uniform rules that restrict States in their interference with economic activities could help to avoid such potential chain reactions and stabilize today's international markets. This justifies the need and interest in uniform standards in international investment protection.

3   Multilateral investment rules and international relations

An additional justification for uniform investment rules could finally result from their contribution to international peace and security, if one accepts the premise that investment treaties not only regulate economic matters, but also form part of a larger framework in ordering international relations between States. By requiring States to order their investment relations based on uniform standards, particularly those

joined by Japan. Only then did the remaining European actors agree to set up a multilateral regime with uniform standards. The bilateral initiative of the United States and the United Kingdom was the trigger that overcame earlier multilateral negotiation deadlocks under the auspices of the Bank for International Settlements. See the literature listed, *supra* footnote 160.

preventing discrimination between investors from different States, uniform rules prevent the emergence of preferential economic treatment between specific States or blocs of States. Uniform principles can thus help to mitigate international conflicts or even undermine the economic basis for military alliances.

That discriminatory economic treatment has, in fact, the potential to generate or aggravate international conflicts is, for example, illustrated by the development of international economic relations in the inter-war period. During that era, systems of preferential economic treatment aggravated international conflicts between States or were even used to prepare military alliances.[162] Discriminatory trade practices have thus been attributed partial responsibility for intensifying the world economic crisis and the international tensions that ultimately discharged in the Second World War.[163] Accordingly, ordering international trade relations on a multilateral basis thereafter was not only a concession to considerations about the economic efficiency of international trade, but also part of an international security architecture in which increasing mutual economic interests would lessen the potential for international conflict.

In fact, theoretical and empirical studies in international political economy have shown that economic cooperation and trade are larger within than across military alliances.[164] International alliances, therefore, seem to cause an increase in international trade relations among allies. Similarly, the reverse claim has been forwarded at least since Kant's *Perpetual Peace* and the classical liberal economists, namely that international economic relations and trade further peace between nations.[165] The mechanisms at play are, first, that trade furthers contact between citizens of different nations and thereby creates mutual respect and harmonious relations and, second,

---

[162] On the discriminatory trade practices in the inter-war period see Pomfret, *Unequal Trade: The Economics of Discriminatory International Trade Policies*, pp. 29 *et seq.* (1988); Kindleberger, *Commercial Policy Between the Wars*, in Mathias and Pollard (eds.), *The Cambridge Economic History of Europe*, vol. VIII, p. 161 (1989); Oye, *Economic Discrimination and Political Exchange*, pp. 71–133 (1992).

[163] *Cf.* also *infra* Ch. IV.A.2 (concerning the development of MFN clauses and their relation to international peace and security).

[164] See Pollins, *Conflict, Cooperation, and Commerce*, 33 Am. J. Pol. Sc. 737 (1989); Gowa, *Allies, Adversaries and International Trade*, pp. 31–78 (1994). Trade is also greater among democracies than between democracies and other regime types; see Mansfield, Milner and Rosendorff, *Why Democracies Cooperate More*, 56 Int'l Org. 477 (2002).

[165] See Oneal and Russett, *The Classical Liberals Were Right*, 41 Int'l Stud. Quart. 267 (1997).

that trade creates economic interdependencies that increase the cost of international conflict.[166] In fact, empirical studies validate this claim that increased international economic relations have a peace-building function between nations.[167]

In the same way as international trade, increased international investment relations between States should have the same effects in stabilizing international relations and in reducing international conflict. Foreign investment activity not only creates personal linkages between citizens from foreign countries, it also increases economic linkages that render conflict more costly and thus less attractive. In particular, ordering investment relations multilaterally, that is, based on notions of non-discrimination and equal rights and obligations, will avoid discriminations among investors from different home States, bilateral isolationism, and the creation of blocs or alliances. Instead of engaging in international conflict, the free play of competition in international investment relations based on unilateral and multilateral rules can, therefore, be viewed as relating to interests beyond pure economics. Uniform and non-discriminatory investment rules do not only play a role in stabilizing of the global economy, but should also contribute to reducing international conflicts and tensions.

D   Conclusion

The failure of multilateral projects for investment protection, coupled with the proliferation of bilateral and regional investment treaties, should have resulted in the diversification and fragmentation not only of the sources of international investment law, but also of its content. In view of the *quid pro quo* bargaining that often occurs in bilateral relations, the shift from multilateralism to bilateralism in investment treaty negotiations should thus have prevented the emergence of uniform standards

---

[166] See Mansfield and Pevehouse, *Trade Blocs, Trade Flows, and International Conflict*, 54 Int'l Org. 775, 776 (2000). See also Arad and Hirsch, *Peacemaking and Vested Interests*, 25 Int'l Stud. Quart. 439 (1981); Arad, Hirsch and Tovias, *The Economics of Peacemaking* (1983).

[167] See Polachek, *Conflict and Trade*, 24 J. Conflict Res. 55 (1980); Gasioroswski and Polachek, *Conflict and Interdependence*, 26 J. Conflict Res. 709 (1982); Oneal *et al.*, *The Liberal Peace*, 33 J. Peace Research 11 (1996); Oneal and Russett (*supra* footnote 165), 41 Int'l Stud. Quart. 267 (1997); Russett, Oneal and Davis, *The Third Leg of the Kantian Tripod for Peace*, 52 Int'l Org. 441 (1998); Gartzke, *Kant We All Just Get Along?*, 42 Am. J. Pol. Sc. 1 (1998); Mansfield and Pollins (eds.), *Economic Interdependence and International Conflict* (2003).

of treatment for foreign investment depending on the relative negotiating power and interests of the States involved. Preferential and discriminatory regimes in international investment protection should, therefore, have been the result.

However, this chapter has shown that the myriad number of BITs converge considerably as regards their function, their object and purpose, and their content. In particular, the principles governing the relations between foreign investors and host States are surprisingly uniform and include standards of non-discrimination and uniform minimum standards of treatment, including the restriction of direct and indirect expropriations, fair and equitable treatment, full protection and security, and free capital transfer. Procedurally, the majority of investment treaties provide for recourse to investor-State arbitration. Furthermore, this convergence of investment treaties regarding the principles of investment protection is independent of whether the treaties are concluded between capital-exporting and capital-importing countries, among developing countries or among developed countries.

Yet, in order to understand the network of BITs as part of a uniform international investment regime, it is necessary to consider why the treaties have developed to display such considerable convergence and show that it is permissible to infer from their textual convergence a convergence in substance and content. By contrast, if their convergence was purely incidental, so that the treaties stand isolated par by par, efforts to understand them as part of an overarching whole would be futile. Accordingly, it would then not be permissible to draw conclusions from the interpretation of the standards of one BIT for the interpretation of an unrelated BIT.

The convergence of BITs is, however, not purely coincidental, but stems from several factors that suggest an intention of States in creating uniform rules governing international investment relations. First, developed countries regularly base the negotiation and conclusion of BITs with capital-importing countries on national model BITs. These model BITs, in turn, converge significantly because they originate from multilateral processes, above all the 1967 OECD Draft Convention for the Protection of Foreign Property. Second, the conclusion of BITs was regularly accompanied by multilateral processes that aimed at ensuring their uniformity, including the conclusion of multilateral treaties as frameworks for the conclusion of BITs as well as informal inter-governmental coordination. This illustrates that the convergence of BITs was not coincidental, but resulted from the intentional planning of capital-exporting countries. For capital-exporting countries the change from multilateralism to bilateralism in international investment relations was, therefore, one of form, not of substance. It was not motivated by the desire for flexible and differentiated rules on investment protection that would enable *quid pro quo* bargains, but served the objective of breaking the negotiation deadlock with capital-importing countries that had occurred earlier in multilateral settings. It was a way of arriving at standards of investment protection that developing countries had opposed in multilateral settings.

Certainly, hegemonic elements were at play in this switch from multilateral to bilateral negotiation. Yet, this hegemonic element did not result in preferential or discriminatory investment protection standards. Instead, investment treaties continued to be based on notions of non-discrimination that subject all States, including capital-exporting States, to the same standards of investment protection. This restriction of the sovereignty of traditional capital-exporting States becomes increasingly effective as investment flows are no longer unidirectional from traditional capital-exporting into capital-importing countries, but materialize in both directions. Furthermore, developing countries started concluding investment treaties with other developing countries without, however, significantly changing their content compared with traditional North–South BITs.

This suggests that capital-importing countries have come to accept the standard content of investment treaties as not only reflecting the interest of capital-exporting States, but also as reflecting their own interests as capital-importers. More generally, States appear to consider BITs as striking an appropriate balance between investment protection and State sovereignty. The aspiration of investment treaties towards universal application is, therefore, a strong counter-argument against the critique that investment treaties constitute instruments of hegemonic domination of developed over developing countries. Instead, they formulate general principles for the relationship between the State and the economy in view of an emerging global economy.

Against this background, this chapter has provided additional arguments as to why States actually have an interest in uniform rules governing the treatment of foreign investment. This interest, it was argued, lies mainly in economic advantages for capital-exporting and capital-importing States that stem from uniform structures reducing political risk and the competition they enable among investors in a global market independent of where investment flows originate from or where they are directed to. Furthermore, uniform rules can lock States into governance structures that prevent them from taking measures that negatively affect not only their national economy, but have spillover effects on the economies of other countries or even destabilize the global economic system. Finally, uniform rules avoid preferential treatment and discrimination among States that negatively affect international relations and the international security architecture. In this perspective, uniform investment rules are in the interest of States because they further non-discriminatory economic cooperation that reduces international conflicts. Uniform rules, it was argued, are therefore in the long-term interest of States and outweigh any benefits of short-term preferential treatments based on *quid pro quo* bargains that discriminate against third countries.

In practical terms, showing that States have an interest in uniform rules demands and justifies that international investment treaties should be interpreted and applied in a uniform manner. The standard of fair and equitable treatment in the BIT between Argentina and Germany, for example, therefore endorses the same concept as the standard of fair and equitable treatment in the BIT between Italy and Tanzania, Egypt and the United States, Canada and Armenia, or China and Peru. The mutual interest in uniform rules, therefore, supports that BITs endorse uniform principles for the protection of foreign investment that function as if the standard were endorsed in a multilateral investment treaty. With respect to the substantive investor rights governing international investment relations, BITs therefore substitute a multilateral regime by not endorsing preferential standards of treatment in bilateral *quid pro quo* bargains, but by establishing uniform standards of investment protection. Although the form of investment treaties remains bilateral, they endorse, with respect to their content and substance, uniform, non-preferential, and non-discriminatory principles that govern international investment relations. Investment treaties are thus not about the domination of developing countries by developed countries, but about establishing a regime that is conducive for market forces to unfold, forces that create economic growth and generate welfare in capital-exporting and capital-importing countries.

IV

Multilateralization through most-favored-nation treatment

The interest of States in a multilateral and non-discriminatory investment regime exists not only on a theoretical level, but positively surfaces in the normative framework that bilateral investment treaties establish. A specific and express normative basis for the multilateralization of investment relations are above all most-favored-nation ("MFN") clauses that are regularly incorporated in bilateral, regional, and sectoral investment treaties as one of the central principles governing international investment relations. MFN clauses in investment treaties are generally reciprocal, unconditional, and indeterminate in nature.[1] A typical MFN clause in a BIT thus provides that:

(1) neither contracting party shall subject investments in its territory owned or controlled by nationals or companies of the other contracting party to treatment less favourable than it accords ... to investments of nationals or companies of any third State; and

(2) neither contracting party shall in its territory subject nationals or companies of the other contracting party, as regards their activity in connection with investments, to treatment less favourable than it accords ... to nationals or companies of any third State.[2]

MFN clauses oblige the State granting MFN treatment to extend to the beneficiary State the treatment accorded to third States in case this treatment is more favorable than the treatment under the treaty between the

---

[1] Acconci, *The Most Favoured Nation Treatment and the International Law on Foreign Investment*, 2(5) Transnat'l Disp. Mgmt. 5 (2005). See further, on the different types of MFN clauses, reciprocal versus unilateral and conditional versus unconditional, and their different formulations, determinate versus indeterminate, Roesner, *Die Meistbegünstigungsklausel in den bilateralen Handelsverträgen der Bundesrepublik Deutschland*, pp. 33–41 (1964); Kramer, *Die Meistbegünstigung*, 35 RIW 473, 474 (1989).

[2] Article 2, Agreement between the Federal Republic of Germany and the People's Republic of Bangladesh concerning the Promotion and Reciprocal Protection of Investments, signed on May 6, 1981, entered into force on September 14, 1986.

granting and the beneficiary State.[3] The clauses break with general international law and its bilateralist rationale that, in principle, permits States to accord differential treatment to different States and their nationals,[4] and instead ensure equal treatment between the State benefiting from MFN treatment and any third State.[5] MFN clauses thus disable States from entering into bilateral *quid pro quo* bargains that extend preferential treatment to certain States and exclude it with respect to others, a behavior which is entirely permissible under customary international law.

Although not all MFN clauses are worded identically, existing differences do not affect the clauses' overall efficacy.[6] Unless the contracting parties made clear that they intended to give an MFN clause in their investment treaty a special and particular meaning, it is widely accepted that even slight differences in the wording of the clauses do not alter their function.[7] Rather, MFN treatment emerges as an overarching principle of international investment law by means of the MFN clauses included in the treaties.[8]

---

[3] See Ustor, *Most-Favoured-Nation Clause*, in Bernhardt and Macalister-Smith (eds.), *Encyclopedia of Public International Law*, vol. III, p. 468 (1997).

[4] See International Law Commission, *Report of the International Law Commission on the Work of its Thirtieth Session 8 May–28 July 1978*, 30 ILC Ybk., vol. II, Part Two, p. 11, para. 50 (1978) (observing that "while States are bound by the duty arising from the principle of non-discrimination, they are nevertheless free to grant special favours to other States on the ground of some special relationship of a geographic, economic, political or other nature"). In particular, entering into specifically advantageous treaty relations in the economic realm constitutes a special favor and does not have to be extended to third States under the duty of non-discrimination under general international law. *Cf.* Schwarzenberger, *Equality and Discrimination in International Economic Law*, 25 Ybk. World Affairs 163, 164 (1971) (stating that "[f]reedom of commerce is a purely optional pattern of international economic law").

[5] See *Rights of Nationals of the United States of America in Morocco (France v. United States)*, Judgment, August 27, 1952, I.C.J. Reports 1952, p. 192 (considering that the rationale of MFN clauses is to "maintain at all times fundamental equality without discrimination among all of the countries concerned"). MFN treatment thus goes beyond the more general duty arising from the principle of non-discrimination connected to the sovereign equality of States under general international law and also extends special benefits granted between States to the State benefiting from MFN treatment.

[6] On varying formulations of MFN clauses in investment treaties and related instruments as well as the various exceptions they contain see Acconci (*supra* footnote 1), 2(5) Transnat'l Disp. Mgmt. 6–16 (2005); Houde and Pagani, *Most-Favoured-Nation Treatment in International Investment Law*, pp. 3–8 (2004).

[7] UNCTAD, *Most-Favoured-Nation Treatment*, p. 6 (1999); Faya Rodriguez, *The Most-Favored-Nation Clause in International Investment Agreements*, 25 J. Int'l Arb. 89, 92 (2008).

[8] *Cf.* Schwarzenberger, *International Law as Applied by International Courts and Tribunals*, vol. I, p. 241 (3rd edn. 1957) (pointing out that "[t]he difference between the most-favoured-nation standard and any particular most-favoured-nation clause corresponds

Complemented by national treatment, the economic rationale of MFN treatment is to create a level playing field for all foreign investors by prohibiting discrimination between investors from different home States.[9] It aims at enabling equal competition among investors by prohibiting the imposition of different transaction costs based on the national origin of investors.[10] Equal competition, in turn, is essential for the functioning of a market economy that helps to allocate resources efficiently. Thus, MFN treatment reflects the crucial importance that competitive structures play in efficient investment and efficient allocation of resources.

Although MFN clauses constitute inter-State obligations, they directly extend the more favorable treatment to covered investors in the context of investment treaties. An investor covered by a BIT with an MFN clause can, therefore, invoke the benefits granted to third-party nationals by another BIT of the host State and directly import them into its relationship with the host State.[11] Consequently, MFN clauses multilateralize the bilateral inter-State treaty relationships and harmonize the protection of foreign investments in a specific host State.[12] MFN clauses thus level differences in the standard of protection offered by varying investment treaties.

to that between principles and rules of international law"). Accordingly, issues surrounding MFN clauses are generally regarded as issues of general international law, in particular the law of treaties. See also 30 ILC Ybk., vol. II, Part Two, p. 14, paras. 59–61 (1978).

[9] Houde and Pagani (*supra* footnote 6), p. 2 (2004) (explaining that "by giving the investors of all the parties benefiting from a country's MFN clause the right, in similar circumstances, to treatment no less favourable than a country's closest or most influential partners can negotiate on the matters the clause covers, MFN avoids economic distortions that would occur through more selective country-by-country liberalisation"); Chukwumerije, *Interpreting Most-Favoured-Nation Clauses in Investment Treaty Arbitrations*, 8 J. World Inv. & Trade 597, 608 (2007); Faya Rodriguez (*supra* footnote 7), 25 J. Int'l Arb. 89 and 91 (2008).

[10] *Cf.* Kurtz, *The MFN Standard and Foreign Investment: An Uneasy Fit?*, 6 J. World Inv. & Trade 861, 873 (2004); UNCTAD (*supra* footnote 7), pp. 8–9 (1999). See also *National Grid* v. *Argentina*, Decision on Jurisdiction, June 20, 2006, para. 92 (observing that "[t]he MFN clause is an important element to ensure that foreign investors are treated on a basis of parity with other foreign investors and with national investors when they invest abroad").

[11] See Article 9(1), ILC's Draft Articles on Most-Favoured-Nation Clauses (clarifying that "the beneficiary State acquires, for itself or for the benefit of persons or things in a determined relationship with it, only those rights which fall within the limits of the subject-matter of the clause"). Questionable, therefore, Faya Rodriguez (*supra* footnote 7), 25 J. Int'l Arb. 89, 99 (2008) (arguing that an importation of more favorable rights could not operate automatically in investment treaties as investment tribunals would only hear claims for breaches of MFN clauses).

[12] See Houde and Pagani (*supra* footnote 6), p. 2 (2004) (describing MFN clauses as "the 'multilateralization' instrument *par excellence*"). Similarly van Aaken, *To Do Away*

Apart from their impact on investor-State relations and beyond their economic rationale, MFN clauses also help to reorder inter-State relations. This was expressed, for example, by the International Court of Justice (ICJ) in *Rights of Nationals of the United States of America in Morocco* when it stated that the purpose of MFN clauses was to "maintain at all times fundamental equality without discrimination among all of the countries concerned."[13] Thus, MFN clauses affect the structure of the international economic order and impact the system of international investment protection by supporting the emergence of a uniform international investment regime. MFN clauses multilateralize and harmonize the level of investment protection by international law in any given host State that orders its international investment relations based on MFN treatment. MFN provisions in BITs thus tend to reduce leeway for specificities in bilateral investment relations and undermine the understanding of BITs as an expression of *quid pro quo* bargains. Instead of limiting BITs to instruments of bilateralism, MFN clauses transform them into instruments of multilateralism in international investment relations. MFN clauses, therefore, serve as a basis for multilateralizing bilateral investment relations.

Yet, while MFN clauses have been used in international commercial treaties for centuries,[14] legal theory and practice have long struggled with their application and interpretation. Thus, literature and decisions by national courts and international tribunals on MFN clauses convey a certain discomfort with clauses' scope and effect. This discomfort stems from the tension the clauses create between multilateralism and bilateralism as conflicting ordering paradigms for international relations. While enshrined in a bilateral treaty, MFN clauses prevent States from shielding future bilateral bargains from multilateralization and from making preferential concessions in order to achieve a desired counter-concession. MFN clauses thus prevent States from assuming certain bargaining positions and from making exclusive promises within the scope of application of an MFN clause in another treaty. They lock States into a framework of multilateralism that is adverse to bilateral alliances.

Parallel to the general discomfort discussed above, investment tribunals struggle with the application and interpretation of MFN clauses in

---

with International Law?, 17 Eur. J. Int'l L. 289, 299 (2006) (designating MFN clauses in international trade law as "multilateralization devices in substantive law").

[13] *Rights of Nationals of the United States of America in Morocco (France v. United States)*, Judgment, August 27, 1952, I.C.J. Reports 1952, p. 192.

[14] For a more detailed account of the history of MFN clauses see *infra* Ch. II.B.

investment treaties. Difficulties in the practice of investment treaty arbitration, above all, relate to the question whether MFN clauses apply to issues of procedure and jurisdiction in investor-State dispute settlement.[15] While one line of argument supports a broad interpretation of MFN clauses, and consequently a comprehensive multilateralization, the opposing view favors a restrictive construction and a narrower function of MFN treatment in international investment law. The more restrictive position particularly denies that MFN clauses can be used to broaden the jurisdiction of treaty-based tribunals.

While this debate is exclusively framed as a doctrinal debate about the scope and the proper interpretation of MFN clauses in investment treaties, the debate has larger implications for the nature of international investment law. It reveals the broader ideological divide between multilateralism and bilateralism as concepts of ordering the relations between States in the economic sector. While expansive approaches to the interpretation of MFN clauses lend support to stronger tendencies of multilateralism, restrictive approaches ideologically align themselves with counter-developments that stress the bilateral elements in international investment relations and view investment treaties as expressions of *quid pro quo* bargains rather than as elements of an emerging international economic order that is based on uniform principles of investment protection. Thus, the bilateralism–multilateralism dichotomy informs the debate over the scope of MFN clauses in international investment law and can serve as an explanatory framework for the development of the arbitral jurisprudence on them.

Yet, as will be argued in this chapter, the restrictive interpretation put forward by some tribunals denies giving MFN clauses their proper effect and disregards the firm stance they take for multilateralism as an ordering principle of international relations that subject States to equal and non-discriminatory rules. Accordingly, this chapter proposes a broad understanding of MFN clauses, save express language to the contrary, as multilateralizing not only substantive investment protection but also the procedural implementation of investment treaties through investment treaty arbitration.

After outlining the historical and doctrinal background of MFN clauses more generally, this chapter will address their application in investment treaties with regard to substantive investor rights and discusses to which extent they apply to issues of investor-State dispute settlement. In this

---

[15] See *infra* Ch. IV.

context, this chapter criticizes that arbitral jurisprudence has developed a distinction between admissibility-related restrictions regarding investor-State dispute settlement, to which MFN clauses are regularly applied, while declining to apply them as a basis of jurisdiction by incorporating the host State's more favorable consent from third-country investment treaties. In making the case that the more convincing arguments militate for a broad application of MFN clauses, this chapter suggests a (rebuttable) presumption that the clauses incorporate more favorable treatment concerning procedure and jurisdiction relating to investor-State dispute settlement just as they apply to substantive standards. MFN clauses are, therefore, portrayed as comprehensively multilateralizing investment treaties. In conclusion, this chapter argues that MFN clauses do not only multilateralize international investment relations as of today, but help project multilateralism into the future.

A Historical and doctrinal background of MFN clauses

In order to understand the debate about the scope and interpretation of MFN clauses in international investment treaties, it is necessary to shed light on the structure, history, and applicable principles of interpretation relating to MFN clauses in general. This background also clarifies that MFN clauses are not particular to international investment law, but rather constitute a traditional instrument for structuring international cooperation in a variety of areas.

1 The structure of MFN clauses

The operation of MFN clauses in international law presupposes a relationship of at least three States (see Figure IV.1): State A (the granting State) enters into an obligation vis-à-vis State B (the beneficiary State) to extend rights and benefits granted in a specific context to any third State C. The consequence of the MFN clause in the treaty between A and B is that State B can invoke and rely on all benefits State A grants vis-à-vis State C as long as the granted benefit is within the scope of application of the MFN clause in the relationship between A and B. The treaty containing the MFN clause between A and B is designated as the "basic treaty" because it contains the basis for incorporating more favorable conditions granted in a third-party treaty into the treaty relationship between A and B.

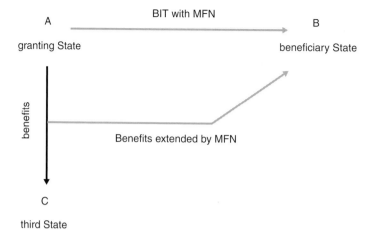

Figure IV.1   General function of MFN clauses

The third-party treaty (between A and C) does not, however, modify the relationship between A and B, the parties to the basic treaty. It does not govern the relationship between the parties of the basic treaty as the applicable international treaty. Rather, the content of the third-party treaty becomes operative by means of the basic treaty's MFN clause. MFN clauses do not, therefore, break with the *inter partes* effect of international treaties. As put by the ICJ in *Anglo-Iranian Oil Company*:

> It is this [i.e., the basic] treaty which established the juridical link between the [beneficiary State] and a third-party treaty and confers upon that State the rights enjoyed by the third party. A third party treaty, independent of and isolated from the basic treaty, cannot produce any legal effect as between the [beneficiary State] and [the granting State]: it is *res inter alios acta*.[16]

The third-party treaty is thus incorporated by reference and *ipso iure* into the relationship between the State parties to the basic treaty without any additional act of transformation.[17] For this reason, MFN clauses have been characterized as "drafting by reference."[18] They function as an automatic treaty adaptation mechanism without the need for the State parties

---

[16] *Anglo-Iranian Oil Company (United Kingdom v. Iran)*, Judgment, July 22, 1952, I.C.J. Reports 1952, p. 109. Decisively also *Suez and InterAguas v. Argentina*, Decision on Jurisdiction, May 16, 2006, para. 58 (clarifying that "[t]he principle of *res inter alios acta* has no application, because the Tribunal is not applying the Argentina–France BIT [presumably the alleged act between third parties] to this case. Rather it is applying the Argentina–Spain BIT's provisions on equality of treatment.").

[17] See *supra* footnote 11.   [18] Schwarzenberger (*supra* footnote 8), p. 243 (1971).

to the basic treaty to negotiate anew in order to include third-country benefits. The MFN clause thus prevents the granting State from entering into bilateral treaty relations that are more preferential to a third State and put the beneficiary State at a relative disadvantage.[19]

The benefits flowing from MFN clauses are closely connected to the benefits from multilateral ordering.[20] First, MFN treatment prevents market distortions stemming from the imposition of differential transaction costs that could arise out of differential standards of protection offered to investors from different States. Second, MFN treatment protects the value of concessions made between the contracting parties to the basic treaty. It upholds the bargain that States struck by preventing either one of them from hollowing out the content of the basic treaty by granting more favorable protection to a third State and thus making investments from the original treaty partner comparably less attractive. Third, MFN treatment allows for a more transparent framework for international investment relations because it dispenses with the necessity to adhere to complicated, and thus costly, rules on the origin of capital in order to ascertain the applicable standard of protection.

Fourth, apart from these primarily economic aspects, MFN treatment also has broader implications for the structure of international relations in implementing equal treatment among nations. It prevents States from forming economic alliances to the detriment and to the exclusion of other States which might, in turn, increase the potential for tension, or even military conflict.[21] In this context, MFN treatment also protects smaller States against the influence of larger and more powerful States, as it precludes hegemonic State behavior in imposing patterns of preferential treatment to the exclusion of other States.[22] MFN treatment thus breaks with bilateralism as an ordering paradigm for international relations by extending rights and benefits from a third-party relationship to the treaty

---

[19] Conversely, once benefits from a third-country treaty cease, they also cease with respect to the basic treaty. See *Rights of Nationals of the United States of America in Morocco (France v. United States)*, Judgment, August 27, 1952, I.C.J. Reports 1952, pp. 190–92, 204–5. In this case, the United States attempted to rely on more the favorable rights that Morocco had granted to the United Kingdom and Spain concerning fiscal immunity and consular jurisdiction. Since these more favorable conditions had ceased to exist, the United States was prevented from incorporating them into their relationship with Morocco based on an MFN clause.

[20] See *supra* Ch. III.C.

[21] See *infra* footnotes 45–50 and accompanying text.

[22] *Cf.* Bileski, *Der Grundsatz der wirtschaftlichen Gleichberechtigung in den Mandatsgebieten*, 16 ZöR 214, 228–29 (1936).

relationship containing the MFN clause. Finally, MFN treatment has a constitutional function, because it locks States into a multilateral framework and makes the abandonment of standards of protection adopted previously more difficult. MFN clauses are, therefore, an instrument with which to push towards an order that is multilateral in substance but bilateral in form.

2 The historical development of MFN clauses

The use and the scope of MFN clauses have varied over time. In fact, their diffusion and scope have varied depending on the prevailing ideologies in international economic and political relations.[23] Originally, MFN clauses primarily operated in matters relating to trade. In this area, they have a long history and have appeared in bilateral commercial treaties since at least the twelfth century.[24] Until approximately the early eighteenth century, these clauses were worded broadly and generally applied to "all privileges, liberties, immunities and concessions ... already granted to foreigners or being granted in the future."[25] The purpose of these early treaties was to put the terms of trade between different nations on an equal footing and to allow in principle for equal competition.

However, the function of MFN clauses changed under the influence of mercantilist ideology in the course of the seventeenth and eighteenth centuries.[26] During that period, MFN clauses were included in commercial treaties in order to safeguard preferential treatments accorded

---

[23] On the dialectic between State-centered theories of foreign trade and liberal theories of foreign trade and their relation to and influence on the diffusion of MFN clauses see Brandt, *Durchbrechung der Meistbegünstigung*, pp. 1 *et seq.* (1933).

[24] See Schwarzenberger, *The Most-Favoured-Nation Standard in British State Practice*, 22 Brit. Ybk. Int'l L. 96, 97 (1945); unilateral grants of MFN treatment can even be traced back to the eleventh century, see Ustor, *First Report on the Most-Favoured-Nation Clause*, 21 ILC Ybk., vol. II, p. 157, paras. 10 *et seq.* (1969).

[25] See. e.g., the MFN provision in a 1679 treaty between the Netherlands and Sweden as quoted in Nolde, *Droits et technique des traités de commerce*, 3 Recueil des Cours 295, 307–8 (1924–II) and translated by the author of this book. Only during the course of the eighteenth century did treaties start differentiating more clearly between political and commercial aspects relating to the presence of foreign merchants. See Ustor (*supra* footnote 24), 21 ILC Ybk., vol. II, p. 157, para. 17 (1969).

[26] Mercantilist economics believed that the wealth of a nation depended upon its supply of capital. It further believed that the volume of trade was unchangeable. Accordingly, mercantilism supported that the wealth of a nation was best furthered by a positive external trade balance where exports outbalanced imports. Accordingly, protectionist measures and high tariffs that discouraged imports were among the instruments of choice of mercantilist politics.

in a bilateral relationship.[27] The automatic extension of more favorable third-party benefits under the MFN clause was thus understood not as an instrument to secure equal competition, but as a punishment for not having adhered to the preferential concession originally made. In aiming to protect an originally discriminatory trade policy, the function of MFN clauses thus differed fundamentally from modern MFN clauses, even though they were similarly formulated as unconditional clauses. Ideologically, MFN clauses during the mercantilist age were not instruments of multilateralism, but an expression of a bilateral and protectionist view on international economic relations.

Yet, the view underlying mercantilist economics changed over time. Starting with the Treaty of Amity and Commerce concluded between the United States and France in 1778, conditional MFN clauses were introduced and subsequently became dominant in international treaty practice.[28] Conditional MFN treatment required that rights and privileges be extended to the beneficiary State under the condition that the beneficiary State grant the same concessions offered by the most-favored-nation in return for the more favorable rights in question. While the conditional form of MFN clauses ensured that the beneficiary State could not benefit from more favorable treatment accorded to third parties without concurrently assuming potential disadvantages incumbent upon the third State,[29] the purpose of conditional MFN clauses was ultimately to arrive at lower tariffs.

The idea behind conditional MFN treatment was to induce the beneficiary State to lower those tariffs that the third party had lowered, as a concession, in order to receive the treatment that was relatively more favorable compared with the treatment originally granted by the granting

---

[27] On this and the following see Brandt (*supra* footnote 23), pp. 2 *et seq.* (1933); Hock, *Was hat man mit der Meistbegünstigung gewollt?*, pp. 8–10 (1931) (both making reference to foundational works by Jastrow, *Die mitteleuropäische Zollannäherung und die Meistbegünstigung* (1915) and Luedicke, *Die Entwicklung des Meistbegünstigungsprinzips* (1925).

[28] Article II of the Treaty stipulated: "The Most Christian King and the United States engage mutually not to grant any particular favour to other nations, in respect of commerce and navigation, which shall not immediately become common to the other party, who shall enjoy the same favour, freely, if the concession was freely made, or on allowing the same compensation, if the concession was conditional." See Malloy, *Treaties, Conventions, International Acts, Protocols and Agreements between the United States of America and Other Powers, 1776–1909*, vol. I, pp. 468, 469 (1910).

[29] The conditional clause, therefore, attempts to solve a free-rider problem; see W. Schwartz and Sykes, *The Economics of the Most Favored Nation Clause*, in Bhandari and Sykes, *Economic Dimensions in International Law*, pp. 43, 59–61 (1997).

State to the beneficiary State.[30] The purpose of conditional MFN clauses, therefore, was not to secure a preferential bilateral bargain, but eventually to arrive at a more liberal system of international trade based on equality of treatment and non-discrimination coupled with increasingly lower tariffs. Conditional MFN treatment was above all supported by the United States, as a then newly independent State, in order to participate more actively in international trade.[31] It formed part of US foreign economic policy until 1923,[32] but also prevailed in Europe until 1860.[33]

The policy of conditional MFN treatment was ultimately abandoned, because it was too complicated and economically inefficient. US Secretary of State Hughes, for example, explained the reasons of the United States for abandoning conditional MFN treatment:

> [T]he ascertaining of what might constitute equivalent compensation in the applications of the conditional most-favored-nation principle was found to be difficult or impracticable. Reciprocal commercial arrangements were but temporary makeshifts; they caused constant negotiation and created uncertainty. Under present conditions, the expanding foreign commerce of the United States needs a guarantee of equality of treatment which cannot be furnished by the conditional form of the most-favored-nation clause.[34]

In addition, conditional MFN treatment also required a complicated system for traders to record the country of origin of a certain product in order to classify it correctly under the proper country-specific tariff. Depending on the product, this could impose significant additional costs by requiring complicated methods to track the country of origin of certain products or separating the same product originating from different countries. Additional problems arose when products were put together from components produced in different countries. This required rules

---

[30] See Lusensky, *Unbeschränkte gegen beschränkte Meistbegünstigung (Reziprozität)*, pp. 12 et seq., 20 et seq. (1918).

[31] Economically, the conditional clause was in the interest of the United States as long as it was a net importer of products, as the conditional form ensured that the beneficiary State that imported products into the United States had to grant, in return, lower tariffs to exported US products in order to benefit from more favorable tariffs for imports into the United States; see Snyder, *The Most-Favored-Nation Clause*, p. 243 (1948). Conversely, the conditionality of MFN treatment in practice hardly mattered for the United States, compared with unconditional MFN treatment, because the United States usually did not grant tariff reductions against compensation, see Lusensky (*supra* footnote 30), pp. 18 et seq. (1918).

[32] Ustor (*supra* footnote 24), 21 ILC Ybk., vol. II, p. 157, para. 26 (1969).

[33] *Ibid.*, para. 28.

[34] See Hackworth, *Digest of International Law*, vol. V, p. 273 (1943).

of origin that were more difficult to handle than non-discriminatory tariffs.[35]

For this reason, the unconditional MFN clause developed to become the prevailing model governing international economic relations. The archetype of such an MFN clause in modern times was Article XIX of the Treaty of Commerce between Great Britain and France of January 23, 1860, also called the Cobden or Chevalier–Cobden Treaty. It stipulated:

> Each of the two High Contracting Powers engages to confer on the other any favour, privilege, or reduction in the tariff of duties of importation on the articles mentioned in the present Treaty, which the said Power may concede to any third Power. They further engage not to enforce one against the other any prohibition of importation or exportation which shall not at the same time be applicable to all other nations.[36]

Unlike under conditional MFN clauses, this clause did not require the beneficiary State to make the same concessions vis-à-vis the granting State as the most favored nation.

Up to the First World War, the unconditional clause became "the almost universal basis of a vast system of commercial treaties"[37] and developed into the "corner-stone" of international commercial relations.[38] Notwithstanding a temporary chill in the aftermath of the First World War,[39] unconditional MFN treatment remained the ordering paradigm for international trade relations until the world economic crisis broke out in 1929. The conclusion of unconditional MFN clauses was recommended, for instance, at several inter-governmental conferences and by organs of the then newly created League of Nations.[40] Furthermore, the

---

[35] On drawbacks of conditional MFN clauses see Lusensky (*supra* footnote 30), pp. 20 *et seq.* (1918).

[36] 50 British and Foreign State Papers 13, 24–25 (1860).

[37] Snyder (*supra* footnote 31), p. 239 (1948).

[38] Hornbeck, *The Most-Favored-Nation Clause*, 3 A.J.I.L. 395 (1909).

[39] See Ustor (*supra* footnote 24), 21 ILC Ybk., vol. II, p. 157, paras. 30–37 (1969).

[40] In 1922, the International Economic Conference "earnestly recommend[ed] that commercial relations should be resumed upon the basis of commercial treaties, resting on the one hand upon the system of reciprocity adapted to special circumstances, and containing on the other hand, so far as possible, the most-favoured-nation clause." In 1927, the International Economic Conference reiterated its position and stressed that it "considers that the mutual grant of unconditional most-favoured-nation treatment as regards custom duties and conditions of trading is an essential condition of the free and healthy development of commerce between States." It went on to emphasize "that the scope and form of the most-favoured-nation clause should be of the widest and most liberal character and that it should not be weakened or narrowed either by express provisions or by interpretation." This position was upheld by the Committee of the League of Nations Assembly throughout the 1930s. In addition, various attempts were made to codify the

United States abandoned its support for conditional MFN clauses after the First World War and henceforth based its commercial treaties on unconditional MFN treatment.[41] The abandonment of the conditional clause was closely connected to the free trade movement in the nineteenth and early twentieth centuries.[42] Ideologically, this reflected liberal ideas about the equality of States and the contribution of the clauses to liberalizing international trade by fostering equal competition.

The movement to base international economic relations on multilateral and, therefore, general and non-discriminatory rules of conduct, however, was not restricted to international trade relations. Instead, the idea of economic equality and equal competition among nations also characterized other areas of international economic cooperation more similar to the modern foreign investment context. Thus, the mandate system established under the auspices of the League of Nations for former colonies enshrined "equal opportunities for the trade and commerce of other Members of the League" as one of its fundamental principles.[43] Similarly, there were other international treaty regimes that endorsed equality of opportunity as an ordering principle before and after the First World War.[44]

The positive attitude towards multilateralism and free trade, however, did change drastically after the world economic crisis broke out in 1929. As a reaction, bilateral trade relations and discriminatory trade surged.[45] The United Kingdom, for instance, abandoned its free trade policy in 1932; the United States raised tariffs; Germany switched to a system of

---

law on MFN clauses at the time, thus illustrating the importance that was accorded to the concept of unconditional MFN treatment. These attempts encompassed one project under the auspices of the Economic Committee of the League of Nations in the 1930s, the work of the Committee of Experts for the Progressive Codification of International Law and a codification by the Institute of International Law. See Ustor (*supra* footnote 24), 21 ILC Ybk., vol. II, p. 157, paras. 65–106 (1969).

[41] Overall, only 9 out of 607 treaties in the inter-war period contained a conditional clause. See Snyder (*supra* footnote 31), p. 41 (1948).

[42] Ustor (*supra* footnote 24), 21 ILC Ybk., vol. II, p. 157, paras. 28–29 (1969); Lusensky (*supra* footnote 30), p. 11 (1918).

[43] *Cf.* Article 22(5), Covenant of the League of Nations governing the so-called B mandates. For other mandates, the so-called A mandates governed by Article 22(4) of the Covenant, the same principle was endorsed in the respective mandates that required the relevant mandatory to accord equal opportunities for trade and commerce to the other League of Nation Member States. See Bileski (*supra* footnote 22), 16 ZöR 214, 221–22 (1936).

[44] See Schwarzenberger (*supra* footnote 4), 25 Ybk. World Affairs 163, 174 *et seq.* (1971).

[45] Ustor (*supra* footnote 24), 21 ILC Ybk., vol. II, p. 157, paras. 38–39 (1969). See also Pomfret, *Unequal Trade: The Economics of Discriminatory International Trade Policies*, pp. 29 *et seq.* (1988).

discriminatory trade based on bilateral relations. International economic relations were no longer based on multilateral ideas and equality of treatment, but instead characterized by discriminatory trade and investment policies.[46] The surging bilateralism in the years before the Second World War not only yielded to economic considerations, but already foreshadowed the preparation of States for the upcoming war.[47] This is particularly true for Germany whose web of bilateralist economic arrangements created dependencies that could easily be transformed into military alliances.[48] Discriminatory trade policies, in turn, required abandoning MFN clauses as the basis for international economic relations.

After the end of the Second World War, however, multilateralism re-emerged as an instrument for ordering international relations, both politically as well as economically.[49] Accordingly, MFN clauses reappeared and became the basis for ordering international trade and investment relations. In view of the fatal consequences of the Second World War, MFN treatment was now considered as a way to prevent international conflicts and to further world peace by prohibiting bilateral alliances and bloc-building in an economic context prone to spill over into military conflicts.[50]

3   Codification on MFN clauses by the International Law Commission

Parallel to the newly emerging receptiveness towards multilateralism and MFN treatment, there was also renewed interest in further studying and

---

[46] See Sommer, *Die Voraussetzungen des staatsideologischen Kampfes gegen die Meistbegünstigungsklausel*, 16 ZöR 265, 268–70 (1936); see also Ruggie, *Multilateralism: The Anatomy of an Institution*, in Ruggie (ed.), *Multilateralism Matters*, pp. 3, 8 *et seq.* (1993). The change in Germany's foreign economic policy can be aligned with the emerging economic ideology of the Nazi regime that defined itself pronouncedly against the ideology of liberalism; see on this Schill, *Der Einfluss der Wettbewerbsideologie des Nationalsozialismus auf den Schutzzweck des UWG*, pp. 7–14 (2004).

[47] See Verbit, *Preferences and the Public Law of International Trade*, in Hague Academy of International Law, *Colloquium 1968: International Trade Agreements*, p. 27 (1969); see also Barnhart, *Japan Prepares for Total War, The Search for Economic Security 1919–1941* (1987).

[48] See Ruggie (*supra* footnote 46), pp. 3, 8–9 (1993) (with reference to Hirschmann, *National Power and the Structure of Foreign Trade* [1945]).

[49] *Cf.* Ruggie (*supra* footnote 46), pp. 3, 24–31 (1993).

[50] In fact, national protectionism and bilateral isolation of markets in the inter-war period were viewed as a supporting factor, if not one of the reasons, for the economic depression in the 1930s and subsequently the Second World War. See Verbit (*supra* footnote 47), pp. 25–31 (1969); see also Curzon, *Multilateral Commercial Diplomacy*, pp. 20–33 (1965). Some States already regarded economic discrimination to be among the factors having caused the First World War; see Verbit (*supra* footnote 47), pp. 19, 26 (1969).

codifying the use and interpretation of MFN clauses. For this purpose, the International Law Commission (ILC) began work in 1967 on the function and interpretation of MFN clauses. In 1978, it submitted Draft Articles on Most-Favored-Nation Clauses to the UN General Assembly and recommended them as a basis for a multilateral convention.[51]

The Draft Articles intended to "apply to most-favoured-nation clauses contained in treaties between States" (Article 1). MFN clauses, in turn, are defined as "treaty provision[s] whereby a State undertakes an obligation towards another State to accord most-favoured-nation treatment in an agreed sphere of relations" (Article 4), that is, "treatment accorded by the granting State to the beneficiary State, or to persons or things in a determined relationship with that State, not less favorable than treatment extended by the granting State to a third State or to persons or things in the same relationship with that third State" (Article 5).

In line with the decision of the ICJ in *Anglo-Iranian Oil Company*,[52] the Draft Articles clarify that the legal basis for MFN treatment "arises only from the most-favoured-nation clause ... in force between the granting State and the beneficiary" and that "[t]he most-favoured-nation treatment to which the beneficiary State, for itself or for the benefit of persons or things in determined relationship with it, is entitled under a clause ... is determined by the treatment extended by the granting State to a third State or persons or things in the same relationship with that third State" (Article 8). The right arises at the moment the more favorable treatment is extended to the third State (Article 20).

Articles 9 and 10 set out the rules of interpretation for determining whether certain treatment by the granting State falls under the scope of application of the MFN clause. Thus, Article 9(1) clarifies that "the beneficiary State acquires, for itself or for the benefit of persons or things in a determined relationship with it, only those rights which fall within the limits of the subject-matter of the clause." Article 10(1) reiterates that "only if the granting State extends to the third State treatment within the limits of the subject matter of the clause" does the beneficiary State acquire the more favorable treatment under the MFN clause.

Both articles endorse the *ejusdem generis* rule,[53] according to which "the most-favoured-nation clause can only attract matters belonging to

---

[51] See Draft Articles on Most-Favoured-Nation Clauses, 30 ILC Ybk., vol. II, Part Two, p. 16, para. 74 (1978).

[52] See *supra* footnote 16 and accompanying text.

[53] 30 ILC Ybk., vol. II, Part Two, p. 27 (1978), Commentary to Articles 9 and 10, para. 1.

the same category of subject as that to which the clause itself relates."[54] For instance, an MFN clause applying to more favorable treatment concerning tariff concessions will not entitle the beneficiary State to more favorable treatment with respect to the extradition of persons charged with crimes.[55] Determining the exact scope of the subject-matter of a clause, therefore, will require the interpretation of the scope of the MFN clause contained in the basic treaty.

The crux of this rule is that the more favorable treatment accorded to the third State concerns the subject-matter of the MFN clause in the basic treaty. In turn, whether the relationship between the third State and the granting State differs from the relationship between the granting and the beneficiary State is irrelevant:

> [t]he granting State cannot evade its obligations, unless an express reservation so provides, on the ground that the relations between itself and the third country are friendlier than or "not similar" to those existing between it and the beneficiary. It is only the subject-matter of the clause that must belong to the same category, the *idem genus*, and not the relation between the granting State and the third State on the one hand and the relation between the granting State and the beneficiary State on the other.[56]

In particular, as Article 11 clarifies, the fact that the third State made certain concessions in order to be granted more favorable treatment is normally irrelevant, unless the MFN clause in the basic treaty is expressly formulated as a conditional clause.[57] Article 11, therefore, establishes a

---

[54] *Ambatielos Claim (Greece v. United Kingdom)*, Award, March 6, 1956, U.N.R.I.A.A., vol. XII, p. 107; *Maffezini v. Spain*, Decision on Objections to Jurisdiction, January 25, 2000, paras. 46–56. The origins of the principle lie in a common law doctrine of interpretation according to which "general words when following (and sometimes when preceding) special words are limited to the *genus*, if any, indicated by the special words," see McNair, *The Law of Treaties*, p. 393 (1961).

[55] See, for this example, McNair (*supra* footnote 54), p. 287 (1961).

[56] 30 ILC Ybk., vol. II, Part Two, p. 30 (1978), Commentary to Articles 9 and 10, para. 12. *Cf. EC – Regime for the Importation, Sale and Distribution of Bananas*, WTO Appellate Body Report, September 25, 1997, paras. 189–191 (emphasizing that Member States of the WTO are not empowered to create different classes by using different regimes for banana imports depending on whether the bananas came from ACP countries or other foreign countries; the *tertium comparationis* for determining discrimination is therefore established from the perspective of international law and through the relevant dispute settlement mechanism, not by the State concerned).

[57] Article 11, ILC Draft Articles on Most-Favoured-Nation Clauses provides: "If a most-favoured-nation clause is not made subject to a condition of compensation, the beneficiary State acquires the right to most-favoured-nation treatment without the obligation to accord any compensation to the granting State."

presumption in favor of the unconditional character of an MFN clause. Consequently, making MFN treatment conditional upon granting either reciprocity or the concession made towards the third State, therefore, has to be stipulated expressly in the MFN clause in question.[58]

Articles 15 to 18 contain clarifications on factors that are irrelevant for the operation of MFN clauses. Thus, Article 15 reiterates that the making of concessions or compensation by the third party is irrelevant for the operation of an unconditional MFN clause. Article 16, in turn, clarifies that the third State and the granting State cannot exclude the extension of rights under the basic treaty between the granting State and the beneficiary State, thus confirming the general rule under Article 34 of the Vienna Convention on the Law of Treaties that international treaties do "not create either obligations or rights for a third State without its consent." Article 17 further stipulates that it is irrelevant whether the more favorable treatment is extended based on a bilateral or a multilateral agreement. Likewise, under Article 18, the granting State cannot avoid the multilateralizing effect of an MFN clause if the more favorable treatment is extended as national treatment to a third State.[59]

After the ILC recommended the adoption of the Draft Articles as a multilateral convention to the UN General Assembly, the latter adopted a decision only on December 9, 1991, bringing the Draft Articles "to the attention of Member States and of intergovernmental organizations for their consideration in such cases and to such extent as they deem appropriate,"[60] without, however, following through to transforming them into a binding legal instrument. Notwithstanding, the Draft Articles retain their value as an interpretative aid for MFN clauses, including those included in investment treaties. The Draft Articles were understood by the ILC as applying to MFN clauses in general. Thus, the Commission's study understood "the clause as a legal institution" that extended beyond the sphere of international trade "to the operation of the clause in as many spheres as possible."[61] Furthermore, the Draft Articles were always considered to constitute guidelines for the interpretation of MFN clauses. Thus, even if the Draft Articles had been formally adopted

---

[58] See also Articles 12 and 13, ILC Draft Articles on Most-Favoured-Nation Clauses.
[59] Apart from that, Articles 21–30, ILC Draft Articles on Most-Favoured-Nation Clauses contain ancillary or specific aspects of MFN clauses, such as specific regimes for developing countries (Articles 23 and 24), exceptions for frontier trade (Article 25) and provisions on the relationship between the Draft Articles and other international agreements.
[60] See Ustor (*supra* footnote 3), p. 473 (1997).
[61] See 30 ILC Ybk., vol. II, Part Two, p. 14, para. 61 (1978).

by States as an international treaty, this treaty would have mainly established rules for the interpretation of MFN clauses in order to contribute, in this context, to more legal stability and predictability.[62]

Finally, the main reasons why the Draft Articles have never been taken further relate to disagreements not about the general interpretative principles the Draft Articles set out, but about two rather narrow issues. These disagreements concerned, on the one hand, the relationship between MFN clauses and customs unions, respectively regional trade agreements,[63] and, on the other hand, the relationship between MFN clauses and general systems of preferences for developing countries.[64] In view of the fact that both of these trade-related issues are meanwhile being addressed within the WTO framework, the ILC decided in 2007 to establish a Working Group in order to examine the possibility of (re-)considering the topic, in particular in view of the problems concerning the interpretation of MFN clauses in investment treaties.

The Working Group, in turn, concluded that "the Commission could play a useful role in providing clarification on the meaning and effect of the most-favored-nation clause in the field of investment agreements ... building on the past work of the Commission on the most-favoured-nation clause."[65] It "therefore recommend[ed] that the topic of the most-favoured-nation clause be included in the long-term programme of work of the Commission"[66] through the establishment of a working group that would study, *inter alia*, State practice and jurisprudence on MFN clauses since 1978 and "a full articulation of the issues arising out of the

---

[62] This was, for example, the express view of Luxemburg that stated that "the sole purpose of the provision of the draft is the establishment of rules of interpretation or presumptions, intended to establish the meaning of the most-favoured-nation clause in default of stipulations to the contrary," see Ushakov, *Report on the Most-Favoured-Nation Clause*, 30 ILC Ybk., vol. II, Part One, p. 1, para. 328 (1978). This view was also shared by the ILC's Special Rapporteur himself (*ibid.*, paras. 330–31) and enshrined in the final recommendation of the Commission's Draft Articles vis-à-vis the UN General Assembly, see 30 ILC Ybk., vol. II, Part Two, p. 14, para. 59 (1978) (stating that "the draft articles on most-favoured-nation clauses, which contain particular rules applicable to certain types of treaty provisions, namely most-favoured-nation clauses, should be interpreted in the light of the provisions of that Convention ... Nevertheless, the draft articles are intended to constitute an autonomous set of legal rules relating to most-favoured-nation clauses").

[63] See International Law Commission, 59th session, *Most-Favoured-Nation Clause*, Report of the Working Group (July 20, 2007), Annex, para. 14, available at: http://untreaty. un.org/ilc/documentation/english/a_cn4_l719.pdf.

[64] *Ibid.*, Annex, para. 15.   [65] *Ibid.*, para. 4.   [66] *Ibid.*, para. 5.

inclusion of most-favoured-nation clauses in investment agreements."[67] The necessary continuity that the Working Group emphasized with the earlier work of the ILC on MFN clauses, which had resulted in the submission of the Draft Articles in 1978, thus reinforces the general value of the Draft Articles as authoritatively informing the understanding and interpretation of MFN clauses, including those in international investment treaties.

As a consequence, the Draft Articles generally remain valuable as an indication of State practice and *opinio juris* on the general understanding and interpretation of MFN clauses in international treaties. They enshrine what can be considered as the ordinary meaning of an MFN clause in the sense of Article 31 of the Vienna Convention on the Law of Treaties. In sum, the Draft Articles favor the understanding of MFN clauses as normally encompassing unconditional MFN treatment, they set out their general function in directly incorporating more favorable treatment into the basic treaty, and they discard several arguments often invoked against the operation of an MFN clause, that do not play a role in the operation and interpretation of the clauses. Furthermore, as the development of MFN clauses in State practice as well as the Draft Articles show, they are generally understood broadly and endorse multilateralism as an ordering paradigm for international relations. This thrust is also material for the application and interpretation of MFN clauses in international investment treaties.

B   Multilateralizing substantive investment protection

In accordance with their economic rationale to create a level playing field and to allow for equal competition among investors from different home countries, MFN clauses, first and foremost, extend the scope of more favorable substantive rights and protection that host States offer to nationals of third countries. This encompasses not only provisions in domestic laws and regulation or administrative practice,[68] but also more favorable conditions offered in third-country investment treaties. For investors,

---

[67] *Ibid.*, para. 6.
[68] *Cf.* 30 ILC Ybk., vol. II, Part Two, p. 25 (1978), Commentary to Article 8, para. 1. MFN treatment under investment treaties, therefore, applies to a broad array of more favorable treatment, whether *de jure* or *de facto*. See also Faya Rodriguez (*supra* footnote 7), 25 J. Int'l Arb. 89, 92 (2008). For the parallel situation in international trade law see *Canada – Certain Measures Affecting the Automotive Industry*, WTO Appellate Body Report, May 31, 2000, para. 78.

MFN clauses therefore harmonize the legal frameworks governing their economic activity and create uniform standards of investment protection in any given host State that bases its investment treaties on MFN treatment. For purposes of illustrating the multilateralization of international investment law, however, the conferral of more favorable conditions in third-country BITs plays the most significant role.

1　Importing more favorable investor rights

The use of MFN clauses to import more favorable conditions from third-country BITs is largely uncontested.[69] In fact, several tribunals have held that MFN clauses in the BITs governing the disputes at hand directly incorporated into the basic treaty more favorable substantive investment protection from BITs between the host State and third countries. They, therefore, accepted that investors covered under the basic treaty could rely directly on the more favorable treatment granted to other foreign investors under their respective BITs.

In the first known investment treaty arbitration, *Asian Agricultural Products* v. *Sri Lanka*, the Tribunal accepted the principle that an investor covered by the basic treaty could rely on more favorable substantive conditions granted under another BIT of the host State.[70] In that case, however, the investor did not prevail on the more favorable conditions because the investor could not show that the Swiss–Sri Lankan BIT provided for a stricter liability standard of the host State compared with the British–Sri Lankan BIT.[71]

The incorporation of substantive rights from third-country BITs through an MFN clause was also accepted in *Pope & Talbot* v. *Canada*. When discussing the scope of Article 1105(1), NAFTA, the Tribunal faced two propositions in interpreting fair and equitable treatment. The first and more restrictive position, invoked by the host State, asserted that the standard was equivalent to the customary international law minimum standard as expressed in the 1920s *Neer* case.[72] The second position

---

[69]　See only *Berschader* v. *Russia*, Award, April 21, 2006, para. 179 (stating that "it is universally agreed that the very essence of an MFN provision in a BIT is to afford to investors all material protection provided by subsequent treaties").

[70]　*Asian Agricultural Products* v. *Sri Lanka*, Final Award, June 27, 1990, para. 54.

[71]　*Ibid.*

[72]　See *Pope & Talbot* v. *Canada*, Award on the Merits of Phase 2, April 10, 2001, paras. 108–9; *Pope & Talbot* v. *Canada*, Award in Respect of Damages, May 31, 2002, para. 57. *Cf. L. F. H. Neer and Pauline E. Neer (United States)* v. *Mexico*, Opinion, October 15, 1926, U.N.R.I.A.A., vol. IV, pp. 61–62 (requiring that for the minimum standard of

supported a free-standing and arguably broader interpretation of fair and equitable treatment as an independent treaty standard.[73]

The Tribunal concluded that the MFN clause in Article 1103, NAFTA would entitle investors to the broader interpretation of fair and equitable treatment, as this was the standard adopted in the respondent's BITs with third countries.[74] Although NAFTA's Free Trade Commission (FTC) had interpreted Article 1105, NAFTA as an expression of the international minimum standard,[75] the Tribunal in *Pope & Talbot* reaffirmed its position that NAFTA's MFN clause could import a more favorable fair and equitable treatment standard from other Canadian BITs.[76] However, the decision turned on other grounds because the Tribunal held that the respondent State's conduct had already violated even the more restrictive interpretation of fair and equitable treatment.[77]

Furthermore, in *MTD* v. *Chile* the Tribunal allowed the investor to incorporate by means of the MFN clause in the Chilean–Malaysian BIT the more favorable rights contained in the Chilean–Croatian and the Chilean–Danish BITs.[78] The more favorable rights concerned the obligation under the third-country BITs to grant necessary permits once an

---

treatment to be violated the State's conduct must "amount to an outrage, to bad faith, to willful neglect of duty, or to an insufficiency of governmental action so far short of international standards that every reasonable and impartial man would readily recognize its insufficiency"). On the international minimum standard see generally Borchard, *The "Minimum Standard" of Treatment of Aliens*, 38 Mich. L. Rev. 446 (1940).

[73] *Pope & Talbot Inc.* v. *Canada*, Award on the Merits of Phase 2, April 10, 2001, paras. 110 *et seq.*

[74] *Ibid.*, para. 117 (observing that "NAFTA investors and investments that would be denied access to the fairness elements untrammeled by the 'egregious' conduct threshold that Canada would graft onto Article 1105 would simply turn to Articles 1102 and 1103 for relief"). Notably, the Tribunal used the argument that third-party BITs contained more favorable expressions of fair and equitable treatment directly in order to interpret Article 1105(1) NAFTA. *Cf.* Vasciannie, *The Fair and Equitable Treatment Standard in International Investment Law and Practice*, 70 Brit. Ybk. Int'l Law 99, 149 (1999) (observing that that "one effect of the growing network of bilateral investment treaties incorporating the most-favourable-nation standard has been to generalize the applicability of the fair and equitable standard among States").

[75] NAFTA Free Trade Commission, *Notes of Interpretation of Certain Chapter 11 Provisions*, July 31, 2001.

[76] See *Pope & Talbot* v. *Canada*, Award in Respect of Damages, May 31, 2002, para. 12 (quoting from one of its written communications with the parties, the Tribunal pointed out that "the Commission's interpretation would, because of Article 1103 ... produce the absurd result of relief denied under Article 1105 but restored under Article 1103.").

[77] *Ibid.*, para. 66.

[78] *MTD* v. *Chile*, Award, May 25, 2004, paras. 100, 197. See also *MTD* v. *Chile*, Decision on Annulment, March 21, 2007, para. 64.

investment has been approved under the host State's foreign investment legislation. Finally, in *Rumeli Telekom* v. *Kazakhstan*, the Tribunal, *inter alia*, held the host State liable for a violation of fair and equitable treatment that the Tribunal had incorporated based on the MFN clause in the Turkish–Kazakh BIT, from the host State's third-party BITs, in particular the UK–Kazakh BIT.[79]

The cases above highlight the role of MFN clauses in both harmonizing and raising the standards of investment protection. Importing more favorable substantive conditions granted in third-country BITs comports with the economic rationale of MFN clauses, as equal investment conditions and standards of treatment for investors of different nationalities are essential to equal competition and to an efficient allocation of resources. Furthermore, the incorporation of more favorable substantive rights based on MFN clauses shows that the clauses are a tool for the multilateralization and harmonization of substantive standards of investment protection. The clauses not only extend and multilateralize more favorable conditions from third-country BITs, but also deter future efforts to contain inter-State investment relations on a bilateral basis. Thus, the reaction of arbitral tribunals to the FTC's interpretation of fair and equitable treatment under Article 1105, NAFTA illustrates that MFN clauses elevate the level of protection in any given host State to the maximum level granted in any of that State's investment treaties. MFN clauses, therefore, harmonize investment protection at the most elevated level available.

2   Limits to the operation of MFN clauses

While acknowledging that MFN clauses enable investors to invoke more favorable conditions offered under third-country BITs, several arbitral awards have also dealt with the limits of MFN clauses. Limitations on the operation of MFN clauses either flow from explicit restrictions of the clause itself or are implied from limitations in the application of the basic treaty containing the clause.

(a)   Explicit restrictions of the scope of application of the MFN clause

Explicit exceptions to MFN clauses are generally an effective means of shielding bilateral bargains against the multilateralizing effect of the clauses. In the NAFTA case *ADF* v. *United States*, for example, the investor

---

[79] *Rumeli* v. *Kazakhstan*, Award, July 29, 2008, paras. 572, 575 (observing that Kazakhstan had conceded that the MFN clause in question applied to incorporate more favorable substantive investor rights granted under the host State's third-country BITs).

took up the principle in *Pope & Talbot* and invoked the more favorable provisions on fair and equitable treatment in the US–Albanian and the US–Estonian BITs. This would have allowed the investor to circumvent the more restrictive interpretation of Article 1105(1), NAFTA pursuant to the FTC Note of Interpretation.[80] The Tribunal, however, rejected the claimant's argument because the dispute related to a procurement decision, a subject-matter explicitly excluded from the scope of operation of NAFTA's MFN clause in Article 1103.[81]

Furthermore, MFN clauses cannot override clauses included in the basic treaty which absolve a party of the obligations under the treaty as a whole. For example, Article XI of the US–Argentine BIT provides that the "Treaty shall not preclude the application by either Party of measures necessary for the maintenance of public order, the fulfillment of its obligations with respect to the maintenance or restoration of international peace or security, or the protection of its own essential security interests."[82] These clauses not only restrict the scope of application of specific substantive provisions, but directly limit, within their scope of application, the application of the entire BIT, including its MFN clause. Such exceptions, therefore, cannot be bypassed by relying on more favorable treatment accorded to investors from third-party States.

In *CMS* v. *Argentina*, the claimant argued that the MFN clause in the US–Argentine BIT would override the emergency clause mentioned above, because other Argentine BITs did not contain comparable clauses. While the Tribunal rightly rejected the claimant's argument, it chose a problematic justification. It concluded that the emergency clause could be bypassed only if the third-country BIT contained a more favorable emergency clause.[83] This justification, however, which purports to draw on the *ejusdem generis* rule, is mistaken in its premise that an MFN clause could

[80] *Cf. ADF* v. *United States*, Award, January 9, 2003, paras. 76–87, 104–7.

[81] *Ibid.*, para. 196 (the Tribunal applied Article 1108(7)(a), NAFTA that provides that Article 1103 does not apply to procurement by a party or a State enterprise). Furthermore, the decision is also noteworthy because the Tribunal confirmed, in line with *Pope & Talbot* v. *Canada*, the general possibility of circumventing the restrictive interpretation the FTC Note has given to Article 1105(1), NAFTA based on NAFTA's MFN clause, provided that the investor is able to show that other host State BITs are actually more favorable. See *ADF* v. *United States*, Award, January 9, 2003, para. 196.

[82] See Article XI of the Treaty between United States of America and the Argentine Republic concerning the Reciprocal Encouragement and Protection of Investment, signed November 11, 1991, entered into force October 20, 1994, 31 I.L.M. 124 (1992).

[83] In the Tribunal's view, this rule of interpretation would only incorporate more favorable treatment of other investors by a more favorable emergency clause, see *CMS* v. *Argentina*, Award, May 12, 2005, para. 377.

only attract more favorable clauses that have the same subject-matter as the clause in the basic treaty that is supposed to be overridden.

Instead, the *ejusdem generis* rule limits the operation of MFN clauses to importing more favorable treatment relating to the same subject-matter as the clause itself, in the case at hand, therefore, the equal treatment of foreign investors with different nationalities. The *ejusdem generis* rule does not, by contrast, require that the more favorable clause concerns the same subject-matter as the treaty provision in the basic treaty that is supposed to be overridden.[84] The Tribunal in *CMS*, therefore, misrepresented the *ejusdem generis* rule. Although it ultimately reached the correct result, the Tribunal should have relied on the limitation of the MFN clause through the treaty's emergency clause. Consequently, exceptions to the scope of application of a BIT as a whole cannot be overridden by the operation of an MFN clause in the same treaty.

(b)   Restrictions to MFN clauses based on the scope of application of the basic treaty

While the *ejusdem generis* rule limits the operation of MFN clauses to incorporating more favorable treatment concerning the subject-matter of the clause itself, the scope of application of MFN clauses is regularly indirectly restricted by the scope of application of the basic treaty itself. Thus, a treaty's scope of application, as regards its subject-matter (*ratione materiae*), its temporal dimension (*ratione temporis*), and its personal applicability (*ratione personae*), can delimit the scope of application of an MFN clause contained in that treaty. As a result, MFN clauses in BITs will not usually operate as procuring favorable treatment, for example, relating to diplomatic immunities. Being outside of the subject-matter applicability of the basic treaty, these or similarly unrelated subject-matter will usually also be outside the subject-matter of the treaty's MFN clause and thus complement the *ejusdem generis* rule.[85] The scope of application of

---

[84] Similarly 30 ILC Ybk. vol. II, Part Two, p. 30 (1978), Commentary to Articles 9 and 10, para. 12 (stating that it is incorrect "to say that the *treaty* or *agreement* including the clause must be of the same category (*ejusdem generis*) as that of the benefits that are claimed under the clause"). Expressly in this sense also *MTD Equity Sdn Bhd. & MTD Chile SA v. Chile*, ICSID Case No. ARB/01/7, Decision on Annulment, March 21, 2007, para. 64.

[85] *Cf. Maffezini v. Spain*, Decision on Objections to Jurisdiction, January 25, 2000, para. 56 (clarifying with respect to the *ejusdem generis* principle that "the third-party treaty has to relate to the same subject-matter as the basic treaty, be it the protection of foreign investments or the promotion of trade, since the dispute settlement provisions will operate in the context of these matters; otherwise there would be a contravention of that

the basic treaty will, therefore, limit the scope of application of its MFN clause, unless the clause is exceptionally broad and explicitly goes beyond the treaty's subject-matter. In other words, an MFN clause, in principle, cannot extend the scope of application of the basic treaty. Likewise, an investor will not be able to extend the meaning of "investor" or "investment" by means of the basic treaty's MFN clause, even if third-country BITs provide for a broader scope of application *ratione personae* or *ratione materiae*.[86]

The same reasoning also holds true with respect to the basic treaty's temporal applicability. In *Tecmed* v. *Mexico* the Tribunal declined to extend the temporal applicability of the Spanish–Mexican BIT based on the treaty's MFN clause. Thus, the claimant could not rely on more favorable provisions in one of Mexico's third-country BITs that arguably protected against governmental acts before that BIT came into force. In the Tribunal's view, the MFN clause could not lead to an extension of the treaty's application over time, since this would "go to the core matter that must be deemed to be specifically negotiated between the Contracting Parties."[87]

While the Tribunal decided correctly in view of the basic treaty serving as a framework and delimiting for the operation of the MFN clause in question, the reference to a "specifically negotiated" bargain between the State parties is problematic. If this is meant to imply that any specifically negotiated provision in a BIT could not be overridden by more favorable clauses in third-party treaties, the Tribunal's reasoning cannot be supported. This would defeat the object of MFN clauses to establish a level playing field for the economic activity of investors from different home States and runs counter to their basic role of multilateralizing bilateral investment relations.

---

principle"). See also *ibid.*, para. 45 (explaining that the "subject-matter to which the clause applies is indeed established by the basic treaty, it follows that if these matters are more favorably treated in a third-party treaty then, by operation of the clause, that treatment is extended to the beneficiary under the basic treaty. If the third-party treaty refers to a matter not dealt with in the basic treaty, that matter is *res inter alios acta* in respect of the beneficiary of the clause.").

[86] See *Société Générale* v. *Dominican Republic*, Award on Preliminary Objections to Jurisdiction, September 19, 2008, paras. 40–41. See also *Yaung Chi Oo Trading* v. *Myanmar*, Final Award, March 31, 2003, para. 83 (where the non-application of MFN treatment to extending the subject-matter application of the basic treaty, i.e., with respect to the definition of the covered investment, should have been the *ratio decidendi*). On this decision see also *infra* footnote 208.

[87] *Tecmed* v. *Mexico*, Award, May 29, 2003, para. 69.

In addition, such a result would be difficult to justify under rules of treaty interpretation.[88] The effect of MFN clauses does not depend on whether the more favorable treatment would override a specifically nego-tiated provision or any other provision of the basic treaty. The sole rele-vant factor is whether MFN treatment applies or whether it is subject to an explicit or implicit exception. Furthermore, distinguishing between specifically negotiated provisions and other provisions would introduce different classes of provisions within the same treaty. Yet, every provision in a BIT emanates from the treaty-making power and consensus of the contracting State parties and has an equally binding force. Treaty provi-sions do not possess different degrees of validity depending on how diffi-cult it was for the parties to agree on them.[89]

Unless the basic treaty specifies that a certain provision cannot be bypassed by means of an MFN clause, it will be difficult for a tribunal to ascertain whether a certain provision was intended to be immune from circumvention by MFN treatment. Therefore, the relationship between the MFN clause and any other clause in the treaty will have to be resolved based on accepted principles of treaty interpretation. Such interpretative resolution could allow for implied exceptions to the general MFN clause. There is, however, no room for creating a specific class of "specifically negotiated" provisions of the basic treaty that is *per se* immune from cir-cumvention by more favorable treatment in third-party BITs, unless these provisions can be read as constituting an exception to MFN treatment.

3   Circumventing restrictions of MFN treatment

While exceptions to MFN clauses *prima facie* appear to curtail the multilateralizing effect of the clauses, the exceptions will have to figure

---

[88] See also Radi, *The Application of the Most-Favoured-Nation Clause to the Dispute Settlement Provisions of Bilateral Investment Treaties*, 18 Eur. J. Int'l L. 757, 773 (2007) (considering that "this criterion appears to provide little guidance on the determination of the provisions of the basic BIT that cannot be replaced"); critical of the reasoning also Chukwumerije (*supra* footnote 9), 8 J. World Inv. & Trade 597, 624 (2007).

[89] Similarly *Siemens* v. *Argentina*, Decision on Jurisdiction, August 3, 2004, para. 106 (observing that "[t]he acceptance of a clause from a model text does not invest this clause with either more or less legal force than other clauses which may had [sic] been more difficult to negotiate. The end result of the negotiations is an agreed text and the legal sig-nificance of each clause is not affected by how arduous was the negotiating path to arrive there ... The Tribunal finds that when the intention of the parties has been clearly expressed, it is not in its power to second-guess their intentions by attributing special meaning to phrases based on whether they were or were not part of a model draft.").

consistently in the host State's BITs to have full effect. Otherwise, MFN clauses might allow investors to circumvent such exceptions and rely on more favorable treatment in third-country BITs, even though the basic treaty contains an explicit exception for MFN treatment in this respect. Hypothetically, such a situation can arise under the circumstances depicted in Figure IV.2.

If State A grants more favorable treatment to State C, such treatment will not extend to State B, if the MFN clause in the basic treaty between A and B contains an exception covering the more favorable treatment extended to C. However, State B will be able to incorporate the benefits granted to C, despite the existence of an exception to MFN treatment, if State A is obliged to extend the benefits granted to C for a fourth State D based on an MFN clause in a treaty with State D that does not contain a comparable exception. State B can thus incorporate the more favorable treatment directly granted to C based on a double incorporation (or double derivation) via the MFN clause in the treaty between A and B together with the more favorable treatment granted to D which is based on the MFN clause in the treaty between A and D.

A practical example of such a constellation is the interplay of benefits arising under the EU and EC Treaties for investments in Germany by investors from other EU Member States. In general, the multilateralization of such benefits under Germany's investment treaties to investors from third countries is excluded by explicit customs union exceptions to the MFN clauses contained in Germany's BITs.[90] Based on these exceptions, foreign investors from non-EU Member States thus generally cannot rely on benefits arising under the EU and EC Treaties. However, some of these benefits

---

[90] See, e.g., Article 3(3), Treaty between the Kingdom of Thailand and the Federal Republic of Germany concerning Encouragement and Reciprocal Protection of Investments, signed June 24, 2002, entered into force October 20, 2004. These exceptions are common not only in BITs of Member States of the European Union, but also in BITs of the United States and various other countries. See, e.g., Article 2(10), Treaty between the Government of the United States of America and the Government of the Republic of Estonia for the Encouragement and Reciprocal Protection of Investment, signed April 19, 1994, entered into force February 16, 1997. Several commentators consider that exceptions from MFN treatment for customs unions are an exception that has risen to the status of customary international law and does not, therefore, have to be mentioned explicitly. See Gruntzel, *Das System der Handelspolitik*, p. 480 (3rd edn. 1928); Riedl, *Ausnahmen von der Meistbegünstigung*, pp. 7–8 (1931); Brandt (*supra* footnote 23), pp. 10 *et seq.* (1933); Strupp and Schlochauer, *Wörterbuch des Völkerrechts*, vol. II, p. 501 (2nd edn. 1961); Vignes, *La clause de la nation la plus favorisée et sa pratique*, 130 Recueil des Cours 207, 264–85 (1970–II); Kramer (*supra* footnote 1), 35 RIW 473, 477 (1989). For the contrary view see *infra* footnote 96.

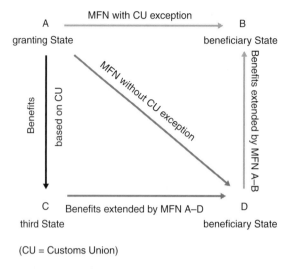

(CU = Customs Union)

Figure IV.2   Circumvention of exceptions to MFN treatment by double-derivation

are in fact extended to US investors based on the MFN clause in the Treaty of Friendship, Commerce, and Navigation (FCN) between Germany and the United States.[91] Thus, in a number of decisions Germany's highest court in civil matters, the *Bundesgerichtshof*, has accepted that US corporations headquartered in Germany were to be recognized as corporations governed by US law, with respect to their internal organization and liability limitation, even though German law traditionally did not recognize

[91] See Article VII(4), Treaty of Friendship, Commerce, and Navigation between the United States of America and the Federal Republic of Germany, signed October 29, 1954, entered into force July 14, 1956. On the debate whether benefits stemming from membership in the EU/EC can be extended by means of the MFN clause in the US–German FCN treaty, although the FCN treaty does not contain an explicit exception in this respect, see Drinhausen and Keinath, *Die grenzüberschreitende Verschmelzung inländischer Gesellschaften nach Erlass der Richtlinie zur grenzüberschreitenden Verschmelzung von Kapitalgesellschaften in Europa*, 52 RIW 81, 87 (2006); Kiem, *Die Regelung der grenzüberschreitenden Verschmelzung im deutschen Umwandlungsgesetz*, 60 WM 1091 (2006) (both supporting an extension of such benefits); differently Frenzel and Axer, *EG-Mitgliedstaat durch die Hintertür?*, 53 RIW 47, 52–54 (2007) (each with further references). See further Lach and Schill, *Anmerkung*, 2005 MittBayNot 243, 244–45 (2005); Dammann, *Amerikanische Gesellschaften mit Sitz in Deutschland*, 68 RabelsZ 607, 629–31 (2004); Sester and Cárdenas, *The Extra-Communitarian Effects of Centros, Überseering and Inspire Art with Regard to Fourth Generation Association Agreements*, 2 Eur. Company & Fin. L. Rev. 398 (2005) (making a similar argument with respect to companies from Chile).

limitations of liability of foreign corporate entities with their corporate seat in Germany.[92] Yet, in the disputes at hand, the *Bundesgerichtshof* accepted the recognition of US corporations, *inter alia* based on MFN treatment granted in the US–German FCN treaty in connection with the benefit of recognition granted to corporate entities from other EU Member States pursuant to Articles 43 and 48, EC Treaty.

These provisions, as interpreted by the European Court of Justice ("ECJ"), require Germany to accept that companies incorporated under the laws of another EU Member State are able to transfer their principal place of business to Germany without having to conform to German company law which often imposed, for example, a higher minimum capital for limited liability companies and may prescribe different rules for director liability. Instead, Articles 43 and 48, EC Treaty require Germany to recognize the internal organization and director liability under the law of the corporate entity's place of incorporation.[93] In effect, Germany therefore had to refrain from applying German company law to companies from other EU Member States.[94]

Based on the MFN clause in the US–German FCN treaty, these benefits also have to be extended to companies incorporated in the United States based on the treaty's MFN clause, because this treaty, unlike most BITs, does not contain an explicit customs union exception. Although several commentators support that MFN clauses contain implicit customs union exceptions as a matter of customary international law,[95] the ILC during its deliberations on the Draft Articles on MFN Clauses was less adamant in this respect.[96] In addition, there is evidence from the negotiating history

---

[92] See BGH, Case No. II ZR 389/02, Judgment, July 5, 2004, BGHZ 153, 353; BGH, Case No. I ZR 245/01, Judgment, October 13, 2004, 42 DStR 2113 (2004). See, for a discussion on these decisions, Lach and Schill (*supra* footnote 91), 2005 MittBayNot 243 (2005); Dammann (*supra* footnote 91), 68 RabelsZ 607 (2004).

[93] *Centros*, C-212/97, Judgment, March 9, 1999, E.C.R I-1459 (1999); *Überseering*, C-208/00, Judgment, November 5, 2002, E.C.R I-9919 (2002); *Inspire Art*, C-167/01, Judgment, September 30, 2003, E.C.R I-10155 (2003).

[94] For the competing theories on the law applicable to the company statute under German conflict of laws rules see Kindler, *Internationales Handels- und Gesellschaftsrecht*, in Rebmann, Säcker and Rixecker, *Münchener Kommentar zum Bürgerlichen Gesetzbuch*, vol. 11, paras. 331–405 (4th edn. 2006).

[95] See, e.g., the literature cited *supra* footnote 90.

[96] See 28 ILC Ybk., vol. II, Part Two, p. 45, Article 15 – Commentary, para. 27 (1976) (stating in a report to the General Assembly that "[m]ost of the members [of the ILC] … admitted that there is no rule of customary international rule which would relieve States upon their entering into a customs union or other association from their obligations under a most-favoured-nation clause"). Similarly, Schwarzenberger (*supra* footnote 24), 22 Brit. Ybk. Int'l L. 96, 109, note 5 (1945); Jahnke, *The European Economic Community*

of the US–German FCN treaty that suggests that the contracting parties did not envisage that the treaty's MFN provision should be subject to a customs union exception.[97] Under the MFN clause in the US–German FCN treaty, US investors in Germany, therefore, have to be accorded treatment as favorable as investors from EU Member States.

While investors from other States that have entered into a BIT with Germany cannot directly rely on the more favorable treatment accorded to EU investors because of explicit customs union exceptions in their respective BITs, such investors could avail themselves of their right to MFN treatment and the more favorable conditions granted to US investors in Germany. Compared with US investors, the MFN exception for customs unions cannot apply since the more favorable conditions for US investors are only indirectly related to the benefits stemming from EU membership.

In particular, the argument that an exception from MFN treatment would also exclude such an indirect multilateralization is not convincing since the rationale of the customs union exception is to exclude the multilateralization of customs union benefits in order to allow for closer economic integration. If such benefits are, however, extended to parties outside the economic union in question, there is no reason why such an exception to MFN treatment should be operative. After all, this would not meet the purpose of the exception to shield closer economic integration against multilateralization. Instead, to the extent competitive advantages are granted to third-country investors, these advantages should equally be multilateralized in view of the economic rationale of MFN clauses.

As this example shows, MFN clauses are a powerful instrument of multilateralism even in the presence of exceptions to their scope of application. An incorporation of more favorable conditions by double derivation enables investors to circumvent exceptions to MFN treatment contained in the basic treaty. Conversely, isolating *quid pro quo* bargains from multilateralization will only be effective if all relevant treaties contain consistent exceptions to MFN treatment.

and the Most-Favoured-Nation Clause, 1 Can. Ybk. Int'l L. 252, 253 *et seq.* (1963); Ustor, *Die Zollunionsausnahme,* in Fischer, Köck and Verdross (eds.), *Völkerrecht und Rechtsphilosophie,* pp. 371, 374–78 (1980); Ustor, *The MFN Customs Union Exception,* 15 J. World Trade L. 377 (1981); Ustor, *Most-Favored-Nation Clauses in Treaties of Commerce,* in Bokor-Szegö (ed.), 3 *Questions of International Law* 225 (1986). See also 30 ILC Ybk., vol. II, Part Two, pp. 13–14 (1978), para. 58 (stating in the final report that the situation was "inconclusive," but that "the silence of the draft articles could not be interpreted as an implicit recognition of the existence or non-existence of such a rule, but should rather be interpreted to mean that the ultimate decision was one to be taken by the States to which that draft was submitted, at the final stage of the codification of the topic").

[97] *Cf.* Dammann (*supra* footnote 91), 68 RabelsZ 607, 629–31 (2004).

C   Multilateralizing procedural investment protection

Unlike the multilateralization of substantive investment protection, the application of MFN clauses to dispute settlement provisions has generated a vibrant debate in academic scholarship and produced seemingly divergent decisions in investment jurisprudence.[98] The general tenor of the arbitral jurisprudence is that MFN clauses allow for the incorporation of more favorable treatment concerning the admissibility of an investor-State claim, but do not allow investors to establish or to expand the jurisdictional basis for investor-State arbitration based on broader consent to arbitration in third-party BITs.[99] In addition, recent BIT practice, specifically that of the United States, has reacted partly with disapproval to the application of MFN clauses to dispute settlement.[100] The

---

[98] See for the jurisprudence *infra* footnotes 106–208 and accompanying text. On this debate see generally Dolzer and Myers, *After Tecmed: Most-Favoured-Nation Clauses in International Investment Protection Agreements*, 19 ICSID Rev. – For. Inv. L. J. 49 (2004); Dolzer, *Meistbegünstigungsklauseln in Investitionsschutzverträgen*, in Bröhmer *et al.* (eds.), *Internationale Gemeinschaft und Menschenrechte*, p. 47 (2005); Fietta, *Most Favoured Nation Treatment and Dispute Resolution under Bilateral Investment Treaties: A Turning Point?*, 8 Int'l Arb. L. Rev. 131 (2005); Freyer and Herlihy, *Most-Favoured-Nation Treatment and Dispute Settlement in Investment Arbitration*, 20 ICSID Rev. – For. Inv. L. J. 58 (2005); Gaillard, *Establishing Jurisdiction through a Most-Favored-Nation Clause*, 233 N.Y. L. J. 2 (June 2, 2005); Hsu, *MFN and Dispute Settlement*, 7 J. World Inv. & Trade 25 (2006); Kurtz (*supra* footnote 10), 6 J. World Inv. & Trade 861 (2004); Kurtz, *The Delicate Extension of Most-Favoured-Nation Treatment to Foreign Investors*, in Weiler (ed.), *International Investment Law and Arbitration*, p. 523 (2005); Newmark and Poulton, *Siemens v. Argentina: Most Favoured Nation Clause (Re)visited*, 3 SchiedsVZ 30 (2005); Teitelbaum, *Who's Afraid of Maffezini?*, 22 J. Int'l Arb. 225 (2005); Essig, *Balancing Investors' Interests and State Sovereignty*, 4(5) Transnat'l Disp. Mgmt. 14–28 (2007); Radi (*supra* footnote 88), 18 Eur. J. Int'l L. 757 (2007); Chukwumerije (*supra* footnote 9), 8 J. World Inv. & Trade 597 (2007); Ben Hamida, *Clause de la nation la plus favorisée et mécanismes de reglement des différends: que dit l'histoire?*, 134 H.J.D.I. 1127 (2007); Vesel, *Clearing a Path through a Tangled Jurisprudence*, 32 Yale J. Int'l L. 125 (2007); Ben Hamida, *MFN Clauses and Procedural Rights*, in Weiler (ed.), *Investment Treaty Arbitration and International Law*, p. 231 (2008); Wong, *The Application of Most-Favored-Nation Clauses to Dispute Resolution Provisions in Bilateral Investment Treaties*, 3 Asian J. WTO & Int'l Health L. & Pol'y 171 (2008); Faya Rodriguez (*supra* footnote 7), 25 J. Int'l Arb. 89 (2008); Valenti, *The Most Favoured Nation Clause in BITs as a Basis for Jurisdiction in Foreign Investor–Host State Arbitration*, 24 Arb. Int'l 447 (2008); Acconci, *Most Favoured Nation Treatment*, in Muchlinski, Ortino and Schreuer, *The Oxford Handbook of International Investment Law*, pp. 361, 387–401 (2008); Paparinskis, *MFN Clauses in Investment Arbitration between Maffezini and Plama: The Third Way?*, ICSID Rev. – For. Inv. L. J. (forthcoming).

[99] See Freyer and Herlihy (*supra* footnote 98), 20 ICSID Rev. – For. Inv. L. J. 58, 82–83 (2005); Chukwumerije (*supra* footnote 9), 8 J. World Inv. & Trade 597, 626–46 (2007).

[100] See Houde and Pagani (*supra* footnote 6), pp. 4–5 (2004). Recent US and Canadian BIT practice concerning MFN treatment in BITs and Free Trade Agreements (FTAs) now

following section examines the multilateralizing effect arbitral jurisprudence has accorded to MFN clauses as regards admissibility-related
access restrictions to investor-State arbitration and contrasts it with the
resistance arbitral jurisprudence has displayed toward the application of
MFN clauses as a basis of jurisdiction.

1   Circumventing admissibility-related access restrictions to investor-State dispute settlement

Access to investor-State arbitration under international investment
agreements often requires the fulfillment of certain preconditions. Most
BITs, for example, require negotiations between investor and host State
prior to submitting the dispute to arbitration.[101] Other treaties require
the expiration of waiting periods prior to arbitration, sometimes as long
as eighteen months,[102] or the exhaustion of local remedies.[103] While these
restrictions may serve to facilitate the amicable settlement of disputes and
to allow the host State's judicial system to redress wrongful conduct,[104]
local remedies and waiting periods can also impede the enforcement of
rights granted under a BIT and delay efficient dispute settlement. In particular, local remedies may be ill-suited to furthering the enforcement of
obligations under investment treaties, either because the treaties are not

---

includes attempts to deliberately limit MFN treatment to substantive investment protection. Thus, the United States introduced a clause in some subsequent negotiations
that specifically intended to exclude the application of MFN clauses to investor-State
dispute settlement. See Article 10.4(2), footnote 1, Draft of the Central America–
United States Free Trade Agreement, January 28, 2004 (stating that the parties agree
that the MFN clause they include in their treaty "does not encompass international
dispute resolution mechanisms such as those contained in Section C of this Chapter
and, therefore, could not reasonably lead to a conclusion similar to that of the *Maffezini*
case").

[101] See, e.g., Article 10(1), Agreement between the Government of the People's Republic
of China and the Government of the Hellenic Republic for the Encouragement and
Reciprocal Protection of Investments, signed on June 25, 1992, entered into force on
December 21, 1993.

[102] See, e.g., Article 10(3)(a), Vertrag zwischen der Bundesrepublik Deutschland und
der Argentinischen Republik über die Förderung und den gegenseitigen Schutz von
Kapitalanlagen, signed on April 9, 1991, entered into force on November 8, 1993.

[103] While the exhaustion of local remedies is generally required before a State espouses a
claim of its national by means of diplomatic protection, BITs only rarely, if at all, contain
this requirement. See Amerasinghe, *Diplomatic Protection*, pp. 334–41 (2008).

[104] See Amerasinghe, *Local Remedies in International Law*, pp. 59–61 (2nd edn. 2004);
Cançado Trindade, *The Application of the Rule of Exhaustion of Local Remedies in
International Law*, p. 11 (1983).

directly applicable in the host State's domestic legal order or because the domestic court system lacks the necessary independence to enforce these obligations effectively against its own government. Thus, to the extent that the different BITs of one host State can contain different "filters" for access to investment treaty arbitration, the question arises whether an investor can rely on more favorable provisions in third-country BITs based on an MFN clause in the basic treaty, just as it is able to benefit from the more favorable substantive treatment granted under the host State's third-party BITs.

In this context, investment tribunals have been faced mostly with the question of whether MFN clauses allow an investor to rely on shorter waiting periods in third-country BITs or to do away with the requirement to pursue local remedies for a limited time before initiating investor-State arbitration. To date, arbitral jurisprudence has rather consistently accepted that investors may circumvent such admissibility-related requirements by relying on more favorable provisions for investor-State dispute settlement under third-country BITs.[105] In this respect, MFN clauses have been held to multilateralize access to investment treaty arbitration. Furthermore, this effect has been accorded even despite differences in the wording of the MFN clauses in question. Rather, MFN treatment in the disputes at issue has been applied like a principle of international investment law that has been incorporated in the pertinent BITs and is independent of the exact wording of the MFN clause in question.

(a)   Shortening waiting periods: *Maffezini* v. *Spain*

Maffezini v. *Spain* was the first ICSID award to apply an MFN clause to circumvent pre-arbitration restrictions by allowing the investor to rely on a shorter waiting period from a third-party BIT. The Tribunal was faced with the question of whether an Argentine investor in Spain was bound by an eighteen-month waiting period before initiating investor-State arbitration under the Spanish–Argentine BIT or whether it could

---

[105] Only the recent award in *Wintershall* v. *Argentina*, Award, December 8, 2008, declined to accept that the investor could shorten an eighteen-month period during which it was to pursue local remedies before initiating investor-State arbitration under the BIT (see *ibid.*, paras. 158–97). However, the Tribunal qualified this requirement as a jurisdictional condition to the host State's consent to arbitration, rather than as an admissibility-related question (see *ibid.*, paras. 108–57). It did not, therefore, contradict the general tenor of arbitral jurisprudence that admissibility-related access restrictions could be circumvented based on an MFN clause. For a more detailed discussion of the decision see also *infra* footnotes 190–99 and accompanying text.

rely, based on the BIT's MFN clause, on more favorable access conditions under the Spanish–Chilean BIT, which required only a six-month waiting period.[106] The Tribunal resorted to first principles in its interpretation of Article IV(2) of the Spanish–Argentine BIT which read:

> In all matters subject to this Agreement, this treatment shall not be less favorable than that extended by each Party to the investments made in its territory by investors of a third country.[107]

Spain as respondent objected to the circumvention on the grounds that more favorable BITs with third countries constituted *res inter alios acta* and could not, therefore, be invoked by the investor. In addition, it argued that, according to the *ejusdem generis* principle, the reference to "all matters" in Article IV(2) referred only to "substantive matters or material aspects of the treatment granted to investors and not to procedural or jurisdictional questions."[108]

The Tribunal, however, declined to limit the MFN clause to matters of substantive investment protection. Instead, it clarified that the MFN clause linked the basic treaty with Spain's third-country BITs and allowed the investor to circumvent the less favorable conditions in the basic treaty under two conditions. First, in order for the third-country BIT not to constitute *res inter alios acta*, the third-party treaty and the basic treaty had to deal with the same subject-matter.[109] This proved unproblematic as both treaties concerned the mutual promotion and protection of foreign investment. Second, within the framework of the same subject-matter of the treaties in question, the *ejusdem generis* rule would serve the purpose of limiting the scope of MFN clauses. Under this rule, an MFN clause only attracts preferential treatment that relates to the subject-matter of the clause itself which, depending on the wording of the MFN clause, may be narrower than the subject-matter of the basic treaty.[110]

---

[106] See *Maffezini* v. *Spain*, Decision on Objections to Jurisdiction, January 25, 2000, paras. 38–64.

[107] *Ibid.*, para. 38.

[108] *Ibid.*, para. 41. With respect to the object and purpose of MFN clauses to avoid discrimination, Spain added that "such discrimination can only take place in connection with material economic treatment and not with regard to procedural matters. Only if it could be established that resort to domestic tribunals would produce objective disadvantages for the investor would it be possible to argue material effects on the treatment owed." (*ibid.*, para. 42).

[109] *Ibid.*, para. 45.

[110] *Ibid.*, paras. 46–56. See also *Ambatielos Claim (Greece* v. *United Kingdom)*, Award of March 6, 1956, U.N.R.I.A.A., vol. XII, p. 107 (stressing that "the most-favoured-nation

On this basis, the Tribunal stressed the importance of investor-State dispute settlement in the protection against undue government interference, highlighted its perceived advantages over dispute resolution in domestic courts and emphasized that procedural enforcement and substantive rights granted under modern BITs were "inextricably related."[111] The Tribunal thus concluded, despite the lack of an express reference to dispute settlement in the MFN clause, that the *ejusdem generis* rule was satisfied:

> [I]f a third-party treaty contains provisions for the settlement of disputes that are more favorable to the protection of the investor's rights and interests than those in the basic treaty, such provisions may be extended to the beneficiary of the most favored nation clause as they are fully compatible with the *ejusdem generis* principle.[112]

The Tribunal, however, qualified its analysis with some exceptions and held that:

> [a]s a matter of principle, the beneficiary of the clause *should not be able to override public policy considerations* that the contracting parties might have envisaged as fundamental conditions for their acceptance of the agreement in question, particularly if the beneficiary is a private investor, as will often be the case. The scope of the clause might thus be narrower than it appears at first sight.[113]

In a non-exhaustive list, the Tribunal recognized possible public policy exceptions to applying MFN clauses to questions of investor-State dispute settlement and determined that the following access restrictions could not be bypassed:

(1) the exhaustion of local remedies (as this constitutes a fundamental rule of international law),
(2) "fork in the road" clauses, which prevent investors from initiating international arbitration where the same cause of action had already been instituted in domestic proceedings or vice versa (as this would upset the finality of settled disputes),
(3) the consent to a particular arbitration forum, and
(4) the establishment of a highly institutionalized system of arbitration.[114]

---

clause can only attract matters belonging to the same category of subject as that to which *the clause* itself relates") (emphasis added).

[111] *Maffezini* v. *Spain*, Decision on Objections to Jurisdiction, January 25, 2000, paras. 54–55.

[112] *Ibid.*, para. 56. [113] *Ibid.*, para. 62 (emphasis added). [114] *Ibid.*, para. 63.

The Tribunal introduced these exceptions in order to avoid perceived negative effects of a broad application of MFN clauses to investor-State dispute settlement, namely "disruptive treaty-shopping that would play havoc with the policy objectives of underlying specific treaty provisions."[115] Regrettably, the Tribunal did not provide a normative basis for these public policy considerations and did not clarify whether they followed from the primacy of specific domestic policy concerns regarding investor-State dispute settlement or whether they should be seen as implicit limitation of MFN clauses.[116]

Notwithstanding these exceptions, the decision of the *Maffezini* Tribunal to allow the circumvention of waiting clauses is convincing. It is not only supported by the wording of the MFN clause in question, but also in conformity with the economic rationale of MFN clauses to create a level playing field for foreign investors from different home States. Certainly, being able to enforce certain obligations under an investment treaty more easily, or more quickly, puts investors at a competitive advantage. Differences in the enforcement mechanisms thus impose different transaction costs upon investors based on their nationality and should, just like differences in the substantive protection of foreign investments, be multilateralized.

(b)   Multilateralizing benefits without extending disadvantages: cherry-picking in *Siemens* v. *Argentina*

Siemens v. *Argentina* built further on the *Maffezini* decision and bolstered the application of MFN clauses by allowing the investor to incorporate benefits from third-country BITs without being bound by the latter treaty's more restrictive provisions.[117] It thus allowed the investor to "cherry-pick" more favorable provisions from third-country BITs without being bound to any less favorable conditions contained in those treaties.

---

[115] *Ibid.*

[116] For criticism of the basis of the "public policy considerations" the Tribunal in *Maffezini* proclaimed, see Dolzer and Myers (*supra* footnote 98), 19 ICSID Rev. - For. Inv. L. J. 49, 52–54 (2004); Gaillard (*supra* footnote 98), 233 N.Y. L. J. 2, 7 (June 2, 2005); Freyer and Herlihy (*supra* footnote 98), 20 ICSID Rev. - For. Inv. L. J. 58, 67 (2005); Hsu (*supra* footnote 98), 7 J. World Inv. & Trade 25, 29 (2006); Radi (*supra* footnote 88) 18 Eur. J. Int'l L. 757, 771–73 (2007); Chukwumerije (*supra* footnote 9), 8 J. World Inv. & Trade 597, 631–32 (2007). See also *Plama* v. *Bulgaria,* Decision on Jurisdiction, February 8, 2005, para. 221 (observing that the Tribunal was "puzzled as to what the origins of these 'public policy considerations'" were). See further *infra* Ch. IV.D.8.

[117] *Siemens* v. *Argentina,* Decision on Jurisdiction, August 3, 2004, paras. 32–110.

After pursuing local remedies, the claimant initiated investor–State arbitration before an eighteen-month waiting period required by the German–Argentine BIT had elapsed. In order to overcome this requirement, the investor invoked the treaty's MFN clause in order to benefit from the six-month waiting period in the Argentine–Chilean BIT.[118] In addition to challenging the applicability of MFN clauses in general to matters relating to investor-State dispute settlement,[119] Argentina also pointed to the allegedly more restrictive wording of Article 3 of the German–Argentine BIT which provided:

(1) None of the Contracting Parties shall accord in its territory to the investments of nationals or companies of the other Contracting Party or to investments in which they hold shares, a less favorable treatment than the treatment granted to the investments … of nationals or companies of third States.

(2) None of the Contracting Parties shall accord in its territory to nationals or companies of the other Contracting Party a less favorable treatment of activities related to investments than granted … to the nationals and companies of third States.[120]

Argentina added that the dispute settlement provisions were "specifically negotiated case by case" and thus could not be overridden by an MFN clause.[121] In addition, the requirement to submit the dispute to domestic courts during the waiting period constituted "an essential element of the exceptional jurisdictional offer made in investment treaties"[122] and was, therefore, immune from circumvention by MFN treatment. Finally, Argentina argued that if the claimant could rely on the shorter waiting period in the Argentine–Chilean BIT, it also should be bound by that treaty's "fork in the road" provision which requires Chilean investors to make a final and binding choice between domestic proceedings or international arbitration.[123] Benefits from third-country treaties should thus not be operative under MFN treatment without their limits and disadvantages.[124]

The Tribunal rejected all of Argentina's arguments. First, it pointed out that the MFN clause in question covered any "treatment" of foreign

---

[118] On the claimant's position see *ibid.*, paras. 60–78.
[119] On the respondent's position, see *ibid.*, paras. 46–59.   [120] *Ibid.*, para. 82.
[121] *Ibid.*, para. 50 (referring to *Tecmed* v. *Mexico*, Award, para. 212).
[122] *Siemens* v. *Argentina*, para. 57.
[123] On "fork in the road" clauses see generally, Schreuer, *Travelling the BIT Route*, 5 J. World Inv. & Trade 231, 239–49 (2004); Dolzer and Schreuer, *Principles of International Investment Law*, pp. 216–17 (2008).
[124] *Siemens* v. *Argentina*, Decision on Jurisdiction, August 3, 2004, paras. 110 and 119.

investors and thus included access to investor-state dispute settlement.[125] Second, the Tribunal turned to the treaty's structure and stressed that the contracting parties had expressly provided for certain exceptions to MFN treatment, without including dispute settlement. *E contrario*, the MFN clause should extend to matters of dispute settlement.[126] Finally, the Tribunal invoked the treaty's object and purpose in order to clarify that the intention of the contracting parties was "to create favorable conditions for investments and to stimulate private initiative."[127] The Tribunal therefore concluded that the BIT:

> ha[d] as a distinctive feature special dispute settlement mechanisms not normally open to investors. Access to these mechanisms is part of the protection offered under the Treaty. It is part of the treatment of foreign investors and investments and of the advantages accessible through an MFN clause.[128]

The Tribunal relied particularly on the decisions in *Rights of Nationals of the United States of America in Morocco* and the *Ambatielos* case in order to support its finding that there is no categorical prohibition in international law against applying MFN clauses to issues concerning access to dispute resolution, nor that there is a specific presumption in favor of a restrictive interpretation of broadly worded MFN clauses.[129] The Tribunal, therefore, followed the reasoning in the *Maffezini* case and allowed the claimant to rely on more favorable dispute settlement provisions in other BITs.[130]

The Tribunal in *Siemens* also stressed that "the purpose of the MFN clause is to eliminate the effect of specially negotiated provisions unless they have been excepted [from the operation of the MFN clause]."[131] In doing so, it was responding to the argument in the *Tecmed* award that every "specifically negotiated" clause in the basic treaty could not be circumvented by MFN treatment.[132] The Tribunal in *Siemens* thus clarified that MFN clauses operate independently of the generality or specificity of the provision that is alleged to be overridden.

Addressing Argentina's argument that the investor would also have to accept less beneficial treatment connected to dispute resolution under the Argentine–Chilean BIT, in particular its "fork in the road" clause, the

---

[125] *Ibid.*, paras. 82–86.   [126] *Ibid.*   [127] *Ibid.*, para. 81.
[128] *Ibid.*, para. 102.   [129] *Ibid.*, para. 97.
[130] Without providing any further justification, the Tribunal also accepted, in line with *Maffezini*, that "the MFN clause may not override public policy considerations judged by the parties to a treaty essential to their agreement" (*ibid.*, para. 109).
[131] *Ibid.*, para. 106.   [132] See *supra* footnote 87.

Tribunal in *Siemens* went beyond the *Maffezini* decision and held that MFN treatment had the effect of selectively importing benefits without concurrently incorporating the limitations of the third-party BIT. It concluded:

> [The Respondent's] understanding of the operation of the MFN clause would defeat the intended result of the clause which is to harmonize benefits agreed with a party with those considered more favorable granted to another party. It would oblige the party claiming a benefit under a treaty to consider the advantages and disadvantages of that treaty as a whole rather than just the benefits. The Tribunal recognizes that there may be merit in the proposition that, since a treaty has been negotiated as a package, for other parties to benefit from it, they also should be subject to its disadvantages. The disadvantages may have been a trade-off for the claimed advantages. However, this is not the meaning of an MFN clause. As its own name indicates, it relates only to more favorable treatment.[133]

As a consequence, the Tribunal viewed the imported more favorable rules as independent from the rest of the third-country BIT. In its view, MFN treatment did not require engaging in a comparison of whether the third-party BIT as a package was more favorable than the basic treaty. Instead, it sufficed that individual clauses were more favorable.

The Tribunal's "cherry-picking" approach has attracted criticism. In particular, some have found it difficult to reconcile the decision with the rationale that MFN treatment ensures equal competition among foreign investors with different nationalities, as the German investor-claimant ultimately seemed to have been put in a more advantageous position compared with Chilean investors in Argentina.[134] On the other hand, what appears to be a selective multilateralization of certain benefits without extending connected disadvantages can also be understood as a stringent application of the unconditional character of MFN clauses that both the historical development[135] and the attempts at codification by the ILC suggest.[136] Consequently, the possibility of cherry-picking from third-party treaties is not a novel and ground-breaking construction by the Tribunal in *Siemens v. Argentina*, but rather reflects both the ordinary meaning as well as the predominant State practice concerning MFN clauses.

The critique that German investors in Argentina would ultimately receive better treatment than Chilean investors is presumably also the background to a somewhat ambiguous paragraph in the *Siemens* decision.

---

[133] *Ibid.*, para. 120; see also para. 108.
[134] Chukwumerije (*supra* footnote 9), 8 J. World Inv. & Trade 597, 621 (2007).
[135] See *supra* Ch. II.B.
[136] See Article 11, ILC Draft Articles on Most-Favoured-Nation Clauses.

In it, the Tribunal pointed out that its understanding of the MFN clause "does not mean that the investor in Argentina will enjoy a more favorable treatment than the investor in Chile. The MFN clause works both ways. The investor in Chile will be able to claim similar benefits under the Chile BIT."[137] Read verbatim, this would mean that a German investor in Chile would be treated as favorably as a German investor in Argentina. Such a conclusion, however would mistakenly assume that the MFN clause in the German–Argentine BIT affected the position of investors *in* Chile. This would violate the *inter partes* effect of the treaty. However, the paragraph makes sense if read as referring to an "investor *from* Chile as being able to claim similar benefits under the Chile BIT." This understanding would merely clarify that a Chilean investor in Argentina could rely on the MFN clause in the Argentine–Chilean BIT and, by its operation, also on the more favorable treatment granted to German investors in Argentina. Chilean investors could thus circumvent the "fork in the road" clause in the Argentine–Chilean BIT based on the more favorable treatment granted under the German–Argentine BIT, even though this treatment is based on a selective multilateralization of benefits stemming from the Argentine–Chilean BIT.

In sum, the Tribunal's decision illustrates that MFN clauses not only can foster equal competition, but might also have an independent multilateralizing effect. Ultimately, the Tribunal augmented the potential of MFN clauses as an instrument of multilateralism by allowing the importation of benefits from third-country BITs independently of the concessions the host State made in the third-country treaty. It allowed the investor to cherry-pick benefits from third-country treaties without taking into account that these treaties constitute a bilateral bargain. The MFN clause in the *Siemens* case, therefore, functioned as a tool of multilateralism that selectively expanded benefits and illustrates a strong decline of the significance of bilateral bargaining under investment treaties.

(c)   Subsequent arbitral jurisprudence

Although the decisions in *Maffezini* v. *Spain* and *Siemens* v. *Argentina* have attracted criticisms in international law scholarship, arbitral jurisprudence, and State practice,[138] several tribunals have affirmed the

---

[137] *Siemens* v. *Argentina*, Decision on Jurisdiction, August 3, 2004, para. 108.
[138] See. e. g., Article 10.4(2), footnote 1, of the Draft of the Central America–United States Free Trade Agreement, January 28, 2004 (stating that the parties agree that the MFN clause they include in their treaty "does not encompass international dispute resolution mechanisms such as those contained in Section C of this Chapter, and therefore could

reasoning and result of these two landmark cases regarding the shortening of waiting periods under Argentine BITs.[139] Furthermore, the criticism of both decisions focuses on the far-reaching consequences the reasoning and rationale of the tribunals might have on what is termed "disruptive treaty-shopping" by foreign investors.[140] Their outcome, by contrast, remains largely uncontested even by tribunals and commentators that take a different and more restrictive approach on the interpretation of MFN clauses in investment treaties.[141] It is thus possible to speak of a generally accepted arbitral jurisprudence holding that MFN clauses are capable of circumventing admissibility-related restrictions, which do not concern the consent to arbitrate, but rather other procedural access restrictions to arbitration, provided, of course, that the clause in question does not expressly exclude such an effect.

A few later decisions do merit attention for reinforcing the multilateralizing effect of MFN clauses and in clarifying points of interpretation. The jurisdictional award in *Gas Natural* v. *Argentina* not only confirmed the result of the decisions in *Maffezini* and *Siemens*,[142] but established a presumption for the interpretation of MFN clauses in investment treaties:

not reasonably lead to a conclusion similar to that of the Maffezini case"). Furthermore Argentina and Panama "exchanged diplomatic notes" after the jurisdictional decision in *Siemens* v. *Argentina* in order to clarify that the MFN clause in the investment treaty between both countries did not extend to dispute resolution provisions; see *National Grid* v. *Argentina*, Decision on Jurisdiction, June 20, 2006, para. 85.

[139] See *Camuzzi* v. *Argentina*, ICSID Case No. ARB/03/2, Decision on Objections to Jurisdiction, May 11, 2005, para. 121; *Gas Natural* v. *Argentina*, Decision on Jurisdiction, June 17, 2005, paras. 26–31; *National Grid* v. *Argentina*, Decision on Jurisdiction, June 20, 2006, paras. 79–94; *Suez and InterAguas* v. *Argentina*, Decision on Jurisdiction, May 16, 2006, paras. 52–66; *AWG* v. *Argentina*, Decision on Jurisdiction, August 3, 2006, paras. 52–56; *Suez and Vivendi* v. *Argentina*, Decision on Jurisdiction, August 3, 2006, paras. 52–68. See also *Camuzzi* v. *Argentina*, ICSID Case No. ARB/03/7, Decisión sobre Jurisdicción, June 10, 2005, para. 28 (noting that Argentina has not objected in this case to extending MFN treatment to circumventing the eighteen-month waiting period in its BIT with the Belgo–Luxemburgian Economic Union).

[140] *Maffezini* v. *Spain*, Decision on Objections to Jurisdiction, January 25, 2000, para. 63; *Salini* v. *Jordan*, Decision on Jurisdiction, November 15, 2004, para. 115; *Plama* v. *Bulgaria*, Decision on Jurisdiction, February 8, 2005, paras. 222–23; *Telenor* v. *Hungary*, Award, September 13, 2006, para. 93; see also Radi (*supra* footnote 88), 18 Eur. J. Int'l L. 757, 771–74 (2007) (criticizing the negative effects of treaty-shopping).

[141] But see *Wintershall* v. *Argentina*, Award, December 8, 2008, paras. 108–97 (disagreeing with the classification of the requirement to pursue local remedies for a specified amount of time as an admissibility-related question that could be circumvented by means of an MFN clause as was done in *Maffezini* and *Siemens*)

[142] *Gas Natural* v. *Argentina*, Decision on Jurisdiction, June 17, 2005, paras. 26–31, 41–49. The Tribunal explicitly affirmed the Decisions on Jurisdiction in *Siemens* and *Maffezini*, *ibid.*, paras. 36–47.

> Unless it appears clearly that the state parties to a BIT or the parties to a particular investment agreement settled on a different method for resolution of disputes that may arise, most-favored-nation provisions in BITs should be understood to be applicable to dispute settlement.[143]

The Tribunal adopted such a presumption because of the importance of the right to have recourse to independent investor-State arbitration. It considered this right to be "perhaps the most crucial element"[144] of the ICSID Convention and the wave of BITs and one that is "universally regarded – by opponents as well as by proponents – as essential to a regime of protection of foreign direct investment."[145] Consequently, the Tribunal considered that doubts in the interpretation of MFN clauses as regards their application to dispute resolution should be resolved in favor of the investor. This further reinforces the potential of MFN clauses as a tool of multilateralism.

Finally, two features stand out in three related cases, *Suez and InterAguas v. Argentina*,[146] *AWG v. Argentina*[147] and *Suez and Vivendi v. Argentina*,[148] that confirmed that MFN treatment generally also applies to circumventing less favorable pre-arbitration requirements. First, the Tribunals emphasized that under the Vienna Convention on the Law of Treaties, the textual interpretation, supplemented by the object and purpose of the treaty in question, had to prevail over those intentions of the parties that did not find textual support.[149] Thus, as the Tribunals emphasized, MFN clauses were not subject to special rules of treaty interpretation under international law, but are to be interpreted objectively like any other treaty provision, whether substantive or procedural. Neither the *ejusdem generis* rule nor the principle of *res inter alios acta* would alter this approach.[150] Thus, no specifically restrictive interpretation of MFN clauses was justified.[151]

---

[143] *Ibid.*, para. 49. Similarly, Radi (*supra* footnote 88), 18 Eur. J. Int'l L. 757, 764–68 (2007).
[144] *Ibid.*, para. 29.   [145] *Ibid.*
[146] *Suez and InterAguas v. Argentina*, Decision on Jurisdiction, May 16, 2006, paras. 52–66.
[147] *AWG v. Argentina*, Decision on Jurisdiction, August 3, 2006, paras. 52–68.
[148] *Suez and Vivendi v. Argentina*, Decision on Jurisdiction, August 3, 2006, paras. 52–68.
[149] *Suez and InterAguas v. Argentina*, Decision on Jurisdiction, May 16, 2006, paras. 53–55; *AWG v. Argentina*, Decision on Jurisdiction, August 3, 2006, paras. 53–57; *Suez and Vivendi v. Argentina*, Decision on Jurisdiction, August 3, 2006, paras. 53–57.
[150] *Suez and InterAguas v. Argentina*, Decision on Jurisdiction, May 16, 2006, paras. 57–58; *AWG v. Argentina*, Decision on Jurisdiction, August 3, 2006, paras. 59–60; *Suez and Vivendi v. Argentina*, Decision on Jurisdiction, August 3, 2006, paras. 59–60.
[151] *Suez and InterAguas v. Argentina*, Decision on Jurisdiction, May 16, 2006, para. 59; *AWG v. Argentina*, Decision on Jurisdiction, August 3, 2006, para. 61; *Suez and Vivendi v. Argentina*, Decision on Jurisdiction, August 3, 2006, para. 61.

Second, as the Tribunals stressed, treatment concerning the scope of MFN clauses did not only comprise substantive investment protection, but equally access to investor-State dispute settlement, as necessary aspects for equal treatment of investors from different home States.[152] In all cases, the Tribunals observed:

> After an analysis of the substantive provisions of the BITs in question, the Tribunal finds no basis for distinguishing dispute settlement matters from any other matters covered by a bilateral investment treaty. From the point of view of the promotion and protection of investments, the stated purposes of the [BITs in question], dispute settlement is as important as other matters governed by the BIT and is an integral part of the investment protection regime that two sovereign states ... have agreed upon.[153]

In affirming the results in *Maffezini* and *Siemens*,[154] these decisions have articulated interpretative principles and economic policies that broaden the reach of MFN clauses to more favorable provisions concerning the admissibility of investor-State arbitration. They particularly stressed the importance of investor-State dispute settlement for the effective protection of foreign investors and thus deny that a valid categorical distinction could be drawn between the grant of substantive rights, to which MFN clauses undoubtedly apply, and their procedural implementation. Accordingly, the Tribunals observed that there is no reason why MFN clauses that are not expressly limited to incorporating more favorable substantive investment protection should be interpreted narrowly. On the contrary, their open wording merits the presumption that they were intended to multilateralize matters of investment protection more generally, including the investor's dispute settlement options.

2 Struggling to base jurisdiction on MFN clauses

While arbitral tribunals have generally accepted the use of MFN clauses to circumvent procedural restrictions on the admissibility of investor-State arbitration, it is debatable as to whether the same reasoning can

---

[152] *Suez and InterAguas* v. *Argentina*, Decision on Jurisdiction, May 16, 2006, para. 55; *AWG* v. *Argentina*, Decision on Jurisdiction, August 3, 2006, para. 55; *Suez and Vivendi* v. *Argentina*, Decision on Jurisdiction, August 3, 2006, para. 55.

[153] *Suez and InterAguas* v. *Argentina*, Decision on Jurisdiction, May 16, 2006, para. 57; *AWG* v. *Argentina*, Decision on Jurisdiction, August 3, 2006, para. 59; *Suez and Vivendi* v. *Argentina*, Decision on Jurisdiction, August 3, 2006, para. 59.

[154] *Suez and InterAguas* v. *Argentina*, Decision on Jurisdiction, May 16, 2006, paras. 60–61; *AWG* v. *Argentina*, Decision on Jurisdiction, August 3, 2006, paras. 62–63; *Suez and Vivendi* v. *Argentina*, Decision on Jurisdiction, August 3, 2006, paras. 62–63.

be applied to broaden the jurisdiction of a treaty-based tribunal. This concerns the question of whether MFN clauses can be used to incorporate more favorable consent to arbitration given by the host State in third-country BITs. It arises, above all, in situations where some BITs of a host State do not contain consent to investor-State dispute resolution at all,[155] while others allow such recourse, where some host State BITs limit recourse to investor-State arbitration to certain causes of action, while others encompass a broader range of causes of action,[156] and where different host State BITs provide for recourse to different dispute settlement fora.[157]

Arbitral practice on this issue has generated diverging decisions. So far, only one decision has applied the reasoning in *Siemens* and *Maffezini* to extend its jurisdictional basis in view of the host State's broader consent to arbitration under its third-country BITs. The majority of cases, by contrast, have refused to accept such an extension. This leads to the seemingly inconsistent result that MFN clauses are applied to some procedural issues but not to others. Yet, the circumvention of pre-arbitration requirements and the incorporation of a host State's broader consent to jurisdiction are distinct issues. While admissibility relates to conditions under which a court or tribunal can render a certain decision, jurisdiction concerns the power that a court or tribunal has over the parties with respect to a specific case.[158] This section, therefore, analyzes the arbitral

---

[155] See, e.g., Treaty between the Federal Republic of Germany and Pakistan for the Promotion and Protection of Investments, signed on November 25, 1959, entered into force on April 28, 1962.

[156] Especially older BITs of formerly socialist countries regularly only provided for recourse to investor-State arbitration for disputes concerning the amount of compensation for expropriation, not however for the violation of other investor rights, such as fair and equitable treatment. See also Schill, *Tearing Down the Great Wall – The New Generation Investment Treaties of the People's Republic of China*, 15 Cardozo J. Int'l & Comp. L. 73, 89–91 (2007) (discussing dispute settlement provisions in older BITs of the PRC).

[157] BITs may allow for a wide range of dispute settlement forums, including ICSID Arbitration, UNCITRAL Arbitration, LCIA Arbitration, SCC Arbitration, and others. Depending on which dispute forum is chosen, the rules on procedure, control by domestic courts, effect and enforcement of awards may differ. See, e.g., on differences between ICSID and UNCITRAL Arbitration, Sacerdoti, *Investment Arbitration under ICSID and UNCITRAL Rules*, 19 ICSID Rev. – For. Inv. L. J. 1 (2004).

[158] See Chukwumerije (*supra* footnote 9), 8 J. World Inv. & Trade 597, 627 (2007). On the distinction between admissibility and jurisdiction see *Interhandel (Switzerland* v. *United States)*, Judgment, March 21, 1959, I.C.J. Reports 1959, p. 26; *Military and Paramilitary Activities in and against Nicaragua (Nicaragua* v. *United States)*, Jurisdiction and Admissibility, Judgment, November 26, 1984, I.C.J. Reports 1984, p. 429, para. 84; *CMS* v. *Argentina*, Decision on Objections to Jurisdiction, July 17, 2003, para. 41; *Enron* v.

jurisprudence denying that MFN clauses can serve as a basis of jurisdiction before arguing, in the following section, that the more expansive application of MFN clauses is backed by more convincing arguments.

(a) *Salini v. Jordan*

In *Salini v. Jordan*, the Tribunal declined to extend its subject-matter jurisdiction to entertain purely contractual claims[159] and rejected the investor's argument that the MFN clause in the Italian–Jordanian BIT would import the host State's broader consent to arbitration from the British–Jordanian and US–Jordanian BITs. These treaties arguably allowed investors to not only bring claims for the violation of the respective BIT, but also contractual claims for the breach of an investor-State contract.[160] The Italian–Jordanian BIT, by contrast, contained a specific provision in Article 9(2) referring contractual disputes to the contractually selected forum.[161]

After an intensive review of prior decisions by international courts and tribunals, the Tribunal declined that the MFN clause in question could incorporate the host State's broader consent to arbitration from the more favorable third-country BITs at issue.[162] It particularly focused on the intentions of the contracting parties to the BIT and

> observe[d] that the circumstances of this case are different [from *Maffezini*]. Indeed, Article 3 of the BIT between Italy and Jordan [i.e. the MFN clause] does not include any provision extending its scope of application to dispute settlement. It does not envisage "all rights or all matters covered by the agreement". Furthermore, the Claimants have submitted nothing from which it *might* be established that the common intention of the Parties was to have the most-favored-nation clause apply to dispute settlement. Quite on the contrary, the intention as expressed in Article 9(2) of the BIT was to exclude from ICSID jurisdiction contractual disputes between an investor and *an* entity of a State Party in order that such

Argentina, Decision on Jurisdiction, January 14, 2004; *SGS v. Philippines*, Decision on Jurisdiction, January 29, 2004, para. 154; *Mondev v. United States*, Award, October 11, 2002, para. 42; *Rompetrol v. Romania*, Decision on Jurisdiction, April 18, 2008, para. 112.

[159] On the differences between contract claims and treaty claims see Cremades and Cairns, *Contract and Treaty Claims and Choice of Forum in Foreign Investment Disputes*, in Horn and Kröll (eds.), *Arbitrating Foreign Investment Disputes*, pp. 325, 327–32 (2004).

[160] *Salini v. Jordan*, Decision on Jurisdiction, November 15, 2004, paras. 102–19.

[161] *Ibid.*, para. 66.

[162] *Ibid.*, para. 119. The MFN clause in question provided that "[b]oth Contracting Parties, within the bounds of their own territory, shall grant investments effected by, and the income accruing to, investors of the Contracting Party no less favourable treatment than that accorded to investments effected by, and income accruing to, its own nationals or investors of Third States" (see *ibid.*, para. 66).

disputes might be settled in accordance with the procedures set forth in the investment agreements.[163]

In addition, the Tribunal referred to the "risk of 'treaty shopping'" as a further argument for denying the application of MFN clauses to incorporate a broader basis of jurisdiction from the host State's third-country BITs.[164]

While the Tribunal, therefore, did not assert that MFN clauses could not, as a matter of principle, broaden the jurisdiction of treaty-based tribunals, it reasoned that such an effect could only be considered if the investor could show and prove that the State parties intended to extend an MFN clause to questions of dispute settlement. For the Tribunal, however, an indication that such an intention was missing was the specific provision in Article 9(2) of the Treaty that relegated contractual disputes to the respective contractual forum.[165]

(b)   *Plama* v. *Bulgaria*

Adopting the approach in *Salini* v. *Jordan*, the Tribunal in *Plama* v. *Bulgaria* also rejected extending its jurisdiction by means of the MFN clause in the Bulgarian–Cypriot BIT.[166] It restricted the claimant to arbitrate disputes concerning the amount of compensation for expropriation as provided under the basic treaty[167] and denied it the right to initiate investor-State arbitration regarding any breach of the treaty as provided in other BITs Bulgaria had concluded. While agreeing with the result, the reasoning and the caveat in the *Maffezini* decision that MFN clauses should not allow for "disruptive treaty-shopping,"[168] the Tribunal diverged from *Maffezini* in basing its analysis on the presumption that the basic treaty must make it sufficiently clear that the MFN clause was intended to apply to issues of investor-State dispute settlement.

---

[163] *Ibid.*, para. 118 (emphasis in the original).   [164] *Ibid.*, para. 115.

[165] *Ibid.*, para. 118.

[166] *Plama* v. *Bulgaria*, Decision on Jurisdiction, February 8, 2005, paras. 183–27. The clause in question provided that "[e]ach Contracting Party shall apply to the investments in its territory by investors of the other Contracting Party a treatment which is not less favourable than that accorded to investments by investors of third states." *Ibid.*, para. 187.

[167] See Article 4, Agreement between the Government of the People's Republic of Bulgaria and the Government of the Republic of Cyprus on Mutual Encouragement and Protection of Investments, signed November 12, 1987, entered into force May 18, 1988, reprinted in *Plama* v. *Bulgaria*, Decision on Jurisdiction, February 8, 2005, para. 26.

[168] *Ibid.*, paras. 222–23.

While the extent of the intention of the contracting parties as regards the interpretation of the MFN clause was only a side issue, the Tribunal emphasized that exercising jurisdiction required the host State's consent to arbitration. After taking note of the widespread emergence of investor-State arbitration, the Tribunal observed:

> [This development] does not take away the basic prerequisite for arbitration: an agreement of the parties to arbitrate. It is a well-established principle, both in domestic and international law, that *such an agreement should be clear and unambiguous*. In the framework of a BIT, the agreement to arbitrate is arrived at by the consent to arbitration that a state gives in advance in respect of investment disputes falling under the BIT, and the acceptance thereof by an investor if the latter so desires.[169]

In determining whether the host State's consent to arbitrate could be incorporated via the Treaty's MFN clause, the Tribunal analogized the situation it faced with one familiar in commercial arbitration, namely, whether non-signatory parties can be bound to arbitrate based on the incorporation of an agreement to arbitrate by reference.[170] The Tribunal held:

> [A] clause reading "*a treatment which is not less favourable than that accorded to investments by investors of third states*" as appears in Article 3(1) of the Bulgaria–Cyprus BIT, cannot be said to be a typical incorporation by reference clause as appearing in ordinary contracts. It creates doubt whether the reference to the other document (in this case the other BITs concluded by Bulgaria) clearly and unambiguously includes a reference to the dispute settlement provisions contained in those BITs.[171]

In the Tribunal's view MFN clauses would usually not fulfil the "clear and unambiguous" requirement to affirm jurisdiction, unless there was specific language to the contrary.

To add support, the Tribunal invoked the difference between substantive rights and their procedural implementation. In this context, it asserted not only a conceptual difference between substance and

---

[169] *Ibid.*, para. 198 (emphasis added).
[170] *Ibid.*, para. 200; see also para. 218. On binding non-signatories see Várady, Barceló and von Mehren, *International Commercial Arbitration*, pp. 197–99 (3rd edn. 2006); Hanotiau, *Complex Arbitrations: Multiparty, Multicontract, Multi-Issue and Class Actions* (2005) (discussing various theories of binding non-signatories); see also Hosking, *The Third Party Non-Signatory's Ability to Compel International Commercial Arbitration: Doing Justice Without Destroying Consent*, 4 Pepp. Disp. Res. L. J. 469 (2004).
[171] *Plama v. Bulgaria*, Decision on Jurisdiction, February 8, 2005, para. 200 (emphasis in the original).

procedure,[172] but also pointed to the principle of separability of arbitration clauses in order to justify the non-application of MFN clauses to dispute settlement provisions.[173] Finally, the Tribunal stressed, in specifically taking issue with the decision in *Siemens v. Argentina*,[174] that an application of MFN clauses to matters of dispute settlement would lead to a peculiar effect:

> [A]n investor has the option to pick and choose provisions from the various BITs. If that were true, a host state which has not specifically agreed thereto can be confronted with a large number of permutations of dispute settlement provisions from the various BITs which it has concluded. Such a chaotic situation – actually counterproductive to harmonization – cannot be the presumed intent of Contracting Parties.[175]

Overall, the Tribunal's primary reason for denying extending its jurisdiction based on the MFN clause in the governing BIT was the requirement that the host State's consent needed to be "clear and unambiguous."[176] *Plama* thus formulated a conceptual approach to the interpretation of MFN clauses in opposition to the jurisprudence in *Maffezini, Gas Natural* and *Suez* and observed:

> [T]he principle with multiple exceptions as stated by the tribunal in the *Maffezini* case should instead be a different principle with one, single exception: an MFN provision in a basic treaty does not incorporate by reference dispute settlement provisions in whole or in part set forth in another treaty, unless the MFN provision in the basic treaty leaves no doubt that the Contracting Parties intended to incorporate them.[177]

(c)   Subsequent jurisprudence

The decision in *Plama v. Bulgaria* was later affirmed by three other tribunals that refined, but mainly repeated, previous arguments. In *Telenor v. Hungary*, the Tribunal faced the issue of whether the claimant could incorporate the host State's broader consent to arbitration under

---

[172] *Ibid.*, para. 209 (pointing out that "[i]t is one thing to add to the treatment provided in one treaty more favorable treatment provided elsewhere. It is quite another thing to replace a procedure specifically negotiated by parties with an entirely different mechanism."). In addition, the Tribunal pointed to subsequent inter-State negotiations between Cyprus and Bulgaria that concerned a revision of the BIT in question. These negotiations had also concerned an explicit expansion of investor-State dispute settlement provisions, a fact that suggested, in the Tribunal's view, that the State parties themselves had never considered an application of the MFN clause in their BIT as applying to investor-State dispute resolution. See *ibid.*, para. 195.

[173] *Ibid.*, para. 212.   [174] *Ibid.*, para. 226.   [175] *Ibid.*, para. 219.
[176] *Ibid.*, para 200.   [177] *Ibid.*, para. 223.

its third-country BITs based on the MFN clause in the Norwegian–Hungarian BIT.[178] The Tribunal "wholeheartedly endorse[d] the analysis and statement of principle furnished by the *Plama* tribunal."[179] It considered the four main arguments against applying MFN clauses as a basis of jurisdiction.[180] First, in its view, the wording of many MFN clauses did not suggest that they applied to dispute settlement; second, treaty-shopping as a consequence of a broad interpretation was undesirable; third, uncertainty and instability would develop because certain limitations of BITs would be overridden; and fourth, the contracting States' practice and their intention would not point to an expansive interpretation. Instead, the Tribunal suggested that the investor either had to have recourse to the host State's domestic courts or ask its home State to grant diplomatic protection.[181]

Similarly, the Tribunal's majority in *Berschader v. Russia* declined to incorporate the Respondent's broader consent to arbitration under third-party BITs based on an MFN clause in the BIT between the Belgo-Luxemburgian Economic Union and Russia. The investor, therefore, remained limited to arbitrating disputes concerning the amount or mode of compensation for expropriation.[182] In interpreting the MFN clause in question, the Tribunal, however, observed that "no general principle exist[ed], according to which arbitration agreements should be construed restrictively."[183] It stressed, however, that "particular care should nevertheless be exercised in ascertaining the *intentions* of the parties with regard to an arbitration agreement which is to be reached by incorporation by reference in an MFN clause."[184] In view of a "fundamental difference [between] material benefits afforded by a BIT, on the one hand, and in relation to dispute resolution clauses, on the other hand"[185] the Tribunal, similar to *Plama*, therefore endorsed the following principle:

---

[178] The MFN clause in question provided that "[i]nvestments made by Investors of one Contracting Party in the territory of the other Contracting Party, as also the returns therefrom, shall be accorded treatment no less favorable than that accorded to investments made by Investors of any third State" (see *Telenor* v. *Hungary*, Award, September 13, 2006, para. 84).

[179] *Ibid.*, para. 90.   [180] *Ibid.*, paras. 91–95.   [181] *Ibid.*, para. 81.

[182] *Berschader* v. *Russia*, Award, April 21, 2006, paras. 151–208. The MFN clause in question provided that "[e]ach Contracting Party guarantees that the most-favored-nation clause be applied to investors of the other Contracting Party in respect of all matters covered by the present Agreement, and in particular its articles 4, 5 and 6" (translation by the author) (see *ibid.*, para. 160).

[183] *Ibid.*, para. 178.   [184] *Ibid.* (emphasis added).   [185] *Ibid.*, para. 179.

[A]n MFN provision in a BIT will only incorporate by reference an arbitration clause from another BIT where the terms of the original BIT
clearly and unambiguously so provide or where it can otherwise be clearly
inferred that this was the intention of the contracting parties.[186]

In a Separate Opinion, Todd Weiler disagreed with the reasoning of
the *Berschader* majority. In contrast to the majority's focus on the parties' intentions,[187] he emphasized the primacy of the textual interpretation of international treaties under Article 31 of the Vienna Convention
on the Law of Treaties. He further criticized that the majority's narrow
application of the MFN clause in question had no basis in the clause and
was incompatible with accepted principles of treaty interpretation.[188] He
concluded:

> The MFN standard is a tried-and-true expression of the international
> economic law principle of non-discrimination. In application, its breadth
> and depth are limited primarily by restrictive language found in the text
> of a treaty (such as general exception clauses and reservation schedules)
> and by the requirement that most favorable treatment be accorded only
> to those who stand in like circumstances. There is simply no reason to
> suppose that – absent some specific treaty language – any given MFN
> provision should be more or less narrowly defined. In other words, MFN
> clauses apply to all aspects of the regulatory environment governed by an
> investment protection treaty, including availability of all means of dis-
> pute settlement.[189]

Finally, the Tribunal in *Wintershall* v. *Argentina* rejected the invest-
or's argument to base its jurisdiction on an MFN clause in the German–
Argentine BIT in order to incorporate the host State's more favorable
consent to arbitration under the US–Argentina BIT.[190] Unlike in *Plama*,
Telenor, or *Berschader*, however, the issue at hand was not whether the
Tribunal could expand its jurisdiction to encompass a broader range of
substantive causes of action, but, much like in *Maffezini*, whether the
investor could circumvent, in view of the quicker access to investor-State
arbitration under the US–Argentine BIT, the requirement to pursue local
remedies in Argentine courts for eighteen months before commencing
international arbitration. Yet, the Tribunal in *Wintershall* qualified this
requirement, as a condition to the host State's consent to arbitration,

---

[186] *Ibid.*, paras. 179–82, quotation at para. 181
[187] *Ibid.*, Separate Opinion by T. Weiler, para. 4.
[188] *Ibid.*, Separate Opinion by T. Weiler, para. 19.
[189] *Ibid.*, Separate Opinion by T. Weiler, para. 20.
[190] *Wintershall* v. *Argentina*, Award, December 8, 2008, paras. 158–97.

not as an admissibility-related obstacle,[191] and consequently adopted an approach mirroring *Plama*'s.

Unlike the Tribunal in *Plama*, however, the Tribunal posited that the interpretation of international treaties under the Vienna Convention on the Law of Treaties had to start with "the elucidation of the meaning of the text, not an independent investigation into the intention of the parties from other sources"[192] and, therefore, left "no room for any presumed intention of the Contracting Parties to a bilateral treaty."[193] Second, it stressed that "international courts and tribunals can exercise jurisdiction over a State only with its consent"[194] and added that "[a] *presumed* consent is not regarded as sufficient, because any restriction upon the independence of a State (not agreed to) cannot be presumed by courts."[195]

On this basis, the Tribunal criticized the interpretative approach to MFN clauses in *Maffezini*, and in cases that endorsed the same approach, which, in its view "proceed[s] on a *presumption*: that dispute-resolution provisions do invariably fall within the scope of an MFN provision."[196] In view of the requirement that actual consent to arbitration is crucial, the Tribunal required that contracting parties, if they intended MFN clauses to serve as a basis of jurisdiction, had to "cho[ose] language in the MFN clause showing an intention to do this."[197] This could only be the case, if the MFN clause "expressly so provide[s]."[198] In line with *Plama*, the Tribunal therefore considered:

> [O]rdinarily and without more, the prospect of an investor selecting at will from an assorted variety of options provided in other treaties negotiated with other parties under different circumstances, dislodges the dispute resolution provision in the basic treaty itself – *unless of course the MFN Clause in the basic treaty clearly and unambiguously indicates that it should be so interpreted.*[199]

Despite certain nuances the decisions in *Telenor, Berschader,* and *Wintershall*, therefore, all accepted the principled approach of the jurisdictional award in *Plama*, namely that MFN clauses could not incorporate the host State's broader consent to arbitration under its third-country BITs.

---

[191] *Ibid.*, paras. 108–57. [192] *Ibid.*, para. 78. [193] *Ibid.*, para. 88.
[194] *Ibid.*, para. 160(3).
[195] *Ibid.* (emphasis in the original) (citing *The Case of the S.S. "Lotus" (France* v. *Turkey),* Judgment, September 7, 1927, P.C.I.J. Series A, No. 10 (1927), p. 18).
[196] *Wintershall* v. *Argentina,* Award, December 8, 2008, para. 179(i) (emphasis in the original).
[197] *Ibid.*, para. 168 (citing *Telenor* v. *Hungary,* Award, September 13, 2006, para. 92).
[198] *Wintershall* v. *Argentina,* Award, December 8, 2008, para. 187.
[199] *Ibid.*, para. 167 (emphasis in the original).

(d) Acceptance of basing jurisdiction on
MFN clauses: *RosInvest Co* v. *Russia*

In stark contrast to the preceding cases, the recent decision in *RosInvest Co* v. *Russia* accepted the multilateralization of the host State's broader consent to arbitration give under a third-country BIT by means of an MFN clause.[200] Faced with an arbitration clause in the basic treaty that was limited to disputes concerning the amount or payment of compensation for expropriation,[201] the Tribunal also asserted jurisdiction in regard to disputes concerning other causes of actions based on the operation of the MFN clause in the BIT between the United Kingdom and the USSR.[202] The MFN clause in question provided:

> (1) Neither Contracting Party shall in its territory subject investments or returns of investors of the other Contracting Party to treatment less favourable than that which it accords to investments or returns of investors of any third State.
>
> (2) Neither Contracting Party shall in its territory subject investors of the other Contracting Party, as regards their management, maintenance, use, enjoyment or disposal of their investments, to treatment less favourable than that which it accords to investors of any third State.[203]

In interpreting this provision and in stressing the crucial importance Article 31 of the Vienna Convention on the Law of Treaties attaches to the clause's wording, the Tribunal first decided that it could not incorporate Russia's broader consent under the Denmark–Russia BIT by means of Article 3(1), UK–Russia BIT because, in its view, the possibility of recourse to international arbitration as compared with dispute settlement in domestic courts "does not directly affect the 'investment.'"[204] In a second step, however, the Tribunal considered that broader consent vis-à-vis third-country nationals to arbitrate disputes about the lawfulness of expropriations related to the claimant's use and enjoyment of its investment and could, therefore, be incorporated as more favorable treatment afforded to investors under Article 3(2), UK–Russia BIT.[205] Furthermore, the Tribunal noted that if the effect of MFN clauses was to extend the protection offered by an investment treaty:

---

[200] *RosInvest Co* v. *Russia*, Award on Jurisdiction, October 2007, paras. 124–39.

[201] See *ibid.*, paras. 105–23.

[202] The BIT applied in *RosInvest Co* v. *Russia* was the BIT between the UK and the USSR, to which Russia, as a successor State to the USSR, is bound.

[203] For the text of Article 3, UK–Russia BIT see *ibid.*, paras. 23 and 126.

[204] *Ibid.*, para. 128.   [205] *Ibid.*, para. 130.

by transferring the protection accorded in another treaty ... the Tribunal sees no reason not to accept it in the context of procedural clauses such as arbitration clauses. Quite on the contrary, it could be argued that, if it applies to substantive protection, then it should apply even more to "only" procedural protection.[206]

Finally, the Tribunal took the existence of explicit exceptions to MFN treatment in Article 7 of the BIT as an indication that the MFN clause was understood broadly by the contracting parties and thus included all subject matters of the basic treaty, unless explicitly excluded.[207]

The Tribunal in *RosInvest Co* v. *Russia*, therefore, accepted that MFN clauses could, in connection with broader consent to arbitration in third-country BITs, form the basis of jurisdiction of an investment tribunal under the basic treaty[208] and thereby accorded a comprehensive multi-lateralizing effect to MFN clauses as regards substantive investment protection, as well as investor-State arbitration. It thereby contradicted the thus far prevailing approach of the tribunals in *Salini, Plama, Telenor, Berschader,* and *Wintershall* to decline the extension of their jurisdiction on the basis of MFN treatment. Overall, the current situation in the practice of arbitral decision-making supports the conclusion that the procedural protection of foreign investors is only partly multilateralized by means of MFN treatment, even though tendencies are visible also to apply MFN clauses in order to serve as a basis of jurisdiction.

D   Multilateralizing arbitral jurisdiction

As discussed in the previous section, arbitral jurisprudence concerning the application of MFN clauses is not consistent on whether matters of dispute resolution can be incorporated as more favorable treatment from third-country BITs. While one line of jurisprudence supports a broad application of MFN clauses, such as the decisions in *Maffezini*,

---

[206] *Ibid.,* paras. 131–32.   [207] *Ibid.,* para. 135.

[208] See also *Yaung Chi Oo Trading* v. *Myanmar,* Final Award, March 31, 2003, para. 83 (declining jurisdiction under the basic treaty's MFN clause in connection with broader consent to arbitration in the host State's third-country BITs by pointing out that "if a party wishes to rely on the jurisdictional possibility affirmed by an ICSID Tribunal in *Maffezini* v. *Kingdom of Spain,* it would normally be incumbent on it to rely on that possibility, and on the other treaty in question, at the time of instituting the arbitral proceedings. That was not done in this case. In any event, in the Tribunal's view there is no indication that there would be arbitral jurisdiction on these facts under any BIT entered into by Myanmar which was in force at the relevant time. Correspondingly, there is no possible basis for such jurisdiction under Article 8 of the Framework Agreement [i.e., the basic treaty's MFN clause].").

Siemens, Gas Natural, RosInvest Co, and others, another line of decisions, namely the ones in *Salini* and *Plama*, takes a more restrictive stance. Notwithstanding the current split, MFN clauses need to be understood broadly as multilateralizing not only substantive investor rights and applying to admissibility-related issues, but equally multilateralizing arbitral jurisdiction by incorporating the host State's broader consent from its third-country investment treaties.

The broad wording of the MFN clauses, their economic rationale of establishing equal competition, the object and purpose of BITs to promote and protect foreign investment, and the positive impact of a broad interpretation of MFN treatment on the compliance of host States with their substantive investment treaty obligations support a broad application of MFN clauses. By contrast, the arguments against such an extension of MFN clauses, in particular by the Tribunal in *Plama*, are problematic, in particular because they disregard accepted methods of interpretation of BITs as international treaties and, instead, import concepts from commercial arbitration into the BIT context, even though such analogies are not tenable. Therefore, the reasoning in *Maffezini* and *Siemens* and their underlying rationale should be extended to matters of jurisdiction, as done by the Tribunal in *RosInvest Co*, while the restrictive approach in *Salini, Plama et al.* should be discarded.

1   *MFN clauses and treaty interpretation*

Whether MFN clauses can be applied to incorporate the host State's broader consent to arbitration is first and foremost a question of interpretation of the specific MFN clause in the basic treaty. Since the clauses may differ, their wording deserves a close look. Several scenarios are possible. When an MFN clause expressly applies to dispute settlement provisions, or is expressly limited to substantive investor rights, their interpretation is straightforward. Difficulties arise, however, when an MFN clause is worded openly, that is, without explicitly excluding or including matters of dispute resolution or consent to arbitration. Notably, such openly worded MFN clauses are those most frequently found in investment treaties.

While aimed at ascertaining the common intention of the contracting parties, the rules of treaty interpretation under Articles 31 and 32 of the Vienna Convention on the Law of Treaties attribute preponderant weight to the "ordinary meaning" of a treaty provision in its context and in light of its object and purpose, instead of engaging in an endeavor to second-guess the parties' mutual intentions.[209] Thus, openly worded MFN clauses, including those examined in *Plama*, *Salini*, *Telenor*, *Berschader*, and *Wintershall*, are usually broad enough to apply not only to more favorable substantive treatment but also to more favorable procedural rights and broader consent to arbitration.

Their ordinary meaning, therefore, allows their application to investor-State dispute settlement provisions. If their scope of application covers "all matters," or simply refers to "treatment of investors" or "treatment of investments" by the host State, their ordinary meaning can be understood, without any terminological contortion, as incorporating more favorable dispute settlement provisions from the host State's third-country BITs, including broader consent to arbitration.[210] Furthermore, the methods of interpretation applicable to MFN clauses remain the same independent of whether the incorporation of substantive investor rights or procedural matters is at issue.[211] The plain wording of such clauses therefore does not mandate a restrictive application.

In light of the existence of BITs that expressly apply MFN treatment to questions of investor-State dispute settlement, it also makes little sense to draw an *e contrario* argument to the effect that MFN clauses ordinarily

---

[209] See Fitzmaurice, *The Law and Procedure of the International Court of Justice*, 28 Brit. Ybk. Int'l L. 1, 7–8 (1951); Fitzmaurice, *The Law and Procedure of the International Court of Justice 1951–4*, 33 Brit. Ybk. Int'l L. 203 (1957); McNair (*supra* footnote 54), pp. 364–82 (1961); Reuter, *Introduction to the Law of Treaties*, p. 96 (2nd edn. 1995) (observing that "[t]he primacy of the text, especially in international law, is the cardinal rule of any interpretation"); I. Sinclair, *The Vienna Convention on the Law of Treaties*, pp. 114 *et seq.* (2nd edn. 1984); Sorel, *Article 31*, in Corten and Klein (eds.), *Les Conventions de Vienne sur le droit des traités*, vol. II, paras. 29 *et seq.* (2006) (stating that "[l]a Convention de Vienne donne priorité à l'interprétation textuelle" – at para. 48); O'Connell, *International Law*, vol. I, pp. 251 *et seq.* (2nd edn. 1970); Schreuer, *The Interpretation of Treaties by Domestic Courts*, 45 Brit. Ybk. Int'l L. 255, 274 (1971); Jacobs, *Varieties of Approach to Treaty Interpretation*, 18 Int'l & Comp. L. Q. 318, 325 *et seq.* (1969); I. Sinclair, *Vienna Convention on the Law of Treaties*, 19 Int'l & Comp. L. Q. 47, 65 (1970); see also *Siemens* v. *Argentina*, Decision on Jurisdiction, August 3, 2004, para. 106. This also becomes clear from the interplay between Article 31(1), Vienna Convention on the Law of Treaties, that provides that "[a] treaty shall be interpreted in good faith in accordance with the ordinary meaning to be given to the terms of the treaty in their context and in the light of its object and purpose," and Article 31(4), Vienna Convention on the Law of Treaties, that stipulates that "[a] special meaning shall be given to a term if it is established that the parties so intended."

[210] See also Radi (*supra* footnote 88), 18 Eur. J. Int'l L. 757, 764–68 (2007).

[211] See *Suez and InterAguas* v. *Argentina*, Decision on Jurisdiction, May 16, 2006, paras. 59 and 64; *AWG* v. *Argentina*, Decision on Jurisdiction, August 3, 2006, paras. 61 and 66; *Suez and Vivendi* v. *Argentina*, Decision on Jurisdiction, August 3, 2006, paras. 61 and 66 (pointing out that "dispute resolution provisions are subject to interpretation like any other provisions of a treaty, neither more restrictive nor more liberal").

do not apply to matters of procedure and jurisdiction.[212] This argument disregards that the inclusion of a reference to dispute settlement in an MFN clause cannot only have the effect of extending the clause's scope of application, but can equally have a declaratory or clarifying effect.[213] Thus, one cannot infer from other States' express inclusion of dispute settlement among the subject matters of MFN clauses that such inclusion is in fact necessary. On the contrary, it is limitations of MFN clauses, as State practice shows, that are usually expressly mentioned.[214] Hence, whenever States wanted to restrict the scope of application of MFN clauses, they explicitly did so.

Tribunals that read MFN clauses restrictively, by contrast, zoom in on the presumed intentions of the contracting parties by asking whether, at the time of conclusion, the State parties positively intended the application of an MFN clause to import more favorable dispute settlement provisions.[215] This emphasis on the subjective intention of States with regard to the interpretation of international treaties, however, is questionable under the approach to treaty interpretation mandated by Articles 31 and 32 of the Vienna Convention. Thus, as the Tribunal in *Wintershall v. Argentina* stressed, the Vienna Convention has to start from "the elucidation of the meaning of the text, not an independent investigation into the intention of the parties from other sources"[216] and, therefore, leaves "no room for any presumed intention of the contracting parties to a bilateral treaty."[217]

Furthermore, arguments that require investors to show that the State parties intended a broad application of MFN treatment to dispute

[212] See *Plama v. Bulgaria*, Decision on Jurisdiction, February 8, 2005, para. 204.

[213] In fact, Article 3(3), UK Model BIT expressly stipulates that MFN treatment applies, "for the avoidance of doubt," to all provisions of the Model BIT, including investor-State dispute settlement. See the 2005 UK Model BIT, reprinted in McLachlan, Shore and Weiniger, *International Investment Arbitration*, p. 379 (2007).

[214] See *Gas Natural v. Argentina*, Decision on Jurisdiction, June 17, 2005, para. 30; *RosInvest Co v. Russia*, Award on Jurisdiction, October 2007, para. 135. This is also reinforced in view of the strictly limited exceptions to MFN clauses recognized by customary international law as implied restrictions. *Cf. supra* footnotes 90 and 96.

[215] See, for example, *Plama v. Bulgaria*, Decision on Jurisdiction, February 8, 2005, paras. 198–224; *Salini v. Jordan*, Decision on Jurisdiction, November 15, 2004, para. 118; *Berschader v. Russia*, Award, April 21, 2006, para. 175; *Telenor v. Hungary*, Award, September 13, 2006, para. 92. This also holds true as regards the decision in *Wintershall v. Argentina*. Even though the Tribunal in that case stressed the objective method of treaty interpretation, it nevertheless considered that the intention of the State was decisive as regards the question of whether it has given consent to arbitration. See, for example, *Wintershall v. Argentina*, Award, December 8, 2008, para. 168.

[216] *Wintershall v. Argentina*, Award, December 8, 2008, para. 78.

[217] *Ibid.*, para. 88.

settlement apply a doubtful concept of the burden of proof, when in fact determining whether an MFN clause can import more favorable consent to arbitration is a question of jurisdiction and thus of interpreting the text of the treaty in question, not a question of proving the intention of the State parties. Accordingly, international courts have frequently stressed that issues of jurisdiction have to be observed by courts *ex officio*.[218] Equally, the ICJ stressed in *Border and Transborder Armed Actions* that "[t]he existence of jurisdiction of the Court in a given case is however not a question of fact, but a question of law."[219] As a consequence, as regards interpretative methodology, it is more convincing to take openly worded MFN clauses at face value and interpret them as encompassing more favorable provisions on dispute settlement, including the host State's consent to arbitration.

2 International jurisprudence supporting a broad application of MFN clauses

The approach focusing on the plain meaning of MFN clauses and concluding on this basis that the clauses can serve as a basis of jurisdiction has also received support in the jurisprudence beyond the investment treaty arbitration context. Thus, numerous jurisprudence from national and international courts and tribunals supports that MFN clauses can incorporate more favorable dispute resolution provisions and thus can serve as a basis of jurisdiction.[220]

For example, in *Rights of Nationals of the United States of America in Morocco* the ICJ was to interpret a provision in a treaty between the United States and Morocco that provided for MFN treatment with respect to commerce in Morocco.[221] Under third-country treaties with Great Britain,

---

[218] See *Rights of Minorities in Upper Silesia (Minority Schools) (Germany v. Poland)*, Judgment, April 26, 1928, P.C.I.J. Series A, No. 15 (1928), p. 23.

[219] *Border and Transborder Armed Actions (Nicaragua v. Honduras)*, Judgment, December 20, 1988, I.C.J. Reports 1988, p. 76, para. 16. This was confirmed in *Fisheries Jurisdiction (Spain v. Canada)*, Judgment, December 4, 1998, I.C.J. Reports 1998, pp. 450–51, para. 38.

[220] On this and the following see also Ben Hamida (*supra* footnote 98), 134 J.D.I. 1127, 1151–59 (2007).

[221] See *Rights of Nationals of the United States of America in Morocco (France v. United States)*, Judgment, August 27, 1952, I.C.J. Reports 1952, p. 190 (Article 14 of the Treaty provided: "The commerce with the United States shall be on the same footing as is the commerce with Spain, or as that with the most favored nation for the time being; and their citizens shall be respected and esteemed, and have full liberty to pass and repass our country and seaports whenever they please, without interruption." Article 24 provided in part that "it is further declared, that whatever indulgence, in trade or otherwise,

Morocco had, *inter alia*, granted "consular jurisdiction in all cases, civil and criminal, when British nationals were defendants."[222] Therefore, the ICJ concluded that "[a]ccordingly, the United States acquired by virtue of the most-favoured-nation clauses, civil and criminal consular jurisdiction in all cases in which United States nationals were defendants."[223] Even though MFN treatment in this context referred to the grant of jurisdiction to the authorities of a foreign State, the ICJ's reasoning indicates no general prohibition against extending MFN clauses to cover matters of jurisdiction.[224] Furthermore, the ICJ's decision in this regard is in line with a significant number of decisions by domestic courts, including the highest courts in France, Italy, Argentina, and the United States, that all accepted that consular jurisdiction could be granted by operation of MFN clauses contained in commercial treaties.[225]

Similarly, a Commission of Arbitration in the *Ambatielos Claim* affirmed that the MFN clause in a treaty between the United Kingdom and Greece could incorporate more favorable procedural treatment accorded to third-party nationals in domestic court proceedings. In the case at hand, the Greek Government alleged that the non-production of evidence by the United Kingdom as a party to court proceedings before her own courts for breach of a contract for the sale of ships between a Greek national and a UK Government Ministry, as well as threats to prosecute the Greek national for tax claims in order to hinder him in initiating judicial proceedings against the government, violated international law. In particular, Greece argued that based on MFN treatment her nationals would have been entitled to more favorable treatment accorded under third-party treaties the United Kingdom had concluded.[226] In accepting this proposition, the Commission observed:

> It is true that "the administration of justice", when viewed in isolation, is a subject-matter other than "commerce and navigation", but this is not necessarily so when it is viewed in connection with the protection of the rights of traders. Protection of the rights of traders naturally finds a place among the matters dealt with by Treaties of commerce and navigation.

---

shall be granted to any of the Christian powers, the citizens of the United States shall be equally entitled to them.").

[222] *Ibid.*   [223] *Ibid.*

[224] *Cf. Siemens v. Argentina*, Decision on Jurisdiction, August 3, 2004, para. 99.

[225] Ben Hamida (*supra* footnote 98), 134 J.D.I. 1127, 1151–53 (2007). Similarly, domestic courts have accepted the application of MFN clauses in respect of other matters relating to procedure and jurisdiction. See *ibid.*, at 1153–54.

[226] *Cf. Ambatielos Claim (Greece v. United Kingdom)*, U.N.R.I.A.A., vol. XII, p. 101.

> Therefore it cannot be said that the administration of justice, in so far as it is concerned with the protection of these rights, must necessarily be excluded from the field of application of the most-favoured-nation clause, when the latter includes "all matters relating to commerce and navigation".[227]

Although the Commission ultimately found that no better treatment had been accorded to other foreign traders in third-country treaties,[228] it held that an MFN clause could apply with respect to access to courts and the procedure they apply even without an explicit reference to cover such issues in the clause in question. While the issue concerned the treatment of foreign nationals in domestic courts, the decision confirms that the application of MFN clauses to matters of dispute settlement holds true as a general matter.[229]

Finally, the dispute resolution mechanism under the GATT offers an illustrative example of how differences in dispute settlement procedures were considered to constitute a violation of the principle of non-discrimination. Although the decision in *United States – Section 337* concerned a violation of the national treatment standard under Article III(4), GATT, because the United States provided different dispute settlement procedures in patent violations cases based on the national origin of a product, the rationale of the decision is equally applicable to MFN treatment. The Panel stated:

> The Panel first addressed the issue of whether only substantive laws, regulations and requirements or also procedural laws, regulations and requirements can be regarded as "affecting" the internal sale of imported products ... The Panel noted that the text of Article III:4 makes no distinction between substantive and procedural laws, regulations or requirements and it was not aware of anything in the drafting history that suggests that such a distinction should be made ... In the Panel's view, enforcement procedures cannot be separated from the substantive provisions they serve to enforce. If the procedural provisions of internal

---

[227] *Ibid.*, p. 107.   [228] *Ibid.*, pp. 108–9.

[229] *Cf. Maffezini*, Decision on Objections to Jurisdiction, January 25, 2000, para. 50. Likewise, the decision in *Suez and InterAguas* v. *Argentina* uttered fundamental criticism with respect to the reasoning in *Plama*, without, however, passing on to evaluating the decision's result. See *Suez and InterAguas* v. *Argentina*, Decision on Jurisdiction, May 16, 2006, para. 63; parallel *Suez and Vivendi* v. *Argentina*, Decision on Jurisdiction, August 3, 2006, para. 65: "Having duly considered the reasons set forth in the *Plama* decision, this Tribunal comes to the conclusion that, *whatever its merits*, it is in any event clearly distinguishable from the present case on a number of grounds" (emphasis added).

law were not covered by Article III:4, contracting parties could escape the
national treatment standard by enforcing substantive law, itself meeting
the national treatment standard, through procedures less favourable to
imported products than to like products of national origin.[230]

In sum, the jurisprudence of national and international courts and tribunals therefore supports the argument that MFN clauses generally have
a broad scope of application and encompass aspects of dispute settlement
and jurisdiction under more favorable third-party treaties. Consequently,
there is also no reason to approach the application and interpretation of
MFN clauses restrictively and limit the clauses to the incorporation of
more favorable substantive rights.

3   The object and purpose of investment treaties

The policies underlying investment treaties further justify the broadening of MFN treatment to incorporate broader consent to investor-State
dispute settlement. Their object and purpose consist in promoting and
protecting foreign investment, often with a particular focus on direct-
ing investment flows into developing countries. A crucial factor for this
objective is the protection of foreign investors by ensuring the stability
and predictability of their investment activities and their investment-
related rights. The enforcement of substantive BIT obligations helps to
transform mere statements of political intent into enforceable rights.
Giving foreign investors recourse to investor-State arbitration, therefore, adds to promoting foreign investment flows and to achieving the
purpose of investment treaties. It would thus be surprising if States,
without providing for an explicit exception, had understood MFN
clauses as inapplicable to that part of investment treaties that gives
muscle to the treaties' purpose. The object and purpose of investment
treaties therefore militates for incorporating more favorable dispute
settlement provisions by means of MFN clauses.

4   Equal competition and investor-State dispute settlement

Furthermore, the rationale of MFN clauses to create a level playing
field for foreign investors independent of their nationality militates for
the more expansive application. Applying MFN clauses to questions of

---

[230] *United States – Section 337 of the Tariff Act of 1930*, GATT Panel Report, November 7,
1989, para. 5.10.

investor-State dispute settlement, including admissibility and jurisdiction, helps to level the playing field for foreign investors because it makes no difference whether two foreign investors face differences as regards their substantive or procedural protection. Thus, an investor who has easier or broader recourse to arbitration has a competitive advantage over other investors who cannot initiate investor-State arbitration on comparable terms. Absent other equally effective means of enforcing BIT obligations (e.g., before domestic courts), the latter's transaction costs, here in the form of enforcement costs, will be higher. If the worst comes to the worst the investor will have to bear the full costs resulting from the host State's violation of BIT obligations, while competitors covered by a different BIT can enforce such obligations. Consequently, investors who cannot enforce rights under their BIT cannot offer services and goods at the same price as investors with broader recourse options to investor-State arbitration.

Thus, substantive investment protection is inseparable from its procedural implementation, which is essential to the conferral of a right.[231] Moreover, it is even questionable whether access to arbitration is a matter of procedural law. Instead, having recourse to law enforcement mechanisms also can be understood as a substantive right of an investor protected under an investment treaty.[232] The investor's right to initiate arbitration, therefore, should not be separated from other substantive treatment standards as regards the operation of an MFN clause. Instead, the broader consent to arbitration in third-country BITs can be construed as an offer by the host State that, although under the more favorable third-country treaty it only extends to investors covered by that treaty, can also be accepted by investors under the basic treaty because the MFN clause in that BIT has the effect of broadening the scope of offerees *ratione personae*. Consent to arbitration given under the more favorable third-country BIT, therefore, extends, by means of the MFN clause in the basic treaty, to the investors covered under that treaty.

Using MFN clauses to incorporate the host State's broader consent to arbitrate under third-country BITs also dampens externalities arising

---

[231] See *Siemens* v. *Argentina*, Decision on Jurisdiction, August 3, 2004, para. 102; *Gas Natural* v. *Argentina*, Decision on Jurisdiction, June 17, 2005, para. 29; *RosInvest Co* v. *Russia*, Award on Jurisdiction, October 2007, para. 132; see also Radi (*supra* footnote 88), 18 Eur. J. Int'l L. 757, 763–64 (2007).

[232] *Cf. Gas Natural* v. *Argentina*, Decision on Jurisdiction, June 17, 2005, para. 29; *RosInvest Co* v. *Russia*, Award on Jurisdiction, October 2007, para. 132; similarly, *Ambatielos Claim (Greece* v. *United Kingdom)*, U.N.R.I.A.A., vol. XII, p. 107.

from imperfect enforcement of the host State's BIT obligations. Instead, being able to make host States comply results in States seeing the full consequences of a potential breach of an investment treaty. A broad construction of MFN treatment, therefore, increases the host State's need to internalize the costs of violating an investment treaty. This will limit governments to breach investment treaties only in cases where the advantage they derive from the breach outweighs the full costs to potentially affected foreign investors. Denying MFN treatment in the context of investor-State dispute settlement, on the other hand, would enable a government to shift consequences of its breach selectively to procedurally less protected investors. An interpretation of MFN clauses that encompasses more favorable dispute settlement provisions thus requires host States to internalize the costs stemming from a violation of investment treaties with respect to investors from any home State.

5   Jurisdiction and compliance with treaty obligations

The internalization of costs due to a broader jurisdictional basis also has additional benefits with regard to the compliance of host States with their obligations under investment treaties. The prospect of being ordered by an arbitral tribunal to pay damages for the violation of BIT obligations not only increases the costs of a violation, but should also lead to fewer violations of investment treaties in the future.[233] Broader jurisdiction of investment tribunals thus goes along with an additional compliance pull regarding the primary BIT obligations. A broad interpretation of MFN clauses, in particular with respect to jurisdictional issues, therefore, makes BITs more efficient and effective in governing international investment relations.

Construing MFN treatment as broadening the jurisdiction of investment tribunals also accords with the structure of international law and the duty it imposes on States to comply with international obligations. In fact, compliance with international law in general and international treaties in particular is central to the fabric of international law. It not only follows from the principle of *pacta sunt servanda* that governs the law of international treaties,[234] but also informs the object and purpose of State responsibility. Thus, resuming compliance with its primary

---

[233] *Cf.* Hylton, *Fee Shifting and Incentives to Comply with the Law*, 46 Vand. L. Rev. 1069 (1993).
[234] See Article 26, Vienna Convention on the Law of Treaties.

obligations is the principal duty of a State that has committed an internationally wrongful act.[235] In view of the general interest of States to effectuate compliance with international law, MFN clauses should be interpreted as broadening the basis of jurisdiction of investment tribunals as investor-State arbitration does not only help to settle disputes, but also functions as a mechanism to make States comply with their investment treaty obligations.

However, if the basic treaty does not provide for investor-State dispute settlement at all, the situation will be different. In such cases, the interpretation of an MFN clause in the treaty will more likely than not bar the incorporation of the consent to dispute settlement from third-party BITs, since it will be difficult to establish that the MFN clause covered issues of dispute settlement, as part of its subject matter. That the subject matter of the basic treaty does not encompass matters of dispute settlement militates against the presumption that the subject matter of the MFN clause is broad enough so as to cover matters that are outside the scope of application of the basic treaty. Instead, under the *ejusdem generis* rule, the basic treaty's MFN clause usually would be limited to importing more favorable substantive investment protection. Likewise, if the basic treaty does not contain provisions on investor-State dispute settlement at all, one would not expect the contracting parties to limit the scope of application of an MFN clause accordingly. By contrast, treaties allowing for limited recourse to investor-State arbitration already account for the possibility that investors are entitled to enforce obligations contained in an investment treaty. Broader consent to arbitration in such cases thus directly relates to the type of protection of foreign investors that was already envisaged in the basic treaty.

Finally, State practice suggests that an MFN clause included in a treaty that does not provide for investor-State dispute settlement at all cannot incorporate more favorable dispute settlement mechanisms that a State has consented to under third-party treaties. Thus, under Article II(1), GATS, which enshrines MFN treatment for the trade in services, the issue arose whether that Article could introduce into the GATS more favorable rights from third-country investment treaties, in particular investor-State dispute settlement mechanisms, and thus extend any more favorable treatment than a State extended under its BITs to all GATS signatories.[236] While

---

[235] See Article 29, ILC Articles on State Responsibility.
[236] On this and the following see Ben Hamida (*supra* footnote 98), 134 J.D.I. 1127, 1159–62 (2007); Ben Hamida, in Weiler (ed.) (*supra* footnote 98), pp. 242–96.

three States have in fact excluded, in exemptions they made to Article II, GATS, the incorporation of investor-State dispute settlement provisions established under investment treaties, the vast majority of States did not adopt any position on such an effect of the MFN clause in GATS. Although it is arguable that, by accepting Article II(1), GATS, all these States agreed to have their consent to investor-State arbitration incorporated from third-country BITs into the GATS, it is more convincing to conclude that these States believed from the outset that Article II(1), GATS would not have such an effect, since investor-State dispute settlement has to be regarded as clearly outside the scope of application of GATS. It, therefore, is not covered by the subject matter of that provision.

6   Must the State's consent to arbitrate be "clear and unambiguous"?

The main argument against incorporating more favorable consent to investor-State arbitration based on MFN treatment is that consent to arbitration must be, similar to the position adopted by domestic courts concerning commercial agreements to arbitrate, "clear and unambiguous."[237] Thus, the US Supreme Court, for example, considers in a long-standing jurisprudence that consent to commercial arbitration has to be "clear and unmistakable."[238] This requirement is, however, not germane to dispute settlement under public international law. Although States under public international law must equally consent to arbitration in order to come under the jurisdiction of an arbitral tribunal, the forms in which such consent can be expressed cannot be measured by the standards that are applicable in the commercial arbitration context. Instead, analogies to commercial arbitration are questionable.

First, if the argument that consent to arbitration had to be "clear and unambiguous" was a resounding requirement of State consent to

---

[237] See *Plama* v. *Bulgaria*, Decision on Jurisdiction, February 8, 2005, paras. 198, 199, 200, 204, 212, 218, 223; *Wintershall* v. *Argentina*, Award, December 8, 2008, paras. 167, 187–189; *Telenor* v. *Hungary*, Award, September 13, 2006, para. 90; *Berschader* v. *Russia*, Award, April 21, 2006, para. 181.

[238] See *First Options of Chicago, Inc.* v. *Kaplan et al.*, 514 U.S. 938, 944 (1995). Courts in the United Kingdom "have struggled with conflicting views on whether or not there must be 'distinct and specific words' specifically referring to the arbitration clause in order for it to be incorporated by reference:" see Hosking, *Non-Signatories and International Arbitration in the United States*, 20 Arb. Int'l 289, 292 (2004). See also *Plama* v. *Bulgaria*, Decision on Jurisdiction, February 8, 2005, para. 198 (stating that this requirement "is a well-established principle, both in domestic and international law").

jurisdiction under international law in general, international courts and tribunals would be required to interpret jurisdictional requirements restrictively and resolve doubts in favor of State sovereignty. They would always have to decline jurisdiction in cases of ambiguity or a lack of clarity. However, neither investment treaty arbitration nor international law dispute resolution more generally show this to be the case. Thus, the Tribunal in *Amco Asia* v. *Indonesia* emphasized:

> [L]ike any other conventions, a convention to arbitrate is not to be construed *restrictively*, nor, as a matter of fact, *broadly* or *liberally*. It is to be construed in a way which leads to find out and to respect the common will of the parties: such a method of interpretation is but the application of the fundamental principle *pacta sunt servanda*, a principle common, indeed, to all systems of internal law and to international law.[239]

Following *Amco Asia*, the Tribunal in *Mondev* v. *United States* held that matters of jurisdiction had to be interpreted neither extensively nor restrictively, but objectively according to the accepted rules of treaty interpretation. It stressed that:

> there is no principle either of extensive or restrictive interpretation of jurisdictional provisions in treaties. In the end the question is what the relevant provisions mean, interpreted in accordance with the applicable rules of interpretation of treaties.[240]

Furthermore, the Permanent Court of International Justice already acknowledged that "there is no rule laying down that consent [to jurisdiction] must take the form of an express declaration rather than that of acts conclusively establishing it."[241] Likewise, the ICJ has never been restrictive in interpreting jurisdictional issues. Instead, the Court clarified that it will "have to consider whether the force of the arguments militating in favour of jurisdiction is preponderant, and to 'ascertain whether an intention on the part of the Parties exists to confer jurisdiction upon it.'"[242] At the same time, it cited the PCIJ in *The Factory at Chorzów* to support that"[t]he fact that weighty arguments can be advanced to

---

[239] *Amco Asia* v. *Indonesia*, Decision on Jurisdiction, September 25, 1983, para. 14(i) (emphasis in the original).

[240] *Mondev* v. *United States*, Award, October 11, 2002, para. 43 (internal citation omitted); see also *Ethyl Corporation* v. *Canada*, Award on Jurisdiction, June 24, 1998, para. 55.

[241] *Rights of Minorities in Upper Silesia (Minority Schools) (Germany* v. *Poland)*, Judgment, April 26, 1928, P.C.I.J. Series A, No. 15 (1928), p. 25.

[242] *Border and Transborder Armed Actions (Nicaragua* v. *Honduras), Jurisdiction and Admissibility,* Judgment, December 20, 1988, I.C.J. Reports 1988, p. 76, para. 16 (making reference to *The Factory at Chorzów (Claim for Indemnity) (Germany* v. *Poland)*, Jurisdiction, Judgment, July 26, 1927, P.C.I.J. Series A, No. 9 (1927), p. 32).

support the contention that it has no jurisdiction cannot in itself create a doubt calculated to upset jurisdiction."[243] Hence, "it is for the Court to determine [its jurisdiction] from all the facts and taking into account all the arguments advanced by the Parties"[244] on the basis of an objective interpretation without any presumption of either restrictive or expansive interpretation.[245] Judge Higgins thus concluded in her Separate Opinion in *Oil Platforms*:

> It is clear from the jurisprudence of the Permanent Court and of the International Court that there is no rule that requires a restrictive interpretation of compromissory clauses. But equally, there is no evidence that the various exercises of jurisdiction by the two Courts really indicate a jurisdictional presumption in favour of the plaintiff ... The Court has no judicial policy of being either liberal or strict in deciding the scope of compromissory clauses: they are judicial decisions like any other.[246]

Yet, a State's consent to arbitration under investment treaties is not different to a State's consent to the jurisdiction of international courts and tribunals in all of these cases. Requiring "clear and unambiguous" consent to arbitration by States therefore would depart from the test generally applied to determine the jurisdiction of international courts and tribunals. Accordingly, the Tribunal in *Suez and InterAguas* v. *Argentina* rejected the requirement that the State's consent had to be "clear and unambiguous" in order for MFN clauses to incorporate broader consent to arbitration from third-party treaties. It emphasized instead "that dispute resolution provisions are subject to interpretation like any other provisions of a treaty, neither more restrictive nor more liberal."[247]

Second, the analogy which tribunals in cases such as *Plama* v. *Bulgaria* draw between investment treaty arbitration and commercial arbitration mischaracterizes the nature of BITs. BITs are not ordinary contracts between private parties, but international treaties the interpretation of which follows rules and rationales different from those in the interpretation and application of commercial contracts. Above all, the distributions of interests in both situations differ. BITs do not constitute private law instruments that solely govern the relations between private and

---

[243] *Ibid.*

[244] *Fisheries Jurisdiction (Spain* v. *Canada)*, Judgment, December 4, 1998, I.C.J. Reports 1998, p. 450, para. 38.

[245] See *ibid.*, para. 44.

[246] *Oil Platforms (Iran* v. *United States)*, Preliminary Objection, Judgment, December 12, 1996, Separate Opinion by Judge Higgins, I.C.J. Reports 1996, p. 857, para. 35.

[247] *Suez and InterAguas* v. *Argentina*, Decision on Jurisdiction, May 16, 2006, para. 64; likewise *AWG* v. *Argentina*, Decision on Jurisdiction, August 3, 2006, para. 66; *Suez and Vivendi* v. *Argentina*, Decision on Jurisdiction, August 3, 2006, para. 66.

theoretically equal parties. Rather, investment treaties order the invest-ment relations between States.

Similarly, the rationale for requiring "clear and unambiguous" consent to arbitrate in commercial settings is not applicable to the investor-State context. Requiring "clear and unambiguous" consent has different rami-fications for commercial and investment arbitrations. In commercial arbitration, such a requirement ensures not only that "commercial arbi-tration agreements, like other contracts, 'are enforced to their terms' … and according to the intentions of the parties."[248] It also protects private parties against forgoing their right to dispute settlement in a State court absent their clear consent. Host States, by contrast, do not need compar-able protection. Indeed, requiring the host State's consent to be "clear and unambiguous" might deny the investor access to efficient, independ-ent and neutral dispute settlement by arbitration and leave them with often less efficient and neutral means, especially in developing countries. Ultimately, a strict interpretation of MFN clauses that shields host States from dispute settlement and enforcement mechanisms under investment treaty arbitration, even though the host State's consent to such mecha-nisms can readily be construed, is, therefore, also questionable from a policy perspective.

7   MFN clauses and treaty-shopping

The second major argument against a broad application of MFN treat-ment is that this would further "undesirable" or "disruptive treaty-shopping."[249] Reflecting the bilateralism paradigm in investment treaty arbitration, this argument contravenes the object and purpose of MFN treatment to prevent States from shielding rights and benefits in bilateral relations from their extension to third-country investors. MFN clauses decisively target such discriminatory behavior and aim at creating a level playing field with equal conditions for competition by foreign investors. Seeking the most favorable protection offered by the BITs of a specific host State is therefore not shopping for unwarranted advantages, but the core objective of MFN clauses. Moreover, the term "treaty-shopping"

---

[248] *First Options of Chicago, Inc.* v. *Kaplan et al.*, 514 U.S. 938, 947 (1995).
[249] See *Maffezini* v. *Spain*, Decision on Objections to Jurisdiction, January 25, 2000, para. 63; *Salini* v. *Jordan*, Decision on Jurisdiction, November 15, 2004, para. 115; *Plama* v. *Bulgaria*, Decision on Jurisdiction, February 8, 2005, paras. 222–23; *Telenor* v. *Hungary*, Award, September 13, 2006, para. 93; see also *Wintershall* v. *Argentina*, Award, December 8, 2008, paras. 167–68, 173–76. Critical on the negative effects of treaty-shopping, also Radi (*supra* footnote 88), 18 Eur. J. Int'l L. 757, 771–74 (2007).

misrepresents investors as co-opting third-party treaties to their relationship with the host State. This, however, is not the case: the treaty governing the investor-State relations always remains the basic treaty, not any more favorable third-party treaty.

Furthermore, the application of MFN clauses to matters of jurisdiction does not harm the investment relations of States. Quite the contrary, such application of MFN clauses harmonizes compliance procedures of host States for their obligations under investment treaties. Arguments about a disharmonizing effect of MFN clauses or complaints about "treaty-shopping" as a problem are thus incompatible with the very rationale of MFN treatment. These arguments express mere unease with MFN treatment as a principle governing international investment relations and disregard the benefits stemming from uniform and non-discriminatory rules. Criticizing "treaty-shopping" is thus merely a cover for policy arguments against the desirability of MFN treatment as such, rather than an independent argument to guide the interpretation of MFN clauses.

8   MFN treatment and public policy restrictions

The Tribunal in *Maffezini* attempted to distinguish between the "legitimate extension of rights and benefits by means of the operation of the [MFN] clause ... and disruptive treaty-shopping that would play havoc with the policy objectives of underlying specific treaty provisions ..."[250] In consequence, it introduced a number of "public policy considerations" in order to prevent circumventing certain restrictions on investor-State dispute settlement.[251] The Tribunal, however, has never explained the legal basis of these exceptions to satisfaction. Yet, two explanations for the Tribunal's reasoning seem possible. Either public policy exceptions to MFN treatment stem from the domestic legal order of the host State or from the consent of the contracting State parties to the BIT and therefore form part of international law.

The term "public policy consideration," as used by the Tribunal, evokes a parallel to exceptions to the enforcement of agreements to arbitrate in commercial arbitration. In fact, the formulation in the *Maffezini* decision resembles the conclusion of the US Supreme Court in *Bremen* v. *Zapata Off-Shore Co.* that "[a] contractual choice-of-forum clause should be held unenforceable if enforcement would contravene a strong public policy of

---

[250] *Maffezini* v. *Spain*, Decision on Objections to Jurisdiction, January 25, 2000, para. 63.
[251] See *supra* footnote 114 and accompanying text.

the forum in which suit is brought, whether declared by statute or judicial decision."[252] "Public policy" in this context is used as an exception to the enforceability of arbitration clauses.

Yet, such exceptions in commercial arbitration serve a purpose that is at odds with the basic framework of investment treaty arbitration as an instrument of public international law. In commercial arbitration, public policy exceptions aim at upholding specific interests of the forum State in preventing private parties from settling disputes outside the forum State's court system. The interests protected by public policy exceptions are either specific interests of the State that insists on public enforcement of certain non-arbitral matters, such as status-related proceedings in family matters, or aims at protecting one of the private parties from forgoing its right to recourse to State courts.

The situation in investment treaty arbitration, by contrast, is fundamentally different. States, unlike private parties, do not have to be protected against the enforcement of obligations under international law. On the contrary, one of the major deficiencies in traditional investor-State relations always has been the lack of effective enforcement mechanisms under general international law.[253] Similarly, in the BIT context, the consequences of not enforcing an arbitration agreement between the State and the investor are fundamentally different from the commercial arbitration context. Instead of being able to have recourse to State courts that – at least in developed countries – effectively and efficiently render justice, an investor would face the courts in the host State that, in many countries, are not sufficiently independent and impartial, or do not settle disputes efficiently.[254] Furthermore, if the public policy considerations proclaimed by the *Maffezini* Tribunal originated from the host State's domestic legal order, their recognition would allow the host State to unilaterally invoke exceptions to the operation of an MFN clause and thus contravene the primacy of international over national law.[255]

Consequently, the only defensible basis for the Tribunal's "public policy considerations" can be the consent of the State parties to the BIT.[256] As such, the "public policy considerations" could be explained as constituting implicit exceptions to the scope of application of MFN clauses. Whether this is properly called a "public policy exception" may be doubted as no

---

[252] *The Bremen et al.* v. *Zapata Off-Shore Co.*, 407 U.S. 1, 15 (1972).
[253] *Cf.* Schill, *Enabling Private Ordering – Function, Scope and Effect of Umbrella Clauses in International Investment Treaties*, 18 Minn. J. Int'l L. 1, 23–26 (2009).
[254] *Cf. ibid.*, at 21–22.   [255] *Cf.* Article 27, Vienna Convention on the Law of Treaties.
[256] See Dolzer and Myers (*supra* footnote 98), 19 ICSID Rev. – For. Inv. L. J. 49, 52–54 (2004).

independent public policy concerns would be involved that override the host State's consent.

Apart from semantics, such implicit exceptions, however, are hardly necessary in the application of MFN clauses to matters of investor-State dispute settlement. Instead, the existing limits to the operation of MFN clauses, in particular the *ejusdem generis* rule, arguably constitute sufficient barriers against what can be considered a "disruptive" effect of the clauses. If the contracting parties mutually agree to limit the scope of application of MFN clauses, they can always spell out exceptions in the text of the respective BIT, such as customs union or benefits stemming from double taxation treaties. In contrast, implicit exceptions to MFN clauses have traditionally only been accepted under limited circumstances.[257] *A fortiori*, there is no place for unilateral public policy considerations, as this would enable one State to escape unilaterally from its obligations under international law.[258] Last, but not least, invoking public policy considerations is implausible if the host State does not uniformly include them in its investment treaties.[259]

Instead, principles of treaty interpretation suffice to determine the scope and the limits of MFN clauses in investment treaties. Thus, one will have to go through accepted modes of treaty interpretation, primarily the text of the instrument in its context and in the light of its object and purpose, in order to reach a conclusion on whether, for example, Article 1103, NAFTA would incorporate more favorable treatment regarding dispute settlement. In this context, one will also have to weigh the consideration that bypassing procedural limitations in a multilateral and "highly institutionalized system of arbitration" may differ from the effect MFN clauses have in a bilateral treaty framework that handles matters of dispute settlement in a less rigid fashion. There is, however, no need and no normative basis for the conclusion that MFN clauses in a multilateral framework should have *per se* different effects and a different scope from MFN clauses in bilateral treaties.

On the other hand, the remaining examples of "public policy considerations", introduced in *Maffezini*, should be discarded. First, the

---

[257] See *supra* footnotes 90 and 96.

[258] This would be contrary to Article 27, Vienna Convention on the Law of Treaties that clarifies that the domestic legal order cannot serve as an excuse for not complying with international treaty obligations.

[259] *Cf. Siemens* v. *Argentina*, Decision on Jurisdiction, August 3, 2004, para. 105 (observing that "[t]he Tribunal would consider an indication of the existence of a policy of the Respondent if a certain requirement has been consistently included in similar treaties executed by the Respondent").

exhaustion of local remedies prior to investor-State arbitration is not a limitation on the jurisdiction of investment tribunals, but a restriction concerning the admissibility of a claim.[260] It should therefore not be treated differently than waiting clauses. Moreover, the contracting parties to BITs usually waive the requirement to exhaust local remedies. This shows that this access requirement to investor-State arbitration is not important enough in general State practice to be covered by an implicit, and thus mutually agreed, exception to MFN treatment. Moreover, an openly worded MFN clause can hardly be understood to contain an implied exception to an instrument that is as suited to distort enforcement opportunities between investors with different nationalities and to negatively affect competition as the exhaustion of local remedies.

Second, the general proposition that MFN clauses could not bypass "fork in the road" clauses seems equally unconvincing. Although the finality of dispute settlement is a legitimate concern of the contracting parties,[261] "fork in the road" clauses can distort competition between investors covered under different BITs. In view of the rationale of MFN treatment it is thus difficult to justify why investors from some home States should be allowed to bring claims both in the domestic legal system and on the international level, while investors from other home States are restricted to one forum. Depending on the circumstances, concepts such as estoppel or *abus de droit* would better prevent multiple proceedings in bad faith against the host State in its domestic courts and in investor-State arbitration. Nonetheless, such precaution does not justify treating "fork in the road" clauses as immune from being circumvented by the operation of MFN clauses.

Finally, under certain circumstances an investor will even be able to replace the dispute settlement provisions in the basic treaty with those from the host State's third-country BITs based on MFN treatment. This, however, will require scrutiny over whether the latter are indeed more favorable and accept jurisdiction over the claim between the investor and the State in question. Thus, it should be possible for an investor to invoke the consent to ICSID arbitration under one of the host State's third-party BITs, even though the basic treaty provides for arbitration under UNCITRAL rules, or conversely, invoke the consent to UNCITRAL arbitration, even

---

[260] See *Interhandel (Switzerland v. United States)*, Judgment, March 21, 1959, I.C.J. Reports 1959, p. 26 (stating that the objection that local remedies have not been exhausted "must be regarded as directed against the admissibility of the Application of the Swiss Government"); see also *SGS v. Philippines*, Decision on Jurisdiction, January 29, 2004, para. 154 (with further references).

[261] See *Maffezini v. Spain*, Decision on Objections to Jurisdiction, January 25, 2000, para. 63.

though the basic treaty provides for ICSID arbitration. Indeed, depending on the circumstances of the case, ICSID or UNCITRAL arbitration may be more favorable for an investor in initiating investment treaty arbitration.[262] While ICSID arbitration, for example, is more favorable than UNCITRAL arbitration regarding recognition and enforcement, UNCITRAL arbitration can be more favorable than ICSID arbitration as it does not require that the jurisdictional requirements of Article 25, ICSID Convention are met, which excludes, for example, claims by dual nationals and may have a stricter scope *ratione materiae* as regards the notion of investment than some investment treaties.

At the same time, however, the more favorable forum under the third-country BIT has to be open to the investor's claim under the basic treaty and accept jurisdiction. For example, an investor whose home State has not ratified the ICSID Convention cannot conduct arbitration under the ICSID Convention based on the MFN clause in the basic treaty, even though the host State may have consented to ICSID arbitration in third-country BITs.[263] Similarly, when the United Kingdom invoked MFN treatment vis-à-vis Iran in the *Anglo-Iranian Oil Company* case to establish the jurisdiction of the ICJ based on the argument that Iran had submitted to such jurisdiction in relation to other FCN treaties, the Court pointed out that its basis for jurisdiction over Iran was limited pursuant to Iran's declaration under Article 36(2) of the Court's Statute to disputes relating to the application of treaties or conventions accepted by Iran after the ratification of said declaration.[264] The Court therefore declined jurisdiction in the case at hand and observed:

> [The] most-favoured-nation clause [the United Kingdom invoked] … is contained in the Treaties of 1857 and 1903 between Iran and the United Kingdom, which are not subsequent to the ratification of the Iranian Declaration. While Iran is bound by her obligations under these Treaties as long as they are in force, the United Kingdom is not entitled to rely upon them for the purpose of establishing the jurisdiction of the Court, since they are excluded by the terms of the Declaration.[265]

---

[262] On relevant differences between ICSID and UNCITRAL arbitration, see Sacerdoti, *Investment Arbitration under ICSID and UNCITRAL Rules*, 19 ICSID Rev. – For. Inv. L. J. 1 (2004).

[263] However, one could consider in such cases whether recourse to arbitration under the ICSID Additional Facility rules is possible.

[264] See *Anglo-Iranian Oil Company (United Kingdom v. Iran)*, Judgment, July 22, 1952, I.C.J. Reports 1952, pp. 107–10.

[265] *Ibid.*, p. 109.

Notably, the Court declined jurisdiction in the case at hand not because it considered that an MFN clause could not incorporate more favorable jurisdiction, but rather because the jurisdiction of the ICJ itself was limited by the Court's Statute in connection with the Iranian declaration. The Court, therefore, did not reject the proposition that MFN clauses could incorporate broader consent to jurisdiction.[266]

E   Conclusion: MFN treatment – securing the future of multilateralism

MFN clauses in investment treaties influence the multilateralization of bilateral investment relations between States. Parallel to international trade law, MFN treatment in the investment context aims at creating non-discriminatory conditions for investors from different home States as a prerequisite for equal competition among them. They aim at preventing a distortion of the market by prohibiting competitive disadvantages for certain investors based on differences in the scope of investment protection that their respective home State BIT offers. MFN clauses thus recognize the value competitive structures bring to an efficient allocation of investment in a market environment. They are thus also in line with the more general thrust of BITs to implement institutions that support economic efficiency, reduce transaction costs in international investment relations and enable host States to attract investment into economic sectors where they have a competitive advantage over other economies.

Against this backdrop, arbitral practice has accepted that MFN clauses incorporate more favorable substantive investment protection from third-country BITs and thus create a uniform level of substantive investment protection for all investors to whom MFN treatment applies. Similarly,

---

[266] Similarly, *Leupold-Praesent* v. *Germany*, 25 ILR 540 (1958). Concerning the recourse of a Swiss national invoking MFN treatment granted in a treaty between Switzerland and Germany before the Arbitral Commission on Property, Rights and Interests in Germany, access to which was restricted to nationals of UN Member States, the Commission held, *ibid.*, p. 542: "It is true that, by agreement with a country which, like the Swiss Confederation, is not a member of the United Nations, the Federal Republic of Germany could grant the nationals of such a country the same concessions as those granted under Article 6 of Chapter Ten, but it has no power to extend the jurisdiction of the Commission to disputes with such nationals without the consent of the other Signatory States. The Commission was established by the Convention and its jurisdiction is defined therein and in the Charter annexed thereto. Any extension of that jurisdiction would constitute a modification of the Convention and of the Charter and, as in the case of any modification of an agreement, may be made only with the consent of all the Parties thereto."

investment tribunals have generally accepted that MFN clauses allow circumvention of access restrictions to investor-State arbitration, in particular less favorable waiting periods, if third-country BITs offer more favorable conditions. By contrast, the operation of MFN clauses to incorporate broader consent to arbitration from third-country BITs has met considerable resistance. Relying on analogies with commercial arbitration that require "clear and unambiguous" consent, arbitral jurisprudence has, so far with one exception, declined to apply MFN clauses as a basis of jurisdiction for investment tribunals.

This chapter, however, has argued that absent any clear indications to the contrary, MFN clauses should be applied broadly to incorporate any more favorable treatment, independent of whether it concerns substantive or procedural matters. Not only are analogies with regard to the interpretation of the consent to arbitrate in commercial matters, on the one hand, and investment treaty arbitration, on the other, misplaced. Restrictive interpretations of either MFN clauses in investment treaties or of the host State's consent to arbitration are also not compatible with accepted modes of treaty interpretation under international law. Rather "dispute resolution provisions are subject to interpretation like any other provisions of a treaty, neither more restrictive nor more liberal."[267]

Excluding MFN clauses from applying to questions of jurisdiction also contravenes the rationale of MFN treatment to create a level playing field for investors from different home States and creates tensions with the object and purpose of investment treaties. Rather, the importance of investor-State arbitration as a dispute settlement and compliance mechanism for the promotion and protection of foreign investment militates for the broad application of MFN clauses to encompass matters of jurisdiction. This does not also remove the fundamental requirement that States need to consent to arbitration or any other dispute resolution mechanism under international law. Instead, the consent they have given under one treaty will be extended, based on the operation of an MFN clause, to the beneficiaries of that clause.

As a consequence, good arguments exist for the proposition that MFN clauses can import the broader consent to arbitration from third-country treaties. Thus, the offer to arbitrate in the third-country BIT does not only extend to the investors covered by the third-party treaty, but also to investors covered under the basic treaty containing the MFN clause. Broader

---

[267] *Suez and InterAguas* v. *Argentina*, Decision on Jurisdiction, May 16, 2006, para. 64; *AWG* v. *Argentina*, Decision on Jurisdiction, August 3, 2006, para. 66; *Suez and Vivendi* v. *Argentina*, Decision on Jurisdiction, August 3, 2006, para. 66.

consent in third-party BITs can include more substantive causes of action as well as refer to different arbitral fora that may, for example, render more easily recognizable and enforceable arbitral awards, or offer fewer or less stringent jurisdictional access restrictions.

The situation, however, may be different, if the basic treaty does not provide for investor-State dispute settlement at all. Then the basic treaty does not encompass investor-State arbitration among its subject matters. This would limit the scope of the treaty's MFN clause to importing more favorable treatment in matters of substantive investment protection. Provisions concerning investor-State dispute settlement, by contrast, would relate to subject matter that is outside the scope of application of the basic treaty.

The debate about the scope of MFN clauses and its application to questions of jurisdiction also illustrates the struggle between bilateralism and multilateralism as ordering paradigms for international investment relations. While the restrictive interpretation of MFN clauses understands BITs as expressions of bilateral *quid pro quo* bargains, the broader approach is closer in line with creating a multilateral order for a single global economy that is based on non-discriminatory and uniform rules for investors in every investment-related aspect. For the broader approach, BITs are committed to non-discrimination and liberalization and constitute elements of a multilateral international order for foreign investment relations with uniform standards of protection.

Yet, MFN clauses do not only have effects on the relationship between investors and States. They also level the inter-State relations between the host State and different home States and advance the system of international investment protection towards multilateralism. In particular, MFN clauses have the effect of reducing leeway for specificities in bilateral investment relations and undermine the possibilities for bilateral *quid pro quo* bargaining. In doing so, MFN clauses do not only affect international economic relations, but more generally transform the idea of ordering international relations on a multilateral basis into actual practice.[268] Thus, similar to the context of international trade, the inclusion of MFN clauses in investment treaties can be seen as yielding also to non-economic objectives in suppressing the type of protectionism and bilateral isolation that constituted at least a supporting factor for the economic depression in the 1930s and subsequently the Second World War.[269]

[268] See Verbit (*supra* footnote 47), pp. 25–31.
[269] See Verbit (*supra* footnote 47), pp. 25–31; see also Curzon (*supra* footnote 50), pp. 20–33 (1965).

Finally, MFN clauses do not only multilateralize existing international investment treaties. By securing that specific bilateral advantages are multilateralized, they also make it harder for States to shift their future international economic policy-making to genuine bilateralism that includes granting preferential treatment on the basis of *quid pro quo* bargains. Instead, MFN clauses secure that a certain level of investment protection that was reached in earlier investment treaties will be more difficult to change by introducing more restrictive BITs in the future. MFN clauses impede attempts to withdraw from the level of investment protection once granted by a host State in its investment treaties as the clauses enable investors to incorporate possibly broader standards of investment protection from older investment treaties the same State has concluded. Only changes in a State's investment treaty practice that are accompanied by restrictions in MFN clauses themselves will enable States to isolate new investment treaties from a multilateralization of earlier agreements. To a certain extent, MFN clauses therefore lock States into the most favorable level of investment protection reached at one point of time and project this level into the future.[270] In doing so, MFN clauses form part of the ongoing process of a multilateralization of international investment relations and constitute one of the explicit normative bases of this development.

---

[270] States are, therefore, only gradually able to change the principles of international investment law enshrined in their BITs, in particular since most BITs are concluded for substantial periods of time of usually at least ten years and also provide for long periods of protection for existing investment after a possible termination (often up to twenty years). See, e.g., Article 15, Agreement between the People's Republic of China and the Federal Republic of Germany on the Encouragement and Reciprocal Protection of Investments, signed on December 1, 2003, entered into force November 11, 2005. Changes to the overall treaty system will, therefore, unless the contracting State parties agree on the changes, require that newly concluded BITs contain limitations of MFN treatment for more favorable treaty provisions than earlier treaties. Canada has therefore amended its Model BIT in this direction. It now includes an annex that exempts MFN treatment with respect to prior BIT obligations and thus gives it more leeway to gradually change the level of investment protection under its investment treaties. See Annex III(1), 2004 Canadian Model BIT, available at: www.sice.oas.org/investment/NatLeg/Can/2004-FIPA-model-en.pdf.

V

Multilateralization and corporate structuring

The multilateralization of international investment law cannot be observed only from the perspective of foreign investors that are able, through the operation of MFN clauses, to rely on uniform rules governing their investment activities in a specific host State. The convergence of bilateral treaties into a multilateral investment regime also becomes apparent from the compliance perspective of States. Even absent the operation of MFN clauses, and even though the bilateral structure of investment treaties would in principle allow for differentiated treatment depending on the investor's national origin, host States are increasingly troubled in applying differentiated treatment to investors from different home States. Instead, compliance with investment treaties, in practice, increasingly resembles compliance with obligations under a multilateral regime as a uniform level of treatment of foreign investors is required of States.

Multilateral regimes are characterized by the existence of identical obligations of one State vis-à-vis at least two other States. These obligations can be either *erga omnes* and owed to the international community as a whole,[1] or *erga omnes partes* (or *inter partes*), that is, owed independently and individually to every participant in a multilateral regime.[2] While the difference between *erga omnes* and *inter partes* obligations relates above all to the question of who is entitled to enforce these obligations in case of their breach – either every single participant in a multilateral regime in case the obligation is *erga omnes,* or only the individual

---

[1] See *Barcelona Traction, Light and Power Company, Limited (Belgium v. Spain)*, Judgment, February 5, 1970, I.C.J. Reports 1970, p. 32, para. 33 (stating that "an essential distinction should be drawn between the obligations of a State towards the international community as a whole, and those arising vis-à-vis another State in the field of diplomatic protection. By their very nature the former are the concern of all States. In view of the importance of the rights involved, all States can be held to have a legal interest in their protection; they are obligations *erga omnes*"). See, comprehensively on *erga omnes* obligations, Tams, *Enforcing Obligations* Erga Omnes *in International Law* (2005).

[2] See Pauwelyn, *A Typology of Multilateral Treaty Obligations*, 14 Eur. J. Int'l L. 907 (2003) (showing with respect to obligation under the WTO Agreement that obligations under a multilateral treaty do not need to be collective in nature, but can consist of a bundle of bilateral relations); see further also Tams (*supra* footnote 1), pp. 117–28.

member that has been harmed by a violation of the obligation in an *inter partes* relationship[3] – the differences are marginal from the perspective of the addressee of the obligations. Independent of whether the obligations addressed to a State in a multilateral regime are *erga omnes* or merely *inter partes*, compliance with them requires the State to live up to a uniform standard in relation to every other Member State. Typical bilateral obligations, by contrast, are fundamentally different. Their enforcement under international law is restricted not only to the one State deriving an entitlement from a bilateral obligation. Above all, bilateral treaty relations allow for differentiated standards depending on the identity of the other contracting party.

Prima facie, BITs clearly form part of the category of bilateral treaty obligations. Unlike obligations under human rights treaties,[4] or obligations under the WTO Agreement,[5] they restrict the behavior of the host State only with respect to the treatment of specific foreign investors covered by the applicable BIT. As such, they do not impose either collective obligations or a bundle of identical obligations. Their scope of application is restricted *ratione personae* to investors that have the nationality of the other contracting party in a bilateral relationship. Inclusion into and exclusion from the protection granted by an investment treaty thus strictly depend on the bond of nationality between the investor and its home State. Such access restrictions to international investment protection based on the nationality of the investor provide a strong counter-argument against the proposition that international investment law can be understood as a multilateralizing system. Instead, the bond of nationality militates for viewing investment protection based on BITs as a typical example of bilateralism in inter-State relations, similar to the ICJ's categorization of obligations concerning the treatment of aliens under customary international law which were enforceable by means of diplomatic protection in the *Barcelona Traction* case.[6]

[3] Pauwelyn (*supra* footnote 2), 14 Eur. J. Int'l L. 907, 908 *et seq.* (2003).
[4] See, for example, Article 1, European Convention on Human Rights that formulates rights and freedoms for everyone within the jurisdiction of the contracting parties. The protection, therefore, extends to anyone, independent of his or her nationality, including nationals of States that are not a party to the Convention. See Frowein and Peukert, *Europäische Menschenrechtskonvention,* Article 1, para. 3 (2nd edn. 1996).
[5] The obligations under the WTO Agreement consist of a bundle of bilateral relations, see Pauwelyn (*supra* footnote 2), 14 Eur. J. Int'l L. 908, 925 *et seq.* (2003).
[6] *Barcelona Traction, Light and Power Company, Limited (Belgium v. Spain),* Judgment, February 5, 1970, I.C.J. Reports 1970, p. 32, para. 35 (observing that "[o]bligations the performance of which is the subject of diplomatic protection are not of the same category

The nationality of an investor is, however, becoming an increasingly drifting criterion that loses its effectiveness in limiting the scope of application of a specific BIT *ratione personae* and thus determining inclusion into or exclusion of a specific investor from the protection offered by investment treaties. On the contrary, States have difficulties in limiting the effect of investment treaties to a specific bilateral relationship. The reasons for this are twofold. First, BITs regularly rely on a broad notion of investment that does not only cover assets in the host State directly owned by an investor. Instead, they also grant protection to the shareholding of foreign investors in a corporate entity that holds assets in the host State. Secondly, BITs not only protect investments by natural persons,[7] but also extend to investments by corporate investors.

The contribution of both factors opens up the possibility for investors to use corporate structuring in order to influence the level of investment protection. For instance, while the nationality of natural persons is a relatively stable criterion that is not subject to quick and frequent changes, corporate structures can change their nationality quickly and at little cost by either migrating to another jurisdiction, or by setting up a corporate vehicle there. As will be shown in this chapter, the interplay between investment protection, corporate law and corporate structuring has a profound influence on the multilateralization of international investment law. Investors are not only in a position to free themselves from bilateral inter-State relations, but corporate structuring also requires host States to treat BIT obligations as if they were part of a multilateral regime. This further mitigates the strict focus on *bilateral* investment protection and contributes to the multilateralization of international investment law.

[i.e., *erga omnes* obligations]. It cannot be held, when one such obligation in particular is in question, in a specific case, that all States have a legal interest in its observance.").

[7] BITs usually define the national of a party as "a natural person who is a national of that Party under its applicable law." See, for example, Article I(c), Treaty between the Government of the United States of America and the Government of the Republic of Georgia concerning the Encouragement and the Reciprocal Protection of Investment, signed on March 7, 1994, entered into force on August 10, 1999. In case of dual nationals, the determination may need to be accompanied by a sufficiently "genuine link" between the person and the State granting nationality; see *Nottebohm (Liechtenstein v. Guatemala)*, Judgment, April 6, 1955, I.C.J. Reports 1955, pp. 20 *et seq.* Such a requirement may not be necessary if the person possesses only one nationality; see *Siag v. Egypt,* Decision on Jurisdiction, April 11, 2007, paras. 195–201; *Micula v. Romania*, Decision on Jurisdiction and Admissibility, September 24, 2008, paras. 98–106.

In order to illustrate the contribution of corporate structuring to the multilateralization of international investment relations, this chapter analyzes the relationship between investment protection and corporate law. In the first section, it addresses how the protection of shareholders under numerous investment treaties leads to a passive multilateralization of BIT obligations, as host States have to conform their behavior vis-à-vis foreign investors to the investment treaty with the most comprehensive level of investment protection that they have entered into with any other State, independent of whether the host State's investment treaties are based on MFN treatment. The protection of shareholders thus *de facto* extends the protection of BITs to non-covered investors and allows them to benefit indirectly and passively from a BIT between the host State and an unrelated third State.

In the second part, this chapter shows how the protection of corporate entities enables investors to actively influence the level of investment protection by selecting the investment treaty of a host State that they consider most beneficial and appropriate for their individual purposes. This not only allows for treaty-shopping by foreign investors, but also eviscerates the possibilities for host States to differentiate between investors depending on their national origin and depending on the respective inter-State relations with the investor's home State.

A   Shareholder protection in international investment law

Most investment treaties do not only protect assets in the host State that are directly owned by foreign investors. Instead, the notion of investment often endorsed by investment treaties rests on a broad definition that includes "shares, debentures, stocks and any other kind of interest in companies."[8] Investment treaties, therefore, take into account the reality of financing and structuring foreign investment activities that are often channeled through several layers of companies in several jurisdictions. In particular, investment treaties usually cover shareholdings in companies as part of their definition of investment, including not only majority shareholdings, but also minority non-controlling shareholdings. In addition, the notion of investor is often understood broadly as covering

---

[8] See Article 1(1), Agreement between the People's Republic of China and the Federal Republic of Germany on the Encouragement and Reciprocal Protection of Investments, signed on December 1, 2003, entered into force on November 11, 2005.

shareholders on multiple levels within corporate structures.[9] This broad coverage of shareholders as investors and shareholdings as investments in many, if not most, investment treaties *de facto* transforms the nature of BIT obligations from strictly bilateral into quasi-multilateral ones, as host States must adapt their behavior in complying with all of their investment treaty obligations to the investment treaty that accords the most comprehensive protection to foreign investors even in the absence of an MFN clause.

1   Companies incorporated in the host State

Foreign investment projects are often implemented through companies incorporated in the host State.[10] Yet, having the nationality of the host State, the locally incorporated company regularly does not qualify as an investor under an investment treaty.[11] Without an independent

---

[9] See on the protection of shareholders Acconci, *Determining the Internationally Relevant Link between a State and a Corporate Investor*, 5 J. World Inv. & Trade 139 (2004); Orrego Vicuña, *Changing Approaches to the Nationality of Claims in the Context of Diplomatic Protection and International Dispute Settlement*, 15 ICSID Rev. – For. Inv. L. J. 340 (2000); Alexandrov, *The "Baby Boom" of Treaty-Based Arbitrations and the Jurisdiction of ICSID Tribunals*, 6 J. World Inv. & Trade 387, 393–407 (2005); Schreuer, *Shareholder Protection in International Investment Law*, in Dupuy *et al.* (eds.), *Common Values in International Law*, p. 601 (2006); McLachlan, Shore and Weiniger, *International Investment Arbitration – Substantive Principles*, pp. 184–96 (2007).

[10] In fact, the foreign investment laws of many countries require foreign investors to channel their investment through a locally incorporated company.

[11] Under the Treaty between the Federal Republic of Germany and the Republic of Bolivia concerning the Promotion and Mutual Protection of Investments, signed on March 23, 1987, entered into force on November 9, 1990, for example, a locally incorporated subsidiary does not qualify as a covered investor. The substantive rights granted by the BIT refer to treatment by the host State of nationals or companies of the other contracting party. Article 1(4) of the Treaty defines German companies as those having their seat in Germany and Bolivian companies as those having been established in conformity with Bolivian law. A locally incorporated subsidiary in the host State does not, therefore, qualify as an investor of the other contracting party and does not come under the protective umbrella of the BIT. The Treaty, however, provides in Article 1(1)(b) that "shares of companies" in a locally incorporated company qualify as an investment of the national of the other contracting party. For a similar structure see Article 1(a)(ii) and 1(b), Treaty between the United States of America and the Argentine Republic concerning the Reciprocal Encouragement and Protection of Investment, signed on November 14, 1991, entered into force on October 20, 1994. However, Article 25(2)(b), ICSID Convention allows locally incorporated companies that are under foreign control to be treated as having the nationality of the controlling shareholder's home State if the parties to the dispute so agree. Some investment treaties by default incorporate this choice. See, for example, Article 1(b)(iii), Agreement on Encouragement and Reciprocal Protection

protection of the company's foreign shareholders, the host State could thus easily escape from its obligations under investment treaties if its measures against a local company were outside the scope of protection of the treaties. For this reason, many BITs provide that the notion of investment encompasses "a company or shares of stock or other interests in a company or interests in the assets thereof."[12] In consequence, the shareholding in the company qualifies as a protected investment and the foreign shareholder accordingly can invoke the substantive obligations of an investment treaty. Against this background, arbitral jurisprudence has uniformly held that a majority shareholding in a locally incorporated subsidiary constitutes an investment in the sense of most BITs.[13] The shareholders can thus rely on the substantive protection of the BIT between their home State and the host State, even if the host State passes measures that directly only affect rights and interests of the local subsidiary.

2   Minority shareholder protection

Under most BITs, the protection of shareholders is not, however, limited to majority or controlling shareholders. Instead, arbitral jurisprudence has unanimously confirmed that investment treaty protection can extend to minority shareholders without a controlling interest in a local subsidiary. In *Lanco* v. *Argentina*, the first decision that expressly commented on this issue, the Tribunal emphasized that the language of the US–Argentine BIT "says nothing indicating that the investor in the capital stock has to have control over the administration of the company, or a

---

of Investments between the Kingdom of the Netherlands and the Republic of Bolivia, signed on March 10, 1992, entered into force on November 1, 1994.

[12] See Article 1(a)(ii), Treaty between the United States of America and the Argentine Republic concerning the Reciprocal Encouragement and Protection of Investment, signed on November 14, 1991, entered into force on October 20, 1994.

[13] See *American Manufacturing & Trading* v. *Zaire*, Award, February 21, 1997, paras. 5.14 *et seq.*; *Alex Genin* v. *Estonia*, Award, June 25, 2001, para. 324; *CME* v. *Czech Republic*, Partial Award, September 13, 2001, paras. 375 *et seq.*; *Antoine Goetz* v. *Burundi*, Sentence, February 10, 1999, para. 89; *Maffezini* v. *Spain*, Decision on Objections to Jurisdiction, January 25, 2000, paras. 65 *et seq.*; *Plama* v. *Bulgaria*, Decision on Jurisdiction, February 8, 2005, paras. 125 *et seq.*; *AES Corporation* v. *Argentina*, Decision on Jurisdiction, April 26, 2005, paras. 75 *et seq.*; *Gas Natural* v. *Argentina*, Decision on Jurisdiction, June 17, 2005, paras. 32 *et seq*; *African Holding* v. *République Démocratique du Congo*, Sentence sur les Déclinatoires de Compétence et la Recevabilité, July 29, 2008, paras. 97–103; see also *Kardassopoulos* v. *Georgia*, Decision on Jurisdiction, July 6, 2007, paras. 123–24.

majority share."[14] Instead, it considered an equity share participation of 18.3 percent as sufficient in order to trigger the protection of the governing BIT.[15]

Along the same line, the Tribunal in *CMS* v. *Argentina* stressed that there was "no bar in current international law to the concept of allowing claims by shareholders independently from those of the corporation concerned, not even if those shareholders are minority non-controlling shareholders."[16] It observed that since the decision of the ICJ in the *Barcelona Traction* case, which determined the entitlement to exercise diplomatic protection depending on whether rights of the company or rights of the shareholder were affected and whether the requisite bond of nationality existed between the affected entity and the State espousing the claim,[17] international law had undergone a profound change as regards the protection of shareholders. With reference to the ICJ decision in the *ELSI* case,[18] various lump-sum agreements, decisions of the Iran–United States Claims Tribunal, and decisions of the UN Compensation Commission, it reached the conclusion that the protection and standing of minority and non-controlling shareholders could be regarded by now

---

[14] *Lanco* v. *Argentina*, Decision on Jurisdiction, December 8, 1998, para. 10. Already in an earlier award the claimant only disposed of a minority shareholding interest in a local joint venture. It was, however, never challenged that this constituted an investment under the applicable BIT between the United Kingdom and Sri Lanka; see *Asian Agricultural Products* v. *Sri Lanka*, Final Award, June 27, 1990, para. 95.

[15] The outcome of this decision was confirmed in a number of further investor-State disputes under various BITs that stressed that non-controlling minority shareholder benefited from investment treaty protection. See *Enron* v. *Argentina*, Decision on Jurisdiction, January 14, 2004, para. 39; *GAMI Investments* v. *Mexico*, Final Award, November 15, 2004, paras. 26 *et seq.*; *LG&E* v. *Argentina*, Decision on Jurisdiction, April 30, 2004, paras. 50 *et seq.*; *Compañia de Aguas del Aconquija* v. *Argentina*, Decision on Annulment, July 3, 2002, paras. 48 *et seq.*; *Camuzzi* v. *Argentina*, ICSID Case No. ARB/03/2, Decision on Objections to Jurisdiction, May 11, 2005, paras. 28 *et seq.*; *Sempra* v. *Argentina*, Decision on Objections to Jurisdiction, May 11, 2005, paras. 38 *et seq.*; *Camuzzi* v. *Argentina*, ICSID Case No. ARB/03/7, Decisión sobre Jurisdicción, June 10, 2005, para. 34(v).

[16] *CMS* v. *Argentina*, Decision on Objections to Jurisdiction, July 17, 2003, para. 48.

[17] See *Barcelona Traction, Light and Power Company, Limited (Belgium* v. *Spain)*, Judgment, February 5, 1970, I.C.J. Reports 1970, pp. 34–38, paras. 39–54. For exceptional cases in which a lifting of the corporate veil regarding the exercise of diplomatic protection was perceivable, see *ibid.*, paras. 55–84. In the case at hand, the Court rejected the entitlement of Belgium to espouse a claim against Spain on behalf of Belgian nationals who suffered loss as shareholders in the Barcelona Traction, Light and Power Company, a company incorporated in Canada, when the company was declared bankrupt pursuant to bankruptcy proceedings in Spanish Courts.

[18] *Elettronica Sicula SpA (ELSI) (United States* v. *Italy)*, Judgment, July 20, 1989, I.C.J. Reports 1989, p. 15.

as a general rule concerning the protection of investors under investment treaties.[19] The Tribunal in *CMS* thus concluded that:

> it is beyond doubt that shareholders have standing in ICSID to submit claims separate and independent from the claims of the corporation. Moreover, this principle applies to all shareholders, no matter whether or not they own the majority of the shares or control the corporation.[20]

3   Indirect investments in multilevel corporate structures

The protection of shareholders under investment treaties has also been accepted in cases where the investment in the company that was directly affected by the host State's measures was held indirectly via an intermediary corporate structure as depicted in Figure V.1. In such cases, arbitral jurisprudence has accepted in most cases that the top-level shareholder or parent company is protected under the BIT in force between its home State and the host State where the subsidiary is actually active despite the existence of intermediary companies.

Corporate structuring via intermediary corporate structures can leave the nationality relations between investor, its home State, and the host State unaffected if the intermediary structure is incorporated in either the investor's home State or the host State. Thus, in *Siemens* v. *Argentina*,

---

[19] *CMS* v. *Argentina*, Decision on Objections to Jurisdiction, July 17, 2003, paras. 47 *et seq.* See also *Sempra* v. *Argentina*, Decision on Objections to Jurisdiction, May 11, 2005, para. 157 (clarifying that the reference in *CMS* v. *Argentina* to a general rule of the protection of shareholders "does not necessarily mean that it refers to the emergence of a customary rule. The general rule is evidenced by the fact that practically all disputes relating to foreign investments are today submitted to arbitration by resorting to the mechanisms of that *lex specialis*, as expressed by means of bilateral or multilateral treaties or other agreements." – note that the President of the Tribunal in the *CMS* and the *Sempra* cases was the same person). Independent from the question of whether BITs have an impact on the formation of customary international law, the *CMS* decision is certainly in line with *Barcelona Traction*, since the ICJ had already pointed out in its decision that the protection of shareholders under international law, independent from the company, was possible in view of specific treaty provisions. *Cf. Barcelona Traction, Light and Power Company, Limited (Belgium* v. *Spain)*, Judgment, February 5, 1970, I.C.J. Reports 1970, p. 47, para. 90. Several Tribunals have confirmed that the *Barcelona Traction* case should be limited to questions relating to the exercise of diplomatic protection, see *GAMI Investments* v. *Mexico*, Final Award, November 15, 2004, para. 30; *LG&E* v. *Argentina*, Decision on Jurisdiction, April 30, 2004, para. 52; *Azurix* v. *Argentina*, Decision on Jurisdiction, December 8, 2003, para. 72; *Sempra* v. *Argentina*, Decision on Objections to Jurisdiction, May 11, 2005, paras. 150–54; *Camuzzi* v. *Argentina*, ICSID Case No. ARB/03/2, Decision on Objections to Jurisdiction, May 11, 2005, paras. 138–42; *Camuzzi* v. *Argentina*, ICSID Case No. ARB/03/7, Decisión sobre Jurisdicción, June 10, 2005, para. 44.

[20] Alexandrov (*supra* footnote 9), 6 J. World Inv. & Trade 387, 395 (2005).

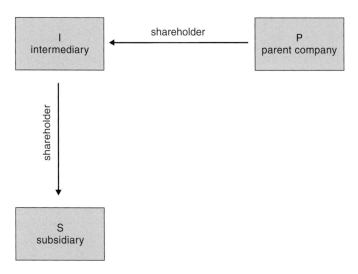

Figure V.1 Three-level corporate structure

the Tribunal held that an intermediary company incorporated in the parent's home jurisdiction, which in turn held a shareholding interest in a company incorporated in the host State, did not exclude the parent company from claiming protection as an investor under the BIT between its home State and the host State of the subsidiary. Instead, as illustrated in Figure V.2, the parent company's indirect shareholding in the local subsidiary was considered to constitute an investment under the governing BIT. Despite the lack of an explicit reference to indirect investments,[21] the Tribunal stressed that:

> [t]he Treaty does not require that there be no interposed companies between the investment and the ultimate owner of the company. Therefore, a literal reading of the Treaty does not support the allegation that the definition of investment excludes indirect investments.[22]

---

[21] For such an explicit reference see, for example, Article 1(1), Agreement between the People's Republic of China and the Federal Republic of Germany on the Encouragement and Reciprocal Protection of Investments, signed on December 1, 2003, entered into force on November 11, 2005.

[22] *Siemens* v. *Argentina*, Decision on Jurisdiction, August 3, 2004, para. 137. Similarly, *Azurix* v. *Argentina*, Decision on Jurisdiction, December 8, 2003, paras. 63 *et seq.* (where the local subsidiary was partly held through an intermediary in the parent's home jurisdiction). Differently, however, the majority in *Berschader* v. *Russia*, Award, April 21, 2006, paras. 124–50, see also *ibid.*, Separate Opinion by T. Weiler, paras. 7–14.

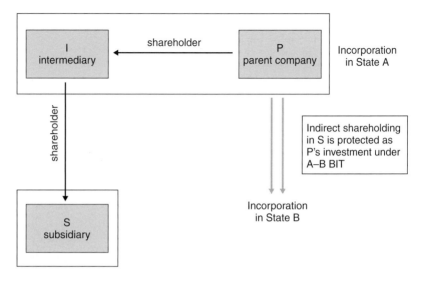

Figure V.2   BIT protection with intermediary in investor's home State

Similarly, arbitral tribunals have accepted that indirect shareholding interests constitute an investment if the parent holds a shareholding in a locally incorporated subsidiary through an intermediary company incorporated under the laws of the host State, as illustrated in Figure V.3. Thus, in *Enron* v. *Argentina*, the Tribunal observed in a case where a US company had invested indirectly in the Argentine gas sector through multiple intermediaries established in Argentina that:

> there is nothing contrary to international law or the ICSID Convention in upholding the concept that shareholders may claim independently from the corporation concerned, even if those shareholders are not in the majority or in control of the company.[23]

However, the Tribunal in *Enron* v. *Argentina* also voiced concerns about the consequences and potential limits of allowing claims by shareholders and observed:

---

[23] *Enron* v. *Argentina*, Decision on Jurisdiction, January 14, 2004, para. 39. Similarly, *Azurix* v. *Argentina*, Decision on Jurisdiction, December 8, 2003, paras. 63 *et seq.*; *Enron* v. *Argentina*, Decision on Jurisdiction (Ancillary Claim), August 2, 2004, paras. 29 *et seq.*; *Sempra* v. *Argentina*, Decision on Objections to Jurisdiction, May 11, 2005, paras. 80 *et seq.*; *Camuzzi* v. *Argentina*, ICSID Case No. ARB/03/2, Decision on Objections to Jurisdiction, May 11, 2005, paras. 54 *et seq.*; *Camuzzi* v. *Argentina*, ICSID Case No. ARB/03/7, Decisión sobre Jurisdicción, June 10, 2005, para. 34; *Gas Natural* v. *Argentina*, Decision on Jurisdiction, June 17, 2005, paras. 9–10, 50–52.

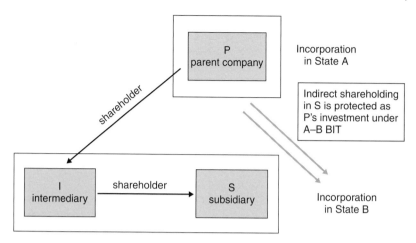

Figure V.3 BIT protection with intermediary in the host State

> The Argentine Republic has rightly raised a concern about the fact that if minority shareholders can claim independently from the affected corporation, this could trigger an endless chain of claims, as any shareholder making an investment in a company that makes an investment in another company, and so on, could invoke a direct right of action for measures affecting a corporation at the end of the chain … The Tribunal notes that while investors can claim in their own right under the provisions of the treaty, there is indeed a need to establish a cut-off point beyond which claims would not be permissible as they would have only a remote connection to the affected company.[24]

While the structuring of investments through subsidiaries in the claimant's home State or the investment's host State does not affect any third-country jurisdictions and thus remains within the confines of one bilateral treaty relationship, the interposition of an intermediary company can also involve a corporate structure that has the nationality of a third State. In such cases, respondent States have regularly raised the objection that indirect investments that were held via third-country subsidiaries were not protected as investments of the parent shareholder under the investment treaty between its home State and the host State. Yet, arbitral jurisprudence to date has regularly rejected such arguments and accepted that third-country intermediaries would not affect the

---

[24] *Enron* v. *Argentina*, Decision on Jurisdiction, January 14, 2004, paras. 50 *et seq.* Similarly, *Noble Energy* v. *Ecuador*, Decision on Jurisdiction, March 5, 2008, paras. 80–82.

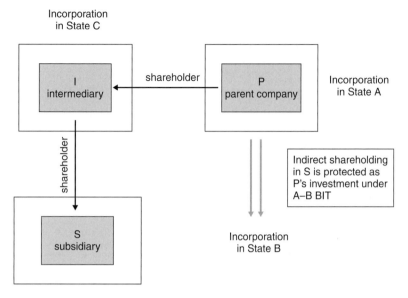

Figure V.4   BIT protection with intermediary in third country

protection available to the parent shareholder under the BIT between its home State and the host State as illustrated in Figure V.4.

The Tribunal in *Waste Management* v. *Mexico*, for instance, accepted that indirect investments between NAFTA investors that were effectuated via a non-NAFTA subsidiary were covered by the notion of investment under Article 1139 NAFTA. Thus, the Tribunal observed that "[t]here is no hint of any concern that investments are held through companies or enterprises of non-NAFTA States, if the beneficial ownership at relevant times is with a NAFTA investor."[25] Instead it emphasized:

> Where a treaty spells out in detail and with precision the requirements for maintaining a claim, there is no room for implying into the treaty additional requirements, whether based on alleged requirements of general international law in the field of diplomatic protection or otherwise. If the NAFTA Parties had wished to limit their obligations of conduct to enterprises or investments having the nationality of one of the other Parties they could have done so. Similarly they could have restricted claims of loss or damage by reference to the nationality of the corporation which itself suffered direct injury. No such restrictions appear in the text. It is not disputed that at the time the actions said to amount to a

---

[25] *Waste Management* v. *Mexico*, Award, April 30, 2004, para. 80.

breach of NAFTA occurred, Acaverde was an enterprise owned or controlled indirectly by the Claimant, an investor of the United States. The
nationality of any intermediate holding companies is irrelevant to the
present claim.[26]

Overall, arbitral jurisprudence in investment treaty cases regularly
supports a broad interpretation of the notion of investor as encompassing the protection of shareholders independent from the existence of
intermediary companies and from their place of incorporation. Equally,
the notion of investment, as adopted by most investment treaties and as
interpreted by arbitral tribunals, is considered to cover direct as well as
indirect shareholdings in companies. The broad understanding of the
notions of investor and investment is, therefore, receptive of the reality of
commercial relations in multinational enterprises with subsidiaries and
inter-linkages within and across several jurisdictions and leaves room for
a broad range of multi-jurisdictional corporate structuring.

4 The scope of protection of shareholders

While the broad protection of shareholders as such is recognized and
firmly established as a matter of standing to initiate investment treaty
arbitration, the nature and the exact scope of the substantive protection
that investment treaties offer to shareholders is less well understood and
still undertheorized.[27] In particular, it remains unclear whether the substantive scope of investor rights, such as fair and equitable treatment or
indirect expropriation, differs depending on whether the host State interfered with rights and interests of the company incorporated in the host
State or whether it interfered with rights and interests of the shareholders
in that company.

---

[26] *Ibid.*, para. 85; similarly, *Sedelmayer* v. *The Russian Federation*, Arbitration Award, July 7,
1998, para. 2.1.5; *Ronald S. Lauder* v. *The Czech Republic*, Final Award, September 3,
2001, paras. 153 *et seq.* (where it was not disputed by the respondent State that the shareholding interest of a US citizen in a company established under the law of the host State
via third-country intermediaries constituted an investment under the BIT between the
United States and the Czech Republic); *Noble Energy* v. *Ecuador*, Decision on Jurisdiction,
March 5, 2008, paras. 77–83; *African Holding* v. *République Démocratique du Congo*,
Sentence sur les Déclinatoires de Compétence et la Recevabilité, July 29, 2008, paras.
85–103 (both concerning cases in which the investment of US investors were channeled
via corporate vehicles incorporated in the Cayman Islands).

[27] *Cf.* Perkams, *Piercing the Corporate Veil in International Investment Agreements*, in
Reinisch and Knahr (eds.), *International Investment Law in Context*, pp. 93, 113 (2008)
(considering that "the question, whether indirect claims are generally admissible ... is
not the end of the story – it is probably not even the beginning of the end").

What is clear and uncontentious, is that direct interference with the rights of shareholders in the management of companies can result in violations of investor rights, including the protection against direct and indirect expropriation, the standard of fair and equitable treatment, etc. For example, the appointment of managers and directors for foreign-owned enterprises directly interferes with the shareholders' rights in the management of a company and thus violates rights that are directly vested in the shareholders.[28]

More difficult to resolve, however, are cases in which the host State does not interfere with the rights of shareholders, but passes measures that directly affect only the locally incorporated company or its assets. The host State can, for instance, expropriate assets belonging to a locally incorporated company or revoke an operating license held by that company. In such cases, the rights and interests of the shareholders are not directly affected. Consequently, it remains unsettled – regarding the procedural as well as the substantive law – how rights and claims by the shareholders under an investment treaty relate to the rights and potential claims by the company they invested in.

Thus, the following questions arise in this context: is the shareholder, who has standing under an investment treaty, merely bringing a claim on behalf of the company or does its claim rely on an independent cause of action for a violation of rights and interests that are vested in the shareholder based on the investment treaty in question? Can the shareholder seek its share of the damage sustained by the company or can it recuperate the decline in value of its shareholding due to an interference by the host State vis-à-vis the company? Finally, are there differences concerning the content of obligations under investment treaties depending on whether the investor is a shareholder or invests directly? Is the protection of shareholders under investment treaties, therefore, a reversed form of "piercing the corporate veil"[29] for the benefit of the foreign investor who can claim protection against host State measures despite the interposition of an intermediary corporate structure, or do differences in the scope of

---

[28] Such direct interferences with rights of shareholders have played a major role in the jurisprudence of the Iran–United States Claims Tribunal, since Iran had in numerous cases appointed managers and directors for foreign-owned enterprises. See C. N. Brower and Brueschke, *The Iran–United States Claims Tribunal*, pp. 394–410 (1998); Aldrich, *The Jurisprudence of the Iran–United States Claims Tribunal*, pp. 174–88 (1996).

[29] On the rationale of the doctrine of piercing the corporate veil and the underlying principle of the distinction between corporations and shareholders, see generally, Morissey, *Piercing All the Veils*, 32 J. Corp. L. 529 (2007).

protection exist depending on whether the host State's conduct result in an interference with the rights and interests of the company or the rights and interests of the shareholders?

On the level of domestic law, these questions have been answered quite clearly based on the differences between the company as a corporate structure and its shareholders. In this context, both the entitlement to a cause of action and the determination of damages depend on whether the affected right or interest is vested in the corporate structure or in the shareholders. This understanding of the separation between company and shareholders is also the conception informing the ICJ's jurisprudence on diplomatic protection for the violation of rights and interests of the alien's home State under customary international law. Thus, in *Barcelona Traction*, the Court drew on the "firm distinction between the separate entity of the company and that of the shareholder, each with a distinct set of rights,"[30] and held that the entitlement of a State to grant diplomatic protection depended, in principle, on whether the rights of the company or the rights of the shareholders were affected and whether the requisite bond of nationality existed between the affected entity and the State espousing the claim.[31]

Accordingly, the Court prolonged the municipal law distinction between corporate entity and shareholders on the level of customary international law. In case a State measure interfered directly with the rights of the shareholders, diplomatic protection could, in principle, be granted by the shareholders' home State; in case a State measure infringed the rights of the company, diplomatic protection could be granted by the company's home State. This conceptual approach has not only been reaffirmed for cases of diplomatic protection under customary international law by the Court in its recent *Diallo* case,[32] it has also been adopted by the International Law Commission in its 2006 Draft Articles on Diplomatic Protection.[33]

International investment law, however, seems to have departed from the strict conceptualization the ICJ considered pertinent for the protection of aliens under customary international law. Thus, several tribunals

---

[30] *Barcelona Traction, Light and Power Company, Limited (Belgium v. Spain)*, Judgment, February 5, 1970, I.C.J. Reports 1970, p. 34, para. 41.

[31] See *ibid.*, paras. 39–54. For exceptional cases in which a lifting of the corporate veil regarding the exercise of diplomatic protection was perceivable, see *ibid.*, paras. 55–84.

[32] *Ahmadou Sadio Diallo (Republic of Guinea v. Democratic Republic of the Congo)*, Preliminary Objections, Judgment, May 24, 2007, paras. 49–96.

[33] See Articles 11 and 12, ILC Draft Articles on Diplomatic Protection.

expressly limited the significance of the Court's ruling to the field of diplomatic protection and declined to apply the judgment's limitations regarding the protection of shareholders to the protection of foreign investment under modern investment treaties.[34] With regard to standing, modern investment treaty jurisprudence has rather given up the strict distinction between the rights and interests of shareholders and companies.[35] Unlike customary international law, modern investment treaties do not, therefore, shield the host State from investment treaty arbitration initiated by shareholders, but grant the latter standing to enforce obligations of the host State under investment treaties.

What is less clear, by contrast, is whether the distinction between the rights of the shareholders and the rights of the corporate structure do not persist on the level of the substantive standards. Without attempting to offer a final resolution to the complex questions arising in this context, it is nevertheless noteworthy to point at some aspects that suggest an emerging investment jurisprudence that does not completely give up the distinction between shareholder and company as regards the substantive obligations under investment treaties. Thus, various decisions of investment tribunals differentiate with respect to the protection of shareholder-investors between the sphere of protection of the corporate structure and the sphere of protection of the shareholder.

---

[34] *Cf. CMS* v. *Argentina*, Decision on Objections to Jurisdiction, July 17, 2003, paras. 43–44; *GAMI Investments* v. *Mexico*, Final Award, November 15, 2004, para. 30; *LG&E* v. *Argentina*, Decision on Jurisdiction, April 30, 2004, para. 52; *Sempra* v. *Argentina*, Decision on Objections to Jurisdiction, May 11, 2005, paras. 151 *et seq.*; *Camuzzi* v. *Argentina*, ICSID Case No. ARB/03/7, Decisión sobre Jurisdicción, June 10, 2005, para. 44; *Azurix* v. *Argentina*, Decision on Jurisdiction, December 8, 2003, para. 72; *Siemens* v. *Argentina*, Decision on Jurisdiction, August 3, 2004, para. 141. In fact, in *Barcelona Traction* the ICJ had already pointed out that the protection of shareholders under international law, independent from the company, was possible in view of specific treaty provisions. *Cf. Barcelona Traction, Light and Power Company, Limited (Belgium v. Spain)*, Judgment, February 5, 1970, I.C.J. Reports 1970, p. 47, para. 90.

[35] See Alexandrov (*supra* footnote 9), 6 J. World Inv. & Trade 387, 406 *et seq.* (2005) (observing "that all the tribunals' decisions … gave little if any credence to the argument that when a shareholder invokes a dispute relating to assets of the local company … such a dispute does not arise directly out of an investment in the stock of the company. Tribunals disposed of this argument in a rather summary fashion. It is clear that they all considered it to be beyond doubt that a shareholder's interest in a company includes an interest in the assets of that company, including its licenses, contractual rights, rights under law, claims to money or economic performance, etc., and that in finding jurisdiction they based that reasoning on the broad definition of investment in the applicable BIT.").

First, arbitral jurisprudence recognizes that the claim by an investor as shareholder is distinct from the claim of the company in which it invested, even though both causes of action may result from the same measure the host State took vis-à-vis the company. Thus, instead of relying on a violation of the rights of the company and bringing a derivative claim,[36] the shareholder-investor has to show that one of its own rights under the applicable investment treaty has been violated.[37] The investor thus has to make out a claim for the violation of rights granted by the BIT under which the investor is covered *ratione personae*. Such a claim might be linked to the interference of the host State with the rights of the investor as a shareholder under domestic corporate law, but this is not necessarily the case.[38] Second, the damages a shareholder-investor can recover are not equivalent to the damages the company incurs from a breach of its rights, but have to result from the breach of the rights of the shareholder-investor under the applicable investment treaty.[39]

Furthermore, arbitral jurisprudence is refining the substantive scope of the various investor rights granted under BITs as well as the elements of a successful claim of shareholder-investors. With respect to direct and indirect expropriation,[40] for example, arbitral jurisprudence increasingly

---

[36] But see the more elaborate provisions under Articles 1116 and 1117, NAFTA that draw a distinction between investors who are bringing a claim on their own behalf and investors who are bringing claims on behalf of a subsidiary that is incorporated in the host State.

[37] *Camuzzi* v. *Argentina*, ICSID Case No. ARB/03/7, Decisión sobre Jurisdicción, June 10, 2005, paras. 43–44.

[38] *GAMI Investments* v. *Mexico*, Final Award, November 15, 2004, para. 33 (pointing out that "[t]he fact that a host state does not explicitly interfere with share ownership is not decisive. The issue is rather whether a breach of NAFTA leads with sufficient directness to loss or damage in respect of a given investment.").

[39] *Cf. Mondev* v. *United States*, Award, October 11, 2002, para. 82; *Maffezini* v. *Spain*, Decision on Objections to Jurisdiction, January 25, 2000, para. 67–70 (stressing that the claimant has to make out a claim for damages sustained in his personal capacity); *Barcelona Traction, Light and Power Company, Limited (Belgium* v. *Spain)*, Judgment, February 5, 1970, I.C.J. Reports 1970, pp. 35–36, paras. 44–47.

[40] Indirect expropriation refers to State measures that do not interfere with the owner's title but rather with the property's substance and thus void the owner's actual power over his property. See Christie, *What Constitutes a Taking of Property under International Law?*, 38 Brit. Ybk. Int'l L. 307 (1962); Weston, *"Constructive Takings" under International Law*, 16 Va. J. Int'l L. 103 (1975); Higgins, *The Taking of Property by the State*, 176 Recueil des Cours 259, 322 *et seq.* (1982); Dolzer, *Indirect Expropriation of Alien Property*, 1 ICSID Rev. – For. Inv. L. J. 41 (1986); Wälde and Kolo, *Environmental Regulation, Investment Protection and "Regulatory Taking" in International Law*, 50 Int'l & Comp. L. Q. 811 (2001); Paulsson and Douglas, *Indirect Expropriation in Investment Treaty Arbitrations*, in Horn and Kröll (eds.), *Arbitrating Foreign Investment Disputes*, p. 145 (2004); Fortier

distinguishes, in cases of shareholder claims, based on whether the host State interfered with the rights of the company or with the rights of the shareholders. The Tribunal in *LG&E* v. *Argentina*, for example, endorsed the "control theory" as a test for determining whether an indirect expropriation of the shareholding in a locally incorporated company has occurred through measures the host State has taken vis-à-vis that company.

In the Tribunal's view, indirect expropriation in such cases occurs only "when governmental measures have 'effectively neutralize[d] the benefit of property of the foreign owner.' Ownership or enjoyment can be said to be 'neutralized' where a party no longer is in control of the investment, or where it cannot direct the day-to-day operations of the investment."[41] The acceptance of the control theory in this context, which is shared by an increasing number of arbitral tribunals,[42] suggests that it is necessary to distinguish, for defining the substantive protection offered to shareholder-investors under the concept of indirect expropriation, between property interests of the company and property interests of the shareholders. Thus, as a rule, in order to show the existence of an interference with a property right as a necessary element of a claim for indirect expropriation, it is insufficient if the host State's measure only affected property rights of the company, rather than property rights of the shareholder.[43]

Only in exceptional cases will tribunals find an indirect expropriation of the shareholders when all or almost all assets of the company in which

---

and Drymer, *Indirect Expropriation in the Law of International Investment,* 19 ICSID Rev. – For. Inv. L. J. 293 (2004); Newcombe, *The Boundaries of Regulatory Expropriation,* 20 ICSID Rev. – For. Inv. L. J. 1 (2005); Kunoy, *Developments in Indirect Expropriation Case Law in ICSID Transnational Arbitration,* 6 J. World Inv. & Trade 467 (2005).

[41] *LG&E* v. *Argentina,* Decision on Liability, October 3, 2006, para. 188 (citing *CME* v. *Czech Republic,* Partial Award, September 13, 2001, para. 604 and *Pope & Talbot Inc.* v. *Canada,* Award on the Merits of Phase 2, April 10, 2001, para. 100); similarly *CMS* v. *Argentina,* Award, May 12, 2005, paras. 260 *et seq.*

[42] See *Feldman* v. *Mexico,* Award, December 16, 2002, paras. 103 *et seq.; Waste Management* v. *Mexico,* Award, April 30, 2004, paras. 141 *et seq.; Tecmed* v. *Mexico,* Award, May 29, 2003, paras. 113 *et seq.; S. D. Myers, Inc.* v. *Canada,* Partial Award, November 13, 2000, paras. 280 *et seq.; Pope & Talbot Inc.* v. *Canada,* Interim Award, June 26, 2000, paras. 100 *et seq.;* decisively supporting the control theory, *GAMI Investments* v. *Mexico,* Final Award, November 15, 2004, paras. 117 *et seq.* and 129 (holding that "GAMI [the claimant] is entitled to invoke the protection of Article 1110 if its property rights (the value of its shares in GAM) were taken by contact in breach of NAFTA ... GAMI's investment in GAM is protected by Article 1110 only if its shareholding was 'taken.'").

[43] See *LG&E* v. *Argentina,* Decision on Liability, October 3, 2006, para. 198 (clarifying that in the case at hand the "true interests at stake here are the investment's asset base").

they invested are expropriated without compensation,[44] or affected in such a way that any business activity has "disappeared; i.e. the economic value of the use, enjoyment or disposition of the assets or rights affected … have been neutralized or destroyed."[45] Consequently, interference with the rights of the company can only have the effect of indirectly expropriating the shareholders in rare circumstances. Normally, however, a claim by a shareholder based on direct or indirect expropriation will require an interference with its property rights and interests, not with those of the company in which it invested.

Similarly, with respect to umbrella clauses, arbitral jurisprudence has made first efforts at distinguishing more precisely as to whether the host State has incurred obligations vis-à-vis the locally incorporated company or the shareholders.[46] Thus, in analyzing whether Argentina had violated its obligations under an umbrella clause in the BIT with the United States when providing for specific guarantees for the calculation of gas tariffs in privatizing the gas sector, the Tribunal in *LG&E* v. *Argentina* distinguished according to whether the host State had entered into an obligation vis-à-vis the shareholder-investor, or solely vis-à-vis the locally incorporated company. It set out a three-step test for determining whether the umbrella clause was violated in such cases. According to the Tribunal, it had to determine:

> whether the provisions of the Gas Law and its implementing regulations constitute (i) "obligations" (ii) "with regard to" LG&E's capacity as a foreign investor (iii) with respect to "its investment," such that abrogation of the guarantees set forth in the Gas Law and its implementing regulations give rise to a violation of the Treaty.[47]

This three-step test clarifies above all that the specific obligations of the host State in question had to be assumed vis-à-vis the foreign investor. Obligations entered into solely with a local subsidiary were, by contrast, not considered to be sufficient.[48] In the Tribunal's view, the tariff

---

[44] See *Compañia del Desarrollo de Santa Elena SA* v. *Costa Rica,* Award of February 17, 2000; *Starrett Housing* v. *Iran,* Award, December 19, 1983, 4 Iran–U.S. C.T.R. 122; see also *GAMI Investments* v. *Mexico,* Final Award, November 15, 2004, paras. 123 *et seq.* (clarifying that even a direct expropriation of assets of a company will not necessarily constitute an indirect expropriation of the shareholder-investor as long as control over the subsidiary was not affected and review and compensation were provided to the subsidiary).

[45] *Tecmed* v. *Mexico,* Award, May 29, 2003, para. 116.

[46] On umbrella clauses generally see *supra* Ch. III.A.2.d.

[47] *LG&E* v. *Argentina,* Decision on Liability, October 3, 2006, para. 172.

[48] *Ibid.,* para. 175. See also *Azurix* v. *Argentina,* Award, July 14, 2006, para. 384 (confirming that obligations entered into solely with local subsidiaries were not obligations in the

guarantees made under the Argentine Gas Law and its implementing regulation constituted, however, such specific obligations.[49] The promises, it argued, were also made specifically with respect to the shareholder-investor and did not concern only the local subsidiaries, because Argentina had advertised the content of the regulatory framework for the gas distribution sector and the tariff regime in order to attract foreign investors to purchase shareholding interests in locally incorporated gas distributing companies. Hence, the specific promises the host State incurred in the case at hand as regards the regulatory framework of the gas sector were extended not only to the local subsidiaries but also to the foreign shareholders.[50] Conversely, claims for the violation of an umbrella clause will be unsuccessful if the host State has incurred only specific obligations vis-à-vis the company in which a shareholder invested.

Despite developments to differentiate between the sphere of shareholders and the sphere of the corporate structure in which they invested in respect of the rules on direct and indirect expropriation and concerning umbrella clauses, such developments are less visible regarding the guarantee of fair and equitable treatment. In this context, the jurisprudence of arbitral tribunals applies the standard rather independently of whether the host State's measure directly affected rights and interests of a company only or also extended to its shareholders.[51]

In fact, tribunals that found a violation of the fair and equitable treatment standard almost exclusively had to deal with cases of shareholder-investors that held an interest in a locally incorporated company. Notwithstanding, tribunals have, for example, found a violation of fair and equitable treatment of the shareholders in cases where the host State had refused to grant or to prolong an operating license for landfills to the local subsidiary.[52] Similarly, in the cases involving Argentina's 2001 economic emergency legislation, various tribunals found a violation of fair and equitable treatment of shareholder-investors because the legislator had fundamentally changed the regulatory regime for investments in the country's energy sector, thereby contravening the stability of the regulatory

sense of the umbrella clause). See also Gallus, *An Umbrella just for Two?*, 24 Arb. Int'l 157 (2008).

[49] *LG&E* v. *Argentina*, Decision on Liability, October 3, 2006, para. 174.

[50] *Ibid.*, para. 175.

[51] On fair and equitable treatment, see *supra* Ch. III.A.2.b.

[52] *Tecmed* v. *Mexico*, Award, May 29, 2003, paras. 152 *et seq.* (concerning the non-prolongation of an operating license for a locally incorporated subsidiary); *Metalclad* v. *Mexico*, Award, August 30, 2000, paras. 74 *et seq.* (concerning the refusal to grant a construction permit for a waste landfill).

regime that was expected by the affected shareholder-investors.[53] Overall, fair and equitable treatment therefore applies not only to direct investors, but also protects shareholder-investors against measures that are primarily directed vis-à-vis the companies they have invested in.

Fair and equitable treatment is thus owed to foreign investors independently of the form of their investment as direct investments or investment in a shareholding in a company. It enables them to seek damages whenever the host State acted in a way contrary to the rule of law standards established under fair and equitable treatment.[54] This does not, however, require a violation of the specific rights of an investor under domestic law in its function as a shareholder. Despite the broad substantive protection granted to shareholder-investors under fair and equitable treatment, the cause of action is independent from any interference with rights and interests of the company and the damages that can be claimed on its basis are those incurred by the shareholder, not damage sustained by the company. Consequently, the substantive protection of shareholders becomes operative primarily through the guarantee of fair and equitable treatment. Investment treaties do not, however, generally overcome the separation between the corporate sphere and the rights and interests of the company, on the one hand, and the sphere of the shareholders, on the other hand.

5 Multilateralization of investment protection through shareholder protection

Even though shareholder-investors may not necessarily dispose of a greater protection under investment treaties as regards expropriatory measures of the host State, the fair and equitable treatment standard coupled with a broad definition of investment offers them substantial protection even if the host State has exclusively taken measures vis-à-vis the locally incorporated corporate entity in which they have invested. This protection of shareholders also has significant influence on the multilateralization of international investment protection. While measures of a host State taken vis-à-vis a corporate entity originally had to be assessed,

---

[53] See *CMS* v. *Argentina*, Award, May 12, 2005, paras. 266–84; *LG&E* v. *Argentina*, Decision on Liability, October 3, 2006, paras. 100–39; *Enron* v. *Argentina*, Award, May 22, 2007, paras. 251–68; *Sempra* v. *Argentina*, Award, September 28, 2007, paras. 290–304; *BG* v. *Argentina*, Final Award, December 24, 2007, paras. 289–310.

[54] See *supra* Ch. III.A.2.b.

absent the protection of shareholders of the company, only against the rules in place between the host State and the company's home State, the protection of shareholders leads to a multiplication of protected interests in relation to a single measure the host State may have taken vis-à-vis the corporate entity. It leads to a multiplication of potential claimants and potentially to a multiplication of applicable investment treaties if the shareholders in the company have different nationalities and are covered by different investment treaties that encompass shareholder protection. As a consequence, the host State's measures vis-à-vis a corporate entity not only have to conform to those BITs with the company's home State, but also to those BITs with the home State of every single shareholder in that company and the shareholders of those shareholders that encompass shareholders as covered investors and shareholdings as investments.

Even if the host State's investment treaties differ in their scope of application and with regard to the substantive protection they offer, the host State has to gauge its behavior vis-à-vis a company according to the most comprehensive investment treaty that is potentially applicable in order not to violate any of its BITs.[55] From the perspective of the host State, compliance with BIT obligations *de facto* requires the host State to comply with the most far-reaching of its investment treaty obligations. Even if the host State does not extend MFN treatment under its investment treaties, the most far-reaching investment treaty obligations nevertheless set the standard to which the host State has to conform its conduct if it wishes to comply with all of its investment treaty obligations. Even though the entitlement to claim a violation of an investment treaty might be limited to those shareholder-investors that can avail themselves of the most far-reaching BIT protection, other shareholder-investors in the same company will nevertheless indirectly benefit from farther-reaching treaty obligations covering third-party shareholder-investors as the host State's actions are indistinguishably directed vis-à-vis the company the various shareholder-investors have invested in. From the host State's compliance perspective, the protection of shareholders, therefore, *de facto*

---

[55] *Cf.* Legum, *Defining Investment and Investor*, 22 Arb. Int'l 521, 524 (2006) (arguing that "although each investment treaty is drafted as a bilateral set of obligations, to comply with those obligations the host state must treat them as obligations *erga omnes*: obligations owed to every state and every company"). Note, however, that the designation of BITs assuming the character of *erga omnes* obligations is imprecise as the breach of such obligations can only be enforced by the investor who has actually incurred damages, irrespective of its home State. The idea behind Legum's characterization is, therefore, better caught by the idea of BIT obligations assuming a multilateral character.

multilateralizes international investment protection even absent the operation of a treaty provision granting MFN treatment.

The multilateralization effect based on the protection of shareholders gains even greater momentum in view of the structure of multinational enterprises and international financial markets. International commercial activity, including foreign investment projects, is often not only operated by enterprises that consist of several layers of corporate shareholdings with various intermediaries in various countries. Much more, the ultimate shareholders of multinational companies are themselves natural and legal persons with various nationalities, given that multinational companies finance themselves on the international financial markets in various locations, such as New York, London, Frankfurt or Tokyo, and may trade their shares among shareholders with innumerable nationalities. Consequently, the protection of shareholders can have the effect of potentially making every investment treaty of a specific host State applicable to a specific measure, even though the host State only takes a single measure vis-à-vis a single company. The protection of shareholders, therefore, renders nationality as a criterion that enables differential treatment between corporate investors from different home States not only impractical, but potentially ineffective.

Measuring its conduct with respect to the most expansive investment treaty obligations when acting vis-à-vis corporate investors is all the more necessary for a host State wishing to comply with its investment treaty obligations, as it will regularly not be possible for the host State to know the nationality of all shareholders in a corporate entity and the nationality of the shareholders behind corporate shareholders. In order to comply with its obligations under investment treaties, the host State therefore has to assume that the most comprehensive of its investment treaties will be applicable in any given situation and it will have to conform its conduct to the most favorable standards even if no MFN clause is operative. Consequently, "[t]he reality that foreign capital is highly fungible and the breadth of the definitions of investor and investment thus combine effectively to transform the facially bilateral obligations of the BIT into an obligation that the host state must consider potentially applicable to all investors."[56]

This protection of shareholders as investors does not only require host States to accord *de facto* to all foreign investors the highest level of investment protection it has granted under any single one of its BITs. It will

---

[56] Legum (*supra* footnote 55), 22 Arb. Int'l 521, 525 (2006).

also prevent host States from availing themselves of instruments that are typically available in international relations coined by bilateral considerations. In bilateral relations, States are, for example, entitled to suspend, in a proportionate manner, treaty obligations vis-à-vis another State as a counter-measure in order to make that State comply with other international obligations.[57] In the investment treaty context, a host State could thus suspend the protection of an investment treaty vis-à-vis those foreign nationals who are citizens of a State that is itself in violation of another, even non-investment-related, international legal obligation vis-à-vis the host State.[58] The host State could thus deny investment treaty protection to investors with a specific nationality in accordance with the bilateral enforcement structure of the law of State responsibility. Yet, BIT obligations vis-à-vis investors with a different nationality cannot be suspended.[59] Thus, in cases of joint investments in one company of investors from the home State against whom counter-measures could be lawfully taken and third-country nationals who are protected under a different BIT, a host State will *de facto* be prevented from imposing counter-measures, similar to regimes of *erga omnes* or *erga omnes partes* obligations under a truly multilateral regime.

The protection of shareholder-investors under investment treaties thus has the effect of *de facto* multilateralizing BIT obligations by making every other shareholder-investor in the same company indirectly benefit from a specific BIT. This indirect protection will, in fact, not be limited to foreign shareholder-investors, but will equally benefit domestic investors to the extent that they hold shares in the same company as a foreign investor who, in turn, is covered by an investment treaty. As a consequence, the conclusion of investment treaties is bound to have effects in transforming the domestic legal system in more general terms. Although nationals cannot directly rely on investment treaties, the host State will likely adapt the forms and procedures of government conduct so as to conform to its international obligations as joint ventures between foreign and domestic investors are one of the most common vehicles for foreign investment projects. In effect, international investment treaties will, therefore, likely lead not only to securing a framework that is conducive

---

[57] See Articles 49–54, Articles on State Responsibility.

[58] See on the application of counter-measures as a defense to a violation of an investment treaty as excluding the wrongfulness of the breach, *Archer Daniels Midland, v. Mexico*, Award, November 21, 2007, paras. 110–80; see also Paparinskis, *Investment Arbitration and the Law of Countermeasures* (2008).

[59] See Article 49(1), ILC Articles on State Responsibility.

to foreign investment, but to investment activities more generally, independent of the source of the capital, be it foreign or domestic.

B   "Hiding behind the corporate veil": corporate structuring and corporate nationality

Nationality, as a gateway that determines the applicability of an investment treaty, is not only becoming increasingly irrelevant in passively determining the conduct of host States due to the protection of shareholders and the multiplication of interests and nationalities that go along with it. Nationality is also becoming increasingly irrelevant for determining the active level of investment protection due to a specific investor and its investment and the investor's right to initiate investment arbitration against the host State. Instead, investors are increasingly able to actively choose the applicability of the investment treaty they consider most beneficial and appropriate for their individual purposes.

The vehicle for such treaty-shopping is the broad applicability many investment treaties offer *ratione personae* to corporate entities as "investors" under the respective treaty. This not only allows for the protection of existing corporate entities as foreign investors, but also enables investors to actively use corporate structuring in order to channel their investment through a corporate vehicle in a third-country jurisdiction and thus bring a specific investment under the protection of a specific BIT with the host State that would otherwise not be applicable *ratione personae*.

Corporate structuring thus allows investors to effectively change their nationality for purposes of investment protection and opt into a "foreign" BIT regime. This section, therefore, addresses how investment treaties regularly define corporate nationality, to what extent they accept corporate structuring for purposes of treaty-shopping, and how this treaty-shopping contributes to the multilateralization of international investment law.

1   Defining corporate nationality

BITs follow different approaches in order to determine the nationality of a corporate investor.[60] Some treaties stipulate that their nationality is

---

[60] See Dolzer and Stevens, *Bilateral Investment Treaties*, pp. 34–42 (1995); Dolzer and Schreuer, *Principles of International Investment Law*, pp. 49–52 (2008). See further Acconci (*supra* footnote 9), 5 J. World Inv. & Trade 139 (2004); Wisner and Gallus, *Nationality Requirements in Investor-State Arbitration*, 5 J. World Inv. & Trade 927, 933–44 (2004); A. Sinclair, *The Substance of Nationality Requirements in Investment*

linked to the place of incorporation, an approach endorsed, for example, in the Dutch–Indonesian BIT that covers as investors "legal persons constituted under the law of that Contracting Party."[61] Other treaties, such as most German BITs, rely on the concept of the corporate seat (or *siège social*). Under this approach, the notion of investor comprises "[a] ny juridical person as well as any commercial or other company or association with or without legal personality having its seat in the area of application of this Treaty."[62] Finally, some treaties determine corporate nationality, under the control theory or some form of it, according to the nationality of its controlling shareholders. The BIT between the United States and the Democratic Republic of Congo, for example, defines a corporate investor as "a company duly incorporated, constituted or otherwise duly organized under the applicable laws and regulations of a Party … in which … natural persons who are nationals of such Party … have a substantial interest."[63]

While the control theory mandates looking behind the corporate veil of a corporate entity in order to determine the corporation's nationality for purposes of investment treaty protection, treaties that determine the nationality of a corporate investor, either in terms of its seat or its incorporation, allow investors from third countries to establish a corporate vehicle in the jurisdiction in question in order to opt into the investment treaty in place between the home State of the corporate vehicle and the host State. Determining corporate nationality with reference to the corporate seat or the place of incorporation thus allows investors to shop for investment treaty protection. As observed by the Tribunal in *Aguas del Tunari v. Bolivia*:

> it is not uncommon in practice, and – absent any particular limitation – not illegal to locate one's operations in a jurisdiction perceived to provide a beneficial regulatory and legal environment in terms, for example, of

---

Treaty Arbitration, 20 ICSID Rev. – For. Inv. L. J. 357, 368–78 (2005). See also Article 9, ILC Draft Articles on Diplomatic Protection (linking the host State's right to grant diplomatic protection to the company's place of incorporation).

[61] Article 1(2)(ii), Agreement between the Government of the Kingdom of the Netherlands and the Government of the Republic of Indonesia on Promotion and Protection of Investment, signed on April 6, 1994, entered into force on July 1, 1995.

[62] Article 1(3), No. 2, Treaty between the Federal Republic of Germany and the People's Republic of Bulgaria concerning the Reciprocal Encouragement and Protection of Investments, signed on April 12, 1986, entered into force on March 10, 1988.

[63] Article 1(b), Treaty between the United States of America and the Republic of Zaire concerning the Reciprocal Encouragement and Protection of Investment, signed on August 3, 1984, entered into force on July 28, 1989.

taxation or the substantive law of the jurisdiction, including the availability of a BIT.[64]

Some treaties, however, restrict the possibilities of investors using corporate vehicles in a third-country jurisdiction to opt into a different BIT regime. They contain so-called "denial of benefits" clauses that allow the host State to deny investment treaty protection to those investors that have merely opted into the treaty regime in question through the establishment of a shell or mailbox corporation.[65] The United States–Georgia BIT, for instance, provides that "[e]ach Party reserves the right to deny to a company of the other Party the benefits of this Treaty if nationals of a third country own or control the company and … the company has no substantial business activities in the territory of the Party under whose laws it is constituted or organized."[66]

"Denial of benefits" provisions thus recognize that corporate entities can be used as vehicles to bring an investment under the applicability *ratione personae* of a third-country investment treaty. They aim at preventing such corporate structuring for purposes of investment treaty protection in case the corporate vehicle has no business activities in the jurisdiction of incorporation and thus no "genuine link" to this jurisdiction. At the same time, "denial of benefits" clauses are also a clear illustration that States are aware of the possibility of investors channeling their investments through third-country corporations in order to benefit from the protection of a specific investment treaty.

Accordingly, in the absence of such clauses, or other specific treaty language that would exclude corporate special purpose vehicles as investors under an investment treaty,[67] arbitral tribunals have uniformly declined to pierce the corporate veil in order to deny a corporate investor standing and protection under an investment treaty because

---

[64] *Aguas del Tunari* v. *Bolivia*, Decision on Jurisdiction, October 21, 2005, para. 330.

[65] On such clauses see A. Sinclair (*supra* footnote 60), 20 ICSID Rev. – For. Inv. L. J. 357, 378–87 (2005); see also *Plama* v. *Bulgaria*, Decision on Jurisdiction, February 8, 2005, paras. 143–70 (attributing, however, to "denial of benefits" clauses the questionable content of only allowing host States to deny benefits of the investment treaty protection prospectively after the invocation of the clause, instead of handling it properly as an objection to jurisdiction or admissibility of a claim).

[66] Article XII, Treaty between the Government of the United States of America and the Government of the Republic of Georgia concerning the Encouragement and Reciprocal Protection of Investment, signed on March 7, 1994, entered into force on August 10, 1999. Similarly, Article 17(1), Energy Charter Treaty.

[67] See, for example, Article I(2), 1987 ASEAN Agreement which requires, in addition to incorporation, effective management of a company. On this provision see also *Yaung Chi Oo Trading* v. *Myanmar*, Final Award, March 31, 2003, paras. 46–52.

of the diverging nationality of its controlling shareholder.[68] Instead, arbitral tribunals have broadly accepted that corporate vehicles qualify as "investors" and, consequently, accepted that foreign investors can structure their investment via third-State intermediaries in order to have access to an investment treaty and its investor-State dispute settlement mechanism.

Thus, arbitral jurisprudence has accepted that an investor can opt into the treaty regime between the host State and another State and hide behind the corporate veil of a third-country corporation. Likewise, arbitral jurisprudence has accepted that dual nationals can hide behind the corporate veil of a company incorporated in the State of one of their nationalities. Finally, several cases have even accepted that investors with the host State's nationality can hide behind the corporate veil of a company established in a third-country jurisdiction and thus bring their investment under the protection of an investment treaty. This underscores how broadly corporate structuring can be used in order to circumvent restrictions in a specific BIT beyond the operation of an MFN clause.

2   Assuming third-country nationality

How ineffective the concept of nationality becomes as a criterion to limit the benefits of a specific investment treaty to investors with a specific nationality is illustrated by a consistent line of jurisprudence that declines to pierce the corporate veil in order to look, in determining nationality and the scope of application of a BIT *ratione personae*, at the nationality of a company's shareholders.[69] Which power this gives to investors can

---

[68] A somewhat different approach was taken in *TSA* v. *Argentina*, Award, December 19, 2008, paras. 133–62, where the Tribunal pierced, in determining "foreign control" under Article 25(2)(b), ICSID Convention, the corporate veil of the parent company in order to determine ultimate control of the claimant, a locally incorporated subsidiary. Arguably, this decision, however, relates to the interpretation of a specific jurisdictional problem under the ICSID Convention and does not concern the determination of nationality of corporate investors under the scope of application of investment treaties more generally. For a closer discussion *infra* footnotes 105–16 and accompanying text.

[69] See *Wena Hotels.* v. *Egypt*, Decision on Jurisdiction, June 29, 1999, 41 I.L.M. 881, 886–89 (2002); *Champion Trading* v. *Egypt*, Decision on Jurisdiction, October 21, 2003, para. 3.4.2; *Tokios Tokelés* v. *Ukraine*, Decision on Jurisdiction, April 29, 2004, paras. 21–70; *Aguas del Tunari* v. *Bolivia*, Decision on Jurisdiction, October 21, 2005, paras. 206–323; *Saluka* v. *Czech Republic*, Partial Award, March 17, 2006, paras. 222–42; *ADC* v. *Hungary*, Award, October 2, 2006, paras. 335–62; *Rompetrol* v. *Romania*, Decision on Jurisdiction, April 18, 2008, paras. 75–110. See also *Soufraki* v. *United Arab Emirates*, Award, July 7, 2004, para. 83 (observing that had the claimant "contracted with the United Arab

be illustrated, for example, with regard to the ICSID case in *Aguas del Tunari* v. *Bolivia*.[70]

The claimant in this case, Aguas del Tunari, whose concession for providing water and sewage services was terminated, was a company incorporated under Bolivian law. A US company owned 55 percent of its shares, originally by means of an intermediary company established in the Cayman Islands. This original corporate structure did not, however, provide investment treaty coverage to the investment, as neither the Cayman Islands nor the United States had entered into a BIT with Bolivia.[71]

Subsequently, the US parent company restructured its participation in Aguas del Tunari, *inter alia*, by migrating the Cayman Island intermediary to Luxemburg and by interposing, on top of the now Luxemburgian intermediary an additional layer of holding companies incorporated in the Netherlands.[72] Based on the interposition of the Dutch companies the claimant argued that it qualified as an investor under the Dutch–Bolivian BIT that provided:

> the term "nationals" shall comprise with regard to either Contracting Party: ... legal persons controlled directly or indirectly, by nationals of that Contracting Party, but constituted in accordance with the law of the other Contracting Party.[73]

The respondent, by contrast, argued that the Dutch intermediaries constituted "mere shells" without any effective control over the claimant and were themselves controlled by companies in Italy and the United States.[74] Hence, in the respondent's view, the protection of the investment under the Dutch–Bolivian BIT was excluded, since the ultimately controlling shareholders did not qualify themselves as covered investors under this treaty. The respondent therefore urged the Tribunal to pierce the corporate veil in order to determine the nationality of the locally incorporated company based on the nationality of the ultimately controlling company, not merely of one element in a corporate chain.

Emirates through a corporate vehicle incorporated in Italy, rather than contracting in his personal capacity, no problem of jurisdiction would now arise").

[70] *Aguas del Tunari* v. *Bolivia*, Decision on Jurisdiction, October 21, 2005.
[71] *Ibid.*, para. 61 (including a diagram of the original ownership structure).
[72] *Ibid.*, paras. 67 *et seq.* (including a diagram of the new ownership structure at para. 71).
[73] See Article 1(b)(iii), Agreement on Encouragement and Reciprocal Protection of Investments between the Kingdom of the Netherlands and the Republic of Bolivia, signed on March 10, 1992, entered into force on November 1, 1994.
[74] *Aguas del Tunari* v. *Bolivia*, Decision on Jurisdiction, October 21, 2005, paras. 206 *et seq.*

The Tribunal's majority, however, accepted that the claimant qualified as an investor under the Dutch–Bolivian BIT because the Dutch holding companies were legally capable of controlling the Bolivian subsidiary, even if they were themselves controlled by a parent company of another nationality.[75] In holding that "[t]he BIT does not limit the scope of eligible claimants to only the 'ultimate controller'"[76] the majority thus accepted that corporate structuring could be legitimately used in order to come under the protection of a specific BIT. However, the Tribunal also added that treaty-shopping should not be accepted in cases of abusive or fraudulent multi-jurisdictional structuring. It "acknowledge[d] that the corporate form may be abused and that the form may be set aside for fraud or on other grounds."[77] Overall, the decision in *Aguas del Tunari* thus illustrates how foreign investors are able to channel their investment through corporate structures incorporated in third-country jurisdictions and hide behind the corporate veils they establish there, provided that the investment treaty of the corporate vehicle chosen does not endorse the control test for determining corporate nationality or contains other instruments for restricting corporate structuring, such as "denial of benefits" clauses.

Similarly, other arbitral decisions have accepted that investors from one State could opt into a different BIT regime by setting up a corporate vehicle in a third-country jurisdiction. Thus, in *ADC* v. *Hungary* the Tribunal decided that, in determining whether a corporate entity was covered *ratione personae* as an investor by the BIT in question, recourse had to be made solely to the criteria figuring in the relevant BIT.[78] It emphasized that a BIT that linked corporate nationality only to the place of incorporation prevented additional criteria from becoming decisive. Consequently, the sources of funds, the potential control by third-party nationals or other criteria establishing an additional "genuine link" were irrelevant.[79] However, similar to the Tribunal in *Aguas del Tunari*, the Tribunal also suggested that the corporate veil could be pierced in order to look at the nationality of the shareholders, if the multi-jurisdictional corporate structuring were abusive, for example, in "situations where the

---

[75] In the Tribunal's view, the exercise of actual control was not necessary under the BIT; instead, the legal capacity to control was sufficient, *ibid.*, para. 264. The dissenting arbitrator by contrast considered that the exercise of actual control was necessary and thus declined to view Aguas del Tunari as a Dutch investor under the Dutch–Bolivian BIT. See *Aguas del Tunari* v. *Bolivia*, Decision on Jurisdiction, October 21, 2005, Declaration of Alberro-Semerena, paras. 19 *et seq.*

[76] *Aguas del Tunari* v. *Bolivia*, Decision on Jurisdiction, October 21, 2005, para. 237.

[77] *Ibid.*, para. 245.　　[78] *ADC* v. *Hungary*, Award, October 2, 2006, paras. 335–62.

[79] *Ibid.*, paras. 358–59.

real beneficiary of the business misused corporate formalities in order to disguise its true identity and therefore to avoid liability."[80]

Equally, the Tribunal in *Saluka* v. *Czech Republic* accepted that a company set up in the Netherlands by a Japanese investor, which would itself not have benefited from an investment treaty with the Czech Republic, for the sole purpose of holding shares in a company in the host State qualified as an investor under the Dutch–Czech BIT.[81] Similar to the decision in *ADC* v. *Hungary*, the Tribunal in *Saluka* stressed that the wording of the BIT was clear in covering every corporate entity established under the laws of the Netherlands and thus prohibited the "Tribunal to import into the definition of 'investor' some requirement relating to such a relationship having the effect of excluding from the Treaty's protection a company which the language agreed by the parties included within it."[82]

While the Tribunal also suggested that in cases of "fraud and malfeasance" the corporate veil could be exceptionally pierced,[83] it extensively addressed the question of whether shell or mailbox companies were covered as corporate investors.[84] First, it shared the concern that the protection of mere shell companies without any substantial business activity in the home State which is controlled by a company from a third State "lends itself to abuses of the arbitral procedure, and to practices of 'treaty shopping' which can share many of the disadvantages of the widely criticized practice of 'forum shopping.'"[85] At the same time, the Tribunal stated clearly that limiting qualifications for being protected as an investor *ratione personae* could not be implied. It argued:

> The parties had complete freedom of choice in this matter, and they chose to limit entitled "investors" to those satisfying the definition set out in Article 1 of the Treaty. The Tribunal cannot in effect impose upon the parties a definition of "investor" other than that which they themselves agreed. That agreed definition required only that the claimant-investor should be constituted under the laws of (in the present case) The Netherlands, and it is not open to the Tribunal to add other requirements which the parties could themselves have added but which they omitted to add.[86]

Arbitral jurisprudence thus allows, in the absence of limiting language, that even mere shell or mailbox companies are protected as investors

---

[80] *Ibid.*, para. 358.
[81] *Saluka* v. *Czech Republic*, Partial Award, March 17, 2006, paras. 222–42.
[82] *Ibid.*, para. 229.   [83] *Ibid.*, para. 230.
[84] *Ibid.*, paras. 239–42. See also, on the protection of mailbox companies as investors, A. Sinclair (*supra* footnote 60), 20 ICSID Rev. – For. Inv. L. J. 357, 378–87 (2005).
[85] *Saluka* v. *Czech Republic*, Partial Award, March 17, 2006, para. 240.
[86] *Ibid.*, para. 241.

under a BIT that determines corporate nationality according to the place of incorporation. This jurisprudence is consistent with the ordinary meaning approach to treaty interpretation under the Vienna Convention on the Law of Treaties.[87] It is also consistent with the determination of corporate nationality under customary international law which, as the ICJ in *Barcelona Traction* observed, "traditional[ly] attribute[d] the right of diplomatic protection of a corporate entity to the State under the laws of which it is incorporated and in whose territory it has its registered office."[88] Consequently, there is also no basis in customary international law to imply the necessity of additional links beyond the incorporation of a corporate entity.[89] Moreover, from a policy perspective, there is no reason to interpret corporate nationality restrictively by requiring substantial links beyond incorporation, and thus to deny the protection of an investment treaty to shell or mailbox companies, as it is not decisive how investment activity is channeled into a foreign country, but rather that such investment activity takes place. In view of the object and purpose of investment treaties to promote foreign investments, it should thus matter little for the host State where the capital for such investments comes from and what relations a corporate investor has to the State of its incorporation.

3   Dual nationals and corporate structuring

Arbitral jurisprudence has, however, not only accepted that corporate structuring allows investors to opt for the nationality of a third country.

---

[87] See *supra* Ch. IV, footnote 209.

[88] See *Barcelona Traction, Light and Power Company, Limited (Belgium* v. *Spain)*, Judgment, February 5, 1970, I.C.J. Reports 1970, p. 42, para. 70.

[89] See *ADC* v. *Hungary*, Award, October 2, 2006, para. 350; *Saluka* v. *Czech Republic*, Partial Award, March 17, 2006, paras. 229, 240–41. However, in certain extreme circumstances even customary international law allows the disregard of the place of formal incorporation, if no connection whatsoever existed between the company and the State of incorporation. See also Article 9, ILC Draft Articles on Diplomatic Protection (stating that "when the corporation is controlled by nationals of another State or States and has no substantial business activities in the State of incorporation, and the seat of management and financial control of the corporation are both located in another State, that State shall be regarded as the State of nationality"). Such cases will, however, be extremely limited. Thus, the German *Bundesgerichtshof*, for example, considered it sufficient for a "genuine link" to exist between the corporate entity and its State of incorporation, when the company disposed of a telephone line with an answering machine or a forwarding service to a call center in its country of incorporation, and had entered into a software licensing agreement there, see BGH, Case No. I ZR 245/01, Judgment, October 13, 2004, 42 DStR 2113, 2114–15 (2004). This ultimately suggests that even a mailbox is sufficient as a "genuine link," all the more the payment of taxes in the State of incorporation, the existence of the registered office, the presence of officers of the corporation, etc.

It has also accepted that dual nationals can strip off one of their nationalities by structuring an investment through a corporate entity and thus benefit from protection under international law, even though they share a bond of nationality with the host State.[90] In *Champion Trading* v. *Egypt*, for example, the Tribunal was faced with a claim for the violation of various investor rights granted under the US–Egyptian BIT.[91] The claim was brought jointly by a company that was incorporated in the United States and its shareholders who were dual US and Egyptian nationals. All claimants, in turn, were shareholders of a company incorporated under Egyptian law that had invested in the local cotton industry.

Regarding the natural claimants the Tribunal declined jurisdiction based on Article 25(2)(a), ICSID Convention that expressly stipulates that no personal jurisdiction under the Convention existed for claims by "any person who … also had the nationality of the Contracting State party to the dispute."[92] Concerning the corporate claimant, by contrast, the Tribunal accepted its standing as an investor both under the ICSID Convention and Article 1(b) of the US–Egyptian BIT, even though it was owned by the same dual nationals who were denied standing in their personal capacity.[93] In this respect, the Tribunal emphasized that neither the ICSID Convention nor the BIT contained "any exclusion of dual nationals as shareholders of companies of the other Contracting State, contrary to the specific exclusion of Article 25(2)(a) of the Convention regarding natural persons."[94] The decision therefore allowed natural persons with a dual nationality who are prevented from bringing investor-State disputes against the host State under the ICSID Convention in their personal capacity to hide behind the corporate veil of a company established in the State of their second citizenship. By structuring their investment through an intermediary corporate structure they are thus able to circumvent restrictions that otherwise result from their dual nationality.

---

[90] Traditionally, general international law followed the concept of effective nationality regarding dual nationals; see *Nottebohm (Liechtenstein* v. *Guatemala)*, Judgment, April 6, 1955, I.C.J. Reports 1955, pp. 21–23; *Iran–United States, Case No. A/18*, Decision, April 6, 1984, 5 Iran–U.S. C.T.R. 251, 259–66. See also Wisner and Gallus (*supra* footnote 60), J. World Inv. & Trade 927, 930–33 (2004).

[91] *Champion Trading* v. *Egypt*, Decision on Jurisdiction, October 21, 2003.

[92] Article 25(2)(a), ICSID Convention. A possibly broader definition of "investor" under the BIT was, therefore, immaterial for purposes of jurisdiction, see *Champion Trading* v. *Egypt*, Decision on Jurisdiction, October 21, 2003, para. 3.4.1.

[93] *Ibid.*, para. 3.4.2.

[94] *Ibid.*, para. 3.4.2.

4   Protecting host State reinvestments

While the decision in *Champion Trading* is an understandable response by an investment tribunal to a loophole in the protection offered by the ICSID Convention to dual nationals,[95] other tribunals went even further and accepted that nationals of the host State could hide behind the corporate veil of a company incorporated in a third country and, therefore, bring their investment under the protection of the BIT between their home State and the company's home State. For instance, the Tribunal's majority in *Tokios Tokelés* v. *Ukraine* had to entertain a claim brought against Ukraine by a company that was incorporated in Lithuania but was fully owned and controlled by Ukrainian nationals.[96] The respondent, therefore, urged the Tribunal "to 'pierce the corporate veil' … and determine the nationality of the company according to the nationality of its predominant shareholders and managers" because "find[ing] jurisdiction in the case would be tantamount to allowing Ukrainian nationals to pursue international arbitration against their own government, which … would be inconsistent with the object and purpose of the ICSID Convention."[97]

That the company was controlled by nationals of the host State, however, did not matter in the view of the Tribunal's majority. It relied on the object and purpose of the investment treaty that aimed at protecting and promoting investments in order to justify a broad interpretation of the notion of investor,[98] and also pointed to the non-existence of a "denial of benefits" clause that other investment treaties used in order to exclude the protection of such investments.[99] Drawing an *e contrario* argument from the practice of third parties, the Tribunal observed:

> These investment agreements confirm that state parties are capable of excluding from the scope of the agreement entities of the other party that

[95] See Shihata and Parra, *The Experience of the International Centre for Settlement of Investment Disputes*, 14 ICSID Rev. – For. Inv. L. J. 299, 308 (1999) (mentioning a case where the Secretariat had to inform an individual with dual nationality that the Centre could not entertain the case even though the individual was covered by the BIT in question. See on the legislative history of Article 25 and its exclusion of dual nationals Schreuer, *The ICSID Convention*, Article 25, paras. 440 *et seq.* (2001).

[96] *Tokios Tokelés* v. *Ukraine*, Decision on Jurisdiction, April 29, 2004, paras. 21 *et seq.*

[97] *Ibid.*, para. 22.

[98] *Ibid.* (para. 31, quoting the decision in *SGS* v. *Philippines*, Decision on Jurisdiction, January 29, 2004, para. 116).

[99] The US–Argentine BIT, for example, provides that "[e]ach Party reserves the right to deny to any company of the other Party the advantages of this Treaty if (a) nationals of any third country, or nationals of such Party, control such company and the company has no substantial business activities in the territory of the other Party." *Ibid.*, para. 35.

are controlled by nationals of third countries or by nationals of the host country. The Ukraine–Lithuania BIT, by contrast, includes no such "denial of benefits" provision with respect to entities controlled by third-country nationals or by nationals of the denying party. We regard the absence of such a provision as a deliberate choice of the Contracting Parties. In our view, it is not for tribunals to impose limits on the scope of BITs not found in the text, much less limits nowhere evident from the negotiating history. An international tribunal of defined jurisdiction should not reach out to exercise a jurisdiction beyond the borders of the definition. But equally an international tribunal should exercise, and indeed is bound to exercise, the measure of jurisdiction with which it is endowed.[100]

As a result, the Tribunal allowed the claim by the corporate investor to proceed despite its being owned and controlled by nationals of the host State. Similar to the decisions in *Aguas del Tunari*, *ADC* and *Saluka*, the Tribunal also accepted the need for exceptions granting treaty protection to corporate structures if this was necessary "to prevent the misuse of the privileges of legal personality, as in certain cases of fraud or malfeasance, to protect third persons such as a creditor or purchaser, or to prevent the evasion of legal requirements or of obligations."[101]

The majority's conclusion was, however, fiercely criticized by the dissenting President of the Tribunal. He considered that the decision contravened the object and purpose of the ICSID Convention and international law more generally. In his view, the majority's decision "rests on the assumption that the origin of the capital is not relevant and even less decisive. This assumption is flying in the face of the object and purpose of the ICSID Convention and system as explicitly defined both in the Preamble of the Convention and in the Report of the Executive Directors."[102] In recurring fashion, the dissent also emphasized that the transaction lacked an international character and did thus not come under the ambit of international law, including the scope of application of the ICSID Convention and any international investment treaty.[103]

---

[100] *Ibid.*, para. 36 (making reference to *Compañia de Aguas del Aconquija* v. *Argentina*, Decision on Annulment, July 3, 2002, para. 112). In addition, the Tribunal argued that its view was consistent with a number of other ICSID awards and the opinions of ICSID scholars; see *Tokios Tokelés* v. *Ukraine*, Decision on Jurisdiction, April 29, 2004, paras. 40 *et seq.*

[101] *Tokios Tokelés* v. *Ukraine*, Decision on Jurisdiction, April 29, 2004, para. 53 (citing *Barcelona Traction, Light and Power Company, Limited (Belgium* v. *Spain)*, Judgment, February 5, 1970, I.C.J. Reports 1970, p. 39, para. 58).

[102] *Tokios Tokelés* v. *Ukraine*, Decision on Jurisdiction, April 29, 2004, Dissenting Opinion by Prosper Weil, para. 6.

[103] Critical on the majority's decision also Burgstaller, *Nationality of Corporate Investors and International Claims against the Investor's Own State*, 7 J. World Inv. & Trade 857 (2006);

The forceful dissent of the Tribunal's President notwithstanding, subsequent jurisprudence has largely continued the trend of the majority decision in *Tokios Tokelés* to allow the protection of host-State reinvestments under investment treaties and to decline looking behind the corporate veil. Recently, for example, the Tribunal in *Rompetrol* v. *Romania* affirmed the rationale of the decision in *Tokios Tokelés* and emphasized that neither general international law, the ICSID Convention, nor the BIT in question would allow the Tribunal to look behind the corporate veil in order to determine the nationality of the corporate investor that was bringing the claim under the Dutch–Romanian BIT based on the nationality of its controlling shareholders, even if this nationality coincided with the nationality of the host State.[104]

An apparently conflicting decision concerning the protection of reinvestments of investors in their home State, via corporate vehicles incorporated abroad, was handed down in the ICSID arbitration in *TSA* v. *Argentina*. The dispute arose under the Dutch–Argentine BIT and involved the claim by a locally incorporated company based on the termination of a concession for the administration, management, and control of the radio spectrum.[105] Since the claimant was fully owned by TSI, a company incorporated in the Netherlands, it argued that it qualified as a Dutch investor under Article 25(2)(b), ICSID Convention and the Dutch–Argentine BIT which provided that "the term 'investor' shall comprise with regard to either Contracting Party: legal persons, wherever located, controlled, directly or indirectly, by nationals of that Contracting Party."[106]

García-Bolívar, *The Teleology of International Investment Law*, 6 J. World Inv. & Trade 751, 759 (2005).

[104] See *Rompetrol* v. *Romania*, Decision on Jurisdiction, April 18, 2008, paras. 75–110 (concluding at para. 110 "that neither corporate control, effective seat, nor origin of capital has any part to play in the ascertainment of nationality under the Netherlands–Romania BIT"). See also *ADC* v. *Hungary*, Award, October 2, 2006, para. 360 (describing the majority opinion in *Tokios Tokelés* as "still represent[ing] good international law"); see already *Wena Hotels* v. *Egypt*, Decision on Jurisdiction, June 29, 1999, 41 I.L.M. 881, 886–89 (2002) (holding that a company incorporated in the United Kingdom could bring a case against Egypt for violation of the UK–Egyptian BIT, even though the British company was owned and controlled by an individual who allegedly was an Egyptian national).

[105] *TSA* v. *Argentina*, Award, December 19, 2008, paras. 1–4.

[106] See *ibid*, para. 21. Furthermore, Article 10(6) of the Dutch–Argentina BIT provides that "[a] legal person which is incorporated or constituted under the law in force in the territory of one Contracting Party and which, before a dispute arises, is controlled by nationals of the other Contracting Party shall, in accordance with article 25(2)(b) of the Convention be treated for the purposes of the Convention as a national of the other Contracting Party."

TSI itself was owned, on the date relevant for determining the claimant's nationality, by an Argentine citizen.[107] The claimant, however, argued that the Tribunal should look only at the corporate nationality of TSI in determining foreign control and claimant's nationality for the purposes of the dispute.[108]

The Tribunal, however, argued that, in order for a company incorporated in the host State to be treated as being under foreign control pursuant to Article 25(2)(b), ICSID Convention, one needed to determine the ultimate controller and thus pierce the corporate veil of TSI.[109] After pointing out that the case turned on the interpretation of the second clause of Article 25(2)(b), ICSID Convention and thus concerned a different constellation than the ones in *Tokios Tokelés* or *Rompetrol*, it held:

> [t]he situation is different, however, when it comes to the second clause of Article 25(2)(b) of the Convention. Here, the text itself allows the parties to agree to lift the corporate veil, but only "because of foreign control", which justifies, but at the same time conditions, this exception. Although the text refers to juridical persons holding the nationality of the host State that the parties have agreed should be treated as nationals of another contracting State "because of foreign control", the existence and materiality of this foreign control have to be objectively proven in order for them to establish ICSID jurisdiction by their agreement. It would not be consistent with the text, if the tribunal, when establishing whether there is foreign control, would be directed to pierce the veil of the corporate entity national of the host State and to stop short at the second corporate layer it meets, rather than pursuing its objective identification of foreign control up to its real source, using the same criterion with which it started.[110]

The Tribunal supported the "piercing of the corporate veil up to the real source of control,"[111] in particular, because "ultimate control [was] alleged to be in the hands of nationals of the host State, whose formal nationality is also that of the claimant corporation."[112] In the end, the Tribunal's majority declined jurisdiction because it found that the claimant could not be treated as a foreign company under Article 25(2)(b), ICSID Convention, because it was ultimately controlled by an Argentine national.[113] Furthermore, the Tribunal considered that the provisions of the Dutch–Argentine BIT could not modify this conclusion as Article 25(2)(b), ICSID Convention had to be viewed as containing "objective limits … which cannot be extended or derogated from even by agreement of the Parties."[114]

---

[107] *Ibid.*, paras. 128–29, 162.   [108] *Ibid.*, para. 129.   [109] *Ibid.*, paras. 133–62.
[110] *Ibid.*, para. 147.   [111] *Ibid.*, para. 153.   [112] Ibid.   [113] *Ibid.*, para. 162.
[114] *Ibid.*, para. 134. Arbitrator Aldonas dissented from the Tribunal decision in this respect and argued that the test for "foreign control" under Article 25(2)(b), ICSID Convention

The decision of *TSA* v. *Argentina* could be interpreted as refuting the approaches taken by the tribunals in *Tokios Tokelés*, *Rompetrol* and others and be viewed as supporting the control theory in determining corporate nationality under investment treaties more generally. It would then constitute a counter-movement to the possibilities of multilateralizing international investment relations through corporate structuring that other tribunals have allowed. However, it is crucial to understand that *TSA* v. *Argentina* concerned only the specific question under which circumstances a company that is incorporated in the host State could be treated as being under foreign control pursuant to the second alternative of Article 25(2)(b), ICSID Convention. The decision, by contrast, did not expressly deal with the question of how the locally incorporated company qualified under the Dutch–Argentine BIT.[115] Notwithstanding the tensions that exist between the approaches in *TSA*, on the one hand, and *Aguas del Tunari*, on the other, which declined to search for the ultimately controlling shareholder,[116] the scope of the decision in *TSA* v. *Argentina* is rather limited and only concerns a specific jurisdictional problem under the ICSID Convention. It does not, by contrast, invalidate the possibilities of corporate structuring in cases of host State reinvestment treaties more genrally, and does not affect procedural frameworks that can govern investment treaty artitrations other than the ICSID Convention.

5　Corporate structuring and treaty-shopping

In general, arbitral tribunals thus usually reject determining corporate nationality for purposes of BIT protection using any form of the control theory, unless the treaty in question explicitly mandates such an approach, and hence allow investment treaty-shopping through corporate structuring. Allowing such treaty-shopping in the case of investment protection is also preferable from a policy perspective. First, linking investment protection to a specific nationality meets considerable practical problems

---

was "expressly dependent on an agreement between 'the parties,' not some putative 'objective test,'" thus, mandating giving effect to the way the BIT in question defined a locally incorporated company under foreign control; see Dissenting Opinion of Arbitrator Grant D. Aldonas, para. 8.

[115] See *TSA* v. *Argentina*, Award, December 19, 2008, para. 162 (stating that "whatever interpretation is given to the BIT between Argentina and the Netherlands, including the Protocol to the BIT, TSA cannot be treated, for the purposes of Article 25(2)(b) of the ICSID Convention, as a national of the Netherlands because of absence of 'foreign control'").

[116] See *supra* footnotes 70–77 and accompanying text.

as regards the protection of investments by corporate investors. While determining corporate nationality according to the nationality of the controlling shareholders under the control theory may still be feasible in simple two- or three-level structures, such determinations will become increasingly difficult, if not impossible, with increasing numbers of shareholders, increasing numbers of overlapping corporate levels, and increasing numbers of nationalities involved.[117] In the case of publicly traded companies that finance themselves over the stock markets, for example, the nationality of the shareholders will often be unknown. Determining the nationality of a company on such a basis therefore entails significant, if not prohibitive, costs for obtaining information about the shareholder structure and the shareholders' nationalities.

Second, from an economic perspective it matters little for a host State from where the capital for investment projects originates. The contribution that economic activity makes to economic growth and development in a host State does not depend on whether capital flows in from State A or State B.[118] Ultimately, even the (re-)investment of nationals of the host State via third-country intermediaries will further economic growth and development in the host State. This is all the more so as channeling investments into many countries, in particular those with developing or transitioning economies, through corporate vehicles that are incorporated in states with major financial and capital markets will facilitate the financing of the respective investment activity and increase the trust the market has in such companies. In addition, the host State's national could also decide to invest elsewhere and divert funds from its home State.

Taking the object and purpose of investment treaties seriously, therefore, suggests that the source of capital does not matter. Accordingly, there is no, at least no economic, reason why investors from one country or another, including investors from the host State, should receive less or more preferable treatment.[119] Instead, uniform treatment and uniform levels of investment protection that meet the institutional requirement that markets need in order to function carry the greatest benefits for host States and home States as investment can flow to wherever it is allocated most efficiently. The corporate structure, by contrast, is merely the vehicle for allowing investments to enter into protection regimes that facilitate and back up their efficient use.

---

[117] *Cf.* Alexandrov (*supra* footnote 9), 6 J. World Inv. & Trade 387, 400 (2005).
[118] On the economic benefits of foreign investment in general see *supra* Ch. III.C.1.
[119] See also *supra* Ch. III.C (on the economic rationales for uniform standards of investment protection).

Consequently, it is not decisive how investment activity is channeled into a country, but rather that such investment activities take place, as it generates economic growth and development and is thus beneficial for the host State as well as the various home States involved. Moreover, the considerations are arguably also different from considerations regarding the taxation of corporate companies. In that context, offshore corporate structuring may involve questions of tax evasion and, therefore, create an interest of the home State in the restriction of treaty-shopping. In the investment context, by contrast, treaty-shopping merely ensures that investments benefit from effective investment protection, an interest that is shared by home and host States alike.[120]

C   Conclusion

Most investment treaties are based on broad notions of investment and investor. Consequently, BITs commonly not only protect assets in the host country that are directly held by foreign investors, but also protect share-holdings in locally incorporated companies. This protection is regularly not restricted to majority shareholders, but equally encompasses minority non-controlling shareholders. Similarly, many, if not most, investment treaties protect shareholdings that are indirectly held through intermediary companies that are incorporated in the investor's home State, the host State, or a third-country jurisdiction.

This protection of shareholders has significant effects in multilateralizing international investment law because it multiplies the application of investment treaties to the measures the host State takes in regulating the conduct of locally incorporated, but foreign-owned, companies. As such companies can be owned, either directly or indirectly, by a potentially infinite number of foreign investors with different nationalities, the host State has to adapt its behavior to the most extensive and far-reaching of its BITs if it wants to avoid engaging its international responsibility under any of its investment treaties. Compliance with all of its BITs, therefore, requires the host State to comply with its most comprehensive and far-reaching investment treaty.

Although shareholder-investors that are not directly protected by an investment treaty do not have standing to hold the host State liable for measures that violate such a treaty, they nevertheless benefit indirectly from the protection of every third-party BIT that covers other

[120]   See *supra* Ch. III.C.

shareholder-investors in the same corporate entity. The protection of shareholders, therefore, passively multilateralizes investment treaty protection by *de facto* extending the effect of BITs *ratione personae* to investors who are not directly protected. From the host State's compliance perspective, there is thus little difference between a regime based on bilateral treaties and a multilateral regime of investment protection as compliance with the most comprehensive regime will comprise compliance with obligations under less favorable BITs. The effect of shareholder protection is, therefore, similar to the effect of MFN clauses in that the host State will have to adapt its behavior to the most favorable investment treaty that could potentially apply. *De facto* the most comprehensive BIT obligations thus have a similar effect as *erga omnes partes* obligations in a multilateral regime.

While the protection of shareholders as investors entails a passive multilateralization, corporate structuring enables investors to influence the level of investment protection actively. By channeling an investment through corporate vehicles in one or several third-country jurisdictions, investors can effectively change their nationality and thereby come under the scope of application of virtually any other of the host State's BITs, provided that the BIT in question defines corporate nationality according to the company's place of incorporation or its corporate seat and does not look at the nationality of the company's shareholders.

Thus, arbitral jurisprudence has consistently accepted treaty-shopping through corporate structuring in a variety of circumstances, allowing not only foreign investors to opt into third-party BIT regimes, but also allowing dual nationals and nationals of the host State to hide behind the corporate veil of a foreign corporation in order to protect their investment. Corporate structuring, in this context, is particularly facilitated if the corporate entity does not have to unfold significant business activity in the home State in order to qualify as a national company of that State. Rather, in many cases establishing mere shell or mailbox corporations is often sufficient, unless the BIT in question contains specific provisions, such as a "denial of benefits" clause, that excludes the protection of such companies.

Corporate structuring opens broad possibilities for investors to bring their investment under the protection of a specific BIT with the host State. They are not only capable of choosing among different levels of treaty protection, but are also able to bring their investment under BIT protection in cases where none had originally existed, either because the investor's home State had not entered into a BIT with the host State at all or because the investor was a national of the host State. Investors are thus able to shop for the best possible protection under investment treaties. In essence, treaty-shopping through corporate structuring, therefore, has similar effects to the operation of MFN clauses by allowing investors to benefit from the host State's most favorable treatment of foreign investors under any one of its BITs. This also multilateralizes investment treaties because virtually any investor from virtually any country is capable of opting into virtually any BIT regime.

In the end, it may even be sufficient for a host State to have signed and ratified one single BIT in order to allow any investment to benefit from the rights and benefits under the BIT, provided that the treaty in question does not require piercing the corporate veil to determine the nationality of corporate investors. Access to investment protection in a specific host State does not, therefore, necessarily require ratification of multiple investment treaties by the host State. With respect to the practicalities of negotiation, conclusion, and ratification of treaties, corporate structuring thus levels differences between multilateral and bilateral approaches. Similar to a multilateral convention, a single act rather than the conclusion of multiple treaties can be sufficient to participate in the regime of international investment protection.

Similarly, investors are able to react flexibly to problems between the host State and their respective home State which might impact the protection granted under their home State BIT, such as the suspension of BIT obligations as counter-measures, or even the termination of the BIT, by restructuring their investment so as to come under the protection of a different BIT. If, for example, State B suspends the protection of investors under the BIT with State A as a counter-measure for State A's violation of another international law obligation vis-à-vis State B, the investor from State A can react by bringing its investment under the protective umbrella of the BIT between State B and State C that is unaffected by the tensions in the relationship between States B and A.[121] Similarly, in case State B terminates its BIT with State A, investors from State A can restructure their investment and bring it under the protection of the BIT between States B and C.[122]

This shows that corporate structuring not only multilateralizes access to the international investment regime, but also restricts the selective

---

[121] See *supra* footnotes 57–59 and accompanying text.

[122] See A. Sinclair (*supra* footnote 60), 20 ICSID Rev. 357 (2005); Deutsch and Tylor, *Options for the Nervous Investor in Venezuela*, 5(2) Transnat'l Disp. Mgmt. (2008).

exit from this regime in relation to specific States. Instead, exit from international investment protection is possible only if the host State terminates all of its bilateral treaty relationships or structures them in a way so as to exclude effectively any possibility of corporate structuring. Similar to the situation in a multilateral regime, access to international investment protection by BITs is thus possible by means of a single ratification; exit from the regime, in turn, similar to the situation under a multilateral convention, requires complete isolation from the entire system by reneging its benefits vis-à-vis all other contracting parties.

Moreover, corporate structuring has a tendency to provide investment protection beyond the classical boundaries of international law as it may allow nationals of the host State to opt into an international legal regime.[123] Thus, corporate structuring is not only a source of the multilateralization, but the universalization of international investment law that sets standards for the relationship between the State and private economic actors more generally, independent of whether foreign or domestic investors are involved.

As a consequence, the possibility of corporate structuring shows that nationality as a criterion to restrict the benefits of an investment treaty to specific nationals is becoming increasingly ineffective in regulating access to, and exclusion from, the protection of bilateral investment treaties. It shows that ordering international investment relations on a truly bilateral basis with rights and benefits only accruing to the nationals of one specific home State is an increasingly illusionary undertaking, since the nationality of corporate investors has become as fungible as capital in global markets. Instead, the possibility for investors to set up multi-level, multi-jurisdictional corporate structures allows them to circumvent remaining bilateral elements in international investment relations because corporate nationality no longer functions effectively as a distinguishing criterion. Ultimately, BIT protection is less a question of the investor's nationality, but rather a question of whether an investment is structured in a specific way.

Ultimately, the possibilities of multi-jurisdictional structuring are a phenomenon of the globalization of financial markets and cross-border economic activities that illustrate not only that the nation-State and the criteria that have traditionally served to separate different spheres of sovereignty over persons and companies are increasingly disintegrating as an ordering paradigm for social relations on the international level, but that the idea of national economies interacting as participants in a global

---

[123] See *supra* Ch. V.B.4.

economy is giving way to the idea of a truly global market economy in which private economic actors with numerous national backgrounds directly interact in a single global market. In line with this transformation of the global economy, the nature of bilateral obligations under BITs is increasingly multilateralizing. While formally remaining attached to the bilateral form of customary international law rules on diplomatic protection that the ICJ contrasted in *Barcelona Traction* with *erga omnes* obligations and that require the determination of whether the host State's conduct violated an obligation that was specifically owed to the investor's home State and caused damage to the investor as their beneficiaries,[124] BIT obligations are losing their strict bilateral focus with the increasing decoupling of capital and nationality. As a consequence, instead of establishing differing rules depending on the nationality of the foreign investor, host States have to adapt their own conduct to uniform standards that result from their most comprehensive BIT obligations.

---

[124] *Barcelona Traction, Light and Power Company, Limited (Belgium* v. *Spain)*, Judgment, February 5, 1970, I.C.J. Reports 1970, pp. 32–33, paras. 33–35.

VI

Multilateral enforcement of international investment law

The multilateralization of international investment law and the emergence of uniform principles of investment protection are not only a matter of the resemblance of treaty texts, of the operation of MFN clauses, and of the effects of corporate structuring. They are also championed by the rules on investor-State dispute settlement. At a time when capital-exporting and capital-importing States were still unable to agree on a common set of substantive rules for international investment relations, above all the appropriate level of protection of foreign investors, they agreed, by concluding the ICSID Convention in the mid-1960s, to establish multilateral rules for the procedural aspects of investor-State disputes. Genuine multilateralism in this context presumably worked because States agreed that investor-State dispute settlement constituted a valuable institution, even though they disagreed on the extent of restrictions to be imposed on States regarding the treatment of foreign investors.

Although the ICSID Convention is not the only procedural framework under which investment treaty arbitration can take place,[1] it remains the most important one, having governed 62 percent of the 290 investment treaty-based disputes known by the end of 2007.[2] Furthermore, the ICSID Convention illustrates best the importance of the procedural framework for the multilateralization of international investment law. For this reason, the following chapter concentrates on investor-State dispute settlement under the ICSID Convention.

Notwithstanding its exclusively procedural scope, the ICSID Convention contributes significantly to the multilateralization of international investment law. Already from a formal perspective, it establishes a uniform framework for the settlement of investor-State disputes. This responds to the objective of creating a level playing field not only in terms

---

[1] Depending on the consent of the host State, investment treaty disputes can also be settled under the rules of the ICSID Additional Facility, UNCITRAL Arbitration Rules or any another agreed upon set of arbitration rules or ad hoc arbitration.

[2] UNCTAD, *Latest Developments in Investor-State Dispute Settlement*, pp. 1–2 (2008).

of the substantive treatment of foreign investors, but also concerning the assertion of breaches and the enforcement of investment treaties as a prerequisite for competition among investors from different home States, which in turn enables a more efficient use of capital.[3] In addition, the ICSID Convention multilateralizes the enforcement of rights and obligations stemming from investment treaties as it requires States to recognize and enforce awards rendered under the Convention.[4] This responds to the objective of implementing an arbitral award effectively across several jurisdictions, but also transforms the effect of an award concerning a specific BIT into an obligation that has to be complied with by all State parties to the ICSID Convention.

The contribution of investor-State dispute settlement to the multilateralization of international investment law is, however, much broader and more significant than the exclusive focus on uniform procedural rules on investor-State arbitration suggests. The ICSID Convention is not only formally a multilateral instrument that establishes a uniform procedural framework which multilateralizes international investment relations by creating uniform dispute settlement rules and by providing for multilateral recognition and enforcement of ICSID awards. Investor-State arbitration also transforms international investment law from an instrument of inter-State diplomacy into a genuinely legal framework. It breaks fundamentally with the traditional bilateral structure of compliance with international law through inter-State negotiation and recourse to counter-measures.[5] Instead, the empowerment of investors to initiate arbitration under investment treaties directly against the host State entails an essential move away from bilateral inter-State compliance toward a multilateral ordering structure. It effectively removes the power of States to both unilaterally defect from investment treaties and bilaterally negotiate around the consequences of breaches of such treaties. This function of

---

[3] See *supra* Ch. III.C.1.

[4] Again, the ICSID Convention is not the exclusive framework governing investor-State disputes. While it contains its own rules for the recognition and enforcement of arbitral awards, other investor-State disputes rendered outside its scope of application can be recognized and enforced beyond the arbitral situs pursuant to the United Nations Convention on the Recognition and Enforcement of Foreign Arbitral Awards, done at New York on June 10, 1958, 330 U.N.T.S. 38 (New York Convention). Parallel to the ICSID Convention, the New York Convention does contain uniform rules concerning the recognition and enforcement of commercial arbitral awards. However, it leaves more leeway to the enforcement-State to refuse enforcement of arbitral awards. See *infra* Ch. VI.A.2.d.

[5] See Articles 49–53, ILC Articles on State Responsibility.

investment treaty arbitration as a compliance mechanism for international investment law that excludes post-breach bilateralism will thus be dealt with in the first part of this chapter.

Furthermore, investor-State arbitration also has another impact on international investment law that adds to its multilateralization. By adjudicating disputes between foreign investors and host States and by interpreting the relevant investment treaty, tribunals not only apply generally framed rules and principles to a specific case and thereby concretize the law in view of specific facts, they also assume a norm-creative function in adjudicating investor-State disputes. Even though this claim is a truism for legal theorists and legal scholars in the domestic realm, it constitutes a *problématique that* is only tentatively reflected upon in international investment law.[6]

By assuming a norm-generative function, the institutionalization of investor-State dispute settlement responds – as will be argued in the second part of this chapter – to the problem of solving uncertainty in international investment relations. Investor-State arbitration thus constitutes a mechanism not only for the *ex post* settlement of investment treaty disputes, but also prospectively helps to "fill gaps" that exist in these treaties. This enables States to enter into stable long-term investment relations without the need for continuous bilateral bargaining. In this regard, investor-State arbitration responds to the need to solve uncertainty and ambiguity in international investment relations, to stabilize them over time, and to adapt them to changing realities. Most notably, the norm-generative function of investment treaty arbitration is not limited to the specific BIT that governs the dispute at hand, but equally affects unrelated third-party BITs.

A   Investment treaty arbitration as a compliance mechanism

Traditionally, enforcement of international law was vested exclusively in the hands of States. In case of a violation of international law, the State that was harmed by the breach could resort to counter-measures, such as reprisals, retaliation, and ultimately even the use of force, in order to make the violating State comply with its obligations. Enforcement, in this context, was essentially bilateral, as only the beneficiary of a

---

[6] See, for example, Paulsson, *International Arbitration and the Generation of Legal Norms,* 3(5) Transnat'l Disp. Mgmt. (2006).

specific obligation under international law was entitled to proceed with enforcement. In addition, enforcement – and thus actual compliance – depended to a large extent on the factual power relationships between States. Consequently, "bilateralism unveils, and even endorses, the crucial dependence of the enforceability of a State's international legal rights upon a favourable distribution of factual power."[7]

Modern investment treaties, by contrast, break with this State-centered mode of enforcement. Instead of laying enforcement exclusively in the hands of States, they provide for the right of foreign investors to have recourse to investor-State arbitration and directly claim for the violation of the respective investment treaty. This constitutes a fundamental shift in the compliance mechanisms under international law and elevates investment treaties from bilateral enforcement rationales towards an objective, law-based order in which the general principles of investment protection can be enforced uniformly independent of the actual power relations between the States concerned. This becomes particularly clear when contrasting the traditional inter-State compliance structure, and the broad leeway it leaves to States in subjecting enforcement to considerations motivated by bilateralism, with the mechanism of investor-State arbitration.

1   Bilateralism in traditional international law compliance structures

Even though customary international law provided for some substantive protection to foreign investment,[8] its compliance mechanism followed essentially bilateral rationales. Above all, it lacked an enforcement mechanism that was independent of the relative power relationship between home and host States. The investor's primary remedy existed in having recourse to the domestic courts of the host State. However, said courts were often not well placed to entertain investor-State disputes because the court system, in particular in developing countries, was underdeveloped, not sufficiently independent vis-à-vis the host government, or even corrupt.[9] Furthermore, an investor could invoke only the customary

---

[7] Simma, *From Bilateralism to Community Interest in International Law*, 250 Recueil des Cours 217, 233 (1994).

[8] See *supra* Ch. II.A.1.

[9] More generally on the problem of corruption in the judiciary, see Buscaglia and Dakolias, *An Analysis of the Causes of Corruption in the Judiciary*, 30 Law & Pol'y Int'l Bus. 95 (1999); Dakolias and Thachuk, *The Problem of Eradicating Corruption from the Judiciary*, 18 Wis. Int'l L. J. 353 (2000).

international law protection of aliens if the host State had transformed international law into its domestic legal order, either by following the monist theory on the relationship of international and national law, or by actively transposing international into domestic law. Otherwise, the investor could only ask its home State for diplomatic protection, the effectiveness of which depended, however, on the home State's relative power and willingness to enforce international law against the host State, and, in case diplomatic protection was sought through means of formal inter-State dispute settlement, required the host State's consent.[10]

This traditional compliance mechanism was insufficient and allowed bilateral rationales to unfold, mainly for two reasons. First, the investor, as the one whose interests were immediately affected, was not vested with the power to enforce its rights directly against the host State and independently from its home State's intervention. Instead, the investor was mediated through an inter-State prism. Second, even in cases where the home State granted diplomatic protection, the available remedies were insufficient to protect foreign investment effectively and to induce the host State to comply with any obligation under international law. As a consequence, traditional international law enforcement mechanisms concerning the protection of foreign investors provided ample space for post-breach bilateral bargaining that could eventually invalidate the pre-existing substantive rules of investment protection.

(a)   The mediation of foreign investors through an
inter-State prism

Traditionally, foreign investors could not directly make host States comply with their obligations under customary international law. Instead, foreign investors were mediated through an inter-State prism that originated in the traditional positivist understanding of international law as *ius inter gentes*. The positivist understanding of international law not only construed a fundamental difference between domestic and international law, but also denied the individual any independent standing.[11] The "essential difference"[12] between international and municipal law was conceived in the most fundamental way. It found its expression not only in a strict voluntarism with

---

[10] On diplomatic protection generally, see Amerasinghe, *Diplomatic Protection* (2008).
[11] *Cf.* Korowicz, *The Problem of the International Personality of Individuals*, 50 A.J.I.L. 533 (1956).
[12] Oppenheim, *International Law*, vol. I, § 20, p. 25 (1905); similarly Triepel, *Völkerrecht und Landesrecht*, p. 9 (1899) (considering international and municipal law as distinct with regard to their sources and distinct with regard to the social relations they govern).

respect to the sources of international law, but also regarding the subject-matter regulated by the respective legal orders: "Municipal Law regulates relations between the individuals under the sway of the respective State and the relations between this State and the respective individuals. International Law, on the other hand, regulates relations between the member States of the Family of Nations."[13] In accordance with the paradigm of international law as *ius inter gentes*, international legal positivism construed the question of legal personality in international law: "States solely and exclusively are the subjects of International Law. This means that the Law of Nations is the law for the international conduct of States, and not of their citizens."[14]

Consequently, obligations under international law could not exist between a host State and a foreign investor. Instead, the idea underlying the customary international law of aliens was that the violation of interests of a foreign investor constituted a violation of the foreigner's home State. This understanding found its classical expression in the *Mavrommatis Palestine Concessions* case that the Permanent Court of International Justice (PCIJ) decided in 1924.

In this case, the Greek Government had brought a claim against Britain alleging that the Palestinian Government, which was under the mandate of Britain at the time, had violated a concession granted to a Greek national for the construction and operation of an electric tramway and the supply of electric light, power, and drinking water in Jerusalem. Concerning the relationship between the Greek investor, Britain as the host State and Greece as the investor's home State, the PCIJ stated:

> In the case of the Mavrommatis concessions it is true that the dispute was at first between a private person and a State – i.e. between M. Mavrommatis and Great Britain. Subsequently, the Greek Government took up the case. The dispute then entered upon a new phase; it entered the domain of international law, and became a dispute between two States ... It is an elementary principle of international law that a State is entitled to protect its subjects, when injured by acts contrary to international law committed by another State, from whom they have been unable to obtain satisfaction through the ordinary channels. By taking up the case of one of its subjects and by resorting to diplomatic action or international judicial proceedings on his behalf, a State is in reality asserting its own rights – its right to ensure, in the person of its subjects, respect for the rules of international law.[15]

---

[13] Oppenheim (*supra* footnote 12), § 20, p. 26 (1905).
[14] *Ibid.*, § 13, pp. 18 *et seq.*
[15] *The Mavrommatis Palestine Concessions (Greece v. Britain)*, Judgment, August 30, 1924, P.C.I.J. Series A, No. 2 (1924), p. 12. Similarly, *The Factory at Chorzów (Claim for*

(b)   Structural insufficiencies of diplomatic protection

Independent of the fact that the host State could not assume obligations under international law vis-à-vis the foreign investor, the enforcement mechanisms for inter-State obligations relied on an embryonic institutional infrastructure. Inter-State adjudication before international courts and tribunals, in particular, was possible only with the consent of both States. This often required bilateral negotiations, the outcome of which depended more on the relative strength of the parties than on the merits of a claim as of right.

Furthermore, the system of diplomatic protection itself was prone to be influenced by specific interests reigning in the bilateral inter-State relationship. First, diplomatic protection is a right of a State vis-à-vis another State to "ensure in the person of its nationals respect for the rules of international law."[16] There is, however, no corresponding duty of the home States towards its own nationals to grant diplomatic protection. Instead, States remain free to exercise this right in a discretionary way.[17]

Indemnity) (Germany v. *Poland)*, Merits, Judgment, September 13, 1928, P.C.I.J. Series A, No. 17 (1928), p. 28; *Payment of Various Serbian Loans Issued in France (France* v. *Kingdom of the Serbs, Croats and Slovenes)*, Judgment, July 12, 1929, P.C.I.J. Series A, No. 20/21 (1929), p. 17; *The Panevezys-Saldutiskis Railway Case (Estonia* v. *Lithuania)*, Judgment, February 28, 1939, P.C.I.J. Series A/B, No. 76 (1939), p. 16; *Nottebohm (Liechtenstein* v. *Guatemala)*, Judgment, April 6, 1955, I.C.J. Reports 1955, p. 24; *Barcelona Traction, Light and Power Company, Limited (Belgium* v. *Spain)*, Judgment, February 5, 1970, I.C.J. Reports 1970, pp. 45–46, para. 85.

[16]   See *supra* footnote 15. There is, however a development in the jurisprudence of the ICJ that suggests that the rules on diplomatic protection constitute less a restriction of the substantive rights of an alien vis-à-vis a foreign State, but exclusively a restriction of the alien's standing in international law dispute settlement mechanisms. See Schill, *Der völkerrechtliche Staatsnotstand in der Entscheidung des BVerfG zu Argentinischen Staatsanleihen*, 68 ZaöRV 45, 52–56 (2008).

[17]   See already Borchard, *The Diplomatic Protection of Citizens Abroad*, pp. 29–30, 354, 356, 363–65 (1915); *Barcelona Traction, Light and Power Company Limited (Belgium* v. *Spain)*, Judgment, February 5, 1970, I.C.J. Reports 1970, p. 44, para. 79 (stressing the discretion States dispose of as a matter of international law in espousing claims of their nationals). Likewise, most domestic legal systems do not oblige the State to pursue claims of their nationals by means of diplomatic protection; see, for example, Hofmann, *Grundrechte und grenzüberschreitende Sachverhalte*, pp. 107 *et seq.* (1994) (regarding the situation in Germany); *Abbasi et al.* v. *Secretary of State* [2002] EWCA Civ 1598 (regarding the situation in the United Kingdom); *Kaunda* v. *President of the Republic of South Africa*, 44 I.L.M. 173 (2005) (regarding the situation in South Africa). See also Vermeer-Künzli, *Restricting Discretion: Judicial Review of Diplomatic Protection*, 75 Nordic J. Int'l L 279 (2006) (discussing national jurisprudence and developments on the international level and observing an emerging development towards a State's obligation to exercise diplomatic protection in cases of serious violations of human rights law). Ultimately, this discretion is the expression of the difference in the legal relation between the investor

Second, as a consequence of the distinction between domestic and international law, the home State is vested, under international law, with exclusive control over the rights of their nationals on the international level and is entitled to settle, waive or modify the rights of their nationals by an international agreement with the host State.[18] In practice, this entitlement has led to the settlement of international claims concerning the violation of the rights of foreigners by lump-sum agreements.[19] These agreements were used particularly to deal with the compensatory framework in the aftermath of armed conflicts or other large-scale events like revolutions and traditionally fixed the compensation of foreign nationals to a fraction of the full claim and ruled out any further compensation. They illustrate the significant influence bilateral inter-State relations have even in cases of clear breaches of international law on the compliance with international obligations.

Finally, in view of the distinction between the rights of the investor and the rights of its home State the entitlement to receive compensation for the violation of international law protecting foreign nationals is not vested in the alien but in its home State. Therefore, compensation did not have to be paid to the investor, but to the home State that espoused the claim.[20] The home State, in turn, is under no obligation to pass the compensation on to the investor who suffered the damage.[21]

(c)   Distinction between State and investor interests

Essentially, the distinction between the municipal and the international legal order results from the distinction between the interests of the foreign investor and the interests of its home State. While the investor's interest involves exclusively economic interests concerning the investment relationship with the host State, its home State may have additional interests that are external to the investor-State relations. In its decision to espouse a

---

and the host State, on the one hand, and the relationship between the two States, on the other hand.

[18] Borchard (*supra* footnote 17), pp. 366–75 (1915). See also Hagelberg, *Die völkerrechtliche Verfügungsbefugnis des Staates über Rechtsansprüche von Privatpersonen*, pp. 49–52 (2006) (arguing, however, that human rights law restricts the home State's disposition of claims of its nationals, *ibid.*, pp. 147 *et seq.*); similarly, Dolzer, *Eigentum, Enteignung und Entschädigung im geltenden Völkerrecht*, pp. 136 *et seq.* (1985).

[19] See Lillich and Weston, *International Claims: Their Settlement by Lump-Sum Agreements* (1975); Weston, Bederman and Lillich, *International Claims: Their Settlement by Lump-Sum Agreements 1975–1995* (1999).

[20] Borchard (*supra* footnote 17), pp. 356–59, 383–88 (1915); Hagelberg (*supra* footnote 18), p. 51 (2006).

[21] See Hagelberg (*supra* footnote 18), p. 51, footnote 110 (with further references) (2006).

claim by one of its nationals, the home State is free to take into account not only economic aspects that play a role, but also considerations that factor into the inter-State relationship. This may include aspects of a broader political nature, such as geo-strategic factors. The actual enforcement of international law on the inter-State level thus depends on numerous political factors that find their origin in bilateral inter-State relations.

To take a recent example: in a situation like the Argentine economic crisis of 2001/2002, a foreign investor will regularly only be interested in recovering damages, without considering the consequences that the payment of such damages may have on the political and economic situation in the country. While the investor presumably cares little if the obligation to pay compensation leads to social unrest or a further political and economic destabilization, foreign States will more likely include such considerations when facing the decision about whether to grant diplomatic protection. Although the rationale for a State's discretion in exercising diplomatic protection is the need to vest States with sufficient flexibility in their foreign relations, this discretion also allows bilateralist considerations to unfold, as the home State will proceed with the enforcement or abstain from it based on its relations to the host State and depending on its own interests. This can eventually lead to discrimination among investors in the same host State in the enforcement of international investment obligations depending on the investor's nationality.

2 The empowerment of investment tribunals

While the traditional inter-State enforcement of obligations under international law was thus subject to a number of extra-legal considerations, modern international investment law has brought a fundamental change in this respect. Instead of retaining power over the enforcement of international investment treaties, States have to a large extent subordinated to external control by arbitral tribunals. This change in the enforcement of international investment law excludes, to a greater extent, the possibilities for States to influence the system of investment protection through post-breach bilateral bargaining.

Four components are critical to understanding the empowerment of arbitral tribunals in this context: (1) the direct right of action by a foreign investor to seek damages for a violation of an investment treaty; (2) the limited influence of States on the arbitral process itself; (3) the limited review of arbitral awards; and (4) the provisions on recognition and enforcement of investment treaty awards. Taken together, these elements transform investor-State arbitration into an effective instrument to compel compliance by States with their obligations under investment treaties independent of specific bilateral considerations.

(a)   The investor's right to seek damages

The introduction of a private right of action fundamentally breaks with the traditional enforcement mechanism of international investment law. Investors under modern investment treaties are no longer mediated through an inter-State prism. Instead of depending upon their home State's power and willingness to espouse their claim, they have an independent right of action to initiate investor-State arbitration and are able to seek redress in their own name against violations by the host State of the applicable investment treaty. The available remedies, in this context, are generally those that are also available on the inter-State level under the law on State responsibility.[22] Yet, the most common remedy – and the only one that is readily enforceable – consists in a claim for damages, even though the investor can also demand non-pecuniary relief.[23]

The investor's right of action to claim damages for the violation of an investment treaty is particularly powerful, since the jurisdiction of investment tribunals does not rest on the dispute-specific consent of the host State. Instead, the State's consent is regularly given in advance, in unconditional and generalized form, in the applicable investment treaty. An investor claiming violations of an investment treaty can invoke this consent and initiate investment arbitration.[24] The host State, in turn, cannot withdraw its consent unilaterally[25] or frustrate arbitration by default.[26]

The introduction of this private right of action has a number of consequences. First, investor-State dispute settlement transforms the way

---

[22] See Articles 34–39, ILC Articles on State Responsibility.

[23] *Cf.* Schreuer, *Non-Pecuniary Remedies in ICSID Arbitration*, 20 Arb. Int'l 325 (2005); Endicott, *Remedies in Investor-State Arbitration: Restitution, Specific Performance and Declaratory Awards*, in Kahn and Wälde (eds.), *New Aspects of International Investment Law*, p. 517 (2007).

[24] See Paulsson, *Arbitration Without Privity*, 10 ICSID Rev. – For. Inv. L. J. 232 (1995); Cremades, *Arbitration in Investment Treaties: Public Offer of Arbitration in Investment-Protection Treaties*, in Briner *et al.* (eds.), *Law of International Business and Dispute Settlement in the 21st Century*, pp. 149 *et seq.* (2001); Bjorklund, *Contract Without Privity: Sovereign Offer and Investor Acceptance*, 2 Chi. J. Int'l L. 183 (2001).

[25] See Article 25(1), ICSID Convention.

[26] *Cf.*, for example, *American Manufacturing & Trading* v. *Zaire*, Award, February 21, 1997, paras. 3.23, 3.26; *Iurii Bogdanov* v. *Moldova*, Arbitral Award, September 22, 2005, para. 3.3, p. 11 (concerning two cases of host State default in participating in the proceedings).

disputes are settled in the realm of international investment relations from a bilateral and dyadic negotiation-based structure into an instrument of triadic dispute settlement.[27] It introduces an independent third party, the arbitral tribunal, and thereby enables the settlement of disputes between foreign investors and host States according to pre-established legal rules.[28]

Second, investor-State arbitration depoliticizes issues of investment protection by disassociating the investor's interests from the potentially conflicting interests of its home State.[29] The decision whether to initiate and proceed with an investor-State claim does not anymore depend on aspects that are extrinsic to the investor-State relationship, such as broader geo-political or strategic interests that influence the bilateral relations between the host State and the investor's home State. Instead, it is the investor's independent decision to pursue its claims in view of its own preferences without being limited by the political interests of its home State.

Third, money damages as a remedy allow the investor to be indemnified for the financial harm resulting from the host State's violation of an investment treaty. This conforms to the fundamental principle of State responsibility that an injured State is entitled to obtain reparation for the internationally wrongful act of another State.[30] As acknowledged by the PCIJ in the *The Factory at Chorzów*, this "reparation must, as far as possible, wipe out all the consequences of the illegal act and re-establish the situation which would, in all probability, have existed if that act had not been committed."[31] Allowing the recovery of money damages, therefore,

---

[27] On the governance structures that emerge from triadic compared to dyadic dispute settlement, see Stone Sweet, *Judicialization and the Construction of Governance*, 32 Comp. Pol. Stud. 147 (1999).

[28] The *travaux préparatoires* of the ICSID Convention mention, at various instances, that the Convention was designed in order to remove the settlement of investment dispute from the realm of politics and diplomacy into the realm of law; see Schreuer, *The ICSID Convention*, Article 27, para. 11 (2001).

[29] *Cf.* Shihata, *Towards a Greater Depoliticization of Investment Disputes: The Roles of ICSID and MIGA*, 1 ICSID Rev. – For. Inv. L. J. 1 (1986).

[30] See Article 34, ILC Articles on State Responsibility. The Articles are generally considered to constitute a codification of the customary international law of State responsibility; see *Gabčíkovo-Nagymaros Project (Hungary/Slovakia)*, Judgment, September 25, 1997, I.C.J. Reports 1997, pp. 40–41, paras. 51–52; *Legal Consequences of the Construction of a Wall in the Occupied Palestinian Territory*, Advisory Opinion, July 9, 2004, I.C.J. Reports 2004, p. 195, para. 140; *CMS v. Argentina*, Award, May 12, 2005, para. 317.

[31] *The Factory at Chorzów (Claim for Indemnity) (Germany v. Poland)*, Merits, Judgment, September 13, 1928, P.C.I.J. Series A, No. 17 (1928), p. 47.

leads to the host State's internalization of the costs of a violation of an investment treaty. This induces governments to breach investment treaties only in cases where the advantage they derive from the breach outweighs the full costs to potentially affected foreign investors. This, in turn, promotes efficient behavior of host States.[32]

In conclusion, the private right of action entails an important power shift from States to tribunals. This is all the more true since the jurisdiction of modern investment tribunals no longer rests on a dispute- or fact-specific consent of the host State. Instead, modern investment tribunals have more extensive jurisdiction than tribunals established in post-conflict situations whose mandates were limited to a certain time period, such as the Iran–United States Claims Tribunal, the Ethiopia–Eritrea Claims Commission or the various Claims Commissions during the pre-Second World War era.[33] Today, the power of States concerning their submission under the jurisdiction of an international tribunal is, therefore, reduced to the one-time act of giving general and advance consent to investor-State arbitration in an investment treaty. This prevents host States from using their consent to investment arbitration as a bargaining chip in the resolution of disputes after a breach of an investment treaty has occurred.

(b)   The limited influence of States on the arbitral process

State control over the arbitral process itself has also been significantly reduced as the host State in investment treaty arbitration is procedurally treated as a party on equal footing with the claimant-investor. Following the model of international commercial arbitration, the power to appoint arbitrators is shared between host State and investor.[34] This excludes the predominant influence of the host State over the arbitral process. Even though investors, like States, have a special interest in appointing an individual who they believe to favor their position, the method of party

---

[32] See, on the theory of efficient breach, Birmingham, *Breach of Contract, Damage Measures, and Economic Efficiency*, 24 Rutgers L. Rev. 273, 284 (1970); Goetz and Scott, *Liquidated Damages, Penalties and the Just Compensation Principle*, 77 Colum. L. Rev. 554 (1977).

[33] See on the specificities of State consent in modern investment treaties compared with more classical investment dispute settlement mechanisms, Legum, *The Innovation of Investor-State Arbitration under NAFTA*, 43 Harv. Int'l L. J. 531 (2002).

[34] Arbitral panels most often consist of three arbitrators, with both parties being entitled to appoint one arbitrator each; the two party-appointed arbitrators then agree on the tribunal's president. The investor's home State also has no say in the appointment of the arbitrators. See, for example, Article 37, ICSID Convention, Article 7, UNCITRAL Arbitration Rules.

appointments aims at securing a balanced assessment of the case and at ensuring the independence and impartiality of the arbitral tribunal.

Investment arbitration under the ICSID Convention also obstructs the collective power of the investor's home State and the host State to influence arbitral proceedings. Arguably, the ICSID Convention removes the power of States to settle claims that arise under an investment treaty once arbitration proceedings have been initiated by the investor. While Article 27, ICSID Convention explicitly only prevents the home State from intervening by means of diplomatic protection,[35] this provision equally will have to be interpreted as preventing other interferences by the investor's home State in the dispute settlement proceedings, including the joint disposal of a claim after it has been submitted to arbitration by the investor.

Although home State and host State are empowered under general international law to dispose of a claim raised by one of the home State's nationals,[36] the ICSID Convention arguably restricts this right to the period *prior* to the commencement of investment arbitration. This flows from the object and purpose of Articles 25–27, ICSID Convention that establish investment arbitration as a self-contained regime to the exclusion of other remedies under international law once an investor-State dispute has begun.[37] In view of the host State's advance consent to arbitration, this *de facto* excludes a settlement of disputes among the States involved without the investor's consent, since the latter can unilaterally exercise its right to recourse to arbitration and thereby move the dispute from the realm of diplomatic protection into the exclusive jurisdiction of an ICSID tribunal.[38]

(c)   Limited review of arbitral awards

The power of States is further weakened in view of the binding force of arbitral awards. This allows investment tribunals to effectively implement

---

[35] Article 27, ICSID Convention provides:

(1) No Contracting State shall give diplomatic protection, or bring an international claim, in respect of a dispute which one of its nationals and another Contracting State shall have consented to submit or shall have submitted to arbitration under this Convention, unless such other Contracting State shall have failed to abide by and comply with the award rendered in such dispute.

(2) Diplomatic protection, for the purposes of paragraph (1), shall not include informal diplomatic exchanges for the sole purpose of facilitating a settlement of the dispute.

[36] See *supra* Ch. VI.A.1.b.

[37] *Cf.* Schreuer, *Investment Protection and International Relations*, in Reinisch and Kriebaum (eds.), *The Law of International Relations*, pp. 345, 349 *et seq.* (2007).

[38] Absent any advance consent to ICSID, the right of States to dispose of a claim will, however, not be affected.

their decisions even against the will of a powerful respondent. Compared with decisions of other international judicial bodies, for example, the WTO Dispute Settlement Body, the awards of investment tribunals take on a particularly strong finality, since they are not subject to approval by the State parties to the investment treaty in dispute. Contrary to the WTO's Dispute Settlement Body,[39] not even the collective agreement of States can overturn the outcome of an investment award. Investor-State arbitration, therefore, constitutes a particularly effective remedy as it allows even investors from relatively weak countries to enforce investment treaty obligations against a powerful host State.

The exclusive remedy against ICSID awards is the initiation of annulment proceedings pursuant to Article 52, ICSID Convention. Yet, the potential of these proceedings to restrict the power of arbitral tribunals is limited.[40] Article 52(1), ICSID Convention allows the annulment of an arbitral award only for the following reasons: improper constitution of the tribunal; corruption on the part of one of the tribunal's members; the tribunal's manifest excess of power; its serious departure from a fundamental rule of procedure; or its failure to state the reasons for the award.

State influence on the outcome of annulment proceedings is also reduced as States cannot intervene in the appointment of ad hoc annulment committees whose members are appointed by the Chairman of the ICSID Administrative Council.[41] Finally, in practice annulment committees have assumed a role as "guardians of the arbitral award" rather than as a control organ of investment tribunals,[42] and thus have strengthened the power of arbitral tribunals vis-à-vis States.

Non-ICSID investment treaty arbitration, by contrast, is less shielded against State interference. Unlike ICSID awards, awards rendered pursuant to UNCITRAL Rules, ICSID Additional Facility Rules or ad hoc arbitration, do not benefit from an equally broad binding force and recognition. While these awards also do not require State approval, they

---

[39] For this so-called "principle of reversed-consensus" see Articles 16(4), 17(14), Understanding on Rules and Procedures Governing the Settlement of Disputes.

[40] See, on annulment proceedings, Schreuer (*supra* footnote 28), Article 52 (2001). See further Broches, *Observations on the Finality of ICSID Awards*, 6 ICSID Rev. – For. Inv. L. J. 321 (1991); Delaume, *ICSID-Arbitration and the Courts*, 77 A.J.I.L. 784 (1983); Feldman, *The Annulment Proceedings and the Finality of ICSID Arbitral Awards*, 2 ICSID Rev. – For. Inv. L. J. 85 (1987).

[41] Article 52(3), ICSID Convention.

[42] *Cf.* E. Schwartz, *Finality at What Cost? The Decision of the* Ad Hoc *Committee in* Wena Hotels v. Egypt, in Gaillard and Banifatemi (eds.), *Annulment of ICSID Awards*, pp. 43, 45 (2004).

are subject to so-called *vacatur* proceedings, that is, procedures for the setting aside of an arbitral award according to the municipal law in force at the place of arbitration.[43] This notwithstanding, *vacatur* proceedings do not necessarily give any control to those States affected by an investor-State dispute, since the place of arbitration is not necessarily in the territory of either the host State or the home State. Instead, the arbitral tribunal itself can freely choose the place of arbitration, unless the parties to the proceedings, investor and host State, jointly choose the arbitral situs.[44] Investment tribunals not subject to the ICSID Convention can, therefore, choose the level of scrutiny they are subject to by State courts. This should allow tribunals to evade any significant control by State courts.

(d) Recognition and enforcement of arbitral awards

Finally, the power of investment tribunals is most apparent in the finality of the awards they render. The ICSID Convention, for instance, provides that an "award shall be binding on the parties and shall not be subject to any appeal or to any other remedy except those provided for in this Convention."[45] In addition, the ICSID Convention provides that "[e]ach Contracting State shall recognize an award rendered pursuant to this Convention as binding and enforce the pecuniary obligations imposed by that award within its territories as if it were a final judgment of a court in that State."[46] Both provisions encapsulate the broad finality of ICSID awards and contribute to the multilateralization of international investment treaties.

Unlike in cases governed by the New York Convention, the State where enforcement of the award is sought is prevented from invoking its public policy against an ICSID award or from otherwise challenging the competence of the arbitral tribunal.[47] The only loophole remaining for the host State to refuse recognition and enforcement of an ICSID award on its own territory is to invoke State immunity.[48] However, given that the

---

[43] In this context, domestic courts have already used the tools available under the New York Convention to set aside investment treaty awards. See, for example, *The United Mexican States* v. *Metalclad Corporation*, 2001 BCSC 644; *cf.* also *Republic of Ecuador* v. *Occidental Exploration & Production Co.* [2006] EWHC 345.

[44] See, for example, Article 16(1), UNCITRAL Arbitration Rules.

[45] Article 53(1), ICSID Convention.

[46] Article 54(1), ICSID Convention.

[47] Schreuer (*supra* footnote 28), Article 54, para. 71 (2001). Article V, New York Convention, by contrast, allows, *inter alia*, denying recognition and enforcement of an award based on the enforcement State's *ordre public*.

[48] See Article 55, ICSID Convention.

award can also be enforced outside the host State's territory against assets belonging to the respondent State, this exception seems to have rather limited effect in preventing the enforcement of investment treaty awards. For example, investment awards can be enforced against a bank account a State holds with a bank in New York or London, even if the State refuses enforcement in its own territory based on State immunity.

Instead, the broad enforceability of ICSID awards ensures that effect is given to the tribunals' decisions and that ICSID Member States recognize the effects of a violation of a bilateral investment treaty on a multilateral level. This allows the enforcement of an ICSID award across several jurisdictions without the contortive effects of post-breach bilateral bargaining between the host State and the enforcement State. The rules on recognition and enforcement, therefore, restrict unilateral defects of the host State with investment treaty awards and also prevent the host State from bilaterally bargaining around the negative consequences of an ICSID award and hence the consequences stemming from the breach of a BIT.

Non-ICSID arbitration is less – but still sufficiently – shielded from State control with respect to recognition and enforcement. Notably, the New York Convention allows the enforcement State to invoke its public policy in order to refuse to honor an arbitral award.[49] It is, however, doubtful whether a third-party enforcement State has any interest in exercising control over arbitral tribunals that have been concerned with a dispute between two unrelated parties.

Overall, the institutional safeguards of investment arbitration with its decentralized enforcement mechanism effectively reduce State control as compared with the situation under traditional inter-State enforcement. It not only restricts unilateral defects of States from rules and principles governing international economic relations, but also constrains the influence of bilateralist rationales that stem from the inter-State relations between home and host States. The influence of States and the control of enforcement of arbitral awards are, therefore, largely reduced.

3   Multilateralizing investment protection through investor-State arbitration

The existence of investor-State arbitration as a mechanism for settling disputes under investment treaties breaks with one of the coining

---

[49] See Article V(2)(b), New York Convention.

characteristics of inter-State bilateralism. In removing sole State control over the enforcement of and compliance with investment treaties, the institutionalization of investor-State arbitration limits the arena for inter-State negotiations about the content and the consequences of breaches of the respective treaty after a dispute has arisen. The investor's right to initiate arbitration against the host State for a violation of an investment treaty, coupled with the limited power of States to interfere in or even dominate investor-State dispute settlement, excludes bilateral post-breach bargaining and ensures that investment treaties are enforced independent of the relative power relations between host and home States. Traditional international law, by contrast, allowed States to flexibly negotiate around the consequences of the breach of an international obligation, if this was in the interest of the States involved and was achievable in view of their relative bargaining power.

The flexibility that existed under traditional international law compliance mechanisms in bargaining around breaches of international law inescapably led to contortions in the competition between foreign investors from different home States. While investors from home States with more negotiating power were presumably in a better position to secure the host State's compliance with "their" BIT, investors from other home States with more limited negotiation power were more likely not to succeed in making the host State comply with "their" BIT. Compared with the traditional system of diplomatic protection, the introduction of a private right of action for foreign investors, therefore, constitutes a "change in paradigm in international investment law"[50] as it breaks with the traditionally bilateralist scheme of compliance under international law. Access to investor-State arbitration therefore ensures that investors are able to enforce investment treaties against States independently of the States' respective power. This not only consolidates international investment law as a functioning legal regime, but also ensures that the general and uniform principles that investment treaties create as a basis of international investment law are implemented without contortions in the enforcement stage.

---

[50] Schreuer, *Paradigmenwechsel im Internationalen Investitionsrecht*, in Hummer (ed.), *Paradigmenwechsel im Völkerrecht zur Jahrtausendwende*, p. 237 (2002). The importance of diplomatic protection, in turn, declined considerably after the introduction of an investor's private right of action, see Kokott, *The Role of Diplomatic Protection in the Field of the Protection of Foreign Investment*, in International Law Association (ed.), *Report of the Seventieth Conference, New Delhi*, p. 259 (2002).

The procedural framework governing investor-State arbitration, above all the ICSID Convention, also has additional effects in multilateralizing international investment relations. First, the uniformity achieved by a multilateral convention for investor-State arbitration has the effect of subjecting investor-State disputes, independent from the governing investment treaty, to the same procedural rules and thus imposes equal transaction costs upon investors concerning the enforcement of investment treaty obligations. This also reflects the fundamental concept, inherent in the idea of a uniform international economic order for the global economy, to establish equal rules in order to enable equal competition among investors from different home States, which, in turn, enables investments to be used as efficiently as possible.[51] Multilateral rules for investment arbitration procedure, therefore, respond to the objective of creating a level playing field not only concerning the substantive treatment of foreign investors by the host State, but also in relation to the assertion of breaches of investment treaties and their enforcement through dispute settlement procedures. The multilateral procedural rules on investor-State arbitration therefore contribute to ensuring that the general principles governing international investment relations are implemented without contortions due to differences in enforcement procedures.

Second, the multilateral rules in the ICSID Convention on the recognition and enforcement of investment treaty awards respond to the necessity of implementing an arbitral award effectively across several jurisdictions. Even though investor-State arbitration could be structured so as to repel State influence on the dispute settlement process in a strictly bilateral setting, an investor that has obtained a favorable award against the host State still faces the problem of enforcement. An unwilling host State would surely find ways to hinder the enforcement of an arbitral award in its territory, if ultimately by passing legislation that would prevent local courts from enforcing the award rendered by an arbitral tribunal. Conversely, enforcement in third-country jurisdictions requires that the award is recognized by the third State, which would – depending on the relationship between the host State and the enforcement State – give rise to possibilities for bilateral negotiations between the host State and the enforcement State. However, the ICSID Convention prevents such bilateralist contortions through its rules relating to the recognition and enforcement of ICSID awards. It provides for the multilateral regulation

---

[51] See *supra* Ch. III.C.1.

of recognition of arbitral awards in all the Member States of the ICSID Convention, and thereby transforms the effect of an award rendered pursuant to the rules of a specific BIT into an obligation that has to be complied with by all Member States of the ICSID Convention. Overall, investor-State arbitration and the rules governing the enforcement of arbitral awards under the ISCID Convention, thus, elevate the enforcement of investment treaties from the bilateral to the multilateral level and ensure that the uniform and general principles established under investment treaties are not contorted due to differences in enforcement depending on the bilateral relations between the host State and the investor's home State, or the host State and the respective enforcement State.

Furthermore, the empowerment of arbitral tribunals and the investor's right to seek damages for a violation of the applicable investment treaty, do more than replacing one bilateral relationship, the one on the inter-State level, with another bilateral relationship, the one between investor and host State. Instead, investment treaty arbitration assumes a function not only in relation to the investor-State relationship, it also plays a significant role for international relations and the system of investment protection as a whole. Unlike its commercial pendant, investment treaty arbitration is not exclusively a mechanism for the settlement of disputes between foreign investors and host States but also a compliance mechanism for the inter-State obligations contained in investment treaties.[52]

When a foreign investor invokes a violation of the rights granted by an investment treaty against a host State, it not only invokes its own rights, but also acts as an agent for its home State in enforcing the State's rights and obligations existing on the inter-State level.[53] Investment treaty

---

[52] On differences between investment treaty arbitration and commercial arbitration see Van Harten and Loughlin, *Investment Treaty Arbitration as a Species of Global Administrative Law*, 17 Eur. J. Int'l L. 121, 139 *et seq.* (2006). Both forms of arbitration differ with respect to the nature of the disputes, the relationship of the parties, and the nature of the obligations that are at the basis of the arbitral proceedings. In addition, investment treaty arbitration is of an increasingly public character and offers, in certain circumstances, the possibility of *amicus curiae* participation. See on this, Zoellner, *Third-Party Participation (NGOs and Private Persons) and Transparency in ICSID Proceedings*, in Hofmann and Tams (eds.), *The International Convention for the Settlement of Investment Disputes (ICSID)*, p. 179 (2007).

[53] See, for example, *Loewen Group v. United States*, Award, June 26, 2003, para. 233 (stating that "claimants are permitted for convenience to enforce what are in origin the rights of Party states"). See also *SGS v. Philippines*, Decision on Jurisdiction, January 29, 2004, para. 154 (stating that "[a]lthough under modern international law, treaties may confer rights, substantive and procedural, on individuals, they will normally do so in order to achieve some public interest" – internal citation omitted). Investment treaties can, on

arbitration can, therefore, properly be viewed as a form of private enforcement of public international law.[54] From this perspective, it becomes clear that investment treaty arbitration does not replace one dyad – the one between host State and home State – with another dyad – the one between foreign investor and host State. Instead, investment treaty arbitration establishes a regime that helps achieve private and public ends that are closely intertwined, namely, the interest of States and investors in promoting and protecting foreign investment.

Beyond effectuating compliance with a specific investment treaty in a specific case, investor-State arbitration also has important systemic effects on host States in general. With respect to the entire system of investment protection, investor-State arbitration also serves as a mechanism to monitor breaches of investment treaties, thereby inducing States to comply with investment treaty obligations. This also deters States from future violations of investment treaties. Because breaches of such treaties will inevitably be discovered and enforced by the affected investor, host States will breach BIT obligations only in cases where the benefits of the breach outweigh the full costs to the investor.[55] This deterrent effect is, however, not limited to compliance by a specific host State that has been convicted for a specific violation in the past (special deterrence), but creates the general sense that host States will not get away with breaches of investment treaties (general deterrence).[56] This effect of investor-State arbitration multilateralizes investment protection, because both the monitoring function and the deterrent effect influence States to abide by the general and uniform principles of investment protection that emerge on the basis of bilateral treaties and that are part of the international economic order

the contrary, also be viewed as vesting rights directly in foreign investors; these investors would, therefore, not only avail themselves of a procedural right that leaves investment treaties as inter-State obligations intact, but would rely on a right that is directly vested in them. See, on both concepts, Douglas, *The Hybrid Foundations of Investment Treaty Arbitrations*, 74 Brit. Ybk. Int'l L. 151, 182 *et seq.* (2003). See also Douglas, *Nothing if Not Critical for Investment Treaty Arbitration*, 22 Arb. Int'l 27, 37 *et seq.* (2006).

[54] Sykes, *Public versus Private Enforcement of International Economic Law*, 34 J. Legal Stud. 631 (2005). Specifically in the context of investment treaty arbitration, see Schill, *Arbitration Risk and Effective Compliance*, 7 J. World Inv. & Trade 653, 681–83 (2006).

[55] See *supra* footnote 32.

[56] On both concepts in the context of criminal law, see Roxin, *Strafrecht – Allgemeiner Teil*, vol. I, § 3, paras. 11 *et seq.* (3rd edn. 1997). The situation is comparable to the debate in antitrust law where actions by private parties are viewed as a way to enforce the law and also deter actors from future violations. See McAfee, Mialon and Mialon, *Private v. Public Antitrust Enforcement* 92, J. Pub. Econ. 1863 (2008); Segal and Whinston, *Public vs. Private Enforcement of Antitrust Law*, 28 Eur. Comp. L. Rev. 306 (2007).

the treaties create. The compliance function is not limited to a specific bilateral treaty relationship. Much to the contrary, they form a constitutive part of the procedural enforcement infrastructure upon which international investment law relies.

B Investment treaty arbitration as a mechanism for resolving uncertainty in international investment relations

Investment treaty arbitration not only leads to an empowerment of investors and tribunals in enforcing investment treaty obligations and in restricting post-breach inter-State bilateralism in favor of multilateral compliance mechanisms. It also provides a solution to the problem of dealing with uncertainty in inter-State investment relations. Although international treaties ideally constitute, by determining the mutual rights and obligations of the contracting parties, instruments for the realization of gains from cooperation, complex agreements, in particular in long-term relationships, are never complete.[57] They are fraught with gaps regarding manifold aspects of the parties' relations, and are also unable to fully anticipate future changes and contingencies. Complex agreements are incomplete because the costs of negotiating and drafting complete contracts are prohibitively high and the future state of the world is difficult, if not impossible, to predict. As a consequence, "all of the relevant contracting action cannot be concentrated on the ex ante incentive alignment but some of it spills over into the ex post governance."[58] Uncertainty in international investment relations results both from uncertainty about the future development of investment activities as well as possible interventions with such activities by the State.

Uncertainty arising from such contingencies can be solved bilaterally through negotiations.[59] In this context, bilateral negotiations facilitate consensus more easily than multilateral negotiations, because achieving consent between two parties is structurally easier than among multiple parties. However, treaty re-negotiation and adaptation to contingencies

---

[57] *Cf.* Aceves, *The Economic Analysis of International Law*, 17 U. Pa. J. Int'l Econ. L. 995, 1002–4 (1996); Trachtman, *The Domain of WTO Dispute Resolution*, 40 Harv. Int'l L. J. 333, 346–50 (1999) (both pointing out that transaction costs make international treaties, like private contracts, incomplete).

[58] Williamson, *Transaction Cost Economics Meets Posnerian Law and Economics*, 149 JITE 99, 102 (1993).

[59] *Cf.* Mnookin and Kornhauser, *Bargaining in the Shadow of the Law: The Case of Divorce*, 88 Yale L. J. 950 (1979); Cooter, Marks and Mnookin, *Bargaining in the Shadow of the Law*, 11 J. Legal Stud. 225 (1982).

are especially difficult to achieve if disputes in specific cases that turn on a point of uncertainty are already pending. If, for example, the contracting States to an investment treaty have left it unresolved whether, and if so under which circumstances, general regulatory measures for the protection of the environment require compensation to foreign investors under an investment treaty, solving such an uncertainty in bilateral negotiations will be considerably different, depending on whether such negotiations take place in the abstract or against the background of a specific dispute. In particular, short-term considerations may trump the parties' long-term interests in situations where specific disputes already exist. Similarly, real or alleged contingencies may be used as a pretext to diverge from the spirit of a treaty regime and from the balance originally struck between State parties to an investment treaty. Ultimately, the solution of such cases of uncertainty in inter-State relations will depend primarily on the relative power relations of the States concerned and therefore yield to bilateralist rationales.

Alternatively, uncertainty in treaty relationships can also be resolved by submitting disputes, relating both to the interpretation of the treaty and to the filling of existing and impending gaps, to a mechanism of triadic dispute settlement. In this manner, investor-State arbitration can be regarded as a mechanism to deal with such uncertainties in a context that is removed from bilateral negotiation of the State parties involved and independent of their relative negotiation power. Instead of dealing with uncertainty on a bilateral basis through negotiation, uncertainty is resolved by means of submitting to an independent adjudicatory body that processes the uncertainty and generates new or concretizes existing rules.[60]

As an illustration of how investment treaty arbitration serves as a mechanism to deal with uncertainty in international investment relations and to fill gaps in investment treaties, this section illustrates how the vagueness of the core investor rights leads to a dissolution of rule making and rule application and transfers significant rule-making power from States to arbitral tribunals. Thus, the possibility of investors having recourse to investor-State arbitration enables tribunals to actively develop international investment law and to join States as the primary rule makers. This is particularly true since this power of arbitral tribunals is

---

[60] Kreps, *Corporate Culture and Economic Theory*, in Alt and Shepsle (eds.), *Perspectives on Positive Political Economy*, pp. 90, 119 (1990) (observing that parties "agree *ex ante* not so much on what will be done in each particular contingency as they do on the procedure by which future contingencies will be met").

not accompanied, unlike in the relationship between the judiciary and the legislator on the domestic level, by strong counter-balancing powers of States.

At the same time, the power investment tribunals assume as a mechanism to resolve uncertainty in international investment relations is a further source of the multilateralization of international investment law as it enables tribunals to resolve uncertainties that are common to most, if not all, investment treaties, in particular those relating to the interpretation and concretization of the vague principles of investment protection, in a uniform manner for various bilateral treaty relationships.

1   The vagueness of investor rights

Modern investment protection does not only empower arbitral tribunals institutionally and procedurally. An equally important factor militating for a power shift from States to tribunals is the vagueness of several of the underlying substantive investor rights. Both wording and concept of standard guarantees, such as indirect expropriation, fair and equitable treatment or full protection and security, are of such indeterminacy that they lack hard and ascertainable normative content. They provide little guidance for their application and fail to limit the jurisprudential activity of investment tribunals. This can be illustrated, for example, with respect to the guarantee of fair and equitable treatment that is generally included in investment treaties. It holds, however, equally true for other investor rights, such as indirect expropriation or full protection and security.

The vagueness of fair and equitable treatment, in fact, goes beyond the commonplace assertions in legal theory that law is inherently vague and indeterminate.[61] Fair and equitable treatment does not have a consolidated and conventional core meaning as such nor is there a definition of the standard that can be applied easily. So far, it is only settled that fair and equitable treatment constitutes a standard that is independent from the national legal order and is not limited to restricting bad faith conduct of host States.[62] Apart from this very minimal concept, however, its exact normative content is contested, hardly substantiated by State practice, and impossible to narrow down by traditional means of interpretative syllogism.

---

[61] See, for example, Kelsen, *The Pure Theory of Law*, p. 354 (1970); H. Hart, *The Concept of Law*, p. 135 (1961); Schroth, *Hermeneutik, Norminterpretation und richterliche Normanwendung*, in Kaufmann, Hassemer and Neumann (eds.), *Einführung in Rechtsphilosophie und Rechtstheorie der Gegenwart*, pp. 270 *et seq.* (7th edn. 2004).

[62] On fair and equitable treatment, see *supra* Ch. III.A.2.b.

Traditional interpretative approaches applying Articles 31 and 32, Vienna Convention on the Law of Treaties,[63] either directly or as an expression of the customary international law of treaty interpretation,[64] are hardly able to clarify the meaning of fair and equitable treatment. An interpretation of the ordinary meaning may replace the terms "fair and equitable" with similarly vague and empty phrases such as "just," "even-handed," "unbiased" or "legitimate,"[65] but does not succeed in clarifying the meaning of the concept. In particular, the semantics of fair and equitable treatment do not clarify against which yardstick the fairness and equitableness of the treatment owed to a foreign investor has to be measured. Fair and equitable could equally refer to notions of equality or some sort of justice, or to less grand notions of procedural due process.

Likewise, a teleological interpretation hardly provides more specific meaning, even if the purpose of investment treaties, as regularly expressed in the preambles of the treaties, points to the protection and promotion of foreign investment and the deepening of the mutual economic relations between the contracting States.[66] Although this narrows down the possible understandings of fair and equitable treatment to an economic framework, a teleological or purposive interpretation does not enable tribunals to translate the broad language into specific guarantees or rights that a host State has to accord to foreign investors.

If, for example, fair and equitable treatment attempts to secure stability and predictability of the domestic legal order – one of the main claims resulting from arbitral jurisprudence[67] – tribunals are faced with the further problem that methods of interpretation do not elicit which degree of stability and predictability is required in a certain context.

---

[63] 1155 U.N.T.S. 331.

[64] See, for example, *Territorial Dispute (Libyan Arab Jamahiriya/Chad)*, Judgment, February 13, 1994, I.C.J. Reports 1994, pp. 21–22, para. 41; *Oil Platforms (Iran v. United States)*, Preliminary Objection, Judgment, December 12, 1996, I.C.J. Reports 1996, p. 812, para. 23; *Kasikili/Sedudu Island (Botswana/Namibia)*, Judgment, December 13, 1999, I.C.J. Reports 1999, p. 1059, para. 18.

[65] See *MTD v. Chile*, Award, May 25, 2004, para. 113; similarly *Saluka v. Czech Republic*, Partial Award, March 17, 2006, para. 297.

[66] On the object and purpose of investment treaties and the statements contained in their preambles see Dolzer and Stevens, *Bilateral Investment Treaties*, pp. 11–13, 20–25 (1995).

[67] See *LG&E v. Argentina*, Decision on Liability, October 3, 2006, para. 124; *CMS v. Argentina*, Decision on Objections to Jurisdiction, July 17, 2003, para. 28; *CMS v. Argentina*, Award, May 12, 2005, para. 274; *Occidental Exploration v. Ecuador*, Final Award, July 1, 2004, para. 183. See also Schill, *Fair and Equitable Treatment under Investment Treaties as an Embodiment of the Rule of Law*, pp. 11–13 (2006).

Interpretation does not inform us about how stable and predictable the legal framework has to be and under which circumstances, if any, a change of the underlying domestic legal framework is permissible. Equally, it is generally difficult to foresee and estimate whether a specific interpretation of an investment treaty will actually encourage investment flows, or whether, on the contrary, an interpretation that may be too onerous for host States will have the effect of chilling the investment climate and result in host States becoming hostile to foreign investment, thereby undermining the very purpose of international investment law.[68]

The two main methods of treaty interpretation, therefore, prove to be relatively ineffective in clarifying the meaning of fair and equitable treatment. Understandably, investment tribunals do not, therefore, follow a uniform, nor necessarily a well-founded methodology. At least three types of reasoning can be distinguished:

> [o]ne line of reasoning derives a definition from the essential elements of the standard on the basis of abstract reasoning. A second approach resists an attempt of a broader definition and will decide ad hoc whether a certain conduct satisfies the requirements of the standard. Yet a third approach will attempt to primarily base its decision on previous decisions or will build upon relevant precedents by way of analogy or by drawing on the same principle.[69]

However, it is not only the concept of fair and equitable treatment which is inherently vague. Similar observations can also be made with respect to other standard investment guarantees, such as indirect expropriation or full protection and security.[70] These investor rights are equally vague in their scope and content and are difficult, if not impossible, to narrow down by traditional means of treaty interpretation.

---

[68] See van Aaken, *Perils of Success?*, 9 Eur. Bus. Org. L. Rev. 1 (2008) (suggesting that a broadening of investment protection by the interpretations given by investment tribunals might result in a weakening of investment protection in the long run if States cease to participate in the system of investment protection).

[69] Dolzer, *Fair and Equitable Treatment*, 39 Int'l Law. 87, 93–94 (2005).

[70] See, for example, Soloway, *NAFTA's Chapter 11: The Challenge of Private Party Participation*, 16 J. Int' l Arb. 1, 3 (1999); Ferguson, *California's MTBE Contaminated Water*, 11 Col. J. Int'l Envt'l L. & Pol'y 499, 503 (2000) (both noting the "vague language" of NAFTA and its "lack of clarity"); Beauvais, *Regulatory Expropriations Under NAFTA: Emerging Principles and Lingering Doubts*, 10 N.Y.U. Envt'l L. J. 245, 257 *et seq.* (2001–2002); Poirier, *The NAFTA Chapter 11 Expropriation Debate through the Eyes of a Property Theorist*, 33 Environmental Law 851, 902 *et seq.* (2003); Been and Beauvais, *The Global Fifth Amendment?*, 78 N.Y.U. L. Rev. 30, 125 *et seq.* (2003) (all noting the vagueness of the expropriation standard under international law).

2   The dissolution of rule making and rule application

The vagueness of many of the core investor rights, however, not only poses difficult problems of treaty interpretation, it also involves a significant transfer of rule-making power from States to tribunals, because the latter are called to apply the vague language of investment treaties to the facts submitted to them. They have the duty (and the authority) to ascertain the meaning of fair and equitable treatment, indirect expropriation or full protection and security and cannot point to the missing clarity of the applicable rules and standards or the lack of clarifying State practice.[71] In this sense, the vague language of fair and equitable treatment, buttressed by the institutional infrastructure offered above all by the ICSID Convention, can be compared with so-called "general clauses" in civil codes, such as *good faith* or *bonos mores*, that allow the judiciary to ascertain, with a certain degree of independence, the normative content and standards that are applicable in certain social circumstances.[72] Similarly, investment tribunals concretize the exact meaning of fair and equitable treatment in the context of the facts of the case and formulate normative standards to which host States have to conform without being constrained much by the wording of the treaties they apply. Consequently, investment tribunals not only apply investment treaties but also engage in considerable investment rule making.

Traditionally, rule making and rule application have been characterized as categorically distinct functions of government. Judges were perceived as limited by the letter of legal provisions and as exclusively concerned with the implementation of abstract norms that were pre-established by the – ideally democratically elected – legislator.[73] Meanwhile, however, it is but a truism that a clear distinction between both functions of government does not withstand closer scrutiny. Instead, rule application necessarily includes elements of rule making; the clear distinction between legislation and adjudication therefore unravels. Yet, the differences between rule application and rule making become even more difficult to draw the broader and increasingly vague the legislative framework for judicial interpretation becomes. Liberal constitutionalism has, therefore,

---

[71] Article 42(2), ICSID Convention explicitly provides: "The Tribunal may not bring in a finding of *non liquet* on the ground of silence or obscurity of the law."

[72] See, on the function of general clauses, Teubner, *Standards und Direktiven in Generalklauseln*, pp. 60 *et seq.* (1971).

[73] See Hassemer, *Rechtssystem und Kodifikation: Die Bindung des Richters an das Gesetz*, in Kaufmann, Hassemer and Neumann (*supra* note 61), pp. 251 *et seq.* (2004).

stressed the importance of implementing mutual checks and balances between legislation and adjudication, between law and politics, in order to domesticate both politics by law, and law by politics.

However, an equilibrium between legislation and adjudication that is comparable with the exercise of municipal public power is difficult to observe in the context of international investment law, where arbitral tribunals are relatively less restricted in making the rules and normative standards under investment treaties that affect domestic policy making, domestic administration, and domestic judicial proceedings. This is particularly true as, unlike in the domestic context where the legislator can correct, regularly by majority vote, misdevelopments in the application of law by the courts, investment treaties do not establish equally balanced power relations between tribunals and States.

On the contrary, once States consent to investment treaty arbitration as a dispute settlement mechanism, they divest themselves, to a considerable extent, of possibilities to interfere with and to control arbitral jurisprudence. This is so not only with respect to a loss of control over the arbitral process and the enforcement of awards,[74] but equally as regards the power of States to amend investment treaties in order to influence the way arbitral tribunals interpret and apply investment treaties, for instance, in order to clarify the meaning of certain principles of investment protection or to oppose certain jurisprudential development that the contracting States did not foresee or approve of.

Certainly, the contracting parties to an investment treaty have the power to amend the treaty in question. However, such amendments require the consent of all States concerned and may, therefore, be difficult to achieve. This is particularly true as the interests of the contracting parties often diverge when it comes to reacting to specific jurisprudential developments the States in question did not foresee when originally concluding an investment treaty. While States might have originally agreed on a specific solution in view of the uncertainty of whether they would have in the future benefited from a specific solution, their interests potentially change once States know whether they concretely draw benefits or disadvantages from the same solution, and with it the willingness and incentive to agree on the same solution. In addition, the relative bargaining power of the parties plays an essential role as to whether agreement on an amendment can be achieved among the contracting States. Consequently, the treaty amending power will, at the most, be

[74] See *supra* Ch. VI.A.2.

an instrument to adjust investment treaties in a long-term perspective, rather than control the activity of arbitral tribunals concerning the conformity of specific host State conduct with an investment treaty, in particular once disputes have arisen or at least crystallized.

As an alternative to formal treaty amendments, the contracting States can also influence the interpretation of an investment treaty by issuing interpretative notes that are binding on an arbitral tribunal pursuant to Article 31(3)(a), Vienna Convention on the Law of Treaties.[75] Some investment treaties, such as NAFTA, have even institutionalized the power to issue interpretative statements by creating a specific treaty organ that has the competence to issue binding interpretations. Under NAFTA, this power has been conferred to the Free Trade Commission (FTC).[76] However, just like the treaty amendment power,[77] such a procedure requires unanimity and might, therefore, be equally limited in counterbalancing the rule-making power of investment tribunals.

In sum, the institutional position of investment tribunals is, therefore, favorable to increasingly displace States as the primary rule makers in international law. This becomes apparent when considering the institutional empowerment of investment tribunals, the vagueness of many provisions in investment treaties, and the insufficiencies of traditional counter-balancing instruments in the hands of States. Taken together, these elements have the effect of shifting power from States to arbitral tribunals and enable them to effectively fulfill not only a gap-filling, but also a norm-generative, function as regards international investment law.

3   NAFTA digression: the effectiveness of Notes of Interpretation

A telling account of the power struggle between States and tribunals can be found in the NAFTA context. It concerns the definition of the

[75] Argentina and Panama, for example, exchanged diplomatic notes after the jurisdictional decision in *Siemens* v. *Argentina* in order to clarify that the MFN clause in the investment treaty between both countries did not extend to dispute resolution provisions. See *National Grid* v. *Argentina*, Decision on Jurisdiction, June 20, 2006, para. 85.

[76] Article 1131(2), NAFTA. Likewise, the new US Model BIT provides for a similar treaty-based body. See Article 30(3), 2004 US Model BIT which provides: "A joint decision of the Parties, each acting through its representative designated for purposes of this Article, declaring their interpretation of a provision of this Treaty shall be binding on a tribunal, and any decision or award issued by a tribunal must be consistent with that joint decision" (reprinted in McLachlan, Shore and Weiniger, *International Investment Arbitration*, p. 393 (2007).

[77] See Article 2001(4), NAFTA.

normative content of the standard of fair and equitable treatment under Article 1105(1), NAFTA and its relations to the minimum standard of treatment under customary international law. It illustrates both the authority arbitral tribunals dispose of and the difficulties States face in influencing the direction of investment treaty jurisprudence by means of instruments like interpretative notes.

(a) The impending threat of institutional conflict: *Pope & Talbot* v. *Canada*

The Tribunal in *Pope & Talbot* v. *Canada*, one of the first cases that dealt with the scope of fair and equitable treatment, discussed at length the relationship between fair and equitable treatment under Article 1105(1), NAFTA and the international minimum standard.[78] The doctrinal background to this discussion is a long-standing and ongoing debate in international investment law as to whether fair and equitable treatment merely codifies the international minimum standard of treatment or whether it is to be construed independently and autonomously from customary international law.[79] Linking fair and equitable treatment to the international minimum standard would suggest a scope of fair and equitable treatment which is more restrictive than an autonomous interpretation, while an independent construction would allow tribunals a closer scrutiny of host State conduct.

Less scrutiny by arbitral tribunals would be the result if the scope of the international minimum standard is viewed as being reflected in the 1920s *Neer* case that required, in order to find a violation of the minimum standard State conduct, what "amount[s] to an outrage, to bad faith, to willful neglect of duty, or to an insufficiency of governmental action so far short of international standards that every reasonable and impartial man would readily recognize its insufficiency."[80] Even today, respondent States regularly invoke this statement as representing the standard of customary international law. They purport that more recent State practice and *opinio juris* are missing in order for the standard, as customary international law standard, to allow for a more comprehensive content.[81] Such attempts to relink the content of investment treaties to customary international law cannot be viewed only as an effort to establish the meaning

---

[78] *Pope & Talbot* v. *Canada*, Award on the Merits of Phase 2, April 10, 2001, paras. 105 *et seq.*

[79] See *supra* Ch. III.A.2.b (with further references).

[80] *L. F. H. Neer and Pauline E. Neer (United States)* v. *Mexico*, Opinion, October 15, 1926, U.N.R.I.A.A., vol. IV, pp. 61–62.

[81] See, for example, *ADF* v. *United States*, Award, January 9, 2003, paras. 121 *et seq.*

of fair and equitable treatment, they are also part of the struggle to deter-mine whether tribunals or States have the ultimate power of interpreting investment treaties and the principles they contain.

When faced with this debate, the Tribunal in *Pope & Talbot* adopted, in a decision in April 2001, the view that fair and equitable treatment under Article 1105(1), NAFTA was independent of the international minimum standard. In relying primarily on a textual approach to treaty interpreta-tion and by drawing a parallel to other BITs in force with third States, it held that Article 1105(1), NAFTA:

> adopt[s] the additive character of the fairness elements. Investors are entitled to those elements, no matter what else their entitlement under international law. A logical corollary to this language is that compliance with the fairness elements must be ascertained free of any threshold that might be applicable to the evaluation of measures under the minimum standard of international law.[82]

In reaching this decision, the Tribunal dismissed submissions by both the respondent, Canada, and by the United States, as the investor's home State, that asserted that fair and equitable treatment was equivalent to the international minimum standard. The Tribunal instead found that "[i] t is difficult to believe that the drafters of NAFTA consciously intended such a result, and, as noted, Canada, Mexico and the United States have provided no evidence whatsoever that they did."[83] By endorsing its broad interpretation of fair and equitable treatment, the Tribunal took away considerable power of interpretation from the contracting States and shifted it to the dispute settlement body.

The NAFTA parties' reaction to the Tribunal's finding, approximately three months later, was the issuance of a binding interpretation by the Free Trade Commission under Article 1131(2) (the FTC Note) that stated:

> **Minimum Standard of Treatment in Accordance with International Law**
> 1. Article 1105(1) prescribes the customary international law minimum standard of treatment of aliens as the minimum standard of treat-ment to be afforded to investments of investors of another Party.
> 2. The concepts of "fair and equitable treatment" and "full protection and security" do not require treatment in addition to or beyond that which is required by the customary international law minimum standard of treatment of aliens.

---

[82] *Ibid.*, para. 111.
[83] *Ibid.*, para. 116.

3. A determination that there has been a breach of another provision of the NAFTA, or of a separate international agreement, does not establish that there has been a breach of Article 1105(1).[84]

The intended effect of this Note was not only to clarify the meaning of fair and equitable treatment under NAFTA, it also aimed at shifting power back from arbitral tribunals to the contracting parties in order to regain control over the interpretation of the obligations under NAFTA. The FTC Note was thus an attempt by the contracting parties to rebalance rule making and rule application under NAFTA and to manifest the power of the States as rule makers. It also attempted to stress the bilateral elements in international investment law, as the theory of interpretative power underlying the FTC Note presupposes that the contracting State parties of every investment treaty can influence and channel the treaty's interpretation depending on their bilateral relations.

At first, it seemed that the mechanism of issuing binding interpretative notes constituted a successful strategy in domesticating arbitral tribunals.[85] In its following decision, the Tribunal in *Pope & Talbot* ultimately accepted, albeit grudgingly, the binding nature and authoritativeness of the FTC Note. Yet, it did so only after having assessed whether the FTC had acted within its powers under NAFTA when issuing the Note.[86] Notably, the Tribunal distinguished whether the interpretative note was a binding interpretation under Article 1131(2), NAFTA, or a modification of the treaty which would have required an amendment pursuant to Article 2202, NAFTA. It thus did not simply consider itself bound to the FTC Note, but assessed whether the Commission remained within the frame of valid interpretation as compared with treaty modification.[87] The Tribunal, therefore, assumed the competence to review the conformity of acts of the FTC with NAFTA.

Even though the Tribunal suggested *obiter dictum* that it considered the Note to constitute an amendment rather than a valid interpretation,[88] it avoided an open institutional conflict with the NAFTA parties and

---

[84] NAFTA Free Trade Commission, Notes of Interpretation of Certain Chapter 11 Provisions, July 31, 2001.

[85] *Cf.* Sampliner, *Arbitration of Expropriation Cases under U.S. Investment Treaties*, 18 ICSID Rev. – For. Inv. L. J. 1, 30 *et seq.*, 43 (2003); Foy, *Effectiveness of NAFTA's Chapter Eleven Investor-State Arbitration Procedures*, 18 ICSID Rev. – For. Inv. L. J. 44, 99 *et seq.*, 108 (2003) (both considering interpretative notes as successful strategies in guiding and limiting investment tribunals).

[86] *Pope & Talbot* v. *Canada*, Award in Respect of Damages, May 31, 2002, paras. 17 *et seq.*

[87] *Ibid.*, paras. 23 *et seq.*   [88] *Ibid.*, para. 47.

decided that even under the more restrictive standard put forward by the FTC and Canada, the respondent had violated Article 1105(1), NAFTA. Instead of pronouncing itself clearly on the question of whether it considered the FTC Note as binding, the Tribunal thus simply denied the relevance of this question for the outcome of the case at hand.

Of equal interest is the approach of the Tribunal in *Pope & Talbot* to the determination of the content of customary international law. While the contracting parties may have assumed that the FTC Note would limit NAFTA tribunals to a standard similar to the one applied in the *Neer* case,[89] the Tribunal interpreted customary international law as an evolving and flexible concept. In its view, a static conception of customary international law was not tenable, since "there has been evolution in customary international law concepts since the 1920s [and] the range of actions subject to international concern has broadened beyond the international delinquencies considered in *Neer* to include the concept of fair and equitable treatment."[90]

In reaction to the FTC's linkage of fair and equitable treatment and customary international law, the Tribunal therefore reacted with a theory of the evolutionary character of customary international law and the content of its minimum standard for the treatment of foreign investors. Furthermore, the Tribunal advanced the argument that fair and equitable treatment itself had become part of customary international law due to its inclusion in, at that time, approximately 1,800 BITs. The Tribunal held that "applying the ordinary rules for determining the content of custom in international law, one must conclude that the practice of States is now represented by those treaties."[91] Both arguments of the Tribunal in *Pope & Talbot* essentially voided the FTC Note of any practical effect for the interpretation of fair and equitable treatment, as the Tribunal implied that an independent and autonomous standard of fair and equitable treatment had already become part of customary international law.

Independent of the question of whether this argumentative move is sound as a matter of international law,[92] it is important to emphasize the effects of the Tribunal's approach on the relationship between arbitral

---

[89] This was the content of customary international law as argued in the case by Canada; see *ibid.*, para. 57.

[90] *Ibid.*, paras. 58 *et seq.*   [91] *Ibid.*, para. 62 (internal citations omitted).

[92] On the debate on whether BITs affect or create customary international law, see Hindelang, *Bilateral Investment Treaties, Custom and a Healthy Investment Climate*, 5 J. World Inv. & Trade 789 (2004).

tribunals and contracting States. In arguing that fair and equitable treatment had become part of customary international law, the Tribunal in *Pope & Talbot* restored the power relationship between States and tribunals to the situation prior to the issuance of the FTC Note, and parried the development towards stricter State control of arbitral activity by shifting the argumentative framework. Ultimately, the notion of evolutionary customary international law ingeniously allowed the Tribunal to reintroduce the content of an autonomous interpretation of fair and equitable treatment under the label of customary international law without effectively imposing the limits on its judicial freedom that would have resulted from a strict application of the FTC Note. The *Pope & Talbot* case, therefore, underscores the radical shift away from States as regards control over the interpretation and application of investment treaties due to the introduction of investor-State dispute settlement.

(b)   Post-*Pope & Talbot*: dynamic adjustments of
       customary international law

In subsequent NAFTA arbitrations, arbitral tribunals were generally less radical than the Tribunal in *Pope & Talbot* and refrained from questioning the binding effect of the FTC Note as such.[93] While formally paying more deference to the institutional relations between States and tribunals, they did, however, continue to endorse the concept of the evolutionary character of customary international law. Similarly to *Pope & Talbot*, some tribunals also supported the view that the conclusion of BITs influenced the content of customary international law. The Tribunal in *Mondev v. United States*, for example, emphasized both aspects, and thereby fostered the interpretative power of arbitral tribunals that had already resulted from the decision in *Pope & Talbot*, by arguing:

> [T]here can be no doubt that, by interpreting Article 1105(1) to prescribe the customary international law minimum standard of treatment of aliens as the minimum standard of treatment to be afforded to investments of investors of another Party under NAFTA, the term "customary international law" refers to customary international law as it stood no

---

[93] See *Mondev v. United States*, Award, October 11, 2002, paras. 100 *et seq.*; *United Parcel Service v. Canada*, Award on Jurisdiction, November 22, 2002, para. 97; *ADF v. United States*, Award, January 9, 2003, paras. 175 *et seq.*; *Loewen v. United States*, Final Award, June 26, 2003, paras. 124 *et seq.*; *Waste Management v. Mexico*, Award, April 30, 2004, paras. 90 *et seq.*; *International Thunderbird Gaming v. Mexico*, Arbitral Award, January 26, 2006, paras. 192 *et seq.*; *Methanex v. United States*, Final Award, August 3, 2005, Part IV, Chapter C, paras. 20 *et seq.*

earlier than the time at which NAFTA came into force. It is not limited to the international law of the 19th century or even of the first half of the 20th century, although decisions from that period remain relevant. In holding that Article 1105(1) refers to customary international law, the FTC interpretations incorporate current international law, whose content is shaped by the conclusion of more than two thousand bilateral investment treaties and many treaties of friendship and commerce. Those treaties largely and concordantly provide for "fair and equitable" treatment of, and for "full protection and security" for, the foreign investor and his investments.[94]

Similarly, the Tribunal in *ADF* v. *United States* noted that "both customary international law and the minimum standard of treatment of aliens it incorporates, are constantly in a process of development."[95]

Both tribunals, therefore, rejected the proposition that fair and equitable treatment was limited to treatment not amounting to "outrage, to bad faith, to willful neglect of duty, or to an insufficiency of governmental action so far short of international standards that every reasonable and impartial man would readily recognize its insufficiency," as required by the 1920s *Neer* case.[96] Accordingly, even to the extent the tribunals accepted that fair and equitable treatment had to be interpreted in accordance with customary international law, the nexus made by the FTC Note between treaty law and custom was likely to have no influence on the concrete outcome of NAFTA arbitrations.

Certainly, not all NAFTA tribunals adopt an equally extensive understanding of fair and equitable treatment and support an equally close scrutiny of host State conduct under international law.[97] However, more deferent approaches appear to be prompted primarily by restrictions the tribunals impose on themselves, rather than due to any external control mechanisms. In sum, the strategy to domesticate arbitral tribunals by linking the interpretation of fair and equitable treatment to customary international law in the NAFTA context can therefore hardly be considered successful. Instead of interpreting fair and equitable treatment as an independent treaty standard that would have directly allowed for a

---

[94] *Mondev* v. *United States*, Award, October 11, 2002, para. 125.
[95] *ADF* v. *United States*, Award, January 9, 2003, para. 179.
[96] Similar views on the relation of fair and equitable treatment and the *Neer* case can also be found outside the NAFTA context. See, for example, *Eureko* v. *Poland*, Partial Award, August 19, 2005, para. 234.
[97] More deferent to national law under NAFTA, for example, *Loewen* v. *United States*, Final Award, June 26, 2003, in particular paras. 241 *et seq.*, and *Methanex* v. *United States*, Final Award, August 3, 2005, Part IV, Chapter C, paras. 13 *et seq.*

broad interpretation, NAFTA tribunals now state that they interpret fair and equitable treatment in accordance with customary international law, yet, at the same time, interpret customary international law as an evolutionary concept.[98] This rhetoric essentially allowed tribunals to comply with the institutional infrastructure of NAFTA, and the apparent will of its contracting States, while, at the same time, allowing them to continuously expand their own power as decision makers. Instead of interpreting fair and equitable treatment directly as a flexible standard, they now make the notion of customary international law itself more flexible and re-introduce their original standards of decision-making through the back door.

C   Conclusion

The institutional structure of investment treaty arbitration coupled with the vagueness of the substantive provisions of investment treaties has to be understood as a fundamental shift in power from States to arbitral tribunals. Investor rights, such as fair and equitable treatment, full protection and security, indirect expropriation, and national treatment can be viewed more as "general clauses" that *de facto* delegate substantial rule-making power to judicial bodies than as legal rules that are ascertainable by means of simple treaty interpretation. Consequently, arbitral tribunals emerge as important rule makers in international investment law. Their function is not restricted to applying pre-existing rules and principles to the facts of a case, but extends to developing the existing principles into more precise rules and standards of conduct.

The power shift from States to tribunals becomes all the more clear when focusing on the restrictive possibilities that States have in order to influence the direction of the jurisprudence of investment tribunals. Limited possibilities for influencing the appointment of arbitrators, the arbitral process, and the enforcement of arbitral awards leave little leeway to counter-balance the rule-making power investment tribunals, now often exercise. Their power is further supported by the limited possibilities States have for influencing investment jurisprudence through their treaty amendment power or the issuance of interpretative notes. This illustrates how powerful investment treaties and investment treaty arbitration can become in limiting State sovereignty.

---

[98] *Cf.* Choudhury, *Evolution or Devolution? – Defining Fair and Equitable Treatment in International Investment Law*, 6 J. World Inv. & Trade 297 (2005).

The institutionalization of investor-State dispute settlement and the empowerment of arbitral tribunals is, however, not necessarily a threat to international investment relations in general. It is also a source of the multilateralization of international investment law. Even though arbitral tribunals function as ad hoc dispute settlement bodies, the rules on investor-State dispute settlement multilateralize the enforcement of investment treaty awards. The ICSID Convention, for example, subjects investor-State arbitration to uniform rules and enables the enforcement of investment treaty awards across multiple municipal jurisdictions as if the arbitral awards constituted judgments of the respective domestic courts. This transforms the effect of an investment award directly into the domestic legal order and ensures that the content of an award and the extent to which it is enforceable remain uniform across various municipal legal orders. The procedural rules therefore contribute to the uniform and non-discriminatory enforcement of investment treaties.

Furthermore, investor-State arbitration and the empowerment of arbitral tribunals restrict bilateral rationales in the enforcement of investment treaty obligations by removing the possibility of States to defect from their investment treaty obligations based on power-backed post-breach bargaining with the investor's home State or the State where enforcement of an award is sought. Instead, because of the investor's right to have recourse to investment arbitration and to enforce an award in numerous jurisdictions, power-based escapes from compliance with investment treaties are to a considerable extent excluded. Investor-State arbitration, therefore, transforms compliance with investment treaties from bilateral to multilateral rationales, because it excludes bilateral post-breach defects and bargaining.

Finally, the norm-generative function of investor-State arbitration adds to the multilateralization of international investment law. It not only retrospectively helps to enforce compliance with their investment treaty obligations, but equally helps prospectively to resolve uncertainty in international investment relations and to "fill gaps" in investment treaties. This enables States to enter into stable long-term investment relations that are not obstructed by continuous bilateral bargaining every time the general principles of investment protection have to be concretized for specific areas of State conduct. Investor-State arbitration thereby responds to the need to solve uncertainty and ambiguity in international investment relations, to stabilize them over time, and to adapt them to changing realities. Moreover, the function of investment tribunals to fill gaps in investment treaties often enough transforms into the function of *de facto* determining the normative content of some of the standard investor rights that are included in investment treaties. Particularly as regards concepts such as fair and equitable treatment, full protection and security or indirect expropriation, tribunals rather than States determine the normative content of international investment treaties.

Although the vagueness of many of the standard investor rights, coupled with the institutional back-up of investment tribunals, entails a considerable shift of rule-making power from States to tribunals, the establishment of investor-State dispute settlement also has a considerable effect on the multilateralization of international investment law. Most notably, the function of concretizing existing and generating new investment law is not limited to a specific investment treaty that governs a dispute submitted to arbitration, but affects the interpretation of investment treaties more generally, including unrelated third-party BITs. Unlike pure ad hoc dispute settlement bodies, investment tribunals rather engage in creating convergence in investment treaty arbitration and in forging a body of international investment law that overarches the individual investment treaties and develops, relatively independently of the underlying bilateral treaties, primarily based on the jurisprudence of investment tribunals. In a sense, therefore, arbitral tribunals develop into legislators for the entire system of international investment law. After setting out the institutional structure of the relations between States and tribunals, the following chapter will therefore focus more precisely on how the practice of investor-State arbitration contributes to the multilateralization of international investment law.

VII

Multilateralization through interpretation: producing and reproducing coherence in investment jurisprudence

Tendencies to a multilateralization of international investment law are also visible in the practice of arbitral tribunals, above all in the way they interpret and construe investment treaties. Unlike their bilateral form suggests, arbitral tribunals do not predominantly interpret and construe BITs according to methods characteristic of the interpretation of bilateral treaties that contain *quid pro quo* bargains, but employ rationales and argumentative structures that suggest the existence of an overarching body of international investment law that has merely found its expression in bilateral treaty relationships. The dynamics at work in this respect are twofold. On the one hand, investment jurisprudence is reflective of the multilateral aspirations of international investment law that have been outlined above and merely applies them in an already multilateralized environment. On the other hand, the jurisprudence of investment tribunals is proactive in transforming investment law into a multilateral (sub-)system of international law. By multilateralizing investment law through interpretation, arbitral tribunals further develop the aggregate of investment treaties into a functional substitute of a multilateral investment instrument and create overarching linkages between seemingly unconnected treaty relationships. Investment tribunals thus translate the similarities of bilateral treaties, backed by the existing elements of multilateralism, into multilateral reality. They produce and reproduce international investment law as a uniform transnational investment regime.

In order to understand investment law as a multilateral system that exists independently from, and at the same time above, bilateral treaty relations, it is necessary to show that investment tribunals develop coherence in their jurisprudence not only with respect to one bilateral treaty relationship but across various BITs. "Cross-treaty coherence" is one of the necessary factors in understanding investment treaties and the jurisprudence based on them as part of a uniform transnational system of investment protection. In contrast, describing and conceptualizing investment law as a system would be of little help if the arbitral decisions were hardly predictable in the light of frequent and fundamental contradictions among them. Actual coherence in the jurisprudence is, however, only one building block in order to understand investment law as a multilateral system. It is not sufficient that coherence in investment jurisprudence occurs merely coincidentally. If one wants to properly describe international investment law as a multilateral system, "cross-treaty coherence" has to be the result of overarching rules and principles of international investment law that have merely coincidentally been embodied in bilateral treaties. Perceiving international investment law as a multilateral and uniform order thus requires the unity of its sources (*Einheit der Rechtsordnung*) as a basis of coherence in the actual decision-making process.[1]

Both criteria, the unity of sources and coherence in application, are the basis for understanding municipal law as a legal system. Under the civil law tradition, the unity of the legal system is traditionally understood in terms of the unity of legal text. It is the unity of the largely codified law that generates coherent judicial decisions. Even though the paradigm of the judge being the "mouth of the law" has been invalidated as an analytically viable concept,[2] the constructive unity of civil law is secured by the reference of the system's components, the single court decisions, to the unity of the codification. Every judicial decision therefore relates to the entire system of law through its reference to a uniform text. In contrast, under the common law tradition the unity of the legal system is realized primarily through the concept of *stare decisis* that, in simplified terms, requires courts to follow earlier decisions.[3] Unity under the common law is, therefore, secured primarily by the prohibition against reaching diverging results in comparable cases. It is a unity catalyzed by tradition, rather than by posited and codified law.[4]

---

[1] See Canaris, *Systemdenken und Systembegriff in der Jurisprudenz*, pp. 11–18 (1969). See also Benvenisti, *The Conception of International Law as a Legal System*, 50 German Ybk. Int'l L. 393 (2008).

[2] See *supra* Ch. VI.B.2.

[3] See, for example, Schauer, *Precedent*, 39 Stan. L. Rev. 571 (1987). See also Hathaway, *Path Dependence in the Law*, 86 Iowa L. Rev. 601, 602 (2001) (observing the path dependence entailed in the doctrine of *stare decisis* that keeps the common law system stable over time by "creat[ing] a seamless web connecting the past to the present and the future").

[4] Civil law systems, therefore, ensure consistency in decision-making and the unity of the legal order based on the idea of the norm; common law systems reach the same result

Under both the civil and the common law systems, unity is, however, not only a function of the empirically coherent application of individual cases in relation to each other, that is to say, the consistency of the system's components on a horizontal level, but also the reproduction of the system's overarching structure, that is to say, the reproduction of overarching legal rules and principles in the individual decision. The unity of the system therefore also has to influence and determine the outcome of individual decisions on a vertical level.[5] Coherence among individual decisions thus has to be the product of the existence of overarching legal rules and principles. This second criterion holds true for both civil and common law. While civil law systems are based on the idea that legal rules and principles are primarily embodied in codified norms that determine individual decisions, common law systems understand judicial decisions as the expression of an unwritten legal rule or principle that, in turn, influences any decision, even in cases of first impression.[6]

In investment treaty jurisprudence both factors play a decisive role. Tribunals presuppose both the unity of the sources of international investment law and create unity through dialogue with and citation of earlier tribunals' decisions. Coherence in investment jurisprudence is achieved through the development of case law that subsequently influences the outcome of other investment disputes and emerges as an independent source of international investment law which, in turn, influences the behavior of States and investors. Unity is further created through the interpretation of BITs in light of other third-party investment treaties. Arbitral tribunals thus produce and reproduce international investment law as a multilateral system through interpretative approaches, namely, the frequent reference to prior arbitral awards and to third-party investment treaties. Taken together, investment treaty arbitration thus operates as part of an autopoietic, self-referential, and normatively closed system

through their concept of binding precedent. Despite these conceptual differences, both common law as well as civil law systems in practice rely on hybrid forms of securing consistency. Under common law, judicial decisions are also perceived as an expression of an, albeit uncodified, rule or principle; in civil law, codifications are not complete and, therefore, require further development and gap-filling by the judicial decisions. Thus, judicial precedent plays an important role even in civil law systems despite the widespread existence of codified law and despite precedent lacking the status of a formal source of law.

[5] See Luhmann, *Das Recht der Gesellschaft*, pp. 38–123, in particular pp. 98–117 (1993) (denominating this as the operative closure of the legal system which is a prerequisite for the emergence of a self-referential autopoietic system of law).

[6] See, on the quest of legal scholarship in the United States to understand common law as a system of law, Reimann, *Historische Schule und Common Law*, pp. 121 *et seq.* (1993).

of law[7] that overarches the myriad number of bilateral investment treaty relations, unites them under common principles governing international investment relations, and contributes to providing a legal framework for the functioning of the global economic system.[8] These principles inform bilateral treaty relations and the interpretation of BITs as if they constituted elements of a multilateral (sub-)system of international law.

In order to show how tribunals contribute, by means of adjudicating disputes between investors and host States, to the multilateralization of international investment law, this chapter analyzes the methods of treaty interpretation arbitral tribunals employ as well as the ways they make use of sources of law. It particularly shows how investment tribunals adapt their interpretative methodology and their use of sources to multilateral rationalities. After outlining the potential for inconsistencies in investment treaty arbitration, this chapter illustrates the specificities in treaty interpretation that suggest that arbitral tribunals perceive international investment law as a uniform body of law despite its fragmentation into a large number of bilateral treaties. Subsequently, this chapter addresses the extensive use that investment tribunals make of precedent as a source of law, thereby creating a genuine treaty-overarching body of law that influences the outcome of investor-State disputes. Yet, the purpose, in this context, is not to provide an exhaustive analysis of all investment treaty awards concerning all issues that can possibly arise, or have arisen in the past, but to address certain argumentative structures that play a coining role in the interpretation of investment treaties in arbitral jurisprudence, above all with respect to the principles of international investment protection.

A   The potential for inconsistencies in investment treaty arbitration

Every legal system that relies on the judicial solution of individual conflicts has to deal with the problem of conflicting or contradictory decisions. Incoherence and inconsistencies are not only problematic with respect to the ability of the law to regulate human behavior and to stabilize mutual expectations. Inconsistencies and incoherence in the judicial decision-making process are also counter-productive for understanding the legal norms they apply as part of a legal system.

---

[7] See *supra* footnote 5.
[8] *cf.* Luhmann (*supra* note 5), pp. 124–64 (1993) (on the function that law serves for society).

While legal systems will not be able to achieve full consistency and perfect coherence, their ability to stabilize expectations and social relations is rendered non-existent if the degree of inconsistencies is too great.

On the domestic level, both internal and external mechanisms ensure the consistency of the legal order. Internal control mechanisms are, for example, the unity of the norm that is applied by the judiciary or the concept of precedent in common law systems.[9] External control mechanisms consist of the institutional structure of the judiciary where conflicts between courts are resolved within a hierarchical structure. The use of precedent in judicial decisions, as well as institutionalized intra-judiciary conflict resolution mechanisms, assure the operative unity of law as a system and secure the development and persistence of a common communicative structure within the system that enables the inter-linkage of single decisions as components of the legal system.

1 Incoherence and fragmentation in international dispute resolution

Unlike in domestic legal systems, for a long time there was no need to address inconsistencies in international dispute resolution due to the scarcity of international dispute settlement bodies and their limited jurisdiction in temporal, substantive, and personal terms.[10] Similarly, it constituted an uncontested rule that decisions by international courts and tribunals had binding effect only between the parties to the dispute without prejudging the resolution of disputes in future cases.[11] The reasons for not endorsing the concept of *stare decisis* in international law were, however, not only due to the scarcity of mechanisms of international dispute resolution, but rooted at a deeper theoretical level, as according judicial decisions the value of a formal source of international law would have contradicted the voluntarist approach to the international law doctrine of sources.[12] If decisions were binding beyond the individual case, States

---

[9] See *supra* footnotes 1–6 and accompanying text.

[10] See *infra* footnote 36.

[11] Article 59 of the ICJ Statute explicitly provides that no *stare decisis* doctrine exists concerning the decisions of the ICJ: "The decision of the Court has no binding force except between the parties and in respect of that particular case." See Verdross and Simma, *Universelles Völkerrecht*, pp. 395 *et seq.* (3rd edn. 1984).

[12] On the linkage between the wills of States and the formation of international law, see already Oppenheim, *International Law*, vol. I, pp. 20 *et seq.* (1905); Schachter *International Law in Theory and Practice*, pp. 35 *et seq.* (1991). See also *The Case of the*

would lose their exclusive position as the creators of international law.[13] For this reason, decisions of international courts and tribunals only constitute "subsidiary means for the determination of rules of [international] law."[14]

The perception that international judicial decisions were of only subsidiary importance in international law did, however, change with the proliferation of international courts and tribunals and the rise in their respective dispute settlement activities.[15] At the same time, the question of consistency in international jurisprudence surfaced as one of the main concerns in the debate about the fragmentation of international law.[16] One of the triggering events for this debate has, in fact, been the tension created by an inconsistent interpretation of general international law in the *Tadić* case, where the Appeals Chamber of the International Criminal Tribunal for the Former Yugoslavia departed from the jurisprudence of the ICJ concerning the question of when the actions of a paramilitary

---

S.S. "Lotus" (France v. Turkey), Judgment, September 7, 1927, P.C.I.J. Series A, No. 10 (1927), p. 18 (stating that "[t]he rules of law binding upon States therefore emanate from their own free will as expressed in conventions or by usages generally accepted as expressing principles of law and established in order to regulate the relations between these co-existing independent communities or with a view to the achievement of common aims."); *Military and Paramilitary Activities in and against Nicaragua (Nicaragua v. United States)*, Merits, Judgment, June 27, 1986, I.C.J. Reports 1986, p. 135, para. 269 (observing that "in international law there are no rules, other than such rules as may be accepted by the State concerned, by treaty or otherwise").

[13] See *supra* Ch. VI.B.2.

[14] Article 38(1)(d), Statute of the International Court of Justice.

[15] A surge of literature has developed that focuses on the implications of this development for the international legal system. See, for example, Helfer and Slaughter, *Toward a Theory of Effective Supranational Adjudication*, 107 Yale L. J. 273 (1997); Kingsbury, *Foreword: Is the Proliferation of International Courts and Tribunals a Systemic Problem?*, 31 N.Y.U. J. Int'l L. & Pol. 679 (1999); Charney, *The Impact on the International Legal System of the Growth of International Courts and Tribunals*, 31 N.Y.U. J. Int'l L. & Pol. 697 (1999); Romano, *The Proliferation of International Judicial Bodies: The Piece of the Puzzle*, 31 N.Y.U. J. Int'l L. & Pol. 709 (1999); Alford, *The Proliferation of International Courts and Tribunals: International Adjudication in Ascendance*, 94 Am. Soc'y Int'l L. Proc. 160 (2000); Spelliscy, *The Proliferation of International Tribunals: A Chink in the Armor*, 40 Colum. J. Transnat'l L. 143 (2001); Reed, *Great Expectations: Where Does the Proliferation of International Dispute Resolution Tribunals Leave International Law?*, 96 Am. Soc'y Int'l L. Proc. 219 (2002). See also the other contributions to a symposium held at New York University School of Law in October 1998 on the proliferation of international courts and tribunals, in 31 N.Y.U. J. Int'l L. & Pol. 679–933 (1999).

[16] See, on the fragmentation debate, Koskenniemi, *Fragmentation of International Law* (2007). See also the contributions to the 25th Anniversary Symposium of the Michigan Journal of International Law, entitled "Diversity or Cacophony? New Sources of Norms in International Law?", in 25 Mich. J. Int'l L. 845–1375 (2004).

group could be attributed to a foreign State.[17] With the increasing judicialization of international law and the creation of various dispute settlement fora, the unity of international law as a whole unavoidably came into perspective. The proliferation of international dispute settlement mechanisms and the lack of intra-organizational institutions that could ensure the unity of the jurisprudence of different courts and tribunals, therefore, produced a threat of inconsistency that not only puts the ability of international law to stabilize expectations and serve as guidelines for inter-State behavior into question, but also endangers the idea of international law as a system more generally.

Similar to the general debate about fragmentation in international law, a debate about the impact of inconsistent decisions in investment treaty arbitration has ensued.[18] One of the triggers for this debate was the occurrence of inconsistent decisions of investment tribunals. The Tribunals in *SGS v. Pakistan* and *SGS v. Philippines*,[19] for example, reached incompatible conclusions concerning the interpretation of very similar umbrella clauses in two different investment treaties. The Tribunals in *CME v. Czech Republic* and *Lauder v. Czech Republic* reached contrary results in two proceedings that related to the same fact pattern, but were brought by different claimants under two different BITs.[20] Likewise, the interpretation of MFN clauses has resulted in incompatible decisions concerning the question of whether these clauses apply to more favorable treatment regarding investor-State dispute settlement.[21]

In fact, within the field of international investment law, there is abundant potential for inconsistent and conflicting decisions. This potential stems from the embryonic institutionalization of investor-State dispute settlement and the lack of a rule of *stare decisis*. Investment treaty arbitration therefore lacks internal as well as external control mechanisms that can ensure uniformity in the outcomes of the tribunals' decision-making processes.

---

[17] See Rao, *Multiple International Judicial Forums*, 25 Mich. J. Int'l L. 929, 956–57 (2004); in detail see also de Hoogh, *Articles 4 and 8 of the 2001 ILC Articles on State Responsibility, the Tadić Case and Attribution of Acts of Bosnian Serb Authorities to the Federal Republic of Yugoslavia*, 72 Brit. Ybk. Int'l L. 255 (2001).

[18] See, for example, Franck, *The Legitimacy Crisis in Investment Treaty Arbitration*, 73 Fordham L. Rev. 1521 (2005); see further the contributions in Sauvant (ed.), *Appeals Mechanism in International Investment Disputes* (2008).

[19] See *infra* footnotes 178–91 and accompanying text.

[20] See *infra* footnotes 28–30 and accompanying text.

[21] See *supra* Ch. IV.C.

2 Fragmentation in international investment law: multiplicity of sources, multiplicity of proceedings

A number of factors rooted in substantive international investment law are responsible for the potential for inconsistent decisions. First, the fragmentation of sources of international investment law plays a role in creating incoherences. Thus, the same State measure that affects two investors with different nationalities might have to be assessed differently under two investment treaties.[22] Second, inconsistencies in investment treaty arbitration can result from differing assessments of law and facts by different tribunals.[23] Two tribunals may agree on the legal elements of a certain standard of investment protection or a defense of the State, but disagree on the assessment of the relevant facts. They may, for example, agree on the elements of necessity in international law but disagree on whether the circumstances prevailing in the host State actually qualify as an emergency.[24] Conversely, tribunals may disagree on the interpretation of certain provisions in the same BIT. The Tribunals in *CMS v. Argentina* and *LG&E v. Argentina*, for example, reached different conclusions in applying the BIT between the United States and Argentina because they assumed a different legal relationship between necessity under customary international law and a specific emergency clause in the treaty, and distributed the burden of proof for limiting elements differently.[25]

Differences in interpretation may also stem from opposing views of different tribunals relating to the proper interpretation and construction of comparable treaty provisions in different treaties. This was, for example, the basis for the conflict between the tribunals in *SGS v. Pakistan* and *SGS v. Philippines* that reached conflicting conclusions concerning the interpretation of comparable treaty provisions in two different BITs. While the Tribunal in *SGS v. Philippines* accepted that a provision in

---

[22] While the BIT with the home State of investor A might entitle investor A to damages, the BIT with the home State of investor B might not sanction the very same behavior. The incoherence in this respect, therefore, stems from the fragmentation of sources. They are, however, mitigated to a great extent by the MFN clauses that are regularly included in the relevant BITs (see *supra* Ch. IV) and the possibility that investors can opt into a treaty regime they desire (see *supra* Ch. V).

[23] Such conflicts can occur contemporaneously as well as consecutively.

[24] See *Sempra v. Argentina*, Award, September 28, 2007, para. 346 (explaining the differences with earlier jurisprudence concerning the Argentine economic crisis with differences in the factual assessment).

[25] See *infra* footnotes 221–33 and accompanying text.

the BIT between Switzerland and the Philippines allowed an investor to bring contractual claims as a violation of the treaty's umbrella clause, the Tribunal in *SGS v. Pakistan* denied this effect to the parallel provisions in the BIT between Switzerland and Pakistan.[26] Similarly, the different interpretations of the scope of MFN clauses concern a question of different interpretations of the same standard of investment protection in different treaties.[27]

Third, inconsistent decisions can also stem from the multiplicity of proceedings relating to an identical set of facts that can arise from independent claims by shareholders at different levels of a corporate structure.[28] Such a constellation led, for example, to the conflicting decisions by two different tribunals in *CME v. Czech Republic* and *Lauder v. Czech Republic*. Here, measures of the host State against a locally incorporated media company resulted in proceedings before two independent investment tribunals under two different BITs: one by CME, the direct shareholder of the locally incorporated media company; the other by Mr. Lauder, the controlling shareholder of CME. While the Tribunal in *CME* found that the respondent's measures violated several provisions of the Dutch–Czech BIT, including fair and equitable treatment, full protection and security, and the obligation not to deprive the investor of its investment, and accordingly ordered it to pay damages of approximately US\$ 270 million,[29] the Tribunal in *Lauder* only found that the Czech

---

[26] See *infra* footnotes 178–91 and accompanying text.

[27] See *supra* Ch. IV.C.

[28] Assume, for instance, that the host State passes a measure against a company that is incorporated locally but owned by a number of foreign shareholders. This fact pattern may, under certain circumstances, entitle the locally incorporated company to initiate investment arbitration against the host State if it qualifies as a foreign investor because of its foreign ownership. At the same time, the shareholders of the locally incorporated company are regularly entitled to bring an independent claim against the host State, because their shareholding in the company qualifies as an investment under most BITs. The existence of several shareholders may thus lead to several shareholder claims, above all since shareholders are usually entitled to initiate investment arbitration independently of whether they are controlling or non-controlling, majority or minority shareholders. To complicate things even further, international investment law not only allows parallel claims of direct shareholders, but also enables indirect shareholders, i.e., shareholders of shareholders in multilevel corporate structures, to initiate investment arbitration independently from each other. This can result in several parallel or subsequent claims that originate from a single measure of the host State against a single locally incorporated company. See more extensively on the protection of shareholders *supra* Ch. V.A.

[29] For the decision determining the grounds of liability, see *CME v. Czech Republic*, Partial Award, September 13, 2001. For the calculation of damages see *CME v. Czech Republic*, Final Award, March 14, 2003.

Republic breached the US–Czech BIT concerning the prohibition of arbitrary and discriminatory conduct with respect to events in 1993, but did not award damages due to remoteness.[30]

In sum, the potential factors for inconsistent decisions pertaining to substantive international investment law are numerous. The multiplicity of sources, the multiplicity of proceedings, and the significant potential for inconsistent interpretations resulting from it create abundant concerns relating to incoherent decisions. These factors in themselves aggravate understanding international investment law as a system of law.

3   Arbitration: an embryonic institutional design

In addition to the fragmentation of sources, the institutional design of investment treaty arbitration itself is a threat to consistent decision-making. Unlike national and international courts, investment treaty disputes are not entertained by a standing judicial institution. Instead, investment arbitration is a form of ad hoc dispute settlement, even if every arbitral tribunal is constituted according to the same (or at least similar) rules and applies the same (or at least similar) procedural law. Unlike judges in national and international courts, arbitrators are called upon to decide investment disputes between States and investors based on the appointment by the parties.[31] This results in a significant number of arbitrators for the resolution of investment disputes in general.[32] The number of decision-makers is an aspect that makes investment treaty arbitration fundamentally different from a standing judicial body, where

---

[30] *Lauder* v. *Czech Republic*, Final Award, September 3, 2001, para. 235.

[31] See, for example, Article 37, ICSID Convention; Article 7, UNCITRAL Arbitration Rules. Even if arbitral institutions maintain rosters with arbitrators nominated by States, the parties are in general free to choose whichever arbitrator they desire. ICSID, for example, maintains such a roster (Articles 3, 12–16, ICSID Convention), without, however, preventing the parties from appointing other individuals as arbitrators (Article 40(1), ICSID Convention).

[32] Even though some arbitrators are appointed more frequently than others, the number of decision-makers in investment arbitration clearly outnumbers the quantity of judges in a standing international court or tribunal. According to a recent quantitative survey, as of December 1, 2006, 115 concluded ICSID arbitrations were decided by 202 arbitrators, 43 of whom accounted for 49 percent of all appointments. Similarly, in pending ICSID arbitrations, 103 cases are being adjudicated by 137 arbitrators, 32 of whom account for 54 percent of all appointments. See Commission, *Precedent in Investment Treaty Arbitration*, 24 J. Int'l Arb. 129, 138–40 (2007).

the continuity and consistency of the jurisprudence is ensured through the personal continuity of the members of the dispute settlement body.[33] Finally, the different ad hoc arbitration panels co-exist without hierarchy. Apart from the possibility of annulling ICSID awards according to Article 52, ICSID Convention and to set aside non-ICSID awards,[34] investment treaty awards are not subject to appeal or any other form of external control by a hierarchically superior body that could ensure consistency in the decision-making process. Investment arbitration therefore lacks an institutionalized infrastructure that is able to preclude inconsistent decision-making. Rather, its embryonic institutional design adds to the risk of producing inconsistent decisions.[35]

4   The non-existence of stare decisis in international investment law

Investment treaty arbitration also does not incorporate the concept of *stare decisis* that could serve as an internal mechanism for producing consistent decisions.[36] While a BIT could in theory provide for the

[33] I would, therefore, also cast doubt on the weight Commission (*supra* footnote 32), 24 J. Int'l Arb. 129, 136–41 (2007), attaches to the development of an *esprit de corps* among international arbitrators as a factor in forging the use of precedent and thereby contributing to continuity. In my view, the number of arbitrators is still too high to be able to view it as a factor in itself that contributes to overall consistency.

[34] See *supra* Ch. VI.A.2.c.

[35] Only in passing should it be noted that the threat of inconsistent decisions was also one of the aspects that militated for the ICSID Secretariat's proposal to establish an appeals facility; see Tams, *An Appealing Option?*, Beiträge zum Transnationalen Wirtschaftsrecht, vol. 57 (2006). See further Ortino, Sheppard and Warner (eds.), *Investment Treaty Law – Current Issues, Volume 1*, pp. 15–143 (2006); Sauvant (ed.), *Appeals Mechanism in International Investment Disputes* (2008) (both containing contributions to conferences on the value of introducing an appeals mechanism for investment treaty disputes). The attempt to introduce an appeals facility under the ICSID Convention, however, failed to materialize. Similar considerations and difficulties also play out in the attempts of the United States to introduce appeals mechanisms for investment treaty awards under its more recent investment treaty practice, see Gantz, *An Appellate Mechanism for Review of Arbitral Decisions in Investor-State Disputes*, 39 Vand. J. Transnat'l L. 39 (2006). Another possibility for ensuring at least some consistency in related or parallel proceedings is to either consolidate several proceedings (*cf.* Articles 1126, 1117(3), NAFTA), or for the parties to agree on the same set of arbitrators. See OECD, *Improving the System of Investor-State Dispute Settlement*, pp. 21–25 (2006); Kaufmann-Kohler *et al.*, *Consolidation of Proceedings in Investment Arbitration*, 21 ICSID Rev. – For. Inv. L. J. 59 (2006); Shany, *Consolidation and Tests for Application*, 21 ICSID Rev. – For. Inv. L. J. 135 (2006).

[36] Prior to the proliferation of international investment treaties and the advent of investor-State dispute settlement, the question for the value of earlier investment decisions has hardly played any significant role. The reason for this is that investor-State arbitration

binding authority of arbitral awards for future investor-State disputes, hardly any treaty contains provisions addressing this question. Instead, some investment treaties explicitly provide for the relative nature of awards and decisions in investor-State disputes. Article 1136(1), NAFTA, for example, provides that: "An award made by a Tribunal shall have no binding force except between the disputing parties and in respect of the particular case." This clearly indicates that awards in investor-State disputes under NAFTA lack any value as precedent. The concept conveyed in Article 1136(1), NAFTA also applies across different investment treaties. In this context, it can be regarded as a specific expression of the *inter partes* effect of international treaties, that is, the principle that treaties create obligations only between the contracting parties.[37]

A principle of *stare decisis* also cannot be based on the operation of the MFN clause that is regularly included in international investment treaties.[38] In order to illustrate such an argument, assume that two investors A and B are affected by the same measure of host State C. They both rely on the obligation of the host State to accord fair and equitable

based on consent to arbitration in BITs radically changes investment arbitration and transforms it into a real enforcement mechanism for the obligations contained in international investment treaties. Although investment disputes did exist prior to the advent of investment treaty arbitration, they were resolved in a different fashion. Either, disputes concerning, for example, nationalization programs or other large-scale crises that negatively affected foreign investors, such as revolutions, war or civil war, were settled through inter-State negotiations, or by means of arbitration commissions or specific tribunals, like the Iran–United States Claims Tribunal, with jurisdiction limited in time and subject matter. These dispute settlement bodies could ensure consistency in their jurisprudence through the limited number of judges sitting in a standing institution and did not have to be substituted by other mechanisms that were capable of ensuring consistency.

Modern investment treaty arbitration, by contrast, relies on general and prospective consent to arbitration by States in international investment treaties and, therefore, enables an unlimited number of prospective disputes on diverse questions arising out of an unlimited number of measures by the host State. In addition, the dynamics of investment arbitration itself change: investors and States increasingly engage in discussions of earlier investment decisions in their submissions and memorials in investor-State disputes. Because of these differences the value of precedent becomes an issue in modern investor-State dispute settlement.

[37] To this extent, Article 34, Vienna Convention on the Law of Treaties (providing that "[a] treaty does not create either obligations or rights for a third State without its consent"). Although this provision directly only refers to the relative nature of the rights and duties resulting from a treaty, it also illustrates that its effects, in the form of an award of an international tribunal rendered on the basis of this treaty, shall remain restricted to the inter-party relationship. The limited effect of an arbitral award, therefore, forms part of the limitations of the scope of the treaty that governs the dispute.

[38] For a closer discussion of MFN clauses see *supra* Ch. IV.

treatment under two different investment treaties between the host State and their respective home State. Investor A initiates investment arbitration under its BIT and obtains an award against host State C based on the application of the principle of fair and equitable treatment. In view of A's success, investor B also initiates investor-state arbitration under his BIT with the host State C and argues that independent from the actual interpretation of fair and equitable treatment under the BIT between States B and C, the Tribunal is bound to follow the earlier award under the BIT between A and C, because B would need to be treated as favorably as A.

Such an argument, if sustained, would result in an obligation to follow earlier awards, at least if two different arbitral proceedings concern the same host State and relate to investors in the same situation. However, applying MFN clauses in this way is not possible because they apply only to more favorable treatment granted by the host State and thus require conduct that is attributable to the host State.[39] The award of an arbitral tribunal, by contrast, is not attributable to the host State. MFN clauses, therefore, cannot operate with respect to decisions by international tribunals and produce the effect of establishing a system of precedent.

A similar conclusion was reached in the *Aroa Mines* case where the British–Venezuelan Mixed Claims Commission declined the argument by the United Kingdom that the MFN clause in a British–Venezuelan treaty would entitle its nationals to receive the same treatment that third-country nationals received in disputes entertained by other Venezuelan Mixed Claims Commissions that entertained disputes relating to the same events brought by third-country nationals. The Commission decided that the MFN clause in question:

> means only that British subjects in Venezuela, just as Venezuelan citizens in England, have the same warranties, securities, and recourses as other aliens for the protection and maintenance of their respective rights before the courts of justice established by the local laws of each nation. Said clause is not applicable to these mixed commissions, which are of a very extraordinary nature; and if it were, other countries which have agreed with Venezuela upon the provision of most-favored nation would already have protested against some of the clauses of the Venezuelan–British protocol. On the other hand, as these mixed commissions proceed separately and absolutely independently of one another, and as the

---

[39] See Articles 5 and 10, ILC Draft Articles on Most-Favoured-Nation Clauses. See also *supra* Ch. IV.A.3.

persons who constitute them must use their own individual judgement in order to render their decisions according to their own belief and conscience, the decisions of other commissions can not be set up to serve as a guide for those which this Commission will have to make.[40]

Finally, the procedural law governing investor-State disputes equally does not furnish a basis for establishing a system of *stare decisis*. Much to the contrary, Article 53(1), ICSID Convention, for example, excludes such an effect by stating:

> The award shall be binding on the parties and shall not be subject to any appeal or to any other remedy except those provided for in this Convention. Each party shall abide by and comply with the terms of the award except to the extent that enforcement shall have been stayed pursuant to the relevant provisions of this Convention.

This provision not only lays down the obligation of the parties to the dispute to comply with the award, but also excludes any binding effect of an ICSID award as binding precedent for other disputes.[41] This conclusion can also be supported by the negotiating history of the Convention that shows that a binding effect of ICSID awards was never intended.[42] Article 53(1), ICSID Convention can therefore be read as establishing that ICSID awards are "binding *only* on the parties." Therefore, the procedural law governing investor-State disputes does not envisage a system of binding precedent upon third parties, nor does it bind the contracting parties to a BIT concerning the interpretation of the treaty beyond the individual case.

The principle of the non-binding nature of decisions by other investment tribunals is also firmly recognized in the investment jurisprudence. The Tribunal in *AES Corporation* v. *Argentina*, for example, stressed that "there is so far no rule of precedent in general international law; nor is there any within the specific ICSID system for the settlement of disputes between one State party to the Convention and the National of another State Party."[43] The Tribunal also emphasized that any other conclusion would violate

---

[40] *Aroa Mines Case*, British-Venezuelan Mixed Claims Commission, Decision, 1903, U.N.R.I.A.A., vol. IX, p. 407.

[41] See *AES Corporation* v. *Argentina*, Decision on Jurisdiction, April 26, 2005, para. 23; *SGS* v. *Philippines*, Decision on Jurisdiction, January 29, 2004, para. 97 (both holding that the ICSID Convention does not impose the binding authority of earlier ICSID decisions).

[42] See Schreuer, *The ICSID Convention*, Article 53, para. 15 (2001) (noting that nothing in the preparatory works for the ICSID Convention implies the applicability of a *stare decisis* rule).

[43] *AES Corporation* v. *Argentina*, Decision on Jurisdiction, April 26, 2005, para. 23.

the autonomy of the will of the Parties to the ICSID Convention as well as that of the Parties to the pertinent bilateral treaty on the protection of investments [and] the rule according to which each decision or award delivered by an ICSID tribunal is only binding on the parties to the dispute settled by this decision or award.[44]

The Tribunal therefore concluded, and is joined in this conclusion by numerous other decisions, that:

[a]n identity of the basis of jurisdiction of these tribunals, even when it meets with very similar if not even identical facts at the origin of the disputes, does not suffice to apply systematically to the present case positions or solutions already adopted in [other] cases. Each tribunal remains sovereign and may retain, as it is confirmed by ICSID practice, a different solution for resolving the same problem.[45]

From a legal point of view arbitral tribunals are, therefore, free to adopt rulings that deviate from prior decisions of other investment tribunals. As illustrated above all by cases of dissent,[46] investment treaty arbitration does not endorse a concept of *de iure* precedent.

---

[44] *Ibid.*, para. 23.

[45] *Ibid.*, para. 30. This conclusion is shared widely by investment tribunals. See *Amco Asia v. Indonesia*, Decision on the Application of Annulment, May 16, 1986, para. 44; *Liberian Eastern Timber v. Liberia*, Award, March 31, 1986, 2 ICSID Reports 343, 352; *Feldman v. Mexico*, Award, December 16, 2002, para. 107; *Enron v. Argentina*, Decision on Jurisdiction, January 14, 2004, para. 40; *SGS v. Philippines*, Decision on Jurisdiction, January 29, 2004, para. 97; *Enron v. Argentina*, Decision on Jurisdiction (Ancillary Claim), August 2, 2004, para. 25; *El Paso v. Argentina*, Decision on Jurisdiction, April 27, 2006, para. 39; *Gas Natural v. Argentina*, Decision on Jurisdiction, June 17, 2005, para. 36; *Camuzzi v. Argentina*, ICSID Case No. ARB/03/7, Decisión sobre Jurisdicción, June 10, 2005, para. 19; *Bayindir v. Pakistan*, Decision on Jurisdiction, November 14, 2005, para. 76; *EnCana v. Ecuador*, Award, February 3, 2006, para. 189; *Suez and InterAguas v. Argentina* Decision on Jurisdiction, May 16, 2006, para. 26; *Jan de Nul v. Egypt*, Decision on Jurisdiction, June 16, 2006, para. 64; *Azurix v. Argentina*, Award, July 14, 2006, para. 391; *Pan American v. Argentina* and *BP America v. Argentina*, Decision on Preliminary Objections, July 27, 2006, para. 42; *Grand River v. United States*, Decision on Objections to Jurisdiction, July 20, 2006, para. 36; *ADC v. Hungary*, Award, October 2, 2006, para. 293 (observing that "[i]t is true that arbitral awards do not constitute binding precedent. It is also true that a number of cases are fact-driven and that the findings in those cases cannot be transposed in and of themselves to other cases. It is further true that a number of cases are based on treaties that differ from the present BIT in certain respects. However, cautious reliance on certain principles developed in a number of those cases, as persuasive authority, may advance the body of law, which in turn may serve predictability in the interest of both investors and host States."); *World Duty Free v. Kenya*, Award, October 4, 2006, para. 16; *Rompetrol v. Romania*, Decision on Jurisdiction, April 18, 2008, para. 85; *Saipem v. Bangladesh*, Decision on Jurisdiction and Provisional Measures, March 21, 2007, para. 67.

[46] See *infra* Ch. VII.C.2.

5 Conclusion

Both the non-existence of external institutions that can check and eventually reverse investment treaty awards and the lack of internal control mechanisms, such as a doctrine of *stare decisis*, contribute to the great potential for inconsistencies in investment treaty arbitration. In view of the multiplicity of sources and the possibility of multiple proceedings based on the same set of facts, one should therefore expect that inconsistencies in investment treaty arbitration abound. Likewise, the design of investor-State dispute settlement based on case-by-case arbitration by party-appointed arbitrators contributes to the potential for inconsistencies. The institutions of international investment law, therefore, are not designed so as to promote intra-BIT or cross-BIT coherence. One should therefore expect a large degree of fragmentation of international investment law, an argument that would counterweigh any effort at systematization.

Overall, the institutional design of investor-State arbitration follows bilateral rationalities. The lack of a concept of precedent reduces the influence of investment jurisprudence as an authoritative source of international law above all for wholly unrelated investment treaties. It ensures, at least in theory, that the contracting parties to a BIT remain in control of the future of their bilateral treaty relations that will not be affected by the application and interpretation of other, unrelated BITs. Likewise, the lack of any hierarchy among investment tribunals and the lack of external control mechanisms, such as a standing appeals facility, aggravate the development of a uniform and consistent jurisprudence in the realm of international investment law. In essence, the potential for inconsistencies in investment treaty arbitration is, therefore, an expression of bilateralism in international investment relations.

It is against the background of these institutional obstacles that the trend toward multilateralism has to be appraised. It is, as submitted in this chapter, strong enough to overcome these internal and external ramifications of bilateralism and helps to generate a largely consistent jurisprudence, above all as regards the principles of investment protection.

B   Interpretation methods and the unity
of the system's sources

In order to perceive the entirety of international investment treaties as constituting a multilateral system, it is necessary to show the existence of an overarching body of rules and principles that informs the construction and application of bilateral investment treaties.[47] That arbitral tribunals presuppose the existence of such an overarching framework can be illustrated with respect to the interpretative methodologies they apply. Various examples show that investment tribunals do not confine themselves to a strictly bilateral interpretation of BITs, but rather interpret them against the background of a treaty overarching framework. This is particularly true with respect to the use of sources in investment treaty interpretation.

Arbitral tribunals do not confine themselves to consulting the bilateral treaty in question, supplemented by customary international law and general principles, but frequently draw conclusions from wholly or partly unrelated third-party BITs. This method of interpretation, the resort to treaties *in pari materia*, that is, the interpretation of a treaty in the light of another treaty of the same or a similar subject matter,[48] suggests that arbitral tribunals presuppose the existence of a system that overarches and comprises both the treaty for interpretation as well as the third-party treaty. Furthermore, references to model treaties and teleological interpretation play a major role in creating uniformity in the interpretation of unrelated investment treaties and contribute to the emergence of a treaty overarching framework of international investment law.

1   *Bilateralism and multilateralism in treaty interpretation*

The permissibility of the use of third-party treaties as an interpretative aid to the interpretation of a bilateral treaty has long played a role in international dispute resolution. The US–Mexican General Claims Commission, for example, held in 1929: "When there is need of interpretation of a treaty it is proper to consider stipulations of earlier or later treaties in relation to subjects similar to those treated in the treaty under consideration."[49] The PCIJ also commented on the issue of such

---

[47] *Cf.* Simma, *From Bilateralism to Community Interest in International Law*, 250 Recueil des Cours 217, 230–33 (1994) (understanding bilateralism in international law as characterized by the lack of a community interest, or, in other words, the lack of an overarching body of rules or principles that define and structure the international community).

[48] O'Connell, *International Law*, vol. I, p. 260 (2nd edn. 1970). See also Haraszti, *Some Fundamental Problems of the Law of Treaties*, pp. 145–150 (1973).

[49] *Genie Lantman Elton (United States)* v. *Mexico*, Opinion, May 13, 1929, U.N.R.I.A.A., vol. IV, p. 533 (citing Pradier-Fodéré, *Traité de Droit International Public*, vol. II, § 1188, p. 895 [1885]).

"cross-treaty interpretation," but took a more restrictive view. In *The Factory at Chorzów*, the Court observed:

> [A]part from the question whether expressions used in conventions between other Powers and at different periods can be *taken into account in interpreting the intention of the signatories* of the Geneva Convention, the Court holds that, in view of the fundamental difference between the nature of arbitration clauses (*clauses compromissoires*) and the object of the classification of disputes in general arbitration agreements, no conclusions can be drawn from the terminology of the one class of provisions in respect of the other.[50]

The theoretical background to the debate is that "cross-treaty interpretation" is problematic in view of the *inter partes* effect of international treaties,[51] since using a third-party treaty as an interpretative aid can amount to either creating additional obligations, or conversely diminishing a right of one of the parties. Denying cross-treaty interpretation therefore upholds the authority and independence of a bilateral treaty and counters tendencies to view such a treaty as part of a larger system of treaties. Having recourse to cross-treaty interpretation, by contrast, embeds treaties into an overarching system or framework of treaties. To a certain extent, the methods of treaty interpretation are, therefore, connected to the view the interpreter takes on bilateralism and multilateralism as institutional choices for ordering international relations.

(a) Bilateralism in treaty interpretation

Various examples exist in the jurisprudence of international courts and tribunals that emphasize that treaties are, in principle, to be interpreted independently from other treaties and that the same wording may have a different meaning in different treaty relationships depending on the respective context of the treaty. The European Court of Justice, for example, stressed that a special agreement between the EEC and a non-Member did not necessarily follow the same interpretation as the EEC Treaty. Instead, it stressed that:

> it must be observed that although Article 21 of the Agreement and Article 95 of the EEC Treaty have the same object inasmuch as they aim at the

---

[50] *The Factory at Chorzów (Claim for Indemnity) (Germany v. Poland)*, Jurisdiction, Judgment, July 26, 1927, P.C.I.J. Series A, No. 9 (1927), p. 22 (emphasis added). But see *infra* footnote 61, where the Court in the same decision actually exhibited a more positive attitude towards viewing a similar treaty in light of the general State practice relating to arbitration clauses.

[51] See Article 34, Vienna Convention on the Law of Treaties (providing that "[a] treaty does not create either obligations or rights for a third State without its consent").

elimination of tax discrimination, both provisions, which are moreover worded differently, must however be considered and interpreted in their own context ... the EEC Treaty and the Agreement on Free Trade pursue different objectives. It follows that the interpretations given to Article 95 of the Treaty cannot be applied by way of simple analogy to the Agreement on Free Trade. ... Article 21 must be interpreted according to its terms and in the light of the objective which it pursues in the system of free trade established by the Agreement.[52]

The independence of different sources of international law also holds true concerning the relation between international treaties and customary international law. In *Military and Paramilitary Activities in and against Nicaragua*, the ICJ emphasized that rules stemming from different international legal sources had to be interpreted independently even if their content was identical. The Court thus observed:

There are a number of reasons for considering that, even if two norms belonging to two sources of international law appear identical in content, and even if the States in question are bound by these rules both on the level of treaty-law and on that of customary international law, *these norms retain a separate existence ... Rules which are identical in treaty law and in customary international law are also distinguishable by reference to the methods of interpretation and application.* A State may accept a rule contained in a treaty not simply because it favours the application of the rule itself, but also because the treaty establishes what the State regards as desirable institutions or mechanisms to ensure implementation of the rule. Thus, if that rule parallels a rule of customary international law, two rules of the same content are subject to separate treatment as regards the organs competent to verify their implementation, depending on whether they are customary rules or treaty rules.[53]

---

[52] *Hauptzollamt Mainz* v. *C A Kupferberg & Cie KG*, Case 104/81, Judgment, October 26, 1982, E.C.R 3641 (1982), paras. 29 *et seq.* This case concerned the interpretation of Article 21 of an Agreement between the EEC and Portugal concerning the taxation of certain goods after the German *Bundesfinanzhof* had referred a case to the ECJ under former Article 177, EEC (now Article 234, EC). The referring court had asked whether the interpretation of this provision followed the same pattern as Article 95, EEC and thus also prevented potential discrimination. Based on the different context, the different objective, and the slightly different wording the Court concluded that the Agreement required actual discrimination; potential discrimination, unlike under the regime of Article 95 EEC, was not sufficient. Although there was also a difference in wording of the two international treaties involved, the observations of the Court would have presumably also been pertinent if the provisions had been worded identically because the main emphasis of the Court was on the difference in object and purpose of the two rules concerned.

[53] *Military and Paramilitary Activities in and against Nicaragua (Nicaragua* v. *United States)*, Merits, Judgment, June 27, 1986, I.C.J. Reports 1986, pp. 95–96, para. 178 (emphasis added).

Similarly, in the *Loizidou* case, the European Court of Human Rights decided that the permissibility of reservations to the Court's jurisdiction under Article 46, European Convention on Human Rights had to be assessed differently from reservations to the jurisdiction of the ICJ under Article 36, ICJ Statute. The Strasbourg Court in this context stated:

> [I]t is not disputed that States can attach restrictions to their acceptance of the optional jurisdiction of the International Court. Nor has it been contested that Article 46 (art. 46) of the Convention was modelled on Article 36 of the Statute. However, in the Court's view, it does not follow that such restrictions to the acceptance of jurisdiction of the Commission and Court must also be permissible under the Convention.
>
> In the first place, the context within which the International Court of Justice operates is quite distinct from that of the Convention institutions. The International Court is called on inter alia to examine any legal dispute between States that might occur in any part of the globe with reference to principles of international law. The subject-matter of a dispute may relate to any area of international law. In the second place, unlike the Convention institutions, the role of the International Court is not exclusively limited to direct supervisory functions in respect of a law-making treaty such as the Convention.
>
> Such a fundamental difference in the role and purpose of the respective tribunals, coupled with the existence of a practice of unconditional acceptance under Articles 25 and 46 (art. 25, art. 46), provides a compelling basis for distinguishing Convention practice from that of the International Court.[54]

The same approach was taken by the International Tribunal for the Law of the Sea which affirmed in a case concerning the request for provisional measures relating to the protection of the marine environment against pollution through radioactive material that:

> the application of international law rules on interpretation of treaties to identical or similar provisions of different treaties may not yield the same results, having regard to, *inter alia*, differences in the respective contexts, objects and purposes, subsequent practice of parties and *travaux préparatoires*.[55]

Likewise, an arbitral tribunal hearing a case under the 1992 Convention for the Protection of the Marine Environment of the North-East Atlantic observed that:

---

[54] *Loizidou* v. *Turkey*, ECtHR, Judgment, March 23, 1995, 103 ILR 622, paras. 83–85.
[55] *The MOX Plant Case (Ireland v. United Kingdom)*, Order on Provisional Measures, December 3, 2001, para. 51, 41 I.L.M. 405, 413 (2002).

the adoption of a similar or identical definition or term in international texts should be distinguished from the intention to bestow the same normative status upon both instruments. The complex of instruments whose wording was used by the drafters may include unilateral statements, position papers, declarations, recommendations, and the like. While the language of such sources might be instrumental to the extent that it allows one to trace and understand the origins of specific treaty terms, their normative value should not be attributed to similarly worded legal obligations imposed by that treaty.[56]

The decisions of international courts and tribunals discussed above therefore illustrate that in the interpretation of treaty provisions comprehensive consideration has to be given not only to the wording but also to the specific context of a treaty. This may require that provisions, even though they are worded in an identical manner, have to be interpreted differently. Interpreting even identical wording differently can also be justified due to the differences, the separateness, of the legal sources that govern the respective relationships between the parties in question. It is thus exclusively the specific international treaty in question that governs the relationship between the parties. Other treaties, by contrast, above all those between unrelated parties, should not, in principle, have a bearing upon the applicable treaty relationship. Differences in the source of obligations therefore, do not, only justify differences in interpretation, but also ensure, from a functional perspective, that the interpretation of a treaty is strictly focused on the relationship of the contracting parties, independent of the way in which third States structure their international treaty relations.

(b)   Multilateralism in treaty interpretation

The contrary position with respect to cross-treaty interpretation is taken by a number of other decisions of international courts and tribunals. They have considered it to be permissible to interpret a treaty in light of other treaties under the condition that these treaties form part of a system of treaties.[57] Cross-treaty interpretation was, for example, employed with respect to the interpretation of Friendship, Commerce and Navigation (FCN) treaties the United States has entered into since the end of the eighteenth century. In this respect, an arbitral tribunal in the *Kronprins Gustaf Adolf* case made frequent reference to other FCN treaties of the

---

[56] *Access to Information under Article 9 of the OSPAR Convention (Ireland v. United Kingdom)*, Final Award, July 2, 2003, 42 I.L.M. 1118, 1144, para. 141 (2003).
[57] O'Connell (*supra* footnote 48), p. 260 (1970).

United States when interpreting the FCN treaty between the United States and Sweden.[58] Similarly, the ICJ in *Rights of Nationals of the United States of America in Morocco* used treaties between Morocco and third countries, such as France and Great Britain, in order to interpret the FCN treaty between the United States and Morocco.[59]

Likewise, the PCIJ used elements of cross-treaty interpretation in *The Factory at Chorzów* with respect to the interpretation of an arbitration clause in a treaty between Poland and Germany, even though it took a more restrictive stance on cross-treaty interpretation elsewhere in the same decision.[60] Notwithstanding, the Court rejected the argument of the respondent to interpret arbitration clauses restrictively by observing:

> [t]o say, therefore, that the *clause compromissoire*, while confessedly providing for the submission of questions of right and obligation, must now be restrictively interpreted as excluding pecuniary reparation, *would be contrary to the fundamental conceptions by which the movement in favour of general arbitration has been characterized*.[61]

The Court therefore embedded its interpretation of the arbitration clause in the bilateral treaty in question into the more general State practice of the late nineteenth and early twentieth centuries which favored arbitration as a method of inter-State dispute resolution. Even though it left open the question of whether cross-treaty interpretation was permissible as a

---

[58] *Kronprins Gustaf Adolf (Sweden* v. *United States)*, Arbitral Decision, July 18, 1932, U.N.R.I.A.A., vol. II, pp. 1258 *et seq.*

[59] *Rights of Nationals of the United States of America in Morocco (France* v. *United States)*, Judgment, August 27, 1952, I.C.J. Reports 1952, p. 189 (arguing that "in construing the provisions of Article 20 [of the treaty between Morocco and the United States] – and, in particular, the expression 'shall have any dispute with each other' – it is necessary to take into account the meaning of the word 'dispute' at the times when the two treaties were concluded. For this purpose it is possible to look at the way in which the word 'dispute' or its French counterpart was used in the different treaties concluded by Morocco: e.g., with France in 1631 and 1682, with Great Britain in 1721, 1750, 1751, 1760 and 1801.").

[60] See *supra* footnote 50.

[61] *The Factory at Chorzów (Claim for Indemnity) (Germany* v. *Poland)*, Jurisdiction, Judgment, July 26, 1927, P.C.I.J. Series A, No. 9 (1927), p. 22 (emphasis added). See also *ibid.*, p. 24. (observing that the treaty's arbitration clause "*which constitutes a typical arbitration clause* (*clause compromissoire*), contemplates all differences of opinion resulting from the interpretation and application of a certain number of articles of a convention" – emphasis added). See also *ibid.*, p. 25 (observing that "[t]his conclusion, which is deducted from the object of a clause like Article 23, and, in general, of any arbitration clause, could only be defeated, *either* by the employment of terms sufficiently clear to show a contrary intention on the part of the contracting Parties, *or* by the fact that the Convention had established a special jurisdiction for claims in respect of reparation due for the violation of the provisions in question, or had made some other arrangement regarding them", emphasis in the original).

matter of principle, the decision suggests that treaties with the same or a similar subject-matter and the same object and purpose should be interpreted in view of the general development they reflect. Similarly, BITs are an expression of a larger movement within the international community to provide protection for foreign investments and to promote international investment flows in order to further economic growth and development.

An even closer entrenchment of bilateral treaties in a multilateral setting can be illustrated with respect to the inter-war minority protection regime that was created under the auspices of the League of Nations.[62] Although formally based on bilateral treaties, this regime "took on a multilateral aspect through its incorporation into the League as well as through the large number of nearly simultaneous treaties and declarations. The whole scheme was informed by multilateral planning, in contrast with the centuries-old examples of sporadic bilateral treaties protecting (usually religious) minorities."[63] The multilateral aspects of this system also had an impact on the interpretation of the bilateral treaties that contained the substantive law of minority protection.

In its Advisory Opinion in *Minority Schools in Albania*, the PCIJ interpreted the declaration by Albania vis-à-vis the League of Nations, by which the country recognized the protection of minorities, not as an isolated instrument of international law, but put it into the context of the inter-war minority protection regime as a whole. In particular, the Court dwelt on differences between the Albanian Declaration and the first of the series of minority protection treaties, the one with Poland, which served as a model for later treaties, but also strongly emphasized the overall object and purpose of the minority protection system as a whole. The Court thus construed the Albanian Declaration as part of a larger multilateral system that was, however, based on bilateral treaties, or treaty-like relationships.[64] In this context, the Court observed that:

---

[62] On the inter-war minorities regime more generally see Macartney, *National States and National Minorities* (1934); Robinson, *Were the Minority Treaties a Failure?* (1943); De Azcarate, *League of Nations and National Minorities* (1945); Berman, *A Perilous Ambivalence*, 33 Harv. Int'l L. J. 353 (1992); Berman, *But the Alternative is Despair*, 106 Harv. L. Rev. 1792 (1993).

[63] Steiner and Alston, *International Human Rights in Context*, p. 103 (2nd edn. 2000). The substantive international law protecting minorities was enshrined in a number of bilateral treaties between the new States and the Great Powers and in various unilateral declarations. The first such treaty was the one with Poland from June 1919. This treaty served as a model for subsequent minority protection treaties. See Robinson (*supra* footnote 62), p. 25 (1943).

[64] The issue the Advisory Opinion confronted was whether Albania was prevented from passing a general prohibition of private schools in its Constitution that also applied to

Albania did accept ... a régime of minority protection substantially the same as that which had been already agreed upon with other States in which there were no "communities". The differences between the text of the Albanian Declaration and the other texts of the same kind do not affect the essential features of that Act ... It follows that any rights and privileges which the Greek communities in Albania may have enjoyed are only recognized in the Declaration of October 2nd, 1921, in so far as they are covered by the analogous régime of the protection of minorities. As the Declaration of October 2nd, 1921, was designed to apply to Albania the general principles of the treaties for the protection of minorities, this is the point of view which, in the Court's opinion, must be adopted in construing paragraph I of Article 5 of the said Declaration.[65]

The Court thus accepted that the general framework of the minority protection regime had to inform the interpretation of the Albanian Declaration. By doing so, the Court emphasized the multilateral implications of the system of bilateral minorities treaties. Three aspects, in particular, militated for a multilateral interpretation in this context: (1) the institutional integration of the bilateral treaties in a multilateral system, namely, the monitoring and complaint regime under the auspices of the League of Nations; (2) the closely related conclusion of a number of bilateral treaties with similar wording; and (3) the multilateral planning of the minorities regime. The fact that the treaties governed bilateral relationships, by contrast, had little bearing upon their construction in the Court's practice.

The tensions between bilateral and multilateral rationalities can also be illustrated in the interpretation of the US–Italian FCN treaty in the *ELSI*

---

private schools of Greek minorities. While Albania argued that it had only promised national treatment to minorities and was not prevented from passing generally applicable legislation prohibiting private schools, the Court held that the Declaration also granted special rights for minorities that allowed them to continue having private minority schools. While a literal interpretation of the Albanian Declaration and the emphasis on the differences with the model treaty with Poland would have yielded the result supported by Albania, namely, that it had only engaged in granting formal equality, the Court observed that existing differences between the Albanian Declaration and the model of the inter-war minorities regime as contained in the treaty with Poland could not defeat the general object and purpose of the minorities regime.

[65] *Minority Schools in Albania*, Advisory Opinion, April 6, 1935, P.C.I.J. Series A/B, No. 64 (1935), pp. 16–17. See also the Joint Dissenting Opinion by Judges Hurst, Rostworowski, and Negulesco who, while dissenting, supported the same interpretative methodology. See *ibid.*, p. 28 (observing that "[b]eing in conformity with the general type of minority instrument, words and phrases which are common both to the Declaration and to other treaties must be interpreted alike in all; otherwise the obligations of the various Powers bound by such treaties would become divergent").

case considered by the ICJ.[66] Unlike the majority vote that interpreted the treaty according to typically bilateral rationales, Judge Oda emphasized the fact that the FCN treaty in question was embedded in a larger network of FCN treaties that had to be viewed as an overarching system rather than as independent and isolated treaties.[67] As a starting point, Judge Oda highlighted that:

> the granting of … rights to foreign corporations is not unique to the 1948 Treaty between Italy and the United States, as similar provisions are to be found (albeit with some variations) in the FCN treaties which the United States concluded successively with other countries in the post-war period. (The 1948 FCN Treaty with Italy was the second of such treaties to be concluded by the United States, being proceeded by the treaty with China (1946) and followed by the treaties with Ireland (1950); Greece, Israel and Denmark (1951); Japan (1953); the Federal Republic of Germany (1954); Iran (1955); the Netherlands and the Republic of Korea (1956) and others.)[68]

As a consequence, Judge Oda developed his interpretation of the rights granted under the US–Italian FCN treaty by generally citing the parallel provisions in other FCN treaties of the United States,[69] thus recognizing that their framing had repercussions for the interpretation of the treaty between Italy and the United States. His approach becomes particularly clear concerning the interpretation of the prohibition of the taking of property. Concerning the question of whether the requisition of a plant and its subsequent liquidation constituted a taking under the treaty, Judge Oda used a literal argument that directly drew on third-country FCN treaties. He argued:

> In this respect I would like to point out, as a supplementary explanation, that the verb "take", as expressed by "espropriare" in the Italian text, is rendered in the 1956 [sic] FCN Treaty between the Federal Republic of Germany and the United States by the German verb "enteignen", which

---

[66] *Elettronica Sicula SpA (ELSI) (United States* v. *Italy)*, Judgment, July 20, 1989, I.C.J. Reports 1989, p. 15. The case concerned the conformity with the FCN treaty of the requisition of an American-owned plant by Italian authorities, in particular the treaty's provisions prohibiting arbitrary and discriminatory conduct and uncompensated expropriations.

[67] *Elettronica Sicula SpA (ELSI) (United States* v. *Italy)*, Judgment of July 20, 1989, Separate Opinion of Judge Oda, I.C.J. Reports 1989, p. 83.

[68] *Ibid.*, p. 87.

[69] *Ibid.*, p. 87 (concerning the "rights and privileges with respect to organization of and participation in corporations"); *ibid.*, p. 88 (concerning the interpretation of the protection against expropriation); *ibid.*, p. 88 (concerning the protection against arbitrary and discriminatory measures); see also *ibid.*, p. 90.

militates against the acceptance of an interpretation of the requisition order of the Mayor of Palermo as amounting to a "taking" of property.[70]

The majority vote, by contrast, exclusively referred to the two authoritative languages of the treaty in question, being English and Italian, in order to interpret the meaning of expropriation, respectively "espropriazione."[71] Judge Oda's approach, thus, recognizes the fact that FCN treaties were embedded in a larger treaty framework that could and should be taken into account in the interpretation of the applicable FCN treaty. He presupposed that the protection offered by the different treaties cannot be ascertained by recourse to the two languages in question, but had to be developed with respect to the legal concepts referenced by all of the treaties. His approach, therefore, endorses the same multilateral interpretation that can also be discerned with respect to the use of cross-BIT interpretation in modern international investment law.

The permissibility of cross-treaty interpretation has also been accepted in a number of other decisions by international courts and tribunals. In this context, the use of third-party treaties as an interpretative aid assumes a number of functions. First, third-party treaties can be used in order to clarify the meaning of a provision of the treaty for interpretation. Thus, the PCIJ observed in *Treatment of Polish Nationals and Other Persons of Polish Origin or Speech in the Danzig Territory*:

> As between Danzig and Poland, the Convention of Paris is the instrument which is directly binding on Danzig; but in case of doubt as to the meaning of its provisions, recourse may be had to the Treaty of Versailles, not for the purpose of discarding the terms of the Convention, but with a view to elucidating their meaning.[72]

Second, third-party treaties can be used in order to infer the intention of the parties to the treaty for interpretation. This was, for example, the reason behind the PCIJ's interpretation of the arbitration clause in *The Factory at Chorzów* where the Court noted:

> [A]part from the question whether expressions used in conventions between other Powers and at different periods can be taken into account in interpreting the intention of the signatories of the Geneva Convention, the Court holds that, in view of the fundamental difference between the nature of arbitration clauses (*clauses compromissoires*) and the object of

---

[70] *Ibid.*, p. 91.

[71] *Elettronica Sicula SpA (ELSI) (United States v. Italy)*, Judgment of July 20, 1989, I.C.J. Reports 1989, pp. 67–71, paras. 113–19.

[72] *Treatment of Polish Nationals and Other Persons of Polish Origin or Speech in the Danzig Territory*, Advisory Opinion, February 4, 1932, P.C.I.J. Series A/B, No. 44 (1932), p. 32.

the classification of disputes in general arbitration agreements, no conclusions can be drawn from the terminology of the one class of provisions
in respect of the other.[73]

Third, the PCIJ has used third-country treaties as an interpretative
aid, if the treaty for interpretation emanated from multilateral planning. In such cases, recourse to treaties governing the multilateral
process at work can be used for purposes of cross-treaty interpretation.
In *Interpretation of the Convention of 1919 concerning Employment
of Women during the Night*, for instance, the Court interpreted in an
Advisory Opinion a provision from the Washington Convention which
had been concluded under the umbrella of the International Labour
Organization ("ILO") in light of the Treaty of Versailles that had constituted the ILO.[74]

Finally, third-party treaties can be used in reasoning by analogy if the
treaty of comparison forms part of a system of treaties with the treaty for
interpretation. Thus, in the *UNESCO Constitution Case*, the Tribunal
explicitly drew analogies to provisions in the UN Charter and the ICJ
Statute when interpreting Article V, Constitution of UNESCO concerning the question of whether an outgoing member of the Executive
Board may stand for re-election, even though he or she is not a member
of his or her country's delegation to the session of the conference when
elections take place. The Tribunal, drawing on treaties that were part
of the UN constitutional system, and thus institutionally related to the
treaty for interpretation, considered this method of interpretation to be
permissible.[75]

Although the examples mentioned above often concerned resort to
treaties that were at least binding on one of the parties, cases like the
interpretation of the Albanian minorities declaration show that recourse
may also be had to treaties that are not binding upon any of the parties in
question. Instead, what is decisive in cases of interpretation *in pari materia* is that the treaty for interpretation and the third-party treaty form
part of a larger framework or system of treaties. The conclusion to be
drawn from the practice of international courts and tribunals, therefore,

---

[73] *The Factory at Chorzów (Claim for Indemnity) (Germany v. Poland)*, Jurisdiction,
Judgment, July 26, 1927, P.C.I.J. Series B, No. 9 (1927), p. 22. See also *supra* footnote 61.
[74] *Interpretation of the Convention of 1919 concerning Employment of Women during
the Night*, Advisory Opinion, November 15, 1932, P.C.I.J. Series A/B, No. 50 (1932),
pp. 374–76.
[75] *UNESCO Constitution Case*, Decision, September 19, 1949, 16 AD 331, 335 (1949) (drawing analogies to Articles 23 and 61, UN Charter and Article 13, ICJ Statute).

is that cross-treaty interpretation is accepted and permissible to the extent that the treaties taken into account form part of a common and treaty-overarching system. Indications for the existence of such a system are the integration of treaties into an institutional monitoring or dispute settlement structure, their close ties in terms of subject matter and object and purpose, and their emanation from multilateral planning.

2 Multilateralization through cross-treaty interpretation in investment arbitration

Similar to some of the approaches to interpretation mentioned above that had recourse not only to factors strictly relating to the treaty for interpretation but also to third-party treaties as an interpretative aid, investment tribunals frequently employ cross-treaty interpretation in applying and construing BITs. This use of cross-treaty interpretation is genuinely multilateral in nature, as it creates uniform structures of reasoning for the interpretation of concepts that are used in different bilateral treaties. Instead of stressing differences between treaties, interpretation by resort to treaties *in pari materia* establishes uniformity in the interpretation of BITs and embeds BITs into a larger, treaty-overarching framework, which is similar to a genuinely multilateral regime. Cross-treaty interpretation suggests that BITs, even though constituting bilateral treaties, yield to common rationales and refer to common concepts of international investment law that exist independent from the individual bilateral treaty relationships. Cross-treaty interpretation comes in two forms: reference to the BIT practice of the States involved in a dispute and reference to the BIT practice of wholly unrelated third countries.

(a) The use of third-country BITs of the contracting States

Cross-treaty interpretation has already been recognized as an accepted method for the interpretation of investment treaties in *Asian Agricultural Products* v. *Sri Lanka*, the first known investment treaty award. Commenting on the available methods of interpretation, the Tribunal, *inter alia*, stated: "When there is need of interpretation of a treaty it is proper to consider stipulations of earlier or later treaties in relation to subjects similar to those treated in the treaty under consideration."[76]

---

[76] *Asian Agricultural Products* v. *Sri Lanka*, Final Award, June 27, 1990, para. 40 (citing the award of the U.S.–Mexican General Claims Commission referred to *supra* footnote 49).

It thereby set the basis for establishing cross-treaty interpretation as a widespread method of interpretation in investment treaty arbitration.

The first more elaborate use of cross-treaty interpretation can be found in the ICSID decision in *Maffezini* v. *Spain*. When interpreting whether the MFN clause in the Spanish–Argentine BIT also applied to more favorable dispute settlement provisions,[77] the Tribunal did not only have regard to the wording of the MFN clause and the object and purpose of the applicable BIT. It also took into account the general BIT practice of the contracting parties as well as other States concerning the specific issue in question.[78] In this context, the Tribunal invoked, for example, the BIT practice of the United Kingdom that expressly provided for MFN treatment to encompass dispute settlement.[79] Although the Tribunal did not explain the purpose of making reference to these third-party treaties, it presumably did so in order to suggest that MFN clauses in investment treaties are usually intended to apply broadly. In any case, the Tribunal undoubtedly attached relevance to the formulations of third-party BITs for the interpretation of the BIT applicable in the dispute at hand.

Apart from having regard to unrelated third-country BITs, the Tribunal extensively focused on Spain's BIT practice[80] and concluded that "[t]hese treaties indicate that Spain's preferred practice is to allow for arbitration, following a six-months effort to reach a friendly settlement."[81] It went on to state that the Spanish–Argentine BIT was "the only one that speaks of 'all matters subject to this Agreement' in its most favored nation clause … All other treaties … omit this reference and merely provide that 'this treatment' shall be subject to the clause, which is of course a narrower formulation."[82] Based on this, in relation to other Spanish BITs, unusually broad wording of the MFN clause in question, the Tribunal applied MFN

---

[77] *Maffezini* v. *Spain*, Decision on Objections to Jurisdiction, January 25, 2000, paras. 38 *et seq.*

[78] *Ibid.*, paras. 52 *et seq.*

[79] It cited Article 3(3), Agreement between the Government of the United Kingdom of Great Britain and Northern Ireland and the Government of the Republic of Albania for the Promotion and Protection of Investments, signed on March 30, 1994, entered into force on August 30, 1995, that provided: "For the avoidance of doubt it is confirmed that the treatment provided for in paragraphs (1) and (2) above shall apply to the provisions of Articles 1 to 11 of this Agreement." The Tribunal noted that this third-country treaty provision stressed that the reference to dispute settlement was included for "the avoidance of doubt." It also referred to the MFN clause in the BIT between Chile and the Belgo–Luxemburgian Economic Union that applied to "all rights contained in the present Agreement." See *Maffezini* v. *Spain*, Decision on Objections to Jurisdiction, January 25, 2000, para. 52).

[80] *Ibid.*, paras. 58 *et seq.*   [81] *Ibid.*, para. 58.   [82] *Ibid.*, para. 60.

treatment to circumventing access restrictions for investor-State dispute settlement. It, therefore, used Spain's general BIT practice as a frame of reference for the interpretation of the specific MFN clause in the specific BIT.

The use of the host State's general BIT practice also played a decisive role in *Aguas del Tunari* v. *Bolivia* with respect to the question of whether foreign control of a locally incorporated company, in order for this company to qualify as a foreign investor under the Dutch–Bolivian BIT, required actual control by a foreign shareholder or merely its legal capacity to control.[83] In resolving this issue, the Tribunal, *inter alia*, compared the provisions of the Dutch–Bolivian BIT to allegedly more precise formulations in the Dutch–Argentine BIT and the Bolivian–Argentine BIT[84] and concluded that these third-party treaties confirmed that the legal capacity to control was sufficient under the Dutch–Bolivian BIT.[85] Although stressing "that the BIT practice of the Netherlands and Bolivia is necessarily of limited probative value to the task of interpreting the BIT between the Netherlands and Bolivia,"[86] the Tribunal went on to explain the significance of the host State's general BIT practice:

> The practice of a state as regards the conclusion of BITs other than the particular BIT involved in a dispute is not of direct value to the task of interpretation under Article 31 of the Vienna Convention. The fact that a pattern might exist in the content of the BITs entered into by a particular state does not mean that a specific BIT by that state should be understood as necessarily conforming to that pattern rather than constituting an exception to that pattern.
>
> The practice of a state as regards the negotiation of BITs may be helpful, however, in testing the assertions of parties as to the general policies of either Bolivia or the Netherlands concerning BITs, and in testing assumptions a tribunal may make regarding BITs.[87]

While the Tribunal stressed that third-party BITs had no "direct" bearing for the interpretation of the BIT in question, it nevertheless suggested a legally relevant connection between the applicable BIT and other BITs of the States involved. Moreover, the very fact that it assessed these third-country treaties suggests that it viewed BITs not as isolated and

---

[83] *Aguas del Tunari* v. *Bolivia*, Decision on Jurisdiction, October 21, 2005, paras. 206 *et seq.*

[84] *Ibid.*, para. 312.

[85] *Ibid.* (stating that the third-party BITs were "consistent with the Tribunal's view that there is no appreciable difference between a company that is 'controlled directly or indirectly' by another company and a company that is 'under the direct or indirect control of' or 'subject to the direct or indirect control of' another company").

[86] *Ibid.*, para. 314.   [87] *Ibid.*, paras. 291 *et seq.*

strictly bilateral treaties but as embedded in a broader framework of investment protection. If, by contrast, the Tribunal had indeed been unaffected by the third-country BITs, it would not have been necessary to expand on them over twenty-six paragraphs in its decision.[88]

The purpose of the reference to the treaty practice of the contracting parties to the BIT governing an investor-State dispute is usually to view the provisions in the applicable BIT in the context of other BITs concluded by the State parties concerned in order to grasp more clearly whether a specific BIT follows the country's general practice or departs from it. As a consequence, tribunals draw either an *e contrario* argument from the fact that the applicable BIT departs from the country's general treaty practice, like the Tribunal in *Maffezini*, or read the provisions of the applicable BIT in the light of the provisions of the third-party BIT, like the Tribunal in *Aguas del Tunari*. In this context, the primary function of having recourse to third-country BITs lies in clarifying the intention of the parties.[89]

(b)   The use of wholly unrelated third-country BITs

Arbitral tribunals, however, do not only use references to third-country BITs of the host or the home States. They also regularly rely on provisions in wholly unrelated BITs in interpreting the applicable BIT. A reference to wholly unrelated third-country investment treaties was used, for example, by the Committee in the ICSID annulment decision in *Compañia de Aguas del Aconquija* v. *Argentina* when interpreting the arbitration clause in the French–Argentine BIT.[90] Thus, the Annulment Committee not only pointed out that the wording of the clause that referred to "[a]ny dispute relating to investments made under this Agreement between one Contracting Party and an investor of the other Contracting

[88]   *Ibid.*, paras. 289–314.
[89]   See *Plama* v. *Bulgaria*, Decision on Jurisdiction, February 8, 2005, para. 195 (considering that "treaties between one of the Contracting Parties and third States may be taken into account for the purpose of clarifying the meaning of a treaty's text at the time it was entered into"); *Aguas del Tunari* v. *Bolivia*, Decision on Jurisdiction, October 21, 2005, para. 292 (considering that "the practice of States as regards the negotiation of BITs may be helpful, however, in testing the assertions of parties as to the general policies of either Bolivia or the Netherlands concerning BITs"); *Suez and Vivendi* v. *Argentina*, Decision on Jurisdiction, August 3, 2006, para. 58 (noting with respect to subsequent BIT practice of the United Kingdom that "[t]he inference to be drawn from this language is that this new paragraph, by its terms, is intended to clarify what had been the United Kingdom's preexisting intention in negotiating its BITs").
[90]   *Compañia de Aguas del Aconquija* v. *Argentina*, Decision on Annulment, July 3, 2002, paras. 53 *et seq.*

Party" was broad enough to encompass both contract and treaty claims. It also supported its construction by drawing a parallel to the dispute settlement clause in Article 1116, NAFTA and argued:

> Read literally, the requirements for arbitral jurisdiction in Article 8 [of the French–Argentine BIT] do not necessitate that the Claimant allege a breach of the BIT itself: it is sufficient that the dispute relate to an investment made under the BIT. This may be contrasted, for example, with Article 11 of the BIT, which refers to disputes "concerning the interpretation or application of this Agreement," or with Article 1116 of the NAFTA, which provides that an investor may submit to arbitration under Chapter 11 "a claim that another Party has breached an obligation under" specified provisions of that Chapter.[91]

The Annulment Committee thus used a provision of NAFTA, a wholly unrelated third-party treaty, in order to draw an *argumentum e contrario* for the construction of the French–Argentine BIT. The purpose of the reference was to clarify the wording of the governing BIT.

A similar argumentative structure played a role in *L.E.S.I. et ASTALDI v. Algeria*.[92] Here, the Tribunal declined its jurisdiction for contract claims because the BIT's arbitration clause covered only the submission of treaty claims.[93] As support for upholding the distinction between contract claims and treaty claims the Tribunal also invoked the non-existence of an umbrella clause in the Italo–Algerian BIT. It observed in this context:

> Cette interprétation est confirmée *a contrario* par la rédaction que l'on trouve dans d'autres traités. Ceux-ci contiennent en effet ce qu'il est convenu d'appeler des clauses de respect des engagements ou "*umbrella clauses*". Ces clauses ont pour effect de transformer les violations des engagements contractuels de l'Etat en violations de cette disposition du traité et, par là même, de donner compétence au tribunal arbitral mis en place en application du traité pour en connaître ... Une telle formule n'a précisément pas été retenue pour l'Accord bilatéral conclu entre l'Algérie et l'Italie, ce qui confirme *a contrario* l'interprétation retenue.[94]

---

[91] *Ibid.*, para. 55.   [92] *L.E.S.I. et ASTALDI* v. *Algeria*, Decision, July 12, 2006.
[93] *Ibid.*, para. 84.
[94] *Ibid.*, para. 84(ii) (citing Article 10(1), ECT, Article 3, Agreement between the Government of Hong Kong and the Government of the Republic of France for the Reciprocal Promotion and Protection of Investments, signed on November 30, 1995, entered into force on May 30, 1997, and Article 11(2), Agreement between the Federal Republic of Germany and the State of Kuwait for the Encouragement and Reciprocal Protection of Investments, signed on March 30, 1994, entered into force on November 15, 1997, as examples of umbrella clauses); see also an earlier award based on the same facts, but brought by the wrong

The Tribunal in *L.E.S.I.* thus used the existence of umbrella clauses in third-country BITs in order to justify its narrow interpretation of the arbitration clause in the Italo–Algerian BIT by way of an *argumentum e contrario.* In this context, the reference to the existence of umbrella clauses in third-party BITs functioned as a systematic argument which presupposes that the BIT in question and the third-country treaties relate to a common *tertium comparationis*, that is, a treaty-overarching body of international investment law.

Similarly, the Tribunal in *Plama* v. *Bulgaria* drew an *argumentum e contrario* from third-country treaties in order to support a narrow interpretation of the MFN clause in the Bulgarian–Cypriot BIT. When faced with the question of whether the Treaty's MFN clause allowed the investor to import broader consent to arbitration from other BITs of the host State, the Tribunal pointed out that MFN clauses in the BIT practice of the United Kingdom were formulated so as to expressly cover more favorable investment provisions in the host State's third-party BITs.[95] In the Tribunal's view, this was evidence that MFN clauses applied to dispute settlement provisions only when explicitly framed in this way.[96] The UK treaty practice was thus used as an *argumentum e contrario* for the interpretation of the Bulgarian–Cypriot BIT.[97] Although this way of invoking the UK BIT practice *e contrario* contrasts with the conclusion by other arbitral tribunals,[98] both lines of argument have in common that they use BITs of wholly unrelated third countries in order to draw systematic

---

claimant *Consorzio L.E.S.I.–DIPENTA* v. *Algeria*, Sentence, January 10, 2005, para. 25(ii) (containing word-for-word the same considerations).

[95] For a closer discussion of this case see *supra* Ch. IV.C.2.b.

[96] *Plama* v. *Bulgaria*, Decision on Jurisdiction, February 8, 2005, para. 204. Similarly, *Salini* v. *Jordan*, Decision on Jurisdiction, November 15, 2004, para. 116.

[97] In the same breath, the Tribunal in *Plama* also rebutted the argument that the explicit exclusion of an extension of MFN clauses to dispute settlement provision could be used as an *argumentum e contrario* for a broad interpretation of the treaty in question. See *Plama* v. *Bulgaria*, Decision on Jurisdiction, February 8, 2005, para. 203 (observing that "[t]his shows that in NAFTA … the incorporation by reference of the dispute settlement provisions set forth in other BITs is explicitly excluded. Yet, if such language is lacking in an MFN provision, one cannot reason *a contrario* that the dispute resolution provisions must be deemed to be incorporated.").

[98] See *Maffezini* v. *Spain*, Decision on Objections to Jurisdiction, January 25, 2000, para. 52. See also *Enron* v. *Argentina*, Decision on Jurisdiction, January 14, 2004, para. 46 (reasoning in relation to the protection of indirect shareholders that "[t]he fact that a treaty may have provided expressly for certain rights of shareholders does not mean that a treaty not so providing has meant to exclude such rights if this can be reasonably inferred from the provisions of such treaty").

arguments which, in turn, presuppose the existence of BITs to a treaty-overarching framework of international investment protection.[99]

Investment tribunals, however, do not make reference only to provisions of third-country investment treaties in order to interpret substantive investor rights. They also have recourse to third-party BITs when determining the scope of application of a specific BIT in question. The use of third-country treaties in this respect suggests that not only the substantive standards of investment protection are subject to interpretation against an overarching body of international investment law, but also their scope of application concerning time, subject-matter and protected investors.[100]

The scope of application *ratione personae* was, for example, at stake in *Tokios Tokelés* v. *Ukraine*.[101] In holding that a company qualified as an investor under the Ukranian–Lithuanian BIT, although its shareholders were nationals of the host State, the Tribunal pointed, *inter alia*, to two unrelated third-country investment treaties, the US–Argentine BIT and the Energy Charter Treaty, in order to justify its decision. Since both of these unrelated third-party treaties contained explicit exceptions for the protection of home State reinvestments, the Tribunal drew an *argumentum e contrario* to the extent that the notion of "investor" in the Ukrainian–Lithuanian BIT also encompassed companies that were controlled by nationals of the host State.[102] Again, such an *argumentum e contrario* presupposes that investment treaties are embedded into a treaty-overarching framework that informs the drafting and interpretation of every single BIT.

Similarly, the Tribunal in *International Thunderbird Gaming* v. *Mexico* was faced with the question of whether the claimant had standing under Article 1117, NAFTA to bring a claim "on behalf of an enterprise of another Party that is a juridical person that the investor owns or controls directly or indirectly."[103] In deciding whether the investor needed to

---

[99] At the same time, however, the adverse results *Maffezini* and *Plama* drew from the same relationship between governing BIT and third-country BIT practice also illustrate the interpretative leeway this type of reasoning leaves for the arbitral tribunals.

[100] Cross-treaty interpretation in these respects is even more noteworthy as questions relating to the applicability of a specific BIT should presumably be even less accessible to normative overlaps between the individual treaty and the overarching investment regime since the scope of application of the specific BIT constitutes the outer limits of the participation of States in the international investment regime.

[101] *Tokios Tokelés* v. *Ukraine*, Decision on Jurisdiction, April 29, 2004, paras. 21 *et seq.*

[102] *Ibid.*, paras. 34 *et seq.*

[103] *International Thunderbird Gaming* v. *Mexico*, Arbitral Award, January 26, 2006, paras. 96 *et seq.*

show *de facto* or legal control of the subsidiary under this provision, the Tribunal also drew an analogy to a more explicit provision from the Energy Charter Treaty.[104] Like other tribunals, it therefore presupposed that international investment treaties in general, including regional and sectoral treaties such as NAFTA and the ECT, formed part of the sources of international law that could be used for guidance in interpreting the scope of application of a specific investment treaty.

In sum, the reference to third-party BITs, both those concluded by the contracting parties to the specific BIT that governs the dispute at hand, as well as those concluded by entirely unrelated States, is not an isolated phenomenon in the interpretation of investment treaties, but a widespread and accepted mode of treaty interpretation. Arbitral tribunals use it not only to clarify the intentions of the parties to a specific BIT, or to ascertain the ordinary meaning of a specific provisions in general State practice, they also use it as part of the systematic method of treaty interpretation that suggests that specific BITs are part of and relate to a framework of reference that overarches BITs as a general system of international investment protection. While such an approach is not incompatible with the Vienna Convention on the Law of Treaties it departs from the strictly bilateral method of treaty interpretation that has regard only to treaty-specific aspects and shields the interpretation of a specific treaty against the influence of other instruments of international law, in particular instruments concluded by wholly unrelated third parties.

3   The use of model treaties in interpretation

Apart from the extensive use of third-party treaties as an interpretative aid, arbitral tribunals occasionally also make reference to model treaties and the common historic origins of BITs in order to support their construction of specific provisions of investment treaties. In addressing the question of whether the shareholding in a company incorporated in the host State constituted an investment under the US–Argentine BIT, the Tribunal in *Enron* v. *Argentina* observed that "the United States model investment treaties are based on a rather broad interpretation of investment that was included with the express intention of overriding the eventual restrictive effects that could result from the *Barcelona Traction* decision."[105] Similarly, the Tribunal in *El Paso* v. *Argentina*

[104] *Ibid.*, para. 106.
[105] *Enron* v. *Argentina*, Decision on Jurisdiction, January 14, 2004, para. 46.

referred to the 2004 US Model Treaty in interpreting the umbrella clause in the US–Argentine BIT, even though the BIT had already been signed in 1991.[106]

While in both the *El Paso* as well as the *Enron* cases, the Tribunals referred to the model treaties of one of the parties, the Tribunal in *Eureko* v. *Poland* went a step further and invoked – as support for its interpretation of an umbrella clause in the Dutch–Polish BIT – the more general influence that model treaties had on the development of BITs. In its construction of said umbrella clause, the Tribunal did not invoke the Dutch model treaty, but instead made reference to the historic background concerning the emergence of umbrella clauses in the Abs–Shawcross Draft in 1959 and later the 1967 OECD Draft Convention on the Protection of Foreign Property in order to clarify the function of the clause. In this context, it observed:

> The provenance of "umbrella clauses" has been traced to proposals of Elihu Lauterpacht in connection with legal advice he gave in 1954 in respect of the Iranian Consortium Agreement … It found expression in Article II of a draft Convention on Investments Abroad ("the Abs–Shawcross Draft") of 1959, which provided: "Each Party shall at all times ensure the observance of any undertakings which it may have given in relation to investments made by nationals of any other Party." It was officially espoused in Article 2 of the OECD draft Convention on the Protection of Foreign Property of 1967, in whose preparation, Lauterpacht, as representative of the United Kingdom, played a part. It provided that: "Each Party shall at all times ensure the observance of undertakings given by it in relation to property of nationals of any other Party." The commentary to the draft Convention stated that, "Article 2 represents an application of the general principle of *pacta sunt servanda* – the maintenance of the pledged word" which "also applies to agreements between States and foreign nationals".[107]

The Tribunal therefore did not view the interpretation of the BIT at hand as a question concerning an isolated bilateral treaty relationship, but as a question relating to the larger framework of international investment protection that shared common origins and was based on attempts

---

[106] *El Paso v. Argentina*, Decision on Jurisdiction, April 27, 2006, para. 80 (arguing that "[t]he view that it is essentially from the State as a sovereign that the foreign investors have to be protected through the availability of international arbitration is confirmed, in the Tribunal's opinion, by the language in the new 2004 US Model BIT, which clearly elevates only the contract claims stemming from an investment agreement *stricte sensu*, that is, an agreement in which the State appears as a sovereign, and not all contracts signed with the State or one of its entities to the level of treaty claims").

[107] *Eureko v. Poland*, Partial Award, August 19, 2005, para. 251.

at multilateral planning. In view of the common heritage of investment treaties, the Tribunal therefore considered that it was permissible to draw conclusions relating to the development of multilateral projects, such as the Abs–Shawcross Draft and the 1967 OECD Draft Convention, even though these instruments never materialized, and themselves never became binding upon the parties to the dispute at hand.

4 Teleological interpretation of BITs

Another method of interpretation that plays a major role in creating unity among the different investment treaties, independent of who the contracting parties are, is the purposive or teleological method of treaty interpretation. Not only the often identical wording and the common historic origin militate for a converging interpretation of different BITs, but also the fact that they all share a common object and purpose. They all aim at protecting and promoting foreign investment flows.[108] This teleology of BITs not only mandates to embed the interpretation of BITs in an economically informed framework that accounts for the actual protection and promotion of foreign investment flows. It is also used by arbitral tribunals to level differences in the wording of BITs as long as the wording does not clearly mandate a departure from the commonly adopted approach to investment protection. The danger, of course, exists that relying on the object and purpose overrides the wording of BIT provisions or the States' intention to the treaty.[109] Notwithstanding, the teleological interpretation of BITs plays a major role in the multilateralization of BIT interpretation.

The teleological method assumes several different functions in the interpretation of investment treaties. First, the teleological interpretation plays a significant role in defining and in clarifying the scope of application of BITs, particularly with respect to their applicability *ratione materiae*, that is, the notion of investment, and their applicability *ratione personae*, that is, the notion of investor. The Tribunal in *Tokios Tokelés* v. *Ukraine*, for example, relied on the object and purpose of the BIT between Lithuania and Ukraine in order to justify its finding that reinvestments of a Lithuanian company in the Ukraine were covered under

---

[108] On the object and purpose of investment treaties and the statements contained in their preambles see Dolzer and Stevens, *Bilateral Investment Treaties*, pp. 11–13, 20–25 (1995).

[109] See I. Sinclair, *The Vienna Convention on the Law of Treaties*, p. 130 (2nd edn. 1984); *Plama* v. *Bulgaria*, Decision on Jurisdiction, February 8, 2005, para. 193.

the Ukrainian–Lithuanian BIT, although the company was controlled by Ukrainian nationals.[110] It held that:

> [t]he object and purpose of the Treaty likewise confirm that the control-test should not be used to restrict the scope of "investors" in Article 1(2)(b). The preamble expresses the Contracting Parties' intent to "intensify economic cooperation to the mutual benefit of both States" and "create and maintain favourable conditions for investment of investors of one State in the territory of the other State." The Tribunal in *SGS* v. *Philippines* interpreted nearly identical preambular language in the Philippines–Switzerland BIT as indicative of the treaty's broad scope of investment protection. We concur in that interpretation and find that the object and purpose of the Ukraine–Lithuania BIT is to provide broad protection of investors and their investments.[111]

Second, several tribunals have relied on the object and purpose of BITs in interpreting the scope of substantive investor rights under BITs broadly. In *MTD* v. *Chile*, for example, the Tribunal supported that "the fair and equitable standard of treatment has to be interpreted in the manner most conducive to fulfill the objective of the BIT to protect investments and create conditions favorable to investments."[112] The Tribunal in *SGS* v. *Philippines*, in interpreting an umbrella clause, went even further and supported that the teleological interpretation would justify "resolv[ing] uncertainties in [the BIT's] interpretation so as to favour the protection of covered investments."[113] It, therefore, suggested that investment treaties should be interpreted *in dubio pro investore*.[114]

The contrary position to an interpretation *in dubio pro investore* is the interpretative doctrine of *in dubio mitius* that mandates the interpretation of international treaties, in case of doubt, in favor of States. This doctrine relies on the principle set out in the *Lotus* case that "restrictions upon

---

[110] See also *supra* Ch. V.B.4.

[111] *Tokios Tokelés* v. *Ukraine*, Decision on Jurisdiction, April 29, 2004, para. 31 (quoting *SGS* v. *Philippines*, Decision on Jurisdiction, January 29, 2004, para. 116).

[112] *MTD* v. *Chile*, Award, May 25, 2004, para. 104. Similarly, *CMS* v. *Argentina*, Award, May 12, 2005, para. 274 (interpreting fair and equitable treatment in the light of the objective contained in the preamble "to maintain a stable framework for investments and maximum effective use of economic resources").

[113] *SGS* v. *Philippines*, Decision on Jurisdiction, January 29, 2004, para. 116 (concerning the construction of the umbrella clause in the BIT between Switzerland and the Philippines).

[114] See also *International Thunderbird Gaming* v. *Mexico*, Arbitral Award, January, 26, 2006, Separate Opinion by T. Wälde, paras 40–53 (arguing that based on transparency requirements doubts should be resolved in favor of the investor).

the sovereignty of States cannot ... be presumed."[115] This interpretative doctrine has also been applied by the Tribunal in *SGS* v. *Pakistan* in order to justify a restrictive interpretation of a provision in the Swiss–Pakistani BIT as not constituting an umbrella clause.[116] The problem with such an approach to treaty interpretation, however, is that treaties not only impose obligations on one of the parties, but correlate with a right vested in the other contracting party. As both States are exercising their sovereignty in entering into a treaty,[117] an interpretation in favor of one State's sovereignty would equally result in a detriment to the other State's sovereignty. Consequently, an interpretation of international treaties *in dubio mitius* has not found support in the Vienna Convention on the Law of Treaties and is, apart from that, rarely endorsed by decisions of international courts and tribunals.[118] Much to the contrary, the majority

[115] See *The Case of the S.S. "Lotus" (France* v. *Turkey)*, Judgment, September 7, 1927, P.C.I.J. Series A, No. 10 (1927), p. 18.

[116] *SGS* v. *Pakistan*, Decision on Jurisdiction, August 6, 2003, para. 171 (pointing out that "[t]he appropriate interpretive approach is the prudential one summed up in the literature as *in dubio pars mitior est sequenda*, or more tersely, *in dubio mitius*", emphasis in the original).

[117] See *Case of the S.S. "Wimbledon" (Britain et al.* v. *Germany)*, Judgment, August 17, 1923, P.C.I.J. Series A, No. 1 (1923), p. 25 (observing that "any convention creating an obligation ... places a restriction upon the exercise of the sovereign rights of the State ... But the right of entering into international engagements is an attribute of State sovereignty.").

[118] Interpretation of international law *in dubio mitius* has, however, played a certain role in the jurisprudence of the PCIJ. See, for example, *Free Zones of Upper Savoy and the District of Gex (France* v. *Switzerland)*, Judgment, June 7, 1932, P.C.I.J. Series A/B, No. 46 (1932), p. 167 (observing that "in case of doubt a limitation of sovereignty must be construed restrictively"); *Article 3, Paragraph 2, of the Treaty of Lausanne*, Advisory Opinion, November 21, 1925, P.C.I.J. Series B, No. 12 (1925), p. 25 (considering as "sound" the principle that "if the wording of a treaty provision is not clear, in choosing between several admissible interpretations, the one which involves the minimum of obligations for the Parties should be adopted"). See also, more recently, *EC – Measures Concerning Meat and Meat Products (Hormones)*, WTO Appellate Body Report, January 16, 1998, paras. 163–65 (observing that "[i]f the meaning of a term is ambiguous, that meaning is to be preferred which is less onerous to the party assuming an obligation"); similarly, *Argentina – Safeguard Measures on Imports of Footwear*, WTO Panel Report, June 25, 1999, para. 7.8. The application of the principle *in dubio mitius* in WTO law has, however, received significant criticism. See, for example, Hughes, *Limiting the Jurisdiction of Dispute Settlement Panels*, 10 Geo. Int'l Envt'l L. Rev. 915, 921–22 (1998); Jackson, *The Changing Fundamentals of International Law and Ten Years of the WTO*, 8 J. Int'l Econ. L. 3, 14 (2005); Jackson, *Sovereignty, the WTO and Changing Fundamentals of International Law*, p. 262 (2006) (arguing that "[s]ome treaty interpretation concepts, such as *in dubio mitius* ... are absurd and destructive of the purposes of institutions like the GATT and WTO. This treaty concept represents 'consent theory gone amok,' and also evokes thoughts about criticism of the famous international law *Lotus Case* as being 'extreme positivism.'").

of international courts and tribunals openly reject the *in dubio mitius* approach as a valid interpretative method.[119]

However, an interpretation that uniformly favors investors in case of doubt is equally too broad. It disregards the fact that it cannot be presumed that States, by entering into an international investment treaty, intended to restrict their sovereignty to the extent that doubts would mitigate in favor of the protection of foreign investors. In other words: it cannot be presumed that the State parties to a BIT wanted to shift to themselves the burden of proof that they acted in conformity with the international law governing investor-State relations. This position does not find any support in the BITs themselves, nor is it an interpretative principle that is accepted by the Vienna Convention.

Even if the treaties aim at promoting and protecting foreign investment flows, one will also have to keep in mind that the interpretation of investor rights that results in overly onerous restrictions of the sovereignty of

---

[119] See, for example, *Ethyl Corporation* v. *Canada*, Award on Jurisdiction, June 24, 1998, para. 55 (stating that the doctrine of *in dubio mitius* "has long been displaced by Articles 31 and 32 of the Vienna Convention"); *Eureko* v. *Poland*, Partial Award, August 19, 2005, para. 258 (stating that "[t]his Tribunal feels bound to add that reliance of the Tribunal in *SGS* v. *Pakistan* on the maxim *in dubio mitius* so as effectively to presume that sovereign rights override the rights of a foreign investor could be seen as a reversion to a doctrine that has been displaced by contemporary customary international law, particularly as that law has been reshaped by the conclusion of more than 2000 essentially concordant bilateral investment treaties"); *Loewen* v. *United States*, Decision on Jurisdiction, January 5, 2001, para. 51 ("not accept[ing] the Respondent's submission that NAFTA is to be understood in accordance with the principle that treaties are to be interpreted in deference to the sovereignty of states"); *United Parcel Service* v. *Canada*, Award on Jurisdiction, November 22, 2002, para. 40 (stating with respect to treaty interpretation that the "general rule ... requires neither a broad nor a restrictive approach"); *Mondev* v. *United States*, Award, October 11, 2002, para. 43 (stating that "there is no principle either of extensive or restrictive interpretation of jurisdictional provisions in treaties. In the end the question is what the relevant provisions mean, interpreted in accordance with the applicable rules of interpretation of treaties."); *Amco Asia* v. *Indonesia*, Decision on Jurisdiction, September 25, 1983, para. 14(i) (stating that "like any other conventions, a convention to arbitrate is not to be construed *restrictively*, nor, as a matter of fact, *broadly* or *liberally*" – emphasis in the original); *Siemens* v. *Argentina*, Decision on Jurisdiction, August 3, 2004, para. 81 (stressing that "the Treaty has to be interpreted neither liberally nor restrictively, as neither of these adverbs is part of Article 31(1) of the Vienna Convention"). In any event, it is important to note that the doctrine of *in dubio mitius* only applied in case there was doubt about the scope of application of a treaty obligation. See *Minority Schools in Albania*, Advisory Opinion, April 6, 1935, P.C.I.J. Series A/B, No. 64 (1935), p. 22; *Free Zones of Upper Savoy and the District of Gex (France* v. *Switzerland)*, Judgment, June 7, 1932, P.C.I.J. Series A/B, No. 46 (1932), p. 167; *Article 3, Paragraph 2, of the Treaty of Lausanne*, Advisory Opinion, November 21, 1925, P.C.I.J. Series B, No. 12 (1925), p. 25.

host States may have an adverse effect on host States in becoming increasingly critical towards admitting foreign investments.[120] An overly broad interpretation of BITs based on their object and purpose may thus lead to effectively reducing investment flows between the States concerned. This was a point addressed by the Tribunal in *Saluka* v. *Czech Republic* that pointed out that:

> [t]he protection of foreign investments is not the sole aim of the Treaty, but rather a necessary element alongside the overall aim of encouraging foreign investment and extending and intensifying the parties' economic relations. That in turn calls for a balanced approach to the interpretation of the Treaty's substantive provisions for the protection of investments, since an interpretation which exaggerates the protection to be accorded to foreign investments may serve to dissuade host States from admitting foreign investments and so undermine the overall aim of extending and intensifying the parties' mutual economic relations.[121]

Although the preamble of the Dutch–Polish BIT in question was more elaborate than usual, and referred not only to the promotion and protection of foreign investment flows, but more broadly aimed at extending and intensifying the parties' economic relations,[122] the approach undertaken in *Saluka* is a more balanced approach to the teleology of international investment treaties than one that unilaterally construes investment treaties in favor of investors. After all, the aim of the treaties is not to unilaterally favor foreign investors over host States, but to create an investment-friendly environment that is characterized by stability and predictability and leads to economic growth and development in both home and host States.

Likewise, a number of other tribunals have accepted that a balanced approach to the teleology of investment treaties should guide the interpretation of BITs. The Tribunal in *Noble Ventures* v. *Romania*, for example, while using the object and purpose of BITs in order to support its broad reading of the umbrella clause in the US–Romanian BIT, also included a caveat against an excessive use of teleological interpretations in this context. It highlighted that "it is not *permissible,* as is too often done regarding BITs, to interpret clauses exclusively in favour of investors."[123] Similarly, the Tribunal in *El Paso* v. *Argentina* stressed that a "balanced

---

[120] *Cf.* van Aaken, *Perils of Success?*, 9 Eur. Bus. Org. L. Rev. 1 (2008).

[121] *Saluka* v. *Czech Republic*, Partial Award, March 17, 2006, para. 300.

[122] For the preamble of the Treaty see *ibid.*, para. 299.

[123] *Noble Ventures* v. *Romania*, Final Award, October 12, 2005, para. 52 (emphasis in the original).

interpretation is needed, taking into account both State sovereignty and the State's responsibility to create an adapted and evolutionary framework for the development of economic activities, and the necessity to protect foreign investment and its continuing flows."[124] Even in light of such balanced approaches to the purposive method of BIT interpretation, the common object and purpose behind international investment treaties channels their interpretation into a uniform direction and is an element that mitigates the potential for fragmentation and inconsistencies that exists in international investment law.

5 Conclusion

As can be seen from the examples given above, investment tribunals liberally use references to other BITs of one of the State parties involved in an investment dispute as well as references to BITs of wholly unrelated parties when interpreting the treaty governing a specific investor-State dispute. The arguments they draw from comparing the governing treaty with third-party treaties take on a variety of forms and can be located on different systematic levels. They occur above all as an interpretative aid to determine the ordinary meaning of the standard provisions of BITs and are applied with respect to construing investor rights as well as the scope of application of BITs.

Tribunals, for example, use the wording of third-party treaties in order to positively support their interpretation of the governing BIT. In such cases, the argument turns on the question of how to understand and interpret the ordinary wording of a specific treaty provision. The reference to third-party treaties of one of the States may also help to clarify the intentions of the contracting State parties when entering into a specific BIT. Third-party treaties may either contain more specific language and, therefore, clarify the intention of the State when concluding a specific treaty provision, or, conversely, may show that a specific meaning was not intended to be attributed to a treaty provision. Comparison of the wording of one treaty with the wording of concurrent third-party treaties may thus allow either to draw analogies or an *argumentum e contrario* as

---

[124] *El Paso* v. *Argentina*, Decision on Jurisdiction, April 27, 2006, paras. 68 *et seq.*; see also *Methanex* v. *United States*, Partial Award, August 7, 2002, para. 105 (observing that "the provisions of Chapter 11 [of NAFTA] should be interpreted in good faith in accordance with their ordinary meaning (in accordance with Article 31(1) of the Vienna Convention), without any one-sided doctrinal advantage built in to their text to disadvantage procedurally an investor seeking arbitral relief").

320 MULTILATERALIZATION THROUGH INTERPRETATION

an expression of the (presumed) intention of the State parties. Similarly, the general treaty practice, including the one of wholly unrelated third countries, may allow drawing inferences as regards the intention of the contracting parties to the BIT that governs the specific dispute at hand.

At the same time, the use of third-country treaties as an interpretative tool entails an important standard-setting function for investment treaties in that the predominant BIT practice informs the interpretation and construction of BITs. In this context, several ICSID tribunals have expressed the view that the provisions of BITs have to be interpreted uniformly unless the meaning in a treaty deviated from the meaning normally given to the provisions in question. Thus, the Tribunal in *Enron* v. *Argentina* addressed this issue as follows:

> Indeed, the interpretation of a bilateral treaty between two parties in connection with the text of another treaty between different parties will normally be the same, unless the parties express a different intention in accordance with international law ... There is no evidence in this case that the intention of the parties to the Argentina–United States Bilateral Treaty might be different from that expressed in other investment treaties invoked.[125]

Finally, tribunals also use references to third-country BITs in order to draw systematic arguments for the interpretation of the BIT governing a dispute. This was, for example, the case in the decision in *L.E.S.I. et ASTALDI* and the annulment decision in *Compañia de Aguas del Aconquija*, where the arbitrators contrasted the formulation of arbitration clauses in the governing BIT with differently drafted clauses in third-country BITs. This way of reasoning suggests that arbitral tribunals view the provisions of BITs as part of a body of norms that overarches the single components of the international investment regime which is composed of bilateral, regional or sectoral investment treaties.

This way of interpreting BITs departs from the classical bilateral method of treaty interpretation, as tribunals not only have regard to the text, the object and purpose, the history, and other relevant circumstances of the investment treaty in question, but take into account third-party treaties and accord them significant weight in the interpretative process. BITs are thus not interpreted as isolated *quid pro quo* bargains,

---

[125] *Enron* v. *Argentina*, Decision on Jurisdiction, January 14, 2004, para. 47. See also *Sempra* v. *Argentina*, Decision on Objections to Jurisdiction, May 11, 2005, para. 144 (confirming that "as the tribunal held in *Enron*, it could be possible that the interpretation of a bilateral treaty between two parties in connection with the text of another treaty between different parties might be the same, unless a different intention is expressed").

but are put in relation to other BITs of the contracting states to a BIT in dispute and to the BITs of other States more generally. What this technique of interpretation suggests is that tribunals perceive the network of bilateral investment treaties as an expression of an overarching legal framework that only happened to find its expression in bilateral treaty relationships. The use of third-party investment treaties as an interpretative tool is, therefore, part of the process by which investment tribunals translate multilateral aspirations into multilateral arbitral practice.

C   The system's operative unity: the emergence of a system of *de facto* precedent in investment treaty arbitration

Investment tribunals not only use third-country BITs as an interpretative tool, they also generate largely coherent decisions based on different BITs. This generally coherent body of law is not a product of mere coincidence, but is fostered by an inter-award dialogue and the widespread practice in investment treaty arbitration of citing and following earlier awards. The use of precedent is, therefore, another element that drives the emergence of international investment law as a multilateral system based on largely uniform principles of investment protection. The way investment tribunals interact with earlier arbitral decisions by other tribunals indicates that they perceive international investment law as a uniform body of law that forms part of an international investment regime. This reliance on precedent in the decision-making process of arbitral tribunals therefore supports the thesis that investment treaty arbitration is in a process of self-institutionalization as a proper (sub-) system of international law.[126]

As will be illustrated, arbitral tribunals actively produce coherent outcomes in their decision-making activity by relying increasingly on common law-type reasoning that takes into account, follows and/or distinguishes earlier investment awards and decisions. In fact,

---

[126] This phenomenon is similar to the one taking place in other international dispute settlement fora, such as the WTO DSB. See Palmeter and Mavroidis, *The WTO Legal System: Sources of Law*, 92 A.J.I.L. 398 (1998); Bhala, *The Myth about* Stare Decisis *and International Trade Law*, 14 Am. U. Int'l L. Rev. 845 (1999); Bhala, *The Precedent Setters: De Facto Stare Decisis in WTO Adjudication*, 9 J. Transnat'l L. & Pol'y 1 (1999), Bhala, *Global Trade Issues in the New Millennium*, 33 Geo. Wash. Int'l L. Rev. 873 (2001); Blackmore, *Eradicating the Long Standing Existence of a No-Precedent Rule in International Trade Law*, 29 N.C. J. Int'l L. & Com. Reg. 487 (2004). For the use of precedent in the jurisprudence of the ICJ see Shahabuddeen, *Precedent in the World Court* (1996).

references to ICSID decisions can be found in virtually any of the more recent investment treaty decisions and awards. A recent quantitative citation analysis, for example, concluded after analyzing the frequency of citations of investment tribunals to earlier investment treaty awards and other sources of international law that "citations to supposedly subsidiary sources, such as judicial decisions, including arbitral awards, predominate."[127] Unlike in the context of commercial arbitration, this development is, above all, made possible due to the publication of decisions and awards on the Internet and in print journals, coupled with the extensive professional and academic critique of awards.

That the citation of earlier awards not only occurs incidentally, but is exercising guidance for subsequent awards, can also be seen from the statements investment tribunals make regarding the value of earlier arbitral decisions. Although tribunals emphasize the non-existence of a rule of legally binding precedent,[128] they nevertheless constantly turn to earlier decisions for guidance. The Tribunal in *El Paso* v. *Argentina*, for example, termed it "a reasonable assumption that international arbitral tribunals, notably those established within the ICSID system, will generally take account of the precedents established by other arbitration organs, especially those set by other international tribunals."[129] Similarly, the Tribunal in *ADC* v. *Hungary* considered that "cautious reliance on

---

[127] Commission (*supra* footnote 32), 24 J. Int'l Arb. 129, 148 (2007). The study illustrates a number of interesting trends. It shows, for example, a "marked increase of citation to ICSID decisions by ICSID tribunals" with citations increasing from an average of approximately two decisions between 1990 and 2001 an average of more than seven between 2002 and 2006. ICSID decisions on jurisdiction even cited an average of nine earlier ICSID decisions or awards (*ibid.*, at 148–50 (2007) (Tables 3, 4 and 5) – quotation at footnote 149). Similar trends can also be observed with regard to decisions under the ICSID Additional Facility and non-ICSID investment treaty awards (*ibid.*, at 150–51 (2007) [Tables 6 and 7]). At the same time, the study suggests that references to other sources, such as non-investment treaty awards, the writings of publicists, general principles of law, and international custom may be declining (*ibid.*, at 151–53).

[128] See *supra* Ch. VII.A.4.

[129] *El Paso* v. *Argentina*, Decision on Jurisdiction, April 27, 2006, para. 39. Similarly, *AES Corporation* v. *Argentina*, Decision on Jurisdiction, April 26, 2005, paras. 27–28 (pointing out that it "nevertheless reject[s] the excessive assertion which would consist in pretending that, due to the specificity of each case and the identity of each decision on jurisdiction or award, absolutely no consideration might be given to other decisions on jurisdiction or awards delivered by other tribunals in similar cases. In particular, if the basis of jurisdiction for these other tribunals and/or the underlying legal dispute in analysis present a high level of similarity or, even more, an identity with those met in the present case, this Tribunal does not consider that it is barred, as a matter of principle, from considering the position taken or the opinion expressed by these other tribunals").

certain principles developed in a number of those cases, as persuasive authority, may advance the body of law, which in turn may serve predictability in the interest of both investors and host States."[130]

Similarly, the parties to investor-State arbitrations are engaging heavily in the discussion of earlier decisions by investment tribunals. In this context, the Tribunal in *AES Corporation* v. *Argentina*, for instance, observed that the investor relied on earlier investment awards "more or less as if they were precedent [tending] to say that Argentina's objections to the jurisdiction of this Tribunal are moot if not even useless since these tribunals have already determined the answer to be given to identical or similar objections to jurisdiction."[131] The way the parties to the disputes rely on precedent, therefore, suggests the emergence of expectations that tribunals will base their decisions not on abstract interpretations of the governing BIT, but embed them into the pre-existing structure and content of the discourse among investment treaty awards.

Despite the absence of a doctrine of binding precedent (or *de iure stare decisis*), arbitral awards exercise significant influence on subsequent decisions in other investment disputes. Even though they are not followed as a matter of law, they exercise, as a matter of fact, strong extra-legal constraints upon subsequent tribunals. The use of precedent and the creation of consistency and coherence within the decision-making processes are an additional factor that illustrates how a multilateral system of investment protection is implemented through interpretation on the basis of bilateral treaty relations. What is particularly striking, beyond the mere fact that arbitral tribunals actively engage in inter-award citation, is the manner in which the precedent-directed reasoning of investment tribunals develops. Thus, the functions of precedent range from cautious reasoning by analogy to rather full-blown law-making by arbitral jurisprudence.

Precedent, therefore, serves an important function in creating coherence in the interpretation of different BITs. Moreover, arbitral jurisprudence not only recognizes the need for and the desirability of coherence in investment treaty arbitration through the use of precedent, it even recognizes the need for unity in cases of conflicting interpretations and inconsistent decisions. Unity in investment treaty arbitration is thus a feature that is present not only when arbitral tribunals follow earlier decisions but also in cases of dissent.

---

[130] See *ADC* v. *Hungary*, Award, October 2, 2006, para. 293. See further the decisions cited *supra* footnote 45.

[131] *AES Corporation* v. *Argentina*, Decision on Jurisdiction, April 26, 2005, para. 18.

1   The functions of precedent in concurring awards

How arbitral tribunals translate the apparent patchwork of international investment treaties into a genuine (sub-)system of international law becomes most obvious with regard to the use of precedent in cases of converging jurisprudence. In this context, arbitral tribunals establish a system of *de facto* precedent not only with respect to the interpretation of the same investment treaty, but across various BIT relationships. By doing this, they translate the similarities, or even identities, in treaty texts into coherent results. The functions of precedent, in this context, vary and evolve qualitatively in its contribution to an emerging body of case law in investment treaty arbitration. It ranges from an auxiliary means of interpretation to the generation of treaty-independent standards in international investment law, and thus reflects evolving stages of increasing system generation and system integration in investment treaty arbitration despite the multiplicity of investment treaties.

(a)   Analogizing with earlier decisions

Analogizing with earlier decisions is one way arbitral tribunals make use of precedent. This approach was taken, for example, by the Tribunal in *Gas Natural* v. *Argentina*, a case concerning an investor in the Argentine gas distribution sector that complained about the incompatibility of Argentina's 2001/2002 emergency legislation with the Spanish–Argentine BIT. While emphasizing that it "rendered its decision independently, without considering itself bound by any other judgments or arbitral awards,"[132] the Tribunal developed its decision based on a two-step reasoning.

In a first step, the Tribunal assessed the dispute solely in view of the applicable BIT and held that the claimant had standing to bring the claim, deciding in particular that the investor could circumvent the BIT's eighteen-month waiting period based on the Treaty's MFN clause and more favorable treatment in other Argentine BITs. The only interpretative means the Tribunal employed in this first step was reference to the wording of the relevant treaty provisions and their context. The Tribunal avoided, however, any allusions as to how other ICSID tribunals had responded to similar issues. It thus purported to be exclusively guided by the methods of treaty interpretation set out in the Vienna Convention on the Law of Treaties.

---

[132] *Gas Natural* v. *Argentina*, Decision on Jurisdiction, June 17, 2005, para. 36.

Prior decisions by other investment tribunals, including those in the *CMS* and the *Siemens* cases, only came into play in a second step, headlined by the Tribunal as "Checking the Tribunal's Conclusions."[133] In this step, the Tribunal compared its decision with earlier investment treaty awards and found – surprisingly? – that they coincided with its own findings in the case at hand. The Tribunal, therefore, seems to claim that the prior ICSID decision did not constitute part of the interpretative methodology, nor, in fact, had formed part of the process of legal interpretation.

The Tribunal justified this additional step by stating that it "thought it useful to compare its conclusion with the conclusions reached in other recent arbitrations."[134] While the method involved apparently refers to reasoning by analogy ("compare"), the question arises as to what the consequences would have been, had the Tribunal found an interpretative conflict between its own and earlier decisions? Would it have reconsidered its position or simply concluded that other awards reached contrary conclusions? In fact, it seems more likely – and actually reflects the process of arguing and reasoning legal decisions more realistically – that the Tribunal knew of the earlier awards and took them into account when hearing the case and giving the reasons for its decision. That it actually ignored other ICSID decisions in its first step of reasoning is difficult to conceive. While the presentation of the Tribunal's reasoning in the decision appears to be driven by a concern to deny any influence of other awards on the process of interpretation in investment arbitration and, therefore, reinforces the principle of non-binding precedent, it is simply make-belief that its interpretation was not influenced by precedent.

In *AES Corporation v. Argentina*, another case concerning the effects of Argentina's emergency legislation, the Tribunal adopted a comparable approach of taking earlier decisions into account as a tool of reasoning by analogy. It considered that arbitral tribunals were permitted to use earlier decisions as a source of "comparison and … of inspiration."[135] In the Tribunal's view, this applied to both interpretation of law as well as interpretation of facts. It observed:

> One may even find situations in which, although seized on the basis of another BIT as combined with the pertinent provisions of the ICSID

---

[133] *Ibid.*, before para. 36.   [134] *Ibid.*, para. 36 (emphasis added).
[135] *AES Corporation v. Argentina*, Decision on Jurisdiction, April 26, 2005, para. 31. See also *ibid.*, para. 30 (stating that "but decisions on jurisdiction dealing with the same or very similar issues may at least indicate some lines of reasoning of real interest; this Tribunal may consider them *in order to compare its own position with those already adopted by its predecessors*" – emphasis added).

Convention, a tribunal has set a point of law which, in essence, is or will be met in other cases whatever the specificities of each dispute may be. Such precedents may also be rightly considered, at least as a matter of comparison and, if so considered by the Tribunal, of inspiration.

The same may be said for the interpretation given by a precedent decision or award to some relevant facts which are basically at the origin of two or several different disputes, keeping carefully in mind the actual specificities still featuring each case. If the present Tribunal concurs with the analysis and interpretation of these facts as they generated certain special consequences for the parties to this case as well as for those of another case, it may consider this earlier interpretation as relevant.[136]

The approach chosen by the Tribunals in *Gas Natural* and *AES Corporation* has a particular appeal for making reference to awards that are based on BITs that are different from the one applicable to the dispute at hand, because it stresses that the source of the earlier decision was different, while integrating the reasoning and the result of an earlier decision into a system of investment treaty arbitration. Reasoning by analogy, therefore, reconciles the principle of non-binding precedent with the persuasive influence of prior investment decisions, in particular in "cross-BIT" cases.

(b)   Precedent as a means of clarification of BIT provisions

Other arbitral tribunals have used precedent as a means to clarify the meaning of provisions of the BIT governing the dispute at hand. This function is the one envisaged in Article 38(1)(d), ICJ Statute that describes "judicial decisions … as subsidiary means for the determination of rules of law." This clarifies that judicial decisions can be used as an auxiliary means of interpretation of international law in general and of international treaties in particular.[137] Accordingly, decisions by international courts and tribunals can be employed as evidence of the existence of a specific rule or principle of international law, or as evidence of a certain interpretation and application of a rule or principle of international law, including international treaties. Furthermore, precedent is a tool for ascertaining the ordinary meaning of specific treaty provisions. As put by the Tribunal in *Azurix* v. *Argentina*: "The Tribunal is required to consider the ordinary meaning of the terms used in the BIT under Article 31 of the Vienna Convention. The findings of other tribunals, and in particular of the ICJ, should be helpful to the Tribunal in its interpretative task."[138]

---

[136] *Ibid.*, paras. 31–32.   [137] See Shahabuddeen (*supra* footnote 126), p. 47 (1996).

[138] *Azurix* v. *Argentina*, Award, July 14, 2006, para. 391 (concerning the interpretation of "arbitrariness" in the BIT between Argentina and the United States).

Thus, arbitral precedent can be used in order to determine the function of a specific treaty provision. This was, for example, the way the Tribunal in *Eureko* v. *Poland* used precedent in its interpretation of an umbrella clause in the Dutch–Polish BIT.[139] The case concerned the question of whether the claimant could invoke the breach of an agreement with the Polish State Treasury as a breach of Article 3(5) of the BIT that provided that "[e]ach Contracting Party shall observe any obligation it may have entered into with regard to investors of the other Contracting Party." While the respondent urged that this clause be interpreted restrictively, as done in respect of a comparable clause in the Swiss–Pakistani BIT by the Tribunal in *SGS* v. *Pakistan*, the claimant relied on the broader interpretation given to a similar clause in the Swiss–Filippino BIT by the Tribunal in *SGS* v. *Philippines*.[140]

In accepting the claimant's reading of the treaty provision in question,[141] the Tribunal's majority in *Eureko* relied not only on the plain meaning of Article 3(5) of the BIT, the principle of effective interpretation and the history of umbrella clauses.[142] It also invoked the other investment awards, in particular the decision in *SGS* v. *Philippines* in order to support its conclusion.[143] Recounting and commenting on the decisions in *SGS* v. *Pakistan* and *SGS* v. *Philippines*, the Tribunal's majority observed:

> This Tribunal finds the foregoing analysis of the Tribunal in *SGS* v. *the Republic of the Philippines*, a Tribunal which had among its distinguished members Professor Crawford, cogent and convincing. While having the greatest respect for the distinguished members of the Tribunal in *SGS* v. *the Islamic Republic of Pakistan*, it is constrained to say that it finds its analysis of the umbrella clause less convincing.[144]

Even though the Tribunal put significant emphasis on the interpretation of the umbrella clause by the Tribunal in *SGS* v. *Philippines*, it did not simply adopt its decision like binding precedent without engaging in its own interpretation of the Dutch–Polish BIT. Instead, it used earlier decisions as an auxiliary means of interpretation, as an interpretative aid without authoritative or binding effect. What primarily counted were the arguments provided in the earlier decisions and their weight

---

[139] *Eureko* v. *Poland*, Partial Award, August 19, 2005. Similarly cautious in its use of precedent *Azurix* v. *Argentina*, Decision on Jurisdiction, December 8, 2003, paras. 73, 89.

[140] See more in detail on both positions *infra* footnotes 178–91 and accompanying text.

[141] *Eureko* v. *Poland*, Partial Award, August 19, 2005, para. 245.

[142] *Ibid.*, paras. 246–49.   [143] *Ibid.*, paras. 252–58.   [144] *Ibid.*, para. 257.

and credibility, not the fact that an earlier decision had reached a specific result.

(c)   Abbreviation of reasoning

Such cautious approaches to the use of precedent are not, however, followed by all investment tribunals. Instead, one can regularly observe that investment treaty awards accord prior decisions a more direct and more significant influence. Thus, the use of precedent is often less embedded in a problem-oriented and deliberative interpretation that deals with the material arguments raised by earlier decisions, but assumes a function that goes beyond such an auxiliary means of interpretation. This more enhanced degree of influence of prior investment treaty awards can be illustrated, for example, in the Decision on Jurisdiction in *Enron* v. *Argentina*, a case that raised several legal questions which had already been addressed by a number of earlier decisions, *inter alia*, the decisions in *CMS* v. *Argentina, Lanco* v. *Argentina,* and *Compañia del Aguas del Aconquija* v. *Argentina*.[145]

Unlike the *Eureko* Tribunal, the Tribunal in *Enron* referred to these earlier awards, and their respective argumentation, not only to support its own reasoning. Instead, it incorporated the reasoning of these earlier awards by reference into its own decision. Although it emphasized that it did not consider such earlier awards as binding precedent,[146] it used these earlier decisions as a way of abbreviating its own reasoning. It noted with respect to various of the objections to jurisdiction Argentina had raised as standard objections that it "does not intend to discuss again questions that have been amply considered in recent decisions and which have been also extensively argued by the parties in this case."[147] Furthermore, it noted that "[t]he reasoning supporting the above holdings will not be repeated for the sake of brevity."[148] For example, with respect to whether shareholders had standing to bring claims under an investment treaty, the Tribunal considered it as sufficient to refer to earlier ICSID decisions, to summarize their findings, and finally to point out that it would only discuss "with particular attention the situation of these claims ... in view of the existence of facts that are specific to this particular case."[149]

---

[145]   *Enron* v. *Argentina*, Decision on Jurisdiction, January 14, 2004, para. 24 footnote 3.
[146]   *Ibid.*, paras. 24, 40.   [147]   *Ibid.*, para. 38.   [148]   *Ibid.*, para. 39.
[149]   *Ibid.*, para. 41. Similarly, the Tribunal chose "not to repeat those considerations" from prior awards that concerned questions of the relationship between treaty claims and forum selection clauses and the operation of a "fork in the road" clause. See *ibid.*, paras. 91, 97.

Without dwelling on the precise content of the issues at hand, the Tribunal thus simply incorporated by reference the reasoning of earlier investment awards into its decision, without presenting an independent interpretation of the applicable BIT and without responding individually to the legal arguments raised by Argentina. Instead, it applied to the case at hand what it designated as "ICSID's case law concerning the Argentine Republic."[150] While the Tribunal stressed that it did not consider "decisions of ICSID or other arbitral tribunals [as] a primary source of rules," and rather used the citations of and references to earlier decisions because it "believe[d] that in essence the conclusions and reasons of those decisions are correct,"[151] the use of precedent in this case assumes a more imposing function compared with cases like *Gas Natural* or *Eureko*.

The reason why the Tribunal considered its approach to be justifiable was that it concurred substantively with the earlier decisions. Even though it seems to have verified the reasoning and the results of the earlier decisions, the abbreviation and the incorporation of the reasoning of precedents illustrate a qualitative step towards an increasing self-reference of the system of investment treaty arbitration and a more direct influence of earlier awards on the decision-making process of arbitral tribunals. While other awards discussed earlier referred to precedent in order to clarify the meaning of a specific BIT provision by illustrating possible meanings, with precedent thus serving the function of narrowing down possible results, references to prior awards in cases like *Enron* are used to incorporate by reference a specific reasoning endorsed by one or several earlier arbitral decisions. Unity of the international investment arbitration system is, therefore, narrowed down from overall consistency in legal reasoning to consistency in the application and generation of the system's operations itself. Likewise, it illustrates that the perception of investment awards within the canon of sources of international law is increasingly changing, despite pronunciations of tribunals to the contrary,[152] from a subsidiary means for the determination of

---

[150] *Ibid.*, before para. 24.   [151] *Ibid.*, para. 40.

[152] *Cf. Camuzzi v. Argentina*, ICSID Case No. ARB/03/7, Decisión sobre Jurisdicción, June 10, 2005, para. 19 (stating in respect of the value of earlier ICSID decisions in disputes relating to Argentina's emergency legislation: "Las referencias a la jurisprudencia de Tribunales CIADI se efectúan en la presente decisíon no porque esa jurisprudencia constituya una fuente vinculante de derecho internacional, sino porque la argumentacíon en que se basan esas sentencias arbitrales se consideran jurídicamente correctas, independientemente de su imperatividad directa. Es pertinente su referencía en cuanto su razonamiento se estima adecuado y en cuanto se refiere a supuestos de hecho similares a los del presente caso. Por ello el Tribunal puede apoyar en ellas su decisíon, usando

rules of law, to a rather primary source for resolving investment treaty disputes.

(d)   The creation of *de facto stare decisis*: precedent and standard setting

In connection with the interpretation of BITs, several arbitral awards go even further and view precedent as constituting a standard that they will depart from only upon the presentation of new facts, new legal aspects or upon showing that the contracting parties had intentions that departed from the common framing of investment treaties. The Tribunal in *Enron* v. *Argentina*, for example, held:

> The key issues raised by the parties in connection with jurisdiction in this case, however, are not really different from those raised in earlier cases. This being the case, the conclusions of the Tribunal follow the same line of reasoning, not because there might be a compulsory precedent but because the circumstances of the various cases are comparable, and in some respects identical ... The parties have not really made any new argument in this respect and, therefore, the Tribunal sees no basis for changing any of the conclusions already reached.[153]

The same line of argument also played a role in the Decision on Jurisdiction in *Camuzzi* v. *Argentina* where the Tribunal *de facto* required the parties to the dispute to provide it with specific reasons to depart from earlier ICSID jurisprudence, particularly the *CMS* and *Enron* cases. It maintained that "the Tribunal has no reason not to concur with that conclusion, even though some of the elements of fact in each dispute may differ in some respects."[154] The perception of precedent in this case thus moves extremely close to the common law system of *stare decisis*. The Tribunal no longer seems to interpret primarily the text of the governing treaty and the ICSID Convention, but confines itself to referring to prior ICSID awards that are considered to constitute an

---

esa jurisprudencía como medio auxiliar en la determinacíon de las reglas de derecho internacional").

[153] *Enron* v. *Argentina*, Decision on Jurisdiction (Ancillary Claim), August 2, 2004, paras. 25 *et seq.* Although this claim was an ancillary claim to a pending proceeding, the Tribunal did not rely on the jurisdictional findings made in the earlier decision, but examined anew the jurisdictional arguments made by the Argentine Republic, see *ibid.*, para. 26.

[154] *Camuzzi* v. *Argentina*, ICSID Case No. ARB/03/2, Decision on Objections to Jurisdiction, May 11, 2005, para. 82; *Sempra* v. *Argentina*, Decision on Objections to Jurisdiction, May 11, 2005, para. 94. Similarly *Camuzzi* v. *Argentina*, paras. 87, 111; *Sempra* v. *Argentina*, paras. 99, 122.

authoritative source and to measuring the legal and factual arguments of the parties against them.

Equally the reasoning of the Tribunal implies that a change in jurisprudence would require the parties to provide reasons for such a change. Ultimately, such reasoning shifts the burden of argumentation and persuasion upon the party wishing to change an existing jurisprudence, even if this jurisprudence has developed based on wholly unrelated BITs.[155] In this context, the use of precedent, therefore, has a standard-setting function in BIT interpretation up to a point where there is, as a matter of fact, little difference between persuasive and binding precedent. Similarly, in *Saipem* v. *Bangladesh* the Tribunal observed, after stressing that it was not bound by arbitral precedent, that:

> it is of the opinion that it must pay due consideration to earlier decisions of international tribunals. It believes that, subject to compelling contrary grounds, it has a duty to adopt solutions established in a series of consistent cases. It also believes that, subject to the specifics of a given treaty and of the circumstances of the actual case, it has a duty to seek to contribute to the harmonious development of investment law and thereby to meet the legitimate expectations of the community of States and investors towards certainty of the rule of law.[156]

---

[155] See also *Gas Natural* v. *Argentina*, Decision on Jurisdiction, June 17, 2005, para. 49 (observing that "unless it appears clearly that the state parties to a BIT or the parties to a particular investment agreement settled on a different method for resolution of disputes that may arise, most-favored-nation provisions in BITs should be understood to be applicable to dispute settlement").

[156] *Saipem* v. *Bangladesh*, Decision on Jurisdiction and Provisional Measures, March 21, 2007, para. 67. On the emergence of expectations in the reference to, application of and justified departure from precedent compare also *Japan – Taxes on Alcoholic Beverages*, WTO Appellate Body Report, October 4, 1996, p. 14 (observing that "[a]dopted panel reports are an important part of the GATT *acquis*. They are often considered by subsequent panels. They create legitimate expectations among WTO Members, and, therefore, should be taken into account where they are relevant to any dispute. However, they are not binding, except with respect to resolving the particular dispute between the parties to that dispute."). See also *International Thunderbird Gaming* v. *Mexico*, Arbitral Award, January 26, 2006, Separate Opinion by T. Wälde, para. 16 (stating that "[w]hile individual arbitral awards by themselves do not as yet constitute a binding precedent, a consistent line of reasoning developing a principle and a particular interpretation of specific treaty obligations should be respected; if an authoritative jurisprudence evolves, it will acquire the character of customary international law and must be respected. A deviation from well and firmly established jurisprudence requires an extensively reasoned justification" – note, however, that the reference to arbitral awards creating customary international law is inaccurate, as customary international law requires a certain consistency in State practice, not in the practice of arbitral tribunals) and *ibid.*, paras. 129–30. See generally on the function of law in stabilizing expectations Luhmann (*supra* note 5), pp. 124–43 (1993).

(e)   Transfer of the law-making function
from States to tribunals

While most of the decisions discussed above concerned the use of precedent in proceedings involving similar factual circumstances, relating above all to the evaluation of Argentina's economic emergency legislation, the use of arbitral precedent also plays an important role in the clarification and judicial development of standard investor rights, such as the concepts of indirect expropriation, fair and equitable treatment or full protection and security. In fact, the interpretation and application of these standards of treatment is driven and normatively influenced more by arbitral precedent than by the texts of the treaties or State practice.

The reason for this is primarily the extreme terminological vagueness of these investor rights. Both wording and concept of guarantees, such as indirect expropriation, fair and equitable treatment, and full protection and security are of such indeterminacy that they lack hard and easily ascertainable normative content and thus provide little guidance for treaty interpreters. Accordingly, the classical interpretative approaches endorsed by the Vienna Convention on the Law of Treaties are hardly able to provide normative guidance.[157] Consequently, arbitral tribunals often exclusively resort to a more precise source of clarification available, that is, the interpretation of these standards in earlier investment decisions which they then apply to the dispute at hand as if they formed part of the governing law, or at the least constituted authoritative restatements or concretizations of it.

How influential precedent in the interpretation and application of investor rights has become, can, for example, be illustrated with respect to the standard of fair and equitable treatment that has been coined primarily through the interpretation of arbitral tribunals. In this context, the NAFTA award in *Waste Management* v. *Mexico* is a good example in which the Tribunal extensively recounted prior investment awards regarding fair and equitable treatment in order to extrapolate a definition of this standard which could then be applied to the facts of the case at hand. It thus defined the standard of fair and equitable treatment by referring to earlier NAFTA decisions and stated:

> Taken together, the *S. D. Myers, Mondev, ADF* and *Loewen* cases suggest
> that the minimum standard of treatment of fair and equitable treatment
> is infringed by conduct attributable to the State and harmful to the claim-
> ant if the conduct is arbitrary, grossly unfair, unjust or idiosyncratic, is

[157]   See also *supra* Ch. VI.B.1.

discriminatory and exposes the claimant to sectional or racial prejudice, or involves a lack of due process leading to an outcome which offends judicial propriety – as might be the case with a manifest failure of natural justice in judicial proceedings or a complete lack of transparency and candour in an administrative process. In applying this standard it is relevant that the treatment is in breach of representations made by the host State which were reasonably relied on by the claimant.[158]

What subsequently primarily mattered for the Tribunal in applying fair and equitable treatment was the application of the facts of the case to the standard as it defined it in view of earlier NAFTA decisions.[159] The Tribunal did not, however, obtain the normative content by interpreting Article 1105, NAFTA or by using the earlier arbitral decisions as a subsidiary means of interpretation. Instead, the earlier decisions were treated as if they constituted an authoritative interpretation by the contracting parties and were binding upon the Tribunal. The importance of precedent in this context is all the more imposing as the Tribunal did not critically analyze earlier decisions and their arguments, but merely endorsed their holdings, in a similar mode to the common law system of *stare decisis*.

While the precedents taken into account in *Waste Management* exclusively related to earlier NAFTA awards, the jurisprudential development relating to fair and equitable treatment through reliance on precedent functions largely identically in cross-treaty cases. This can be illustrated, for example, with respect to the interpretation of fair and equitable treatment in the Spanish–Mexican BIT in *Tecmed* v. *Mexico* and its progeny. In fact, the interpretation of fair and equitable treatment that this decision endorsed has subsequently been adopted by several tribunals as if it were binding precedent for BITs between Chile and Malaysia, Ecuador and the United States, the Netherlands and Poland and others.

In *Tecmed* v. *Mexico*, the Tribunal had to assess the conformity of the non-renewal of an operating license for a hazardous waste landfill with the Spanish–Mexican BIT. Although the investor only disposed of a temporary operating license that was subject to an annual extension on a discretionary basis, the Tribunal, *inter alia*, found a violation of fair and equitable treatment because the host State had created legitimate expectations in the foreign investor that its operating license would be extended. In its application of fair and equitable treatment, the Tribunal merely posited that the standard endorsed the protection of legitimate expectations rather than engaging in a proper normative deduction that explained its

---

[158] *Waste Management* v. *Mexico*, Award, April 30, 2004, para. 98.
[159] *Ibid.*, paras. 99 *et seq.*

premises and grounded them in accepted international legal instruments. It simply outlined its understanding of the meaning of fair and equitable treatment as follows:

> The Arbitral Tribunal considers that this provision of the Agreement, in light of the good faith principle established by international law, requires the Contracting Parties to provide to international investments treatment that does not affect the basic expectations that were taken into account by the foreign investor to make the investment. The foreign investor expects the host State to act in a consistent manner, free from ambiguity and totally transparently in its relations with the foreign investor, so that it may know beforehand any and all rules and regulations that will govern its investments, as well as the goals of the relevant policies and administrative practices or directives, to be able to plan its investment and comply with such regulations. Any and all State actions conforming to such criteria should relate not only to the guidelines, directives or requirements issued, or the resolutions approved thereunder, but also to the goals underlying such regulations. The foreign investor also expects the host State to act consistently, i.e. without arbitrarily revoking any preexisting decisions or permits issued by the State that were relied upon by the investor to assume its commitments as well as to plan and launch its commercial and business activities. The investor also expects the State to use the legal instruments that govern the actions of the investor or the investment in conformity with the function usually assigned to such instruments, and not to deprive the investor of its investment without the required compensation. In fact, failure by the host State to comply with such pattern of conduct with respect to the foreign investor or its investments affects the investor's ability to measure the treatment and protection awarded by the host State and to determine whether the actions of the host State conform to the fair and equitable treatment principle. Therefore, compliance by the host State with such pattern of conduct is closely related to the above-mentioned principle, to the actual chances of enforcing such principle, and to excluding the possibility that state action be characterized as arbitrary; i.e. as presenting insufficiencies that would be recognized "... by any reasonable and impartial man," or, although not in violation of specific regulations, as being contrary to the law because: "... (it) shocks, or at least surprises, a sense of juridical propriety."[160]

As becomes clear from this passage, the Tribunal simply posited that the protection of the investor's expectations formed part of the standard of fair and equitable treatment. The justification for this far-reaching standard, by contrast, is surprisingly thin. The Tribunal relied mainly

---

[160] *Tecmed* v. *Mexico*, Award, May 29, 2003, para. 154 (quoting *Elettronica Sicula SpA (ELSI)* (*United States* v. *Italy*), Judgment, July 20, 1989, I.C.J. Reports 1989, p. 65).

on the principle of effective interpretation of treaty provisions and the object and purpose of the BIT. In this light, it justified its interpretation as follows:

> If the above were not its intended scope, Article 4(1) of the Agreement would be deprived of any semantic content or practical utility of its own, which would surely be against the intention of the Contracting Parties upon executing and ratifying the Agreement since, by including this provision in the Agreement, the parties intended to strengthen and increase the security and trust of foreign investors that invest in the member States, thus maximizing the use of the economic resources of each Contracting Party by facilitating the economic contributions of their economic operators. This is the goal of such undertaking in light of the Agreement's preambular paragraphs which express the will and intention of the member States to "… intensify economic cooperation for the benefit of both countries …" and the resolve of the member States, within such framework, "…to create favorable conditions for investments made by each of the Contracting Parties in the territory of the other …"[161]

While the result of the Tribunal's view on fair and equitable treatment is solid and widely accepted, its reasoning displays serious weaknesses. In particular, the Tribunal did not acknowledge that the arguments it used could also have been invoked to justify a different interpretation of the standard, for instance, in light of the *Neer* case that required conduct by the host State that "amounts to an outrage, to bad faith, to willful neglect of duty, or to an insufficiency of governmental action so far short of international standards that every reasonable and impartial man would readily recognize its insufficiency."[162] The interpretation of fair and equitable treatment in *Tecmed* is therefore a possible, but not a necessary interpretation. Thus, additional arguments would have been needed to buttress the decision in the sources of international law that are available, such as general principles of law, on which the Tribunal could have relied in order to justify its reasoning.

In any case, given the vagueness of fair and equitable treatment and the lack of guiding State practice, the "interpretation" offered by the Tribunal in *Tecmed* effectively constitutes an act of delegated law-making that decided to apply a certain normative standard as part of fair and equitable treatment, rather than an interpretation based on deductive legal reasoning. Conversely, the Tribunal could have just as well endorsed a

---

[161] *Tecmed* v. *Mexico*, Award, May 29, 2003, para. 156.
[162] *L. F. H. Neer and Pauline E. Neer (United States)* v. *Mexico*, Opinion, October 15, 1926, U.N.R.I.A.A., vol. IV, pp. 61–62.

completely different standard as the normative content of fair and equitable treatment with equally convincing arguments and applied this standard to the facts of the case.

Consequently, the vague language of fair and equitable treatment can be compared with the phenomenon of general clauses in civil codes, such as *good faith* or *bonos mores*, that allow the judiciary to ascertain, with a considerable degree of independence, the normative content and the standards applicable to certain social situations.[163] Parallel to this model, the vagueness of fair and equitable treatment involves a substantive delegation of power from States to tribunals.[164] As a consequence, it is much more the jurisprudence of investment tribunals that concretizes the meaning of fair and equitable treatment and the standards to which host States have to conform rather than the contracting states through their treaty-making power.

Notwithstanding the weaknesses in its reasoning, it is noteworthy that the decision in *Tecmed* v. *Mexico* has since been endorsed by a number of arbitral tribunals as if it were an authoritative determination of the content of fair and equitable treatment. Instead of pointing to shortcomings of the justification or attempting to provide further normative support for the "interpretation" of fair and equitable treatment in *Tecmed*, subsequent arbitral jurisprudence often simply endorsed and refined the standard by applying it to the facts of the case at hand. The Tribunal in *MTD* v. *Chile*, for example, applied the *Tecmed* standard to fair and equitable treatment in the Chilean–Malaysian BIT. After explaining that a literal interpretation of the fair and equitable treatment would mean that foreign investors would have to be treated in an even-handed manner,[165] the Tribunal in *MTD* v. *Chile* quoted the passage from the *Tecmed* award above and simply declared without any further justification: "This is the standard that the Tribunal will apply to the facts of this case."[166]

Similarly, the Tribunal in *Eureko* v. *Poland* did not engage in an interpretation of fair and equitable treatment, but concluded on little less than one page in an award comprising eighty-six pages that "[i]t is abundantly clear to the Tribunal that Eureko has been treated unfairly and inequitably by the Republic of Poland." The basis for this quick conclusion was obviously the understanding given to fair and equitable

---

[163] On the function of general clauses in the domestic context see Teubner, *Standards und Direktiven in Generalklauseln*, pp. 60 *et seq.* (1971).
[164] See *supra* Ch. VI.B.   [165] *MTD* v. *Chile*, Award, May 25, 2004, paras. 113 *et seq.*
[166] *Ibid.*, para. 115.

treatment in the *Tecmed* award which the Tribunal in *Eureko* found "apposite."[167] Its extremely brief reasoning suggests that the Tribunal was heavily influenced by the *Tecmed* decision in its conclusion. As the award in *Eureko* shows, decisions of earlier tribunals, therefore, assume essential influence on the decision-making process in investment treaty arbitration.[168]

The Tribunal in *Saluka* v. *Czech Republic*, by contrast, has found a more balanced and refined approach to the interpretation of fair and equitable treatment, but also did not manage to escape the discursive framework created by the *Tecmed* award.[169] Thus, the decision also relied on arbitral precedent that considered the protection of the investor's expectations to be part of fair and equitable treatment in, *inter alia,* the *Tecmed* case, but stressed that this protection would need to be balanced against the legitimate interests of the host State in regulating economic affairs. While in principle following the *Tecmed* award, the Tribunal in *Saluka* observed:

> while it subscribes to the general thrust of these and similar statements, it may be that, if their terms were to be taken too literally, they would impose upon host States' obligations which would be inappropriate and unrealistic. Moreover, the scope of the Treaty's protection of foreign investment against unfair and inequitable treatment cannot exclusively be determined by foreign investors' subjective motivations and considerations. Their expectations, in order for them to be protected, must rise to the level of legitimacy and reasonableness *in light of the circumstances.*
>
> No investor may reasonably expect that the circumstances prevailing at the time the investment is made remain totally unchanged. In order to determine whether frustration of the foreign investor's expectations was justified and reasonable, the host State's legitimate right subsequently to regulate domestic matters in the public interest must be taken into consideration as well. As the *S. D. Myers* tribunal has stated, the determination of a breach of the obligation of "fair and equitable treatment" by the host State "must be made in the light of the high measure of deference that international law generally extends to the right of domestic authorities to regulate matters within their own borders."
>
> The determination of a breach of [fair and equitable treatment] by the Czech Republic therefore requires a weighing of the Claimant's legitimate

---

[167] *Eureko* v. *Poland*, Partial Award, August 19, 2005, paras. 231 *et seq.*

[168] The *Tecmed* standard was also endorsed and applied in *Occidental Exploration* v. *Ecuador*, Final Award, June 1, 2004, para. 185; *CMS* v. *Argentina*, Award, May 12, 2005, para. 279; *Azurix* v. *Argentina*, Award, July 14, 2006, paras. 371–73; *LG&E* v. *Argentina*, Decision on Liability, October 3, 2006, paras. 127–28; *PSEG* v. *Turkey*, Award, January 19, 2007, para. 240; *Enron* v. *Argentina*, Award, May 22, 2007, para. 262; *Sempra* v. *Argentina*, Award, September 28, 2007, para. 298.

[169] *Saluka* v. *Czech Republic*, Partial Award, March 17, 2006, paras. 301 *et seq.*

and reasonable expectations on the one hand and the Respondent's legitimate regulatory interests on the other.[170]

While confirming the importance of precedent in investment treaty arbitration for the concretization of fair and equitable treatment, the award in *Saluka* also illustrates that tribunals should not blindly endorse the decisions and definitions of earlier tribunals, but assess such decisions and their reasoning critically as to whether it is not only a possible interpretation, but also one that is sustainable and acceptable to both States and investors. Notwithstanding, what the decision in *Saluka* shows is that investment treaty arbitration develops path dependencies that are typical for a precedent-oriented system. Thus, tribunals frame their reasoning, even if they do not, or do not fully, agree with earlier awards, as part of the discursive framework established by earlier decisions. As a consequence, even if precedent in investment treaty arbitration does not manage to bind future tribunals, it nonetheless frames their reasoning and their intellectual grasp of the rules and principles of international investment law.

(f)   Conclusion

Making reference to earlier investment treaty awards represents a standard method in the practice of parties arguing investment disputes and of the tribunals deciding them. Although tribunals do not consider themselves to be legally bound by earlier investment decisions, they still take them into account as a primary basis for their decisions. Notably, it is regularly irrelevant whether an earlier decision has interpreted the same or a different investment treaty. While references to earlier awards can often be explained and justified by traditional methods of legal exegesis and interpretation, such as clarifying the ordinary meaning of a clause, the function of precedent goes beyond constituting a simple means for the determination of a rule of law or an auxiliary aid for treaty interpretation. Instead, references to prior decisions, in particular to cases that concern the interpretation of wholly unrelated BITs, underline that investment treaty arbitration is in a state of self-institutionalization and self-constitutionalization as a system of investment protection in which the resolution of individual disputes is interconnected and embedded into a treaty-overarching system of dispute settlement.

This self-institutionalization through the use of precedent is particularly striking with respect to the concretization of vague substantive

[170] *Ibid.*, paras. 304–6 (quoting *S. D. Myers* v. *Canada*, Partial Award, November 13, 2000, para. 263) (emphasis in the original).

standards of treatment, such as the concepts of fair and equitable treatment or indirect expropriation. While these investor rights were initially not well-defined by either the texts of investment treaties or general State practice, tribunals first posited their normative content and later turned to arbitral precedent as the primary source that indicated the direction for interpretation and application of these rights. By doing so, the normative content of these rights became characterized by investment jurisprudence, with every decision containing concretizations not only for the specific investment treaty in question, but for the treaty-overarching concepts of fair and equitable treatment or indirect expropriation. Investment jurisprudence thus assumes and fulfills a law-making function in concretizing the normative content of the core investor rights for the entire system of investment protection.[171] This multilateralizes international investment law considerably as the treaty-overarching use of precedent ensures that standards like fair and equitable treatment, full protection and security, or the concept of indirect expropriation, are applied consistently across various bilateral treaties.

2   Unity of investment law and conflicting decisions

The trend to generate the unity of the system of investment treaty arbitration can, however, not only be observed with respect to the use of precedent in concurring decisions. The fact that investment tribunals presuppose that they operate within the confines of a uniform system of investment protection can equally be illustrateted with respect to cases of conflicting and incoherent decisions. Certainly, conflicting decisions are most critical in the reconstruction of arbitral jurisprudence as reflecting the existence of a system of law because they cast doubt on the unity of law and instead stress its fragmentation. However, the occurrence of open dissent with prior investment treaty awards, even with respect to disputes arising under unrelated treaties, is surprisingly rare, in particular if one takes into account the lack of safeguards against inconsistencies. In fact, only a few cases of direct and open dissent as regards the principles of investment protection can be spotted in the existing jurisprudence.

Certainly, not every investment decision is always and completely consistent with every other decision, nor does arbitral jurisprudence as

---

[171] See *supra* Ch. VI.B.

a whole always create a doctrinally fully consistent and coherent picture of the state of international investment law. Notwithstanding, by and large investment tribunals are not only generating mostly consistent and predictable jurisprudence, but actively recognize consistency as a value in investment treaty arbitration. Thus, arbitral tribunals generally avoid conflicting views about the proper interpretation of international investment law. Instead of openly disagreeing with the reasoning or the holding of an earlier decision, they often seek – like in a system of binding precedent – to substitute open dissent by other strategies that uphold the unity of the system of international investment law, for example, by stressing the differences in fact of the dispute at hand in relation to earlier cases, or by referring to the existence of meta-rules that allow the reconcilation of seemingly incompatible outcomes.

Even if tribunals do not employ such strategies, which are constructive of a treaty-overarching system, open dissent is rarely framed with respect to strict bilateral rationales that stress, for example, the limited scope and function of investor-State arbitration as solely aimed at the resolution of a specific dispute, or that resolve disputes wholly outside the argumentative framework established by the use of precedent in investment treaty arbitration.[172] Instead, open dissent often has the aspiration of influencing, in the long term, the development of a consistent and treaty overarching jurisprudence concerning matters that are common to investment treaties more generally. Instead, as this section will discuss, even the way arbitral tribunals deal with conflicting views on the proper interpretation of investment treaties suggests, parallel to the strong emphasis on precedent in concurring awards, that they perceive investment law as an overarching system, even if they occasionally depart from earlier awards and create conflict.

---

[172] But see *RosInvest Co v. Russia*, Award on Jurisdiction, October 2007, para. 137 (observing in a case of open dissent with regard to the interpretation of MFN clauses: "After having examined them [i.e., decisions of arbitral tribunals regarding MFN clauses and their application to matters of arbitration clauses in other treaties], the Tribunal feels there is no need to enter into a detailed discussion of these decisions. The Tribunal agrees with the Parties that different conclusions can indeed be drawn from them depending on how one evaluates their various wordings both of the arbitration clauses and the MFN clauses and their similarities in allowing generalisations. However, since it is the primary function of this Tribunal to decide the case before it rather than developing further the general discussion on the applicability of MFN clauses to dispute-settlement-provisions, the Tribunal notes that the combined wording in [the MFN clause] and [the clause containing exceptions to MFN treatment] of the [applicable] BIT is not identical to that in any of such other treaties considered in these other decisions.").

(a) Cases of open dissent

Open dissent between arbitral tribunals concerning the interpretation of substantive investment law, that is, the clear and unambiguous rejection of an earlier decision, occurs only rarely. While inconsistencies in the arbitral jurisprudence exist relating to some minor issues, such as the distribution of costs,[173] the construction of the core investor rights tends to generate largely consistent results not only with respect to the same BIT, but across various investment treaties.[174] With respect to the construction of umbrella clauses, however, the arbitral jurisprudence has developed a manifest and open split in jurisprudence. While the exact function and scope of umbrella clauses is not settled in investment jurisprudence and academic scholarship, the general thrust of the clauses is to grant investment treaty protection to investor-State contracts and other specific undertakings of the host State vis-à-vis foreign investors. It allows an investor to bring a claim for the breach of an investment-related contract as a breach of the umbrella clause in the applicable investment treaty. Umbrella clauses thus "seek to ensure that each Party to the treaty will respect specific undertakings towards nationals of the other Party."[175] What is, however, less clear is whether umbrella clauses allow investors to initiate investment arbitration for any, including minor, breaches of investment contracts and similar undertakings,[176] and whether they are restricted to acts of a sovereign nature or equally comprise breaches based on the State's commercial activity.[177]

---

[173] Decisions on costs in investment treaty arbitration are not always completely coherent, but can, by and large, be squared into a consistent framework and a consistent theory; see Schill, *Arbitration Risk and Effective Compliance*, 7 J. World Inv. & Trade 653 (2006). In addition, the distribution of costs is not a question that concerns the core of the international investment system, i.e., the substantive standards of protection of foreign investment. For further, however minor, inconsistencies see Schreuer and Weiniger, *A Doctrine of Precedent?*, in Muchlinski, Ortino and Schreuer (eds.), *The Oxford Handbook of International Investment Law*, pp. 1188, 1197 (2008).

[174] Note that the conflicting decisions in the cases *CME* v. *Czech Republic* and *Lauder* v. *Czech Republic* mentioned above cannot be counted as cases of open dissent as such because they were handed down independently within a matter of only ten days and, therefore, did not have a chance of interacting with one another. Furthermore, the cases, even though concerning the same factual situation triggering the arbitration procedures, were brought by claimants having a different relationship to the host State, one being a direct, the other being an indirect investor.

[175] See *supra* Ch. III.A.2.d.

[176] *Cf.* Schreuer, *Travelling the BIT Route*, 5 J. World Inv. & Trade 231, 255 (2004).

[177] For the more restrictive view, see Wälde, *The "Umbrella" Clause in Investment Arbitration*, J. World Inv. & Trade 183 (2005). Differently Schill, *Enabling Private Ordering: Function,*

The split in the construction and application of umbrella clauses was triggered by two openly conflicting ICSID decisions and has since been fostered with subsequent tribunals aligning themselves with either the more restrictive approach to the construction of umbrella clauses in *SGS v. Pakistan*[178] or the broader approach in *SGS v. Philippines*.[179] The broader approach allows foreign investors to use investment treaty arbitration in order to seek relief for any breach of an investment contract with the host State, independent of the nature of the breach, and thus goes beyond the protection of investor-State contracts by customary international law.[180] The competing approach, by contrast, attributes a narrower scope to umbrella clauses and restricts their operation to breaches resulting from sovereign acts. This narrower approach views umbrella clauses as a declaratory codification of customary international law which merely clarifies that rights of a foreign investor under an investor-State contract can form the object of a compensable expropriation.[181]

Not focusing here on the question of which of the two approaches is more convincing,[182] the main point of interest is the way in which arbitral tribunals created and handled the jurisprudential conflict involved in the application of umbrella clauses. Unlike other cases of conflicting interpretation discussed later in this section, the second Tribunal in *SGS v. Philippines* did not try to avoid conflict or to reconcile its interpretation with the interpretation put forward in the earlier decision in *SGS v. Pakistan*. Instead, the Tribunal in *SGS v. Philippines* explicitly disagreed with, and directly criticized the reasoning in *SGS v. Pakistan*, even though it did not have to apply and interpret the Swiss–Pakistani BIT but the Swiss–Filipino BIT.

In both cases, the same claimant had entered into "Pre-Shipment Inspection Agreements" with Pakistan and the Philippines under which

Scope and Effect of Umbrella Clauses in International Investment Treaties, 18 Minn. J. Int'l L. 1, 35–58 (2009).

[178] See *SGS v. Pakistan*, Decision on Jurisdiction, August 6, 2003, paras. 163–74; *El Paso v. Argentina*, Decision on Jurisdiction, April 27, 2006, paras. 71–88; *Pan American v. Argentina* and *BP America v. Argentina* (consolidated claims), Decision on Preliminary Objections, July 27, 2006, paras. 100–16.

[179] See *SGS v. Philippines*, Decision on Jurisdiction, January 29, 2004, paras. 113–29; *Eureko v. Poland*, Partial Award, August 19, 2005, paras. 244–60; *Noble Ventures v. Romania*, Final Award, October 12, 2005, paras. 46–62; *LG&E v. Argentina*, Decision on Liability, October 3, 2006, paras. 169–75; *Siemens v. Argentina*, Award, February 6, 2007, paras. 204–6.

[180] See Schill (*supra* footnote 177), 18 Minn. J. Int'l L. 1, 6 (2009).

[181] *Ibid.*, 18 Minn. J. Int'l L. 1, 6–7 (2009).

[182] See comprehensively *ibid.*, 18 Minn. J. Int'l L. 1 (2009).

it had to inspect goods for import into both countries in order for them to be classified under the proper customs heading. In both cases, the claimant alleged breaches of the BITs in question and initiated investment arbitration, invoking, *inter alia*, a breach of a provision the claimant classified as an umbrella clause which thus would have allowed it to bring claims for breaches of the investor-State contract involved.

In the first of the two proceedings, the Tribunal in *SGS v. Pakistan* was faced with the issue of whether the investor could bring contract claims as a violation of Article 11 of the Swiss–Pakistani BIT that provided that "[e]ither Contracting Party shall constantly guarantee the observance of the commitments it has entered into with respect to the investments of the investor of the other Contracting Party."[183] The Tribunal considered, however, that the wording of this provision was not sufficiently clear to constitute an umbrella clause which would have allowed the investors to bring claims for the breach of contract and concluded:

> [W]e do not find a convincing basis for accepting the Claimant's contention that Article 11 of the BIT has had the effect of entitling a Contracting Party's investor, like SGS, in the face of a valid forum selection contract clause, to "elevate" its claims grounded solely in a contract with another Contracting Party, like the PSI Agreement, to claims grounded on the BIT, and accordingly to bring such contract claims to this Tribunal for resolution and decision.[184]

The main reason for not following the claimant's argument that Article 11 of the Swiss–Pakistani BIT elevated breaches of contract to breaches of the BIT was the Tribunal's preoccupation with the potential effects that such a broad interpretation could have.[185] It pointed out that the clause would not be limited to contractual claims, but would allow claims for the violation of any commitment of the host State. In addition, it considered that a broad interpretation would render other BIT provisions, such as national treatment or fair and equitable treatment, inoperative, as an umbrella clause would already cover all claims relating to breaches of investor-State contracts. Finally, the Tribunal was concerned that a broad interpretation of the clause would override contractual forum selection clauses and, therefore, upset the contractual equilibrium of the investor-State contract. It therefore concluded that Article 11 of the Swiss–Pakistani BIT did not constitute an umbrella clause and declined its jurisdiction for contract claims while retaining the investor's claims for the breach of other treaty provisions.

---

[183] *SGS v. Pakistan*, Decision on Jurisdiction, January 29, 2004, para. 160.
[184] *Ibid.*, para. 165.   [185] See *ibid.*, paras. 166–68.

The Tribunal in *SGS v. Philippines*, by contrast, reached the directly opposite conclusion concerning the interpretation of a very similar provision in the Swiss–Filipino BIT that provided that "[e]ach Contracting Party shall observe any obligation it has assumed with regard to specific investments in its territory by investors of the other Contracting Party."[186] It decided that this clause constituted a genuine umbrella clause which granted protection against the breach of the contract between the host State and the investor and, as a consequence, allowed the claimant to bring not only breaches of treaty but also breaches of contract in the treaty-based forum established under the BIT.[187]

Yet, instead of disregarding the earlier interpretation of a similar clause in *SGS v. Pakistan* as concerning a different bilateral treaty, or justifying its conflicting decision primarily with differences in the wording of the applicable treaties, the Tribunal in *SGS v. Philippines* emphasized that it considered the interpretation in *SGS v. Pakistan* as unconvincing and ultimately mistaken. Rather than trying to avoid conflict, the Tribunal in *SGS v. Philippines* therefore sought an open conflict with the preceding decision. It noted that its interpretation was "contradicted by the decision of the Tribunal in *SGS v. Pakistan*,"[188] and explicitly criticized the earlier decision as "failing to give any clear meaning to the 'umbrella clause.'"[189] Furthermore, it is noteworthy that the Tribunal in *SGS v. Philippines* considered whether it should, nonetheless, "defer to the answers given by the *SGS v. Pakistan* Tribunal" for the sake of consistency.[190] However, it observed:

> [A]lthough different tribunals constituted under the ICSID system should in general seek to act consistently with each other, in the end it must be for each tribunal to exercise its competence in accordance with the applicable law, which will by definition be different for each BIT and each Respondent State. Moreover there is no doctrine of precedent in international law, if by precedent is meant a rule of the binding effect of a single decision. There is no hierarchy of international tribunals, and even if there were, there is no good reason for allowing the first tribunal in time to resolve issues for all later tribunals. It must be initially for the control mechanisms provided for under the BIT and the ICSID Convention, and in the longer term for the development of a common legal opinion or *jurisprudence constante*, to resolve the difficult legal questions discussed by the *SGS v. Pakistan* Tribunal and also in the present decision.[191]

---

[186] *SGS v. Philippines*, Decision on Jurisdiction, January 29, 2004, para. 115.
[187] *Ibid.*, para. 128.   [188] *Ibid.*, para. 119.   [189] *Ibid.*, para. 125.
[190] *Ibid.*, para. 97.   [191] *Ibid.*, para. 97.

The Tribunal, therefore, clearly recognized that coherence among decisions was desirable, but pointed out that the mechanism for achieving this consistency could not lie in requiring subsequent tribunals to follow earlier decisions, especially if they considered these to be ultimately unpersuasive or wrong. Instead, it considered that the method for arriving at consistency should rather be one of dialogue between investment tribunals and annulment committees under the ICSID Convention. Consequently, the decision in *SGS* v. *Philippines* explicitly recognized the existence of a treaty-overarching system of investment protection and stressed the importance of generating unity and consistency within this system. The divergence of *SGS* v. *Philippines* from the earlier *SGS* v. *Pakistan* decision cannot, therefore, be seen as an indication of the lack of a uniform system of investment protection that is based on disparate and diverging standards of investment protection. Instead, the divergence between both *SGS* cases merely reflects disagreement about how a certain investor right in the system of international investment protection should be properly applied and thus about the direction the entire system should take.

While, at first, the decision in *SGS* v. *Philippines* has generally received support in subsequent arbitral jurisprudence,[192] more recently, it has not been followed by several arbitral decisions which were all entertained by nearly the same set of arbitrators.[193] These decisions, including the one in *El Paso* v. *Argentina*, explicitly endorsed the interpretative approach to the application of umbrella clauses adopted by the Tribunal in *SGS* v. *Pakistan* and thus placed themselves into a position of open conflict with the jurisprudential line started by *SGS* v. *Philippines*. Again, what is interesting to note is how these subsequent decisions dealt with the way they interpreted the umbrella clause in the US–Argentine BIT compared with the interpretation of the umbrella clause in the Swiss–Filippino BIT in *SGS* v. *Philippines*.

When approaching the interpretation of the umbrella clause in Article II(2)(c) of the US–Argentine BIT that provided that "[e]ach Party shall observe any obligation it may have entered into with regard to investments,"[194] the Tribunal in *El Paso* did not primarily engage in an interpretation of the clause itself, but instead extensively discussed the different arguments provided for by the tribunals in *SGS* v. *Pakistan* and *SGS* v. *Philippines* for their respective positions.[195] After weighing the

---

[192] See *supra* footnote 179.   [193] See *supra* footnote 178.
[194] See *El Paso* v. *Argentina*, Decision on Jurisdiction, April 27, 2006, para. 70.
[195] *Ibid.*, paras. 71–78.

competing justifications given in these two decisions, it ultimately found the arguments in *SGS v. Pakistan* to be more convincing and concluded in very general terms that "an umbrella clause cannot transform any contract claims into a treaty claim."[196]

While the Tribunal in *El Paso* could have simply based its decision on the fact that it was concerned with the application of a different BIT, it considered it to be necessary to provide arguments as to why it did not follow the decision in *SGS v. Philippines*. In addition, it provided systemic arguments by referring to the scope and function of umbrella clauses in the system of investment protection in general, instead of focusing on the specific clause in the governing BIT.[197] Furthermore, it did not criticize the decision in *SGS v. Philippines* as an unpersuasive interpretation of the Swiss–Filippino BIT, but rather designated it as a mistaken approach to the interpretation of umbrella clauses in international investment law as such.

The Tribunal thus based its reasoning on generalized arguments about the approach taken in *SGS v. Philippines* instead of declining any relevance of the decision as being based on a different BIT that was not binding on the parties in the dispute at hand. The reasoning in *El Paso*, therefore, reflects the Tribunal's assumption of a treaty-overarching concept of umbrella clauses which is less concerned with the interpretation of an individual clause in a specific bilateral treaty. This is further supported by the Tribunal's statement that it was "not convinced that the clauses analysed so far really should receive different interpretations."[198] The decision is therefore another illustration of how arbitral tribunals make use of system-oriented arguments instead of focusing on the interpretation of the governing bilateral treaty, even in cases of conflicting interpretations.

Although contradicting interpretations of core investor rights are undesirable from the point of view of legal certainty and predictability of international investment law, jurisprudential conflict is also one of the driving forces behind the development of the system of precedent in common law because it enables tribunals to engage in a critical discourse about the proper interpretation of investor rights in view of different hypotheses relating to the proper interpretation of a legal rule or principle. In addition to the fact that even in cases of open conflict tribunals

---

[196] *Ibid.*, para. 82. See also *ibid.*, para. 85 (concluding that "the Tribunal, endorsing the interpretation first given to the so-called 'umbrella clause' in the Decision *SGS v. Pakistan*, confirms ... that it has jurisdiction over treaty claims and cannot entertain purely contractual claims").

[197] *Cf. El Paso* v. *Argentina*, Decision on Jurisdiction, April 27, 2006, para. 76.

[198] *Ibid.*, para. 70.

reason in a generalized form with reference to a treaty-overarching framework, divergence in investment arbitration should not be seen as defying the idea of a uniform system of investment protection, but can be squared into an evolutionary theory of case law that views different jurisprudential lines as a possibility or even necessity for the law to evolve towards a *jurisprudence constante*. Furthermore, it is necessary to recognize that conflicting decisions of different dispute settlement bodies also exist under domestic legal systems. Splits between courts of appeal in different circuits are, for example, a phenomenon with which many domestic legal systems are familiar. Yet, doubts that domestic law for this reason does not constitute a system of law that is based on uniform rules and principles are rather rare.

(b)   Distinction of facts as an instrument to uphold unity

Cases of open dissent in investment treaty arbitration are, however, rather exceptional. Instead, in most cases of conflicting decisions arbitral tribunals attempt to uphold the unity of investment law by applying strategies that avoid open conflict. The Tribunal in *Sempra* v. *Argentina*, for example, explained the inconsistencies in arbitral jurisprudence concerning the question of whether Argentina was exempted from its international responsibility based on the plea of necessity with differences concerning the assessment of facts. Equally, it distinguished its own decision, which diverged from one line of earlier jurisprudence, based on an alleged difference in the appreciation of facts, and thus suggested that at least the law in this regard was not uncertain, unpredictable or inconsistent. Instead, it observed:

> [W]hile the *CMS* and *Enron* tribunals have not been persuaded by the severity of the Argentine crisis as a factor capable of triggering the state of necessity, *LG&E* has considered the situation in a different light and justified the invocation of emergency and necessity, albeit for a limited period of time. This Tribunal, however, is not any more persuaded than the *CMS* and *Enron* tribunals about the crisis justifying the operation of emergency and necessity.[199]

Distinguishing cases on the basis of the facts, and thereby creating the illusion of a consistent framework of investment protection, is sometimes also used in order to avoid directly criticizing the interpretation of an earlier tribunal and explicitly departing from it. Thus, instead of challenging the decision of an earlier tribunal and its legal ruling directly, some

---

[199] *Sempra* v. *Argentina*, Award, September 28, 2007, para. 346.

tribunals have, in the reasoning of their decision, restricted the scope of application of the earlier decision on the basis of the underlying facts or based on differences in the governing BIT. This way of reasoning transforms potential conflicts about the content of legal principles into mere differences of fact. It avoids open conflict and upholds the consistency of a treaty-overarching principle in question, even if the underlying conflict between tribunals relates to a disagreement about the scope or proper interpretation of the principle or rule itself.

This method of creating consistency in international investment law was used, for example, in *Salini* v. *Jordan* with respect to the question of whether the MFN clause in the Italian–Jordanian BIT also incorporated more favorable dispute settlement provisions.[200] While the claimant relied mainly on the decision in *Maffezini* v. *Spain* which held that an MFN clause could, in principle, allow an investor to import more favorable dispute settlement provisions from the host State's third-country BITs,[201] the Tribunal did not adopt the reasoning and the result of this earlier decision. Instead, it declined to apply the MFN clause in the Italian–Jordanian BIT to matters of dispute settlement.[202]

While the Tribunal "share[d] the concerns that have been expressed in numerous quarters with regard to the solution adopted in the *Maffezini* case,"[203] it did not, however, enter into open conflict with the *Maffezini* decision. Instead, it distinguished its case from the *Maffezini* decision based on differences in the MFN clauses in the two BITs.[204] It stressed "that the circumstances of this case are different. Indeed, Article 3 of the BIT between Italy and Jordan does not include any provision extending its scope of application to dispute settlement."[205] While the Spanish–Argentine BIT simply referred to "all rights or all matters covered by the agreement," the MFN clause in the Italian–Jordanian BIT distinguished

---

[200] *Salini.* v. *Jordan*, Decision on Jurisdiction, November 15, 2004, paras. 102 *et seq.* Similarly, *Suez and InterAguas* v. *Argentina*, Decision on Jurisdiction, May 16, 2006, para. 63 ("Having duly considered the reasons set forth in the *Plama* decision, this Tribunal comes to the conclusion that, whatever its merits, it is in any event clearly distinguishable from the present case on a number of grounds").

[201] *Maffezini* v. *Spain*, Decision on Objections to Jurisdiction, January 25, 2000, paras. 38 *et seq.* See also *supra* Ch. IV.C.1.a.

[202] *Salini* v. *Jordan*, Decision on Jurisdiction, November 15, 2004, para. 119.

[203] *Ibid.*, para. 115.

[204] This way of distinguishing cases is similar to distinguishing based on differences of facts in domestic legal systems, even if differences in investment treaties are concerned.

[205] *Salini* v. *Jordan*, Decision on Jurisdiction, November 15, 2004, para. 118.

between equal treatment vis-à-vis investments and treatment of investors and provided:

1. Both Contracting Parties, within the bounds of their own territory, shall grant investments effected by, and the income accruing to, investors of the other Contracting Party, no less favourable treatment than that accorded to investments effected by, and income accruing to, its own nationals or investors of Third States.

2. In case, from the legislation of one of the Contracting Parties, or from the international obligations in force or that may come into force in the future for one of the Contracting Parties, should come out a legal framework according to which the investors of the other Contracting Party would be granted a more favourable treatment than the one foreseen in this Agreement, the treatment granted to the investors of such other Parties will apply also for outstanding relationships.[206]

Based on the textual differences of both clauses, the Tribunal in *Salini* concluded that the MFN clause in the BIT that governed the dispute at hand applied only to substantive investor rights. However, invoking the differences in wording seems somewhat superficial, because it is difficult to see to what extent the formulation of the MFN clause in the Italian–Jordanian BIT differs in scope from the parallel clause in the Spanish–Argentine BIT, applied in the *Maffezini* case.[207] Instead, offering recourse to investment treaty arbitration to some but not to all foreign investors may well be interpreted as according different treatment to investors based on different nationalities.[208] This suggests that the disagreement concerning the interpretation of MFN clauses and their application to questions of dispute settlement was a disagreement relating to the scope of MFN clauses as such rather than a difference in the wording of the specific clauses involved. Nevertheless, by distinguishing its case on this basis, the Tribunal in *Salini* upheld the unity of international investment law as a coherent system and avoided open conflict.[209]

---

[206] *Ibid.*, para. 104.

[207] *Cf. Plama* v. *Bulgaria*, Decision on Jurisdiction, February 8, 2005, para. 190 (stating that "the difference between the terms 'treatment ... accorded to investments,' as appearing in Article 3(1) of the Bulgaria–Cyprus BIT, and 'treatment... accorded to investors,' as appearing in other BITs, is to be noted. The Tribunal does not attach a particular significance to the use of the different terms, in particular not since Article 3(1) contains the words 'investments by investors.'"); *Siemens* v. *Argentina*, Decision on Jurisdiction, August 3, 2004, paras. 91 *et seq.* Similarly, Radi, *The Application of the Most-Favoured-Nation Clause to the Dispute Settlement Provisions of Bilateral Investment Treaties*, 18 Eur. J. Int'l L. 757, 764–68 (2007).

[208] See further *supra* Ch. IV.D.1.

[209] See also *Berschader* v. *Russia*, Award, April 21, 2006, paras. 151–208 (while framing the question of whether MFN clauses apply to more favorable treatment regarding

(c) Reconciling conflicts through conflict rules

Investment tribunals do not, however, only create unity in interpreting and applying investment treaties by distinguishing earlier cases based on the facts or the different wording of the applicable BIT. Tribunals that diverge from earlier arbitral decisions also employ other genuinely systemic techniques in order to produce unity in investment treaty arbitration. An example of such techniques is the decision in *Plama* v. *Bulgaria*.[210] The issue at hand concerned the application of an MFN clause to incorporate the host State's broader consent to arbitration under third-country BITs into the basic treaty. The claimant argued that the reasoning in *Maffezini* v. *Spain* should apply and thus broaden the basis of jurisdiction of the Tribunal.

The Tribunal in *Plama*, however, strongly disagreed with the soundness of the reasoning in *Maffezini*.[211] Not only was it critical that the Tribunal in *Maffezini* had misinterpreted earlier decisions by the ICJ and other arbitral awards concerning the application of MFN clauses,[212] it also disagreed explicitly with the starting point of legal analysis in *Maffezini*. In this respect, it criticized that the Tribunal in *Maffezini* should have pigeonholed the issue not as a question of the scope of the MFN clause at hand, but as a question of whether the host State was bound, similar to a non-signatory party in a commercial arbitration, by an agreement to arbitrate which is incorporated by reference. Against this background, the Tribunal considered the *Maffezini* Tribunal's "basis for analysis in principle to be inappropriate for the question whether dispute resolution provisions in the basic treaty can be replaced by dispute resolution provisions in another treaty."[213] Furthermore, the Tribunal in *Plama* also disagreed with the policy behind the solution in

---

investor-State dispute settlement as a question of principle, *ibid.*, para. 179, the Tribunal also distinguished the specificities of the MFN clause governing the dispute at hand from MFN clauses that were operative in cases like *Maffezini*, *Siemens*, or *Gas Natural*; see *Berschader* v. *Russia*, Award, April 21, 2006, paras. 175, 183–94. However, rather than stressing exclusively bilateral rationales concerning the specificities of individual investment treaties, the Tribunal's reasoning is also framed, similar to the decision in *El Paso*, in terms of an interpretation of MFN clauses in investment treaties in general. See, in particular, *Berschader* v. *Russia*, Award, April 21, 2006, paras. 177–82).

[210] *Plama* v. *Bulgaria*, Decision on Jurisdiction, February 8, 2005. See also *supra* Ch. IV.C.2.b.

[211] *Ibid.*, paras. 217 *et seq.*

[212] *Ibid.*, para. 217 (considering that the precedent cited by *Maffezini* did "not provide a conclusive answer to the question").

[213] *Ibid.*, para. 218.

Maffezini and disagreed that a broad application of MFN clauses would harmonize international investment law.[214] Finally, the Tribunal in *Plama* also disagreed with the "public policy exceptions" the Tribunal in *Maffezini* set up as limitations on MFN treatment.[215] Overall, the language and the general tone of the *Plama* decision, therefore, express deeply rooted dissent with the decision in *Maffezini* that departed from an "inappropriate basis for analysis" with respect to the question at hand.[216] The conflict between *Plama* and *Maffezini* was, therefore, one regarding the legal principles governing the interpretation of MFN clauses rather than one pertaining to differences of facts or the governing BIT.

Nevertheless, the Tribunal in *Plama* endeavored to reconcile its decision with the decision in *Maffezini*, apparently in an attempt to avoid open dissent. After advancing its critique against the reasoning in the *Maffezini* decision, it pointed out that the decision in *Maffezini* was "understandable"[217] and expressed its "sympath[y] with a tribunal that attempts to neutralize such a provision [i.e., one requiring recourse to domestic courts for 18 months before turning to international arbitration] that is nonsensical from a practical point of view."[218] The Tribunal in *Plama*, therefore, expressed the view that the result of *Maffezini* was less reproachable than its reasoning. The reason for such sympathy may simply be seen as a matter of courtesy among different tribunals. It can, however, also be understood as an expression of the more fundamental quest to ensure consistency in the application of standard provisions in investment treaties, such as MFN clauses, and to uphold the unity of investment treaty arbitration as a legal system.

This can, in particular, be inferred from the way the Tribunal in *Plama* argued and how it attempted to reconcile its decision with the earlier *Maffezini* decision. Namely, the Tribunal in *Plama* read down the grounds of the *Maffezini* decision to an exception in order to reconcile its own decision with this earlier jurisprudence and its progeny. In its view, the situation underlying the *Maffezini* case constituted "exceptional circumstances [that] should not be treated as a statement of general principle guiding future tribunals in other cases where the circumstances are not present."[219] In its view

> the principle with multiple exceptions as stated by the tribunal in the
> *Maffezini* case should instead be a different principle with one, single

---

[214] *Ibid.*, para. 219.   [215] *Ibid.*, para. 221.   [216] *Cf. ibid.*, para. 218.
[217] *Ibid.*, para. 224.   [218] *Ibid.*, para. 224.   [219] *Ibid.*, para. 224.

exception: an MFN provision in a basic treaty does not incorporate by reference dispute settlement provisions in whole or in part set forth in another treaty, unless the MFN provision in the basic treaty leaves no doubt that the Contracting Parties intended to incorporate them.[220]

It thus relied on a standard technique in legal reasoning employed in order to reconcile seemingly conflicting rules. Instead of supporting *Maffezini* as the expression of a principle, it depicted it as an exception to a principle established by its own decision. Relying on the meta-logic about rules and exceptions, the *Plama* decision thus upheld unity and consistency in investment treaty arbitration. Despite its fundamental discontent with the *Maffezini* decision, *Plama* did not base its decision on its independent competence as an arbitral tribunal and the lack of a system of binding precedent, as did the Tribunal in *SGS v. Philippines*, but on a legal argument that allowed it to reconcile its conclusion with a conflicting precedent. This illustrates that consistency in investment jurisprudence, and thus a systemic and treaty-overarching factor, was a significant concern for the Tribunal in *Plama* in grounding its decision.

(d)   Unity in investment jurisprudence by concealing dissent

Another method used by tribunals that are faced with earlier investment jurisprudence with which they disagree is to conceal the existence of conflicting interpretations instead of engaging with them and justifying their departure from them. The most notable proponent of this approach is the Decision on Liability in *LG&E v. Argentina*[221] which departed from the earlier award in *CMS v. Argentina*[222] with respect to the plea of necessity as an excuse for the breach of the US–Argentine BIT. The contradictory outcome of both decisions is all the more surprising as both disputes related to almost identical fact patterns, concerned the identical conduct of the same host State, and were brought under the same investment treaty.

In both cases, the claimants had participated in the privatization of Argentina's gas sector and purchased shareholding interests in local gas distributing companies. Those companies were then granted long-term licenses with the right to calculate gas tariffs in US dollars and to convert them into Argentine pesos at the prevailing exchange rate. In addition, the tariff regime included the right to have tariffs adjusted every six

---

[220] *Ibid.*, para. 223.   [221] *LG&E v. Argentina*, Decision on Liability, October 3, 2006.
[222] *CMS v. Argentina*, Award, May 12, 2005. See on this decision Schill, *From Calvo to CMS*, 3 SchiedsVZ 285 (2005); van Aaken, *Zwischen Scylla und Charybdis*, 105 ZVglRWiss 544 (2006).

months based on the US Producer Price Index.[223] As part of Argentina's larger approach to create economic stability and prosperity, the country had also pegged its local currency to the US dollar with an exchange rate of one-to-one.[224]

After the country's economic crisis began to unfold in the late 1990s, a further increase of the gas tariffs was considered to be detrimental to the national economy and social peace in Argentina.[225] After first agreeing on a temporary tariff freeze, Argentina finally adopted an Emergency Law[226] that lifted the peso's convertibility, transformed all internal US dollar denominated claims at a one-to-one ratio into peso, and abrogated the tariff adjustment clauses granted to the claimants. Both companies then initiated ICSID arbitrations against the changes in the governing regulatory framework and claimed for damages due to a violation of the US–Argentine BIT. Argentina's main defense, in this context, was necessity under customary international law and reliance on an emergency clause in the US–Argentine BIT.

While the decision in *LG&E* largely followed the earlier award in *CMS v. Argentina* concerning the assessment of Argentina's conduct under the substantive BIT obligations, such as fair and equitable treatment, indirect expropriation and the umbrella clause, it departed from the *CMS* decision with respect to the plea of necessity.[227] Whereas the *CMS* award had denied the operation of necessity in the case submitted to it, since Argentina, in its view, had contributed to the crisis and could have taken less restrictive measures,[228] the decision in *LG&E* accepted that

---

[223] The framing of the tariff regime was particularly designed against the backdrop of Argentina's major currency instability and hyperinflation in the 1980s and early 1990s and aimed at attracting foreign capital for the privatization of the State-owned gas sector.

[224] See the "Convertibility Law" No. 23.928, March 27, 1991, modified by Law No. 25.445, June 21, 2005.

[225] For the background of Argentina's economic crisis see Bickel, *Die Argentinien-Krise aus ökonomischer Sicht*, Beiträge zum Internationalen Wirtschaftsrecht, vol. 38 (2005); Di Rosa, *The Recent Wave of Arbitrations against Argentina under Bilateral Investment Treaties*, 36 U. Miami Inter-Am. L. Rev. 41, 44 *et seq.* (2004).

[226] Law No. 25.561, January 6, 2002, B.O. No. 29.810.

[227] See, for a more detailed comparison of both decisions, Schill, *Auf zu Kalypso?*, 5 SchiedsVZ 178 (2007); Schill, *International Investment Law and the Host State's Power to Handle Economic Crises*, 24 J. Int'l Arb. 265 (2007); see also Reinisch, *Necessity in International Investment Arbitration – An Unnecessary Split of Opinions in Recent ICSID Cases?*, 8 J. World Inv. & Trade 191 (2007); Waibel, *Two Worlds of Necessity in ICSID Arbitration*, 20 Leiden J. Int'l L. 637 (2007).

[228] *CMS v. Argentina*, Award, May 12, 2005, paras. 323–31; see also *ibid.*, paras. 353–94 (concerning the interpretation of the BIT's emergency clause and the question of compensation in case of necessity).

Argentina was excused from complying with its BIT obligations during a period of approximately eighteen months.[229] As a consequence, the claimant in *LG&E* was required to bear the financial consequences stemming from the emergency legislation and was not fully entitled to damages or compensation, whereas the claimant in *CMS* was able to recover damages for the entire period during which Argentina's emergency prevailed.

The differences between both decisions are not only substantial as regards the outcome, they also rely on squarely different legal reasoning. While the *CMS* award applied necessity under customary international law, as codified in Article 25, ILC Articles on State Responsibility, the decision in *LG&E* gave precedence to a non-precluded measures clause in the US–Argentine BIT, the interpretation of which led it to exempt Argentina from liability under the BIT. The outcomes of both decisions are, therefore, clearly contradictory, even though they were based on different sources of law, customary international law, and treaty law, respectively.

Yet, it is noteworthy how the *LG&E* decision dealt with this conflict in jurisprudence. Notably, the Tribunal in *LG&E* frequently concurred with the award in the *CMS* case as regards the assessment and interpretation of the substantive BIT obligations. In this context, it even cited the *CMS* award as support for its interpretation of fair and equitable treatment and the Treaty's umbrella clause.[230] It did not, however, mention that the *CMS* award fundamentally differed with respect to the assessment of the plea of necessity under international law. Instead, it concealed the existing divergence and justified its decision without rebutting the arguments provided in the *CMS* award against the operation of necessity.

Even if one considers the decision in *LG&E* as the appropriate application of the defense of necessity,[231] it is objectionable to use precedent in such a selective way.[232] Whenever it concurred with the award in *CMS v. Argentina*, the Tribunal in *LG&E* invoked its support, whenever it disagreed with the earlier decision, it did not even mention, let alone rebut, existing counter-arguments. This suggests that concealing differences in interpretation and selectively citing the *CMS* award was a method by which the Tribunal in *LG&E* upheld the unity of the system of investment

---

[229] *LG&E* v. *Argentina*, Decision on Liability, October 3, 2006, paras. 226–66.

[230] *Ibid.*, paras. 125, 128, 171.

[231] See, however, for a critical analysis of the treatment of the defense of necessity in *LG&E* Schill (*supra* footnote 227), 24 J. Int'l Arb. 211, 226 *et seq.* (2007).

[232] Similarly, Shahabuddeen (*supra* footnote 126), pp. 130–31 (1996).

arbitration without needing to dwell on inconsistencies with earlier decisions.[233]

3 Conclusion

Even though decisions by arbitral tribunals constitute only a subsidiary source of international law from the perspective of the traditional State-centered theory of international law, they have advanced to one of the primary sources of consultation and reference in the practice of investment treaty arbitration. This is true above all for concurring decisions where arbitral tribunals take earlier decisions into account in order to clarify the meaning of certain provisions in investment treaties, to clarify the intention of the parties, or to draw analogies. Although investment tribunals emphasize, time and again, that they are not legally bound by earlier decisions, they increasingly use precedent as embodying the standard interpretation of investment treaties that tribunals will diverge from only if the parties to a dispute provide specific reasons to do so, or establish that the governing treaty diverges from standard BIT practice. Precedent, therefore, assumes a standard-setting function for the interpretation of investment treaties. Finally, some of the standard investor rights, such as indirect expropriation or fair and equitable treatment, are actually primarily forged by precedent, not by reference to other sources of international law or State practice. Far from constituting merely a subsidiary source of international law, precedent in these cases assumes the function of a primary source of international law.

Most notably, it is of little importance whether an earlier decision was based on the same or a different investment treaty. The use of precedent, therefore, is also a source of the multilateralization of international investment law as it transposes a solution adopted under one treaty to a different treaty relationship. Even if some arbitral decisions emphasize the independence of every treaty relationship, and thus seemingly favor bilateral rationales, the predominant approach is to use precedent as a

---

[233] The same observation holds true with respect to the subsequent decision in *Enron* v. *Argentina*, Award, May 22, 2007, that frequently cited the earlier *LG&E* award as support for its own interpretation of investor rights, such as fair and equitable treatment, or the interpretation of the Treaty's umbrella clause, see *Enron* v. *Argentina*, Award, May 22, 2007, paras. 260, 262–63, 274, without, however, mentioning that it did not concur with this precedent regarding the assessment of Argentina's necessity defense; see *ibid.*, paras. 288–345.

source of investment law in intra-treaty and cross-treaty interpretation alike. The use of precedent thus generates uniformity in the application of investment treaty concepts within and across various treaty relationships. The danger that exists in this respect is, of course, that differences between treaties are leveled, although this was not intended by the contracting parties. Tribunals will, therefore, have to pay close attention to the question of whether divergent wording has to be understood as intending a divergent result, or whether different wordings nevertheless allude to the same legal concept.

The creation of a system of *de facto* precedent and, more generally, the contribution precedent makes towards a multilateralization of international investment law, is also not countered by decisions that diverge from earlier arbitral decisions or by the development of conflicting lines of investment jurisprudence. Certainly, these cases illustrate most strikingly the absence of a system of binding precedent and demonstrate the potential for inconsistencies in investment treaty arbitration. The rarity of such awards nonetheless shows that investment jurisprudence is largely consistent. Moreover, already the fact that prior decisions are dealt with demonstrates the self-institutionalization through self-reference of investment treaty arbitration as a system. Furthermore, tribunals regularly apply methods well-known in common and civil law to distinguish cases on the basis of facts and by reading down a decision on a point of law from a rule to a principle and/or from a principle to an exception.

Finally, the way investment tribunals handle even openly conflicting decisions confirms that they presuppose the existence of a framework of international investment law that overarches the individual bilateral treaties. More often than not, they frame their disagreement in systemic terms, arguing not that they diverge because their function is restricted to solving a specific dispute under a specific treaty, but that a certain interpretation or application of investment treaty principles is unpersuasive as a general proposition in the system of international investment protection. Cases of dissent therefore show, despite the disagreement about the interpretation of certain issues at hand, that investment tribunals have a deeply rooted perception of the unity of international investment arbitration. In their reasoning, they do not confine themselves to the solution of the individual dispute, but have regard to the idea of an overarching international legal order for the regulation and protection of foreign investment. Even cases of dissent, therefore, support the conclusion that – from the perspective of the tribunals' self-description and self-perception – international investment protection does not consist of a fragmented aggregate of individual decisions based on isolated bilateral treaties, but is embedded in an overarching framework with a multilateral character.

What splits in investment jurisprudence therefore clarify, much more than the lack of multilateral rationalities at play, are the deficiencies of a dispute settlement system that is based on ad hoc dispute settlement bodies, instead of a more institutionalized structure that is able to properly address inconsistencies in the application of international investment law, such as an appeals mechanism similar to the WTO Dispute Settlement Understanding, or a preliminary judgment procedure similar to Article 234, EC Treaty. Instead, only time and the development of arbitral jurisprudence will show which of two (or more) conflicting approaches will prevail on the long run or be favored in future treaty practice.

D   Conclusion: the emergence of a system of international investment law through interpretation

Tendencies towards a multilateralization of international investment law cannot only be traced in the structure of investment treaties. They are also visible in the jurisprudence of investment tribunals when deciding investor-State disputes and enforcing the rights and obligations arising under BITs. Investment tribunals use a number of mechanisms to create uniformity in the application of investment treaties and thereby mitigate differences that exist between a genuinely multilateral system that is based on a single international treaty and the current system that is based on more than 2,500 bilateral treaty relationships.

First, tribunals frequently use cross-treaty interpretation, that is, reference to third-party treaties that are not binding upon the parties involved in an investment dispute, in order to interpret and to apply the governing treaty. This has the effect of creating uniformity in treaty interpretation and embeds BITs in a treaty-overarching framework. Even though the third-party treaties do not become the applicable law, they nevertheless inform the interpretation of the governing treaty. This has a multilateralizing effect as the strict emphasis on the bilateral relationship in treaty-interpretation is abandoned. Instead, cross-treaty interpretation increasingly has the effect of treating investment treaties as if they emanate from a single source that is applicable rather independently from the governing BIT.

Second, investment tribunals use arbitral precedent in an extensive way. Far from constituting a subsidiary source of international law, precedent has become, both quantitatively as well as qualitatively, the premier determinant for the outcome of investor-State disputes. Even though precedent is considered to be non-binding, it has a considerable influence on the outcome of investment disputes to the extent that divergences in investment jurisprudence become a rather rare phenomenon. Notably, even in cases of conflicting decisions, tribunals employ various strategies to uphold the overall consistency of international investment law, even though the governing treaty constitutes a different source which should *prima facie* not trigger concerns about incoherences. System consistency is thus clearly a concern that influences and drives investment treaty jurisprudence.

Comparable with the use of cross-treaty interpretation, the use of precedent reinforces the view that investment law is based on a uniform framework that overarches individual bilateral treaties. The use of precedent also creates intra-system communication and consistency and ensures that differences in jurisprudence are addressed and dealt with. This method resembles the method of common law reasoning and will arguably lead not only to largely consistent decision-making but also to the further systemic refinement of investment jurisprudence. In this respect, investment arbitration contributes to a further self-institutionalization and self-constitutionalization of international investment law as a system of law that functions largely similar to a genuinely multilateral regime.

The contribution that the jurisprudence of investment tribunals makes toward a multilateralization of international investment law is most apparent when juxtaposing it with the traditional view of the effects of bilateral treaties and bilateral methods of treaty interpretation. From a bilateralist perspective, making use of precedent in cross-treaty cases and referring to third-party treaties as an interpretative aid would be seen as a violation of the *inter partes* effect of international treaties, since the third-party treaty is indirectly accorded normative weight for the legal assessment of the investment relationship between two different States. Clearly, if third-party treaties are used as an interpretative aid, this can amount to creating additional obligations of States if the interpretation is supported by the language of third-country BITs. Conversely, reliance on third-party treaties can reduce existing obligations under investment treaties.

Likewise, the extensive reliance on precedent would be opposed, from a bilateralist perspective, as a violation of the traditional doctrine of sources of international law, because precedent is not applied as a subsidiary source of international law, but as the primary framework of reference in investment treaty arbitration. In particular, the use of precedent would be viewed critically in this perspective as it entails a manifest power transfer from States to tribunals concerning the interpretation and application of investment treaties. If BITs were purely bilateral bargains, both the interpretation of BITs by recourse to third-country BITs and the use of precedent would indeed be highly problematic, if not plainly impermissible.

Apart from the fact that a purely positivistic critique of the practice of investment tribunals would have difficulty in changing the behavior of tribunals, and thus fail to have an actual impact, the multilateral interpretation of BITs that takes into account the wording of third-country BITs and uses precedent based on wholly unrelated BITs, however, can be justified even under traditional methods of treaty interpretation. It not only finds precursors in the jurisprudence of the PCIJ, various international arbitral tribunals, and the jurisprudence of the ICJ, it can also be reconciled with the principles of treaty interpretation endorsed by Article 31, Vienna Convention on the Law of Treaties. Although as a general rule treaties have to be interpreted according to their specific context, BITs dispose of a number of convergence criteria that militate for the appropriateness and legitimacy of a multilateralization by interpretation through the use of precedent and cross-treaty interpretation. These criteria are the treaties' common teleology to promote and to protect foreign investment flows, the archetype structure of BITs that are negotiated and concluded against the background of model BITs and multilateral draft Conventions, the common intention and the common interest that can be presumed to exist as a justification for the conclusion of investment treaties, and their implementation and compliance procedures that are based, to a large extent, on a multilateral procedural framework.

The use of third-country BITs and of precedent relating to the interpretation of such treaties is relevant in order to ascertain the ordinary meaning of treaty provisions commonly used in investment treaties. The meaning of fair and equitable treatment or the notion of "investor" or "investment" can thus be ascertained in view of the understanding that prevails among the majority of States that enter into BITs. If it was, for instance, commonly understood that a complete disregard of the investor's legitimate expectations was a violation of fair and equitable treatment or that national treatment did not only prohibit direct, but encompassed indirect discriminations of foreign investors, the use of standard treaty language in a specific BIT would signal adherence to this standard content of these investor rights. Deviation from the standard understanding of such concepts, by contrast, would require a specific wording of a BIT. Even though BITs do not constitute a uniform text, it is legitimate, and in conformity with the Vienna Convention on the Law, of Treaties, if tribunals refer not only to third-country BITs and related precedent, but use an emerging line of jurisprudence as a legal standard that they will deviate from in case the host State concerned can show that a meaning of the BIT was intended that differed from the ordinary understanding.

Apart from the same teleology, the use of unrelated precedent as well as the comparison with third-country BITs is also justified in view of the archetype structure of BITs and their common historic pedigree. The treaties are not negotiated and concluded in a vacuum, but go back to model treaties that themselves form part of genuinely multilateral projects. As the pedigree of international investment treaties suggests, the conclusion of BITs can be seen as a reaction to the failure of several multilateral approaches. Instead of pursuing multilateral approaches, capital-exporting States shifted forums to bilateral relationships and rooted the content of what was intended to become a multilateral instrument in bilateral treaties. The content, however, was supposed to be identical to the content of the proposed multilateral frameworks for investment protection. Against this background, it is thus appropriate to view BITs in connection with other BITs of the countries directly affected by an investor-State dispute (that is, the host State as well as the investor's home State) as well as in connection with the BITs between wholly unrelated countries. They share a common historic background and accordingly use wording that refers to the same rules and concepts. Similarly, the close resemblances in the wording of BITs reflect a common intention of States in establishing uniform rules that govern international investment relations.[234]

Close attention, however, has to be paid to differences in the wording of investment treaties. Such differences may be material as a divergence of a bilateral treaty from the general treaty practice and from its multilateral aspirations. Yet, the question also has to be addressed whether differences in wording merely confirm standard concepts of international investment law or customary international law (and thus occur *ex abundante cautela*) or whether differences in wording are included

---

[234] See *supra* Ch. III.C.

in order to modify existing general international law or the standard meaning of the concepts used under international investment law.

Overall, the way arbitral tribunals interpret and apply international investment treaties, in particular by presupposing the unity of the sources of international investment law and by employing styles of common law reasoning, supplements the existing normative bases of a multilateralization of international investment law in the form of MFN clauses and the possibility that investors can pick and choose their preferred regime of investment protection. In essence, arbitral tribunals and their jurisprudence reproduce and, more importantly, put into practice a system that behaves and functions according to multilateral rationales and does not, despite the existence of innumerable bilateral investment relationships, dissolve into infinite fragmentation.

VIII

Conclusion: multilateralization – universalization – constitutionalization

Most international treaties order the relations between two States only. They create mutual rights and obligations and coordinate State behavior on a bilateral basis. While allowing for flexible solutions depending on the specific situation and interests of the States involved, bilateralism also inhibits the emergence of an international community that is ordered on the basis of general and uniform principles. Bilateralism puts the State, its sovereignty, and its consent to the creation of international law center stage and secures the precedence of State interests over interests outside or beyond its realm. This fortification of the State coined the traditional understanding of international law as it developed throughout the nineteenth and most of the twentieth century. It characterized its doctrine of sources by strictly focusing on State consent, it denied international law subjectivity to non-State actors, and *de facto* coupled the enforcement of international law to a favorable distribution of power in a non-hierarchical order. Within this framework, the international treaty was essentially a "workhorse of bilateralist international law"[1] that coordinated State behavior by entering into *quid pro quo* bargains based on the underlying power relations and national interests.

Multilateralism, by contrast, assumes the existence and legitimacy of interests of an international community beyond the interests of States. It does not order inter-State relations on the basis of bilateral bargains, but rather on the basis of general principles that establish a general framework for the interactions among States and their citizens. It aspires toward universal validity and application and views States as being embedded within the structure of an international community. Following the Second World War, multilateralism became increasingly important as an ordering paradigm for international relations in a number of fields, in particular international human rights, international security, and international trade. It left its imprint on the structure and nature of international law

---

[1] Simma, *From Bilateralism to Community Interest in International Law*, 250 Recueil des Cours 217, 322 (1994).

362

by recognizing the limitations of State sovereignty in view of interests and values of an international community. The recognition of *ius cogens*, the development of international criminal law, or the increasing importance of humanitarian and peace-keeping interventions, are just a few examples that illustrate the emergence of an international community that possesses values that are independent from, and claim precedence over, the sovereignty of States. What is characteristic for multilateralism is less the fact that at least three States participate in the negotiation and conclusion of an international agreement, but more that international relations are ordered on the basis of general and non-discriminatory principles. Multilateralism is, therefore, an alternative model to imperial and hegemonic international law.

Typically, multilateralism is implemented on the basis of multilateral treaties that "serve as the vehicle *par excellence* of community interest."[2] They base relations of States on general non-discriminatory principles and create legal institutions around which the expectations and conduct of States and their citizens can evolve. Multilateralism is closely connected to moving power away from States and creating compliance mechanisms that are based on legal forms of order. In the realm of international economic relations, the paramount example for this development is the WTO, which orders international trade based on principles of non-discrimination and controls its imposition by providing for a dispute settlement system. It establishes institutions that structure and stabilize the international economy in an interest that can no longer be clearly attributed to specific States, but is a function of an emerging international society with individuals and corporations forming its constituent parts.

Even though multilateralism usually emerges on the basis of multilateral treaties, it can also develop on the basis of bilateral treaties. In the realm of international investment protection, bilateral rather than multilateral treaties are creating the institutions necessary for the development and stabilization of the global economy. Even though direct and open multilateralism has failed in the context of foreign investment protection, bilateral treaties have filled the remaining gap by serving as a substitute for genuine multilateralism in this field.[3] Similar to multilateral treaties, BITs order international investment relations on the basis of general principles that are relatively uniform across the myriad number of bilateral treaty relationships. Unlike typical bilateral treaties, they do not

---

[2] *Ibid.*, 250 Recueil des Cours 217, 323 (1994).   [3] See *supra* Ch. II.

constitute *quid pro quo* bargains, but establish a uniform legal framework that stabilizes and structures the economic activity of foreign investors and requires host States to conform their behavior to rule of law standards that enable market forces to unfold.

Along these lines, this thesis has argued that international investment law is evolving towards a multilateral system based on bilateral treaties. While bilateralism describes the form of international investment relations, it does not capture their content. BITs establish a largely uniform regime for the protection of foreign investment that is based on identical principles independent from the specific bilateral treaty relationship in question. In this respect, international investment law is developing towards an increasingly multilateralized system.

A   Summary: the multilateralization of international investment law

The thesis that international investment law is progressively multilateralizing departed from the observation that the myriad number of investment treaties are similar, and often identical, in structure, content, and objective.[4] The treaties do not contain contract-like distributive bargains that consist of the exchange of specific performances, but intend to reduce the political risk for foreign investors and converge above all with respect to the principles of investment protection they contain, including provisions on non-discrimination, fair and equitable treatment and full protection and security, the protection against direct and indirect expropriation, and investor-State dispute settlement. This holds true not only for investment treaties between developed and developing countries, but also for the increasing number of South–South BITs and the investment treaty relations among developed countries, such as under NAFTA or the ECT.[5] This convergence is surprising since the bilateral form should suggest an almost infinite fragmentation into disorderly two-party relationships.

The guiding question has, therefore, been whether this convergence is the expression of a uniform system of investment protection that structures the expectations and guides the actions of investors and States in an emerging global investment space. That this convergence can in fact be interpreted as an expression of the intention of States to establish a framework based on uniform standards is justified in view of

---

[4] See, in particular, *supra* Ch. III.A.   [5] See *supra* Ch. II.C.

the economic rationale for the conclusion of BITs and the standards of investment protection contained therein.[6] The interest in uniform rules, it was argued, stems from the interest in establishing standards of investment protection that would allow market forces to allocate investments efficiently in an increasingly globalized market. Investment treaties, in this view, endorse principles, including national and MFN treatment and government according to the concept of the rule of law, that constitute the necessary legal framework for a market to function. Uniformity in this context refers to the general principles and institutions structuring the relationship between the State and the economy, not, however, to the regulatory framework governing economic activities in their entirety. It was argued that uniform principles ordering the relations between investors and host States were necessary to enable global competition, which in turn results in the efficient allocation of resources and enables States to play out their competitive advantage. In this view, States have a genuine interest in uniform standards because market competition is the driving force for economic growth and development.

By contrast, the continuing failure to conclude a multilateral investment treaty is not inconsistent with the assumption that States have an interest in uniform rules. While earlier attempts at establishing multilateral investment protection indeed failed because of a lack of agreement on the appropriate level of investment protection,[7] the more recent attempts failed not because of differences on the principles of international investment law, but rather due to the complexities of multilateral negotiations with different parties seeking different exceptions and exemptions from general principles.[8] For instance, under the MAI the quest of various States for exceptions from national treatment provisions effectively prevented consensus among the negotiating parties, even though there was no disagreement about the general principles of investment protection. Similarly, the failure to begin negotiations on a multilateral investment treaty under the auspices of the WTO was due primarily to disagreements on non-investment-related issues of international trade. Thus, the more recent failures of direct multilateralism in international investment relations do not contradict the suggestion that a general interest exists among States in having uniform investment rules and principles of investment protection.

That States have an interest in uniform rules regarding the standards of treatment for foreign investment is particularly reflected in the MFN

---

[6] See *supra* Ch. III.C.   [7] See *supra* Ch. II.B.   [8] See *supra* Ch. II.E.

clauses contained in virtually every BIT.[9] These clauses lead to creating a level playing field for foreign investments in any given host State. They make it impossible to base international investment relations on preferential, and thus discriminatory, treatment. Instead, investors always benefit from the most comprehensive level of investment protection in a given host State by availing themselves of the most beneficial protection in any one of the host State's BITs. In this context, this book argued that MFN clauses not only multilateralize the level of substantive investment protection,[10] but also have a multilateralizing impact on dispute settlement procedures available to foreign investors.[11] As a consequence, access to investor-State arbitration, and to a certain extent the scope of a tribunal's jurisdiction, are based on the most comprehensive investment treaty concluded by the host State in question. MFN clauses, therefore, create a uniform regime for the protection of foreign investors in any given host State independent of the investor's nationality.

Even in the absence of an investment treaty between the investor's home State and the host State, corporate structuring allows investors to influence the level of investment protection.[12] Investors can channel their investment by setting up subsidiaries in a third country that has entered into a BIT with the State where the investment is to be located. Even though the actual investor does not directly benefit from the protection of a BIT, it can opt into the protective regime of an investment treaty between the host State and a third country as long as a subsidiary within a chain of corporate structures has the nationality of a State that has entered into a BIT with the host State. In sum, multi-jurisdictional corporate structuring has an effect similar to MFN clauses as it *de facto* extends the level of investment protection to investors that would otherwise be at a competitive disadvantage vis-à-vis investors from other States that are covered by one of the host State's BITs. This often even allows investors who are themselves not covered by a BIT with the host State to opt into the regime of international investment protection. The possibility of opting into BITs by means of multi-jurisdictional corporate structuring thus illustrates that BITs cannot be regarded as instruments of genuine bilateralism, given that there is effectively only limited leeway for creating preferential treatment for investors from specific home States.

The procedural law that governs investor-State disputes also contributes to the multilateralization of international investment law.

---

[9] See *supra* Ch. IV.   [10] See *supra* Ch. IV.B.   [11] See *supra* Ch. IV.C.
[12] See *supra* Ch. V.

Procedural rules, above all those of the ICSID Convention, furnish uniform rules for investor-State arbitration. Moreover, by allowing investors to pursue rights granted under investment treaties through arbitration, international investment law provides for an effective dispute settlement mechanism that does not depend on compliance through bilateral inter-State negotiation and enforcement, but relies on a right of action of the affected economic actors.[13] Engaging the investor in enforcing international investment law constitutes a fundamental transformation of this field of law, away from an order that is based on power, diplomacy, and negotiation, towards a formalized order that is based on the application of legal principles to individual cases. This effectively disables States from deviating from their original agreement *ex post*. Investor-State arbitration as a compliance mechanism therefore contributes to understanding international investment law as an objective order that provides stable institutions for the functioning of a global market economy.

The tendencies to understand investment treaties as an expression of a treaty-overarching framework with uniform standards of investment protection is also visible in the way in which investment tribunals resolve disputes between States and investors. Arbitral tribunals regularly do not apply investment treaties as if they were bilateral treaties, but interpret them in a genuinely multilateral fashion.[14] They recognize that the treaties have common historical origins, follow the same object and purpose, and contain similar, if not identical, language. They also employ interpretative strategies that reflect an understanding of these treaties as part of a uniform regime. Above all, they do not interpret them as isolated bilateral bargains, but rather view them in connection with other third-party treaties. For example, they frequently draw analogies to the provisions of treaties between wholly unrelated State parties or draw *e contrario* arguments from differences in formulation between different BITs. This has the effect of embedding BITs into a framework for ordering international investment relations that overarches the individual bilateral treaty relations. Instead of isolating BITs, tribunals, thus, interpret and apply them as part of a system of treaties.

Similarly, arbitral tribunals make frequent reference to earlier awards in investment treaty arbitrations and accord an ever-increasing weight to precedent.[15] Reference to earlier awards is used independently of whether these awards concerned the same or a different investment

---

[13] See *supra* Ch. VI.A.   [14] See *supra* Ch. VII.B.   [15] See *supra* Ch. VII.C.

treaty. Although tribunals deny that precedent is formally binding under a *de iure* rule of *stare decisis*, the use of precedent creates a body of case law that is applied independently from the governing treaty relationship. In particular, with respect to investor rights, such as fair and equitable treatment or indirect expropriation, precedent is used to concretize the rather broad and openly worded principles of international investment protection.

The use of precedent also entails a transfer in the law-making power from States to tribunals, as it is not so much the States who decide *ex ante* whether certain conduct violates the legal standards on which they agreed.[16] Instead, it is primarily the tribunals that interpret and concretize these standards *ex post* and thus fill the very general principles with more precise normative content. In view of the increasing influence of precedent in investment arbitration, this approximates arbitral tribunals to international legislators who make rules for every bilateral investment treaty relation, not only the one that governs the specific dispute at hand.

To a large extent, the regime established by bilateral investment treaties therefore approximates a truly multilateral system which is based on a single multilateral treaty. It is based on rather uniform general principles and disposes of a compliance mechanism that ensures their implementation. While the argument is not that all BITs are identical, one can observe a significant convergence on the level of the texts of the treaties that is complemented by various mechanisms that mitigate differences in scope and wording, including MFN clauses, the possibility of corporate structuring, and the modes of treaty interpretation and application by arbitral tribunals. The convergence and multilateralization of BITs, therefore, lies mostly in a convergence of general investment law principles like non-discrimination, fair and equitable treatment, the protection against direct and indirect expropriation, and investor-State dispute settlement, rather than in a convergence of all minor details contained in investment treaties.

In certain respects, however, the existing international investment regime falls short of a truly multilateral system. Because of the bilateral form of investment treaties, diversions are possible and not every host State adheres to exactly the same standards of investment protection. Host States have the competence to determine a different level of investment protection if they choose. Depending on the negotiation power, host

---

[16] See *supra* Ch. VI.B.

States can tailor investment treaties so as to diverge from the standard content and scope of investment protection. This has, for example, been the case with the old generation investment treaties of the People's Republic of China.[17] In addition, the possibilities of multiple proceedings under different investment treaties, depending on the corporate structure of a foreign investment project, constitute a factor that is due to the bilateral form of investment treaties. Finally, because of the lack of a hierarchically structured dispute settlement mechanism, the danger of inconsistent decisions by arbitral tribunals persists. This danger also recollects the bilateral pedigree of international investment treaties. In order to constitute a purely multilateral system, investment treaties and investment treaty arbitration would, therefore, require a change in the form of the sources of investment law from the current bilateral form into a truly multilateral treaty. Notwithstanding, divergences and inconsistencies in treaty practice and arbitral jurisprudence are generally rather insignificant and do not counter the claim that the existing framework is progressively multilateralizing and yields multilateral rather than bilateral rationales, despite the predominance of bilateral treaty instruments.

B Toward a universal regime of investment protection

The choice between bilateralism and multilateralism in international investment relations was not conditioned by the desire and need to establish flexible and differentiated standards for different countries and different bilateral relationships. In fact, this flexibility for *quid pro quo* bargaining would have prevented investment treaties from effectively establishing institutions for the functioning of market structures on a global level. The proliferation of BITs was also not conditioned by potential enforcement advantages of bilateral obligations nor by advantages in resolving uncertainty in the interpretation of bilateral treaties. Both of these issues are resolved through investor-State dispute settlement that serves as an enforcement mechanism for BIT obligations and constitutes a procedure for resolving uncertainty in international investment law.

Instead, the institutional choice in favor of bilateralism resulted from the negotiation deadlock between capital-exporting and capital-importing States in multilateral negotiations. Even though an interest in uniform rules existed, States initially could not agree on the distribution of

---

[17] See *supra* Ch. III footnotes 129–30 and accompanying text.

investor rights and State sovereignty. While capital-exporting countries aimed at establishing strong and stable institutions for the protection of their investors abroad, capital-importing countries were primarily concerned with the perceived encroachment of investment protection schemes on their sovereignty. Accordingly, the failure of multilateral negotiations until the 1970s was due to the politico-ideological conflict about the function of the State in relation to the economy and the potential limits of its power to interfere in the economic activities of private actors. While capital-exporting countries were largely guided by liberal ideals about the relationship between the State and the market and focused on the State's limitation, capital-importing countries emphasized the sovereignty of the State in organizing its economy and in the treatment of foreign investors. This reflected to a large extent the East–West conflict between socialism and liberalism, but also the concern of decolonized, newly independent States to uphold their independence in economic matters.

Capital-exporting countries finally resolved the resulting negotiation deadlock in multilateral settings by abandoning such projects and shifting their endeavors to the conclusion of BITs without, however, altering the standards of investment protection at which they aimed. Although this negotiation strategy was more time-consuming and more costly than negotiating and concluding a multilateral treaty, it ultimately proved to be more conducive towards reaching the desired result. The triggering factor in changing the form of ordering international investment relations from multilateralism to bilateralism can, therefore, be explained by the ability of capital-exporting countries to forge bilateral treaties with a content they could not achieve in multilateral negotiations. Consequently, there were elements of hegemonic behavior at play concerning the dissection of the negotiation process into bilateral segments.

Yet, over time BITs were not only adopted between developed and developing countries but also amongst developing countries and amongst developed countries, without however involving different principles of investment protection. This suggests that even those developing countries that were initially opposed to foreign investment protection accepted BITs as appropriate for governing international investment relations, independent of whether developed or developing countries are involved as contracting parties. The same conclusion has to be drawn when considering that traditional capital-exporting countries enter into investment treaties with other capital-exporters. In sum, the patterns of investment treaty practice suggest that there is an increasingly stable and lasting consensus among States that BITs strike an appropriate balance between, on the one hand, sovereign rights and, on the other hand, the protection of foreign investors.

Even though elements of hegemonic behavior of capital-exporting countries were at play in switching from multilateral to bilateral negotiations of investment treaties, a strong counter-argument against this hegemonic critique stems from the claim that BITs establish a regime that aspires toward general validity and subjects all States to the same set of rules. It is, thus, particularly noteworthy that BITs are based on general principles that apply independently of the nature of States as capital-importing or capital-exporting countries. Certainly, investment treaties initially focused on attracting foreign investment into developing countries and *de facto* only imposed restrictions on capital-importing countries.

Yet, this perspective is gradually changing as traditional capital-exporting countries are becoming, with progressing globalization, targets of foreign investment flows from developed and developing economies. Accordingly, the effect of BITs on developed countries is increasingly felt as they become respondents in investor-State disputes. Moreover, investors in developed countries can avail themselves of investment treaty protection by structuring their investments through subsidiaries in third-country jurisdictions that have entered into an investment treaty with the respective target State. Overall, international investment law, is therefore, not only multilateralizing but also developing toward an increasingly universal regime that can come into play independently of the sources and targets of foreign investment flows. This suggests a change in paradigm in viewing investment treaties less as part of development politics, but as instruments for the stabilization of the global economy that limits the leeway of developing and developed countries in interfering with economic activities.

BITs are, thus, not about dominating developing countries, but about establishing a regime that supports international investment cooperation and aims at implementing structures that are essential for the functioning of a global market economy. National and MFN treatment aim at ensuring a level playing field for foreign and domestic economic actors and are a prerequisite for competition. The protection against uncompensated expropriation guarantees respect for property rights as an essential institution for market transactions. Capital transfer guarantees ensure the free flow of capital and contribute to the efficient allocation of resources in a global market. Umbrella clauses back up private ordering between foreign investors and host States. Fair and equitable treatment and full protection and security ensure basic due process rights for foreign investors, enshrine the concept of the rule of law, and require adequate protection against threats to investors by private parties. Finally, the availability of recourse to investor-State arbitration represents a mechanism that allows foreign investors to enforce compliance with investment treaty obligations.

Finally, another development is noteworthy that suggests the emancipation of international investment law from transborder investment flows and its development toward a universal framework for structuring the relation between the State and the economy in general. Although investment treaties directly apply only to foreign investors – possibilities of corporate structuring notwithstanding – they indirectly also affect government conduct vis-à-vis domestic investors. Arguably, the limits that investment treaties impose on government conduct vis-à-vis foreign investors will gradually also become available to domestic actors as a matter of domestic law as separate systems for local and foreign investors will be more costly, or even impossible, to maintain compared with a uniform system. Consequently, distinctions between foreign and national investors should progressively disappear with respect to the treatment they actually receive. BITs thus create an incentive for States to support legal reform developments that ensure good governance standards not only vis-à-vis aliens but investment activities in general.

C   The constitutional function of international investment law

Understanding international investment protection as a multilateral system has implications for construing a general theory of international investment law. It suggests that we can understand international investment law as a system that behaves according to uniform rationales and establishes a uniform order for international investment relations. This also has implications for the application of BITs by arbitral tribunals and provides a genuine justification for interpreting investment treaties based on multilateral rationales. Instead of understanding them as contract-like *quid pro quo* bargains, they should be viewed as instruments establishing uniform principles for the protection of foreign investment. Accordingly, the standards of fair and equitable treatment, national treatment, indirect expropriation, etc., in any of the more than 2,500 BITs have to be understood as referring to the identical principles that impose identical obligations on the State parties involved. Consequently, BITs have to be interpreted like a multilateral treaty by emphasizing the objective content of such principles, not by engaging in a quest for the (often presumed) intention of the two contracting State parties to a specific BIT.

Unlike contracts, international investment law can thus be understood as serving a constitutional function for the emerging global economy.[18] Like constitutions, they restrict State action and, as part of an international public order, create and safeguard the interests of an international community in the functioning of the global economic system. Investment treaties comprise constitutional traits by establishing legal principles that serve as a yardstick for the conduct of States vis-à-vis foreign investors. Furthermore, investment treaties establish standards that can be effectively implemented by means of investor-State arbitration. This constitutional function is, however, subject to two limitations: first, investment treaties constitute a special regime for foreign investors; and, second, only entitle to damages in case the host State violates its obligations without assuming normative supremacy. Nevertheless, damages as a remedy sufficiently pressure States into complying with and incorporating the normative guidelines of investment treaties into their domestic legal order. Finally, opting out of the system is rather difficult, as it is not sufficient to terminate one single BIT. Instead, a country will have to sever all of its investment treaty relations, given that investors can restructure their investments so as come under the protective umbrella of a different BIT of the same host State.

Stressing the constitutional function of investment treaties also helps to shift focus in a critical analysis of investment arbitration. Instead of focusing exclusively on the dichotomy between investor rights and State sovereignty as a paradigm for structuring the debate about international investment law, the focus should equally be directed towards the relationship between the State and the global economy. In this context, one should not only ask how the interests of investors and host States are balanced, but also how international investment law and its compliance mechanisms affect the position of States vis-à-vis the economy as a whole and which concept of the State serves as a guiding paradigm in the era of globalization.

Against this backdrop, the relationship between States and investment tribunals has to be addressed. The institutional structure of investment arbitration, coupled with the vagueness of the substantive provisions of

---

[18] See, for the understanding of the "constitutional function" referred to in this context, *supra* Ch. I footnote 41.

investment treaties, has to be understood as a shift in power from States to arbitral tribunals. The function of investment tribunals is not restricted to applying pre-existing principles to the facts of a case, but rather involves developing more precise rules that govern international investment relations. Standards like fair and equitable treatment or the concept of indirect expropriation serve as "general clauses" that effectively transfer substantial rule-making power to arbitral bodies that are established on a case-by-case basis and that lack genuine democratic legitimacy to develop restrictions for public acts of States under international law. The power shift from States to tribunals becomes all the more clear when considering the restrictions States face in influencing the direction of the jurisprudence of investment tribunals. Limitations in influence regarding the appointment of arbitrators, the arbitral process, and the enforcement of arbitral awards essentially leave States little room to counterbalance the authority investment tribunals exercise. Above all, unlike in the domestic context, there is no legislator for international investment law that could easily counteract mis-developments of the arbitral jurisprudence.[19]

The considerable power that has been conferred upon investment tribunals has led several commentators to question the suitability of investor-State arbitration as a mechanism by which to review public acts of host States.[20] While this critique raises salient concerns with respect to the accountability of arbitrators for the power they exercise over States and suggests the establishment of a standing judicial body,[21] it seems unlikely that the general features of the system of international investment protection, including its compliance mechanism through inter-State arbitration, are going to change fundamentally in the foreseeable future. Despite the emergence of new hesitances vis-à-vis investment treaties both in developing and developed countries,[22] they are still being concluded at a remarkable pace and – almost without exception – rely on investor-State dispute settlement as a compliance mechanism.

With the current system of investment protection and dispute resolution likely to stay in place it, therefore, seems more viable to consider

---

[19] Cf., in the context of WTO law, von Bogdandy, *Law and Politics in the WTO*, 5 Max Planck U.N. Ybk. 609 (2001).

[20] See, for example, Been and Beauvais, *The Global Fifth Amendment?*, 78 N.Y.U. L. Rev. 30 (2003); Poirier, *The NAFTA Chapter 11 Expropriation Debate through the Eyes of a Property Theorist*, 33 Environmental Law 851 (2003). Most recently Van Harten, *Investment Treaty Arbitration and Public Law*, pp. 152 *et seq.* (2007).

[21] See van Harten (*supra* footnote 20), pp. 180 *et seq.* (2007).

[22] See van Aaken, *Perils of Success?*, 9 Eur. Bus. Org. L. Rev. 1 (2008).

ways of improving the system and of legitimizing its activity from within. The aim must be to develop concepts that enhance the predictability of investment arbitration and make the decisions of investment tribunals comprehensible and acceptable for States and investors alike. Part of this effort must be to balance the power of tribunals and those of the States that established and support the current system of investment treaty arbitration.

One prong to enhancing the legitimacy of investment arbitration by restraining the power of tribunals over States can consist in defining more closely the tribunals' standard of review for State action in a way that accommodates the need for State regulation and allows States to pursue legitimate policy goals. An approach to defining the appropriate standard of review could be fueled by drawing analogies with domestic legal frameworks regarding the scrutiny by constitutional courts of the conduct of the *pouvoirs constitués* or the standard of review used by courts regarding the conduct of administrative bodies. Similarly, comparisons with other international law regimes that encompass judicialized dispute settlement procedures, such as human rights regimes or the WTO, can be helpful in this context.

One possible option could consist in developing, parallel to other dispute settlement bodies that decide on the conformity of State conduct with international law, a margin of appreciation doctrine in investment treaty arbitration.[23] This could fulfill the dual purpose of subjecting States to judicially monitored compliance with investment treaties, while allowing for a certain degree of deference towards the decisions taken on the domestic level.[24] This allows developing mechanisms to balance the distribution of power between States and investment tribunals and can result in "less intrusive and, by implication, more politically acceptable and cost-effective standards of review of national decisions."[25] Developing a margin of appreciation doctrine in investment treaty arbitration seems particularly suitable because it could help mitigate the

---

[23] See Yourow, *The Margin of Appreciation Doctrine in the Dynamics of European Human Rights Jurisprudence* (1996); Arai-Takahashi, *The Margin of Appreciation Doctrine and the Principle of Proportionality in the Jurisprudence of the ECHR* (2002); see also Shany, *Toward a General Margin of Appreciation Doctrine in International Law*, 16 Eur. J. Int'l L. 907, 926 *et seq.* (2005).

[24] Shany (*supra* footnote 23), 16 Eur. J. Int'l L. 907, 908 (2005). Furthermore, the heightened democratic legitimacy of domestic institutions militates for the development of a margin of appreciation doctrine. See *ibid.*, at 918 *et seq.*

[25] *Ibid.*, 16 Eur. J. Int'l L. 907, 909 (2005).

reproach that investment tribunals are exercising unpredictable *ex post facto* control of host State conduct. A margin of appreciation doctrine could procedurally rebalance the power relationship between States and tribunals and accommodate sufficient leeway for substantive policy-making of host States. While States would generally be free to organize their polity according to self-determined standards, investment tribunals would be charged with ensuring that States do not surpass the outer limits imposed by investment treaties on the means of their policy-making. Although some tentative strategies to develop such a doctrine already exist in the arbitral jurisprudence, such an approach should receive stronger emphasis in order to draw the line between the domain of investment tribunals and the power of States.[26]

Apart from procedurally rebalancing the relations between tribunals and States, another aspect of enhancing the legitimacy of investment treaty arbitration consists in efforts to concretize and conceptualize the normative content of the substantive investor rights. This task would most appropriately be addressed by developing a theory of investment law principles that is based on the insight that investment law is a body of law not isolated to bilateral treaty relationships, but one that forms part of an overarching system of investment protection. Developing a theory of principles would contribute to reducing the perceived unpredictability of many of the concepts of investment protection and would thus strengthen the legitimacy of international investment law.[27] This is a task not only for investment tribunals, but also, and maybe foremost, for scholarship and doctrine.

A methodological approach for achieving this aim could consist in concretizing the principles of international investment protection like fair and equitable treatment, indirect expropriation, or national treatment, on the basis of a comparative law approach that focuses on the contribution of legal institutions to the functioning of a market economy and is supplemented by interdisciplinary approaches, such as economic analysis and institutional economics. Comparative approaches in this respect can draw on both domestic legal systems, in particular constitutional

---

[26] See *Pope & Talbot* v. *Canada*, Award on the Merits of Phase 2, April 10, 2001, para. 155; *S. D. Myers* v. *Canada*, Partial Award, November 13, 2000, paras. 261, 263; *Tecmed* v. *Mexico*, Award, May 29, 2003, para. 122; *ADF* v. *United States*, Award, January 9, 2003, para. 190; *Mondev* v. *United States*, Award, October 11, 2002, para. 136; *Azinian* v. *Mexico*, Final Award, November 1, 1999, para. 99.

[27] Cf. von Bogdandy, *Europäische Prinzipienlehre*, in von Bogdandy (ed.), *Europäisches Verfassungsrecht*, p. 149 (2003) (for the related claim in the context of a theory of principles of European constitutional law).

principles that structure the State–market relationship, such as domestic property rights, contract enforcement, and the rule of law, as well as cross-regime comparisons with other international law regimes that govern aspects of the emerging global economy, including the WTO regime and human rights treaties. Drawing analogies to these seemingly unrelated fields of law is justified if one understands investment treaties as part of a larger international law structure that establishes institutions for the functioning of a global society. As part of this larger framework, investment treaties reflect and share certain commonalities with other international regimes that organize the relationship between States, the international community (or international society), and specific functional sub-systems, such as the global economy.

A way of re-injecting legitimacy and normative content into the system of international investment protection also has to take into account how investment treaties are situated in the politico-ideological debate about the relation between the State and its economy. Arguably, the model that has been at the core of the movement towards introducing international investment protection from the very start was the liberal model that departed from a rights-based approach to the relation between the State and society and that endorsed a market-based approach to organizing the economic system. Parallel to the traditions of liberal constitutionalism and its take on the relationship between the State and the market, between society as a whole and the individual, the basic purpose of investment treaties is therefore twofold. First, they aim at restraining governments with respect to interference in the economic activity of private actors and restrict the State's sovereign power. Second, investment treaties aim at binding States into a legal framework that gives them an incentive and a yardstick for transforming their legal systems into ones that are conducive to market-based investment activities and provide the institutions necessary for the functioning of such markets. The underlying goal, in this context, is the establishment of a legal infrastructure that creates economic growth and development.

In serving as a substitute for the inability of many States to establish such legal institutions, BITs are informed by, and ultimately aim at, transforming the relationship between the State and the market along the lines of a liberal perspective that is based on notions of property protection and rule of law standards. This does not, however, mean that market considerations will or should dominate over legitimate interests of host States and their respective constituencies. Rather, the order that investment treaties aim at requires that investment protection is given due regard in situations of conflict between public and private interests. Investment protection, therefore, does not take precedence over competing public interests of host State policy-making, but requires a reasonable balance between them. In order to achieve and operationalize this balance and to illustrate how property protection and the requirement of government according to the rule of law interact with competing public welfare aspects, such as environmental protection, human rights protection, labor standards, or the protection of public morals, an apposite analogy can again be drawn to constitutional principles in domestic legal orders, such as proportionality analysis and reasoning.

On this basis and with this perspective in mind, investment treaties are less threatening to State sovereignty than is often assumed. Instead, investment treaties and the substantive standards of treatment they establish are able to accommodate a balanced relationship between investment protection and competing public interests. While a theory of investment law principles is in a position to develop more closely the concrete balances that are to be struck, the multilateralization of investment relations, which is outlined in the present contribution, furnishes the framework in which to perceive investment treaties as constituting a uniform system of investment protection that is developing into an increasingly universal scope of application and that is able to serve a constitutional function for a global economy in requiring States to furnish and abide by the legal institutions necessary for this objective.

BIBLIOGRAPHY

Aaken, Anne van, *To Do Away with International Law?*, 17 E.J.I.L 289 (2006).
Zwischen Scylla und Charybdis: Völkerrechtlicher Staatsnotstand und Internationaler Investitionsschutz, 105 Zeitschrift für Vergleichende Rechtswissenschaft (ZVglRWiss) 544 (2006).
Perils of Success? The Case of International Investment Protection, 9 Eur. Bus. Org. L. Rev. 1 (2008).

Abbott, Frederick M., *A New Dominant Trade Species Emerges: Is Bilateralism a Threat?*, 10 J. Int'l Econ. L. 571 (2007).

Abs, Hermann J., *Proposals for Improving the Protection of Private Foreign Investments* (1958).

Acconci, Pia, *Determining the Internationally Relevant Link between a State and a Corporate Investor – Recent Trends Concerning the Application of the "Genuine Link" Test*, 5 J. World Inv. & Trade 139 (2004).
The Most Favoured Nation Treatment and the International Law on Foreign Investment, 2(5) Transnat'l Disp. Mgmt. (2005).

Acemoglu, Daron, Simon Johnson and James Robinson, *Institutions as the Fundamental Cause of Long-Run Growth*, in Philippe Aghion and Steven N. Durlauf (eds.), *Handbook of Economic Growth*, vol. 1A, p. 385 (2005).

Aceves, William J., *The Economic Analysis of International Law: Transaction Cost Economics and the Concept of State Practice*, 17 U. Pa. J. Int'l Econ. L. 995 (1996).

Afilalo, Ari, *Constitutionalization Through the Backdoor: A European Perspective on NAFTA's Investment Chapter*, 34 N.Y.U. J. Int'l L. & Pol. 1 (2001).
Towards a Common Law of International Investment: How NAFTA Chapter 11 Panels Should Solve Their Legitimacy Crisis, 17 Geo. Int'l Envt'l L. Rev. 51 (2004).
Meaning, Ambiguity and Legitimacy: Judicial (Re-)construction of NAFTA Chapter 11, 25 Nw. J. Int'l L. & Bus. 279 (2005).

Aldrich, George H., *The Jurisprudence of the Iran–United States Claims Tribunal* (1996).

Alenfeld, Justus, *Die Investitionsförderungsverträge der Bundesrepublik Deutschland* (1971).

Alexandrov, Stanimir A., *Breaches of Contract and Breaches of Treaty*, 5 J. World Inv. & Trade 555 (2004).

The "Baby Boom" of Treaty-Based Arbitrations and the Jurisdiction of ICSID Tribunals: Shareholders as "Investors" under Investment Treaties, 6 J. World Inv. & Trade 387 (2005).

Alford, Roger P., *The Proliferation of International Courts and Tribunals: International Adjudication in Ascendance*, 94 Am. Soc'y Int'l L. Proc. 160 (2000).

Alsop, Richard B., *The World Bank's Multilateral Investment Guarantee Agency*, 25 Colum. J. Transnat'l L. 101 (1986).

Altieri, Laura, *Trade and Economic Affairs: NAFTA and the FTAA: Regional Alternatives to Multilateralism*, 21 Berkeley J. Int'l L. 847 (2003).

Alvarez, José E., *Critical Theory and the North American Free Trade Agreement's Chapter Eleven*, 28 U. Miami Inter-Am. L. Rev. 303 (1996–1997).

Multilateralism and Its Discontents, 11 Eur. J. Int'l L. 393 (2000).

Alvarez, Guillermo Aguilar and William Park, *The New Face of Investment Arbitration: NAFTA Chapter 11*, 28 Yale J. Int'l L. 365 (2003).

Amerasinghe, Chittharanjan F., *Local Remedies in International Law* (2nd edn. 2004)

Diplomatic Protection (2008).

Anderlini, Luca and Leonardo Felli, *Incomplete Written Contracts: Undescribable States of Nature*, 109 Quart. J. Econ. 1085 (1994).

Arad, Ruth and Seev Hirsch, *Peacemaking and Vested Interests: International Economic Transactions*, 25 Int'l Stud. Quart. 439 (1981).

and Alfred Tovias, *The Economics of Peacemaking: Focus on the Egyptian–Israeli Situation* (1983).

Arai-Takahashi, Yutaka, *The Margin of Appreciation Doctrine and the Principle of Proportionality in the Jurisprudence of the ECHR* (2002).

Avramovich, Michael P., *The Protection of International Investment at the Start of the Twenty-First Century: Will Anachronistic Notions of Business Render Irrelevant the OECD's Multilateral Agreement on Investment?*, 31 John Marshall L. Rev. 1201 (1998).

Axarloglou, Kostas and Mike Pournarakis, *Do All Foreign Direct Investment Flows Benefit the Local Economy?*, 30 World Econ. 424 (2007).

Baklanoff, Eric N., *Expropriation of U.S. Investments in Cuba, Mexico, and Chile* (1975).

Baldwin, Richard E., *Multilateralising Regionalism: Spaghetti Bowls as Building Blocs on the Path to Global Free Trade*, 29 World Econ. 1451 (2006).

Banz, Michael, *Völkerrechtlicher Eigentumsschutz durch Investitionsschutzabkommen – insbesondere die Praxis der Bundesrepublik Deutschland seit 1959* (1988).

Barnhart, Michael A., *Japan Prepares for Total War, The Search for Economic Security 1919–1941* (1987).

Battigalli, Pierpaolo and Giovanni Maggi, *Rigidity, Discretion, and the Costs of Writing Contracts*, 92 Am. Econ. Rev. 798 (2002).

Baumann, Rainer, *Der Wandel des deutschen Multilateralismus* (2006).

Beauvais, Joel C., *Regulatory Expropriations Under NAFTA: Emerging Principles and Lingering Doubts*, 10 N.Y.U. Envt'l L. J. 245 (2001–2002).

Beck, Ulrich, *What is Globalization?* (2000).

Been, Vicki L. and Joel C. Beauvais, *The Global Fifth Amendment? NAFTA's Investment Protections and the Misguided Quest for an International "Regulatory Takings" Doctrine*, 78 N.Y.U. L. Rev. 30 (2003).

Behrens, Peter, *Wirtschaftsverfassungsrechtliche Ansätze im völkerrechtlichen Investitionsschutz*, in Christoph Engel and Wernhard Möschel (eds.), *Recht und spontane Ordnung – Festschrift für Ernst-Joachim Mestmäcker zum achzigsten Geburtstag*, p. 53 (2006).

Towards the Constitutionalization of International Investment Protection, 45 Archiv des Völkerrechts (AVR) 153 (2007).

Ben Hamida, Walid, *Clause de la nation la plus favorisée et mécanismes de règlement des différends: que dit l'histoire?*, 134 Journal du Droit International (J.D.I.) 1127 (2007).

MFN and Procedural Rights: Solutions from WTO Experience?, in Todd Weiler (ed.), *Investment Treaty Arbitration and International Law*, p. 231 (2008).

Bénassy-Quéré, Agnès, Maylis Coupet and Thierry Mayer, *Institutional Determinants of Foreign Direct Investment*, 30 World Econ. 764 (2007).

Benvenisti, Eyal, *The Conception of International Law as a Legal System*, 50 German Ybk. Int'l L. 393 (2008).

Benvenisti, Eyal, and George W. Downs, *The Empire's New Clothes: Political Economy and the Fragmentation of International Law*, 60 Stan. L. Rev. 595 (2007).

Berman, Nathaniel, *A Perilous Ambivalence: Nationalist Desire, Legal Autonomy, and the Limits of the Interwar Framework*, 33 Harv. Int'l L. J. 353 (1992).

But the Alternative is Despair: European Nationalism and the Modernist Renewal of International Law, 106 Harv. L. Rev. 1792 (1993).

Bhagwati, Jagdish, *The New International Economic Order: The North–South Debate* (1978).

The World Trading System at Risk (1991).

Regionalism and Multilateralism: An Overview, in Jaime de Melo and Arvind Panagariya (eds.), *New Dimensions in Regional Integration*, p. 22 (1993).

Preferential Trade Agreements: The Wrong Road, 27 L. & Pol'y Int'l Bus. 865 (1996).

Why Multinationals Help Reduce Poverty, 30 World Econ. 211 (2007).

Bhala, Raj, *The Myth about Stare Decisis and International Trade Law (Part One of a Trilogy)*, 14 Am. U. Int'l L. Rev. 845 (1999).

The Precedent Setters: De Facto Stare Decisis *in WTO Adjudication (Part Two of a Trilogy)*, 9 J. Transnat'l L. & Pol'y 1 (1999).

Global Trade Issues in the New Millennium: The Power of the Past: Towards de Jure Stare Decisis *in WTO Adjudication (Part Three of a Trilogy)*, 33 Geo. Wash. Int'l L. Rev. 873 (2001).

Bickel, Matthias, *Die Argentinien-Krise aus ökonomischer Sicht: Herausforderungen an Finanzsystem und Kapitalmarkt*, Beiträge zum Internationalen Wirtschaftsrecht, vol. 38 (2005), available at: www.telc. uni-halle.de/Heft38.pdf.

Bileski, Moritz, *Der Grundsatz der wirtschaftlichen Gleichberechtigung in den Mandatsgebieten*, 16 Zeitschrift für öffentliches Recht (ZöR) 214 (1936).

Birmingham, Robert L., *Breach of Contract, Damage Measures, and Economic Efficiency*, 24 Rutgers L. Rev. 273 (1970).

Bjorklund, Andrea K., *Contract Without Privity: Sovereign Offer and Investor Acceptance*, 2 Chi. J. Int'l L. 183 (2001).

Blackmore, Dana T., *Eradicating the Long Standing Existence of a No-Precedent Rule in International Trade Law – Looking Toward* Stare Decisis *in WTO Dispute Settlement*, 29 N.C. J. Int'l L. & Com. Reg. 487 (2004).

Bloomfield, Arthur I., *Patterns of Fluctuation in International Investment Before 1914* (1968).

Bogdandy, Armin von, *Law and Politics in the WTO – Strategies to Cope with a Deficient Relationship*, 5 Max Planck U.N. Ybk. 609 (2001).

Europäische Prinzipienlehre, in Armin von Bogdandy (ed.), *Europäisches Verfassungsrecht – theoretische und dogmatische Grundzüge*, p. 149 (2003).

Globalization and Europe: How to Square Democracy, Globalization, and International Law, 15 Eur. J. Int'l L. 885 (2004).

Böhmer, Alexander, *The Struggle for a Multilateral Agreement on Investments*, 41 German Ybk. Int'l L. 268 (1998).

Borchard, Edwin, *The Diplomatic Protection of Citizens Abroad or the Law of International Claims* (1915).

The "Minimum Standard" of Treatment of Aliens, 38 Mich. L. Rev. 446 (1940).

Bradlow, Daniel D. and Alfred Escher (eds.), *Legal Aspects of Foreign Direct Investment* (1999).

Braithwaite, John, *Methods of Power for Development: Weapons of the Weak, Weapons of the Strong*, 26 Mich. J. Int'l L. 297 (2004).

Brand, Ronald A., *GATT and the Evolution of United States Trade Law*, 18 Brook. J. Int'l L. 101 (1992).

Brandon, Michael, *An International Investment Code: Current Plans*, 3 J. Bus. L. 7 (1959).

Recent Measures to Improve the Investment Climate, 9 J. Pub. L. 125 (1960).

Survey of Current Approaches to the Problem, in *The Encouragement and Protection of Investment in Developing Countries*, Int'l & Comp. L. Q. Suppl. No. 3, p. 1 (1962).

Brandt, Helmut, *Durchbrechung der Meistbegünstigung – Ein Beitrag zu den Gegenwartsfragen der zwischenstaatlichen Wirtschaftsbeziehungen* (1933).

Brewer, Thomas L. and Stephen Young, *The Multilateral Investment System and Multinational Enterprises* (1998).

Broches, Aron, *The Convention on the Settlement of Investment Disputes between States and Nationals of Other States*, 136 Recueil des Cours 331 (1972–II).

Observations on the Finality of ICSID Awards, 6 ICSID Rev. – For. Inv. L. J. 321 (1991).

Brower, Charles H., *Structure, Legitimacy, and NAFTA's Investment Chapter*, 36 Vand. J. Transnat'l L. 37 (2003).

A Crisis of Legitimacy, Nat'l L. J., October 7, 2002

Brower, Charles N. and Jeremy K. Sharpe, *The Coming Crisis in the Global Adjudicative System*, 19 Arb. Int'l 415 (2003).

and Jason D. Brueschke, *The Iran–United States Claims Tribunal* (1998).

and John B. Tepe, *The Charter of Economic Rights and Duties of States: A Reflection or a Rejection of International Law?*, 9 Int'l Law. 295 (1975).

Burgstaller, Markus, *Nationality of Corporate Investors and International Claims against the Investor's Own State*, 7 J. World Inv. & Trade 857 (2006).

Burt, Eric M., *Developing Countries and the Framework for Negotiations on Foreign Direct Investment in the World Trade Organization*, 12 Am. U. Int'l L. Rev. 1015 (1997).

Buscaglia, Edgardo and Maria Dakolias, *An Analysis of the Causes of Corruption in the Judiciary*, 30 Law & Pol'y Int'l Bus. 95 (1999).

Buscaglia, Edgardo, William Ratcliff and Robert Cooter, *The Law and Economics of Development* (1997).

Büthe, Tim and Helen V. Milner, *The Politics of Foreign Direct Investment into Developing Countries: Increasing FDI through International Trade Agreements?*, 52 Am. J. Pol. Sc. 741 (2008).

Canaris, Claus-Wilhelm, *Systemdenken und Systembegriff in der Jurisprudenz* (1969).

Cançado Trindade, A. A., *The Application of the Rule of Exhaustion of Local Remedies in International Law* (1983).

Canner, Stephen J., *The Multilateral Agreement on Investment*, 31 Cornell Int'l L. J. 657 (1998).

Carkovic, Maria and Ross Levine, *Does Foreign Direct Investment Accelerate Economic Growth?*, in Theodore H. Moran, Edward M. Graham and Magnus Blomström, *Does Foreign Direct Investment Promote Development?*, p. 195 (2005).

Charney, Jonathan I., *The Impact on the International Legal System of the Growth of International Courts and Tribunals*, 31 N.Y.U. J. Int'l L. & Pol. 697 (1999).

Chatterjee, S. K., *The Convention Establishing the Multilateral Investment Guarantee Agency*, 36 Int'l & Comp. L. Q. 76 (1987).

Chimni, B. S., *Marxism and International Law – A Contemporary Analysis*, Economic and Political Weekly, p. 337 (February 6, 1999).

International Institutions Today: An Imperial Global State in the Making, 15 Eur. J. Int'l L. 1 (2004).

Choudhury, Barnali, *Evolution or Devolution? – Defining Fair and Equitable Treatment in International Investment Law*, 6 J. World Inv. & Trade 297 (2005).

Chowdhury, Abdur and George Mavrotas, *FDI and Growth: What Causes What?*, 29 World Econ. 9 (2006).

Christie, George C., *What Constitutes a Taking of Property under International Law?*, 38 Brit. Ybk. Int'l L. 307 (1962).

Chukwumerije, Okezie, *Interpreting Most-Favoured-Nation Clauses in Investment Treaty Arbitrations*, 8 J. World Inv. & Trade 597 (2007).

Chung, Olivia, *The Lopsided International Investment Law Regime and Its Effect on the Future of Investor-State Arbitration*, 47 Va. J. Int'l L. 953 (2007).

Civello, Paul, *The TRIMs Agreement: A Failed Attempt at Investment Liberalization*, 8 Minn. J. Global Trade 97 (1999).

Clagett, Brice M., *Title III of the Helms–Burton Act is Consistent with International Law*, 90 A.J.I.L. 434 (1996).

Commission, Jeffrey P., *Precedent in Investment Treaty Arbitration – A Citation Analysis of a Developing Jurisprudence*, 24 J. Int'l Arb. 129 (2007).

Compa, Lance, *The Multilateral Agreement on Investment and International Labor Rights: A Failed Connection*, 31 Cornell Int'l L. J. 683 (1998).

Cone III, Sydney M., *The Promotion of Free-Trade Areas Viewed in Terms of Most-Favored-Nation Treatment and "Imperial Preference"*, 26 Mich. J. Int'l L. 563 (2005).

Cooter, Robert, Stephen Marks and Robert Mnookin, *Bargaining in the Shadow of the Law*, 11 J. Legal Stud. 225 (1982).

Cooter, Robert and Thomas Ulen, *Law and Economics* (4th edn. 2004).

Corbridge, S. E. (ed.), *International Debt* (1999).

Corten, Olivier and Pierre Klein (eds.), *Les Conventions de Vienne sur le droit des traités – Commentaire article par article*, vol. II (2006).

Cremades, Bernardo, *Arbitration in Investment Treaties: Public Offer of Arbitration in Investment-Protection Treaties*, in Robert Briner, L. Yves Fortier, Klaus Peter Berger and Jens Bredow (eds.), *Law of International Business and Dispute Settlement in the 21st Century – Liber Amicorum Karl-Heinz Böckstiegel*, p. 149 (2001).

Curzon, Gerard, *Multilateral Commercial Diplomacy* (1965).

Dakolias, Maria and Kimberley L. Thachuk, *The Problem of Eradicating Corruption from the Judiciary: Attacking Corruption in the Judiciary: A Critical Process in Judicial Reform*, 18 Wis. Int'l L. J. 353 (2000).

Dammann, Jens C., *Amerikanische Gesellschaften mit Sitz in Deutschland*, 68 RabelsZ 607 (2004).

Dattu, Riyaz, *A Journey from Havana to Paris: The Fifty-Year Quest for the Elusive Multilateral Agreement on Investment*, 24 Fordham Int'l L. J. 275 (2000).

De Azcarate, P., *League of Nations and National Minorities* (trans. Eileen E. Brooke) (1945).

de Hoogh, André J. J., *Articles 4 and 8 of the 2001 ILC Articles on State Responsibility, the Tadić Case and Attribution of Acts of Bosnian Serb Authorities to the Federal Republic of Yugoslavia*, 72 Brit. Ybk. Int'l L. 255 (2001).

Delaume, Georges R., *ICSID-Arbitration and the Courts*, 77 A.J.I.L. 784 (1983).

Demaret, Paul, Jean-François Bellis and Gonzalo García Jiménez (eds.), *Regionalism and Multilateralism after the Uruguay Round: Convergence, Divergence and Interaction* (1997).

Denza, Eileen and Shelagh Brooks, *Investment Protection Treaties: United Kingdom Experience*, 36 Int'l & Comp. L. Q. 908 (1987).

Desai, Mihir A., C. Fritz Foley and James R. Hines Jr., *Foreign Direct Investment and the Domestic Capital Stock*, 95(2) Am. Econ. Rev. 33 (2005).

Domestic Effects of the Foreign Activities of U.S. Multinationals, 1 Am. Econ. J.: Econ. Pol'y 181 (2009).

Deutsch, Richard D. and Timothy Tylor, *Options for the Nervous Investor in Venezuela: Structuring for BIT Protection and Preserving the ICSID Option*, 5(2) Transnat'l Disp. Mgmt. (2008).

Di Rosa, Paola, *The Recent Wave of Arbitrations against Argentina under Bilateral Investment Treaties: Background and Principal Legal Issues*, 36 U. Miami Inter-Am. L. Rev. 41 (2004).

Diebold, William Jr., *The End of the ITO*, in Kym Anderson and Bernard Hoekman (eds.), *The Global Trading System, Vol. I: Genesis of the GATT*, pp. 81–111 (2002) (reprint of William Diebold Jr., *The End of the ITO*, Princeton Essays in International Finance No. 16 [1952]).

DiMascio, Nicholas and Joost Pauwelyn, *Nondiscrimination in Trade and Investment Treaties: Worlds Apart or Two Sides of the Same Coin?*, 102 A.J.I.L. 48 (2008).

Dolzer, Rudolf, *Eigentum, Enteignung und Entschädigung im geltenden Völkerrecht* (1985).

Indirect Expropriation of Alien Property, 1 ICSID Rev. – For. Inv. L. J. 41 (1986).

Indirect Expropriation: New Developments?, 11 N.Y.U. Envt'l L. J. 64 (2002).

Fair and Equitable Treatment: A Key Standard in Investment Treaties, 39 Int'l Law. 87 (2005).

Meistbegünstigungsklauseln in Investitionsschutzverträgen, in Jürgen Bröhmer, Roland Bieber, Christian Calliess, Christine Langenfeld, Stefan Weber and

Joachim Wolf (eds.), *Internationale Gemeinschaft und Menschenrechte – Festschrift für Georg Ress zum 70. Geburtstag*, p. 47 (2005).

The Notion of Investment in Recent Practice, in Steve Charnovitz, Debra P. Steger and Peter von den Bossche (eds.), *Law in the Service of Human Dignity: Essays in Honour of Florentino Feliciano*, p. 261 (2005).

Dolzer, Rudolf and Terry Myers, *After Tecmed: Most-Favoured-Nation Clauses in International Investment Protection Agreements*, 19 ICSID Rev. – For. Inv. L. J. 49 (2004).

and Christoph Schreuer, *Principles of International Investment Law* (2008).

Dolzer, Rudolf and Margrete Stevens, *Bilateral Investment Treaties* (1995).

Douglas, Zachary, *The Hybrid Foundations of Investment Treaty Arbitrations*, 74 Brit. Ybk. Int'l L. 151 (2003).

Nothing if Not Critical for Investment Treaty Arbitration: Occidental, Eureko *and* Methanex, 22 Arb. Int'l 27 (2006).

Drahos, Peter, *BITs and BIPs – Bilateralism in Intellectual Property*, 4 J. World Int. Prop. 791 (2001).

Drinhausen, Florian and Astrid Keinath, *Die grenzüberschreitende Verschmelzung inländischer Gesellschaften nach Erlass der Richtlinie zur grenzüberschreitenden Verschmelzung von Kapitalgesellschaften in Europa*, 52 Recht der Internationalen Wirtschaft (RIW) 81 (2006).

Dunoff, Jeffrey L., *Constitutional Conceits: The WTO's "Constitution" and the Discipline of International Law*, 17 Eur. J. Int'l L. 675 (2006).

Dye, Ronald A., *Costly Contract Contingencies*, 26 Int'l Econ. Rev. 233 (1985).

Easterly, William R., *The Elusive Quest for Growth: Economists' Adventures and Misadventures in the Tropics* (2002).

Ebenroth, Carsten Thomas, *Code of Conduct – Ansätze zur vertraglichen Gestaltung internationaler Investitionen* (1987).

Ebenroth, Carsten Thomas and Joachim Karl, *Die multilaterale Investitions-Garantie-Agentur* (1989).

Egger, Peter and Valeria Merlo, *The Impact of Bilateral Investment Treaties on FDI Dynamics*, 30 World Econ. 1536 (2007).

Egger, Peter and Michael Pfaffermayr, *The Impact of Bilateral Investment Treaties on Foreign Direct Investment*, 32 J. Comp. Econ. 788 (2004).

Elkins, Zachary, Andrew T. Guzman and Beth A. Simmons, *Competing for Capital: The Diffusion of Bilateral Investment Treaties, 1960–2000*, 60 Int'l Org. 811 (2006).

Engering, Frans, *The Multilateral Investment Agreement*, 5 Transnat'l Corp. 147 (December 1996).

Epstein, Richard A., *Takings: Private Property and the Power of Eminent Domain* (1985).

Escobar, Alejandro A., *Introductory Note on Bilateral Investment Treaties Recently Concluded by Latin American States*, 11 ICSID Rev. – For. Inv. L. J. 86 (1996).

Essig, Holger, *Balancing Investors' Interests and State Sovereignty: The ICSID-Decision on Jurisdiction* Plama Consortium Ltd. *v.* Republic of Bulgaria, 4(5) Transnat'l Disp. Mgmt. (2007).

Fatouros, Arghyrios A., *An International Code to Protect Private Investment – Proposals and Perspectives*, 14 U. Toronto L. J. 77 (1961).

Faya Rodriguez, Alejandro, *The Most-Favored-Nation Clause in International Investment Agreements – A Tool for Treaty Shopping?*, 25 J. Int'l Arb. 89 (2008).

Feldman, Mark B., *The Annulment Proceedings and the Finality of ICSID Arbitral Awards*, 2 ICSID Rev. – For. Inv. L. J. 85 (1987).

Ferguson, Julia, *California's MTBE Contaminated Water: An Illustration of the Need for an Environmental Interpretative Note on Article 1110 of NAFTA*, 11 Col. J. Int'l Envt'l L. & Pol'y 499 (2000).

Fietta, Stephen, *Most Favoured Nation Treatment and Dispute Resolution under Bilateral Investment Treaties: A Turning Point?*, 8 Int'l Arb. L. Rev. 131 (2005).

Fitzmaurice, Gerald, *The Law and Procedure of the International Court of Justice: Treaty Interpretation and Other Treaty Points*, 28 Brit. Ybk. Int'l L. 1 (1951).

The Law and Procedure of the International Court of Justice 1951–4: Treaty Interpretation and Other Treaty Points, 33 Brit. Ybk. Int'l L. 203 (1957).

Foighel, Isi, *Nationalization: A Study in the Protection of Alien Property in International Law* (1957).

Fortier, L. Yves and Stephen L. Drymer, *Indirect Expropriation in the Law of International Investment: I Know It When I See It, or Caveat Investor*, 19 ICSID Rev. – For. Inv. L. J. 293 (2004).

Foy, Patrick G., *Effectiveness of NAFTA's Chapter Eleven Investor-State Arbitration Procedures*, 18 ICSID Rev. – For. Inv. L. J. 44 (2003).

Franck, Susan D., *The Legitimacy Crisis in Investment Treaty Arbitration: Privatizing Public International Law through Inconsistent Decisions*, 73 Fordham L. Rev. 1521 (2005).

Frenzel, Ralf and Georg Axer, *EG-Mitgliedstaat durch die Hintertür?*, 53 Recht der Internationalen Wirtschaft (RIW) 47 (2007).

Freyer, Dana H. and David Herlihy, *Most-Favored-Nation Treatment and Dispute Settlement in Investment Arbitration: Just How "Favored" is "Most-Favored"?*, 20 ICSID Rev. – For. Inv. L. J. 58 (2005).

Frick, Helmut, *Bilateraler Investitionsschutz in Entwicklungsländern – ein Vergleich der Vertragssysteme der Vereinigten Staaten von Amerika und der Bundesrepublik Deutschland* (1975).

Friedman, Samy, *Expropriation in International Law* (1953).

Frowein, Jochen A. and Wolfgang Peukert, *Europäische Menschenrechtskonvention* (2nd edn. 1996).

Füracker, Matthias, *Relevance and Structure of Bilateral Investment Treaties – The German Approach*, 4 Zeitschrift für Schiedsverfahren / German Arb. J. (SchiedsVZ) 236 (2006).

Furubotn, Eirik G. and Rudolf Richter, *Institutions and Economic Theory: The Contribution of the New Institutional Economics* (1997).

Gaffney, John P. and James L. Loftis, *The "Effective Ordinary Meaning" of BITs and the Jurisdiction of Treaty-Based Tribunals to Hear Contract Claims*, 8 J. World Inv. & Trade 5 (2007).

Gagné, Gilbert and Jean-Frédéric Morin, *The Evolving American Policy on Investment Protection: Evidence from Recent FTAs and the 2004 Model BIT*, 9 J. Int'l Econ. L. 357 (2006).

Gaillard, Emmanuel, *Establishing Jurisdiction through a Most-Favored-Nation Clause*, 233 N.Y. L. J. 2 (June 2, 2005).

Gallagher, John and Robald Robinson, *The Imperialism of Free Trade*, 6 Econ. Hist. Rev. 1 (1953).

Gallagher, Kevin P. and Melissa B. L. Birch, *Do Investment Agreements Attract Investment? – Evidence from Latin America*, 7 J. World Inv. & Trade 961 (2006).

Gallus, Nick, *An Umbrella just for Two? BIT Obligations Observance Clauses and the Parties to a Contract*, 24 Arb. Int'l 157 (2008).

Ganguly, Samrat, *The Investor-State Dispute Mechanism (ISDM) and a Sovereign's Power to Protect Public Health*, 38 Colum. J. Transnat'l L. 113 (1999).

Gantz, David A., *Potential Conflicts Between Investor Rights and Environmental Regulation under NAFTA's Chapter 11*, 33 Geo. Wash. Int'l L. Rev. 651 (2001).

The Evolution of FTA Investment Provisions: From NAFTA to the United States–Chile Free Trade Agreement, 19 Am. U. Int'l L. Rev. 679 (2004).

An Appellate Mechanism for Review of Arbitral Decisions in Investor-State Disputes: Prospects and Challenges, 39 Vand. J. Transnat'l L. 39 (2006).

García-Bolívar, Omar E., *The Teleology of International Investment Law*, 6 J. World Invest. & Trade 751 (2005).

Gartzke, Erik, *Kant We All Just Get Along? Opportunity, Willingness, and the Origins of the Democratic Peace*, 42 Am. J. Pol. Sc. 1 (1998).

Gasioroswski, Mark and Solomon W. Polachek, *Conflict and Interdependence: East–West Trade and Linkages in the Era of Détente*, 26 J. Conflict Res. 709 (1982).

Geiger, Rainer, *Towards a Multilateral Agreement on Investment*, 31 Cornell Int'l L. J. 467 (1998).

Regulatory Expropriations in International Law: Lessons from the Multilateral Agreement on Investment, 11 N.Y.U. Envt'l L. J. 94 (2002).

Geist, Michael A., *Toward a General Agreement on the Regulation of Foreign Direct Investment*, 26 L. & Pol'y Int'l Bus. 673 (1995).

Genschel, Philipp and Thomas Plümper, *Wenn Reden Silber und Handeln Gold ist – Kooperation und Kommunikation in der internationalen Bankenregulierung*, 3 Zeitschrift für Internationale Beziehungen 225 (1996).

Regulatory Competition and International Co-operation, 4 J. Eur. Pub. Pol'y 626 (1997).

Gerig, Benjamin, *The Open Door and the Mandates System: A Study of Economic Equality Before and Since the Establishment of the Mandates System* (1930).

Gess, Karol N., *Permanent Sovereignty over Natural Resources: An Analytic Review of the United Nations Declaration and Its Genesis*, 13 Int'l & Comp. L. Q. 398 (1964).

Gilette, Clayton and Robert E. Scott, *The Political Economy of International Sales Law*, 25 Int'l Rev. L. & Econ. 446 (2005).

Ginsburg, Tom, *International Substitutes for Domestic Institutions: Bilateral Investment Treaties and Governance*, 25 Int'l Rev. L. & Econ. 107 (2005).

Glaeser, Edward L., Rafael La Porta, Florencio Lopez-de-Silanes and Andrei Shleifer, *Do Institutions Cause Growth?*, 9 J. Econ. Growth 271 (2004).

Goetz, Charles J. and Robert E. Scott, *Liquidated Damages, Penalties and the Just Compensation Principle: Some Notes on an Enforcement Model and a Theory of Efficient Breach*, 77 Colum. L. Rev. 554 (1977).

Gowa, Joanne S., *Allies, Adversaries and International Trade* (1994).

Graham, Edward M., *Regulatory Takings, Supernational Treatment, and the Multilateral Agreement on Investment: Issues Raised by Nongovernmental Organizations*, 31 Cornell Int'l L. J. 599 (1998).

Fighting the Wrong Enemy: Antiglobal Activists and Multinational Enterprises (2000).

Griebel, Jörn, *Jurisdiction over "Contract Claims" in Treaty-Based Investment Arbitration on the Basis of Wide Dispute Settlement Clauses in Investment Agreements*, 4(5) Transnat'l Disp. Mgmt. (2007).

Gruntzel, Josef, *Das System der Handelspolitik* (3rd edn. 1928).

Gudgeon, K. Scott, *United States Bilateral Investment Treaties: Comment on Their Origin, Purposes, and General Treatment Standards*, 4 Int'l Tax & Bus. L. 105 (1986).

Gudofsky, Jason L., *Shedding Light on Article 1110 of the North American Free Trade Agreement (NAFTA) Concerning Expropriations: An Environmental Case Study*, 21 Nw. J. Int'l L. & Bus. 243 (2000).

Gurudevan, Naveen, *An Evaluation of Current Legitimacy-based Objections to NAFTA's Chapter 11 Investment Dispute Resolution Process*, 6 San Diego Int'l L. J. 399 (2005).

Guzman, Andrew T., *Why LDCs Sign Treaties that Hurt Them: Explaining the Popularity of Bilateral Investment Treaties*, 38 Va. J. Int'l L. 639 (1998).

Hackworth, Green H., *Digest of International Law*, vol. III (1942).

Digest of International Law, vol. V (1943).

Hagelberg, Juliane, *Die völkerrechtliche Verfügungsbefugnis des Staates über Rechtsansprüche von Privatpersonen* (2006).

Hallward-Driemeier, Mary, *Do Bilateral Investment Treaties Attract Foreign Direct Investment? Only a bit ... and they could bite*, World Bank Policy Research, Working Paper Series No. WPS 3121 (2003).

Hanotiau, Bernard, *Complex Arbitrations: Multiparty, Multicontract, Multi-Issue and Class Actions* (2005).

Hansen, Henrik and John Rand, *On the Causal Links between FDI and Growth in Developing Countries*, 29 World Econ. 21 (2006).

Haraszti, Györgi, *Some Fundamental Problems of the Law of Treaties* (1973).

Hart, H. L. A., *The Concept of Law* (1961).

Hart, Jeffrey A., *The New International Economic Order: Conflict and Cooperation in North–South Economic Relations, 1974–77* (1983).

Hart, Oliver and John Moore, *Foundations of Incomplete Contracts*, 66 Rev. Econ. Stud. 115 (1999).

Hathaway, Oona A., *Path Dependence in the Law: The Course and Pattern of Legal Change in a Common Law System*, 86 Iowa L. Rev. 601 (2001).

Hawkins, Henry C., *Commercial Treaties and Agreements: Principles and Practice* (1951).

Helfer, Laurence R. and Anne-Marie Slaughter, *Toward a Theory of Effective Supranational Adjudication*, 107 Yale L. J. 273 (1997).

Henderson, David, *The MAI Affair: A Story and Its Lessons* (1999).

Herdegen, Matthias, *Investitionsschutz in Lateinamerika: Neuere Entwicklungen im Verfassungs- und Völkervertragsrecht*, 94 Zeitschrift für Vergleichende Rechtswissenschaft (ZVglRWiss) 341 (1995).

Higgins, Rosalyn, *The Taking of Property by the State: Recent Developments in International Law*, 176 Recueil des Cours 259 (1982).

Hilaire, Alvin and Yongzheng Yang, *The United States and the New Regionalism/ Bilateralism*, 38 J. World Trade 603 (2004).

Hilf, Meinhard and Ernst-Ulrich Petersmann (eds.), *National Constitutions and International Economic Law* (1993).

Hindelang, Steffen, *Bilateral Investment Treaties, Custom and a Healthy Investment Climate – The Question of Whether BITs Influence Customary International Law Revisited*, 5 J. World Inv. & Trade 789 (2004).

Hirschmann, Albert O., *National Power and the Structure of Foreign Trade* (1945).

Hock, Helmut, *Was hat man mit der Meistbegünstigung gewollt?* (1931).

Hofmann, Rainer, *Grundrechte und grenzüberschreitende Sachverhalte* (1994).

Horn, Norbert and Stefan Kröll (eds.), *Arbitrating Foreign Investment Disputes* (2004).

Hornbeck, S. K., *The Most-Favored-Nation Clause*, 3 A.J.I.L. 395 (1909).

Hosking, James M., *Non-Signatories and International Arbitration in the United States: The Quest for Consent*, 20 Arb. Int'l 289 (2004).

The Third Party Non-Signatory's Ability to Compel International Commercial Arbitration: Doing Justice Without Destroying Consent, 4 Pepp. Disp. Res. L. J. 469 (2004).

Houde, Marie-France and Fabrizio Pagani, *Most-Favoured-Nation Treatment in International Investment Law*, OECD Working Papers on International Investment 2004/2, available at: www.oecd.org/dataoecd/21/37/33773085. pdf.

Hsu, Locknie, *MFN and Dispute Settlement – When the Twain Meet*, 7 J. World Inv. & Trade 25 (2006).

Hughes, Layla, *Limiting the Jurisdiction of Dispute Settlement Panels: The WTO Appellate Body Beef Hormone Decision*, 10 Geo. Int'l Envt'l L. Rev. 915 (1998).

Hurrell, Andrew and Amrita Narlikar, *A New Politics of Confrontation? Brazil and India in Multilateral Trade Negotiations*, 20 Global Society 415 (2006).

Hylton, Keith N., *Fee Shifting and Incentives to Comply with the Law*, 46 Vand. L. Rev. 1069 (1993).

Jackson, John H., *Global Economics and International Economic Law*, 1 J. Int'l Econ. L. 1 (1998).

The Changing Fundamentals of International Law and Ten Years of the WTO, 8 J. Int'l Econ. L. 3 (2005).

Sovereignty, the WTO and Changing Fundamentals of International Law (2006).

Jacobs, Francis G., *Varieties of Approach to Treaty Interpretation: With Special Reference to the Draft Convention on the Law of Treaties Before the Vienna Diplomatic Conference*, 18 Int'l & Comp. L. Q. 318 (1969).

Jahnke, L. G., *The European Economic Community and the Most-Favoured-Nation Clause*, 1 Can. Ybk. Int'l L. 252 (1963).

Jastrow, Ignaz, *Die mitteleuropäische Zollannäherung und die Meistbegünstigung* (1915).

Jawara, Fatoumata and Ailee Kwa, *Behind the Scenes at the WTO: The Real World of International Trade Negotiations – the Lessons of Cancun* (updated edition 2004).

Jayasuriya, Kanishka, *Globalization, Sovereignty, and the Rule of Law: From Political to Economic Constitutionalism?*, 8 Constellations 442 (2001).

Jennings, Robert, *State Contracts in International Law*, 37 Brit. Ybk. Int'l L. 156 (1961).

Juillard, Patrick, *Lomé III et l'investissement international*, 29 Revue du Marché Commun 217 (1986).

Le reseau français des conventions bilatérales d'investissements: à la recherche d'un droit perdu?, 13 Droit et Pratique du Commerce International 9 (1987).

L'évolution des sources du droit des investissements, 250 Recueil des Cours 9 (1994–VI).

Kahn, Philippe and Thomas W. Wälde (eds.), *Les aspects nouveaux du droit des investissements internationaux – New Aspects of International Investment Law* (2007).

Kalicki, Jean and Suzana Medeiros, *Fair, Equitable and Ambiguous: What Is Fair and Equitable Treatment in International Investment Law?*, 22 ICSID Rev. – For. Inv. L. J. 24 (2007).

Kantor, Mark, *The New Draft Model U.S. BIT: Noteworthy Developments*, 21 J. Int'l Arb. 383 (2004).

Karl, Joachim, *The Promotion and Protection of German Foreign Investment Abroad*, 11 ICSID Rev. – For. Inv. L. J. 1 (1996).

Das multilaterale Investitionsabkommen (MAI), 44 Recht der Internationalen Wirtschaft (RIW) 432 (1998).

Internationaler Investitionsschutz – Quo vadis?, 99 Zeitschrift für Vergleichende Rechtswissenschaft (ZVglRWiss) 143 (2000).

On the Way to Multilateral Investment Rules – Some Recent Policy Issues, 17 ICSID Rev. – For. Inv. L. J. 293 (2002).

Kaufmann, Arthur, Winfried Hassemer and Ulfrid Neumann (eds.), *Einführung in Rechtsphilosophie und Rechtstheorie der Gegenwart* (7th edn. 2004).

Kaufmann-Kohler, Gabrielle, Laurence Boisson de Chazournes, Victor Bonnin and Makane Moïse Mbengue, *Consolidation of Proceedings in Investment Arbitration: How Can Multiple Proceedings Arising from the Same or Related Situations Be Handled Efficiently?*, 21 ICSID Rev. – For. Inv. L. J. 59 (2006).

Kelley, Glen, *Multilateral Investment Treaties: A Balanced Approach to Multinational Corporations*, 39 Colum. J. Transnat'l L. 483 (2001).

Kelsen, Hans, *The Pure Theory of Law* (trans. Max Knight) (1970).

Kenen, Peter B., *The International Economy* (4th edn. 2000).

Kennedy, Kevin C., *A WTO Agreement on Investment: A Solution in Search of a Problem?*, 24 U. Pa. J. Int'l Econ. L. 77 (2003).

Kerber, Wolfgang and Ulrich Schwalbe, *Economic Foundations of Competition Law*, in Franz-Jürgen Säcker, Frank Montag and Gunter Hirsch (eds.), *Competition Law: European Community Practice and Procedure*, p. 202 (2007).

Khalil, Mohamed I., *Treatment of Foreign Investment in Bilateral Investment Treaties*, 7 ICSID Rev. – For. Inv. L. J. 339 (1992).

Khandelwal, Padamja, *COMESA and SADC: Prospects and Challenges for Regional Trade Integration*, IMF Working Paper WP/04/227 (December 2004), available at: www.imf.org/external/pubs/ft/wp/2004/wp04227.pdf.

Kiem, Roger, *Die Regelung der grenzüberschreitenden Verschmelzung im deutschen Umwandlungsgesetz*, 60 Wertpapiermitteilungen / Zeitschrift für Wirtschafts-und Bankrecht (WM) 1091 (2006).

Kim, Sokchea, *Bilateral Investment Treaties, Political Risk, and Foreign Direct Investment*, 11 Asia Pac. J. Econ. & Bus. 1 (2006), also available at: http://ssrn.com/abstract=909760.

Kindleberger, Charles, *Commercial Policy between the Wars*, in Peter Mathias and Sidney Pollard (eds.), *The Cambridge Economic History of Europe*, vol. VIII, p. 161 (1989).

Kindler, Peter, *Internationales Handels- und Gesellschaftsrecht*, in Kurt Rebmann, Franz Jürgen Säcker and Roland Rixecker, *Münchener Kommentar zum Bürgerlichen Gesetzbuch*, vol. 11 (4th edn. 2006).

Kingsbury, Benedict, *Foreword: Is the Proliferation of International Courts and Tribunals a Systemic Problem?*, 31 N.Y.U. J. Int'l L. & Pol. 679 (1999).

Klein Bronfman, Marcela, *Fair and Equitable Treatment: An Evolving Standard*, 10 Max Planck U.N. Ybk. 609 (2006).

Kline, John M., *International Regulation of Transnational Business: Providing the Missing Leg of Global Investment Standards*, 2 Transnat'l Corp. 153 (February 1993).

Kobrin, Stephen, *The MAI and the Clash of Globalizations*, 112 Foreign Pol'y 97 (1998).

Kodama, Yoshi, *Asia-Pacific Region: APEC and ASEAN*, 30 Int'l Law. 367 (1996).

Koehane, Robert O., *Multilateralism: An Agenda for Research*, 45 Int'l J. 731 (1990).

Kojima, Kiyoshi, *Direct Foreign Investment: A Japanese Model of Multinational Business Operations* (1978).

Kokott, Juliane, *The Role of Diplomatic Protection in the Field of the Protection of Foreign Investment*, in International Law Association (ed.), *Report of the Seventieth Conference New Delhi*, p. 259 (2002).

Kolo, Abba, *Investor Protection vs Host State Regulatory Autonomy during Economic Crisis: Treatment of Capital Transfers and Restrictions under Modern Investment Treaties*, 8 J. World Inv. & Trade 457 (2007).

Kolo, Abba, and Thomas W. Wälde, *Economic Crises, Capital Transfer Restrictions and Investor Protection under Investment Treaties*, 3 Capital Markets L. J. 154 (2008).

Kooijmans, Pieter, *The ICJ in the 21st Century: Judicial Restraint, Judicial Activism, or Proactive Judicial Policy*, 56 Int'l & Comp. L. Q. 741 (2007).

Korowicz, Marek St., *The Problem of the International Personality of Individuals*, 50 A.J.I.L. 533 (1956).

Koskenniemi, Martti, *International Law in a Post-Realist Era*, 16 Australian Ybk. Int'l L. 1 (1995).

Fragmentation of International Law: Difficulties Arising from the Diversification and Expansion of International Law – Report of the Study Group of the International Law Commission (2007).

Krajewski, Markus and Jan Ceyssens, *Internationaler Investitionsschutz und innerstaatliche Regulierung – Eine Untersuchung anhand der bilateralen Investitionsschutzabkommen Deustchlands*, 45 Archiv des Völkerrechts (AVR) 180 (2007).

Kramer, Stefan, *Die Meistbegünstigung*, 35 Recht der Internationalen Wirtschaft (RIW) 473 (1989).

Kreps, David M., *Corporate Culture and Economic Theory*, in James E. Alt and Kenneth A. Shepsle (eds.), *Perspectives on Positive Political Economy*, p. 90 (1990).

Kunoy, Bjørn, *Developments in Indirect Expropriation Case Law in ICSID Transnational Arbitration*, 6 J. World Inv. & Trade 467 (2005).

Singing in the Rain – Developments in the Interpretation of Umbrella Clauses, 7 J. World Inv. & Trade 275 (2006).

Kurtz, Jürgen, *A General Investment Agreement in the WTO? Lessons from Chapter 11 of NAFTA and the OECD Multilateral Agreement on Investment*, 23 U. Pa. J. Int'l Econ. L. 713 (2002).

The MFN Standard and Foreign Investment: An Uneasy Fit?, 6 J. World Inv. & Trade 861 (2004).

The Delicate Extension of Most-Favoured-Nation Treatment to Foreign Investors, in Todd Weiler (ed.), *International Investment Law and Arbitration*, p. 523 (2005).

Lach, Sebastian and Stephan Schill, *Anmerkung*, 2005 Mitteilungen des Bayerischen Notarvereins (MittBayNot) 243 (2005).

Leathley, Christian, *International Dispute Resolution in Latin America: An Institutional Overview* (2007).

Leben, Charles, *La liberté normative de l'etat et la question de l'expropriation indirecte*, in Charles Leben (ed.), *Le contentieux arbitral transnational relatif à l'investissement international: nouveaux développements*, p. 163 (2006).

Legum, Barton, *The Innovation of Investor-State Arbitration under NAFTA*, 43 Harv. Int'l L. J. 531 (2002).

Lessons Learned from the NAFTA: The New Generation of U.S. Investment Treaty Arbitration Provisions, 19 ICSID Rev. – For. Inv. L. J. 344 (2004).

Defining Investment and Investor: Who is Entitled to Claim?, 22 Arb. Int'l 521, 524 (2006).

Lillich, Richard B. and Burns H. Weston, *International Claims: Their Settlement by Lump-Sum Agreements* (1975).

Lipstein, Kurt, *The Place of the Calvo-Clause in International Law*, 22 Brit. Ybk. Int'l L. 139 (1945).

Lowenfeld, Andreas F., *Congress and Cuba: The Helms–Burton Act*, 90 A.J.I.L. 419 (1996).

Investment Agreements and International Law, 42 Colum. J. Transnat'l L. 123 (2003).

International Economic Law (2nd edn. 2008).

Luedicke, H., *Die Entwicklung des Meistbegünstigungsprinzips* (1925).

Luhmann, Niklas, *Grundrechte als Institution* (1965).

Die Weltgesellschaft, 57 Archiv für Rechts- und Sozialphilosophie 1 (1971).

Die Wirtschaft der Gesellschaft (1988).

Das Recht der Gesellschaft (1993).

Die Gesellschaft der Gesellschaft (1997).

Lusensky, F., *Unbeschränkte gegen beschränkte Meistbegünstigung (Reziprozität)* (1918).

Macartney, Carlile A., *National States and National Minorities* (1934).

Malloy, William M., *Treaties, Conventions, International Acts, Protocols and Agreements between the United States of America and Other Powers, 1776–1909*, vol. I (1910).

Mann, F. A., *State Contracts and State Responsibility*, 54 A.J.I.L. 572 (1960).

Mann, Howard, Konrad von Moltke, Luke E. Peterson and Aaron Cosbey, *The IISD Model International Agreement on Investment for Sustainable Development*, 20 ICSID Rev. – For. Inv. L. J. 84 (2005).

Mansfield, Edward D., Helen V. Milner and B. Peter Rosendorff, *Why Democracies Cooperate More: Electoral Control and International Trade Agreements*, 56 Int'l Org. 477 (2002).

Mansfield, Edward D., and Jon C. Pevehouse, *Trade Blocs, Trade Flows, and International Conflict*, 54 Int'l Org. 775 (2000).

Mansfield, Edward D., and Brian M. Pollins (eds.), *Economic Interdependence and International Conflict: New Perspectives on Enduring Debate* (2003).

Mashayekhi, Mina and Murray Gibbs, *Lessons from the Uruguay Round Negotiations on Investment*, 33(6) J. World Trade 1 (1999).

Maskin, Eric and Jean Tirole, *Unforeseen Contingencies and Incomplete Contracts*, 66 Rev. Econ. Stud. 83 (1999).

Mayeda, Graham, *Playing Fair: The Meaning of Fair and Equitable Treatment in Bilateral Investment Treaties*, 41 J. World Trade 273 (2007).

McAfee, R. Preston, Hugo M. Mialon and Sue H. Mialon, *Private v. Public Antitrust Enforcement: A Strategic Analysis*, 92 J. Pub. Econ. 1863 (2008).

McDonald, Jan, *The Multilateral Agreement on Investment: Heyday or Mai-Day for Ecologically Sustainable Development?*, 22 Melbourne U. L. R. 617 (1998).

McKinstry Robin, Patricia, *The BIT Won't Bite: The American Bilateral Investment Treaty Program*, 33 Am. U. L. Rev. 931 (1984).

McLachlan, Campbell, Laurence Shore and Matthew Weiniger, *International Investment Arbitration – Substantive Principles* (2007).

McNair, Arnold D., *The Law of Treaties* (1961).

Merrill, Thomas W., *Incomplete Compensation for Takings*, 11 N.Y.U. Envt'l L. J. 110 (2002).

Metzger, Stanley D., *Multilateral Conventions for the Protection of Private Foreign Investment*, 9 J. Pub. L. 133 (1960).

Miller, Arthur S., *Protection of Private Foreign Investment by Multilateral Conventions*, 53 A.J.I.L. 371 (1959).

Minor, Michael S., *The Demise of Expropriation as an Instrument of LDC Policy, 1980–1992*, 25 J. Int'l Bus. Stud. 177 (1994).

Mnookin, Robert and Lewis Kornhauser, *Bargaining in the Shadow of the Law: The Case of Divorce*, 88 Yale L. J. 950 (1979).

Morin, Jean-Frédéric and Gilbert Gagné, *What Can Best Explain the Prevalence of Bilateralism in the Investment Regime?*, 36 Int'l J. Pol. Econ. 53 (2007).

Morissey, Daniel J., *Piercing All the Veils: Applying an Established Doctrine to a New Business Order*, 32 J. Corp. L. 529 (2007).

Mosoti, Victor, *Bilateral Investment Treaties and the Possibility of a Multilateral Framework in Investment at the WTO: Are Poor Countries Caught in Between?*, 26 Nw. J. Int'l L. & Bus. 95 (2005).

Muchlinski, Peter T., *The Rise and Fall of the Multilateral Agreement on Investment: Where Now?*, 34 Int'l Law. 1033 (2000).

    The Rise and Fall of the Multilateral Agreement on Investment: Lessons for the Regulation of International Business, in Ian Fletcher, Loukas Mistelis and Marise Cremona (eds.), *Foundations and Perspectives of International Trade Law*, p. 114 (2001).

Muchlinski, Peter T., Federico Ortino and Christoph Schreuer (eds.), *The Oxford Handbook of International Investment Law* (2008).

Müller, Edgar Felix, *Der völkerrechtliche Eigentumsschutz – Eine historisch-systematische Darstellung unter Berücksichtigung der internationalen Ökonomie und Politik* (1981).

Müller-Graff, Peter-Christian, *Die konstitutionelle Rolle der binnenmarktrechtlichen Grundfreiheiten im neuen Europäischen Verfassungsvertrag*, in Heribert Franz Köck, Alina Lengauer and Georg Ress (eds.), *Europarecht im Zeitalter der Globalisierung – Festschrift für Peter Fischer*, p. 363 (2004).

Navaretti, Giorgio Barba and Anthony J. Venables, *Multinational Firms in the World Economy* (2004).

Newcombe, Andrew, *The Boundaries of Regulatory Expropriation*, 20 ICSID Rev. – For. Inv. L. J. 1 (2005).

Newman, Edward, Ranesh Thakur and John Tirman (eds.), *Multilateralism under Challenge? Power, International Order, and Structural Change* (2006).

Newmark, Chris and Edward Poulton, *Siemens -v- Argentina: Most Favoured Nation Clause (Re)visited*, 3 Zeitschrift für Schiedsverfahren / German Arb. J. (SchiedsVZ) 30 (2005).

Neumayer, Eric and Laura Spess, *Do Bilateral Investment Treaties Increase Foreign Direct Investment to Developing Countries?*, 33 World Development 1567 (2005).

Nolde, B., *Droits et technique des traités de commerce*, 3 Recueil des Cours 295 (1924–II).

North, Douglass C., *Structure and Change in Economic History* (1981).

Institutions, Institutional Change, and Economic Performance (1990).

Norton, Patrick, *A Law of the Future or a Law of the Past? Modern Tribunals and the International Law of Expropriation*, 85 A.J.I.L. 474 (1991).

Nouvel, Yves, *L'indemnisation d'une expropriation indirecte*, 5 Int'l L. FORUM du droit int. 198 (2003).

Nov, Avi, *The "Bidding War" to Attract Foreign Direct Investment: The Need for a Global Solution*, 25 Va. Tax Rev. 835 (2003).

O'Connell, D. P., *International Law*, vol. I (2nd edn. 1970).

OECD, *Open Markets Matter – The Benefits of Trade and Investment Liberalisation* (1998).

Improving the System of Investor-State Dispute Settlement: An Overview, Working Papers on International Investment No. 2006/1, available at: www.oecd.org/dataoecd/3/59/36052284.pdf.

Okediji, Ruth, *Back to Bilateralism? Pendulum Swings in International Intellectual Property Protection*, 1 U. Ottawa L. & Tech. J. 125 (2003–2004).

Oneal, John R., Frances H. Oneal, Zeev Maoz and Bruce Russett, *The Liberal Peace: Interdependence, Democracy, and International Conflict, 1950–85*, 33 J. Peace Res. 11 (1996).

Oneal, John R. and Bruce M. Russett, *The Classical Liberals Were Right: Democracy, Interdependence and Conflict*, 41 Int'l Stud. Quart. 267 (1997).

Oppenheim, Lassa, *International Law – A Treatise*, vol. I (1905).

Orakhelashvili, Alexander, *The Normative Basis of "Fair and Equitable Treatment": General International Law on Foreign Investment?*, 46 Archiv des Völkerrechts (AVR) 74 (2008).

Orrego Vicuña, Francisco, *Changing Approaches to the Nationality of Claims in the Context of Diplomatic Protection and International Dispute Settlement*, 15 ICSID Rev. – For. Inv. L. J. 340 (2000).

Ortino, Federico, Audley Sheppard and Hugo Warner (eds.), *Investment Treaty Law – Current Issues Volume 1* (2006).

Oschmann, Friedrich, *Calvo–Doktrin und Calvo-Klauseln* (1993).

Investitionsschutz durch internationale Investitionsversicherung – Die wachsende Rolle der MIGA in Recht und Praxis, 41 Recht der Internationalen Wirtschaft (RIW) 972 (1995).

Investitionsschutzverträge in Lateinamerika, 42 Recht der Internationalen Wirtschaft (RIW) 494 (1996).

Ostry, Sylvia, *Looking Back to Look Forward: The Multilateral Trading System After 50 Years*, in WTO Secretariat (ed.), *From GATT to the WTO: The Multilateral Trading System in the New Millennium*, p. 97 (2000).

Oye, Kenneth A., *Economic Discrimination and Political Exchange: World Political Economy in the 1930s and 1980s* (1992).

Palmeter, David and Petros C. Mavroidis, *The WTO Legal System: Sources of Law*, 92 A.J.I.L. 398 (1998).

Paparinskis, Martins, *Investment Arbitration and the Law of Countermeasures*, Society of International Economic Law (SIEL) Inaugural Conference 2008, Online Proceedings Working Paper No. 23/08, available at: http://ssrn.com/abstract=1152338 (June 27, 2008).

MFN Clauses in Investment Arbitration between Maffezini *and* Plama: *The Third Way?*, ICSID Rev. – For Inv. L. J. (forthcoming)

Paulsson, Jan, *Arbitration Without Privity*, 10 ICSID Rev. – For. Inv. L. J. 232 (1995).

Denial of Justice in International Law (2005).

International Arbitration and the Generation of Legal Norms: Treaty Arbitration and International Law, 3(5) Transnat'l Disp. Mgmt. (2006).

Pauwelyn, Joost, *A Typology of Multilateral Treaty Obligations: Are WTO Obligations Bilateral or Collective in Nature?*, 14 Eur. J. Int'l L. 907 (2003).

Perkams, Markus, *Piercing the Corporate Veil in International Investment Agreements – The Issue of Indirect Shareholder Claims Reloaded*, in August Reinisch and Christina Knahr (eds.), *International Investment Law in Context*, p. 93 (2008).

Peters, Paul, *Dispute Settlement Arrangements in Investment Treaties*, 22 Neth. Ybk. Int'l L. 91 (1991).

Peters, Paul, and Nico Schrijver, *Latin America and International Regulation of Foreign Investment: Changing Perceptions*, 39 Neth. Int'l L. Rev. 355 (1992).

Petersmann, Ernst-Ulrich, *International Economic Theory and International Economic Law: On the Tasks of a Legal Theory of International Economic Order*, in Ronald St. J. Macdonald and Douglas M. Johnston (eds.), *The Structure and Process of International Law*, p. 227 (1983).

Constitutional Functions and Constitutional Problems of International Economic Law (1991).

Constitutionalization and WTO Law, in Daniel L. M. Kennedy and James D. Southwick (eds.), *The Political Economics of International Trade Law*, p. 32 (2002).

Petersmann, Hans G., *Die Multilaterale Investitions-Garantie-Agentur (MIGA)*, 46 Zeitschrift für ausländisches öffentliches Recht und Völkerrecht/ Heidelberg J. Int'l L. (ZaöRV) 758 (1986).

Picciotto, Sol, *Linkages in International Investment Regulation: The Antinomies of the Draft Multilateral Agreement on Investment*, 19 U. Pa. J. Int'l Econ. L. 731 (1998).

Picherack, J. Roman, *The Expanding Scope of the Fair and Equitable Treatment Standard: Have Recent Tribunals Gone Too Far?*, 9 J. World Inv. & Trade 255 (2008).

Platteau, Jean-Philippe, *Institutions, Social Norms, and Economic Development* (2000).

Poirier, Marc R., *The NAFTA Chapter 11 Expropriation Debate through the Eyes of a Property Theorist*, 33 Environmental Law 851 (2003).

Polachek, Solomon W., *Conflict and Trade*, 24 J. Conflict Res. 55 (1980).

Pollins, Brian M., *Conflict, Cooperation, and Commerce: The Effect of International Political Interactions on Bilateral Trade Flows*, 33 Am. J. Pol. Sc. 737 (1989).

Pomfret, Richard, *Unequal Trade: The Economics of Discriminatory International Trade Policies* (1988).

Is Regionalism an Increasing Feature of the World Economy?, 30 World Econ. 923 (2007).

Porter, Michael E., *The Competitive Advantage of Nations* (1990).

Porterfield, Matthew C., *An International Common Law of Investor Rights?*, 27 U. Pa. J. Int'l Econ. L. 79 (2006).

Posner, Richard A., *The Constitution as an Economic Document*, 56 Geo. Wash. L. Rev. 4 (1987).

Pradier-Fodéré, P., *Traité de Droit International Public*, vol. II (1885).

Prasad, Eswar, Kenneth Rogoff, Shang-Jin Wei and M. Ayan Kose, *Effects of Financial Globalization on Developing Countries: Some Empirical Evidence*, IMF Occasional Paper 220 (2003).

Price, Daniel M. and P. Bryan Christy, III, *Agreement on Trade Related Investment Measures (TRIMS): Limitations and Prospects for the Future*, in Terence P. Stewart (ed.), *The World Trade Organization: The Multilateral Trade Framework for the 21st Century and U.S. Implementing Legislation*, p. 439 (1996).

Quillin, Scott S., *The World Trade Organization and Its Protection of Foreign Direct Investment: The Efficacy of the Agreement on Trade-Related Investment Measures*, 28 Okla. City U. L. Rev. 875 (2003).

Radi, Yannick, *The Application of the Most-Favoured-Nation Clause to the Dispute Settlement Provisions of Bilateral Investment Treaties: Domesticating the "Trojan Horse"*, 18 Eur. J. Int'l L. 757 (2007).

Rao, Pemmaraju Sreenivasa, *Multiple International Judicial Forums*, 25 Mich. J. Int'l L. 929 (2004).

Ratchik, Jonathan R., *Cuban Liberty and the Democratic Society Act of 1995*, 11 Am. U. J. Int'l L. & Pol'y 343 (1996).

Reading, Michael, *The Bilateral Investment Treaty in ASEAN: A Comparative Analysis*, 42 Duke L. J. 679 (1992).

Reed, Lucy, *Great Expectations: Where Does the Proliferation of International Dispute Resolution Tribunals Leave International Law?*, 96 Am. Soc'y Int'l L. Proc. 219 (2002).

Reimann, Mathias, *Historische Schule und Common Law* (1993).

Reinisch, August, *Necessity in International Investment Arbitration – An Unnecessary Split of Opinions in Recent ICSID Cases? Comments on CMS v. Argentina and LG&E v. Argentina*, 8 J. World Inv. & Trade 191 (2007).

(ed.), *Standards of Protection in International Investment Law* (2008).

Reisman, W. Michael and Robert D. Sloane, *Indirect Expropriation and its Valuation in the BIT Generation*, 74 Brit. Ybk. Int'l L. 115 (2003).

Reuter, Paul, *Introduction to the Law of Treaties* (2nd edn. 1995).

Riedl, Richard, *Ausnahmen von der Meistbegünstigung* (1931).

Rixen, Thomas and Ingo Rohlfing, *The Institutional Choice of Bilateralism and Multilateralism in International Trade and Taxation*, 12 Int'l Negotiation 389 (2007).

Robinson, Jacob, *Were the Minority Treaties a Failure?* (1943).

Rodrik, Dani, Arvind Subramanian and Francesco Trebbi, *Institutions Rule: The Primacy of Institutions over Geography and Integration in Economic Development*, 9 J. Econ. Growth 131 (2004).

Roesner, Peter, *Die Meistbegünstigungsklausel in den bilateralen Handelsverträgen der Bundesrepublik Deutschland* (1964).

Romano, Cesare P. R., *The Proliferation of International Judicial Bodies: The Piece of the Puzzle*, 31 N.Y.U. J. Int'l L. & Pol. 709 (1999).

Root, Elihu, *The Basis of Protection to Citizens Residing Abroad*, 4 A.J.I.L. 517 (1910).

Roth, Andreas H., *The Minimum Standard of International Law Applied to Aliens* (1949).

Rourke, Kevin H. O. and Jeffrey G. Williamson, *Globalization and History: The Evolution of a Nineteenth-Century Atlantic Economy* (1999).

Rowat, Malcolm D., *Multilateral Approaches to Improving the Investment Climate of Developing Countries: The Cases of ICSID and MIGA*, 33 Harv. Int'l L. J. 103 (1992).

Roxin, Claus, *Strafrecht – Allgemeiner Teil*, vol. I (3rd edn. 1997).

Ruggie, John G., *Multilateralism Matters: The Theory and Praxis of an Institutional Form* (1993).

Russett, Bruce M., John R. Oneal and David R. Davis, *The Third Leg of the Kantian Tripod for Peace: International Organizations and Militarized Disputes, 1950–1985*, 52 Int'l Org. 441 (1998).

Sacerdoti, Giorgio, *Bilateral Treaties and Multilateral Instruments on Investment Protection*, 269 Recueil des Cours 251 (1997).

Investment Arbitration under ICSID and UNCITRAL Rules: Prerequisites, Applicable Law, Review of Awards, 19 ICSID Rev. – For. Inv. L. J. 1 (2004).

Salacuse, Jeswald W. and Nicholas P. Sullivan, *Do BITs Really Work? An Evaluation of Bilateral Investment Treaties and Their Grand Bargain*, 46 Harv. Int'l L. J. 67 (2005).

Sampliner, Gary H., *Arbitration of Expropriation Cases under U.S. Investment Treaties – A Threat to Democracy or the Dog that Didn't Bark?*, 18 ICSID Rev. – For. Inv. L. J. 1 (2003).

Sauvant, Karl P. (ed.), *Appeals Mechanism in International Investment Disputes* (2008).

Sauvant, Karl P. and Lisa E. Sachs (eds.), *The Effect of Treaties on Foreign Direct Investment: Bilaterial Investment Treaties, Double Taxation Treaties, and Investment Flows* (2009).

Sauvé, Pierre, *Multilateral Rules on Investment: Is Forward Movement Possible?*, 9 J. Int'l Econ. L. 325 (2006).

Schachter, Oscar, *International Law in Theory and Practice* (1991).

Schauer, Frederick, *Precedent*, 39 Stan. L. Rev. 571 (1987).

Schill, Stephan, *Der Einfluss der Wettbewerbsideologie des Nationalsozialismus auf den Schutzzweck des UWG* (2004).

From Calvo to CMS: Burying an International Law Legacy – Argentina's Currency Reform in the Face of Investment Protection: The ICSID Case CMS v. Argentina, 3 Zeitschrift für Schiedsverfahren/German Arb. J. (SchiedsVZ) 285 (2005).

Arbitration Risk and Effective Compliance: Cost-Shifting in Investment Treaty Arbitration, 7 J. World Inv. & Trade 653 (2006).

Fair and Equitable Treatment under Investment Treaties as an Embodiment of the Rule of Law, IILJ Working Paper 2006/6 (Global Administrative Law Series) (2006), available at: www.iilj.org/publications/2006–6Schill.asp.

Revisiting a Landmark: Indirect Expropriation and Fair and Equitable Treatment in the ICSID Case Tecmed, 3(2) Transnat'l Disp. Mgmt. (2006).

Auf zu Kalypso? Staatsnotstand und Internationales Investitionsschutzrecht, 5 Zeitschrift für Schiedsverfahren / German Arb. J. (SchiedsVZ) 178 (2007).

Do Investment Treaties Chill Unilateral State Regulation to Mitigate Climate Change?, 24 J. Int'l Arb. 469 (2007).

International Investment Law and the Host State's Power to Handle Economic Crises, 24 J. Int'l Arb. 265 (2007).

Tearing Down the Great Wall – The New Generation Investment Treaties of the People's Republic of China, 15 Cardozo J. Int'l & Comp. L. (2007).

Der völkerrechtliche Staatsnotstand in der Entscheidung des BVerfG zu Argentinischen Staatsanleihen – Anachronismus oder Avantgarde?, 68 Zeitschrift für ausländisches öffentliches Recht und Völkerrecht / Heidelberg J. Int'l L. (ZaöRV) 45 (2008).

Enabling Private Ordering – Function, Scope and Effect of Umbrella Clauses in International Investment Treaties, 18 Minn. J. Int'l L. 1 (2009).

Schittecatte, Catherine, *The Politics of the MAI*, 1 J. World Inv. 329 (2000).

Schneiderman, David, *Investment Rules and the New Constitutionalism*, 25 L. & Soc. Inquiry 757 (2000).

Investment Rules and the Rule of Law, 8 Constellations 521 (2001).

Constitutionalizing Economic Globalization (2008).

Schöbener, Burkhard and Lars Markert, *Das International Centre for Settlement of Investment Disputes (ICSID)*, 105 Zeitschrift für Vergleichende Rechtswissenschaft (ZVglRWiss) 65 (2006).

Schreuer, Christoph, *The Interpretation of Treaties by Domestic Courts*, 45 Brit. Ybk. Int'l L. 255 (1971).

The ICSID Convention – A Commentary (2001).

Paradigmenwechsel im Internationalen Investitionsrecht, in Waldemar Hummer (ed.), *Paradigmenwechsel im Völkerrecht zur Jahrtausendwende*, p. 237 (2002).

Travelling the BIT Route – Of Waiting Period, Umbrella Clauses and Forks in the Road, 5 J. World Inv. & Trade 231 (2004).

Fair and Equitable Treatment in Arbitral Practice, 6 J. World Inv. & Trade 357 (2005).

Non-Pecuniary Remedies in ICSID Arbitration, 20 Arb. Int'l 325 (2005).

Shareholder Protection in International Investment Law, in Pierre-Marie Dupuy, Bardo Fassbender, Malcolm N. Shaw and Karl-Peter Sommermann (eds.), *Völkerrecht als Wertordnung – Festschrift für Christian Tomuschat (Common Values in International Law) – Essays in Honour of Christian Tomuschat*, p. 601 (2006).

Investment Protection and International Relations, in August Reinisch and Ursula Kriebaum (eds.), *The Law of International Relations – Liber Amicorum Hanspeter Neuhold*, p. 345 (2007).

Schularick, Moritz, *Finanzielle Globalisierung in historischer Perspektive: Kapitalflüsse von Reich nach Arm, Investitionsrisiken und globale öffentliche Güter* (2006).

Schuyler, Eugene, *American Diplomacy and the Furtherance of Commerce* (1886).

Schwartz, Eric, *Finality at What Cost? The Decision of the Ad Hoc Committee in Wena Hotels v. Egypt*, in Emmanuel Gaillard and Yas Banifatemi (eds.), *Annulment of ICSID Awards*, p. 43 (2004).

Schwartz, Warren F. and Alan O. Sykes, *The Economics of the Most Favored Nation Clause*, in Jagdeep S. Bhandari and Alan O. Sykes, *Economic Dimensions in International Law*, p. 43 (1997).

Schwarzenberger, Georg, *The Most-Favoured-Nation Standard in British State Practice*, 22 Brit. Ybk. Int'l L. 96 (1945).

International Law as Applied by International Courts and Tribunals, vol. I (3rd edn. 1957).

Foreign Investments and International Law (1969).

Equality and Discrimination in International Economic Law (I), 25 The Year Book of World Affairs 163 (1971).

Schwebel, Stephen M., *The Story of the U.N.'s Declaration on Permanent Sovereignty over Natural Resources*, 49 Am. Bar Ass. J. 463 (1963).

The United States 2004 Model Bilateral Investment Treaty: An Exercise in the Regressive Development of International Law, 3(2) Transnat'l Disp. Mgmt. (2006).

Segal, Ilya R. and Michael D. Whinston, *Public vs. Private Enforcement of Antitrust Law: A Survey*, 28 Eur. Comp. L. Rev. 306 (2007).

Sester, Peter and José Luis Cárdenas T., *The Extra-Communitarian Effects of Centros, Überseering and Inspire Art with Regard to Fourth Generation Association Agreements*, 2 Eur. Company & Fin. L. Rev. 398 (2005).

Shahabuddeen, Mohamed, *Precedent in the World Court* (1996).

Shan, Wenhua, *The Legal Framework of EU–China Investment Relations – A Critical Appraisal* (2005).

Shany, Yuval, *Toward a General Margin of Appreciation Doctrine in International Law*, 16 Eur. J. Int'l L. 907 (2005).

Consolidation and Tests for Application: Is International Law Relevant?, 21 ICSID Rev. – For. Inv. L. J. 135 (2006).

Shea, Donald R., *The Calvo Clause, A Problem of Inter-American and International Law and Diplomacy* (1955).

Shenkin, Todd S., *Trade-Related Investment Measures in Bilateral Investment Treaties and the GATT: Moving Towards a Multilateral Investment Treaty*, 55 U. Pitt. L. Rev. 541 (1994).

Shihata, Ibrahim F. I., *The Multilateral Investment Guarantee Agency*, 20 Int'l Law. 487 (1986).

Towards a Greater Depoliticization of Investment Disputes: The Role of ICSID and MIGA, 1 ICSID Rev. – For. Inv. L. J. 1 (1986).

The Multilateral Investment Guarantee Agency (MIGA) and the Legal Treatment of Foreign Investment, 203 Recueil des Cours 95 (1987–III).

MIGA and Foreign Investment – Origins, Operations, Policies and Basic Documents of the Multilateral Investment Guarantee Agency (1988).

Legal Treatment of Foreign Investment: The World Bank Guidelines (1993).

Shihata, Ibrahim F.I. and Antonio R. Parra, *The Experience of the International Centre for Settlement of Investment Disputes*, 14 ICSID Rev. – For. Inv. L. J. 299 (1999).

Simma, Bruno, *From Bilateralism to Community Interest in International Law*, 250 Recueil des Cours 217 (1994).

Sinclair, Anthony C., *The Origins of the Umbrella Clause in the International Law of Investment Protection*, 20 Arb. Int'l 411 (2004).

The Substance of Nationality Requirements in Investment Treaty Arbitration, 20 ICSID Rev. – For. Inv. L. J. 357 (2005).

Sinclair, Ian M., *Vienna Convention on the Law of Treaties*, 19 Int'l & Comp. L. Q. 47 (1970).

The Vienna Convention on the Law of Treaties (2nd edn. 1984).

Smythe, Elisabeth, *Your Place or Mine? States, International Organizations and the Negotiation of Investment Rules*, 7 Transnat'l Corp. 85 (December 1998).

Snodgrass, Elizabeth, *Protecting Investors' Legitimate Expectations – Recognizing and Delimiting a General Principle*, 21 ICSID Rev. – For. Inv. L. J. 1 (2006).

Snyder, Richard. C., *The Most-Favored-Nation Clause: An Analysis with Particular Reference to Recent Treaty Practice and Tariffs* (1948).

Södersten, Bo and Geoffrey Reed, *International Economics* (3rd edn. 1994).

Sohn, Louis B. and Richard R. Baxter, *Responsibility of States for Injuries to the Economic Interests of Aliens*, 55 A.J.I.L. 545 (1961).

Solow, Robert M., *Technical Change and the Aggregate Production Function*, 39 Rev. Econ. & Stat. 312 (1957).

Soloway, Julie A., *NAFTA's Chapter 11: The Challenge of Private Party Participation*, 16 J. Int'l Arb. 1 (1999).

Sommer, Louise, *Die Voraussetzungen des staatsideologischen Kampfes gegen die Meistbegünstigungsklausel*, 16 Zeitschrift für öffentliches Recht (ZöR) 265 (1936).

Sornarajah, M., *Protection of Foreign Investment in the Asia-Pacific Economic Co-operation Region*, 29(2) J. World Trade 105 (1995).

The International Law on Foreign Investment (2nd edn. 2004).

Spelliscy, Shane, *The Proliferation of International Tribunals: A Chink in the Armor*, 40 Colum. J. Transnat'l L. 143 (2001).

Spero, Joan Edelman and Jeffrey A. Hart, *The Politics of International Economic Relations* (6th edn. 2003).

Steiner, Henry J. and Philip Alston, *International Human Rights in Context – Law, Politics, Morals* (2nd edn. 2000).

Stewart, Terence P. (ed.), *The GATT Uruguay Round: A Negotiating History* (1993).

Stone, Madeleine, *NAFTA Article 1110: Environmental Friend or Foe?*, 15 Geo. Int'l Envtl. L. Rev. 763 (2003).

Stone Sweet, Alec, *Judicialization and the Construction of Governance*, 32 Comp. Pol. Stud. 147 (1999).

Strazzeri, Joseph A., *A Lucas Analysis of Regulatory Expropriations under NAFTA Chapter Eleven*, 14 Geo. Int'l Envtl. L. Rev. 837 (2002).

Strupp, Karl and Hans-Jürgen Schlochauer, *Wörterbuch des Völkerrechts*, vol. II (2nd ed. 1961).

Stumberg, Robert, *Sovereignty by Subtraction: The Multilateral Agreement on Investment*, 31 Cornell Int'l L. J. 491 (1998).

Swenson, Deborah L., *Why Do Developing Countries Sign BITs?*, 12 U.C. Davis J. Int'l L. & Pol'y 131 (2005).

Sykes, Alan O., *Public versus Private Enforcement of International Economic Law. Standing and Remedy*, 34 J. Legal Stud. 631 (2005).

Tams, Christian J., *Enforcing Obligations* Erga Omnes *in International Law* (2005).

An Appealing Option? The Debate about an ICSID Appellate Mechanism, Beiträge zum Transnationalen Wirtschaftsrecht, vol. 57 (2006), available at: www.telc.uni-halle.de/Heft57.pdf.

Konstitutionalisierungstendenzen im Recht des internationalen Investitionsschutzes, in Christian Tietje and Karsten Nowrot (eds.), *Verfassungsrechtliche Dimensionen des Internationalen Wirtschaftsrechts,* p. 229 (2007).

te Velde, Dirk Willem and Miatta Fahnbulleh, *Investment Related Provisions in Regional Trade Agreements* (October 2003), available at: www.odi.org.uk/ iedg/Projects/Inv%20Prov%206.pdf.

Teitelbaum, Ruth, *Who's Afraid of* Maffezini? *Recent Developments in the Interpretation of Most Favored Nation Clauses,* 22 J. Int'l Arb. 225 (2005).

Teubner, Gunther, *Standards und Direktiven in Generalklauseln: Möglichkeiten und Grenzen der empirischen Sozialforschung bei der Präzisierung der Gute-Sitte-Klauseln im Privatrecht* (1971).

Tirole, Jean, *Incomplete Contracts: Where Do We Stand?,* 67 Econometrica 741 (1999).

Tobin, Jennifer and Susan Rose-Ackerman, *Foreign Direct Investment and the Business Environment in Developing Countries: The Impact of Bilateral Investment Treaties,* Yale Law and Economics Research Paper No. 293 (2005), available at: ssrn.com/abstract=557121.

When BITs Have Some Bite: The Political-Economic Environment for Bilateral Investment Treaties, in Roger P. Alford and Catherine Rogers (eds.), *The Future of Investment Arbitration,* p. 131 (2009).

Trachtman, Joel P., *The Domain of WTO Dispute Resolution,* 40 Harv. Int'l L. J. 333 (1999).

The Constitutions of the WTO, 17 Eur. J. Int'l L. 646 (2006).

Triepel, Heinrich, *Völkerrecht und Landesrecht* (1899).

Tschofen, Franziska, *Multilateral Approaches to the Treatment of Foreign Investment,* 7 ICSID Rev. – For. Inv. L. J. 384 (1992).

Tudor, Ioana, *The Fair and Equitable Treatment Standard in the International Law of Foreign Investment* (2008).

UNCTAD, *Bilateral Investment Treaties in the Mid-1990s* (1998).

Most Favoured-Nation Treatment, UNCTAD Series on Issues in International Investment Agreements, vol. III (1999).

Lessons from the MAI (2000).

International Investment Agreements: Key Issues, vol. I (2004).

Investor-State Disputes Arising from Investment Treaties: A Review (2005), available at: www.unctad.org/en/docs/iteiit20054_en.pdf.

South–South Cooperation in International Investment Arrangements (2005), available at: www.unctad.org/en/docs/iteiit20053_en.pdf.

Investment Provisions in Economic Integration Agreements (2006), available at: www.unctad.org/en/docs/iteiit200510_en.pdf.

Investor-State Dispute Settlement and Impact on Investment Rulemaking (2007), available at: www.unctad.org/en/docs/iteiia20073_en.pdf.

Recent Developments in International Investment Agreements (2006–June 2007) (2007), available at: www.unctad.org/en/docs/webiteiia20076_en.pdf.

World Investment Report 2007 – Transnational Corporations, Extractive Industries and Development (2007), available at: www.unctad.org/en/docs/wir2007_en.pdf.

Latest Developments in Investor-State Dispute Settlement (2008), available at: www.unctad.org/en/docs/iteiia20083_en.pdf.

US Department of State, *Commercial Treaty Program of the United States*, Publication 6565, Commercial Policy Series No. 163 (1958).

Ushakov, Nikolai, *Report on the Most-Favoured-Nation Clause*, 30 ILC Ybk., vol. II, Part One, p. 1 (1978) (International Law Commission, *Most-Favoured-Nation Clause*, UN Doc. A/CN.4/309).

Ustor, Endre, *First Report on the Most-Favoured-Nation Clause*, 21 ILC Ybk., vol. II, p. 157 (1969) (International Law Commission, *Most-Favoured-Nation Clause*, UN Doc. A/CN.4/213 [April 18, 1969]).

Die Zollunionsausnahme, in Peter Fischer, Heribert Franz Köck and Alfred Verdross (eds.), *Völkerrecht und Rechtsphilosophie – Internationale Festschrift für Stephan Verosta zum 70. Geburtstag*, p. 371 (1980).

The MFN Customs Union Exception, 15 J. World Trade L. 377 (1981).

Most-Favored-Nation Clauses in Treaties of Commerce: The Question of an Implied Customs Union Exception, in Hanna Bokor-Szegö (ed.), 3 *Questions of International Law* 225 (1986).

Most-Favoured-Nation Clause, in Rudolf Bernhardt and Peter Macalister-Smith (eds.), *Encyclopedia of Public International Law*, vol. III, p. 468 (1997).

Valenti, Mara, *The Most Favoured Nation Clause in BITs as a Basis for Jurisdiction in Foreign Investor–Host State Arbitration*, 24 Arb. Int'l 447 (2008).

Valliantos, Mark, *De-Fanging the MAI*, 31 Cornell Int'l L .J. 713 (1998).

van Harten, Gus, *Private Authority and Transnational Governance: The Contours of the International System of Investor Protection*, 12 Rev. Int'l Pol. Econ. 600 (2005).

Investment Treaty Arbitration and Public Law (2007).

van Harten, Gus and Martin Loughlin, *Investment Treaty Arbitration as a Species of Global Administrative Law*, 17 Eur. J. Int'l L. 121 (2006).

Vandevelde, Kenneth J., *The Bilateral Investment Treaty Program of the United States*, 21 Cornell Int'l L. J. 201 (1988).

U.S. Bilateral Investment Treaties: The Second Wave, 14 Mich. J. Int'l L. 621 (1993).

Investment Liberalization and Economic Development: The Role of Bilateral Investment Treaties, 36 Colum. J. Transnat'l L. 501 (1998).

Sustainable Liberalism and the International Investment Regime, 19 Mich. J. Int'l L. 373 (1998).

The Political Economy of a Bilateral Investment Treaty, 92 A.J.I.L. 621 (1998).

The Economics of Bilateral Investment Treaties, 41 Harv. Int'l L. J. 469 (2000).

A Brief History of International Investment Agreements, 12 U.C. Davis J. Int'l L. & Pol'y 157 (2005).

Várady, Tibor, John J. Barceló III and Arthur T. von Mehren, *International Commercial Arbitration – A Transnational Perspective* (3rd edn. 2006).

Vasciannie, Stephen, *The Fair and Equitable Treatment Standard in International Investment Law and Practice,* 70 Brit. Ybk. Int'l Law 99 (1999).

Verbit, G. P., *Preferences and the Public Law of International Trade: The End of Most-Favoured-Nation Treatment?,* in Hague Academy of International Law, *Colloquium 1968: International Trade Agreements,* p. 19 (1969).

Verdross, Alfred and Bruno Simma, *Universelles Völkerrecht* (3rd edn. 1984).

Verhoosel, Gaëtan, *Foreign Direct Investment and Legal Constraints on Domestic Environmental Policies: Striking a "Reasonable" Balance between Stability and Change,* 29 L. & Pol'y Int'l Bus. 451 (1998).

Vermeer-Künzli, Annemarieke, *Restricting Discretion: Judicial Review of Diplomatic Protection,* 75 Nordic J. Int'l L. 279 (2006).

Vesel, Scott, *Clearing a Path through a Tangled Jurisprudence: Most-Favored-Nation Clauses and Dispute Settlement Provisions in Bilateral Investment Treaties,* 32 Yale J. Int'l L. 125 (2007).

Vignes, Daniel, *La clause de la nation la plus favorisée et sa pratique contemporaine – Problèmes poses par la Communauté Économique Européenne,* 130 Recueil des Cours 207 (1970–II).

Wagner, J. Martin, *International Investment: Expropriation and Environmental Protection,* 29 Golden Gate U. L. Rev. 465 (1999).

Waibel, Michael, *Two Worlds of Necessity in ICSID Arbitration: CMS and LG&E,* 20 Leiden J. Int'l L. 637 (2007).

Wälde, Thomas W. (ed.), *The Energy Charter Treaty – An East–West Gateway for Investment and Trade* (1996).

A Requiem for the "New International Economic Order" – The Rise and Fall of Paradigms in International Economic Law and a Post-mortem with Timeless Significance, in Gerhard Hafner and Gerhard Loibl (eds.), *Liber Amicorum: Professor Ignaz Seidl-Hohenveldern in Honour of his 80th Birthday,* p. 771 (1998).

The "Umbrella" Clause in Investment Arbitration: A Comment on Original Intentions and Recent Cases, 6 J. World Inv. & Trade 183 (2005).

Wälde, Thomas W. and Abba Kolo, *Environmental Regulation, Investment Protection and "Regulatory Taking" in International Law,* 50 Int'l & Comp. L. Q. 811 (2001).

Walker, Herman Jr., *Treaties for the Encouragement and Protection of Foreign Investment: Present United States Practice*, 5 Am. J. Comp. L. 229 (1956).

Modern Treaties of Friendship, Commerce and Navigation, 42 Minn. L. Rev. 805 (1958).

Wallace, Day, *The Legal Environment for a Multilateral Framework on Investment and the Potential Role of the WTO*, 3 J. World Inv. 289 (2002).

Wendrich, Claudia, *Ten Years After: The World Bank Guidelines on Foreign Direct Investment – In Need of Revision?*, 3 J. World Inv. 831 (2002).

The World Bank Guidelines as a Foundation for a Global Investment Treaty: A Problem-Oriented Approach, 2(5) Transnat'l Disp. Mgmt. (2005).

Weston, Burns H., *"Constructive Takings" under International Law: A Modest Foray into the Problem of "Creeping Expropriation"*, 16 Va. J. Int'l L. 103 (1975).

The Charter of Economic Rights and Duties of States and the Deprivation of Foreign Owned Wealth, 75 A.J.I.L. 437 (1981).

Weston, Burns H., David J. Bederman, and Richard B. Lillich, *International Claims: Their Settlement by Lump-Sum Agreements 1975–1995* (1999).

White, Gillian, *Nationalisation of Foreign Property* (1961).

Wilcox, Clair, *A Charter for World Trade* (1949).

Williamson, Oliver E., *The Economic Institutions of Capitalism: Firms, Markets, and Relational Contracting* (1985).

Transaction Cost Economics Meets Posnerian Law and Economics, 149 J.I.T.E 99 (1993).

Wilson, Robert R., *Postwar Commercial Treaties of the United States*, 43 A.J.I.L. 262 (1949).

Property-Protection Provisions in United States Commercial Treaties, 45 A.J.I.L. 83 (1951).

The International Law Standards in Treaties of the United States (1953).

A Decade of Commercial Treaties, 50 A.J.I.L. 927 (1956).

Wisner, Robert and Nick Gallus, *Nationality Requirements in Investor-State Arbitration*, 5 J. World Inv. & Trade 927 (2004).

Witherell, William H., *The OECD Multilateral Agreement on Investment*, 4 Transnat'l Corp. 1 (August 1995).

Wolf, Sebastian, *Welthandelsrechtliche Rahmenbedingungen für die Liberalisierung ausländischer Direktinvestitionen*, Beiträge zum Transnationalen Wirtschaftsrecht, vol. 61 (2006), available at: www.telc.uni-halle.de/Heft61.pdf.

Wolters, Yves G. L., *The Meaning of "Investment" in Treaty Disputes: Substantive or Jurisdictional? Lessons from* Nagel v. Czech Republic *and* S. D. Myers v. Canada, 8 J. World Inv. & Trade 175 (2007).

Wong, Jarrod, *Umbrella Clauses in Bilateral Investment Treaties: Of Breaches of Contract, Treaty Violations, and the Divide between Developing and*

Developed Countries in Foreign Investment Disputes, 14 Geo. Mason L. Rev. 135 (2006).

The Application of Most-Favored-Nation Clauses to Dispute Resolution Provisions in Bilateral Investment Treaties, 3 Asian J. WTO & Int'l Health L. & Pol'y 171 (2008).

World Bank, *World Development Report 1997: The State in a Changing World* (1997).

Wortley, B. A., *Expropriation in Public International Law* (1959).

Yackee, Jason Webb, *Conceptual Difficulties in the Empirical Study of Bilateral Investment Treaties*, 33 Brook. J. Int'l L. 405 (2008).

Yala, Farouk, *The Notion of "Investment" in ICSID Case Law: A Drifting Jurisdictional Requirement? – Some "Un-Conventional" Thoughts on* Salini, SGS *and* Mihaly, 22 J. Int'l Arb. 105 (2005).

Yannaca-Small, Catherine, *Fair and Equitable Treatment Standard in International Investment Law*, OECD Working Papers on International Investment, No. 2004/3, available at: www.oecd.org/dataoecd/22/53/33776498.pdf.

"Indirect Expropriation" and the "Right to Regulate" in International Investment Law, OECD Working Paper on International Investment, No. 2004/4, available at: www.oecd.org/dataoecd/22/54/33776546.pdf.

Yourow, Howard C., *The Margin of Appreciation Doctrine in the Dynamics of European Human Rights Jurisprudence* (1996).

Zagel, Gudrun, *Auslandsinvestitionen in Lateinamerika* (1999).

Zeitler, Helge E., *The Guarantee of "Full Protection and Security" in Investment Treaties Regarding Harm Caused by Private Actors*, Stockholm Int'l Arb. Rev. 1 (2005).

Zoellner, Carl-Sebastian, *Third-Party Participation (NGOs and Private Persons) and Transparency in ICSID Proceedings*, in Rainer Hofmann and Christian J. Tams (eds.), *The International Convention for the Settlement of Investment Disputes (ICSID) – Taking Stock after 40 Years*, p. 179 (2007).

INDEX